Downtown Washington, D.C.

Central Washington, D.C.

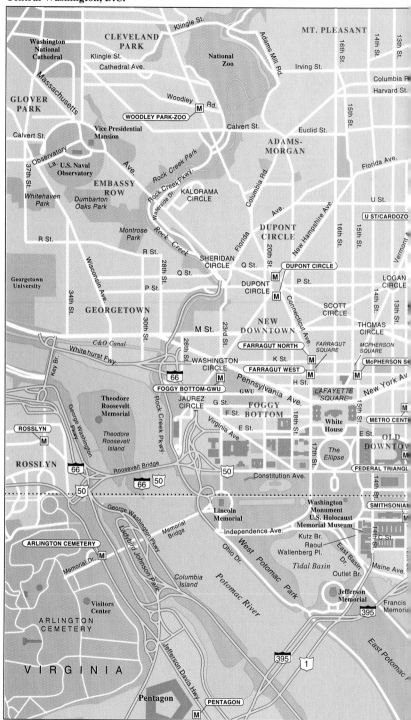

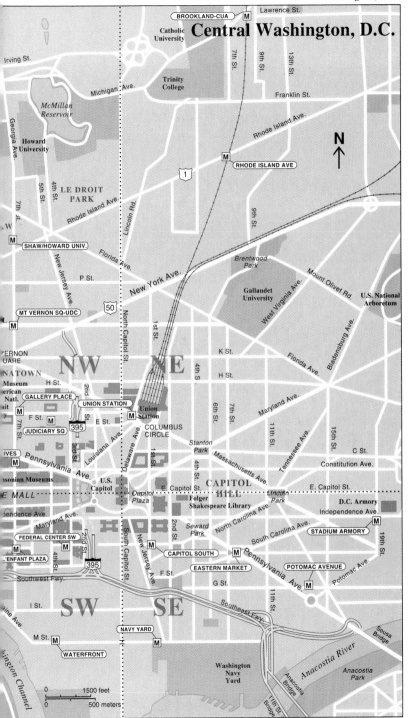

Central Washington, D.C.

The Mall Area, Washington, D.C.

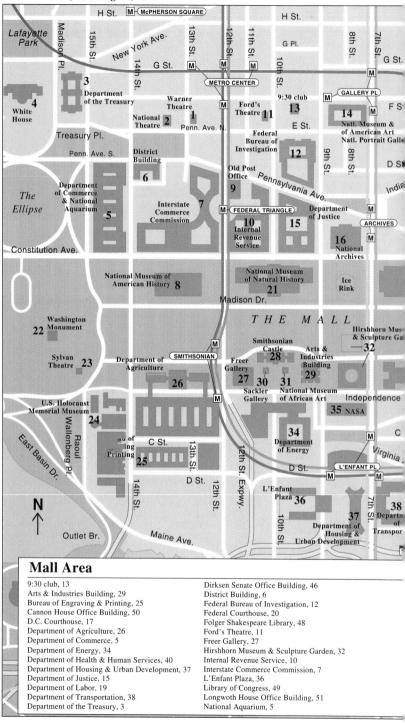

Mall Area

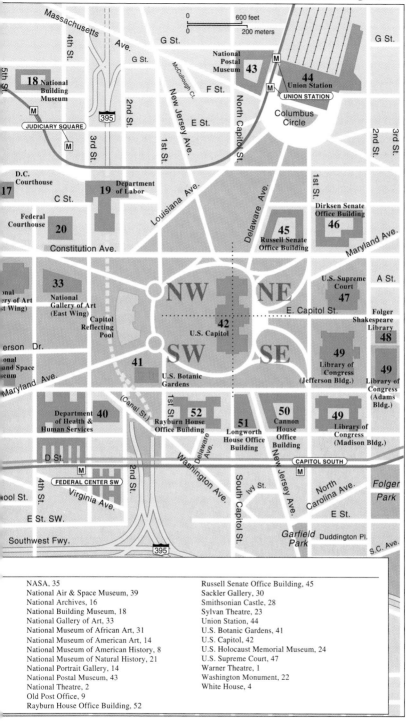

The Mall Area, Washington, D.C.

White House Area, Foggy Bottom, and Nearby Arlington

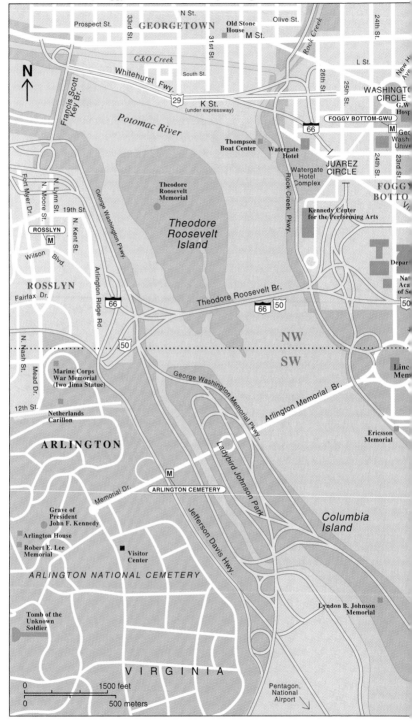

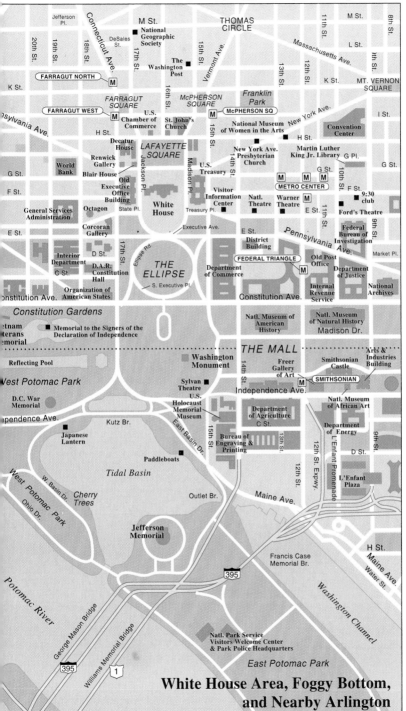

White House Area, Foggy Bottom, and Nearby Arlington

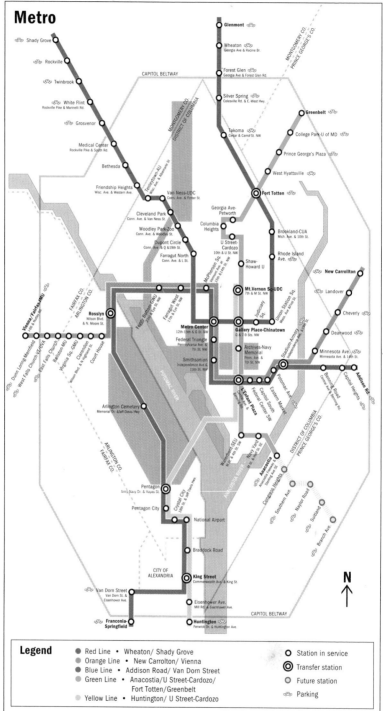

Let's Go writers travel on your budget.

"Guides that penetrate the veneer of the holiday brochures and mine the grit of real life."

—*The Economist*

"The writers seem to have experienced every rooster-packed bus and lunar-surfaced mattress about which they write."

—*The New York Times*

"All the dirt, dirt cheap."

—*People*

Great for independent travelers.

"The guides are aimed not only at young budget travelers but at the independent traveler; a sort of streetwise cookbook for traveling alone."

—*The New York Times*

"Flush with candor and irreverence, chock full of budget travel advice."

—*The Des Moines Register*

"An indispensible resource, *Let's Go*'s practical information can be used by every traveler."

—*The Chattanooga Free Press*

Let's Go is completely revised each year.

"Only *Let's Go* has the zeal to annually update every title on its list."

—*The Boston Globe*

"Unbeatable: good sightseeing advice; up-to-date info on restaurants, hotels, and inns; a commitment to money-saving travel; and a wry style that brightens nearly every page."

—*The Washington Post*

All the important information you need.

"*Let's Go* authors provide a comedic element while still providing concise information and thorough coverage of the country. Anything you need to know about budget traveling is detailed in this book."

—*The Chicago Sun-Times*

"Value-packed, unbeatable, accurate, and comprehensive."

—*Los Angeles Times*

Let's Go

Washington, D.C.

2001

Terry E-E Chang editor

researcher-writers
Randy Gomes
John Mazza
Morgan Rodman

Thea Sakata map editor
Luke Marion photographer

Macmillan

HELPING LET'S GO
If you want to share your discoveries, suggestions, or corrections, please drop us a line. We read every piece of correspondence, whether a postcard, a 10-page email, or a coconut. Please note that mail received after May 2001 may be too late for the 2002 book, but will be kept for future editions. **Address mail to:**

> Let's Go: Washington, D.C.
> 67 Mount Auburn Street
> Cambridge, MA 02138
> USA

Visit Let's Go at **http://www.letsgo.com,** or send email to:

> feedback@letsgo.com
> Subject: "Let's Go: Washington, D.C."

In addition to the invaluable travel advice our readers share with us, many are kind enough to offer their services as researchers or editors. Unfortunately, our charter enables us to employ only currently enrolled Harvard students.

Published in Great Britain 2001 by Macmillan, an imprint of Macmillan Publishers Ltd, 25 Eccleston Place, London, SW1W 9NF, Basingstoke and Oxford.
Associated companies throughout the world
www.macmillan.com

Maps by David Lindroth copyright © 2001, 2000, 1999, 1998, 1997, 1996, 1995, 1994, 1993, 1992, 1991, 1990, 1989, 1988 by St. Martin's Press.

Published in the United States of America by St. Martin's Press.

ISBN: 0-333-90153-3
First edition
10 9 8 7 6 5 4 3 2 1

Let's Go: Washington, D.C. is written by Let's Go Publications, 67 Mount Auburn Street, Cambridge, MA 02138, USA.

Let's Go® and the thumb logo are trademarks of Let's Go, Inc.
Printed in the USA on recycled paper with biodegradable soy ink.

ABOUT LET'S GO

FORTY-ONE YEARS OF WISDOM

As a new millennium arrives, *Let's Go: Europe*, now in its 41st edition and translated into seven languages, reigns as the world's bestselling international travel guide. For over four decades, travelers criss-crossing the Continent have relied on *Let's Go* for inside information on the hippest backstreet cafes, the most pristine secluded beaches, and the best routes from border to border. In the last 20 years, our rugged researchers have stretched the frontiers of backpacking and expanded our coverage into Asia, Africa, Australia, and the Americas. This year, we've introduced a new city guide series with titles to San Francisco and our hometown, Boston. Now, our seven city guides feature sharp photos, more maps, and an overall more user-friendly design. We've also returned to our roots with the inaugural edition of *Let's Go: Western Europe*.

It all started in 1960 when a handful of well-traveled students at Harvard University handed out a 20-page mimeographed pamphlet offering a collection of their tips on budget travel to passengers on student charter flights to Europe. The following year, in response to the instant popularity of the first volume, students traveling to Europe researched the first full-fledged edition of *Let's Go: Europe*, a pocket-sized book featuring honest, practical advice, witty writing, and a decidedly youthful slant on the world. Throughout the 60s and 70s, our guides reflected the times. In 1969 we taught travelers how to get from Paris to Prague on "no dollars a day" by singing in the street. In the 80s and 90s, we looked beyond Europe and North America and set off to all corners of the earth. Meanwhile, we focused in on the world's most exciting urban areas to produce in-depth, fold-out map guides. Our new guides bring the total number of titles to 51, each infused with the spirit of adventure and voice of opinion that travelers around the world have come to count on. But some things never change: our guides are still researched, written, and produced entirely by students who know first-hand how to see the world on the cheap.

HOW WE DO IT

Each guide is completely revised and thoroughly updated every year by a well-traveled set of nearly 300 students. Every spring, we recruit over 200 researchers and 90 editors to overhaul every book. After several months of training, researcher-writers hit the road for seven weeks of exploration, from Anchorage to Adelaide, Estonia to El Salvador, Iceland to Indonesia. Hired for their rare combination of budget travel sense, writing ability, stamina, and courage, these adventurous travelers know that train strikes, stolen luggage, food poisoning, and marriage proposals are all part of a day's work. Back at our offices, editors work from spring to fall, massaging copy written on Himalayan bus rides into witty, informative prose. A student staff of typesetters, cartographers, publicists, and managers keeps our lively team together. In September, the collected efforts of the summer are delivered to our printer, who turns them into books in record time, so that you have the most up-to-date information available for your vacation. Even as you read this, work on next year's editions is well underway.

WHY WE DO IT

We don't think of budget travel as the last recourse of the destitute; we believe that it's the only way to travel. Living cheaply and simply brings you closer to the people and places you've been saving up to visit. Our books will ease your anxieties and answer your questions about the basics—so you can get off the beaten track and explore. Once you learn the ropes, we encourage you to put *Let's Go* down now and then to strike out on your own. You know as well as we that the best discoveries are often those you make yourself. When you find something worth sharing, please drop us a line. We're Let's Go Publications, 67 Mount Auburn St., Cambridge, MA 02138, USA (email: feedback@letsgo.com). For more info, visit our website, www.letsgo.com.

Contents

 accommodations 269

services 291

living in d.c. 281

index 298

maps 305

✚ Hospital	✈ Airport	🏨 Hotel/Hostel	▲ Mountain	
Police	🚌 Bus Station	Camping		Park
✉ Post Office	🚂 Train Station	Food & Drink		
ⓘ Tourist Office	Ⓜ METRO STATION	♪ Arts & Entertainment		Beach
$ Bank	⚓ Ferry Landing	Nightlife		
Embassy/Consulate	✝ Church	Services		Water
▪ Sight or Point of Interest	✡ Synagogue	◯ Sights labeled in key		
P Parking	Mosque	Gravesites of Interest		The Let's Go thumb always points NORTH.
Theater	🏛 Museum	⸺ Pedestrian Zone		

HOW TO USE THIS BOOK

I love to go to Washington—if only to be near my money.
  —Bob Hope

You said it, Bob. Chances are, Washington D.C. already has enough of your money—why give it more? The expensive cuisine and four-star suites can melt away a budget traveler's pocket change only too fast. But there's no need to crack open the nest egg. Instead, whip out this little savvy guide for good times on mere nickels 'n' dimes.

Discover D.C. scopes the city's **top 20 sights** and furnishes the reader with **suggested itineraries** and **walking tours.** Take a crash-course in Washington's history, art, and culture by skimming the **Life & Times** chapter. **Planning Your Trip** reveals the 411 on preparing documents for your urban trek, from visas and plane tickets to bank cards and insurance. Those planning to shack up in Washington will find tips on job and apartment hunting in the **Living in D.C.** chapter.

After you've landed on District turf, **Once in D.C.** dishes the dirty on each of the city's neighborhoods, deciphers the urban streetplan, and spells out the nitty-gritty on maneuvering the Metro. The **Sights, Museums, Shopping, Food & Drink, Nightlife,** and **Accommodations** chapters are all divvyed up by neighborhood; listings are also broken down by type and by price. The **Daytripping** chapter suggests choice weekend getaways to beaches and historic alcoves in Maryland, Virginia, and Delaware.

If you want to call a taxi, groom your poodle, lift weights, or sun at a fake 'n' bake salon; the **Service Directory** has got your vital digits. The **map appendix** clapped onto the end of the book plots out all the neighborhoods—replete with icons for hotels, museums, monuments, restaurants, bars, and subway stops.

Keep your eyes peeled, too, for **Inside Secrets.** These irreverent gems boxed in black will give you the scoop on senator wateringholes, singles' pick-up joints, all-night raves, paintballing jungles, indigenous food, D.C. vogue, and more. They will help you make friends and influence people. No, not quite. But at least, no one will deem you gauche in the ways of the District. Absolute necessities are highlighted in white **Essentials** sidebars found on right-hand pages.

Scattered through this guide are also listings branded with a ▨. These are the creme de la creme of Budgetland. Veer towards the ▨'s for affordable indulgences, and you'll never go hungry again.

And remember, anything you can't find is probably in the **Index.**

RESEARCHER-WRITERS

Randy Gomes   *Washington, D.C. and environs*

From yuppie vogue to senator spotting, from police scandals to warehouse raves—this slick gumshoe with the mad reporting skills scooped *all* of Washington's dirty hidden mysteries, creating the *Inside Secrets* gems you hold in your hand right now. Never one to rest for long, he covered "cultchah" by day and tracked down the hippest hotspots at night. By strategically flashing his pearly whites, Randy tricked his way past the velvet ropes into nightclubs and shows all over Georgetown and Dupont Circle. Randy's copy was awaited with delight back in the office, for we knew it contained not only mountains of razor-sharp research, but also devastatingly clever prose keeping us entertained through the long hours. A sharp eye, smartly sarcastic wit, and mod fashion sense to-die-for; Randy delightfully skewered the nightlife, art, and theatre scenes of D.C.

John Mazza   *Daytrips throughout MD, DE, and VA*

Relentlessly pursued by brazen Southern belles through several states, John used his rugby skills to dodge cheek-pinching grandmums and other would-be femme fatales. Along with charming everything below the Mason-Dixon line, John relived Civil War skirmishes at Manassas and Fredericksburg, feasted on crabcakes along the Bawlmer shores, and mudstomped through colonial Williamsburg. We set John on difficult tasks: a 6-week-long daytrip, a whirlwind tour of colonial American history, and a hunt for the smallest of islands along Maryland's shore. And John proved more than man enough for these challenges, producing clever bits of travel art from dusk to dawn, as he came, saw, and conquered town after town.

Morgan Rodman   *Washington D.C. and environs*

Morgan, our homegrown Tulsa boy *cum* international man of mystery, survived a blistering hot Washington summer surrounded by a cosmopolitan posse of interns. In his sparkling prose, Morgan went house on the Mall's marbled museums and galleries, sampled the ethnic delights of Adams-Morgan, survived Anacostia, and rocked out in the U District. Morgan, through his Native American roots, brought a careful, sensitive perspective to our capital city. He went from politico-ridden Capitol Hill to hipster Adams-Morgan to the more dangerous area around the Southeast without blinking an eye, unfailingly sending us copy so good it blinded the editors around us.

ACKNOWLEDGMENTS

To my whip-smart, 100%-pure fabulous writers—John, Morgan, and Randy: for all your grueling legwork and wicked good prose, I am forever indebted. It was a joy working with such talent. Bravo, boys! I applaud you with all my heart.

To Alice, my managing editor and cross-referencing demon: thank you a thousand times over for your hilarious dry wit, red ink, and unrelenting faith in this book.

To Thea, map goddess: a giant thumbpick for all your hard work, mad spatial skills, and stylin' (real) slim shadies. Now when our readers say, "let's go," they know how to go.

To the ever-nocturnal, well-tanned patrons of the 24hr. Café de la Cité—Val, Brady, Lucy, John, Mel G., Olivia, and Nora: long live caffeinated insanity, tone-deaf sing-a-long, and the mystical derrière-stabbing chicken cow.

A very special thanks to the life-savers who put the final polish on the chrome: Kevin, Aarup, Anup, Cordell, Val, Nate, Kristen, Kaitlin, Beth, Julie, Amy, Vicky, Jeff, Marc, Kate D., Bede, Chris, and all at 67 Mount Auburn.

Tomo, you were far away in Africa this summer, but your letters and postcards kept me afloat with the promise of your return.

To Uyen-Khanh, my purple-streaked friend, you're an angel for burning the midnight oil with me. What a kRaZy time it's been, girl, since we met way-back-when in Cali. You're the wind beneath my wings, sweetie.

To Mom, Dad, Megan, and Allie, I wouldn't be anywhere without you. I love and miss you so very much.

Editor
Terry Chang
Managing Editor
Alice Farmer
Map Editor
Thea Sakata

Publishing Director
Kaya Stone
Editor-in-Chief
Kate McCarthy
Production Manager
Melissa Rudolph
Cartography Manager
John Fiore
Editorial Managers
Alice Farmer, Ankur Ghosh, Aarup Kubal, Anup Kubal
Financial Manager
Bede Sheppard
Low-Season Manager
Melissa Gibson
Marketing & Publicity Managers
Olivia L. Cowley, Esti Iturralde
New Media Manager
Jonathan Dawid
Personnel Manager
Nicholas Grossman
Photo Editor
Dara Cho
Production Associates
Sanjay Mavinkurve, Nicholas Murphy, Rosa Rosalez, Matthew Daniels, Rachel Mason, Daniel Visel
(re)Designer
Matthew Daniels
Office Coordinators
Sarah Jacoby, Chris Russell

Director of Advertising Sales
Cindy Rodriguez
Senior Advertising Associates
Adam Grant, Rebecca Rendell
Advertising Artwork Editor
Palmer Truelson

President
Andrew M. Murphy
General Manager
Robert B. Rombauer
Assistant General Manager
Anne E. Chisholm

IAM L LOCKHART ·
SEPH M SALVO ·
ANDREYKA Jr ·
NT R CAPODANNO ·
NIER ·
LARENCE E DRAKES ·
R ·
D LJ GAUTHIER ·
N L GRANT ·
GELS · KEITH F SHA
NNIE W KELLEY ·
O GARZA LEAL
AMIN H MAS
TCHELL ·
AMES C M
RLES A P
LLARD
BERT V
III ·
RENCE D
RNANDEZ
OWNING
GEORGE W H

RAY COLLINS
JOHN M HAS
DAVID E RAL
BARRY H WIL
DAVID E GOS
RONALD E PE
WILLIAM A W
JEDH C BARK
TROY W COK
THOMAS F D
ERLIN C STE
HARD A JA
ERT A KED
E HARR
TH L PL
TS W R
CHA
SW
W

Discover D.C.

This is a city where romance means wonks in love discussing policy late into the night.
—*The New York Times*

Washington's strange experiment—an infant nation scratching together a capital—has matured into one of America's most celebrated cities. Its marbled monuments and museums suck in millions of visitors for a brush with lunar landers or a peek at the president.

Political Washington hovers in a haze churned by endless press conferences and power lunches, potent memorials and presidential intrigues. Senators and spin doctors conjure magic, rhetoric, and policy as lobbyists and journalists pay court. D.C.'s carnival-like milieu reveals the vigorous—and often scandalous—child of American democracy.

Outside the federal enclave, Washington's neighborhoods flaunt cultural delights. There's more to the Beltway than double-talk and more along Pennsylvania Ave. than the White House. Dupont Circle showcases easels of the masters and budding artists, while Adams-Morgan embraces a banquet of multi-ethnic offerings. High culture bows and pirouettes on the Kennedy Center stage almost every night, while local ska and punk groups rock their youth audience in the U Street grotto. Political powerhouse, bloated metropolis, and vigorous urban center all rolled into one, D.C. thrives as a highly schizophrenic modern city.

WHEN TO GO

Washington in the **summer** is notoriously hot—so hot that a French foreign minister in Washington in the 1890s attributed his despair to the summer weather and promptly killed himself. Despite the hellish heat, millions of tourists descend on Washington in the summer to visit the monuments and museums, stroll through miles of green parks,

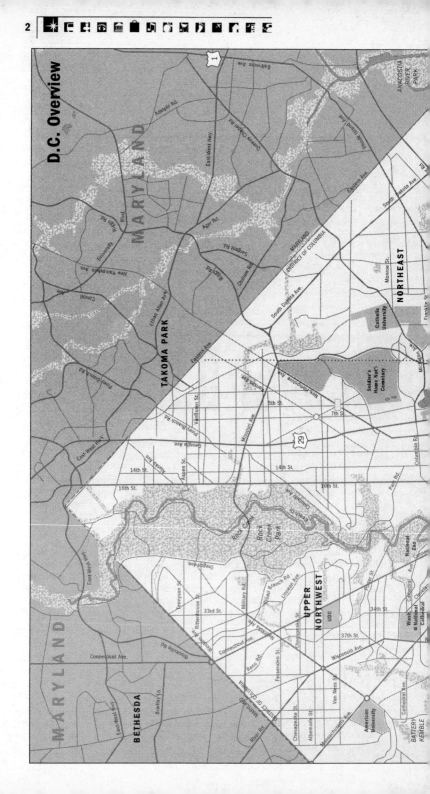

D.C. Overview

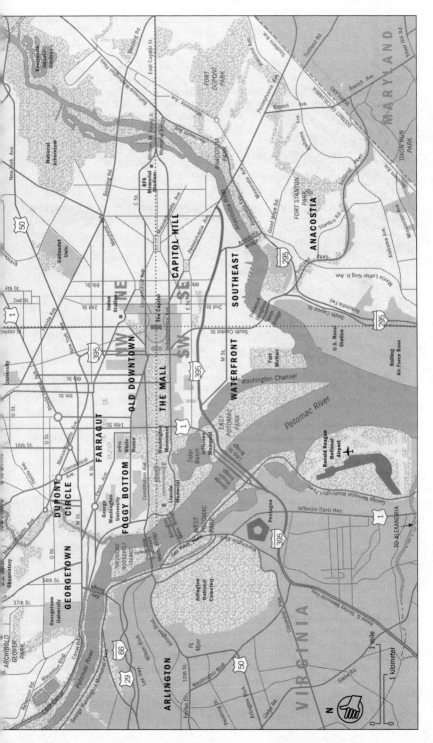

the on dopedc

d.c. trivia

Metro. D.C.'s Metro has 522 escalators, more than any other transit system in the world.

Cosmopolitan Capital. A truly international city, D.C. brings in over 20,000 diplomats and staff from 170 countries.

Libraries. D.C. houses the Library of Congress, the world's largest library, with 532 mi. of bookshelves.

Education. The D.C. area has the highest percentages of adults with graduate degrees (17%) and undergraduate degrees (39%) in the USA.

The Outdoors. Within D.C., there are 50mi. of hiking, biking, and horse trails by streams, woods, and ravines.

Nature. Chesapeake Bay contains the world's largest estuary, with 2,500 plant species by 7,000 mi. of tidal shoreline.

Relics. The George Washington Masonic National Temple displays the world's largest hand-woven Persian rug.

Cold War Leftovers. The Taylor Model Basin contains the World's Longest Bathtub, once used to test submarines. Today, Olympic whitewater canoeists train in the mammoth tub.

d.c. facts

Population: 4,563,123

Sunny Days in a Year: 207

Average Snowfall: 16in.

Average commute time: 28.8min.

Recent unemployment rate: 2.6%

and witness the hundreds of free concerts, festivals, and parades going on in June, July, and August. To avoid the summer's crowds, heat, and high hotel rates, you can visit D.C. in the offseason, although you'll also miss out on all of summer's outdoor freebies and gala events. For a complete listing of Washington's festivals and celebrations year-round, see the **Calendar of Events**, p. 10. Notable events include the **National Cherry Blossom Festival** (Mar. 28-Apr. 9) and the gala **Fourth of July** celebration.

CLIMATE

Average high and low temperatures (in degrees Fahrenheit) and the average yearly rainfall (in inches):

MONTH	TEMPERATURE	PRECIPITATION
January	43°F/28°F	2.8 in.
April	67°F/46°F	2.8 in.
July	88°F/70°F	4.0 in.
October	69°F/50°F	3.0 in.

THE MANY FACES OF D.C.

POLITICAL D.C.

Follow the trail of starched shirts and press passes and you'll stumble into the rabbithole of D.C.'s political wonderland. Want to see democracy in action? Most committee hearings in **The Capitol** (p. 48) and the **House and Senate Office Buildings** (p. 50) are open to the public. Just check out *The Washington Post's* **Today in Congress** for listings of rooms. Weigh justice in the marble grandeur of the **Supreme Court** (p. 51) during oral argument sessions. Don't neglect the **White House,** either, and if you cross your fingers, you might catch a rare glimpse of the President, surrounded by a bevy of aides. Get spread-eagled at the **FBI,** gawk as millions of dollars roll by at the **Bureau of Engraving and Printing,** and get vicarious over the luscious diplomatic mansions along **Embassy Row.** For tips on schmoozing with politicos and their ilk during their off hours, check out **inside secrets to senator spotting,** p. 188.

HIGHBROW D.C.

Art connoisseurs and dilettantes alike won't miss the **Dupont Circle Galleries** (p. 82) on R St., as well as the **Phillips** (p. 122), **Corcoran** (p. 119), **Renwick Galleries** (p. 123). Of course, the **National Gallery of Art** (p. 116) and the **Hirshhorn Museum and Sculpture Garden** (p. 114) are no-brainers. Theater buffs soak in an earful of Elizabethan-speak at the **Folger Shakespeare**

Library (p. 53) on certain midsummer nights. For more modern theater, get thee to the **14th St. District** (p. 141), where small repertory companies will delight you with their experimental antics. At the **Kennedy Center** (p. 142), the **Washington Opera** (p. 140), the **Washington Ballet** (p. 144), and the **National Symphony Orchestra** impress those with a love for classical music.

COUNTER CULTURE D.C.

So you say you're anti-establishment and aren't quite sure how to cut it in the yuppiezoid capital of the universe? No sweat. **U St.** (p. 138) has the answer. If you're grungy and **alternative,** rock out at **9:30 Club, 2:K:9,** or the **Black Cat.** Hardcore **punks** can kick it at the **Velvet Lounge.** If you were born wielding glowsticks with colorful ponybeads at your wrists, roll right on over to **Nation** (p. 139) by the Navy Yard for **Buzz** Fridays, raverkid. See **inside secrets to raves,** p. 184. If you're a sadomasochist with a penchant for leather, whip up a good time at **Club de Sade** (p. 191), which would sate the naughtiest marquis.

WILD THING D.C.

If the birds and the beasts and the little fishies in the sea make your heart sing, stampede toward the **National Zoo** (p. 89) and the **National Aquarium** (p. 73) where they'll do it like they do it on the Discovery Channel. The **Reston Zoo** is a bit further out, in neighboring Vienna, VA, but it comes with such exotic creatures as giraffes and camels (p. 108).

D.C. BRASS

More than any other American city, D.C. honors military men and women. Within the district, be sure to pay respects at the solemn yet elegant **Vietnam Veterans Memorial** (p. 56) or contemplate amid the cascading fountains and flags of the **Navy Memorial** (p. 71). At the **Navy Yard** (p. 93), scope out the **Marine Corps Historical Museum** and **Navy Museum.** Climb all over the destroyer **U.S.S. Barry,** peer into the **submarines,** and ponder the surplus shells of the **Little Boy** and the **Fat Man** atomic bombs. Further out, **Manassas National Battlefield Park** (p. 108) holds reenactments of the bloody Civil War battle where brother fought brother, while **Arlington National Cemetery** (p. 97) marks the graves of America's fallen soldiers.

GREEN D.C.

Pruned or wild, vegetation springs up everywhere in the District. In fact, studies rate Washington as the greenest metropolitan region in the United States. The **US Botanical Gardens** (p. 50) grows exotic foliage right in front of the Capitol, while **Constitution Gardens** (p. 55) harbors a lovely weeping willow-draped island. In the Northeast, the **National Arboretum** (p. 95) covers over 44 acres with foreign and domestic flora ranging from crapemyrtles to bonsai, while nearby waterlily pads coat the nearby **Kenilworth Aquatic Gardens** (p. 95). Hikers will relish the leafy tree-shaded trails along **Roosevelt Island** (p. 100) and **Rock Creek Park** (p. 85).

AFRICAN-AMERICAN D.C.

As a port city between two plantation states, Washington brought over slaves in the 18th-century. During the next two centuries, free African-Americans and slaves played a vital role in shaping the district. Historical sites in African-American D.C. include **Lincoln Park** and the **Martin Luther King Jr. Library** (p. 67). In Georgetown, visit **Herring Hill** (p. 77), the **Mount Zion Methodist Church** (p. 78), and the **Mount Zion Cemetery. Shaw U,** once the stomping grounds of such African-American luminaries as **Langston Hughes** and **Jean Toomer,** houses **Howard University** (p. 91), originially founded in 1867 for newly freed slaves and now home of the **African-American Civil War Memorial** (p. 91).

Center of Town

Flower

Dumbarton Oaks Mansion

THE TOP 15 OF MUST-SEE D.C.

15. U St. (p. 138). Feeling edgy? For late-night moshing and mayhem, sashay over to the U St. scene, D.C.'s mecca for punk and alternative rock.

14. Embassy Row (p. 83). It's fun to traipse down this grand avenue, lined with embassies and diplomatic mansions, and pick out and identify foreign countries by the flags fluttering overhead. The Indonesian Embassy and the Islamic Center are particularly exquisite.

13. MCI Center (p. 68). This 20,000-seat arena is home to the NBA's Washington Wizards, the NHL's Washington Capitals, the WNBA's Washington Mystics, and the NCAA's Georgetown Hoyas. Sports fans, take a guided tour through the team locker rooms, then stop by the National Sports Gallery to record your own play-by-play sportscaster video.

12. Mount Vernon (p. 106). Home and plantation of the nation's first president, George Washington, Mount Vernon lathers on the charm of old school Southern comfort. At the Mount Vernon Museum, ogle such carefully preserved relics as Georgie's very own toothbrush.

11. US Holocaust Memorial Museum (p. 120). A vivid and chilling reminder of the atrocities visited on the Jews by the Nazis during World War II.

10. National Gallery of Art (p. 116). da Vinci. Renior. Fra Angelico. Vermeer. Rembrandt. Rubens. Dali. Calder. Picasso. Matisse. Miro. Man Ray. Giacometti. Rothko. Magritte. Need we say more? The 6-acre sculpture garden, opened only a couple of years ago, is a delight.

9. Kennedy Center (p. 142). Home to the spectacular National Symphony Orchestra, the Washington Opera, and the Washington Ballet. The Millenium Stage concert series holds free performances every day at 6pm.

8. National Zoo (p. 89). The much-loved pandas, Hsing-Hsing and Ling-Ling, have regrettably passed away. The biggest draws now at the zoo are the Reptile Discovery Center, the Great Ape House, and the Elephant and Giraffe House.

7. Arlington National Cemetery (p. 97). 612 acres of rolling green hills hold the bodies of Purple Heart and Silver Star veterans, from five-star generals to unidentified soldiers. Visit the Tomb of the Unknowns, as well as the gravesites of such celebrities as the Kennedys.

6. National Archives (p. 70). Pack rats will think that they've died and gone to heaven. The archives have everything you can dream up and more. Junk treasures include a portrait of Nixon painted on a grain of rice and JFK's doodles during the Cuban Missile Crisis. You'll also find such national treasures as the Declaration of Independence, the Constitution, and the Bill of Rights.

5. Vietnam Veterans Memorial (p. 56). The polished black stone wall contains the names of the 58,214 Americans who died or are still missing in Vietnam. Visitors leave flowers and offerings, or take rubbings of the names from the Memorial.

4. Jefferson Memorial and the Tidal Basin (p. 58). Rimmed by cherry trees, this shrine to TJ overlooks the man-made Tidal Basin. Paddle around the serene artificial lake in a rented boat.

3. White House (p. 61). Home and headquarters of the American President. Take the visitors' tour through the East Wing, and sneak a peek at the Rose Garden which Jackie O. made famous.

2. Smithsonian Museums (p. 111). So much and so free. Our favorites: the Wright brothers' biplane at the National Air and Space Museum, the dino skeletons at the National Museum of Natural History, and Dorothy's red ruby slippers at the National Museum of American History. Art lovers will go house on the Freer Gallery, the Hirshhorn Museum and Sculpture Garden, and the African Art and Sackler Complex.

1. The Capitol (p. 48). Consider this splendid domed building the epicenter of American democracy. Inside, check out the House and Senate Chambers, Statuary Hall, and the Crypt containing Washington's empty tomb. Out front, the US Botanical Gardens brims with exotic flora.

SUGGESTED ITINERARIES

Check out our day-by-day breakdown of D.C. below. Or, if you're feeling energetic, try our walking tours (p. 9). And don't be afraid to strike out on your own!

THREE DAYS

DAY ONE: CAPITOL HILL & MONUMENTS. Kick off your Washington pilgrimage with a sweep of **Capitol Hill.** Start your morning at the **Capitol** (p. 48) building, perhaps eavesdropping on a committee hearing if you're curious. On your way out, stroll briskly through the **US Botanical Gardens** (p. 50). Then, stomp on over to either the **Supreme Court** (p. 42) or the **Library of Congress** (p. 43) to marvel at more marble. A bit farther north, window-shop briefly at **Union Station** (p. 45) before lunching at its international fast food court. Take the Metro from Union Station to the Smithsonian stop. From there, hit up the monuments in the afternoon. Begin with the **Washington Monument** (p. 46) and its famous **Reflecting Pool** (p. 47), and the leafy **Constitution Gardens** (p. 47) nearby. From there, head west toward the **Vietnam Veterans Memorial** (p. 47), and then south toward the **Lincoln Memorial** (p. 48), the **Korean War Veterans Memorial** (p. 49), and the **Franklin Delano Roosevelt Memorial** (p. 50). Cool off in the shade of the **cherry trees** lining the **Tidal Basin** (p. 51) by the Jefferson Memorial. For dinner on the cheap, feast on all-you-can-eat pasta at **Il Radiccho** (p. 153) along Pennsylvania Ave., or tapas and stuffed plantains at the **Banana Cafe and Piano Bar** (p. 153) by Eastern Market.

DAY TWO: MALL & WATERFRONT. Get to the **Mall** (p. 111) early for a whirlwind museum tour. Start with the **National Gallery of Art** (p. 116) and its **sculpture garden.** Next, work your way down Madison Dr. with either the **National Museum of Natural History** (p. 113) or the **National Museum of American History** (p. 112). Lunch at any of the **Smithsonian Eateries** (p. 113). In the afternoon, take your pick between the **Freer Gallery** (p. 116), the **Sackler** (p. 115), the **National Museum of African Art** (p. 115), or the **Arts and Industries Building** (p. 115). The **Hirshhorn Museum and Sculpture Garden** (p. 114) or the **National Air and**

Dupont Circle Park

D.C. at Night

C&O Canal

Space Museum (p. 114) are definite visits. After you're thoroughly spent, head south to the Waterfront (p. 60) for a fresh crab and lobster dinner at the Wharf Seafood Market. In the summer, roam the fairs by the Gangplank Marina or board a river cruise for dancing, dining, and drinks.

DAY THREE: FOGGY BOTTOM & GEORGETOWN. Line up early to tour the White House (p. 61). Then, putz around Foggy Bottom at smaller sites such as the Renwick Gallery (p. 123), St. John's Church (p. 63), the American Red Cross (p. 64), or the Corcoran Gallery (p. 119). Be sure to drop in and roam around at the massive Kennedy Center (p. 66). As you're walking out, catch a glimpse of the notorious Watergate Complex (p. 66), a super-ugly monstrosity. For lunch, head over to Georgetown for quiche and cream-puffs at Cafe La Ruche (p. 168). Amble along the C&O Canal (p. 77) or board a canal boat for a floating tour. Shop the afternoon away at the Georgetown Park Mall (p. 132), schmooze with comely coeds at Georgetown University (p. 79), or visit historical sites in African-American Georgetown (US). Before dusk, head up to the Dumbarton Oaks Estate (p. 78) for a tour of the mansion and the gorgeous garden. If you're feeling particularly romantic, stroll around Lovers' Lane (p. 78) with a special someone. For dinner and entertainment, check out Blues Alley (p. 140) for cool jazz with Creole cuisine or any of Georgetown's tasty M St. restaurants.

FIVE DAYS

In addition to the previous three days, round out your itinerary with these regions:

DAY FOUR: OLD DOWNTOWN. Spend the morning visiting either the National Archives (p. 70), the FBI (p. 71), Ford's Theater (p. 72), or the National Aquarium (p. 73). Grab lunch to-go in the food court of the Ronald Reagan Building (p. 73) and eat near the fountains of Pershing Park. Or, you can do like the senators do, and lunch at the Old Ebbit Grill (see inside secrets to senator spotting, p. 188). Complete the afternoon by visiting the National Building Museum (p. 121). Dine along H St. in nearby Chinatown (p. 163) for spicy Asian fare. After dinner, head toward the nearby 14th St. Theater District (p. 141) to catch a Mamet play. Alternatively, go clubbing at such hot nightspots as Zei (p. 187) and Fado (p. 187).

DAY FIVE: ROCK CREEK PARK & DUPONT CIRCLE. Spend the morning hiking around leafy Rock Creek Park. Hop on the Metro to Dupont Circle and grab a Japanese Bento box lunch at Teaism (p. 166). Walk past the circle down Embassy Row and visit the Phillips Collection (p. 122) and the R and 21st St. galleries (p. 82). Dinner is to be had at any number of the culinary motherlode of ethnic eateries around the Circle. Gyrate the rest of the night away to techno at the ultra-sleek-and-très-mod club Dragonfly (p. 183).

SEVEN DAYS

In addition to the above, tack on these neighborhoods to explore:

DAY SIX: UPPER NORTHWEST & THE SOUTHEAST. Spend the morning in the Upper Northwest with the wild things at the National Zoo (p. 89). Lunch around the Woodley Park Metro stop. Then, metro it down to the Southeast for a tour of Barracks Row and the Navy Yard (p. 93). There, climb aboard the former torpedo-laden destroyer, the U.S.S. Barry. Dine in around Eastern Market (p. 161)—may we suggest crabcakes, an indigenous D.C. specialty?—before heading out to a concert or all-night rave at Nation (p. 139).

DAY SEVEN: ARLINGTON, ALEXANDRIA & FAIRFAX. At the buttcrack of dawn, catch the sunrise at Arlington National Cemetery (p. 97). Next, board the metro to visit the Pentagon (p. 99), the pinnacle of WWI and Cold War military bureaucracy and the world's largest office building. Next, take the Metro to the King St. stop in Old Town Alexandria (p. 103). There, visit historic homes and the shops along Washington and King Sts. Midday, feast on a slice of colonial pie or 18th-century stew at Gadsby's Tavern (p.

157) as costumed waiters in period dress serve you. Learn all about the Old Town on a 45-minute **Potomac Riverboat Tour** (p. 106) along the **Alexandria Waterfront.** Complete your day by touring **Mount Vernon** (p. 106), plantation home of **George Washington,** a short bus ride away from the Huntington Metro. Go home happy—'cuz you're spent, and Washington still isn't sure what kind of whirling dervish hit it.

WALKING TOURS

TOUR #1—MALLRATS (OR D.C. WITH KIDS)

A tour for: those with little ones or the perpetually young at heart. *Duration:* A day.

Start off from the **Smithsonian Metro** and head east along the Mall to the **Smithsonian Castle** (p. 115). The exterior of this big red castle and the surrounding garden are fun for tots, but don't go inside—the exhibits will surely bore your babies to sleep. Next, continue east toward the **Hirshhorn Sculpture Garden** (p. 114), whose large bronzes are perfect for running around and close looking. After the kids have burned some energy outdoors, they're ready to head indoors into the **National Air and Space Museum** (p. 114). **Rockets** and **planes** suspended in mid-air are a major draw, as is whatever film is playing the **IMAX theater.** Feeling hungry? Look no further but to the **National Air and Space Museum Flight Line Cafe,** with futuristic decor straight out of the Jetsons, for a cheap and nourishing buffet lunch. After resting up the legs and filling the tummy, cut northwest across the grassy Mall for the **National Museum of Natural History** (p. 113). Guaranteed hits here are the **dino skeletons,** the **moon rocks,** the outrageous bauble that is the **Hope Diamond,** and the **hands-on displays** in the **Discovery room.** Exit the **National Museum of Natural History** onto **Constitution Ave.** Walk west to cap off the day at **National Aquarium** (p. 73), the nation's first. There, kids will admire scary fish such as sharks, pirahnas, and eels. **Touchtanks** let kids get up close and personal with marine creatures such as **horseshoe crabs.**

TOUR #2—MONUMENTS BY MOONLIGHT

A tour for: couples, poets, incurable romantics, and vampires. For safety and plain old common sense, do not attempt this night tour alone. *Duration:* 3hr. See **Sights,** p. 47.

Pick an evening when the moon is full and bright for this nocturnal trek. Emerge from **Union Station** and walk around the semi-circle by the **Christopher Columbus Memorial Fountain** to **Delaware Ave.** Walk south down Delaware Ave., past the row of regal state flags. This path takes you alongside **Union Station Plaza,** a green, tree-lined patch of park. Continue straight toward the **Capitol.** Admire the tranquil dome, the **reflecting pool** which mirrors it, and the **Peace Monument** before it. Stroll west down the mall toward the glowing **Washington Monument.** Notice the interesting buildings on either side of the mall, including the **Smithsonian Castle** and the **National Gallery of Art.** The **Hirshhorn Sculpture Garden** is not open at this late hour, but you can faintly make out the dark figures by **Rodin** in the garden. Walk to the right of the monument and you can glimpse the White House and its Ellipse in the distance, as well as federal buildings blinking north of the Mall. Passing by the Washington Monument, head west for the glimmering **Reflecting Pool.** The green landscape is full of trees and quiet remembrance. Steal a private romantic moment in the willowy **Constitution Gardens,** beside the small pond, luminous in moonlight. The black walls of the **Vietnam Veterans Memorial** are stark and heavy with emotion. Other statues memorializing the Vietnam War include the **Three Servicemen** sculpture and the **Vietnam Women's Memorial.** Rest on the steps of the **Lincoln Memorial** and stare back at the Washington Monument and the Capitol for a breathtaking view. Amble down Daniel French Drive toward the **Tidal Basin** to luxuriate under the cherry trees and to glimpse the **Jefferson Memorial** across the water. End the tour at the **Smithsonian Metro stop.**

TOUR #3—GAY BOY'S NIGHT OUT IN DUPONT CIRCLE

A tour for: the pretty boys & co. **Duration:** *from dusk till dawn.*

Catch dinner at **Lauriol Plaza** (p. 164) to prepare for a raunchy good time. Warm up at 10pm at the **Fireplace** (p. 191), order drinks by 10:30pm from one of **Omega**'s (p. 191) four bars, catch the tail end of drag lip-synching by 11pm at **Mr. P's** (p. 191), and hit up the ever-popular **J.R.'s** (p. 190) by 11:30pm. Finish off the evening at **J.R's** on Mondays and Tuesdays, at **Club Chaos** (p. 191) on Wednesdays (Lesbian Night), at **Badlands** (p. 190) or **Club Chaos** on Thursdays through Saturdays, and at the **Lizard Lounge** (p. 191) on Saturdays. If all that dancing has worked up an appetite, **Afterwords Café** (p. 166) invites late-night revelers to indulge in white chocolate mochas and munchables until 3am Sunday through Thursday, or 4am Friday and Saturday.

CALENDAR OF EVENTS

JANUARY
Martin Luther King's Birthday (☎ 708-1005), observed Jan. 15. Wreaths laid, "I Have a Dream" speech recited at the Lincoln Memorial. Choirs, speakers, etc. Free.

FEBRUARY
Chinese New Year Parade (☎ 638-1041), early Feb. Metro: Gallery Place. Firecrackers, lions, drums, and dragons. Free.

Abraham Lincoln's Birthday (☎ 619-7222), observed Feb. 12. Laying down of wreaths and recitation of the Gettysburg address at the Lincoln Memorial. Free.

George Washington's Birthday Parade (☎ (703) 838-4200), Feb. 19 at 1pm, through Old Town Alexandria. Pageantry and excitement. Free.

Mount Vernon Open House (☎ (703) 780-2000), Feb. 19. Free admission to Mount Vernon, fife and drums on the green, and the obligatory wreath-laying.

MARCH
St. Patrick's Day Parade, Mar. 17, downtown on Constitution Ave. NW. A celebration of all things green. Dancers, bands, bagpipes, and floats. Free.

Smithsonian Kite Festival (☎ 357-3244), late March on the Mall. Watch kite designers compete for prizes on the Washington Monument grounds. Call for exact date.

APRIL
National Cherry Blossom Festival (☎ 547-1500), Mar. 25-Apr. 8, all over town. Parade, fireworks, fashion show, ball, concerts, and Japanese Lantern Lighting Ceremony.

White House Spring Garden Tours (☎ 456-2200), mid-Apr. at the White House Gardens. Free music, flowers, and festivities highlight the blooming gardens.

White House Easter Egg Roll (☎ 456-2200), Apr. 24, on the White House South Lawn. For kids 6 and under. Famous morning egg roll brings out the President and the press.

American College Theater Festival (☎ 416-8000), Apr. 23-29 at the Kennedy Center. A jury chooses the best college shows from around the country. All shows are free.

MAY
Department of Defense/Joint Services Open House (☎ (301) 568-5995 or (301) 981-4424), mid-May, at Andrews Air Force Base, Camp Springs, MD. Fabulous air aerobatics.

National Symphony Orchestra Memorial Day Weekend Concert (☎ 467-4600), May 27 at 8pm on the West Lawn of the Capitol. Free.

Memorial Day Ceremonies at Arlington Cemetery (☎ (703) 607-8052), May 28. Wreaths at J.F.K.'s tomb and the Tomb of the Unknown Soldier. Services in Memorial Amphitheater.

Memorial Day Ceremonies at the Vietnam Veterans Memorial (☎ 619-7222), May 28. Wreath-laying, speeches, bands, and a keynote address.

Memorial Day Jazz Festival (☎(703) 838-4844), May 28 from noon-8pm, in Old Town Alexandria. Local big bands swing all afternoon. Free.

JUNE
Dupont-Kalorama Museum Walk Day (☎667-0441), 1st weekend in June. 10 museums north of Dupont Circle seek publicity. Music, tours, food, crafts, etc.
Dance Africa D.C. (☎269-1600), 1st week of June at Dance Place. Traditional dance, food.
Festival of American Folklife (☎357-2700), June 27-July 1 and July 4-8, on the Mall. Huge Smithsonian fair demonstrates the crafts, customs, food, and music of D.C.

JULY
Virginia Scottish Games (☎(703) 912-1943), late July, in Alexandria, VA, on the grounds of Episcopal High School. 2-day annual Scottish festival is one of America's largest.
Hispanic Festival (☎835-1555), in late July at the Washington Monument. Food, music, and dance from 40 Latin American nations. Free.
Latin and Jazz Festival (☎331-9404), in July or Aug., at Freedom Plaza. Continuous live jazz and ethnic food by the people who organize the Duke Ellington Birthday tribute.

AUGUST
National Frisbee Festival (☎(301) 645-5043), late Aug. on the Washington Monument Grounds. The largest non-competitive frisbee festival in the US.

SEPTEMBER
African Cultural Festival, early Sept., at Freedom Plaza. African cooking, music.
D.C. Blues Festival (☎828-3028), early Sept., at the Carter-Barron Amphitheater near Rock Creek Park. Blues, folk, twang, wail, and moan. Free.
Kennedy Center Open House (☎467-4600), early Sept. A 1-day medley of classical, jazz, folk, and ethnic music, dance, drama, and film from D.C. performers. Call for date.
Adams-Morgan Day (☎332-3292), Sept. 9. Live music on 3 stages, stuff for sale, and a kaleidoscope of ethnic food. Free.

OCTOBER
White House Fall Garden Tours (☎456-2200), mid-Oct. Like the spring garden tours.

NOVEMBER
Veteran's Day Ceremonies (☎ (703) 607-8052), Nov. 11, around Arlington Cemetery. Solemn ceremony with military bands.

DECEMBER
Kennedy Center Holiday Celebration (☎467-4600), throughout Dec. Free concerts include choral, chamber, "Tubachristmas," and a sing-along to Handel's Messiah.
National Christmas Tree Lighting/Pageant of Peace (☎619-7222), mid-Dec. to Jan. 1, on the Ellipse south of the White House. Christmas trees, menorahs, music, yule logs.
Washington National Cathedral Christmas Celebration and Services (☎537-6247), Dec. 24-25 at the Cathedral. Christmas service and music.
White House Christmas Candlelight Tours (☎208-1631), 3 days after Christmas. The President's extravagant Christmas decorations go on display.

NATIONAL HOLIDAYS

DATE	HOLIDAY	DATE	HOLIDAY
January 1	New Year's Day	September 3	Labor Day
January 15	Martin Luther King Day	October 8	Columbus Day
February 19	Presidents Day	November 11	Veterans Day
May 28	Memorial Day	November 29	Thanksgiving Day
July 4	Independence Day	December 25	Christmas Day

Pet a bottom dweller (like a horseshoe crab) in the
National Aquarium touchpools. Feedings at 2pm. (p. 73)

F St.

M METRO CENTER

10th St.

Ford's Theatre

✉

Old Post Office

M FEDERAL TRIANGLE

5

finish

4

Madison Dr.

14th St.

15th St.

Let the kids burn off some extra energy running
around the garden of the **Smithsonian Castle.** (p. 115)

ylvan eatre

The

1

M SMITHSONIAN

start

C St.

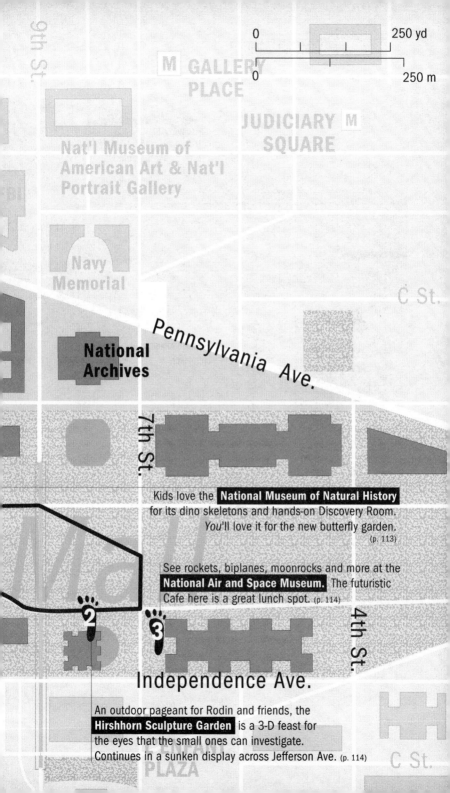

0 250 yd
0 250 m

M GALLERY PLACE

JUDICIARY M SQUARE

Nat'l Museum of American Art & Nat'l Portrait Gallery

9th St.

Navy Memorial

C St.

Pennsylvania Ave.

National Archives

7th St.

Kids love the **National Museum of Natural History** for its dino skeletons and hands-on Discovery Room. *You*'ll love it for the new butterfly garden. (p. 113)

See rockets, biplanes, moonrocks and more at the **National Air and Space Museum.** The futuristic Cafe here is a great lunch spot. (p. 114)

4th St.

Mall

2

3

Independence Ave.

An outdoor pageant for Rodin and friends, the **Hirshhorn Sculpture Garden** is a 3-D feast for the eyes that the small ones can investigate. Continues in a sunken display across Jefferson Ave. (p. 114)

PLAZA

C St.

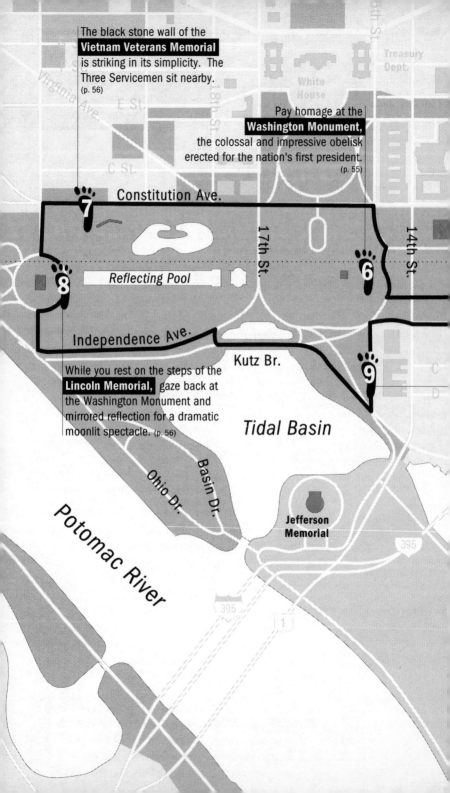

The black stone wall of the **Vietnam Veterans Memorial** is striking in its simplicity. The Three Servicemen sit nearby. (p. 56)

Pay homage at the **Washington Monument,** the colossal and impressive obelisk erected for the nation's first president. (p. 55)

Constitution Ave.

7

Virginia Ave.

E St.

C St.

18th St.

White House

Treasury Dept.

6th St.

Reflecting Pool

17th St.

14th St.

8

6

Independence Ave.

Kutz Br.

9

While you rest on the steps of the **Lincoln Memorial,** gaze back at the Washington Monument and mirrored reflection for a dramatic moonlit spectacle. (p. 56)

Tidal Basin

Ohio Dr.

Basin Dr.

C

D

Jefferson Memorial

Potomac River

395

395

1

start
COLUMBUS
CIRCLE Ⓜ

Wish upon a well at the **Christopher Columbus Memorial Fountain.**

Although the **Hirshhorn Sculpture Garden** is closed at this ungodly hour, you can still sneak a peek at the Maillol and Matisse figures. (p.114)

Traverse **Union Station Plaza,** a small, grassy pocket-park. (p. 53)

Pennsylvania Ave.

Louisiana Ave.

Delaware Ave.

Madison Dr.

Capitol Building

Ⓜ SMITHSONIAN

inish

Maryland Ave.

Independence Ave.

New Jersey Ave.

South Capitol St.

The **Constitution Gardens** will sweep you off your feet. 'ith its romantic weeping willows and pretty lake, the ultimate trysting ground for lovers. (p. 55)

The **Peace Monument** marks serene vistas from which to gaze at the Capitol and its **Reflecting Pool.** (p. 55)

SW

I St.   I St.

Ⓜ WATERFRONT

M St.

'ashington Channel

MOONLIT MONUMENTS
For couples, poets, incurable romantics, and vampires.
EST. TIME 3hrs. EST. DIST. 5km

Ⓜ **PLEASE DO NOT ATTEMPT THIS NIGHT TOUR ALONE.**

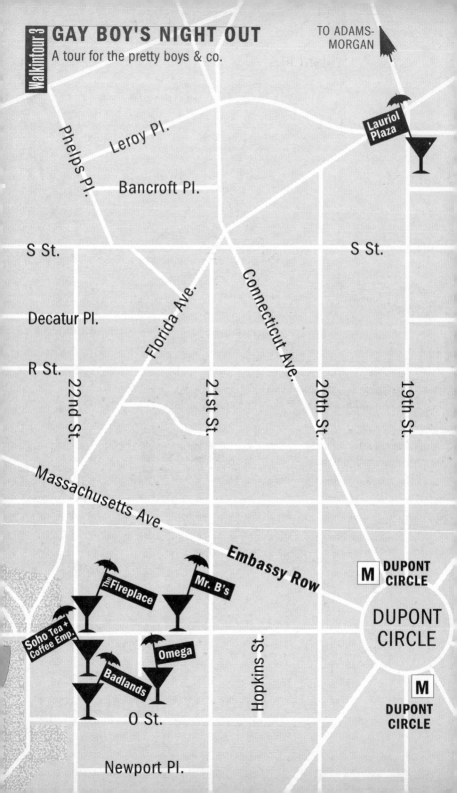

Walkintour 3
GAY BOY'S NIGHT OUT
A tour for the pretty boys & co.

TO ADAMS-
MORGAN

Lauriol
Plaza

Phelps Pl.

Leroy Pl.

Bancroft Pl.

S St.

S St.

Florida Ave.

Connecticut Ave.

Decatur Pl.

R St.

22nd St.

21st St.

20th St.

19th St.

Massachusetts Ave.

Embassy Row

M DUPONT
CIRCLE

The Fireplace

Mr. B's

DUPONT
CIRCLE

Soho Tea +
Coffee Emp.

Omega

Hopkins St.

Badlands

M
DUPONT
CIRCLE

O St.

Newport Pl.

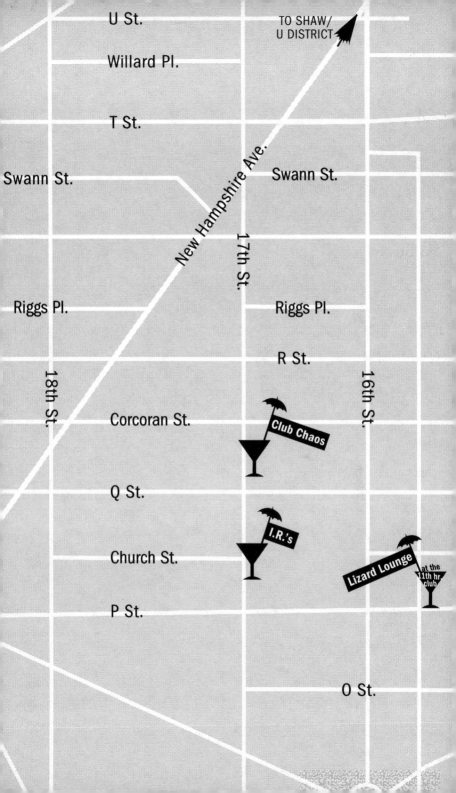

Once in D.C.

Never before was such a compact jam in front of the White House—all the grounds fill'd, and away out to the spacious sidewalks. I was there in the rush inside with the crowd—surged along the passageways, the blue and other rooms, and through the great east room. Crowds of country people, some very funny.
—Walt Whitman, *Specimen Days*

ORIENTATION

Diamond-shaped D.C. stretches its tips in the four cardinal directions. The **Potomac River** forms the jagged southwest border, its waters flowing between the district and Arlington, VA. **North Capitol St., East Capitol St.,** and **South Capitol St.** splice up the city into four quadrants: NW, NE, SE, and SW. These four quadrants are named for where they stand vis-à-vis the Capitol. The **Mall,** stretching west of the Capitol, makes a "West Capitol St." unnecessary. The suffixes of the quadrants distinguish otherwise identical addresses. For instance, you might find both an 800 G St. NW *and* an 800 G St. NE.

Washington's streets lie in a simple grid. Streets that run **east-to-west** are labeled **alphabetically** in relation to the north-south division, which runs through the Capitol. Since the street plan follows the Roman alphabet, in which "I" and "J" are the same letter, there is no J St. After W St., east-west streets take on **two-syllable names,** then **three-syllable names,** then the names of **trees and flowers.** The names run in alphabetical order, but sometimes repeat or skip a letter; discrepancies multiply as you shift farther from the downtown. Streets running **north-south** are **numbered** (1st St., 2nd St...) all the way out to 52nd St. NW and 63rd St. NE. Numbered and lettered streets sometimes disappear for a block, then resume as if nothing happened. Addresses on lettered streets indicate the number of the cross street. For instance, 1100 D St. SE is on the corner of

inside
SECRETS TO...

vogue

D.C. fashion reeks of **conservatism**, with the classic uniform of khakis, polo shirts, and button-down cardigans. So what's a glam-girl from NYC to do? Avoid anything over the top such as bright colors, big hair, big logos, or extensive jewelry. As any fashion mogul will tell you, success lies in the details. Work within the uniform.

For the fellas...stay with the khakis, but try a plain-front, straight leg style. Opt for a one tone, stretch material button-down over tired, plaid, cotton versions. Spice it up with a flashy pair of shoes and a slight spritz to the hair.

For the ladies...think simple but elegant. Leave the stilettos, hard candy makeup, and diamond jewelry at home. Less is definitely more in the District. Match a tight pair of khakis with a dark sleeveless top and add a flashy pair or sunglasses for the final touch.

Note to tourists...fanny packs may be functional but are considered very passé within the district; opt for a chic messenger bag instead.

Note to interns...we all know how proud you are of your job in Senator So-and-So's office but off of the Hill, ditch the neckpass—it draws more snickers than admiration.

D and 11th. The same trick works with addresses on some avenues, like Pennsylvania, but not others, like Massachusetts or Wisconsin.

Avenues named for states radiate outward from the Capitol **(Pennsylvania, New Jersey, Delaware, Maryland)** and the White House **(New York, Connecticut, Vermont)**, and criss-cross downtown **(Massachusetts, New Hampshire, Virginia)**. Downtown avenues meet at circles and squares, notably **Dupont Circle, Washington Circle,** and **Scott Circle.**

THE NEIGHBORHOODS

POLITICAL WASHINGTON

CAPITOL HILL. Postcard-perfect and colored pristine white, Capitol Hill caches the democratic dream into the neoclassical **Capitol** building, **Supreme Court,** and the **Library of Congress.**

MALL. The **Smithsonian Museums** and the **National Gallery of Art** flank this long grassy strip. Monuments and memorials stipple the Mall's west end, as cherry trees bud and blossom along the brink of the **Jefferson Memorial's Tidal Basin.**

SOUTH OF THE MALL. A fresh seafood aroma saturates this stretch of Potomac waterfront. Crustacean-mongers pile into the **Wharf Seafood Market,** while riverboat cruises rev their engines at the marina's docks.

FOGGY BOTTOM. The **State Department** and non-profit organizations make this scenic swampland their stomping grounds. Despite its hideous nickname, lovely gardens and columns drape the Bottom's avenues. Rounding out the Bottom is the **White House,** the executive mansion where a former president got some intern bottom.

OLD DOWNTOWN. It's a celebrity death match in this borough between Big Business and Big Brother. Commercial-plexes like the **International Trade Center** and the **Ronald Reagan Building** muscle for breathing space here with federal agencies like the **FBI.**

CHINATOWN. A tiny enclave crunched into Old Downtown, Chinatown's **H St.** still cooks up the best Chinese, Burmese, and Mongolian cuisine in the District.

FARRAGUT. It's a wonderful (corporate) life in glass-walled Farragut. Legend has it that every time a cell-phone rings, a yuppie just got a new pair of wingtips.

THE SECOND CITY

GEORGETOWN. *The* premier place in the District to eat, to shop, to drink, to see, and to be seen. Delicious **M St.** and **Wisconsin St.** restaurants could turn waifs into gluttons in a pinch. **Georgetown Park,** a waterfall-laden mall, induces occasional fits of consumer euphoria. Other key sights are the **historic homes** and the world-class **Georgetown University.**

DUPONT CIRCLE. This cosmo circle harbors D.C.'s gay scene, its art world, and its foreign diplomats. Glam queens and pretty boys rendezvous nightly in Dupont's flashy gay clubs. Art sophisticates jet in for the **R St. galleries** and **installations.** Diplomats and ambassadors from all parts of the world live and work along **Embassy Row.**

ADAMS-MORGAN. The international party posse stampedes toward the very mod, multiethnic Adams-Morgan for its **ethnic eateries** and raging **dance** and **world-beat clubs.**

UPPER NORTHWEST. Filthy rich bluebloods, like the Rockefeller scions, make their nests in the **Upper Northwest.** Some **mansions,** transformed into museums, are open to the public. Visitors also flock to the **National Zoo** and the **Washington National Cathedral.**

SHAW/U DISTRICT. African-American Washington once ruled Shaw/U, in the years before desegregation. Nowadays, electric **U St.** rocks out nightly—and deafens passersby—as its clubs blast **punk** and **techno** until indecent hours.

BEYOND THE NORTHWEST QUADRANT

SOUTHEAST. The **Navy Yard** and battleship tour of the **U.S.S. Barry** here will excite anyone with a penchant for brass and torpedoes. The Southeast also hosts the rowdiest **concerts** and the wildest **raves** in the entire District.

ANACOSTIA. Pock-marked with urban decay and riven with drug crimes, Anacostia is a very dangerous place. *Let's Go* does not recommend exploring Anacostia alone.

NORTHEAST. Tree-huggers and Green Party members alike adore the Northeast's **National Arboretum** and the **Kenilworth Aquatic Gardens,** with their leafy allure. **Catholic University** has a magnificent onion-domed basilica, the largest in North America. Crack-related violence plagues the Northeast, so be sure to travel in groups when exploring.

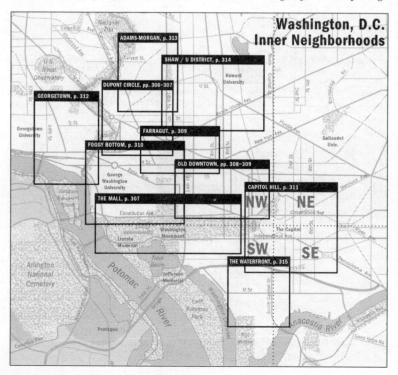

SUBURBS

BETHESDA. This suburb knows what's up with **food**—whether it be ethnic or American—*and* **fashion**—be it retail or vintage.

TAKOMA PARK. A former **hippie** bastion, urban migration has watered down the granola taste of the place. Still, some specialty **boutiques** and a healthy **Farmer's Market** retain the crunchy flavor of this park o' peace-and-love.

ARLINGTON COUNTY. Across the Potomac from the District, America's distinguished military veterans are buried in the vast green hills of **Arlington National Cemetery.** This county also houses the **Pentagon,** Defense Department HQ, which is open for tours.

FAIRFAX COUNTY. Also across the Potomac, Fairfax County features **Old Town Alexandria,** the **Potomac Plantations,** and various **parks.** Preserved homes and shops line ye olde King St. in Old Town **Alexandria. Mount Vernon,** plantation home of George Washington, and **Manassas Battlefield Park** are Fairfax's major draws.

GETTING INTO D.C.

RONALD REAGAN NATIONAL AIRPORT. Driving from the downtown to **National Airport** is easy. Just drive south down **I-395** to the **George Washington Pkwy.** southbound and follow signs for the airport. The ride takes 15 minutes without traffic. **Metrorail's** Blue and Yellow Lines are a short walk or shuttle ride from the airport. The **SuperShuttle** (☎ (800) 258-3826) bus runs between National and the city every 30 minutes on weekdays. **Cabs** cost $10-15 for a ride into the downtown and are a convenient way to access the city.

DULLES INTERNATIONAL AIRPORT. Driving to downtown Washington from Dulles usually takes about 40 minutes—but more during rush hour. To reach the airport, take I-

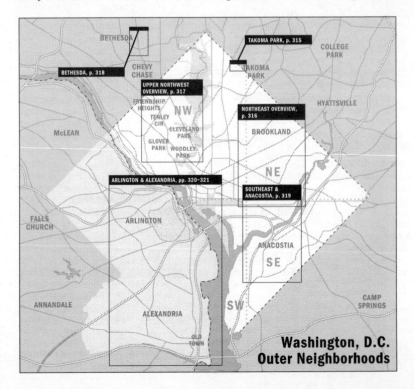

**Washington, D.C.
Outer Neighborhoods**

66 to **Exit 67.** Follow signs to the airport, which lies 16 mi. from Exit 67. Taxis to Dulles from downtown cost over $40. The **Washington Flyer Dulles Express Bus** (☎ (888) 927-4359) leaves frequently to **West Falls Church Metro.** The Flyer Dulles Express ($8, round-trip $14) runs every 30min. from 6-10am, every 20min. 10am-2pm, every 15min. 2-6pm, and every 30min. 6-10:30pm. **Buses** to downtown (**15th** and **K St. NW**) take about 45min. and leave every 30min. from 5:20am to 10:20pm on weekdays; on weekends they leave every hour from 5:20am to 12:20pm, and every 30min. from 12:50pm to 10:20pm ($16, round-trip $26, 3 or more $13 each, under 6 free). For the same prices, buses run between National and Dulles every hour on the hour from 5am-11pm. **SuperShuttle** (☎ (800) 258-3826) also runs buses to downtown ($17-22, $10 additional person).

BALTIMORE-WASHINGTON INTERNATIONAL. BWI lies 10mi. south of Baltimore. From D.C., take **I-295N** to **I-195E,** or take **I-95N** to **Exit 47A;** follow airport signs for both. From Baltimore, take **I-695** to **Exit 22A** (the **Baltimore-Washington Pkwy.**) or take **I-295S** to **I-195E;** follow signs for the airport. Driving time is about 50min. from D.C. The **MARC** is the cheapest way to get from the airport to D.C. ($5 to **Union Station,** round-trip $8.75; M-F only). **Amtrak** also provides train service (40min., $10-11) and **SuperShuttle** (☎ (800) 258-3826) buses run daily every hour at 10min. past the hour, 6:10am through 11:10pm ($28, under 6 free, each additional person $5).

GETTING AROUND D.C.

BY METRORAIL

Metrorail, the Washington subway system, along with **Metrobus,** is the backbone of the D.C. public transportation system. The subway is almost always just called the **Metro** for short. Barely 20 years old, the Metro stations are everything you'd expect from Big Brother: sterile, monumental, and relentlessly beige, with high curved ceilings and no decoration. Even the ceilings—parallel disks which look like beehives—are mainly functional, keeping echoes under control. The metro cars are quiet, carpeted, air-conditioned, and clean. Between the profusion of brown-capped Metro cops and the stations themselves, which leave no place to hide, the system has remained nearly crime-free. The **Wheaton Station** has the world's second-longest escalator, which at 230ft. takes 5min. to ride up. Metro system route maps and rail and bus passes are sold at the sales office at **Metro Center** (☎ 636-3425; open M-F 7:30am-1pm and 2-6:30pm). For general Metro information call ☎ 637-7000 (TDD 638-3780; www.wmata.com; M-F 6am-10:30pm, Sa-Su 8am-10:30pm). For detailed fare information, send a self-addressed stamped envelope to **Washington Metropolitan Area Transit Authority,** 600 5th St. NW, Washington, D.C. 20001 with a note requesting the *All About Metro Fares* pamphlet.

HOURS AND FARES. The Metro runs Monday to Friday 5:30am to midnight, and Saturday and Sunday 8am to midnight. Parking is available in Metro lots around the city and is free on weekends. The Metro operates on a computerized "farecard" system; your fares are based on the distance you wish to travel and the time of day you are traveling. Peak hours are Monday through Friday 5:30-9:30am and 3-8pm, when fares then range from $1.10 to $3.25; at all other times, fares range from $1.10 to $2.10. To get your ticket, purchase a card from the vending machines in the station in front of the turnstiles. Be sure to note the appropriate rate: rush hour or regular. You can credit your farecard with any amount from $1.10 to $45, but the machines give at most $4.95 in change. Note that you must use your ticket in an electronic turnstile to enter and leave the Metro; save your ticket during the ride. If you don't have enough money to cover the fare on your card, you can add money to your card at your destination. Exact-fare cards are eaten up by the exit turnstiles; cards with money left on them are returned. If you plan to connect with a bus after you ride, get a transfer pass from machines on the train platform.

SPECIAL PASSES. If you plan to ride the subway several times, buy a **One-Day Pass** ($5). This is undoubtedly the most economical choice for a day's sightseeing. The pass offers

inside
SECRETS TO...

go-go

Go-go sprouted over two decades ago in Washington D.C., when late seventies' bands like **Trouble Funk** began borrowing from funk and disco. These D.C. bands threw in some more horns and percussion, producing **go-go,** otherwise known as the final evolution of funk.

The beauty of go-go lies in its visual and spontaneous nature as a collection of drummers comes together in an unprepared yet strangely synchronized manner requiring audience participation in the form of call and response. Thus, go-go is perfect for the streetcorner, but totally unsuitable for the studio. Through the 80s, the music of **Chuck Brown and the Soul Searchers,** the **Junkyard Band,** and **Rare Essence** filled the streets of D.C., but gained little acclaim elsewhere until **E.U.** scored a nationwide hit with **"Da Butt"** in 1988. Today, go-go is still D.C.'s most popular music form and can be found playing on streetcorners and in clubs like **Deno's** (2335 Blandensburg Rd. NE). Attitude-wise, go-go is everything political D.C. is not: raucous, spontaneous, and infectiously participatory.

unlimited Metro usage from 9:30am to closing. Also available are **Flash Passes,** which offer two weeks' worth of unlimited bus rides for $20, unlimited Metro rides for $50, and unlimited bus and Metro rides for $65. Passes are available at the main office, Metro Center station, other Metro sales offices, some grocery stores and banks, and through TicketMaster (☎432-7328). Call☎962-1326 for information about advance fare purchases for groups. You will get a 10% bonus on farecards of $20 or more (max. farecard value $45). Up to two children four years old or younger ride free with each paying passenger. Qualified senior citizens and persons with disabilities use $3 or $10 specially encoded farecards and pay half the peak fare, not to exceed $1.60, regardless of the time of day. You must show your Metro ID card to buy the $3 and $10 farecards, and you must have your Metro ID card with you when using the system. The special farecards are available at all Metro sales offices and other retail locations but are not sold at Metro stations. Call☎637-7000 for more information; disabled persons can call ☎962-1245 (TDD 628-8973). Elevators are available. The lost and found (☎962-1195) is open weekdays 11am to 3pm.

BY METROBUS

The extensive **Metrobus** (same address, phone, and hours as Metrorail) system reliably serves **Georgetown, downtown,** and the **suburbs.** Downtown, the bus stops every few blocks. Regular fare in the District is $1.10 (exact change required); fares may vary in Maryland. Seniors and disabled persons are entitled to discounts. Up to two children four years old or younger ride free when accompanied by a paying passenger. Schedules and route maps for buses operating near Metrorail stations are available in those stations. A comprehensive bus map is available from the main Metro office; call or write for availability and price. Alexandria **(DASH)** and Montgomery County **(Ride-On)** also have their own, smaller bus systems; these routes are included in the Metro maps. Both accept Metro **Flash Passes,** though DASH only does during peak hours. **Metro Information** (☎637-7000) describes the exact buses and trains needed to reach any destination.

ROUTES. Bus routes with a letter followed by a number (like D4, S2) or with a two-digit number make stops in D.C. and Maryland, or sometimes (like the J buses) only in Maryland. Some routes (like the thirty-something buses) run only in D.C. If the number precedes the letter (18L, 5D), the route runs in Virginia. Most Virginia routes connect through the Pentagon Metro stop. Thirty-odd buses run only in D.C. The following list gives some useful bus routes for tourists.

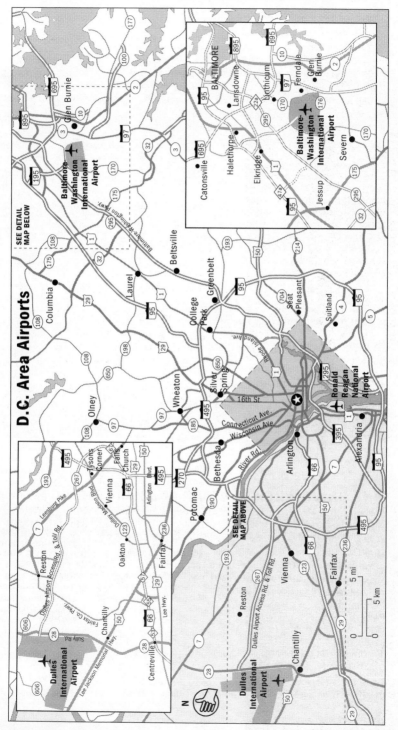

D.C. Area Airports

30-series (30, 32, 34, 35, 36) go downtown up Pennsylvania Ave. NW to Georgetown and then drive up Wisconsin to Upper Northwest.

42 goes from Metro Center to Farragut and then up Connecticut Ave., through Dupont Circle to Columbia Rd., on which it passes through Adams-Morgan.

DS2 and **D4** go from Glover Park in far NW, down Q St. in Georgetown, to Dupont Circle, Farragut, Metro Center, Union Station, and the Greyhound bus terminal, before ending in far NE.

L2 runs from McPherson Sq. in downtown up Connecticut Ave. to Chevy Chase.

N2 and **N4** run from Farragut and Dupont Circle up Massachusetts Ave., past Embassy Row and the Observatory, to American University and Friendship Heights.

BY TAXI

Washington taxi pricing is probably not what you're used to. Within the city, fares are based on a map that splits the city into **eight zones** and a number of subzones. Zone prices are fixed, and the basic cost of your cab ride is determined by the zones in which you begin and end—but not the route in between. Prices between subzones within a particular zone vary only slightly; it's the major zone prices that really matter.

A zone map and a fare chart are posted in every legal cab. To ensure honesty in billing, ask your driver to calculate your fare in advance. In general, within the subzones that surround the **Capitol** your fare will be about $4-5. Fares for other zones range from $4 to $12.50. Exceptions and special charges include a $1 surcharge during rush hours (M-F 7-9:30am and 4-6:30pm). Each additional passenger may incur a $1.50 charge. After the first piece of luggage, baggage costs 50¢ or $2 for "trunk-sized" suitcases. If you call a taxi service and have a cab dispatched, there is an added $1.50 charge. Taxi rides to, from, and within Maryland and Virginia are priced differently than those within the city, and vary based on local rules. The fee is $2.25 for the first ½ mi. and 75¢ for each additional ½ mi. During the day, the Metro makes taxis mostly unnecessary. At night, in subwayless Adams-Morgan or unsafe areas like the Southeast, taking a taxi to a Metro station or bus stop is advisable. A cab ride from the club districts in Adams-Morgan or Dupont Circle to Metro Center costs about $4-5.

If you can't hail a taxi, either because it's too late or because of the neighborhood, call **Yellow Cab** (☎ 544-1212). Call the **Transit Office** (☎ 331-1671) for more info. If you think you're being overcharged or have a complaint, get a receipt, write down the cab number, and call the **D.C. Taxicab Commission** (☎ 645-6005), who will help you lodge a formal complaint.

BY CAR

WHY DRIVE WHEN YOU CAN TAKE THE METRO?

Driving in D.C.—as in any large city—is a royal pain. Don't exacerbate your road rage with needless traffic and parking woes. If you're just putzing around the District and not venturing into the 'burbs, we'd recommend using the very nice Metro instead.

TRAFFIC. Rush-hour traffic will squeeze you in gridlock for ages. Traveling downtown—especially from Virginia—from 7am to 9:30am or leaving the city from 4pm to 6:30pm, you'll see gridlock that would make Congress blush. Lunchtime is also a jam, and Friday afternoon a nightmare. For better access to downtown sights, use the Metro or the bus.

PARKING. Expect to pay $10 or more for garage parking. The most widespread provider is **Colonial Parking** (☎ 452-9600), which runs lots all over the city. Finding on-street parking during the day is almost impossible, especially near the Smithsonian. During afternoon rush hours (M-F 4-6:30pm) most downtown spaces are temporarily illegal. Nighttime parking is tough in Georgetown and Adams-Morgan.

TICKETS. To pay a D.C. **traffic ticket,** go to the Bureau of Adjudication at 65 K St. NE (☎ 727-5000; open M-F 8:30am-7pm; Metro: Union Station). Hearings close at 2pm each day. Pay with cash or credit card (V, MC). Otherwise, make a check payable to the D.C. Treasurer and send it to the Bureau of Adjudication, Washington, D.C. 20002. If your car is towed, go to the Bureau of Adjudication to pay for your towing fee and request directions to the Brentwood lot. Towing will cost you $75 plus a $10 daily storage fee.

CAR RENTAL

Renting a car for days at a time can be prohibitively expensive, but renting for local trips is often reasonable, especially if several people share the cost. Renting is often cheapest in **Arlington, VA.** When dealing with any car rental company, make certain the price includes insurance against theft and collision. **American Express** automatically insures any car rented with its card. Although rental charges run $18-55 per day for an economy car, plus 10-30¢ per mi., most companies have special deals—especially on weekends. If you have a credit card, you can avoid leaving a cash deposit. Most companies charge 21-24 year olds an extra $10-20 per day and will not rent to anyone under 21. See p. 291 for car rental listings.

C&O Canal

BY TOUR

Although walking is a fine way to see the city, tours on wheels might be just the thing for weary monument-trekking feet.

BUS AND TROLLEY TOURS

Tourmobile Sight-seeing, 1000 Ohio Dr. SW (☎554-7950, ☎554-5100, or ☎(888) 868-7707; www.tourmobile.com), runs its blue-and-white buses between 9:30am and 6:30pm from mid-April to mid-Sept. and between 8:30am and 4:30pm in the off-season. For the standard 18-sight loop, get on at any stop, marked by blue-and-white signs, and buy tickets from the driver. Tickets $14, children 3-11 $7. Special routes travel to the Frederick Douglass home (a 2½hr. loop leaving at noon; $7, children $3.50) and to Mount Vernon (daily 10am, noon, and 2pm; $22, children $11; price includes admission). These tours leave from the Washington Monument, Lincoln Memorial, and Arlington Cemetery; purchase tickets up to an hour prior to departure from booth. A Washington-by-night tour is also available.

Wisconsin Ave & M Street

Discover Downtown D.C. tour, sponsored by the Discovery Channel Destination Store (see p. 68), winds through Old Downtown for an hour and a half, stopping at some well-known and a few fairly obscure sights ($7.50, children and seniors $5; tours leave daily 10:30am and 1pm).

Capitol Entertainment Services (☎636-9203) runs standard tours of major sights, but specializes in a three-hour **Black History Tour** through Lincoln Park, Anacostia, and the Frederick Douglass home. Tours begin from area hotels during the summer. Call for winter group tours. Tickets $22, children 3-11 $15.

WALKING TOURS

Anthony S. Pitch (☎(301) 294-9514; www.dcsightseeing.com). These nationally recognized walking tours guide you on a stroll around Adams-Morgan, Lafayette Square, Georgetown, or Political Washington. Group tours $200, individuals $10.

Woodlawn Plantation

SECRETS TO...

yuppiedom

Spot yuppies (young urban professionals) in **Farragut** (p. 74) and **Capitol Hill** (p. 47) by their ultra-conservative, almost uniform manner of dress. Men wear khakis, pressed button-down shirts, non-descript shoes, and short, kempt hair. Women display a little more variety in their shirt types and skirt lengths, but can be identified by a reserved choice of colors, short to shoulder length hair, a scarcity of jewelry, and scant makeup. The real sign of a yuppie, though, are the accessories he or she sports.

Telltale traces of a true-blue **Ikea** kid: look for a **Tumi** computer bag, a **Kate Spade** bag on girls, a **Palm Pilot**, a **Nokia cell phone,** or a **Volkswagen Jetta** key chain.

To purchase yuppie paraphernalia, it's Georgetown all the way. Check out the array of shops along Wisconsin Ave., as well as in the **Georgetown Park Mall** (p. 132) on M St. There, find such yuppie staples as **Banana Republic, J. Crew, Brooks Brothers, Polo,** and **Country Road.**

Tour D.C. (☎(301) 588-8999) leads 90-min. walking tours through historic Georgetown every Saturday and Thursday at 10:30am. Book these popular tours well in advance, as they almost always sell out completely. $12, special group rates and times available.

BIKE TOURS
Bike the Sites, Inc., 3417 Quesada St. NW (☎966-8662; www.bikethesites.com), offers tours complete with bicycles, helmets, equipment, water, and snacks. Tours lead two to 15 people, and leave from and return to major hotels or near Metro stations. Designed for a variety of skill levels. Call ahead as prices, start times, and locations vary seasonally. $35 for a 3hr. Capitol sites tour to $85 for a day-long Civil War battlegrounds ride.

ODDBALL TOURS
Scandal Tours (☎(800) 758-8687), a comedy show on wheels, hires actors to impersonate disgraced politicians as they steer tourists from one place of infamy to the next. In good weather, the 75-minute tour whizzes past Gary Hart's townhouse, Watergate, and the Vista Hotel, where Mayor Barry was caught smoking crack. Tours depart from the 12th St. entrance of the Old Post Office. Apr.-Sept., Sa at 1pm. Reservations required. ($27, methadone not included).

D.C. Ducks, 1323 Pennsylvania Ave. NW (☎832-9800), provides an entertaining land-and-water tour of the monuments and Mall sights. Kids ogle when the van transforms into a boat. Tours leave from Union Station Apr.-Oct. each hour, daily 10am-3pm. Tickets $24, children 4-12 $12.

KEEPING IN TOUCH
MAIL

SENDING AND RECEIVING MAIL
Airmail letters under 1 oz. between North America and the world cost US$1. Envelopes should be marked "airmail" or "par avion" to avoid having letters sent by sea. There are several ways to arrange pick-up of letters sent to you by friends, relatives, and lovers while you are abroad. Mail can be sent to D.C. through **General Delivery.** Unfortunately, all mail sent General Delivery in D.C. goes to the sorting facility on **Brentwood Rd. NE,** miles from everywhere and not served by Metrorail (the closest stop is Rhode Island Ave.). If you must receive mail at Brentwood, bring a passport or other ID with you. Label the letters like this:

Tomohiro <u>HAMAKAWA</u> (capitalize and underline last name
  for accurate filing)
c/o General Delivery
900 Brentwood Rd. NE
Washington, D.C. 20066
USA (if from another country)
HOLD FOR 30 DAYS

American Express's travel offices will act as a mail service for cardholders if you contact them in advance and will hold mail for up to 30 days and forward upon request. Address the letter in the same way as shown above. Some offices will offer these services to non-cardholders, but call ahead to make sure. A complete list is available free from AmEx (☎ (800) 528-4800). If regular airmail is too slow, **Federal Express** (US tel. for international operator ☎ (800) 247-4747) can get a letter from D.C. to Sydney in two days for a whopping $30. By **US Express Mail,** a letter from D.C. arrives within four days and costs $15. **Surface mail** is by far the cheapest and slowest way to send mail. It takes one to three months to cross the Atlantic and two to four to cross the Pacific—appropriate for sending large quantities of items you won't need to see for a while. When ordering books and materials from abroad, always include one or two **International Reply Coupons (IRCs)**—a way of providing the postage to cover delivery. IRCs should be available from your local post office and those abroad ($1.05).

SENDING MAIL HOME FROM THE USA

Aerogrammes, printed sheets that fold into envelopes and travel via airmail, are available at post offices. It helps to mark "airmail" if possible, though "par avion" is universally understood. Most post offices will charge exorbitant fees or simply refuse to send aerogrammes with enclosures. Airmail from the USA averages four to seven days, although times are more unpredictable from smaller towns.

TELEPHONES

CALLING THE USA FROM HOME

To call direct from home, dial:

1. The international access code of your home country. **International access codes** include: Australia 0011; Ireland 00; New Zealand 00; South Africa 09; U.K. 00; US 011. Country codes and city codes are sometimes listed with a zero in front (e.g., 033), but after dialing the international access code, drop successive zeros (with an access code of 011, e.g., 011 33).

2. 1 (USA and Canada's country code).

3. The area code (see chart below) and local number.

CALLING WITHIN THE USA

The simplest way to call within the country is to use a coin-operated phone. You can also buy **prepaid phone cards,** which carry a certain amount of phone time depending on the card's denomination. The time is measured in minutes or talk units (e.g. one unit/one minute), and the card usually has a toll-free access telephone number and a personal identification number (PIN). To make a phone call, you dial the access number, enter your PIN, and at the voice prompt, enter the phone number of the party you're trying to reach. A computer tells you how much time or how many units you have left on your card. Be careful about the type of card you buy: some operate with a PIN number you must know beforehand, while others write the pin on the card itself. Phone rates are highest in the morning, lower in the evening, and lowest on Sunday and late at night.

OVER THE AIRWAVES

AM

570 (WWRC) Business Talk.

630 (WMAL) News, talk, sports.

730 (WBZS) Financial news.

780 (WABS) Contemporary Christian.

820 (WXTR) Classic Country.

930 (WFMD) News Talk.

980 (WWRC) Talk, sports.

1120 (WUST) Multicultural.

1260 (WWDC) Big band, Lounge.

1390 (WZHF) Health and fitness talk.

1450 (WWOL) Current event talk radio.

1460 (WKDV) Children's music.

1500 (WTOP) News, sports.

1504 (WACA) Spanish music and news.

1580 (WPGC) Gospel.

1600 (WINX) Rock 'n' Roll (oldies).

FM

88.5 (WAMU) National Public Radio.

89.3 (WPFW) Jazz/blues, Third World.

90.1 (WCSP) C-SPAN radio.

90.5 (WJYJ) Contemporary Country.

94.7 (WARW) Classic rock.

95.5 (WPGC) R&B, hip-hop.

96.3 (WHUR) Urban contemporary.

97.1 (WASH) Soft rock.

98.7 (WMZQ) Hit country.

99.1 (WHFS) Alternative rock.

99.5 (WGAY) Oldies.

100.3 (WBIG) Oldies.

101.1 (WGMS) Classical.

104.1 (WWZZ) Top 40.

105.9 (WJZW) Smooth Jazz.

106.7 (WJFK) Talk radio, Howard Stern.

107.3 (WRQX) 80s, 90s mix.

107.7 (WTOP) Nonstop news.

inside
SECRETS TO...

police

Over the past ten years, public scrutiny and criticism of police actions have increased tremendously. Ironically though, the accusations of racial profiling and police brutality that plague other large city police forces have been few and far between within the District. Instead, the D.C. police force has been accused of **political infighting** and gross mismanagement, which can be equally destructive forces. **Police Chief Larry Soulsby** and **Lt. Jeffrey Stowe** have faced accusations of impropriety, embezzlement, and extortion. One prominent example of racial profiling did occur in 1991, when a rookie officer shot an innocent Salvadoran man, an event which was followed by prolonged riots in Washington's Mt. Pleasant neighborhood. Ever since that event, citizens have noticed an increased reluctance for police officers to engage citizens and have been increasingly unaware of day-to-day police presence. Recognizing the necessity of a strong and visible police force, police leaders have recently called for a **"zero tolerance" campaign** which will feature more aggressive efforts to police minor offenses.

AREA CODES

Unless otherwise noted, all telephone numbers in this book have a **202** area code. To dial a local number in Maryland, you must dial 1 + area code.

COUNTRY CODES	
Australia	61
Austria	43
Canada	1
Ireland	353
New Zealand	64
South Africa	13
United Kingdom	44
United States	1
AREA CODES	
Arlington and Alexandria, VA	703
Annapolis, MD	410
Baltimore, MD	410
Charlottesville, VA	804
Fairfax County, VA	703
Harpers Ferry, WV	304
Jamestown and Yorktown Plantations, VA	757
Richmond, VA	804
Shenandoah Park, VA	540
Virginia Beach, VA	757
Washington, D.C.	202
Williamsburg, VA	757

THE MEDIA

D.C. is a veritable ant farm of journalists. Eager reporters scurry all over the city, meet mysterious "sources close to the President," dredge up dirt wherever they can get it, and constantly try to tap into new veins of information. The powers that be never disappoint them—something spectacular (or sordid) is always looming.

IN PRINT

THE WASHINGTON POST. The Washington Post (www.washingtonpost.com), D.C.'s major newspaper, contains comprehensive political, national, and international coverage. Founded in 1877, it floundered until 1933, when Republican financier **Eugene Meyer** purchased it at a bankruptcy sale. His daughter, **Katherine Graham,** assumed control of the paper after his suicide in 1963, leading the paper through its Watergate glory days. Today the paper that coined the term "McCarthyism" and published the Pentagon Papers remains one of the most influential in the country, covering everything from world crisis to art and fashion in the metro area.

THE WASHINGTON TIMES. The Washington Times
(www.washtimes.com), a conservative daily founded in
1982 during the "Reagan Revolution," has since lost momen-
tum due to staff shake-ups and hard-right columnists. But
the *Times* is still known for its investigative reporting and
does sometimes find local stories that the *Post* has missed.
The smaller, more wonkish **Washington Monthly** (www.wash-
ingtonmonthly.com) likes to boast that it broke famous stories, like Mayor Barry's corruption, National Security
Council misdeeds, and design flaws in the space shuttle,
years before better-known pages got hold of them. The
scrappy *Monthly* is a favorite of aspiring policymakers; the
magazine keeps tabs on the bureaucracy, but not always on
the city as a whole. If it's Congress you're interested in, read
Roll Call (www.rollcall.com), which prints gossip and news
for members of the House, the Senate, and their lucky staffers twice a week.

THE WASHINGTON CITY PAPER. The Washington **City Paper**
(www.washingtoncitypaper.org) is a thick, free, "alternative" weekly distributed on Thursdays to vending machines
and stores around town. *City Paper* provides excellent
local investigative reporting, features, and comprehensive
listings of the arts in D.C., especially regarding theater and
popular music. (Use the *Post*'s movie listings, but look to
the *City Paper* for the best nightlife listings in town.) The
paper occasionally offers special coupons for clubs. *City
Paper* also has a Classifieds section, including apartments
and personals.

NEIGHBORHOOD PAPERS. Away from the bright lights of
national news, Washington's communities run their own
papers. The daily **Washington Afro-American** covers black D.C.
in a friendly, earnest way, with attention to individual citizens' achievements. The free, weekly **Washington Blade**
(www.washblade.com), stacked in various stores (especially
around Dupont Circle), is the gay and lesbian community's
paper, with articles, listings, and an events calendar. **Washington Jewish Weekly** offers up community news, editorials,
kosher dining information, and a synagogue directory; look
for it in vending machines all over town. **The Washingtonian**
(www.washingtonian.com) is the neighborhood monthly
magazine of the affluent suburbs, mixing plenty of articles on
celebrities and real estate and D.C. trivia, surprising money-
saving tidbits, and lots of lists ("top 10 delis," etc.).

The Capitol Hill neighborhood cleans up weekly with **Hill
Rag,** an area paper distributed all over downtown. The **In
Towner** (www.intowner.com) covers local issues (zoning
and crime, for example) for Dupont Circle, Adams-Morgan,
and points east (Scott and Logan Circles) and west (Cleveland Park). Claiming no relation to the contrived Pepsi ad
campaign of the same name, **Generation Next** is nothing
short of a brilliant representation of 20-something interests
and concerns; free copies infest Dupont Circle. Event listings congregate in **Go** and **Where,** free magazines distributed
at hotels and libraries.

FBI

Horse Statue Outside White House

Roosevelt Island

ON THE TUBE

Political junkies can get their fix 24 hours a day from the **Cable Satellite Public Affairs Network** (C-SPAN), which broadcasts "live gavel-to-gavel" coverage of all full Congressional proceedings. The service consists of three channels: C-SPAN, which covers the House; C-SPAN 2, which covers the Senate; and C-SPAN EXTRA, which covers other live events in Washington. Due to their proximity to government activity, local television networks and radio stations sometimes beat national ones to newsworthy stories. National political programs like the *MacNeil/Lehrer News Hour* and the *McLaughlin Group* are filmed in D.C. Washington's TV stations are: Channel 4, **WRC/NBC;** Channel 5, **WTTG/FOX;** Channel 7, **WJLA/ABC;** Channel 9, **WUSA/CBS;** Channel 20, **WDCA/UPN;** Channel 26, **WETA/ PBS;** Channel 30, **WMDO/Univision;** Channels 38-39, **C-SPAN;** Channel 41-42, **CNN;** Channel 50, **WB.** For complete listings of what's showing daily, check the *Washington Post* (www.washingtonpost.com).

PROTOCOL AND LAWS

TIPPING AND BARGAINING

It's customary to tip cab drivers and waiters about 15%; exceptionally good waiters—or those who work at exceptionally good restaurants—are often tipped 20% of the tab. Tip hairdressers 10% and bellhops around $1 per bag. Bartenders usually expect between 50¢ and $1 per drink. Bargaining is generally frowned upon and fruitless in the US, unless you are buying from a flea-market vendor.

TAXES

The prices quoted throughout *Let's Go: Washington, D.C.* are the amounts before sales tax has been added. Sales tax in D.C. is 6%. Hotel tax is 13%, with an additional $1.50 occupancy tax per room per night. Restaurant, car rental, and liquor taxes are all 10%. Parking in commercial lots (as opposed to Metro lots) incurs a 12% tax.

DRUGS AND ALCOHOL

You must be 21 to purchase **alcoholic beverages** legally in D.C. Many bars and stores will want to see a photo ID before selling you alcohol. Popular drinking spots, as well as upscale liquor stores, are likely to check your card: be forewarned that if they suspect your ID is fake, they may confiscate it. It is extremely dangerous to wander through bad neighborhoods looking for stores that will sell you alcohol underage. Bars and clubs are allowed to serve alcohol until 3am. Beer and wine—but no hard liquor—are sold in D.C. on Sunday. Attempting to purchase **illegal drugs** in Washington is extremely dangerous. Possession of marijuana, cocaine, and other drugs is punishable by imprisonment. Driving under the influence of alcohol or drugs is stupid and punishable by law. If you carry **prescription drugs,** have a copy of the prescriptions ready for Customs.

SAFETY AND SECURITY

Outside of the killings, Washington has one of the lowest crime rates in the country.
   —Mayor Marion Barry

In 1942, D.C. doubled New York City's murder rate and, according to *Newsweek,* became the "Murder Capital of the US." Exactly 50 years later, the title was resurrected, thanks to widespread crack addiction and the increasing availability of assault weapons. The murder epidemic, while mostly an affair of drug dealers shooting one another, sometimes catches innocents in its crossfire. Most crime occurs in places that do not get many visitors, primarily the Northeast and Southeast neighborhoods, and east of 14th St. NW. Try to enter these regions only in a car, and always exercise extreme caution. Throughout the book, *Let's Go: Washington, D.C.* mentions when sights and establishments are located in potentially dangerous areas.

PERSONAL SAFETY

BLENDING IN AND EXPLORING. Tourists are vulnerable to crime because they often carry large amounts of cash and are not as street-savvy as locals. Extra vigilance is always wise, but there is no need for panic when exploring D.C. Find out about unsafe areas from the D.C. tourist office, from the manager of your hotel or hostel, or from a local whom you trust. Whenever possible, *Let's Go: Washington, D.C.* warns of unsafe neighborhoods and areas, but there are some good general tips to follow. When walking at night, stick to busy, well-lit streets and avoid dark alleyways. Do not attempt to cross through parks, parking lots, or other large, deserted areas. Buildings in disrepair, vacant lots, and unpopulated areas are all bad signs. The distribution of people can reveal a great deal about the relative safety of the area; look for children playing, women walking in the open, and other signs of an active community. Keep in mind that D.C. neighborhoods can change character drastically between blocks. If you feel uncomfortable, leave as quickly and directly as you can.

SELF DEFENSE. There is no sure-fire way to protect yourself from all of the situations you might encounter when you travel, but a good self-defense course will give you more concrete ways to react to different types of aggression. **Impact, Prepare, and Model Mugging** can refer you to local self-defense courses in the US (☎ (800) 345-5425). Workshops (2-3hr.) start at $50 and full courses run $350-500. Both women and men are welcome.

FINANCIAL SECURITY

PROTECTING YOUR VALUABLES. To prevent easy theft, don't keep all your valuables (money, important documents) in one place. **Photocopies** of important documents allow you to recover them in case they are lost or filched. Carry one copy separate from the documents and leave another copy at home. Label every piece of luggage both inside and out. **Don't put a wallet with money in your back pocket.** Keep some money separate from the rest to use in an emergency.

PICKPOCKETS AND CON-ARTISTS. In D.C.'s massive city crowds and especially on public transportation, **pickpockets** are amazingly deft at their craft. Rush hour is no excuse for strangers to press up against you on the metro. If someone stands uncomfortably close, move to another car and hold your bags tightly. Also, be alert in public telephone booths. If you must say your calling card number, do so quietly; if you punch it in, make sure no one can look over your shoulder.

ACCOMMODATIONS AND TRANSPORTATION. Never leave your belongings unattended; crime occurs in even the most demure-looking hostel or hotel. Be particularly careful on **buses:** carry your backpack in front of you where you can see it and don't trust anyone to "watch your bag for a second." If you travel by **car,** try not to leave valuable possessions—such as radios or luggage—in it while you are away. If your tape deck or radio is removable, hide it in the trunk or take it with you. Hide baggage in the trunk—although thieves can often tell if a car is loaded by the way it sits on its tires.

Life & Times

HISTORY

FOUNDING AND EARLY YEARS

...this Embryo Capital, where fancy sees,
Squares in morasses, obelisks in trees,
Which second-sighted seers, even now adorn
With shrines unbuilt and heroes yet unborn.
  —Thomas Moore

Rivals **Alexander Hamilton** and **Thomas Jefferson** finalized plans to hatch Washington, D.C. during a 1790 dinner in Manhattan. After American independence, the US government had slid between Philadelphia, Baltimore, Lancaster, York, Princeton, Annapolis, Trenton, and New York. Debates between **North and South** thickened over where to build the permanent capital. Each side wanted the capital city—America's symbolic center—within its own boundaries. One observer wondered whether or not the capital should simply be constructed on wheels and rolled back and forth.

The dinner deal eventually boiled down to **debt assumption.** Hamilton argued that Congress should pay for state war debts, which the South opposed and the North favored. Jefferson agreed to debt assumption in exchange for a Southern capital. The two parties decided to build the capital along the **Potomac River,** bordering Virginia and Maryland.

The bill gave **President George Washington** the task of selecting a site along the Potomac. Washington picked a wilderness area next to the small city of Georgetown, MD. Virginia and Maryland each agreed to donate land contiguous to Georgetown to create the

District of Columbia, from which the capital would sprout. By February of 1791, **Andrew Ellicott,** the US Geographer General, had etched boundaries for the 100 square mile district.

Washington hired 36-year-old French engineer **Pierre L'Enfant** to design and to build the **"Permanent Seat."** L'Enfant envisioned a nexus of grand avenues silhouetted by a pristine Capitol building. From its **Jenkins Hill** base, the Capitol would look over a long mall, culminating in an equestrian statue of George Washington (now the Washington Monument).

L'Enfant was a brilliant designer but a poor politician. He offended his superiors by his "artistic temperament" and outraged area landowners by seizing land for roads without compensation. When L'Enfant tore down an aristocrat's porch because it stood in the way of New Jersey Ave., not even George Washington's influence could save him. He was fired and replaced by his associates, geographer **Andrew Ellicott** and African-American astronomer **Benjamin Banneker.**

Under Ellicott and Banneker, buildings rose quickly. Construction began on the Capitol building, designed by physician **William Thornton,** and the White House, designed by Irishman **James Hoban.** Yet even when Congress moved to the city in 1800, Washington was still a small town; in the middle of that year, D.C. contained a meager 84 brick houses, 151 wooden houses and 3210 people. A visiting Englishmen, journalist Isaac Weld, noted that there were so few buildings in the city that "a spectator can scarcely perceive anything like a town." Washington, "the city of magnificent distances," was yet far from magnificent and far from a city.

The Capitol building's paint had hardly dried when **British troops** set Washington ablaze in August 1814, near the end of the **War of 1812.** British soldiers sacked the White House, setting books and furniture afire. The Brits did not loot much else of value, thanks to the President James Madison's wife Dolley, who fled the burning city with the most important documents and works of art. With the assistance of the White House gardener, Mrs. Madison rescued the famous **Gilbert Stuart** portrait of George Washington that hangs in the White House today.

When the rain put out the blaze that the Brits lit, Congress was almost ready to throw in the towel; one postwar proposal to move the capital from Washington lost by only eight votes. The capital stayed, but so did the problems. As a port city between two plantations, the District made a logical first stop for **slave traders,** whose shackled captives awaited sale in the crowded pens on the Mall and near the White House. Foreign diplomats were properly disgusted, disdainfully deeming D.C. as "Southern." Elected officials understandably decided crude and undeveloped D.C. was no place for families: politicians left wives and children at home and lived in boarding houses where they smoked cigars, chewed tobacco, and dueled.

Though subject to severe racial prejudice, a town-within-a-town of free African-Americans was growing faster than the rest of the city. By 1850 Washington held 2000 slaves, 8000 free blacks, and 30,000 whites. White fear of uprisings gave rise to discriminatory laws and social unrest such as the **Snow Riots** of 1835. However, the thriving community near the **upper South plantations** continued to draw African-American migrants. Enterprising black residents established 15 schools in Georgetown and Washington City before the Civil War.

During the 1830s and 40s, many British travelers published their Washington journals—long records of unpaved streets, half-erected buildings, naked vistas, and horrifying slave traffic. **Charles Dickens,** who dropped by in 1842, said that D.C., the "City of Magnificent Distances," should be renamed the "City of Magnificent Intentions." It had the skeleton of a great city but was still almost a ghost-town.

CIVIL WAR TO WORLD WAR I

The Civil War's outbreak in 1861 turned the capital from the Union's appendix to its jugular vein. The **Union** quickly erected a system of 68 forts around the city. **Abraham Lincoln** had an area in the Treasury Building converted into a bunker where officials could flee, and Congress ordered government buildings—including the Capitol itself—converted into barracks.

Washington was only actually attacked by the Confederates once, in July 1864, when **Gen. Jubal Early** marched on the city. Early came within five miles of the city line before Union general **Ulysses S. Grant** thwarted his advance. Allegedly, Lincoln himself attended the skirmish in his trademark stovepipe hat. When he stood for a better view of the battle, a Union officer shouted, "Get down, you fool!"

The Civil War fueled a period of explosive growth for Washington. By the war's end, the population had increased by 50,000 to 125,000. California journalist **Noah Brooks** wrote that new construction was proceeding so quickly by the end of the war that he feared Washington's "magnificent distances" might be filled up if the building boom continued. Though every other building housed troops, Lincoln directed that work continue on the Capitol dome. "It is a sign," he reasoned, "that the Union shall go on."

The Civil War and Reconstruction sent tens of thousands of former slaves north for a better life. Some found a similarly harsh life, however, in spontaneous shanty towns like **Murder Bay,** a few blocks from the White House. After Lincoln's assassination in 1865, the postwar Republican ascent spelled better times for blacks. The five years after 1868 were called the **Golden Age of Black Washington,** with new enforced civil rights laws, black senators and congressmen, a black public school system, an African-American at the helm of Georgetown University, and the founding of Dunbar High School and Howard University. President Grant appointed former slave and abolitionist **Frederick Douglass** as the District's recorder of deeds.

In May 1870, Congress gave Washington the right to choose a mayor. Holdover official Sayles J. Bowen kicked off a program of public works beginning with an awfully brilliant move: paving Pennsylvania Ave. with wooden blocks which sank into the mud when walked on. **Alexander "Boss" Shepherd,** a handsome former plumber on the Board of Public Works, became the city's *de facto* mayor. Protected by his friendship with President Ulysses S. Grant, Shepherd embarked on an ambitious and costly city improvement program. He paved the city's roads, installed streetlights and sidewalks, built sewers, tore down decrepit buildings, and financed the construction of grand new buildings. It was during this construction boom that Washington was finally modernized. Shepherd's lavish spending, however, quickly sent

1824

Celebrations erupt in D.C. during the visit of the Marquis de Lafayette.

1832

Cholera plagues the city.

1835

The Baltimore and Ohio Railroad reaches D.C.

1846

Congress establishes the Smithsonian Institution.

1862

Congress emancipates all slaves in the District.

1865

Confederate general Robert E. Lee surrenders to Gen. Grant at Appomattox.

1865

Lincoln is assassinated at Ford's Theater by John Wilkes Boothe.

D.C. into debt. In 1874, Congress fired Shepherd for over-spending by $22 million, prompting him to go into exile in Mexico. A board of three commissioners assumed control of the city. It would be over 100 years before self-government returned to D.C.

Despite Shepherd's improvements, late 19th-century Washington hardly resembled today's city in its appearance. The modern landscape developed under **Senator James McMillan,** chairman of the Senate's district committee during **President Theodore Roosevelt's** administration. In 1901, McMillan convened a beautification commission including such notables as **Frederick Law Olmsted,** designer of **New York's Central Park,** and **Augustus Saint-Gaudens,** a sculptor. After an architectural tour of European capitols, the Commission submitted a proposal for landscape improvements to the Senate in 1902. The plan sketched out the district along the lines of L'Enfant's original vision. It required reclaiming **the Mall,** then a railroad bed. After beautifiers moved the trains to a grand new station, the Mall emerged from its century-old chrysalis as a promenade of museums, monuments, and government buildings.

Washington's landscape grew increasingly modern as the **McMillan Plan** was implemented and Presidents ordered further improvements. The tubby but strangely attractive President **William Howard Taft** set the maximum height for buildings within the city limits at 110 feet, so that the Capitol would be visible from every point in the city. Taft's wife made her own contribution to the cityscape, securing the donation of Washington's famous **cherry blossom trees** from Japan.

Meanwhile, D.C.'s African-Americans were losing economic power, even as their numbers and artistic achievements increased. As employment segregation tightened, most became obliged to work in service industries (e.g. driving taxis and catering). Roosevelt himself listened to the black community, but Georgia-born Woodrow Wilson supported a segregation so thorough that black leader **"Lady Mollie" Mary Church Terrell** couldn't get young poet **Langston Hughes** considered for a job at the **Library of Congress**—not even as a page. Cafeterias and even public parks became segregated facilities; at the 1922 dedication of the Lincoln Memorial, world famous educator **Booker T. Washington** was made to sit in a "colored" section. Black Washington in these years was almost an autonomous city, with its own movie houses, theaters, shops, social clubs, and political leaders. The city-within-a-city was hardly unified, though; middle class blacks in **LeDroit Park** had little to do with the impoverished **alley dwellings** in SW and SE.

FDR AND WWII

After the stock market **crash of 1929,** President Herbert Hoover reacted to the **Great Depression** with platitudes instead of money. The **Bonus Army** of unemployed veterans marched to the Mall to demand new benefits, but Hoover answered only with the National Guard. In 1932, newly elected President **Franklin Delano Roosevelt** arrived in D.C. accompanied by his herd of idealistic liberals anxious to make the **Alphabet Soup** of new agencies and relief programs work. NRA, WPA, AAA, YCC, FHA, and SEC were just a few of the novel acronyms FDR's "try anything" philosophy spawned. Roosevelt's posse transfigured the city from a sleepy Southern town into a metropolis eternally envious of New York's sophistication.

What the New Deal began, **World War II** finished. As the US entered the War, Washington's bureaucracy germinated. The War Department seized hotels for office space, and civilians poured into D.C. as clerical jobs opened up daily. This era saw the construction of the Federal Triangle, the government buildings between Pennsylvania and Constitution Ave. A 1943 guidebook called the District the **"Cinderella City."**

Black Washington was changing, too, but more slowly. The city's segregation came to national attention when the Daughters of the American Revolution barred African-American opera star **Marian Anderson** from singing at Constitution Hall. Anderson sang instead, on **Easter Sunday, 1939,** on the steps of **Lincoln Memorial** to an adoring audience of 75,000.

FDR's successor, **Harry S. Truman,** dropped a reality bombshell on the city when his appointed commission released its 1947 report on racism. The Supreme Court's 1953 **"Lost Laws"** ruling (that civil rights laws from 1872 could still be enforced) essentially desegregated most of the city. Paradoxically, the integration of movie theaters, stores, and eating establishments destroyed many black-owned businesses, and the African-American commercial districts north of Massachusetts Ave. began to deteriorate. In a similar vein, Dunbar High School—so good that black families moved to D.C. from the Deep South just to send their kids there—became nothing special after 1954's **Brown v. Board of Education** Supreme Court decision integrated America's schools.

THE COLD WAR AND BEYOND

Sen. Joseph McCarthy's witch hunts for Communists traumatized the bureaucracy in the early 50s, but the government and its city kept growing. A crew of **Cold Warriors** conducted affairs of state throughout the 50s and 60s. **John F. Kennedy's** narrow victory in **1960** and his lovely wife **Jacqueline** enchanted the press and brought a new cultural savvy to the still-provincial capital. His Texan successor, **Lyndon B. Johnson,** bullied Congress into civil rights action, then steered the nation deep into the **Vietnam War.** Even still, the District grew till it spilled past its borders—the area's population doubled from 1950 to 1970s, ballooning in the suburbs where the 1950s bourgeoisie nested.

Scandal around Washington held the nation rapt during the **Watergate** years of 1973-4, when the break-ins **President Richard Nixon** authorized and the White House audiotapes he made led to his disgrace and resignation. The **Carter** administration (1977-81) brought in Democratic outsiders from Georgia, while the **Reagan** administration (1981-89) imported Conservative outsiders and smooth operators, many from his native California. The two Reagan inaugurals were the most expensive ever. During these years, conservative appointees clashed with moderate federal workers, pro-business attitudes paralyzed regulators, and the Pentagon's $1000 toilet seats had their fifteen minutes of fame. While the **Teflon President's** popularity cowed Congress for several years, the **Iran-contra scandals** of 1986-88 showed either astounding disregard for the law

1917
The US enters WWI.

1918
WWI ends.

1919
Race riots and white "negrophobia" convulse the city.

1931-32
Hunger marchers demonstrate on Washington.

1941
After the bombing of Pearl Harbor, America enters WWII.

1945
WWII ends with Allied victory.

1953
Supreme Court's Lost Laws ruling desegregates most of the city.

or incredible ignorance at the top. **President George Bush's** administration bore witness to the passing of **communism** in Eastern Europe and Soviet Union, and fought a high-profile war in the **Middle East.** Amid the pomp and circumstance of the victory parade, scandals sent voter confidence plummeting.

With Fleetwood Mac's "Don't Stop Thinking About Tomorrow" playing in the background, **Democrat Bill Clinton** headed into the White House in 1993. Clinton spent much of his first term waging an unsuccessful campaign for health care reform, scuttled by a Congress too timid to ask employers to pay for universal health care coverage. Clinton suffered another defeat when the House failed to pass his crime bill, which would have banned certain types of assault weapons and helped cities to hire additional police officers.

Buoyed by a rebounding economy, however, Clinton bounced back and won re-election in 1996. His approval ratings remained high, even as he confronted public censure and an impeachment trial after admitting to having "improper sexual relations" with former White House intern **Monica Lewinsky.** Initially claiming in the courts that he "did not have sexual relations with that woman—Miss Lewinsky," Clinton later recanted that statement after significant contrary evidence was presented to the Supreme Court. Claiming that the President had committed perjury by consciously lying to the courts, the Judiciary Committee opened his impeachment hearings on November 19, 1998. On December 19, Clinton became the second President in history to be impeached by the House of Representatives (following Andrew Johnson's **impeachment** by the House in 1868) when the House approved two articles of impeachment against Clinton and sent the articles on to the Senate for approval. The biggest political scandal since Watergate ended on February 13th, 1999 when the Senate acquitted Clinton after failing to achieve the two-thirds majority vote needed to convict him. The most recent presidential election (with primary contenders Democrat Al Gore and Republican George W. Bush) will have taken place in November of 2000, as this book was going to press.

HOME RULE FOR D.C.

I may not be perfect, but I'm perfect for Washington.
   —Marion Barry

Downtown developers kept Washington D.C.'s economy moving from the late 70s to the late 80s, though often at the expense of residential areas. While the city's population dropped to 617,000 in 1988, the suburbs ballooned, producing pseudo-urban areas like Rockville, Maryland—the state's second largest city. While the 70s produced flight to suburban outposts, the 80s lured many back to the townhouses of formerly run-down or blue-collar neighborhoods. Hopeful immigrants continue arriving in the city and suburbs, especially in Mount Pleasant, Adams Morgan, Arlington, and Montgomery County. These groups fuel the metropolitan area with plenty of cultural and commercial vitality.

Congressional rule came to an end in 1973 with the passage of the **Home Rule Act,** which gave D.C. a mayor, a city council, and a non-voting delegate to Congress. The winning mayoral candidate, **Walter E. Washington,** represented the black middle-class.

Washington, who had been the city's appointed mayor for the previous seven years, was too entrenched in the establishment to clean house. He was replaced in 1978 by **Marion Barry,** a prominent 60s civil-rights leader. Barry replaced two-thirds of the city government's staff and initiated a series of programs that turned Washington into a mini-welfare state. By the end of his third term, D.C. employed 48,000 workers.

By the mid-80s, however, the shine had worn off the Barry administration. Corruption was widespread, and crack cocaine use was rampant. The grand finale came when Barry himself was caught using crack in January 1990. Political outsider **Sharon Pratt Kelly** campaigned with a broom in her hand and was elected mayor the following November. Yet, her promises of security and stability proved hollow, and she was defeated in 1994 by Barry himself, fresh from detox.

Upon assuming office again, Barry inherited a deficit of around $700 million, but he didn't have to worry about it for long. A month after he took over, Congress created a **Financial Control Board** with total control over district spending. During the first year of Congressional fiscal control, D.C. ran a surplus of $186 million. Legislation in June of 1997 took away most power that Barry had left, prompting the Mayor to protest "the rape of democracy." His cries fell on deaf ears; the Financial Control Board retains control over the city indefinitely, although power may be returned as soon as 2001 if the city's budget remains balanced.

On January 2, 1999, former Chief Financial Officer of the District of Columbia, **Anthony A. Williams,** took office as the city's mayor. His agenda contains five principal goals, including improving customer service, cleaning up the city, helping residents find employment, bringing in more businesses, and nurturing strong communities.

Historic Home

ARCHITECTURE

At its formal best...Washington has a solemn full-blown beauty...In the Venetian light the art of politics recedes into the art of architecture. The eye rejoices and the soul expands. The experience is more than the pleasurable recognition of an impressive vista or a successful dialogue between structures and spaces. It is an act of love between citizen and stone.
      —Ada Huxtable

Woodlawn Plantation

Early D.C. architects were self-consciously designing for a **republic**—in their eyes, the most important one since the Romans. Their federal style unapologetically echoed **Athens** and **Rome** with columns, pediments, friezes, and marble. Many of the early designs—including those for the Capitol and the White House—were selected in anonymous competitions entered mostly by amateur architects. The mid-1800s saw the advent of the professional architect. The outstanding designer of the period was **Benjamin Latrobe,** who designed two models of sophistication, **St. John's Church** and **Decatur House.**

Hirshhorn Museum

D.C.'s architecture became **Victorian** and excessive in the 1870s under **Boss Shepherd,** who authorized A. B. Mullet's State, War, and Navy Building (now the **Old Executive Office Building,** see p. 62). The building's gingerbread windows delight tourists today, but severe Neoclassicists of the early 1900s hated the building and repeatedly tried to get it demolished. Whereas the Old Executive Office Building goes overboard on ornaments, the Smithsonian's **Arts and Industries Building** is a garish flood of contrasting colors—fun to look at but hard to imagine wanting to build. The Library of Congress's **Jefferson Building** (see p. 52), the magnificent Pension building (now the **National Building Museum,** see p. 121), and the **Old Post Office** (see p. 72) are dignified examples of the Victorian style.

The budget-inspired freeze on building that followed "Boss" Shepherd's fall from power thawed around the turn of the century, when **Daniel Burnham** brought the **Beaux Arts** style to Washington. The McMillan Commission funded Burnham's **Union Station,** which is now a station-*cum*-shopping-mall (see p. 53). The Commission also proposed the **Lincoln Memorial** (see p. 56), which heralded a return to a bigger and sparser variety of Neoclassicism. **John Russell Pope,** the undisputed master of 30s and 40s Greco-Roman building, designed the domed **West Building** of the **National Gallery of Art** (see p. 116).

When the dust of **World War II** cleared, D.C. began striving to blend **International Modernism's** clean lines and brutal simplicity with the monumental marbleness of existing construction; some buildings, like the **Kennedy Center,** do this fairly successfully. In this, it heralded the **postmodern** architecture that moved here in earnest from New York in the late 80s. Postmodern buildings rewrite old styles in a plainer, more modern vocabulary; the **Canadian Embassy** (see p. 70), which puts **Greek** elements where the Greeks would never think to put them, is certainly the best postmodern building now standing in D.C. A few especially nice postmodern offices stand among mediocre older buildings at 20th and M St. NW (at the northwest corner) and along K St.

VISUAL ARTS

MEMORIALS. The body politique's craze to commemorate has filled D.C. with a profusion of public art. Eagles squint from cornices, workers labor heroically from the neo-Hellenic friezes above public buildings, and generals and statesmen gesture from horseback in almost every traffic circle. Most public statues date from between the 1870s, when public art remembered Civil War figures, and World War II, when the government found more urgent ways to spend its money. Some statues bear curious anecdotes (like **General Winfield Scott** in Scott Circle or **Benito Juarez** on Virginia Ave. NW), others have curious inscriptions (like the modern memorial on Roosevelt Island, see p. 100), and still others might actually teach you some history. Some of the city's best monuments are the **Ulysses S. Grant Memorial** near the Capitol, the statue of **Robert Emmet** near Dupont Circle, and the hard-to-get-to **Adams Memorial** in Rock Creek Cemetery.

The public memorial, its own art form, half sculpture and half architecture, may have reached its apex in Washington. Memorials give designers more room to innovate and viewers more space to contemplate than simple sculptures. D.C.'s memorials reach their highest concentration west of the Mall (see p. 55), where the **Washington Monument** and the **Lincoln Memorial** and **Jefferson Memorial** lurk. Designs range from the copycat Greek of the **Lincoln Memorial** to the spare self-reflection of the **Vietnam Veterans Memorial,** the simplest and most affecting piece of outdoor art in Washington.

MUSEUM COLLECTIONS. Though not a hotbed of visual innovation, Washington still boasts world-class museum collections. The **West Wing** of the **National Gallery of Art** is filled to the brim with **Raphaels** and **Vermeers.** The **Hirshhorn's cylinder** is powered by two engines: contemporary art and 20th-century sculpture. Away from the mall, check out the **Phillips Collection,** the **Corcoran Gallery** (for 19th-century Americana and 1980s art), the **Renwick** (for American crafts), and the **National Museum of American Art.** Collector **Duncan Phillips'** museum was showing off modern art while New York's MOMA was still just a building fund, but D.C. had no indigenous painters until a generation later, when **Kenneth Noland's** clean-lined abstracts, **Gene Davis's** parallel trips, and the experimental canvases of critical darling **Morris Louis** were said to form the **Washington Color School.** For more information on Washington's museums, see **Museums,** p. 111.

MUSIC

Washington's indigenous music began with **John Philip Sousa,** who led the **Marine Corps Marching Band** from the 1880s to the 1900s. Sousa taught the band to play, then initiated the bevy of **military brass** concert parades that stomp and honk by the Mall to this day. Things later began to swing: the **Howard Theater** and other jazz venues cultivated a string of Washington artists, most notably the immortal band leader, jazz composer, and pianist **Duke Ellington.** D.C. celebrated Ellington's legacy last year, as the centennial of his birth in 1899 swung into motion on the stages of D.C. in hundreds of tribute concerts. One of America's most prolific composers of all time (he wrote well over 2000 pieces), Ellington travelled through virtually the entire history of jazz, from **ragtime** and **big-band swing** in the **20s** and **30s** to experimental in the **1960s** and **70s**. Jazz song-stresses from D.C. include **Roberta Flack** and **Shirley Horne.**

D.C. **rock 'n' roll** didn't get off the ground until punk touched down in the early 80s. In 1981 hardcore and straight edge were born when a bunch of D.C. kids with guitars listening to **Bad Brains** decided to play as fast and as loud as possible, while consciously abstaining from the violence and drug-use that typically characterized life in music's fast-lane. Bands such as **Teen Idles** and **SOA** led this trend. In 1985, they proclaimed the **Revolution Summer of '85.** The **9:30 Club** and **The Black Cat** pick up much of the slack, hosting big and small acts nightly (after a show at the latter, you can join the performers during their 3am snacks at **Dante's on 14th St.**; see **Rock and Pop,** p. 137, for more live music venues).

The indigenous sound of D.C. is **go-go,** a genre of **raw, rhythmic dance music** that was born in Washington's African-American community in the **late 1960s.** Go-go music blends funk rhythms, African percussion, and instrumental virtuosity with hypnotic rap vocals. The best go-go bands include nine or ten players, mostly percussionists. According to legend, the father of go-go, **Chuck Brown,** got his first guitar in prison in exchange for five packs of cigarettes. After his release in 1962, he put together the **Soul Searchers,** whose **"Bustin' Loose"** became a national hit. The band soon had many imitators, such as **Experience Unlimited** (later E.U.), who went national with their hit song, **"Da Butt,"** and **Rare Essentials,** arguably the hottest go-go band of the 1980s. Repeated attempts to take go-go national have failed. Some say promoters have failed to do it justice, while others maintain that the experience of live go-go just can't be copied on vinyl. Though go-go died down for a while in the early 90s, it's tribal pulse and pure, raw beat is back in style again. Keep your ears open for the go-go groove at clubs around town and at festivals like **Malcolm X Day, Marvin Gaye Day,** or **Adams-Morgan Day** (see **Calendar of Events,** p. 10).

Ska and **Swing,** two current music movements with close ties to the big-band sounds of the **30s** and **40s,** also have a strong presence. Ska, a blend of funk beats, jazz horns, and raucous energy, is meant to be experienced live. **"Skanking,"** the sort of running-in-place, energetic dance done to ska, can be seen at clubs around town, as D.C.-based bands like the jazzy **Eastern Standard Time** and hyper-insane **Decepticonz** rev up crowds to frenzied pitches. Check out the album *DC-Ska* for a sampling of D.C.'s ska-masters.

Dumbarton Oaks

Sculpture Garden at National Gallery

Washington Post

inside
SECRETS TO...

local bands

Vertical Horizon finally gave D.C. fans "everything they wanted" when the alternative group gained nationwide recognition in 1999. Formed by two Georgetown students, **Keith Kane** and **Matt Scannell** in 1991, the group managed to work odd jobs after graduation and scrape together enough cash to record their first album in 1992 entitled *There and Back Again*. The band soon developed a following among Georgetown students and alums and recorded two more albums, *Running on Ice*, and *Live Stages*, before attracting the attention of major label RCA and recording *Everything You Want* in 1998. The title track off that CD curried the band critical favor and solidified their future as a major mover and shaker in the music industry. Looking to follow in their footsteps are local bands such as **Absolutely Boxspring** which plays a quirky mix of blues, pop, and hard rock, and **Laughing Colors,** an alternative band which has opened for the likes of **Dishwalla** and **Marcy Playground.**

Meanwhile, hipsters are donning their saddleshoes and fedoras to swing to the sounds of big-band jazz from D.C. based ensembles like the **J Street Jumpers, Swing Shift,** and **The Tom Cunningham Orchestra.** For more info on the swinging, rocking, and crooning going on nightly in D.C., see **Entertainment, p. 137.**

LITERATURE

More than any other US city, Washington is a place of temporary inspirations: poets, lecturers, novelists, and journalists have lived briefly in D.C., producing some of their best and brightest works during their stay. Before the late twentieth century, however, Washington claimed no true indigenous literary center. Even today, Washington reputedly has more writers per population than any other city in the US.

The earliest writer to settle in the capital was poet **Walt Whitman,** who lived in D.C. from 1862 to 1873. He originally came to find and nurse his wounded brother: he stayed to volunteer as a Union Army nurse. During his time in Washington, he also published two editions of his watershed book, *Leaves of Grass*, shocking the literary world with his spontaneous and whimsical poetics.

In 1880, historian **Henry Adams** invented the city's only native literary genre, the **Washington Novel,** with *Democracy*. Centering on politics and scandal, corrupt politicians, and noble truth-seekers, Washington novels are still written today by authors like Tom Clancy and John Grisham. Among the strangest of the writers that ventured to D.C. in the 1880s was poet **Joaquin Miller,** the namesake of the Joaquin Miller Poetry Festival held annually in Rock Creek Park (see p. 85). Always looking stellar in high-heels and a sombrero, Miller built a small cabin on Meridian Hill in which he holed himself away for years while writing streams of verse.

Literature emanated from the African-American community in the early 20th century, when the famous Harlem Renaissance established a D.C. outpost around U St. through Shaw and in LeDroit Park. Ballad-poet **Paul Dunbar's** move to D.C. was emulated by **Langston Hughes** and **Jean Toomer.** The **MuSoLit Club** gave black intelligentsia a gathering place.

Other poets made strange pilgrimages to see *Cantos* verse-maker **Ezra Pound,** who was confined in St. Elizabeth's for criminal insanity (see **Pound Impounded,** below). Literary lions and doves converged on D.C. for the **1968 March on the Pentagon,** led by novelist **Norman Mailer** and by **Robert Lowell,** whose poem "July in Washington" may be the best ever written about the city. Since World War II, the **Library of Congress** has attracted important poets for the two-year position as **Poetry Consultant;** in the mid-80s the title changed to Poet Laureate (held now by **Robert Pinsky**).

THE WASHINGTON NOVELS

Democracy, by Henry Adams (1880). Written on the corner of 16th and H St., this political novel introduced the genre. Corruption, scandal, and intrigue 19th-century style.

District of Columbia, by John Dos Passos (1952). A series of novels highlighting the dog-eat-dog world of politics from an author whose spared-down style is oft-compared to Ernest Hemingway.

Washington, D.C., by Gore Vidal (1967). Surprise, surprise. The American government shamelessly degrades itself yet again in a fast-paced novel that the *New Yorker* called "the finest of contemporary novels about the capital."

THEATER

From 1964 to 1973, Washington was the only city in the country outside of New York with two professional resident theater companies. The **Arena Stage** was the first professional resident theater in D.C., followed shortly after by the now defunct **Washington Theater Club,** a small theater devoted to producing new and experimental works. The Washington Theater Club imported famous actors like Gene Hackman and Billy Dee Williams to premiere new works by aspiring playwrights: plays like **Harold Pinter's** *The Birthday Party* and works by **Eugene Ionesco** and **Lanford Wilson** were produced on the club's stage sometimes years before they arrived in New York. For a listing of D.C. theaters, see **Theater and Dance,** p. 141. The construction of the **John F. Kennedy Center for the Performing Arts** (see p. 142) in 1971 provided a much-needed cultural center. Today, the Kennedy Center is home to the **Washington Ballet** (see p. 144), the **Washington Opera** (see p. 140), the **American College Theater Festival** (see **Calendar of Events,** p. 10), and scores of other productions annually. The dance scene in Washington has also grown dramatically in the past two decades. The **Washington Ballet,** a company that has primarily focused on classical works, received a hyperactive and extremely creative new Artistic Director, **Septime Webre,** in 1999. For information on dance venues in town, see **Theater and Dance,** p. 141.

FILM

Hollywood, for better or worse, has always had an obsession with the monument-strewed streets and political intrigues of the US capital. Over the years, moviemakers have focused their cameras here in over 170 films, from the classic silent film *Birth of a Nation* in 1915 to 90s blockbusters like *Forrest Gump* (1994) and *Deep Impact* (1998).

WASHINGTON FILMS

The Exorcist (1973). Spinning heads! Shrieking priests! Satan would kill to see this movie! Oh, yeah, and it was filmed in Georgetown.

All the President's Men (1976). Pre-wrinkly Robert Redford and Dustin Hoffman as the reporters who broke the Watergate scandal. Even Nixon gave it 2 thumbs up.

In the Line of Fire (1992). Assassin John Malkovich asks Secret Service agent Clint Eastwood, "Would you take a bullet for the President?"

Forrest Gump (1995). Reflecting Pool scene makes you "happy to be in our nation's capital." This film is like a box of chocolates.

The American President (1995). Toxically insipid but strangely charming film with Michael Douglas and Annette Bening.

Sights

Saw Washington Monument. Phallic. Appalling. A national catastrophe.
   —British writer Arnold Bennett

Washington's true colors don't reveal much subtlety in hue along the Mall, where even the buildings are white. So, although you shouldn't miss the classic sights of **Political Washington,** be sure to also scope the diverse offerings in the **Second City,** where D.C's ethnic restaurants, nightclubs, and galleries roost. Despite their poverty, the dilapidated areas **Beyond the Northwest Quadrant** reward cautious, streetwise visitors with a dose of D.C.'s reality. For a complete breakdown of neighborhoods, see **Once in D.C.,** p. 20.

POLITICAL WASHINGTON

CAPITOL HILL

◪ Highlights: *Capitol, Supreme Court, Library of Congress.* **Museums:** *National Postal Museum, Children's Museum, Sewall-Belmont House.* **Food & Drink:** *p. 161.* **Nearby:** *Mall, Old Downtown, South of the Mall.* **See also:** *Southeast Capitol Hill, p. 92.*

Capitol Hill is the heart of American government, Washington's principal tourist attraction, and one of democracy's most potent icons. Prepare to spend at least a day here exploring the halls of power, but **be cautious in this area at night.** The Hill's approximate boundaries are North and South Capitol streets to the southwest, H Street NE to the north, Lincoln Park to the east, and the Southeast-Southwest Freeway to the south. Most major sights, including the Library of Congress, the Folger Shakespeare Library, and the Supreme Court, cluster close to the Capitol building itself. At dusk, night owls head for the bars and restaurants that line Pennsylvania Ave. between 2nd and 7th St. SE. Use Metro: Capitol South, Eastern Market, Federal Center, or Union Station.

THE CAPITOL

🛈 Contact: *Tourist information* ☎ 225-6827, *Senate offices* ☎ 224-3121, *House offices* ☎ 225-3121; *www.aoc.gov.* **Metro:** *Capitol South or Union Station.* **Hours:** *Daily Mar.-Aug. 9am-8pm; Sept.-Feb. 9am-4:30pm. Closed Thanksgiving, Christmas, and New Years Day.* **Tours:** *Mar.-Aug. M-F 9am-7pm, Sa 9am-4pm; Sept.-Feb. M-Sa 9am-4pm.* **Avoiding the line:** *If you do not want to take the guided tour, do not wait in the line in front of the building. Between mid-Mar. and mid-June, the wait may be as long as 2hr. Instead, enter the building under the steps on the East Front. The entrances here are occasionally closed. If so, head to any House or Senate Office Building and take the subway into the Capitol.* **Accessing closed areas:** *Capitol Police will tell you if you have strayed out of the visitor areas. Pages and interns are allowed to take visitors with them to closed areas of the building. When Congress is not meeting you can access the cloakrooms, where Congressmen linger near the floor, or even the smelly corridors where the garbage is collected, in the company of an intern.* **Viewing the proceedings:** *Americans must get a pass from their senator or representative. Passes can easily be obtained at the House or Senate Office Buildings with proof of residence and are valid for an entire 2-year session of Congress. Foreign nationals may get passes valid for a single day at either the House or Senate appointments desks in the crypt level. Visitors are often disappointed to find that Congress is not meeting during their visit; call ahead to check.* **Accessibility:** *Handicapped accessible. Wheelchairs available. Tours and special assistance for visitors with disabilities are available from the Congressional Special Services Office (☎ 224-4048, TDD 224-4049) in the central crypt area.*

The US Capitol may be an endless font of cynicism, but the structure's scale and style still evoke the glory of the republican ideal. In the spirit of all things Congressional, the Capitol was built by committee. A design by amateur architect **William Thornton** was selected in an anonymous competition in 1793. Thornton resigned in 1800 amid politicking among the project's architects, and **Benjamin Latrobe** took over. The Brits, on a path of destruction, burned down the whole shebang in 1814, using books from the Library of Congress as kindling. **Charles Bullfinch** replaced Latrobe as Congress's interior designer in 1818, finishing the Capitol's central section with a dome made of copper-plated wood. By 1850, the building could no longer contain the expanding Congress, and President Fillmore tapped **Thomas U. Walter** to expand the edifice and erect the Rotunda. Assisted by **Montgomery Meigs,** Walter oversaw the 1860s construction of the awe-inspiring cast-iron dome that stands today.

THE EXTERIOR. The three-tiered **East Front** stands opposite the Supreme Court and the Library of Congress Jefferson Building. From Jackson (1829) to Carter (1977), most US presidents took their inaugural oath on the East Front. Reagan's 1981 inauguration ceremony was the first administered on the **West Front,** whose grand entrance overlooks the National Mall. At night the West Front is deserted but patrolled by Capitol Police officers, and makes for a romantic stroll.

The **Senate** and **House of Representatives** are located in the north and south wings, respectively; a US flag over either wing denotes that the corresponding body is in session. At the apex of the dome stands Thomas Crawford's statue *Freedom;* a full-size, plaster model in the basement of the Russell Senate Office Building lets you get a close-up view of the statue without uncomfortable neck craning.

Outside the East Front, at 1st St. NW, the 1922 **Grant Memorial** is encircled by driveways and barricades. A weary General Ulysses S. Grant contemplates war in a sea of equine chaos. Near the entrance, note the female trio of America, Hope, and Justice in the true 19th-century spirit of representing women as abstract objects. The East Portico displays Randolph Rogers's huge bronze **Columbus Doors,** which mimic Ghiberti's Gates of Paradise in Florence.

THE ROTUNDA. Inside the doors, the 180ft. high, 96ft. wide Rotunda stretches and yawns. A frieze of condensed history encircles the collar of the dome. The frieze was largely executed by **Constantino Brumidi,** but was finished by others after Brumidi fell off his scaffold in 1877 and died three months later; one of his successors paid him tribute by painting his face on a tree (look behind the two rows of soldiers over the door to the corridor leading south towards the House Chamber). In the overhead **Apotheosis of George Washington,** George occupies the center of a giant allegory, as Liberty, Victory, the 13 states, and countless virtues look on.

Eight enormous paintings from the early years of the United States hang below the fresco at ground level. Among them is John Trumbull's **The Declaration of Independence,** featured on the rare $2 bill. An enormous sculpture by Adelaide Johnson was recently moved nearby after protests over the lack of sculptures of women in the Capitol. It depicts the heads of women suffragists **Elizabeth Cady Stanton, Susan B. Anthony,** and **Lucretia Mott** emerging from a huge block of marble. The uncut marble jutting up behind the heads is for a bust of the first woman president.

Statesmen from Lincoln to JFK have lain in state in the Rotunda center for a day prior to burial, but only those to be buried in the Tomb of the Unknown Soldier are required by law to do so. Recently, in his much-publicized "Living Will," the late President Richard Nixon opted to forego this highest of national honors. **Andrew Jackson** was the target of an assassination attempt when he was viewing a body lying in state. The would-be assassin's bullets just missed him; to this day, luck-seekers still rub the feet of a bronze Jackson located in the Rotunda.

The Capitol

OLD HOUSE CHAMBER (STATUARY HALL). Just south of the Rotunda, still on the second level, is the Old House Chamber, the first meeting place of the House of Representatives. **John Quincy Adams** (the only President to serve in Congress after being President) was the first to realize that the room was a rather effective echo chamber. Legend has it that Adams used to lie on his desk "sleeping," as he listened to his political adversaries converse on the other side of the room (ironically, Adams had a stroke at the same desk, and died shortly afterwards). The growing House was eventually forced to move down the hall to the current House Chamber. Since then, the raising of the floor by 12ft. has eliminated the acoustic idiosyncrasies of the room. Only one disturbingly clear whisper tunnel remains. After the House moved, a joint resolution of Congress renamed the chamber Statuary Hall and asked each state for statues of two famous natives. The statues quickly became too much weight for the floor to bear, and the figures were dispersed throughout the building.

Lincoln Memorial

OLD SENATE CHAMBER. North of the Rotunda is the Old Senate Chamber, former stomping ground of such renowned blabbermouths as **Daniel Webster, John C. Calhoun,** and **Henry Clay.** The chamber was restored in 1976 for the American bicentennial celebration to look as it did when last occupied in 1859.

THE CRYPT. The designers of the Capitol had planned to bury George and Martha Washington in a tomb below the crypt. The architects commissioned a statue of **George Washington** to sit above the tomb, but the Washingtons' descendants thwarted the plans when they refused to allow the couple's bodies to be exhumed from Mount Vernon. The statue of Washington eventually found its way to the Smithsonian National Museum of American History. An enormous bust of **Abraham Lincoln** now keeps watch over Washington's empty tomb. Lincoln's head has no left ear—the sculptor (Gutzon Borlgun, who later sculpted Mount Rushmore) claimed that the absent feature is representative of Lincoln's unfinished life.

The crypt also contains the **compass stone,** originally the exact center of Washington, D.C.; it is from this point of origin

Inside the Library of Congress

that the District's quadrants (NW, NE, SW, SE) are drawn. The stone ceased to be the center of the city in 1847 when Arlington was given back to Virginia. On the house side of the crypt rests Hawaii's statue honoring **Father Damien,** who contracted leprosy on an island colony he founded for the state's lepers. Since clothes irritated his skin, a cage was built to hold his clothes away from his body. The statue, located on the ground floor on the House side, shows his contorted face and the cylindrical shape the cage gave him. Nearby is Colorado's statue of Apollo XIII astronaut **Jack Swigert,** the newest statue in the collection and the only statue in color.

OLD SUPREME COURT CHAMBER. Also on the crypt level is the Old Supreme Court Chamber, where the justices supreme met from 1810-1859. The Chamber has a somewhat sinister history: in 1806, the ceiling gruesomely crushed one of Latrobe's assistants, effectively ending an ongoing argument Latrobe had been having over what kind of support was necessary for the Capitol's walls. Latrobe's cat disappeared at the same time, and ghost stories of the **Demon Cat** have haunted the Capitol ever since.

HOUSE AND SENATE CHAMBERS. To reach the galleries of the House and Senate chambers, climb up from the crypt levels on the respective sides of the Capitol. Visitors must check all bags and electronic equipment and then go through metal detectors before being allowed in the galleries. In the House and Senate Chambers, expect a few bored-looking elected officials failing to listen to a speaker talking straight to home-district cable TV viewers. The House Chamber packs in official Washington every January for the President's State of the Union Address.

The real business of Congress is conducted in committee hearings all over the Capitol and in the House and Senate office buildings. Most hearings are open to the public. *The Washington Post's* "Today in Congress" box in the paper's A-section lists hearings and their assigned rooms. Especially interesting and controversial hearings can get very crowded; the few seats are usually reserved for lobbyists and other hangers-on. Potential visitors should show up early and keep their fingers crossed.

US BOTANICAL GARDENS

◪ Location: *At 1st St. and Maryland Ave. SW.* **Metro:** *Federal Center.* **Contact:** *☎ 225-8333.*
In front of the Capitol, exotic foliage from all continents and climates vegetates inside and outside the US Botanical Gardens. Most of the gardens will be closed through the fall of 2000 for renovation, but **Bartholdi Park,** across the street at 1st and Independence St. SW, has exhibits from the botanical gardens that will remain open to the public. Auguste Bartholdi, who designed the Statue of Liberty, is also author to the 40-ton cast-iron fountain that is the park's centerpiece. Purchased by Congress in 1877, the greenish fountain has feral turtles heartily spewing water, while live ducks express bewilderment.

TAFT MEMORIAL

◪ Location: *Northwest of the Capitol, between Constitution, New Jersey, and Louisiana Ave. NW.*
This 1958 statue of Ohio senator **Robert A. Taft** (son of President Taft) assiduously defends a large concrete obelisk. Twenty-seven bells set into the obelisk ring like church chimes every 15 minutes. The statue marks the beginning of **Union Station Plaza,** a park running from the Capitol to the Station.

HOUSE AND SENATE OFFICE BUILDINGS

◪ Location: *On Constitution and Independence Ave.* **Metro:** *Capitol South for the House, and Union Station or Capitol South and the Capitol subway system for the Senate.* **Hours:** *M-F 8am-7pm.*
Flanking the Capitol are the House and Senate Office Buildings. Although the cramped Capitol is the site for all formal meetings of the House and Senate, the real work of legislating is done here, where Congressmen have their offices. Americans should be able to find the offices of their Congressmen without much trouble; consult the directories posted near all entrances and elevators. The receptionist in your Congressman's office will give you passes to the House and Senate galleries with proof of residence in your state or district. You can always ride the underground subway (a.k.a. **"the capitol choochoo"**) to the Capitol from any of the buildings.

Notice the gigantic sculpture by Alexander Calder, *Mountains and Clouds,* in the Hart Senate Office Building (the actual buildings are uninteresting for visitors). Calder's sculpture occupies nine stories of the building's atrium and may be viewed in its natural light from the ground floor or from the building's various open balconies. The stable black "mountains," sculpted from sheet metal, weigh 39 tons; the mobile "clouds," made from aircraft aluminum, weigh 4300 lb. A computer controls the mobile's rotation.

SEWALL-BELMONT HOUSE

🏛 *Location:* 144 Constitution Ave. NE. *Metro:* Union Station. *Contact:* ☎ 546-3989.

Nestled beside the Hart building is the Sewall-Belmont House, which was built in 1798 by **Robert Sewall** but incorporates parts of a house dating back to 1680. The British set the house ablaze in 1814 but restorations returned it to tip-top shape. In 1929, the **National Woman's Party** bought the building for its headquarters, a function the house still serves today. The house showcases a small museum on the women's movement by tour only (see p. 123).

Washington Monument

THE SUPREME COURT

🏛 *Location:* 1 1st St. NE. *Metro:* Capitol South or Union Station. *Contact:* ☎ 479-3000. *Hours:* Courtroom open M-F 9am-4:30pm. *Tours:* The court is in session from Oct.-June, and hears oral arguments Oct.-Apr. M-W 10am-noon and 1-3pm for about 2 weeks of each month. Arguments open to the public, on a first-come, first-served basis. Seating begins at 9:30am with a line usually beginning to form at 8:30am. Everyone is cleared out of the courtroom and the Great Hall during the lunch break (noon-1pm); lines form again for the 1pm session. The "3-minute line" shuffles visitors through the courtroom for a brief glimpse of the hearings. Check the Washington Post for case listings. *Admission:* Free.

Even though they're not looking for votes, the nine appointed justices of the nation's highest court graciously open their courtroom to the touristing masses. From 1800 to 1935, the justices met in the Capitol, first in any empty office they could find and later in the room now known as the **Old Supreme Court Chamber.** This chamber was so poorly illuminated that when some justices complained that a newly arrived statue of Justice depicted the abstract female without the traditional blindfold, Chief Justice **John Marshall** replied that it was fine— she couldn't possibly see anything in the room anyway. In 1935, the court decided to take the nation's separation of powers literally and moved into its current location.

Supreme Court

The grand staircase leading to the entrance on 1st St. is flanked by James Earle Fraser's sculptures *Contemplation of Justice* and *Authority of Law*. Nearby, nine impressive figures strike a pose in the pediment (3 former Chief Justices, 3 classical Greek virtues, 1 former Senator, Cass Gilbert, the building's architect, and Robert Aitken, the pediment's sculptor). The entrance leads to a marble chamber with busts of former chief justices. Straight ahead, behind the red curtain, is the Supreme Court Chamber, where the court meets to hear cases.

To visit the Court, enter from the Maryland Ave. entrance. Below the court, a larger-than-life statue of John Marshall, the "Great Chief Justice," presides over an exhibit on the history of the court and the building. Around the corner from the exhibit hall, a small theater screens an interesting 24-minute film that walks visitors through the judicial process via intimate interviews with many of the justices. Any time the court is not sitting, visitors can file into the courtroom for 30-minute lectures on the

Hirshorn Museum

the on dopedc

Light Reading

The **smallest book** in the Library of Congress is a copy of *Old King Cole*, which is only one millimeter square (the size of a period at the end of a sentence), making it the smallest book in the world. Its tiny pages can only be turned using a needle. The **largest book** in the library is John James Audubon's *Birds of America*, which measures 1m in height and contains life-size illustrations of birds.

court (every hr. on the half-hour 9:30am-3:30pm). When the court is in session, visitors can observe entire oral argument sessions, or walk through the chambers for a brief three-minute glimpse.

THE LIBRARY OF CONGRESS

Location: *1st St. SE between E. Capitol St. and Independence Ave.* **Metro:** *Capitol South.* **Contact:** *Operator ☎ 707-5000, exhibition information ☎ 707-4604, treasures exhibit ☎ 707-3834, research ☎ 707-6400; www.loc.gov.* **Hours:** *Great Hall open M-Sa 8:30am-5:30pm, but areas of interest not fully accessible until 10am. Visitors Center open 10am-5:30pm. Treasures gallery open M-Sa 10am-5pm.* **Tours:** *Leave from the Visitors Center M-Sa 11:30am, 1, 2:30, and 4pm. Tours in Spanish available, call ahead for times.* **Events:** *A host of activities began in mid-1999 and will continue throughout 2000 to celebrate the library's bicentennial in 2000; call for details.* **Research:** *Researchers should enter the Jefferson Building on the 2nd St. side and go to Room G-40 to pick up a reader registration card. The Main Reading Room is open M, W, and Th 8:30am-9:30pm, Tu, F, and Sa 8:30am-5pm; most special collection reading rooms open M-F 8:30am-5pm.*

With 113,026,742 million objects stored on 532 miles of shelves, the Library of Congress is the largest library in the world. The original library was founded in 1800, when Congress began to assemble mostly law and history books for members' personal use. The British torched them all in 1814 (using some, legend has it, as kindling when they set the Capitol on fire). After the war, Congress bought Thomas Jefferson's personal collection of 6487 volumes to replace those that were lost. A fire in 1851 wiped out two-thirds of Jefferson's collection, at which point the surviving volumes were moved to a fire-proof iron room in the Capitol. The collection mushroomed after an 1870 copyright law guaranteed the library two free copies of every book registered in the United States. Today the library holds 26 million books in 460 languages.

When the Italian Renaissance **Jefferson Building,** the heart of today's library complex, opened in 1897, it was praised as a suitably grand home for one of the grandest collection of books in the world. In 1939, the library constructed the Art Deco **John Adams Building** (across 2nd St. from the Jefferson) to accommodate the growing collection, and added the enormous, marble **James Madison Building** in 1980. The Madison's 34.5 acres of floor space are packed almost exclusively with books, but the lobby hosts a small rotating exhibit.

JEFFERSON BUILDING. The Jefferson Building, whose green copper dome and gold-leafed flame seals a spectacular octagonal reading room, is one of the most beautiful edifices in the city. Visitors can wander the Great Hall and peer into the reading room on their own, but the guided tours are excellent. The Visitors Center provides maps and screens a jazzy 12-minute film, narrated by James Earl Jones, which runs continuously beginning at 10am. In the **Treasures Gallery** on the second floor of the Great Hall, a rotating exhibition, "Treasures of the Library of Congress," showcases the library's holdings. The famous Gutenberg Bible, one of three copies of the original 1455 edition, is in a protective case in the Great Hall.

Outside of the Jefferson Building, the **Fountain of Neptune** splish-splashes in the plaza. Wildly twisting horses flank the central figure of Neptune, turtles spit water at Nereids (high-class mermaids), Tritons (mermen) recline half-hidden in water, and twisting snakes spit water at tourists in this homage to Rome's Trevi Fountain.

The octagonal **Main Reading Room** has 250 desks, spread out under a spectacular dome whose apex hovers 160ft. above the floor; visitors can peer in on researchers from a sound-proof gallery. On the top of the dome, Edwin Bashfield's painting *Human Understanding* depicts the major civilizations of history and their primary contributions to mankind; America is represented by a syncretic depiction of Abraham Lincoln's head on a body of Rodin's *Thinker* with wings grafted to its back. The dome's windows feature the seals of each state in the Union. At the gallery level, sculptures represent major academic disciplines flanked by statues of individuals who have distinguished themselves in that field. On the ceiling of the hall are mosaics honoring Americans who have excelled in a variety of professions. Three medallions representing Medicine, Law, and Theology—considered to be the three most educated professions at the time of the library's construction—are at the center. The best way to see the library is to do research there, and tourists have been known to feign scholarly interests to gain access to some of the library's inner reaches. The huge collection, including the rarest items, is open to anyone of college age or older with a legitimate research purpose. The stacks are closed—they bring the books to you. The collection is non-circulating.

FOLGER SHAKESPEARE LIBRARY

⚑ Location: *201 E. Capitol St. SE, next to the Adams Building or the Library of Congress.* **Contact:** *Operator ☎544-4600, box office ☎544-7077; www.folger.edu.* **Hours:** *Exhibits open M-Sa 10am-4pm. Garden tours Apr.-Oct. every 3rd Sa of each month at 10 and 11am. Library open for researchers M-F 8:45am-4:45pm. The restricted portions of the library are open to the public annually on the Su closest to Apr. 23, Shakespeare's birthday.* **Admission:** *Free.* **Events:** *Performances, readings, and concerts in the Elizabethan Theater; call for details.*

The Folger Shakespeare Library houses the world's largest collection of Shakespeareana—over 280,000 books and manuscripts. Alas, unless you're a graduate student with research to do, you can't see any of it. Visitors can go inside the building, though, and see the Great Hall exhibition gallery, a re-created Tudor gallery with dark oak panels and carved Elizabethan doorways. Exhibitions usually feature drawings sampled from the library's collection. During the day, you can peek at the theater, which imitates the Elizabethan "innyard" theaters, like the Blackfriars, where Shakespeare's company performed. Outside, on the 3rd St. side of the building, tourists can stop for a rest or a quiet read in the small but cozy Elizabethan "knot" garden, so named because the different plants—chosen based on their popularity in Shakespeare's day—are arranged in intertwining patterns. The research areas of the library are open to the public one April weekend a year in celebration of Shakespeare's birthday.

UNION STATION

⚑ Location: *50 Massachusetts Ave. NE. Walk northeast down Delaware Ave. from the Capitol or take the Metro to Union Station.* **Contact:** *☎371-9441.* **Hours:** *Retail shops open M-Sa 10am-9pm, Su 10am-6pm.*
Two blocks north of the Capitol grounds, Union Station draws nearly three times as many visitors each day—70,000—as the Capitol itself. Most are there to use the Metro or hop an Amtrak train, but many come to admire **Daniel Burnham's** monumental Beaux Arts design, which cost $25 million to erect from 1905 to 1908. The station has welcomed visitors with 120 shops and a glitzy food court since its 1988 renovation. The train concourse is so expansive that it could fit the Washington Monument horizontally. The station also houses the **National Map Gallery** and a cavernous movie theater. A sculpture of Christopher Columbus stands in the circle outside the station. Across the street, Union Station plaza runs from the Capitol to the station.

NATIONAL CAPITOL POSTAL STATION

⚑ Location: *Corner of 1st St. and Massachusetts Ave.* **Hours:** *M-F 7am-midnight, Sa-Su 7am-8pm.*
Directly west of Union Station is the National Capitol Postal Station, another of Burnham Beaux Arts buildings, which was completed in 1914. The post office still operates

(enter on N. Capitol St.) but the building's new focus is playing host to the subterranean **National Postal Museum** (see p. 121).

GOVERNMENT PRINTING OFFICE

Location: *Bookstore entrance on N. Capitol St.* **Contact:** *☎512-0132.* **Hours:** *M-F 8am-4pm.*
The large, red-brick building farther up North Capitol St. houses the Government Printing Office. Although it has quietly served the government's printing needs for decades, the GPO skyrocketed to national recognition after its web site published the **Starr Report,** which scandalized the nation with President Clinton's intimate confessions of sexual indecency with one-time intern Monica Lewinsky. Tourists are restricted to the **bookstore,** which stocks such entertaining tomes as NATO Handbook of Emergency War Surgery, and the National List of Plant Species that Occur in Wetlands. Across the hall, the Congressional Sales Office sells Congressional publications.

CAPITAL CHILDREN'S MUSEUM

Location: *800 3rd St. NE, enter on 3rd St. between H and I St. NE.* **Metro:** *Union Station.* **Contact:** *☎675-4120; www.ccm.org.*
Northeast of Union Station is the Capital Children's Museum, housed in a large red-brick building that was once a convent. From Union Station, a trail of brilliantly colored mosaics called the **Hopscotch Kids** leads to the museum (see p. 118).

STANTON PARK

Location: *3 blocks southeast of Union Station down Massachusetts Ave. NE.*
Stanton Park offers benches, lots of shade, and a playground. The eclectic mix of white-collar lunchers, homeless loungers, and children frolicking in the playground here will give you an instant sense of Capitol Hill's diversity. The park's visual anchor is a skillful equestrian statue of **Nathaniel Greene, Esq.,** a Revolutionary War Major General.

CARING INSTITUTE

Location: *316-318 A St. NE.* **Contact:** *☎547-4273.* **Hours:** *Open by appt. only.* **Admission:** *$3.*
When he first moved to D.C. after the Civil War, black abolitionist and statesman Frederick Douglass lived at this house two blocks east of the Supreme Court. Once the site of the Smithsonian Museum of African Art, the three-story gray house now houses the museum of the Caring Institute, which honors benevolent Americans.

LINCOLN PARK

Location: *An 11-block walk from the Capitol down E. Capitol St.*
The first memorial statue of **Abraham Lincoln** in Washington stands in this park; it was constructed largely through donations from former slaves. One of the only statues of black women in D.C., a memorial to **Mary McLeod Bethune,** founder of the National Council of Negro Women, also stands in the park. **This area is dangerous after dark.**

THE MALL

YOU ARE HERE — SEE MAP P. 307 — U.S. Capitol Building

Highlights: *Smithsonian (see p. 111), National Gallery of Art (see p. 116).* **Nearby:** *Memorials, Old Downtown, South of the Mall.*
America's national backyard, the Mall was a railway yard and vacant lot until the early-20th century. The first of the large museum complexes was constructed in 1911 and the last above ground complex was finished in the 80s. With the exception of the Washington Monument, the memorials were not constructed until the 20th century, and the bulk were built post-World War II. Today's Mall is a hub of activity, home to the **Smithsonian Institute** and many of the memorials. The US Capitol, the White House, and the rest of the memorials all stand adjacent. Hundreds of people use the Mall's grassy lawn to sunbathe, frolic, and fly squadrons of kites, while die-hard runners pound the gravel paths throughout the year. The Mall and the Tidal Basin are the best places to welcome spring, when hundreds of cherry blossoms burst to life. These delicate flowers only last a week or two, so be sure to look for "blossom" updates on local news programs if you are in town in the early spring. Use the Smithsonian, L'Enfant Plaza, or Archives-Navy Memorial Metro stops to access the area.

The portions of the Smithsonian Institute on the Mall constitute the world's largest museum complex. They are joined on the Mall by a close cousin, the National Gallery of Art, which is technically separate from the Smithsonian.

THE MONUMENTS

WASHINGTON MONUMENT

⚑ Location: *Just west of the Smithsonian museums, between 15th and 17th St.* **Metro:** *Smithsonian.* **Contact:** *☎ 426-6840.* **Hours:** *Daily Apr.-Aug. 8am-midnight, ticket kiosk open 7:30am until all tickets are distributed; Sept.-Mar. 9am-5pm, ticket kiosk open from 8:30am.* **Admission:** *Free. Obtain same-day timed tickets at the 15th St. ticket kiosk; limit of 6 per person. Purchase advance tickets through Ticket-Master (☎ 432-7328 or (800) 551-7328; www.ticketmaster.com) before 3pm the day before you wish to visit the monument ($1.50 per ticket plus one-time 50¢ handling fee). Arrive 30min. before the appointed time.* **Accessibility:** *Handicapped accessible.*

The Washington Monument, at 555ft. tall and 90,854 tons, is the largest free-standing obelisk of its kind and a gargantuan, phallic shrine to America's first president. No cement holds the loose granite blocks together, but the monument is incredibly stable, capable of withstanding a tornado blowing at 145mph. A healthy sway of an eighth of an inch in 30mph winds helps to maintain stability. The monument tilts about 3 in. to the north on hot sunny days, as the stones on the sunlit side expand and those on the cooler, shaded side contract.

L'Enfant's original plan for D.C. called for the erection of an equestrian statue of Washington in the center of the Mall. Congress bickered over the plan for the monument for years. In 1833, prominent Washingtonians formed the **Washington National Monument Society,** a private organization dedicated to the construction of the monument. The society accepted a design by Treasury Building architect **Robert Mills** that called for a variation of the present obelisk with a one-story, 30-column temple around the base. Construction began on July 4, 1848, but the project soon ran out of money. Alabama couldn't afford a cash contribution to a fund aimed at sustaining construction, so the state sent a stone instead, starting a trend that saved the monument. Over 100 nations, states, towns and individuals sent stones; donors ranged from the Cherokee Nation to the American residents of Fu-Chow Fu, China. When the Vatican sent a block of marble in 1854, the Know-Nothings, an anti-Catholic political party, protested by stealing "the Pope's stone." During the Civil War, the half-finished monument was nicknamed the **Beef Depot Monument** in honor of the cattle that Army quartermasters herded on the grounds. When construction resumed after the war, builders switched to a different quarry because they had exhausted the stone in the original quarry. Consequently, the hue of the monument's stones change about 150ft. up from the base. Today, a 70-second elevator ride brings visitors to a gallery with spectacular views of D.C.

After a recent multi-million dollar restoration, the monument re-opened its doors to the public for the 2000 July 4th celebration. Countering the strains of over 100 years of rain, sleet, and snow, the renovation included a complete restoration of exterior masonry, a renovated observation level, and an expanded interpretive exhibit area. Now jutting upwards with a shiny new fervor, the monument clearly arouses a sense of patriotism or awe from onlookers.

REFLECTING POOL

⚑ Location: *Between the Washington Monument and Lincoln Memorial.*

The Reflecting Pool, between the Washington Monument and Lincoln Memorial, reflects the famed obelisk in seven million gallons of water. Modeled after similar pools at **Versailles** and the **Taj Mahal,** the Reflecting Pool's design minimizes wind ripples, and sharpens the watery visage of the monument. Swarms of people surround the 2000ft. by 160ft. pool at civil rights marches, war protests, and the yearly Fourth of July fireworks display.

CONSTITUTION GARDENS

⚑ Location: *North of the Reflecting Pool.*

The rather romantic Constitution Gardens was created in the 1970s to beautify the area between the Washington Monument and the Lincoln Memorial. Trees and paths surround a picturesque lake, at the center of which lies a willow-draped island commemorating the 56 signers of the **Declaration of Independence.** To reach the island, take the small bridge from the northern side of the lake.

VIETNAM VETERANS MEMORIAL

⚑ Location: *Northeast of the Lincoln Memorial, north of the Reflecting Pool, and south of Constitution Ave. at 22nd St.* **Metro:** *Foggy Bottom or Smithsonian.* **Contact:** *☎634-1568.* **Hours:** *24hr. Park rangers on staff daily 8am-midnight.* **Events:** *On Father's Day, children and grandchildren of veterans wash the wall.* **Accessibility:** *Handicapped accessible. Wheelchairs available upon request.*

The reflective black-granite wall offers somber contemplation and remembrance on one of the darker and more recent stains on American history: the Vietnam War. A public competition selected the design for the memorial in 1981. **Maya Ying Lin,** a Yale senior who originally received a "B" when she submitted her memorial concept to a professor at Yale, beat the other 1,421 entrants, including her professor, with the monument dedicated in 1982. She described her design as a "rift in the earth—a long, polished black stone wall, emerging from and receding into the earth...to be understood as one moves into and out of it." The walls bear the names of the 58,214 Americans who died or are still missing in Vietnam in chronological order of their death. A diamond adjacent to each name denotes that the death was confirmed, while a cross signals that the person remains unaccounted for.

When Maya Lin's design for the memorial was chosen, many veterans, citizens and politicians criticized the design for its lack of pomp and circumstance. Less artistic minds prevailed in the negotiations and a compromise was reached in which an alternate memorial would be erected alongside Lin's design. Noted sculptor **Frederick Hart** was commissioned to design a sculpture of troops emerging from an unknown battlefield. To this day, however, the powerful Lin memorial overshadows the **Three Servicemen** sculpture. Nonetheless, the argument led to an upsurge in special interest groups desiring their own memorials. To this end, a **Vietnam Women's Memorial** was also commissioned and stands southeast of the "men's" memorial. Sculpted by **Glenna Goodacre** in 1993, the touching memorial depicts three women around a wounded soldier. Eight yellowwood trees surround the statues, honoring the eight servicewomen killed in action in Vietnam.

Brilliant flowers, haunting pictures, poems, toys, and other memorabilia line the wall and compose makeshift shrines to the deceased. Veterans, friends, and families come to leave these personal offerings and trace the names of the deceased. Rangers collect the offerings daily and move them to a government warehouse. A small sample is on view at the **National Museum of American History** (see p. 112). Park rangers stationed at the west end of the memorial (the end nearest the Lincoln Memorial) answer questions and provide a printout with the full name, date of birth, date of death, and location on the memorial of the fallen or missing soldiers. Directories are available at either side of the memorial. Rangers provide paper for rubbings.

LINCOLN MEMORIAL

⚑ Location: *Southwest of the Vietnam Memorial, in line with the Reflecting Pool and Washington Monument at 23rd St.* **Metro:** *Smithsonian or Foggy Bottom.* **Contact:** *☎426-6895.* **Hours:** *24 hr. Park rangers on staff daily 8am-midnight. Bookshop open daily 7:30am-10:30pm.*

Modeled after the Parthenon, the commanding Lincoln Memorial looms over the reflecting pool in dramatic stone splendor. Though the nation demanded a memorial to Lincoln almost immediately after his assassination in 1865, the public had to wait 50 years before witnessing the memorial's completion. The grandiose memorial was designed by American architect **Henry Bacon,** who finally laid the cornerstone in 1915. During World War II, anti-aircraft shell hit the memorial during a misfire, knocking out a chunk of marble near the "Maryland" engraving on the front right of the upper level. **Daniel Chester French** was chosen to design the sculpture of Lincoln, which depicts him seated, keeping a stern watch over the city. **Picirrili brothers** stonecutting firm, which performed the actual sculpting, couldn't find a block of marble big enough for Lincoln; instead, they joined 28 blocks so tightly that visitors can barely see the seams.

Lincoln's stirring Gettysburg Address appears on the wall to the left of the statue as you enter. His second inaugural address, given 63 days prior to his assassination, appears on the right. Look for the word "future," not too subtly corrected from the erroneously carved "euture." Looming above Lincoln's famous words are **Jules Guerin's** allegorical, gold-detailed canvas murals. To the left, in *Emancipation*, the Angel of Truth frees slaves, flanked by Justice and Immortality. To the right, in *Reunion*, the Angel of Truth brings North and South together after the Civil War, with help from Fraternity and Charity. The elevation of the murals presents viewing difficulties, but the subject matter nevertheless captures the spirit of Lincoln that the memorial was designed to celebrate. Thirty-six simple Doric columns, each 44 ft. high, surround the building and commemorate the states in the Union when Lincoln was assassinated; their names are inscribed into a frieze directly above. The names of the 48 states in existence when the memorial was dedicated in 1922 wrap around its roof (a small plaque at the bottom of the enormous 130 ft. wide stairway footnotes Alaska and Hawaii). The memorial's interior looks best early in the morning, when the rising sun shines through the marble roof (builders soaked it in paraffin to enhance the effect). At night, Lincoln glows in electric lights, and memorial-goers often pause on the steps to watch the Washington Monument's image shimmer in the Reflecting Pool.

Take the elevator down from the statuary or walk to the left of the steps from the bottom to enter the exhibit era. Excerpts from some of Lincoln's famous speeches and writings as well as renderings of rejected memorial designs resembling Egyptian and Aztec pyramids are on display. There is also a photographic history of the many famous events that occurred on the memorial's steps, including Martin Luther King, Jr.'s "I Have a Dream" speech, a Nazi Party vigil, and the 1995 Million Man March.

KOREAN WAR VETERANS MEMORIAL

⚑ Location: *South of the Reflecting Pool and southeast of the Lincoln Memorial.* **Metro:** *Foggy Bottom-GWU or Smithsonian.* **Contact:** *☎ 632-1002.* **Hours:** *24hr. Park rangers on staff daily 8am-midnight.*

Composed of 19 larger-than-life stainless steel statues, the Korean War Veterans Memorial honors the 54,000 American troops who died in the Korean conflict from 1950 to 1953. Rather late in the making, the memorial was dedicated on July 27, 1995, 42 years after the armistice was signed. The $18 million tribute received 60% of its funding from Korean War veterans and made no use of federal money.

The statues, sculpted by World War II veteran **Frank Gaylord,** depict a platoon on patrol with monstrous rain ponchos and roughly cut, grizzled faces. The patrol forms a triangle which intersects a circle of trees, flowers, and a central fountain. A black granite wall emerges from the fountain, representing the Korean peninsula protruding into the Pacific Ocean. Etched on the wall closest to the center of the fountain are the words "Freedom is not free," a chilling reminder of the hardships American forces endured in war. The remainder of the wall is covered with over 2000 hazy, etched images of troops, tanks, helicopters, and nurses, symbolizing the Korean conflict's common nickname, the "Forgotten War." Visit at night for a particularly haunting perspective on the memorial; the gray statues and images etched on the black wall manifest a spectral quality.

FRANKLIN DELANO ROOSEVELT MEMORIAL

⚑ Location: *West Potomac Park. From the Korean War Memorial, head across Independence Ave. towards the southwest bank of the Tidal Basin.* **Metro:** *A long walk from Smithsonian.* **Contact:** *☎ 376-6704.* **Hours:** *24hr. Rangers on site daily 8am-midnight. Bookstore open daily 8am-10pm.* **Tours:** *A 72min. audiotape tour is available from the bookstore.*

The Franklin Delano Roosevelt Memorial deviates from the grand tributes to early presidents surrounding it, replacing their imposing marble statuary with sculpted gardens, cascading fountains, and thematic alcoves. Congress established the **FDR Memorial Commission** in 1955, dropped a controversial 1960 memorial plan, selected the current design in 1974, and then was mired in controversy over funding and design issues for the two ensuing decades. The early 90s saw a heated debate over whether or not to place FDR in a standing position (the way voters knew him) or in his wheelchair (which he cleverly hid from the public thanks to a tacit agreement with a then-cooperative press). A compromise was reached when the commission agreed to display him seated, covered in his Navy cape, a pose based on a famous image of FDR at the 1945 Yalta conference. However, if one looks closely at the back of the chair, a small wheel peeks out from behind the cloak, a discreet nod to the reality of his condition. A replica of Roosevelt's wheelchair, which he designed himself, is located in the gift shop.

The $52 million memorial is divided into a series of four thematically organized outdoor "rooms" depicting Roosevelt's presidency. The first and second rooms focus on the **New Deal,** Roosevelt's revolutionary scheme of social programs designed to lift America out of the Great Depression. They feature bronze sculptures of a breadline, a rural couple, and a

the dope on dc

Cherry Poppin' Daddies

Tidal Basin's famous Yoshino **cherry trees** found themselves in tragic circumstances again two years ago when three beavers decided to build their dam near the Jefferson Memorial. By the time federal wildlife officials found and captured the delinquent beavers, the animals had already felled five cedar trees and four of the much-beloved cherry trees. Now national celebrities, the beavers have been taken to an undisclosed wilderness area where they will, hopefully, build slightly more politically correct accommodations.

man listening to one of the President's trademark "fireside chats." The third and fourth rooms focus on FDR's response to World War II and include a statue of his wife, Eleanor, the first U.S delegate to the United Nations. Waterfalls, pools, and fountains cascade throughout the rooms as a reminder of FDR's love of water and his belief in the efficacy of the therapy he received at Warm Springs, GA, for his polio. Don't try swimming in the memorial's pools yourself: the Park Service banned swimming in 1997 after entire classes of schoolchildren arrived with bathing suits.

JEFFERSON MEMORIAL

🚩 **Location:** *South across the Tidal Basin from the Washington Memorial. From the last room of the FDR Memorial, follow the path over the bridge to East Potomac Park.* **Metro:** *A long walk from L'Enfant Plaza or Smithsonian.* **Contact:** ☎ *426-6821.* **Hours:** *24hr. Park rangers on site daily 8am-midnight.* **Note:** *The usually serene setting is currently disturbed by a massive restoration effort, expected to be completed by the beginning of 2001.*

Finished in 1942, The Jefferson Memorial is the coolest of D.C.'s memorials due to the cross-breezes off of the Potomac. A 19 ft. hollow bronze statue of **Thomas Jefferson** stands enshrined in a domed, open-air rotunda encircled by massive Ionic columns. The building sits on the shore of the picturesque Tidal Basin, surrounded by cherry blossom trees donated by Japan in 1912. Jefferson himself designed a number of Neoclassical buildings during his life, including the Virginia state capitol; his home, Monticello; and the quadrangle and library at the University of Virginia. The memorial's design by National Gallery of Art architect **John Russell Pope** pays homage to Jefferson's designs. Corn and tobacco, Virginia's cash crops, are visible under his coat as reminders of Jefferson's agrarian ideal. The interior walls quote from Jefferson's writings: the Declaration of Independence, the Virginia Statute of Religious Freedom, his Notes on Virginia, and an 1815 letter. The carved squares on the dome grow smaller near the top, creating the illusion that the ceiling is higher than 30 ft. The displays under the memorial highlight Jefferson's role in the formation of the United States.

TIDAL BASIN

🚩 **Location:** *By the Jefferson Memorial.*

Tidal Basin is a lovely man-made lake as polluted as it is popular. Despite the unsavory waters, the shady paths along the lake provide visitors with an escape from the overpopulated memorials. The sea-faring type can brave the waters in rented paddleboats (see **Entertainment,** p. 147).

Too famous for their own good, the Japanese **cherry blossom trees** along the Tidal Basin's rim are surrounded by tourists during the two weeks in late March or early April when most of the trees are in bloom. The original trees, sent in 1909 from Japan as a symbol of trans-Pacific friendship, arrived bearing insects and fungi and were immediately destroyed by the Department of Agriculture. The current trees, received in

1912, represent Japan's more successful second try. After Japanese bombers attacked Pearl Harbor in 1941, irate Washingtonians took buzz saws to several of the trees.

POTOMAC PARKS

↱ Location: *Either side of the Tidal Basin along Ohio Dr. SW.*

The mellow **West Potomac** and **East Potomac Parks** are lush with trees, lawns, and sculptures. The latter is bigger, the former more popular.

SOUTH OF THE MALL

SEE MAP
P. 315

YOU ARE
HERE

U.S.
Capitol
Building

↱ Highlights: *The Mint, Wharf Seafood Market.* **Museums:** *Holocaust Memorial Museum.* **Food and Drink:** *p. 174.* **Nearby:** *Mall, Monuments, Potomac River Parks, Capitol Hill.*

NEAR THE SMITHSONIAN

VOICE OF AMERICA

↱ Location: *330 Independence Ave. SW. Enter on C St. between 3rd and 4th Sts.* **Contact:** *☎ 619-3919.* **Tours:** *M-F except holidays, at 10:30am, 1:30, and 2:30pm; reservations suggested.*

Over 80 million listeners on every continent besides North America tune in regularly to the Voice of America, the US government's overseas radio and TV organ. Ever since 1942, the VOA has been willing to tell the good and the bad about America to the rest of the world, broadcasting objective stories about such controversial headliners as Vietnam and Watergate. Guided tours take visitors into surprisingly vital areas of the building at a rapid pace. A corridor of radio broadcast rooms invites tourists to watch and listen as broadcasters tell the world the latest breaking stories in English and 51 other languages from Dari to Uzbek. Tours vary in focus and length depending on the career interests of the tour guide, and end in the lobby with a mural entitled **The Meaning of Social Security,** by Ben Sahn, a New Dealer and social activist. The tour is popular with nostalgic American ex-pats and international visitors who grew up on VOA. The biggest allure of the VOA today is its **live phone-in interviews** with American leaders; the international clientele has the privileged chance to interrogate the likes of Madeleine Albright or Mario Cuomo on the air. The VOA also airs entertainment programs aimed at propagating American pop culture overseas.

BUREAU OF ENGRAVING AND PRINTING

↱ Location: *14th St. and C St. SW.* **Metro:** *Smithsonian.* **Contact:** *☎ 847-2808.* **Hours:** *Fluctuate, but ticket booth usually open M-F 8am-2pm with tours 9am-2pm. Additional hours 3:30-7pm during the summer. Obtain timed tickets but expect to wait.* **Admission:** *Free.*

Just southeast of the Washington Monument, the Bureau of Engraving and Printing offers guided tours of the presses that annually print over $20 billion in money and stamps. The real place where the buck starts, the bureau is the largest producer of currency, stamps, and security documents in the world. The tour begins with a million bucks conspicuously displayed in a glass case near the entrance, but the narcotic effect of the color of money is irritated by a long wait and TV screens musically accompanied by a none-too-quick elevator. Visitors walk through a claustrophobic, one-way maze, and peer through windows at workers printing, inspecting, and cutting new bills. The occasional employee may wave while a leafy fortune streams through his or her hands. Watching the whole process, with millions of dollars cascading in the next room, proves rather frustrating (yet oddly fantastical), especially with a sign gloating, "I make $128 million a day. I take home $14.95 after taxes." This sardonic effect is amplified by the bureau's recent installation of the Offline Currency Inspection System (OCIS) that inspects 10,000 sheets of money per hour ($440 million a day). Nevertheless, the sight of millions of dollars stacked in your immediate vicinity is somewhat exhilarating and provides a tangible incentive for aspiring tycoons.

L'ENFANT PLAZA

↱ Location: *Just below the intersection of 10th and D St.*

Named for D.C.'s original urban planner Pierre L'Enfant, this bright concrete plaza is aflutter with yuppies, tourists, and derelicts. At the top of the plaza on 10th St., the compact **Benjamin Banneker Park** (named after the first free black person in Maryland) permits a rather chaotic glimpse of the city in all directions.

WATERFRONT

George Washington chose the precise location for Washington, D.C. with an eye to its suitability as a port. Although shipping on the Potomac may have been possible in the 18th century, its narrow stretches and windy bends keep today's large ships out of the area. The waterfront district is home to recreational boaters, a thriving seafood wharf, and excellent views of the Washington Channel, Potomac River, and East Potomac Park. The area extends roughly from Water St. and the 12th St. Expwy. along Maine Ave. and the parallel, smaller Water St. SW, to Fort McNair at the mouth of the Washington Channel and the Anacostia River. Metro: L'Enfant Plaza or Waterfront.

WHARF SEAFOOD MARKET

❚ Location: *Between 9th and 11th St. SW and Maine Ave. NW (next to the Memorial Bridge).* **Metro:** *L'Enfant Plaza. From there, walk through the elevated concrete plaza, over the bridge, and down the sidewalk on the grassy hill, away from the Mall, to Maine Ave.* **Hours:** *daily 8am-9pm.*

Aproned vendors sell seafood year-round on colorful floating platforms tied to the dock. In operation since 1794, the wharf is the oldest open-air seafood market in the US, beating out even New York's famous Fulton Fish Market. The seafood, primarily from the Chesapeake Bay, couldn't be fresher. Be warned, however: the markets do not furnish seating, and the fishy smell may offend. Although some dedicated seafood connoisseurs are willing to scarf recently massacred shrimp, crabs, and lobster at stand-up tables right next to the market, benches and other spots along the waterfront provide more pleasant areas for picnicking and are well worth the walk.

GANGPLANK MARINA

❚ Location: *600 Water St. SW, south of the wharf and across the street from the Arena Stage.* **Contact:** ☎ *554-5000; www.gangplank.com.*

Recreational boats (including a few veritable yachts) tie up at the Gangplank Marina. This rather exclusive boating community is strictly occupied with charming events like a self-conscious recipe exchange or the presentation of "Boater of the Month" awards to prestigious members. In summer, fairs reel in Washingtonians with kids in tow to check out the t-shirts and food and to ogle the boats. A few high-priced seafood restaurants and a two-tiered walkway loom above the marina.

BOAT TOURS

❚ Location: *At the end of Water St.*

Three touring ships offer an even closer look at the surrounding waters. **Spirit Cruises** (☎ 554-8000; www.spiritcruises.com), located at 6th and Water St. SW (Metro: Waterfront), dock two boats at **Pier 4. The Spirit of Washington** offers lunch and dinner year-round (lunch: Tu-Su noon-2pm $32-37, dinner: Tu-Su 7-10pm $62-77). Occasional Midnight Dance Parties to Oldies and Top 40. The ship ambles down the Potomac River and returns without stops. **The Potomac Spirit** has daily trips from mid-March to early October to Washington's home, **Mount Vernon** ($30, seniors $28.50, ages 6-11 $19.50; prices include Mount Vernon admission). Cruises depart at 9am and return at 2:30pm, including 2½ hours at Mount Vernon.

The curious, low-lying boats of **Odyssey Cruises** (☎ 488-6000; www.odysseycruises.com) resemble cabins of a floating monorail. Passengers dress up for an upscale lunch (M-F 11am-2pm, $34; Sa 11am-2pm, $38), dinner (Su-Th 6-10pm, $72; F 7-11pm, $81; Sa 7-11pm, $85), Sunday jazz brunch (11am-2pm; $44), or moonlight cruise (hors d'oeuvres only, F-Sa midnight-2:30am; $34).

PEDESTRIAN PATHWAY

❚ Location: *South of Water St.*

The touring ships mark the beginning of one of the cleanest, most beautiful, and least populated walking/jogging/biking spots in D.C. The pedestrian pathway runs between the quiet condominiums and the **Washington Channel.** At the end of the peaceful walkway stands the **Titanic Statue,** dedicated to the men who "gave their lives that women and children might be saved." Sculpted by **Gertrude Vanderbilt Whitney** in 1931, the androgynous figure extends forward, arms outstretched, and evokes the same vertigo as nearby waves drifting against the docks.

FOGGY BOTTOM

YOU ARE HERE SEE MAP P. 310 U.S. Capitol Building

◪ Highlights: White House, Kennedy Center. **Museums:** Corcoran, Renwick. **Food & Drink:** p. 168. **Nearby:** The Mall, Farragut, Dupont Circle, Georgetown.

Though unscrupulous writers claim all of D.C. was "built on a swamp," only Foggy Bottom can truthfully carry that banner. The misty, low-lying swamp air gave the neighborhood its name, before heavy industry and fog-like pollutants made the moniker even more appropriate in the early 1900s. During World War II, the **State Department** took up quarters here at 23rd and C St. NW. Today the area is closely associated with the department, as well as the locally brewed beer that bears its name. Foggy Bottom extends from 15th St. NW west to the Potomac River, and from I St. south to Constitution Ave.

Near the Mall, government departments and national organizations like the **Daughters of the American Revolution** and the **American Red Cross** form an unbroken sprawl of gardens, columns, and statues. Above F St., the neighborhood is dominated by **George Washington University** and is sprinkled with hotels, townhouses, and the hulking, mirrored buildings of the **World Bank,** located along 19th and G St. The Metro runs along the northern edge of the neighborhood with the Foggy Bottom stop providing easy access to the western half (including Washington Circle dedicated to the first president), while the Farragut West stop brings tourists near the White House in the east. The 30 series of buses also runs along the northern edge.

L'Enfant Plaza

Before the Civil War, when most of Washington remained undeveloped, the **White House** anchored its own neighborhood: socialite circles and Cabinet secretaries lived around Lafayette Square, across from the President's House, or slightly farther up 16th St. NW. Since World War II, development has turned the White House from a center into a boundary: the blocks it occupies separate Farragut to the north, Old Downtown to the east, Foggy Bottom to the west, and the Mall south of the Ellipse.

U.S. Holocaust Museum

THE WHITE HOUSE

◪ Location: 1600 Pennsylvania Ave. NW. **Metro:** McPherson Square, Vermont Ave. exit. **Contact:** ☎ 456-7041, TTY 456-2121; www.whitehouse.gov. **Hours:** By tour only. Tu-Sa 10am-noon. **Tours:** Obtain tickets for the 20min. tour at the White House Visitors Center, 1450 Pennsylvania Ave. NW, at the corner of 15th and E St. Tickets distributed starting at 7:30am until the supply runs out (max. 4 tickets per person). **Admission:** Free. **Accessibility:** Handicapped accessible. Disabled visitors can go straight to the Pennsylvania Ave. entrance without a ticket.

In 1792, after Pierre L'Enfant had been decommissioned, Thomas Jefferson proposed a contest to design the President's residence. President George Washington judged the anonymous competition, choosing **James Hoban's** more regal plan over Jefferson's own modest design. John Adams was the first chief executive to live in Hoban's structure, although the building was still unfinished and lacked furniture at the time of his occupancy; in fact, the Adamses hung laundry to dry in what is now the **East Room.** Jefferson made the building habitable and became the first to build additions.

Wharf Seafood Market

The British burned down the house, along with much of D.C., in 1814; First Lady **Dolley Madison** interrupted her dinner to flee the flames, taking with her one of **Gilbert Stuart's** famous portraits of Washington. The building was rebuilt shortly thereafter and since then technical alterations and advances have been a regular occurrence: lights were installed in 1848, running water and central heating in 1853, electricity in 1891, and telephones in 1902. The White House was made wheelchair-accessible and had a swimming pool installed in 1933 to adapt to the needs of **Franklin D. Roosevelt,** a victim of polio. However, despite remodeling in 1902 and 1948, the central third of the mansion still looks more or less as Hoban planned it. Today, whenever the President is in town, an American flag flies over the house. The President's personal staff works in the West Wing, while the First Lady's staff shares the East Wing with a variety of offices. The Oval Office is the official office of the President and the site of many televised speeches, but his working office is in a room next door.

The tour is guarded but unguided. Visitors start on the ground floor of the East Wing and cover the next two floors; the top two floors are entirely private. The two middle floors contain the state rooms, which are used 250 times a year for events and press conferences. The **China Room** is filled with presidential place-settings from across the decades; not every president is represented because new china is only ordered every 17 years. Upstairs, the **East Room** has been used for the wakes of those Presidents who died in office. It also held boxing and wrestling matches during Theodore Roosevelt's administration and hosted Susan Ford's senior prom.

Three colorful rooms lie between the East Room and the State Dining Room. **The Green Room,** named for the wallpaper selected by John Quincy Adams, the **Blue Room,** named for its blue-upholstered furniture, and the **Red Room,** named for its red- and gold-embroidered sofas. Dolley Madison held Wednesday-night socials here—all it took to be admitted was "proper attire." **The State Dining Room** is used for entertaining large groups of guests. Its gold elegance served as a hall of trophies for hunter Teddy Roosevelt.

The surrounding grounds grew up in much the same fitful way as the house: **John Adams** was the first to plant seedlings, and his son John Quincy Adams fenced off the grounds. One hundred twenty years later, **Jacqueline Kennedy** made the Rose Garden famous; journalists later called Gerald Ford's stay-at-home re-election effort the **"Rose Garden Campaign."** An obsolete bomb shelter under the Treasury building, built during World War II, connects to the White House by a tunnel under the East Lawn; aides in-the-know use the tunnel as a quick exit to 15th St. NW. Big lawns, fences, long driveways, and closed gates discourage terrorists, though four or so unruly people try to jump over the fences each year.

ELLIPSE

⚐ Location: South of the White House.

This grassy area was once used to raise cattle. The **National Christmas Tree,** planted by Jimmy Carter, has also put down roots here. Where the green grass meets E St. NW is **Washington's Zero Milestone.** Distances within the district are officially measured from this stone.

OLD EXECUTIVE OFFICE BUILDING

⚐ Location: 17th St. and Pennsylvania Ave. NW. **Contact:** ☎ 395-5895, TDD 395-9103. **Metro:** Farragut West. **Tours:** Guided tours Sa mornings; space limited. Call in advance to schedule a tour. Note: tours often fill up two months in advance. **Admission:** Free.

The Old Executive Office Building is an explosion of architectural superfluity. Trendsetting when it was erected in Grant's era, its frills regularly go out of fashion; President Truman called it "the greatest monstrosity in America," and the building barely managed to escape demolition in the latter half of the 20th century. Today the building houses the bulk of the White House staff, the Vice-President's office, and a few lucky interns.

LAFAYETTE PARK

⚐ Location: Across Pennsylvania Ave. from the north side of the White House. **Metro:** Farragut North or Farragut West.

Clark Mills's statue of Andrew Jackson stands in the center of the park, the first equestrian statue in America. Legend has it that Mills bought a Virginia thoroughbred and trained it to rear on demand in order to have a model for the unprecedented work. The other statues in the Square represent Revolutionary War heroes and serve as reminders that the US could not have won its independence without help from foreign lands. In 1891, a statue of the Marquis de Lafayette joined Jackson on the southeast corner of the park, near 15th and Pennsylvania. A half-dressed woman, perhaps representing France, hands him his sword; an old joke has the lady saying, "Give me back my clothes, and I'll give you back your sword." At the southwest corner of the park, near 16th St., is a statue of Lafayette's compatriot Rochambeau, surrounded at the base by figures of the American Eagle and Lady Liberty brandishing her sword. Polish Brigadier Thaddeus Kosciuszko, who fortified West Point and Saratoga for the Continental Army, defends the northeast corner. At the northwest corner stands the Prussian Baron Von Steuben, who trained American troops at Valley Forge. Lafayette Park's location across the street from the White House makes it a prime spot for protests. Rainbow covered billboards optimistically tag the area as Peace Park; a 24-hour anti-nuclear vigil has been continuously held in the park since 1981.

White House

ST. JOHN'S CHURCH

🚩 Location: At 16th and H St. NW on the north end of Lafayette Park. **Metro:** Farragut West or Farragut North. **Contact:** ☎ 347-8766. **Hours:** daily 9am-3pm. **Tours:** tour after Su service. Su service 10:30am; Spanish service 12:30pm.

One of the architects responsible for the restoration of the US Capitol after the War of 1812, Benjamin Latrobe also created St. John's Church. St. John's forms a subtle cross whose arms have the triangular pediment of a Greek temple with Latrobe's signature half-moon windows; the facade has columns as well as a triangular pediment. The building is known as the Church of Presidents: each president since Madison has dropped in at least once, all sitting in the same reserved pew. President Clinton sometimes attends an early morning service.

DECATUR HOUSE

🚩 Location: 748 Jackson Pl. NW. Entrance on H St. **Metro:** Farragut West or Farragut North. **Contact:** ☎ 842-0920. **Hours:** Tu-F 10am-3pm (last tour 2:30pm), Sa-Su noon-4pm (last tour 3:30pm). **Tours:** every 30min. **Admission:** $4; seniors, students, and children $2.50.

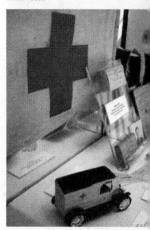
American Red Cross

At the northwest corner of Lafayette Park, Decatur House, also designed by Latrobe, was home to **Stephen Decatur,** the Navy's youngest captain. A dashing military hero who defeated the Barbary Pirates and captured the top British frigate during the War of 1812, Decatur spent only one year in the house before experiencing a gruesome and untimely death in a duel. During the 1830s and 40s, hotelier **John Gadsby** entertained Washington's elite in the ballrooms while running an infamous slave market in the back. He kept slaves chained in the attic and in the mansion's extension along H St., and conducted slave auctions in the backyard. Contemporaries reported that "at night you could hear [the slaves'] howls and cries." In 1871, the house was purchased by **Edward Beale,** best remembered for carrying official news of the California Gold Rush to Washington in a frontiersman's disguise. The Beales were responsible for most of the later renovations, including the elegant inlaid floors and "Romantic eclectic" furnishing seen in the upper drawing room. Tours of the house last 40 minutes.

Kennedy Center of Performing Arts

RENWICK GALLERY

🔎 Location: *at the corner of 17th St. and Pennsylvania Ave. NW.* **Metro:** *Farragut West.* **Contact:** ☎ 357-2700. **Hours:** *daily 10am-5:30 pm.* **Admission:** *Free.*

The Renwick Gallery (see p. 123) of the **National Museum of American Art** devotes itself to "American craft." The building was designed by **James Renwick, Jr.,** also the architect of the Smithsonian Castle, and is in the style of the French Second Empire with its red-brick exterior capped by a slate mansard roof. Most of the interior furniture once belonged to Richard Rush, a Smithsonian regent who personally carried James Smithson's bags of gold from England to the United States.

AMERICAN RED CROSS

🔎 Location: *430 17th St. NW, between D and E St.* **Metro:** *Farragut West.* **Contact:** ☎ 639-3300; www.redcross.org. **Hours:** *Building open M-F 8:30am-4pm.* **Admission:** *Free.*

The American Red Cross has small changing exhibits on the history of the service founded by **Clara Barton** during the Civil War. Display cases in the assembly room and the hall exhibit Clara Barton's glasses and sewing kit, as well as the famous quilt on which the Red Cross sold space for signatures to raise money for relief during WWII. Signatures from notables such as Helen Keller, Theodore Roosevelt, Charlie Chaplin, Mary Pickford, Thomas Edison, and Woodrow Wilson are on it, as well as uniforms created for the movie *In Love and War*, which documents American journalist Ernest Hemingway's affair with a Red Cross nurse.

CORCORAN GALLERY OF ART

🔎 Location: *17th St. between E St. and New York Ave. NW, just north of the Red Cross building.* **Metro:** *Farragut West.* **Contact:** ☎ 639-1700.

Once housed in the Renwick Gallery, the Corcoran Gallery of Art, Washington's oldest art museum, shows works from the 18th through 20th centuries (see p. 119).

ORGANIZATION OF AMERICAN STATES

🔎 Location: *at 17th St. and Constitution Ave. NW, across the street from the southwest corner of the Ellipse.* **Metro:** *Farragut West. OAS open M-F 9am-5:30pm; museum open Tu-Su 10am-5pm.* **Contact:** ☎ 458-3000, museum ☎ 458-6016. **Admission:** *Free.*

The Organization of American States is a red terracotta marriage of North and South American architectural styles. A climate-controlled interior is dominated by a skylit patio with abundant tropical plants and a fountain with Aztec and Mayan elements. The Hall of Americas displays flags of member nations while upstairs formal sessions are held in the OAS meeting rooms. (Sessions are in Spanish and are open to tourists; non-Spanish-speakers can hook up to translation machines. Call to ask when the OAS is in session.) Outside, a sculpture garden features Brazilian artist Nair Kremer's file cabinet sculpture, the *Archives of Memory.* Behind the OAS building is the beautifully landscaped **Aztec Garden** which leads to the **Museum of the Americas,** whose main entrance is on 18th St. The museum displays temporary exhibits of modern art from Mexico, Peru, Brazil, and other nations.

THE OCTAGON

🔎 Location: *1799 New York Ave. NW.* **Metro:** *Farragut West.* **Contact:** ☎ 638-3105. **Hours:** *Tu-Su 10am-4pm.* **Tours:** *every hr. on the half-hour.* **Admission:** *$5, students and seniors $3.*

Designed by William Thornton in 1799 as a house for rich Virginian John Tayloe III, the Octagon isn't remotely octagonal at all. Thornton's design, which more closely resembles a hexagon, was a response to the awkward triangular lot upon which it was built. Architectural elements added for symmetry and order, like fancy doors that go into small closets and hidden doors that lead to passageways and back stairs, partially contributed to the ghost stories that grew up around the house. Of course, a skeleton of a young girl found buried in a wall in the house by workmen, and a century of mysterious thumping noises probably didn't hurt either.

Legend has it that tunnels lead from the house to the White House and the Potomac, though guides assert that this is untrue. The Madisons did manage to quickly flee here when British troops torched the White House in 1814 and for a short period the building became the official presidential residence. Today the house serves as a museum highlighting Tayloe family pieces and period furniture as well as rotating special exhibits.

DEPARTMENT OF THE INTERIOR

🚩 *Location:* on the square between C and D St. NW between 18th and 19th St. *Contact:* ☎ 208-4743. *Metro:* Faragut West. *Hours:* M-F 8:30am-4:30pm. Call in advance to schedule tours. New Deal murals open by appt. only. Native-American murals open M-F 11am-2pm or by appt.

The Department of the Interior brings a unique Art Deco feel to government office space. Franklin Roosevelt laid the cornerstone for the building in 1936, using the same trowel George Washington used to lay the Capitol's cornerstone in 1793. Secretary of the Interior Harold Ickes experimented with the possibilities of employee comfort in the design of the department; this was the first government building to have escalators, a gymnasium, and central air conditioning. Primarily concerned with the history of Native Americans and the American West, exhibits include Kenji Kawano's compelling photos of Navajos, a beautifully woven, traditional Apache rug and a mounted American Bison head, the unofficial symbol of the department. As part of the revitalization efforts of the New Deal, the Department of the Interior commissioned realist and regionalist such artists as William Gropper and John Stuart Curry to create the first set of murals. The more recent murals, painted by Native American artists Woodrow Crumbo and Gerald Nailor, humorously sketch scenes from 1930s Native-American life; donkeys gaze thirstily at the room's water fountain and deer jump over doorways. Spontaneous visitors are restricted from office areas where the murals are located; call ahead for a glimpse of these spectacular works.

St. John's Church

NATIONAL ACADEMY OF SCIENCES

🚩 *Location:* on the block between Constitution Ave. and C St. Enter from Constitution Ave. *Metro:* Farragut West. *Contact:* ☎ 334-2000. *Hours:* M-F 7am-5:30pm.

The National Academy of Sciences features a fantastic gold-tiled dome decorated with representations of ancient Greek philosophers. Dangling from its center is a version of **Foucault's pendulum,** which swings over a pedestal with sun symbols from various cultures; documentation explaining the art is available at the front desk. During most of the day, massive bronze doors in this room are left open to reveal eight panels, each of which depicts an important scientific personality, from Aristotle to Einstein. Rotating exhibits occupy the academy's small gallery; 2001 will feature Natural Domain, a collection of paintings highlighting various insects. Outside the building at the corner of 22nd St. NW and Constitution Ave., a surprisingly 21-foot statue of Einstein sits on a large semicircular bench around a 28-foot field of emerald pearl granite studded with metal chips that represent 55% of the entire sky: galaxies, planets, sun, moon, and stars. The celestial map shows the position of the stars at the time the statue was dedicated: noon, April 22, 1979.

Blair House

STATE DEPARTMENT

🚩 *Location:* on the other corner of 21st and C St. *Metro:* Foggy Bottom-GWU. *Contact:* ☎ 647-3241. *Tours:* M-F at 9:30, 10:30am, and 2:45pm by appt.; call for reservations.

In the 60s, Secretary of State Dean Rusk redecorated the State Department's unflattering avocado-green interior with Chippendale chairs and Boston highboys. While the decor is still a unique flavor of grotesque, fine arts and Americana on display

State Department

include a portrait of Thomas Jefferson in a toga, a highboy capped by a bust of John Locke, a Gilbert Stuart portrait of John Jay, and the desk where Jefferson wrote the Declaration of Independence. The State Department offers a guided tour of its eclectic innards.

GEORGE WASHINGTON UNIVERSITY

🛈 *Location:* visitors center located at 801 22nd St. NW. ☎994-4949. *Hours:* M-F 9am-5pm, Sa 9am-4pm. *Tours* M-F 10am, 2pm; Sa 10am, 1pm.

George Washington University stretches north of F St. in Foggy Bottom. The visitors desk in the Academic Center gives away brochures, newspapers, and *The Big To Do*, an entertainment calendar. Dance, theater, and music flourish at GWU's **Lisner Auditorium** (see p. 139) and the GWU Colonials play basketball from November to March. The campus is sprinkled with rose bushes, statues, and red bricks engraved with the details of GWU graduates.

THE WATERGATE COMPLEX

🛈 *Location:* near the intersection of G St. and Virginia Ave., near 25th St. and New Hampshire Ave.

Composed of black-and-white half-cylinders that scream horrific, the monstrously ugly complex that gave the Watergate scandal its name contains offices and apartments of the rich and famous as well as a luxury hotel. The Watergate's office space housed the Democratic National Committee's headquarters when President Richard Nixon ordered them burgled in 1972. Across the street at the Howard Johnson's, co-conspirator G. Gordon Liddy watched the burglary from a room that cost him only $50, including breakfast and valet parking. Today, Liddy's room rents for over $200; inflation, plus a bit of Watergate-induced notoriety, has placed it beyond the budget traveler's reach.

THE KENNEDY CENTER

🛈 *Location:* 2700 F St. The center rises above Rock Creek Pkwy. just off 25th St. at the end of New Hampshire Ave. NW. *Metro:* Foggy Bottom-GWU, then walk away from downtown on H St. and turn left onto New Hampshire Ave. Free shuttle runs to and from the Metro every 15min. M-F 7am-midnight, Sa 8am-midnight, Su 11am-midnight. *Contact:* ☎467-4600, TDD 416-8524; www.kennedy-center.org. *Hours:* Daily 10am-midnight. *Admission:* Free tours 1hr. on the hour M-F 10am-5pm, Sa-Su 10am-1pm (call ☎416-8340, TTY 415-8524). *Accessibility:* All theaters are wheelchair accessible. *Performance Information:* See p. 142.

Completed in the late 1960s, the John F. Kennedy Center for the Performing Arts is a living monument to John F. Kennedy, entirely analogous to the Washington, Jefferson, Roosevelt, and Lincoln Memorials. The center represents a Congressional imperative to present the finest performing arts in the country, and the $78 million edifice boasts four major stages, a film theater, sumptuous wall-to-wall red carpets, mirrors, crystal chandeliers, and 3,700 tons of Carrara marble. Many pieces of free-standing art and much of the interior furnishings were donated by various nations in memory of JFK. Art scattered about the center ranges from blast-damaged sheet metal to tapestries depicting the Creation.

Visitors enter through the flag-lined **Hall of States** or **Hall of Nations** which lead to the **Grand Foyer,** one of the largest rooms in the world. The foyer is marked by a 7ft. bronze bust of JFK, 18 Swedish chandeliers shaped like cubical grape clusters, and first-class views of the Potomac. The foyer is used to access the **Concert Hall,** the **Opera House,** and the **Eisenhower Theater.** The stage in the Concert Hall was a gift from over 692 high school, college, and community organizations from the US, Canada, Britain, and Japan. In return, the stage frequently hosts high school and youth ensembles, as well as serving as home of the **National Symphony Orchestra.** The President's box includes a reception room and a banner with his seal, which hangs from the balcony when he is in attendance. The **Roof Terrace Restaurant** is very expensive, but a walk along the outdoor roof terrace is free. Exquisite fountains and make this one of the most romantic spots in the city.

OLD DOWNTOWN (PENN QUARTER)

🛈 *Highlights:* National Archives, MCI Center, FBI Building, ESPNZone. *Food & Drink:* p. 171. *Museums:* National Building Museum, National Museum of American Art, National Portrait Gallery, National Museum of Women in the Arts. *Nearby:* White House, North Mall, Farragut. *Metro:* Metro Center, Gallery Place-Chinatown, Judiciary Square, Archives-Navy Memorial, or Federal Triangle.

The Old Downtown, sometimes referred to as Penn Quarter, includes the area north of the Mall bounded by Constitution Ave., 2nd St., New York Ave., and 15th St. NW. Today, the neighborhood primarily hosts a phalanx of regulatory agencies and government offices, but in its heyday it was the nexus of D.C. capitalism. During the 1800s, Old Downtown boasted the city's largest outdoor market, the country's first elevator, and the colossal **Patent Office Building.** The neighborhood remained the city's commercial hub until World War II but lost its importance as a business district after the war. In 1968, riots centered in the former commercial areas of the neighborhood cemented its reputation as one of the most dangerous and seedy sections of the city. In 1972, Congress invented the Pennsylvania Avenue Development Corporation to encourage private enterprise in Old Downtown. In the early 1980s, a series of large construction projects infused the area with new life. Within the past two years, three brand new additions—the **MCI Center** sports complex, **Techworld,** and the **International Trade Center** in the **Ronald Reagan Building**—have brought even more commercial energy to the neighborhood. The city also recently broke ground with the **New Washington Convention Center,** a 2.3 million square foot venue which will open in 2003.

Pennsylvania Avenue, the main thoroughfare traversing Old Downtown, runs from the White House to the Capitol building, along the way hitting all of the finest hotels and restaurants the city has to offer. New presidents traverse this avenue in the Inaugural Parade, giving it its nickname: **The Street of Presidents.** L'Enfant originally planned for the street to stretch uninterrupted from the White House to the Capitol, but President Andrew Jackson impulsively ordered the Treasury Building constructed in the middle of its projected path, spoiling L'Enfant's plan. Pennsylvania Ave. was largely residential until the 1820s, when it began to evolve into a commercial district. During the Civil War, the street and its environs became the city's red-light district after **Union General Joseph Hooker** restricted prostitution in the city to the area. (Although the red-light district became known as **Hooker's Division,** the usage of "hooker" as a slang term for prostitute probably originated elsewhere, most likely in New York City's old Red Hook district.) After the war, the avenue's status declined even further as the remaining houses of commerce closed and moved elsewhere. Construction of the Federal Triangle government building complex after the turn of the century finally restored the avenue's reputation, placing it once again in the very center of national government.

Construction work constantly occurs in Old Downtown. Newly-renovated office suites opposite dilapidated, abandoned housing strike a peculiar contrast, albeit one that is becoming increasingly familiar to D.C. natives. Despite the urban renewal, walking through parts of Old Downtown may still be unsafe at nights.

MARTIN LUTHER KING, JR. LIBRARY

▶ Location: *901 G St.* **Metro:** *Metro Center, entrance on G St. between 9th and 10th.* **Contact:** *☎ 727-0321; www.dclibrary.org. Hours: M-Th 10am-9pm, F-Sa 10am-5:30pm, Su 1-5; closed on Su during the summer; call for extended hrs.* **Admission:** *Free.*

The flagship of D.C.'s library system, this brick and black-glass building represents the Bauhaus style of famed architect Ludwig Mies van der Rohe. Note painter Don Miller's mural of Dr. King, leader of the black civil rights movement of the 1960s. The third floor of the library houses a non-circulating Black Studies Room and the Washingtoniana Room, containing resources for local historians. The library hosts concerts, author talks, readings, and book signings; call for details.

OLD PATENT OFFICE BUILDING

▶ Location: *8th and G St.*

Walt Whitman described this colossal stone landmark as "the noblest of Washington buildings", although tourists might find it hard to determine why. A major tourist attraction and once the largest office building in the United States, an 1877 fire destroyed its collection of patent models. The patent office removed all patents from the building in 1932, and in 1958 it took an act of Congress to save the building from demolition. **The**

the on
dopedc

Ghoulish

Washington has a number of reputed haunted houses, but few are as populated by ghouls as the **Octagon House** (p. 64), whose architecture and history have long fascinated the public imagination. Among the thumping, creaking, door-slamming, moaning, and sighing, and miscellaneous 19th-century figures, several individual ghosts stand out. **Dolley Madison** only lived here a few months, but is still supposed to come back to throw parties periodically and is identified by a mysterious cloud of lilac, her favorite perfume. Two other ghosts belong to the daughters of **John Tayloe III**, the original resident, and center on the most striking architectural feature of the house: its freestanding, three-story spiral staircase. One daughter is said to have thrown herself down the stairwell because Tayloe refused to let her marry as she wished. The other, after eloping with a suitor of whom her father disapproved, was rumored to have been pushed down the staircase by an enraged Tayloe when she returned to beg his forgiveness. For the record, no one from *Let's Go* has ever seen, heard, or felt traces of these ghosts—but then again, we've only visited during the day.

National Museum of American Art (enter at 8th St. and G St.), the **Archives of American Art,** and the **National Portrait Gallery** (enter at 8th St. and F St.) moved here in 1968. (See **Museums,** p. 121.)

MCI CENTER

🚩 *Location: 601 F St. Metro: Gallery Place-Chinatown. Contact:* ☎ 628-3200; www.mcicenter.com.

Constructed over objections that it would create traffic and encroach on Chinatown's boundaries, the 20,000-seat arena opened in 1997 as D.C.'s premier sports venue. It hosts the NBA's Washington Wizards, the NHL's Washington Capitals, the WNBA's Washington Mystics, and the NCAA's Georgetown Hoyas (see **Entertainment,** p. 149). Group tours of the stadium (½ hour) are offered by request.

NATIONAL SPORTS GALLERY

🚩 *Location: In the MCI Center, take the elevator to the 3rd fl. Contact:* ☎ 661-5133. *Hours: Tu-Su 11am-6pm and during all MCI Center events. Admission: $5; $9 player card has enough credit to sample 8 attractions. Additional credit available throughout the gallery.*

Catering exclusively to the hard-core sports fan, the gallery celebrates the storied past of American sports through memorabilia and interactive computer games. Items include the only known autographed bat from notorious Black Sox Shoeless Joe Jackson, the last touchdown ball thrown by Joe Montana, and a Ty Cobb uniform. You can even touch a bat used by Babe Ruth. After soaking up the memories, run up a hefty tab playing life-sized computer games that run on a credit system. For $10, make like Marv Albert in the gallery's broadcaster's booth: pick a two- to four-minute clip from famous sporting events, put on a broadcaster's blazer, and give a play-by-play analysis. The screen offers prompts, or you can make your own calls. When you're done, you get a VHS recording of the commentary with your voice-over and a shot of you in the booth.

DISCOVERY CHANNEL DESTINATION STORE

🚩 *Location: In the MCI Center. Contact:* ☎ 783-5751; www.flagship.discovery.com. *Hours: M-Sa 10am-7pm, Su 10am-6pm.*

This $20-million, four-story attraction located inside the MCI Center is an adventure in creative merchandising as part-store, part-museum. The "Sonic Elevator" pipes in sound effects as visitors explore themed levels crammed with oddities like a 42 ft. cast of the largest assembled **Tyrannosaurus rex** in the world and a restored B-25 bomber. Items for sale range from a fossilized tortoise shell ($8,000) to small precious stones such as Jade and Jasper ($2-3). Beware! The Discovery Channel Theater on the fourth floor no longer shows the popular film "Destination DC."

CHINATOWN

⚑ Location: *Entrance archway at the corner of 7th and H St.*

"Chinatown is so tiny that many Washingtonians don't know it exists."
—The Washington Post

Chinatown's gilded archway boldly announces a cultural crisis: the signs and storefronts for CVS and Starbucks, decorated with traditional Chinese characters, reveal the ever increasing global monoculture that waters down distinctive communities like Chinatown. While the entire street is crammed with interesting grocery stores and restaurants, in this part of town all signs point to the ultra-modern MCI Center. Elsewhere in tiny Chinatown, a Texas barbecue restaurant and a yuppie Irish pub try to lure sports fans and fit in next to traditional Chinese restaurants. The designers of the MCI Center tried to blend the building into Chinatown by including Chinese elements in its architecture, but the very location of the center smack in the middle of the neighborhood makes this effort fairly futile.

Navy Memorial

The area's history resembles that of Chinese districts across the nation: after the Chinese Exclusion Act of 1882 restricted immigration and barred Chinese aliens from most jobs, the persecuted immigrants lived and worked near 4th St. and Pennsylvania Ave. NW. Two rival *tongs* (merchants' associations) formed to offer protection to Chinese-owned businesses. When government buildings displaced the old Chinatown, the *tongs* led the move to today's neighborhood.

A string of excellent restaurants (see **Food & Drink,** p. 163) and Chinese grocers can still be found on the 600 block of H St. and on the 700 block (between G and H St.) of 6th St. Less interesting tourist shops on the outskirts blend Chinatown back into downtown. The streets in this area swarm around noon with the professional lunch crowd from downtown and beyond. **Be careful in the surrounding area at night.**

National Aquarium

NATIONAL BUILDING MUSEUM

⚑ Location: *401 F St.* **Metro:** *Judiciary Sq.*

The National Building Museum honors great American achievements in architecture, design, and urban planning. In 1881, Congress asked military engineer Montgomery Meigs to design a cheap brick building for the 1500 clerks of the Pension Bureau. Meigs's beautiful, Italian-inspired edifice exceeded all expectations—at a cost of $886,614.04. President Grover Cleveland held his Inaugural Ball here in 1885, a tradition that lasted until Woodrow Wilson in 1913 and was reinstated by Richard Nixon in 1973. A grayish-white 1200-ft.-long frieze encircles the building between the first and second floors. Designed by sculptor Casper Buberl, the frieze depicts a parade of Civil War military units. (See **Museums,** p. 121.)

NATIONAL LAW ENFORCEMENT OFFICERS MEMORIAL

⚑ Location: *E St. between 4th and 5th St. at the center of Judiciary Sq.* *Metro: Judiciary Sq. Contact: www.1nleomf.com. Hours: 24hr. Admission: Free.*

Dedicated by President George Bush in October 1991, the three-acre memorial honoring law enforcement officers killed

FBI

the on
dopedc

Hippo hooray

According to local legend, the Potomac River was once inhabited by hippopotami. **George Washington** loved to watch them cavort in the shallows from his porch on Mount Vernon, and his children tried to rub the hippopotami's noses for good luck. Is it coincidence that his false teeth were made in part from hippo ivory or that the National Zoo was well known for its success at breeding pygmy hippopotami? You decide. In any case, there hasn't been a hippo sighting in the D.C. area for quite a while, but George Washington University honors the great "river horse" with a 4 ft. bronze hippo statue at the corner of H and 21st St. The inscription reads: "Art for wisdom, Science for joy, Politics for beauty, and a Hippo for hope."

on the job since 1794 displays the influence of Michelangelo's *Piazza del Campidoglio* in Rome and Maya Ying Lin's Vietnam Veterans Memorial in D.C. (see p. 56). Over 1100 names of slain officers are engraved in concrete along opposing curved and tree-lined "pathways of remembrance." Fourteen thousand daffodils make the memorial a spectacular sight in early April. Rubbing-pads for transferring names are available on-site and at the National Building Museum. Every year on May 13 at 8pm, new names are added to the memorial during a candlelight vigil. The **Visitors Center** details the history of the memorial and the officers it honors. (*605 E St., right past the AARP building.* ☎ *737-3400; www.1nleomf.com. Open M-F 9am-5pm, Sa 10am-5pm, Su noon-5pm.*)

CANADIAN EMBASSY

🚻 *Location: 501 Pennsylvania Ave. Metro: Judiciary Square or Archives-Navy Memorial. Contact:* ☎ *682-1740. Hours: M-F 9am-5pm. Admission: Free.*

The building is a stunning blend of neoclassical and modern architectural concepts designed by Canadian architect Arthur Erickson. Its smooth, unpolished Canadian marble and blue-tinted windows interject architectural vitality into the gloomy conglomeration of federal buildings that make up this section of downtown. Worth a quick stop, the **Rotunda of Provinces** is majestically serene, with twelve 50-foot aluminum columns (representing Canada's twelve provinces) towering over a cascading fountain. Bill Reid's sculpture *The Spirit of Haidi Gwaii* depicts a canoe brimming over with legendary figures from early Canadian Haidi mythology. The small but pleasant gallery inside occasionally hosts rotating exhibits by leading Canadian artists.

NATIONAL ARCHIVES

🚻 *Location: 700 Pennsylvania Ave. Wheelchair accessible entrance on Constitution Ave., between 7th St. and 9th St. Metro: Archives-Navy Memorial. Contact:* ☎ *501-5000, research* ☎ *501-5400, TDD 501-5404; www.nara.gov. Hours: Daily April through Labor Day 10am-9pm; Sept.-Mar. 10am-5:30pm. Research hours M and W 8:45am-5pm, Tu and Th-F 8:45am-9pm, Sa 8:45am-4:45pm. Tours:* ☎ *501-5205 in advance for Archives tour reservations. No reservation required to view Rotunda. US citizens can arrange tours through their representative. Tours M-F 10:15am and 1:15pm (1hr.). Admission: Free.*

If the federal government has an attic, this is it. The Archives are home to everything the government thinks is worth saving ("permanently valuable" is how they like to put it). This select collection amounts to only 2 to 5% of the documents generated by the government every year. The numbers are still staggering: 14 million pictures and posters, 15 million maps, and billions of pages of text. The collection includes all sorts of unusual objects—wacky contributions from the Nixon years include a tiny portrait of Tricky Dick painted on a grain of rice and a red wig worn by Watergate burglar Howard Hunt. The building's long-tiered steps, stone friezes, fluted columns, and mammoth bronze doors (1 ft. thick and 40 ft. high) are indicative of architect John Russell Pope's work and can also be seen in his design of the National Gallery (see **Museums,** p. 111).

The three biggies—the **Declaration of Independence,** the **Constitution,** and the **Bill of Rights**—draw crowds. These "Charters of Freedom" are exhibited in the Rotunda (enter on Constitution Ave.) and are displayed in humidity-controlled, helium-filled cases made of glass and bronze. The refractive property of the glass, and the protective filters that shield the documents from harmful light, give them a greenish tinge. Every night the cases sink 22 feet into a 55-ton steel and concrete basement vault, insuring their contents against theft and nuclear attack.

Largely ignored by tourists is a copy of the **Magna Carta.** Originally signed and issued in 1215, the document detailed King John I of England's guarantee of rights to his angry noblemen. On display is one of four extant copies of the 1297 version. Eccentric billionaire and former presidential hopeful **H. Ross Perot** purchased the famous document in 1984 and loaned it to the Archives indefinitely. **"Picturing the Century, Part 2"** is a collection of photographs capturing social changes in the 20th century featuring portfolios from **Ansel Adams, Danny Lyon,** and **Lewis Hine,** on display until July 4, 2001. Highlights include one of two known photos of **FDR** in a wheelchair and a photo of **Nixon** with **Elvis.**

Chinatown Gilded Archway

The guided tour gives a more in-depth look at some interesting lesser-known holdings such as **President John F. Kennedy's** doodles during the Cuban Missile Crisis and a wall of unlabeled presidential baby pictures. Scholars can access the research room here and at Archives II, a two-million cubic foot storage monster *(8601 Adelphi Rd. College Park, MD. ☎(301) 713-6400. Hours: M,W 8:45am-5pm; Tu,Th,F till 9pm; limited access Sa 12pm-5pm. Both locations also hold special document viewings, films, and lectures).*

NAVY MEMORIAL AND HERITAGE CENTER

🗹 *Location: Across Pennsylvania Ave. from the National Archives. Metro: Archives-Navy Memorial. Contact: ☎ 737-2300; www.lonesailor.org. Hours: 24 hrs. Admission: Free.*

Chinese Lanterns

The United States Navy Memorial is a popular outdoor rest and lunch spot. The memorial's cascading fountains and naval flags suggest the deck of a ship. An engraving of the naval hymn and Bleifeld's statue "The Lone Sailor" create an atmosphere conducive to serene contemplation. In the summer, the Navy Band hosts weekly concerts at the memorial (T, 8pm), and the US Navy Ceremonial Guard performs a drill (T, 1pm).

Located at the rear of the memorial on the northern side, the **Naval Heritage Center** is a hidden treasure. Exhibits include magnificent paintings from the Navy Art Collection, the Navy Log (a video record of Navy veterans), the Naval Heritage Library, and interactive video kiosks. The Presidents' Room shows portraits of presidents who have served. *(Visitors Center open Mar.-Oct. M-Sa 9:30am-5pm; Nov.-Feb. Tu-Sa 10:30am-4pm. Film M-Sa at 11am and 1pm with some special screenings. Admission for film $3.75, seniors and under 18 $3.)*

FEDERAL BUREAU OF INVESTIGATION (FBI)

🗹 *Location: 935 Pennsylvania Ave. NW, enter on E St. between 9th and 10th St. Metro: Federal Triangle or Archives-Navy Memorial. Contact: ☎ 324-3447;*

Go-Los

www.fbi.gov. **Hours:** *M-F 8:45am-4:15pm.* **Tours:** *Visitors permitted by tour only. Get advance, timed tickets from your congressperson (visitors should contact their congressperson at least 4 months in advance), or line up early in the morning to wait 1½hr.+ for tickets at the door.* **Admission:** *Free.*

While the FBI building itself is something of an architectural monstrosity, most tourists eventually succumb to the appeal of espionage and an X-Files curiosity. The building is named after J. Edgar Hoover, controversial leader of the organization during the mid-20th century and reputed cross-dresser, who directed the agency through decades of political espionage and scandal. Employees with a strange resemblance to flight attendants lead visitors through a series of waiting rooms, culminating in a corny movie. The tour then begins with cardboard cutouts of "gangsters," confiscated drug paraphernalia, and the **"Tools of the Spy"** exhibit—a puny, glass-enclosed case containing a camera, a floppy disk, and chalk. Be sure not to snooze through the 10 most wanted criminals exhibit; two tourists have led the FBI to criminals after recognizing their faces during the tour. The tour continues past a mostly empty, working DNA lab, and a display of 5000 illicit guns including one disguised as a cane. At the end of the tour, an agent blows away a sinister cardboard evil-doer with two pistols and a fully automatic rifle, a finale that invariably gets applause.

FORD'S THEATER

⚐ Location: *511 10th St.* **Metro:** *Metro Center.* **Contact:** *☎ 426-6924, TDD 426-1749; www.nps.gov/ foth.* **Hours:** *daily 9am-5pm. Hourly talks 15 min. past the hour except during matinees. Call for details.* **Admission:** *Free.*

Except for the sets of the constantly changing short run productions (see **Entertainment,** p. 141), the poorly lit theater looks much as it did on April 14, 1865 when actor **John Wilkes Booth** snuck into **Abraham Lincoln's** box and shot him in the head with a Derringer pistol. The assassin then leapt clumsily to the stage breaking a bone in his left leg as he shouted out "Sic semper tyranis." That phrase, "thus always to tyrants," the state motto of Virginia, was symbolic of Booth's plan to rid the South of Lincoln's nuisance. National Park Rangers describe the events with animated gusto during a 20-minute talk in the theater. Downstairs, artifacts related to the assassination are displayed. Every sitting President since 1868 has taken his chances and seen a play at the theater at least once a year. Of course, they avoid the unlucky box and sit front row center. Lines to see the theater can wind all the way up the street, so plan on going in the morning.

PETERSEN HOUSE

⚐ Location: *516 10th St.* **Metro:** *Metro Center.* **Contact:** *☎ 426-6830.* **Hours:** *daily 9am-5pm. Closed when the theater is closed to tourists for productions.* **Admission:** *Free.*

The mortally wounded Lincoln was carried across the street to the Petersen House, where he died the next morning in a bed too small for his ungainly frame. The tiny room where he passed away (rumored to be the size of the log cabin where the entire Lincoln family lived when Abe was a boy) is an impeccable historic reconstruction, with the original interior structure and moldings. The intimacy of the room gives visitors the unnerving impression that they are strangers at a wake. Lines are long, so arrive early.

OLD POST OFFICE

⚐ Location: *Pennsylvania Ave. and 11th St.* **Metro:** *Federal Triangle.* **Contact:** *☎ 289-4224; www.old- postofficedc.com.* **Hours:** *Tower open daily mid-Apr. to mid-Sept. 8am-10:45pm; off-season 10am-6pm. Tower closes during inclement weather and Washington Ringing Society performances Th 6:30-9:30pm. Shops open M-Sa 10am-9pm, Su noon-7pm.*

The infamous architecture of the Old Post Office Building was criticized upon as "a cross between a cathedral and a cotton mill." Today, however, its Romanesque style remains a delightful rebuke to its sleeker contemporary neighbors.

The first few floors of the building are home to the "Pavilion," which consists of a stage hosting local entertainment and a touristy collection of shops and ethnic eateries. High above, the **clock tower** allows visitors to perch 270 feet above downtown with unobstructed views of the Capitol, the White House, and the Lincoln Memorial without the wait or tiny windows of the Washington Monument.

RONALD REAGAN BUILDING

🚩 Location: *1300 Pennsylvania Ave.* **Metro:** *Federal Triangle.* **Contact:** *☎ 312-1300; www.itcdc.com* **Hours:** *daily 6am-2am, food court open M-Sa 7am-7pm.*

At a whopping 3.1 million square feet, The Reagan Building stands as the second largest US government building, smaller only than the Pentagon. Inside is a massive atrium, reaching heights of 125 feet and covering an acre in glass. Sculptures and artifacts, including an immense chunk of the Berlin wall, are scattered across the atrium. The basement houses a new and spotless food court with over 20 vendors. The rest of the building contains offices for the International Trade Center.

NATIONAL AQUARIUM

🚩 Location: *14th St. and Constitution Ave., in the basement of the Department of Commerce.* **Metro:** *Federal Triangle.* **Contact:** *☎ 482-2825.* **Hours:** *daily 9am-5pm. Feedings daily 2pm: sharks M, W, Sa; piranhas Tu, Th, Su.* **Admission:** *$3, ages 2-10 75¢.*

The aquarium proudly notes that it is the nation's first over 125 years old, and its antiquated facilities are indicative of its age. Nevertheless, a few sharks, piranhas, touch tanks, and hip island music can still generate ooohs and aaahs from monument-weary kids. The alligator exhibit recently tripled in size, and new touch tanks are constantly being added.

ESPNZONE

🚩 Location: *Corner of E and 11th St.* **Metro:** *Metro Center or Federal Triangle.* **Contact:** *☎ 783-3776* **Hours:** *M-Sa 11:30am-11pm, arcade until midnight. Su 11:30am-10:30pm, arcade until 11pm.*

This is the sports fan's mecca, offering jumbotron screens as well as personal tabletop televisions showing virtually every game being played in every sport at that particular moment. Watch the game while you chomp on the grille's selection of burgers, steaks, and sandwiches. Then head downstairs to the arcade, where you can compete in a number of virtual sports video games as well as climb a mechanical rock wall or test your skills at landing a parachute.

PERSHING PARK

🚩 Location: *14th and E St., across from the White House Visitors Center.* **Metro:** *Federal Triangle.*

A tranquil park and memorial to General John "Black Jack" Pershing, leader of US forces in World War I. A 20-foot statue of Pershing stands next to massive stone walls detailing Pershing's victories overseas, while the various fountains and tables make for a natural picnicking spot. Another statue of Pershing is located down the street at the end of Freedom Plaza, a concrete enormity and popular hangout for the homeless.

NEW YORK AVENUE PRESBYTERIAN CHURCH

🚩 Location: *At the intersection of H St. and New York Ave.* **Metro:** *Metro Center.* **Contact:** *☎ 393-3700.* **Tours:** *after Su services, 9:45am and noon. Visitors also welcome on T-Th from 9am-6pm, F 9am-5pm, Sa 9am-1pm. 10+ visitors should call in advance.*

Inside, the original manuscript of the Emancipation Proclamation hangs in a room below the sanctuary, above the settee where Lincoln drafted the proposal to free the slaves. Blasphemy? The display of the document within a church possibly deifies Lincoln, as more people visit the attraction than attend the Sunday services.

NATIONAL MUSEUM OF WOMEN IN THE ARTS

🚩 Location: *1250 New York Ave.* **Metro:** *Metro Center. Contact:* *☎ 783-5000; www.nmwa.org.* **Hours:** *M-Sa 10am-5pm, Su noon-5pm, Admission: Free.*

Located in the former Masonic Grand Lodge, this museum is the only one in the world dedicated solely to celebrating the achievements of women in the visual, performing, and literary arts. Founded by Wilhelmina and Wallace Holladay, the museum displays paintings, illustrations, and sculptures done by women artists such as Lavinia Fontana and Mary Cassatt from the 16th century to the present day. Look for Dale Kennington's painting "The Debutantes," a beautiful portrayal of the African-American bride.

FARRAGUT

SEE MAP P.309 YOU ARE HERE

🚩 **Highlights:** Washington Post. **Museums:** The Bethune Museum and Archives, B'nai B'rith Klutznick Museum. **Food & Drink:** p. 166. **Nearby:** White House, Foggy Bottom, Georgetown, Dupont Circle.

This is the territory of bureaucrats. E.J. Applewhite described Farragut as "a monotonous uniformity of office buildings poured out like ice cubes," and indeed, walking alongside the regiments on cookie-cutter streets really does call for a whiskey on the rocks. The 13-story height limit prevents New York-style claustrophobia in this glass-walled business district, but white-collar joggers, businessmen in $100 ties, and honking taxicabs point to its corporate soul. Amid the professional clamor there lie a few scenic circles, residential areas, and small museums worthy of attention. Farragut is bounded roughly by N, I, and 15th St. NW on the north, south, and east (respectively), and by 21st St. on the west. Use Metro: Farragut North, Farragut West, or McPherson Square to access the neighborhood.

THOMAS CIRCLE AND ENVIRONS

For a kaleidoscopic glimpse of Washington old and new, take the Vermont Ave. exit from the McPherson Square Metro and walk northeast (toward N St. NW) on Vermont Ave. A short walk brings you to Thomas Circle, which features an amusing statue of **Union General Thomas** sticking his chin out indignantly as his horse sneezes. North of the circle, Vermont Ave. flows into a quiet neighborhood that is home to the **Bethune Museum and Archives,** 1318 Vermont Ave. NW (☎332-1233; Metro: McPherson Square), which chronicles the life of civil rights activist Mary McLeod Bethune (see **Museums,** p. 118).

RHODE ISLAND AVENUE

Budding from Rhode Island Ave., the beautiful red-bricked **St. Matthew's Cathedral** (1725 Rhode Island Ave. NW, ☎347-3215, Metro: Farragut North) offers some architectural diversity from its otherwise boxy neighbors. The cathedral's interior is equally impressive; the central altar, donated by the Archbishop of Agra, espouses stylistic influences from the Taj Mahal. On November 25, 1963, President John F. Kennedy's funeral Mass was held at St. Matthew's Cathedral. The cathedral's mosaics are modeled after the style of churches in Ravenna, Italy. St. Matthew's vibrant, vaulted ceiling frescoes and candle-filled chapels embrace worshipers for Sunday Mass in Latin (7, 8:30, and 10am) and Spanish (11:30am, 1, and 5pm). Down the street from St. Matthew's sits the architecturally inconspicuous **B'nai B'rith Klutznick National Jewish Museum** (1640 Rhode Island Ave. NW, ☎857-6583, see p. 118). The museum provides intriguing and emotional exhibits on Jewish history, the Holocaust, and Jews in modern society.

THE WASHINGTON POST

🚩 **Location:** 1150 15th St. **Metro:** Farragut North. **Contact:** ☎334-7969. **Tours:** 1hr. tours M 9am-3pm. Reservations necessary; tours fill up months in advance. No children under 11. **Admission:** Free.

The domineering tan building at 1150 15th St. houses *The Washington Post,* one of the most influential newspapers in the world and the paper responsible for uncovering the Watergate Scandal. If you can land a spot on the popular tour, you'll see the *Post*'s hectic news room, enormous printing presses, and a small museum. Guides detail the complicated, time-consuming printing process of yore and explain how the paper is printed today. If you can't get a tour, wander into the lobby, where four light-board pillars display photographs of recent newsworthy events.

EXPLORER'S HALL

🚩 **Location:** On the corner of M and 17th St. NW. **Metro:** Farragut North. **Contact:** ☎857-7588, group tours ☎857-7689, Grosvenor Auditorium ☎857-7588; www.nationalgeographic.com. **Hours:** M-Sa and holidays 9am-5pm, Su 10am-5pm. **Admission:** Free. **Accessibility:** Wheelchair accessible.

The **National Geographic Society Explorers Hall** makes exploring (and learning) easy and fun with addicting interactive computer screens and movies, realistic dinosaur displays, and fantastic photos from National Geographic Magazine's best photographers. Passport Fridays are live presentations in Explorers Hall, featuring anything from live rabbits or reptiles to storytelling. Gilbert H. Grosvenor Auditorium hosts live lectures, films, and performances.

FARRAGUT AND MCPHERSON SQUARES

Picnickers enjoy the summer sounds of occasional street musicians in **Farragut Square,** adjoining the Farragut North and Farragut West Metro Stations. A statue of Civil War Admiral David Farragut stares off into the distance, spyglass in hand. Farragut, who coined the phrase "Damn the torpedoes, full speed ahead!" during the 1864 Battle of Mobile Bay, Alabama, is now patron to a regular crowd of homeless and yuppies who lounge and lunch in the park. On summer Thursdays, Farragut Square hosts free lunch-hour jazz. Nearby **McPherson Square** promotes the memory of Gen. James McPherson, who commanded the Union army during Sherman's march through Georgia.

THE SECOND CITY
GEORGETOWN

YOU ARE HERE

U.S. Capitol Building
SEE MAP P. 312

◪ Highlights: Shops and eateries along M St. and Wisconsin Ave., Dumbarton Oaks Estate, C&O Canal. **Museums:** Dumbarton Oaks. **Food & Drink:** p. 168. **Nearby:** Upper Northwest, Adams-Morgan, Dupont Circle, Foggy Bottom.

Georgetown's quiet historical homes are balanced by raucous bars. The tree-lined streets of boxy, brick rowhouses are home to politicos like Secretary of State Madeline Albright, a world-class university, and blocks and blocks of shopping, dining, and drinking. One of few areas in the District which predate the United States of America, Georgetown now preserves its colonial look. Today, both high-income and high-status, Georgetown now attracts a strange blend of students, suburban goths, and tourists.

THE FOUNDING OF GEORGETOWN. Anacostan Indians were the first people to live in the Georgetown area, but were pushed out in the late 17th century by other Native Americans and their Anglo allies. Eventually George Gordon and Ninean Beall came to own much of the Anancostan land, thanks to Scottish land grants. In the early 1700s, however, immigrants fleeing Scotland's social unrest flocked to the lands owned by Gordon and George Beall (Ninean's heir) and eventually forced those estates to relinquish some of their property to form a new town. This became "Georgetown" although it is unknown whether the town was named for the two Georges who reluctantly gave up their land or for England's monarch, King George II.

GROWTH OF GEORGETOWN. Located on the Potomac, at the border of Virginia and Maryland, the town immediately thrived as a center of trade as tobacco and African slaves poured through the area. In the 1750s, Georgetown's bustle attracted **George Washington,** who envisioned the potential for a canal through the city that linked the Potomac with the Ohio River. Washington would later select a parcel of land adjacent to the city for the site of the nation's capital, Washington City. From 1780 to 1830, while Washington City was still a minimally developed swamp, Georgetown became the fashionable and civilized residence of many government officials and foreign ambassadors as many large estates and federal-style buildings were erected. Visitors can still distinguish the smaller rowhouses below Dumbarton St., built for the workers and African-Americans, from the larger, aristocratic houses of upper Georgetown (around R and S Sts.).

FROM RICHES TO RAGS AND BACK AGAIN. In 1871 an act of Congress took away the region's self-government, absorbing it into Washington. The late 19th and early 20th centuries saw Georgetown become less rich and fashionable, as more blue-collar workers and minorities moved into the city. After the Civil War, African-American neighborhoods grew tremendously as droves of ex-slaves joined existing communities of freedmen. Georgetown's fate seemed sealed with the death of the canal which was deemed too shallow for modern steamships and struggled against the competition of the Baltimore and Ohio Railroad.

During the New Deal and World War II, federal jobs in Washington ballooned. The influx of academics-turned-bureaucrats renewed Georgetown at a ferocious pace. In order to form new, wealthier (white) communities, a federal agency expelled African-Americans from Georgetown, and real estate developers bought out longtime home-

the dope on dc

Assassins

Lincoln's assassination was actually part of a larger conspiracy that included plans to kill Secretary of State William Henry Seward and Vice President Andrew Johnson. The conspirators met in Mary Surratt's boardinghouse (now **Go-Lo's,** a Chinese restaurant; see p. 164). While they planned to murder all three government officials simultaneously, Booth was the only assassin to carry through on the staged directions. Lewis Powell's knife was foiled by Seward's neck brace, the result of a recent riding accident. At the last minute, George Atzerodt had stage fright (performance anxiety?). Despite their singularly unequal talents, the company's reception was notably the same: Booth was shot to death by Union soldiers, and Surratt, Powell, and Atzerodt were tried, convicted, and hung.

owners. Once remodeled and spiffed up, the properties were then sold to the new army of white-collar civil servants, creating modern Georgetown.

Today, only the rich can afford the inflated real estate prices in Georgetown. **John F. Kennedy** lived here as a US Senator (at 3260 N St.), as did **Senator John Warner** and then-wife **Liz Taylor.** Hollywood has also found the area compelling, using it as a backdrop for films like *True Lies, The Exorcist,* and *St. Elmo's Fire.* Georgetown is visited less by history buffs than by tourists craving shopping and bar-hopping. Perhaps drawn to the energy of college students and interns, tourists have helped transform Georgetown's image of itself from a collection of staid federal-style buildings and rowhouses into one of booming bars and bustling shops that cater to everyone. Despite the emphasis on traditional tourist activities, visitors with an interest in Georgetown's past will be happy to know that historical sights are busting out all over town. Places like the Dumbarton Oaks Mansion and Garden, Mount Zion Methodist Church, Tudor Place, Dumbarton House, and the C&O Canal are worth a visit. Unfortunately, many of Georgetown's historic homes are closed to the public.

ORIENTATION. Wisconsin Avenue and **M Street** are the main thoroughfares of Georgetown, and their intersection (Washington's oldest) marks the center of this consumer-driven universe. Address numbers on Wisconsin Ave. start below M St. and go up as the avenue goes north (in this area, uphill). Numbered streets run parallel to Wisconsin Ave. and perpendicular to M St., increasing east to west. For most of its Georgetown length, K St., which turns into Water St., is directly under the Whitehurst Fwy. and thus hard to find on maps. Because Rock Creek Park cuts through the city on one side of Georgetown, M St., Pennsylvania Ave., P St., and Q St. are the only routes to Georgetown for pedestrians coming from downtown or Dupont Circle. West of Key Bridge, M St. becomes Canal Rd. (leading to Bethesda, MD) as neon and brick abruptly yield to the trees of Glover Archibold Park.

The nearest Metro stop, Foggy Bottom-GWU, is about five blocks from the center of Georgetown. When you exit the station, you'll be facing 23rd St. NW and the George Washington University Hospital. Turn left down 23rd St. and walk clockwise around Washington Circle until you reach Pennsylvania Ave.; turn left onto Pennsylvania and trudge down over the bridge to M St. Metrobuses #30, 32, 34, 35, and 36 run from Washington Circle (at 24th St. and Pennsylvania Ave.); get a transfer before exiting the Metro and ride to Georgetown for a quarter. Buses run down M St. and up Wisconsin Ave. past Dumbarton Oaks up to the Friendship Heights Metro and the Maryland border. From Dupont Circle, just follow P St. west, past Rock Creek Park. P St. dead-ends in Wisconsin. Turn left to get to the intersection of Wisconsin and M St. Alternatively from Dupont Circle, walk southwest on New Hampshire Ave. and take a right onto M St. Metrobuses D2 and D4 travel from Union Station to Georgetown via Dupont Circle. From Adams-Morgan, take the #42 bus (at Columbia Rd.) to Dupont Circle, then switch to the G2 bus (at 20th and P St.) to Georgetown.

TOWARD THE C&O CANAL

THE OLD STONE HOUSE

🛤 *Location:* 3051 M St. *Contact:* ☎ 426-6851. *Hours:* House open W-Su 12pm-5pm. Garden open W-Su 10am-5pm. *Admission:* Free.

Built in 1765, the Old Stone House is generally accepted to be the oldest house in Washington. Preserved within the house are the original cooking, bread-baking, candle-making, and fabric-spinning tools. Lovely gardens make this a nice place to stop and literally smell the roses in late spring. Guided tours are given every Sunday at 2pm.

C&O CANAL

🛤 *Location:* 1057 Thomas Jefferson St. NW, south of M St. on the towpath. *Contact:* ☎ 653-5190. *Hours:* Open W-Su 9am-4:30pm. Boats leave Apr.-Oct. at 11am, 1:30pm, and 3pm. *Admission:* Adults $7.50, seniors $6, children $4.

Historic Homes

For decades, George Washington agitated for construction of a canal in Georgetown. Expanding on Washington's ideas, **President John Quincy Adams** in 1828 began construction of the C&O canal, which he intended to reach the source of the Ohio River in **Pittsburgh,** some 360 miles away, although in the end the canal only went to **Cumberland,** 185 miles away. Today the canal and adjacent towpath, which run parallel to M St., two blocks south, exist as merely a historic landmark administered by the National Park Service. In some areas, the still water and stone walls of the canal make for quite an attractive stroll or lunchtime spot; near Georgetown, however, the stagnant water trapped by the locks can make the ride considerably rank smelling. To reach the canal's relatively unspoiled bits without straying too far from public transportation, take the D5 bus from Union Station through Upper Northwest to MacArthur Blvd., and walk left through the subdivisions until the canal.

Georgetown University

As a a reminder of the canal's original function, the canal boat **Georgetown** takes tourists through the locks of the canal, pulled from the towpath by huge mules.-Board the 1½hr. ride at the Visitors Center. Information on fishing, ranger-led hiking, biking, tours, and upcoming events is also available at the Visitors Center.

AFRICAN-AMERICAN GEORGETOWN

HERRING HILL

🛤 *The area above M St., around 28th and 30th St.*

Herring Hill was named after the hordes of fish that haunted nearby waterways, providing a staple in the local diet even into the 19th century. This was a historically African-American neighborhood until the 1940s and 50s, when blacks were forced out. The building at 1239 30th St., a private residence known as Spite House, is the **skinniest house** in Georgetown. A converted alley, about 11 ft. wide, the building has room for but one window and one door across the width of its facade—though the interior is comfortable in its coziness.

Skinniest House in Georgetown

MOUNT ZION METHODIST CHURCH

⏺ Location: *1334 29th St.* **Contact:** ☎ *234-0148.* **Hours:** *Services Su 11am. Call ahead for tours.* **Admission:** *Free.*

Washington's oldest African-American congregation, the Mount Zion Methodist Church was founded in 1816 by 125 African-Americans who angrily broke away from the segregated **Montgomery Street Methodist** congregation. In 1880, the original church located at what is now 27th and P St. burnt down. The current church building was constructed from 1880 to 1884 and the carved balcony, the cast-iron pillars, and the pressed tin roof display the skill of early black artisans. Urban renewal and rising housing prices in the 1940s and 50s forced many longtime residents and families to relocate throughout the city, so that even today there are few African-American families in Georgetown. Services, however, draw many former residents back, and the **cemetery** is moving.

HISTORIC ESTATES ALONG Q STREET

DUMBARTON HOUSE

⏺ Location: *2715 Q St., between 27th and 28th St.* **Contact:** ☎ *337-2288.* **Hours:** *Gardens open Tu-Sa 10:15am-12:15pm.* **Tour:** *House open by guided tour only; Sept.-July Tu-Sa 10:15, 11:15am, and 12:15pm. Reservations required for large groups 10+.* **Admission:** *Suggested donation $3. Free.*

Not be confused with the entirely separate Dumbarton Oaks Mansion. This federal-style building is the headquarters for the **National Society of the Colonial Dames of America,** an exclusive group of ladies who can trace their ancestry before 1750 and who have ancestors who made "positive contribution to the colonies." Their mission is preserving historic sites and encouraging educational programs. Dumbarton House was completed by Joseph Nourse, treasurer to the first six Presidents; in 1813, Charles Carroll (who later founded Rochester, NY) moved in and hosted **Dolley Madison** as she fled the British in 1814 (see **Founding and Early Years,** p. 35). The house is decorated with furniture and decorative arts primarily from the federal period (1790-1840). Although most of the furniture is not original to the building, it still gives a sense of how wealthy families in the early 19th century lived. Of special interest is a painting by Charles Wilson Peale, one of the forefathers of American painting, and the dinnerware specially ordered from China, based on a family member's drawing.

TUDOR PLACE ESTATE

⏺ Location: *1644 31st St.* **Contact:** ☎ *965-0400; www.tudorplace.com* **Hours:** *Gardens open to visitors M-Sa 10am-4pm.* **Tours:** *1hr. tours of the house Tu-F 10, 11:30am, 1, and 2:30pm, Sa every hr. 10am-3pm.* **Admission:** *Suggested donation garden alone $2, tour $6, seniors $5, students with ID and under 12 $3. Reservations suggested for groups of 10+.*

Martha Custis Peter used the $8000 willed to her by her step-grandfather, **George Washington,** to build Tudor Place, the Neoclassical mansion, designed by William Thornton. During the Civil War, Mrs. Peter's daughters used to signal to their cousins, **Robert E. Lee** and siblings, by waving petticoats like flags out of the upstairs window. Confederate supporters to the end, Martha's daughter Britannia Peter cleverly rented the estate to Union officers in order to preserve the building during the Civil War. Through dedication (and cousin marriages) subsequent generations ensured that the house and estate remained intact. The tours are an interesting peek into the family's love of their own history, as well as the different eras in which the house was occupied.

DUMBARTON OAKS ESTATE AND ENVIRONS

⏺ Location: *Mansion entrance at 1703 32nd St. NW between R and S St. Garden entrance at 31st and R St.* **Contact:** ☎ *339-6401, tour info* ☎ *339-6409.* **Hours:** *Mansion open Tu-Su 2-5pm. Garden open Apr.-Oct. 2-6pm, Nov.-Mar. 2-5pm.* **Admission:** *For mansion, suggested donation $1. For garden, $5, seniors and children $3; Nov.-Mar. free. Season passes $25, families $40.*

The beautiful, but little known, Dumbarton Oaks Estate is a short walk from the Tudor Place Estate. The **Dumbarton Oaks Mansion,** now a museum, should not be confused with the entirely separate Dumbarton House. This estate is part of the remains of the original **Rock of Dumbarton** property, upon which Georgetown was founded. The mansion has switched names and architectural styles frequently since its construction in 1801. Among the local and national figures who have lived here is **John Calhoun,** who stayed in the mansion while he was Secretary of War, Vice President, and Senator from South Carolina.

Robert and Mildred Bliss purchased the building in 1920 and renovated it to accommodate the library and collections. They then donated the house and gardens to **Harvard University**, Mr. Bliss's alma mater, in 1940. In 1963, Harvard added the stunning gallery designed by **Phillip Johnson** for the pre-Colombian art collection. The attractive displays of the museum housed in the old mansion mainly showcase Byzantine art. See **Museums,** p. 119 for information on the collections.

The 10-acre absolutely stunning **Dumbarton Oaks Gardens** have a separate entrance. Each season reveals different facets of the garden, from the spring explosion of flowers such as the bearded iris, foxglove, lily of the valley, and southern magnolia, to the winter bare "bones" of arched tree limbs. Warning: no picnicking or pets allowed.

Immediately to the east of Dumbarton Oaks is **Lover's Lane,** officially recognized as such in 1900. The beautiful canopied path winds behind the tennis courts of Dumbarton Oaks Park and heads north to where it connects to Rock Creek Park, beginning a two-mile trail that leads through **Rock Creek Park** (see p. 85) up to the **National Zoo.** Unfortunately this path becomes very unsafe at night and should be avoided after dark.

GEORGETOWN UNIVERSITY

🔢 *Location: 37th and O St. Contact: ☎687-1457, for the Information Center. Tours: Campus tours begin at the Office of Undergraduate Admissions, White-Gravenor Hall, Rm. 103, ☎687-3600. Shops: Bookshop open M-F 9am-8pm, Sa-Su 10am-6pm. Transportation: shuttle bus stop outside Leavey Center runs every 15min. to nearby Metro stops, including Rosslyn and Dupont Circle. $1, free for Georgetown students. ☎687-4417.*

Archbishop John Carroll was fully aware of Georgetown's lively nature when he chose to found his university there instead of on then-rural **Capitol Hill.** The first building of Georgetown University was constructed in 1788, and the university opened in 1789, becoming the United States' first Catholic institution for higher learning. Today, approximately 50% of Georgetown's 6000 undergraduates are Catholic, and a Jesuit brother resides in every dorm, although students of many creeds attend.

Georgetown's College of Arts and Sciences is just one of five undergraduate programs—the other four are somewhat more pre-professional: Business, Foreign Service, Language and Linguistics, and Nursing. The distinctions are purely academic, however; students of the several schools live, study, and party together. In addition to the five undergraduate schools, the University has an additional 6,500 graduate students in their graduate schools—Law, Medicine, Business, and the Graduate School of Arts and Sciences. All facilities are located on the main Georgetown campus with the exception of the Law School, which is near Capitol Hill.

Georgetown certainly boasts a long list of rich and powerful graduates, such as Supreme Court Justice **Antonin Scalia,** the late New York prelate **John Cardinal O'Connor,** television journalist and author **Maria Shriver,** and top dog **Bill Clinton** himself, although the student body is much more diverse than its preppy image would suggest. The much-worshipped men's basketball team, which launched the careers of **Patrick Ewing, Alonzo Mourning,** and **Allen Iverson,** is a perennial NCAA tournament contender (they won the national title in 1984).

ESSENTIAL INFORMATION

PARKING IN GEORGETOWN

Finding **parking** is difficult in Georgetown, and you may waste the whole day trying to find a spot. Try **35th St.** near the university (particularly good in the summer), the northern sections near **R** and **S St.,** or Georgetown's eastern edge near **28th St.**

Garages like **Georgetown Parking** (1044 Wisconsin Ave., ☎333-1890) are expensive at $4 per hour but are conveniently near the center of town.

the on dopedc

Nixon Resigns

They now play at the **MCI Center** (see p. 68). Buy tickets through TicketMaster (☎ 432-7328) for these games; purchase other sporting event tickets through the campus Ticket Office (☎ 687-4692).

THE CAMPUS. Through the main gate (at 37th and O St.) lie the prominent Gothic curlicues of **Healy Hall,** named after **Father Patrick Healy,** an African-American priest who was President of Georgetown University in the 1870s. Check out the hands of the clock mounted on Healy Hall tower—if they're there. Most years, seniors attempt to steal them and ship them to the President of the University—or, rumor has it, to destinations as exotic as the Vatican. Don't partake of this tradition; climbing on the outside of the tower is extremely dangerous, not to mention illegal.

In front of the Hall, in the center of Healy Circle, stands a statue of the University's founder, Archbishop **John Carroll.** Maps and directions are available from the information booth to the left of the gate. **Healy** and **Copley Lawns** (on your left and right respectively) host major social gatherings in warm weather.

DUMBARTON OAKS

🖪 *Address: 1703 32nd St. NW, in Georgetown, between R and S St. Contact: Recorded info ☎ 339-6401, tour info ☎ 339-6409, www.doaks.org. Hours: Tu-Su 2-5pm. Admission: Suggested contribution $1.*

Built by **Robert** and **Mildred Bliss** in the Dumbarton Oaks Mansion, this fine museum houses superbly documented exhibits focusing on Byzantine and pre-Colombian art. The **Byzantine Collection** contains floor mosaics, bronzes, ivories, and jewelry, mostly from the Byzantine Empire, but also includes some interesting Coptic (Egyptian Christian) works. Peruvian weavings bridge the passage from the Byzantine mosaics to the pre-Colombian gallery, a series of eight circular glass pavilions arranged around a fountain. The pavilions hold Robert Bliss's pre-Colombian art collection, which spans the Mayan, Olmec, and Aztec cultures. Between the Byzantine and pre-Colombian galleries is the Music Room, the site of Igor Stravinsky's Dumbarton Oaks Concerto which premiered here for the Bliss's 30th wedding anniversary in 1934. Subscription concerts from the Dumbarton Oaks Friends of Music are held every winter (☎ 339-6436 for info).

DUPONT CIRCLE

YOU ARE HERE

U.S. Capitol Building ●

SEE MAP P. 306

🖪 *Highlights: Galleries, Embassy Row, Nightlife. Museums: Phillips Collection, Textile Museum. Food & Drink: p. 164. Nearby: Georgetown, Adams-Morgan, Farragut, Foggy Bottom.*

Once one of Washington's more swanky neighborhoods, Dupont Circle attracted many embassies because of its stately townhouses and large tracts of land. Later, as politicians left for Georgetown and Upper Northwest, Dupont traded in the ritz for the glitz of Washington's large gay community, which now dominates the neighborhood. With crowded restaurants, raucous bars and clubs, a boisterous art scene, and streets full of beautiful people expressing themselves fully, Dupont is both loud and proud.

Dupont's main drag is the section of **Connecticut Avenue,** along which an array of restaurants, bookstores, and small boutiques serve eager customers. West of Connecticut Ave. along **Massachusetts Avenue,** embassies flap their flags, while lobbyists flap their mouths in nearby townhouse offices. Upscale galleries cluster around **21st Street** and **R Street,** just a few blocks away from the Phillips Collection, one of the finest art museums in the city. The area along 17th and 18th St. east of Connecticut Ave. remains quieter than the main drags around Dupont, but is slowly becoming more developed as restaurants, cafes, shops, and bars spring up. The neighborhood is bounded by **16th St., 24th St., N St.,** and **T St.** NW. Side streets west and northeast of Connecticut often have parking spaces. During the day, Massachusetts Ave. might have parking. At night, park as far west as you can and make sure your car has absolutely nothing in it; break-ins are common. Use Metro: Dupont Circle to access the area.

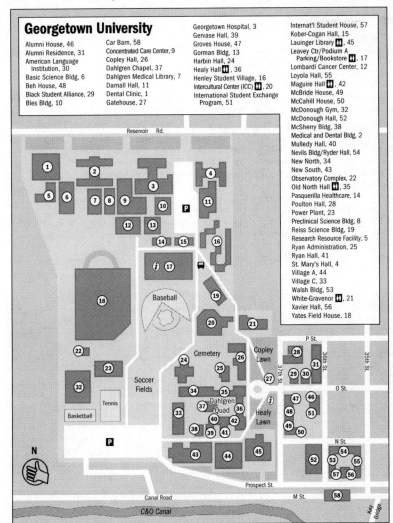

Georgetown University

Alumni House, 46
Alumni Residence, 31
American Language Institution, 30
Basic Science Bldg, 6
Beh House, 48
Black Student Alliance, 29
Bles Bldg, 10

Car Barn, 58
Concentrated Care Center, 9
Copley Hall, 26
Dahlgren Chapel, 37
Dahlgren Medical Library, 7
Darnall Hall, 11
Dental Clinic, 1
Gatehouse, 27

Georgetown Hospital, 3
Gervase Hall, 39
Groves House, 47
Gorman Bldg, 13
Harbin Hall, 24
Healy Hall, 36
Henley Student Village, 16
Intercultural Center (ICC), 20
International Student Exchange Program, 51

Internat'l Student House, 57
Kober-Cogan Hall, 15
Lauinger Library, 45
Leavey Ctr/Podium A Parking/Bookstore, 17
Lombardi Cancer Center, 12
Loyola Hall, 55
Maguire Hall, 42
McBride House, 49
McCahill House, 50
McDonough Gym, 32
McDonough Hall, 52
McSherry Bldg, 38
Medical and Dental Bldg, 2
Mulledy Hall, 40
Nevils Bldg/Ryder Hall, 54
New North, 34
New South, 43
Observatory Complex, 22
Old North Hall, 35
Pasquerilla Healthcare, 14
Poulton Hall, 28
Power Plant, 23
Preclinical Science Bldg, 8
Reiss Science Bldg, 19
Research Resource Facility, 5
Ryan Administration, 25
Ryan Hall, 41
St. Mary's Hall, 4
Village A, 44
Village C, 33
Walsh Bldg, 53
White-Gravenor, 21
Xavier Hall, 56
Yates Field House, 18

DUPONT CIRCLE AND ENVIRONS

DUPONT CIRCLE

⚑ Location: *The intersection between Massachusetts Ave., Connecticut Ave., and New Hampshire Ave.*

The heart of the neighborhood is Dupont Circle itself, a small park inside a traffic rotary that joins the incoming spokes of six avenues and streets. Admiral **Samuel F. Dupont's** millionaire descendants moved his statue from the center of this park to Delaware. A fountain adorned by semi-nude goddesses now graces the circle, watching over the chess players, lunching office workers, drug dealers, and spandex-clad bikers who populate the park. The circle is perfectly safe during the day, but **exercise caution late at night and walk around, rather than through, the park.**

CHRISTIAN HEURICH MANSION

⚑ Location: *1307 New Hampshire Ave. NW., on the corner of 20th St. Contact:* ☎ *785-2068, www.hswdc.org. Hours: M-Sa 10am-4pm; library open W-Sa 10am-4pm. Tours: 30min., self-guided, unless pre-arranged for groups. Admission: $3; students, seniors, and ages 5-12 $1.50; under 5 free.*

Sneak a peek into the lives of German immigrant and beer baron Christian Heurich and his family in their former home, which now houses the **Historical Society of Washington, D.C.** Construction began on the impressive 40-room mansion in 1892, finishing in 1895. The house exemplifies turn-of-the-century bourgeois opulence with indoor plumbing, electricity, gorgeous mosaic floors, and German influences like the heavy carved wood ceiling in the dining room. The garden in back is a lovely and quiet retreat. After marveling at the splendor, raise a mug of **Old Heurich's** in a neighborhood tavern and imagine the good life for yourself.

GALLERIES OF DUPONT CIRCLE

Many visitors are startled to discover that Washington is home to a thriving arts community and many galleries and art spaces. The Dupont Circle community has fostered Washington's gallery scene since its heyday in the 1980s when virtually everyone and his mother was an art collector. Today, over two dozen galleries displaying everything from contemporary photographs to tribal crafts reside in the Dupont Circle area: most of the oldest and best-known galleries lie on **R Street.**

Twenty-one galleries have organized themselves into the **Galleries of Dupont Circle.** Together they hold a joint open house the first Friday of each month from 6-8pm (☎ 232-3610; www.artlineplus.com). These "First Fridays" are the best way to discover D.C.'s local art scene. Six times a year the organization also publishes the **Gallery Guide,** which provides a list of local galleries, current shows, and area maps. You can explore the contents of the galleries almost any afternoon of the week, although many galleries are traditionally closed Mondays and have variable hours (or are closed) in August; call ahead. Most galleries will also schedule appointments outside of regular hours.

For Dupont Circle, the following are some of the more interesting galleries; refer to the Gallery Guide for detailed information on each gallery. The **Washington Printmakers Gallery,** 1732 Connecticut Ave. NW, 2nd fl., is the only D.C. gallery devoted exclusively to prints. (☎ 332-7757; open Tu-Th noon-6pm, F noon-9pm, Sa-Su noon-5pm.) Along R St., **Gallery K,** 2010 R St. NW (☎ 234-0339; open Tu-Sa 11am-6pm), **Marsha Mateyka Gallery,** 2012 R St. NW (☎ 328-0088; open W-Sa 11am-5pm), **Robert Brown Gallery,** 2030 R St. NW (☎ 483-4383; open Tu-Sa noon-6pm), and **Anton Gallery,** 2108 R St. NW (☎ 328-0828; open Tu-Sa noon-5pm) are all quality galleries showing some of the most well-known regional and national artists. Anton and Marsha Mateyka Galleries both show work by a number of women artists. Some of the cooperative galleries are hodgepodges of great and not-so-great work, but two worth checking out are the **Studio Gallery** (2108 R St. NW, downstairs; ☎ 232-8734; open W-Sa 11am-5pm, Su 1-5pm) and the **Foundry Gallery** (9 Hillyer Ct. NW; ☎ 387-0203; open W-Sa 11am-5pm, Su 1-5pm). **Fondo del Sol Visual Arts Center,** 2112 R St. NW (☎ 483-2777), is a bilingual, alternative museum devoted to the culture and art of Latin America, and hosts daily video programs and occasional special programs (open W-Sa noon-5:30pm; requested donation $3, students $1, children free).

POINTS OF INTEREST IN DUPONT CIRCLE

NATIONAL MUSEUM OF AMERICAN JEWISH MILITARY HISTORY

🎫 *Location:* 1811 R St. NW. *Contact:* ☎ 265-6280. *Hours:* M-F 9am-5pm, Su 1-5pm. *Admission:* Free.

The rather bare and unimaginative layout of the museum is compensated for by the fascinating war stories told in the various exhibits. "Rescue and Renewal" documents through photographs and letters the efforts of Jewish-American GIs to help restore the survivors of concentration camps to their countries of origin after WWII. For 2001 the museum will open a new exhibit called "Hall of Heroes," honoring Jewish recipients of the Congressional Medal of Honor. Contact them directly or through their web site for exhibition dates.

THE SCOTTISH RITE FREEMASONRY TEMPLE

🎫 *Location:* 1733 16th St. NW. *Contact:* ☎ 232-3579. *Hours:* M-F 8am-4pm. *Admission:* Free.

Dupont Circle Park

Fourteen presidents from George Washington to Gerald Ford have been Masons, members of a fraternal order devoted to the promotion of good citizenship which, given its list of past members, has had an undeniable power in US politics. Completed in 1915, the temple of the Scottish Rite Masons is flanked by 33 ft. columns and guarded by two sphinxes with eyes open ("Power") and half-open ("Wisdom"). Inside the temple, the outstanding architecture alone is worth the lengthy tour. Based on John Russell Pope's design, which copies the ancient Mausoleum at Halicarnassus in Bodrum, Turkey, the temple is incredible in structure and interior detail. Tour guides are wonderfully thorough and accommodating. If you are pressed for time, ask for a short version of the tour—say, 30 minutes—to see the grand, Gotham City-style meeting rooms, hear the king of spooky organs play, and marvel at the Hall of Masonic Heroes.

EMBASSY ROW

The stretch of Massachusetts Ave. between Dupont and Observatory Circles is also called **Embassy Row.** Before the 1930s, Washington socialites lined the avenue with their extravagant edifices. Status-conscious diplomats later found the mansions perfect for their prestigious purposes, and embassies moved in by the dozen. You can identify an embassy by the national coat of arms or flag out front, and small plaques near the door name the country. Major nations have designed their own compounds (Great Britain and Japan) and some have moved away from downtown for more space (France and Germany), but smaller countries still occupy the grand townhouses. Tucked among the various embassies are several cultural and historic landmarks.

Rock Creek Park

INDONESIAN EMBASSY

🎫 *Location:* 020 Massachusetts Ave. *Contact:* ☎ 775-5200. *Hours:* M-F 9am-5pm, open for tours.

The ornate embassy once belonged to the Walsh family, whose daughter Evelyn Walsh McLean was the last private owner of the infamous **Hope Diamond** (now housed at the National Museum of Natural History, see p. 113). The building's swirling

Belmont Bed & Breakfast

curves, two symmetrically rounded bay windows, and iron grating are exquisite. Other embassies of note, although closed to tourists, include The **Brazilian Embassy,** designed by John Russell Pope, who also designed the National Gallery and the National Archives *(3006 Massachusetts Ave. ☎ 745-2700.)* and the **British Embassy** which has a working red box telephone booth just inside its northern gates. *(3100 Massachusetts Ave. ☎ 462-1340.)*

ISLAMIC CENTER

⊓ Location: *2551 Massachusetts Ave. NW.* **Contact:** *☎ 332-8343.* **Hours:** *daily 10am-5pm; prayers 5 times daily.* **Admission:** *Free.*

Flags line the entrance to this brilliant white building, whose stunning tile and intricately carved designs stretch to the tips of its spired ceilings. Ambassadors of several Islamic nations (Egypt, Iran, Turkey, and Afghanistan) founded the mosque after World War II. Visitors may enter the mosque, but note that shorts are not allowed and women must cover their heads and wear sleeved shirts. Ask at the **bookstore** if you've forgotten your head covering; they may have extra scarves. The bookstore has many books on Islam in addition to novelty gifts like keychains and mosque-shaped clocks.

SHERIDAN CIRCLE

⊓ Location: *23rd St. NW and Massachusetts Ave.*

Sheridan Circle features an equestrian statue of **General Philip Sheridan,** the Civil War cavalry leader who participated in the Southern surrender at Appomatox. His famous words are often misquoted in letter but not in spirit as "the only good Indian is a dead Indian"; it was Sheridan that ordered Custer to kill Black Kettle and his band of Southern Cheyennes. A small, raised plaque on the sidewalk of the Q St. side of the Circle commemorates Chilean ambassador **Orlando Letelier,** who was killed near the Circle in 1976 by a car bomb along with Ronni K. Moffitt. Letelier represented the Marxist government of Salvador Allende, which dictator Pinochet overthrew with CIA help in the same year. Two top generals in the Pinochet government were convicted of planning the assassination and are now imprisoned in Chile. They continue to maintain that the attack was CIA-planned.

WOODROW WILSON HOUSE

⊓ Location: *2340 S St. NW.* **Contact:** *☎ 387-4062.* **Hours:** *Tu-Su 10am-4pm.* **Admission:** *$5, students $2.50, seniors $4, under 7 free.* **Accessibility:** *Wheelchair accessible.*

The Woodrow Wilson House preserves the memory of Wilson in the fragile and embittered years after he lost the White House in 1920. Wilson, partially paralyzed after a stroke, lived out the last two years of his life here, and is still the only President to retire to the District of Columbia after his tenure. As a tribute to his second wife, Edith Bowling, Wilson lavishly decorated the house with gifts bestowed upon the President by foreign dignitaries and adoring admirers. The one-hour tour given by well informed guides is preceded by a 25-minute tape, so plan to spend a bit of time here. The gardens have been relandscaped to reflect what is believed to have been in the Wilsons' garden. Next door is the **Textile Museum,** 2320 S St. NW, which exhibits many rare, antique textiles (see **Museums,** p. 123).

PHILLIPS COLLECTION

⊓ Location: *1600 21st St.* **Contact:** *☎ 387-2151.*

Just off Massachusetts Ave. on 21st St. is the **Phillips Collection.** The first museum of modern art in the US, the Phillips still sits on the cutting edge (see **Museums,** p. 122).

ADAMS-MORGAN

YOU ARE HERE

U.S. Capitol Building●

SEE MAP P. 312

⊓ Highlights: *Dining, nightlife, shopping.* **Food & Drink:** *p. 154.* **Nearby:** *Rock Creek Park, Shaw, Dupont Circle, Upper Northwest.*

Adams-Morgan rules with multicultural hipness. Long a mixed community, its name came from residents' organizations which planned to integrate the neighborhood by mixing students from the largely white Adams School and the predominantly black Morgan School. Immigrants from Mexico, El Salvador, and Ethiopia add to the diversity in Adams-Morgan, sealing its reputation for international restaurants, bars, and clubs. Slick dance,

Call the USA

"feel free to call"

1-800-COLLECT

1 800

COLLECT

**When in Ireland
Dial: 1-800-COLLECT (265 5328)**

**When in N. Ireland, UK & Europe
Dial: 00-800-COLLECT USA (265 5328 872)**

Member of
Dublin Tourism

Australia	0011	800 265 5328 872
Finland	990	800 265 5328 872
Hong Kong	001	800 265 5328 872
Israel	014	800 265 5328 872
Japan	0061	800 265 5328 872
New Zealand	0011	800 265 5328 872

world beat, and do-it-yourself punk venues start up, change names, and collapse yearly in Adams-Morgan. A wreath of fantastic ethnic restaurants circles Columbia Rd., 18th St., and Calvert St., while quirky second-hand stores, swank boutiques, and small bodegas line 18th St. south of Columbia Rd.

ORIENTATION. Florida Avenue NW divides Dupont Circle from Adams-Morgan on the south; **Rock Creek Park** lines its western side. Adams-Morgan's eastern edge, near 16th St., is peppered with churches and embassies but has unsafe areas to its south and east. **Harvard Street** forms a vague north boundary and separates Adams-Morgan from **Mount Pleasant,** a heavily Hispanic and slightly less prosperous neighborhood. Although Adams-Morgan is generally one of the safer areas in the city, **use caution in the area at night, especially around the parks and the eastern and southern edges.**

With no Metro stop, Adams-Morgan is poorly served by public transportation. The neighborhood also suffers from a lack of parking, especially at night. To reach Adams-Morgan from the **Woodley Park-Zoo Metro,** walk south for about five minutes on **Connecticut Ave.** to the intersection with **Calvert St.** Turn left and cross **Rock Creek Park** on the **Duke Ellington Bridge,** and you'll be about three blocks away from Adams-Morgan's center, the five-pronged intersection of **Columbia Rd.** and **18th St.** The entire walk takes about 15 minutes. To reach the neighborhood from the **Dupont Circle Metro,** walk up **18th St.** for about 15 minutes. Alternatively, the **#42 bus** runs north on **Connecticut Ave.** from Farragut and Dupont Circle until it reaches **Columbia Rd.,** on which cuts through Adams-Morgan to **Mt. Pleasant.**

ROCK CREEK PARK

*Attractions: Jogging, hiking, biking, horseback riding, tennis, golf, historical sites. **Nearby:** Georgetown, Upper Northwest, Dupont Circle, Adams-Morgan. **Directions:** Board either the E2, E3, or E4 buses from the Friendship Heights Metro stop. From the stop, walk up the hill to Rock Creek Park.*

Once mistaken by Charles De Gaulle for the French Embassy's backyard, Rock Creek Park offers city-weary travelers a shady recess from the hustle and bustle of D.C. life. More like a managed forest than a landscaped city park, the 2100-acre green stretches 5 miles from the Kennedy Center on the Potomac to D.C.'s border with Maryland, providing 15 miles of hiking, biking, and horse paths. **Rock Creek Parkway,** which becomes **Beach Drive** north of Klingle Rd., winds through the park from north to south alongside its watery namesake. Be attentive driving, as parts of the parkway change direction during rush hour and most roads feature sharp, winding curves.

Some of the forest trails run near the parkway, but on the whole are surprisingly isolated from the surrounding city. Nature lovers can feast their eyes on the tiny bridges and sporadic creeks that claim sole ownership of the picturesque, wilder sections of the park. The trails have few directional signs or markers—visitors should pick up a park map from the Nature Center, Pierce Mill, or the Rock Creek Gallery.

Thanks to the thick canopy of leaves overhead, it's always 10 degrees cooler inside the park than outside—a natural air-conditioner for those utilizing the park's abundant recreational resources. Along Rock Creek Pkwy., starting at 24th St. and Rock Creek Pkwy. below Calvert St., stretches a 1½ mile **exercise trail,** complete with 18 workout stations where you can push-up, pull-up, and sit-up to your heart's content and benefit (use Metro: Woodley Park). A 4 mile **run** starts where Rock Creek Pkwy. crosses under Connecticut Ave. Cyclists will find plenty of **bicycle trails** criss-crossing the park with signs pointing them out. Remember that bicycles are not allowed on foot paths or horse paths. Cyclists also compete with **rollerbladers** for control of Beach Dr. from 7am Saturdays until 7pm Sundays, when the park closes its gates to motorized vehicles for most of its length north of Broad Branch Rd.

Parking is plentiful in lots throughout the park, and sporadic grassy knolls along Beach Dr. are designated as daytime picnic spots. Camping in the park, however, is always illegal, probably dangerous, and mostly impossible anyway. While the park stays open late, it is **unsafe at night;** unless you're there for an evening event, it is wise to leave before the sun sets. **In an emergency, call park police** (☎ 619-7300).

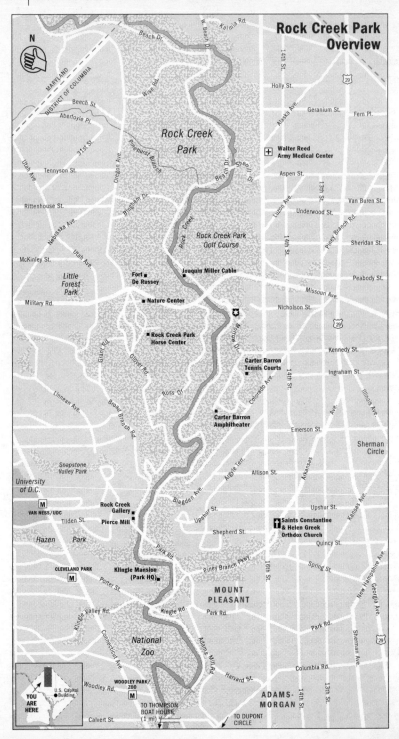

Rock Creek Park Overview

N

W. Beach Dr.
Kalmia Rd.
Beach Dr.
14th St.
Holly St.
29
MARYLAND
DISTRICT OF COLUMBIA
Wise Rd.
Beech St.
Geranium St.
Fern Pl.
Aberfoyle Pl.
Alaska Ave.

31st St.

Pinehurst Branch

Rock Creek Park

Beach Dr.
Sherrill Dr.

Aspen St.

13th St.

Van Buren St.

Walter Reed Army Medical Center

Oregon Ave.

Tennyson St.

Lucon Ave.

Underwood St.

14th St.

Piney Branch Rd.

Rittenhouse St.

Bingham Dr.

Sheridan St.

Nebraska Ave.

Rock Creek

Rock Creek Park Golf Course

Utah Ave.

McKinley St.

Missouri Ave.

Peabody St.

Fort De Russey

Joaquin Miller Cabin

Nicholson St.

Little Forest Park

Military Rd.

■ Nature Center

29

■ **Rock Creek Park Horse Center**

Grant Rd.

Glover Rd.

Morrow Dr.

Kennedy St.

Ingraham St.

Carter Barron Tennis Courts

14th St.

Illinois Ave.

Linnean Ave.

Ross Dr.

Colorado Ave.

Broad Branch Rd.

■ **Carter Barron Amphitheater**

Emerson St.

Sherman Circle

Soapstone Valley Park

Arkansas Ave.

Argyle Terr.

Allison St.

Upshur St.

Kansas Ave.

University of D.C.

Blagden Ave.

M

VAN NESS/UDC

Rock Creek Gallery ■

Upshur St.

Saints Constantine & Helen Greek Orthdox Church

New Hampshire Ave.

Tilden St.

Pierce Mill ■

Shepherd St.

Quincy St.

Hazen Park

Spring St.

Georgia Ave.

CLEVELAND PARK

M

Klingle Mansion (Park HQ) ■

Park Rd.

Piney Branch Pkwy.

16th St.

Porter St.

MOUNT PLEASANT

Park Rd.

Park Rd.

Sherman Ave.

13th St.

Klingle Valley Rd.

Kingle Rd.

29

Connecticut Ave.

National Zoo

Adams Mill Rd.

Harvard St.

Columbia Rd.

U.S. Capitol Building

YOU ARE HERE

Woodley Rd.

WOODLEY PARK/ ZOO

M

ADAMS-MORGAN

14th St.

13th St.

Calvert St.

TO THOMPSON BOAT HOUSE (1 mi)

TO DUPONT CIRCLE

PARK ATTRACTIONS

Pierce Mill, 3545 Williamsburg Ln. NW (☎426-6908), at the corner of Tilden St. and Beach Dr. Rangers are extremely helpful in explaining the history behind this restored gristmill and the development of the mill industry in general. Pierce Mill was the last running mill in the District and fundraising is currently underway to restore it to operation. Tours give an interesting glimpse into the beginning of early industry in the US. Open W-Su 10am-4:30pm.

Rock Creek Gallery, 2401 Tilden St. (☎244-2482), across the street from the Pierce Mill. Also known as the Art Barn. Shows works of mostly obscure local artists. Open Th-Su noon-6pm.

Carter Barron Amphitheater (☎426-6837), at 16th and Colorado St. NW. Outdoor theater offering summertime concerts and popular, free Shakespeare performances in June. For concert and performance info see **Free Music,** p. 138.

Joaquin Miller Cabin Poetry Series (☎726-0971), at the Miller Cabin in the park off of Beach Dr. north of the Military Rd. overpass; park in picnic area #6 lot. Miller, an eccentric and renowned 19th-century poet, retreated to writer's seclusion in a cabin near what is now Meridian Hill Park. When he moved to California, he donated the cabin to the Sierra Club, who gave it to the National Park Service, who then moved it to its present location in Rock Creek Park. Outdoor reading series features 15 poets, mostly from the area. Readings June-July Tu 7:30pm. Call for rain locations.

Nature Center, 5200 Glover Rd. NW (☎426-6829). Happily distributes park info. Exhibits on local flora, fauna, and wildlife, ranging from chestnut laurels to an impressive stuffed bald eagle. Also offers a planetarium show for ages 4 and up (W 4pm, Sa-Su 1 and 4pm). Informal program, *Exploring the Sky,* offers telescope viewings monthly, but dates vary so call in advance. Various "Ranger's Choice" events Sa-Su. Monthly schedules available from the Nature Center. Open W-Su 9am-5pm.

Rock Creek Park Horse Center, 5110 Glover Rd. NW (☎362-0117). The only place in the District for riding without required lessons. Must be 12 years of age for trail rides ($25 per hr.) and a minimum of 30 inches tall for weekend pony rides ($10 per 15min.). Reservations recommended as rides are popular. There are a few designated equestrian trails. Open Tu-Su 9am-6pm. Pick up a map at the Nature Center for more specific info.

Carter Barron Tennis Courts, (☎722-5949), at 16th and Kennedy NW. 10 hard and 15 clay courts. Reservations necessary M-Sa 7-11pm, Sa morning, and in winter. Summer rates $3.25-12. Winter rates $22-31 for heated indoor courts. Senior discounts available to 60+ only during winter. Abundant parking available.Open daily 7am-11pm. Same prices and times at their East Potomac Park tennis courts, 1090 Ohio Dr. SW (554-5962).

Rock Creek Park Golf Course, (☎882-7332), at 16th St. and Rittenhouse NW. Renowned for its lack of par 5 holes and quirky layout, Mother Nature poses many obstructions to the link-goers. Beautiful grounds, especially the more challenging back 9. Offers golf lessons and golf camps for Tiger Woods-wannabes. M-F 9 holes $9, 18 holes $15; Sa-Su 9 holes $12.25, 18 holes $19. Senior (60+) discount price M-F $8 for 9 holes, $10.50 for 18. Club rentals $6-8.75. Course par is 65. Open daily dawn to dusk.

Fletcher's Boat House, 4940 Canal Rd. NW (☎244-0461), at Reservoir and Canal Rd. Canoes $18 per day; rowboats $16 per day. Single-speed bike $8 for 2hr. No rentals after 5pm. Also sells fishing supplies and bait. Open summers M-F 9am-7pm, Sa-Su 7:30am-7pm; hrs. vary with season.

Thompson Boat House, 2900 Virginia Ave. NW. (☎333-4861). Rowing classes available. Canoes $8 per hr., $22 per day. Ocean kayaks $8 per hr., $24 per day. Double kayaks $10 per hr., $30 per day. Bicycles from $4 per hr., $15 per day. No rentals after 5pm. Open M-Sa 6am-8pm, Su 7am-7pm.

UPPER NORTHWEST

◩ Highlights: *National Zoo, National Cathedral.* **Museums:** *Kreeger, Dolls' House Museum, Hillwood.* **Food and Drink:** *p. 175.* **Nearby:** *Rock Creek Park, Adams-Morgan, Dupont Circle, Georgetown.*

Within a city known for its large minority populations, Upper Northwest proves that despite demographics, the city is far from integrated. The neighborhood's homogenous white population, drawn to the area's quiet, clean streets and lack of crime, often draws disinterest from a city council composed mainly of blacks and hispanics, and disdain from private citizens residing elsewhere who call the area "Upper Caucasia." Located west of Rock Creek Park and north of Georgetown in a sort of twilight zone between Downtown D.C. and Maryland, the neighborhood's small communities are linked by the parallel north-south axes of **Wisconsin** and **Connecticut Avenues.** For all its size, Upper Northwest has only a few notable sights: the National Zoo, the Kreeger Museum, and the National Cathedral. The Metro serves Upper Northwest with stops at Woodley Park-Zoo, Cleveland Park, Van Ness-UDC, Tenleytown-AU, and Friendship Heights.

GETTING THERE AND GETTING AROUND. The L1 and L2 Metrobuses shuttle up and down Connecticut Ave., linking Chevy Chase, MD with Dupont Circle and Farragut; the Van Ness-UDC, Cleveland Park, and Woodley Park-Zoo Metro stations are all stops along the bus route. The N2 and N4 buses from Dupont Circle run up Massachusetts Ave. to the National Cathedral. The #30, 32, 34, 35, or 36 buses can shuttle you all the way up Wisconsin Ave. from Georgetown; at the District line in Friendship Heights, a central Metrobus terminal allows travelers to change buses to travel into Maryland. Metro stations are located at Woodley Park, Cleveland Park, Van Ness (on Connecticut Ave.), Tenley Circle (Tenleytown), and Friendship Heights. The neighborhoods are easy to navigate. Most of the cross streets fit into D.C.'s alphabetical scheme: letters, then two-syllable names, then three-syllable names.

FOXHALL ROAD TO GLOVER PARK. Ask someone to "Show me the money" and a D.C. local is most likely to point you towards the far west section of Upper Northwest, along **Foxhall Road.** A favorite hood of the filthy rich, folks like the Rockefellers, the Duncan Phillipses, and the Kreegers make their homes, or rather estates, here. One of the most impressive testaments to wealth is the **Kreeger Museum,** on Foxhall Rd. several miles from any public transportation. (See **Museums,** p. 120, for further information.) East of Foxhall Rd. stretching from the 2300 block of Wisconsin Ave north to the Cathedral is **Glover Park,** an almost indistinguishable extension of upscale, brick-laden Georgetown.

Wish upon a star at the **US Naval Observatory** (3450 Massachusetts Ave., recorded information ☎762-1467, group reservations ☎762-1438). The Observatory opens up for guided tours on Monday nights (except federal holidays) at 8:30pm, although only the first 90 people are allowed in and up to 30 of those spots may be reserved; plan on showing up by 7:30pm to get a spot. Visitors must remain for the entire 1½-hour tour, which has three parts: a 30-minute video, a gander at celestial objects through a 12 in. refracting telescope if the night is clear, and a look at the atomic clock which keeps official US time. **Note:** the tour involves walking over rough grounds and is therefore not wheelchair accessible. Enter the South Gate on Observatory Circle across from the New Zealand Embassy. Parking is available outside the gate on Observatory Circle, near the British Embassy. The grounds of the observatory are closed to the public at all other times, in part for the security and privacy of the Circle's other tenant: the Vice President. The looming **Vice Presidential Mansion** is best viewed from the intersection of Massachusetts Ave. and 34th St., though high fences and dense foliage effectively conceal it.

Across from the Observatory, diplomats beat the heat in the green glass and copper **Finnish Embassy,** which looks as if it's been gift-wrapped in a chain-link fence. The embassy of the **Vatican** next door marks the end of the stretch of Massachusetts Ave. known as **Embassy Row,** which begins southeast of Dupont Circle (see p. 83).

TENLEY CIRCLE AND FRIENDSHIP HEIGHTS. Tenley Circle is the residential neighborhood north of Glover Park on Wisconsin Ave., which extends through condominium complexes and apartment buildings to its northern border along Fessenden St. Tenley Circle serves its residents with a number of both public and private schools, including the **Sidwell Friends School,** an elite, expensive, liberal institution that has educated the kids of big-shots like Bob Woodward, David Brinkley, Bill Bradley, and Bill Clinton. **American University** fans out from **Ward Circle** between Massachusetts Ave. and Nebraska Ave., and offers many affordable performing arts events and free film screenings. Above Fessenden St. on Wisconsin Ave. is **Friendship Heights,** straddling the border between D.C. and Maryland. Primarily the land of the big department stores (Nieman Marcus, Hecht's, Lord & Taylor, etc.), Friendship Heights also plays home to the **Washington Dolls' House and Toy Museum** (see p. 123).

CLEVELAND PARK AND WOODLEY PARK. Running north along Connecticut Ave., east of 34th St. and west of Rock Creek Park, are the neighborhoods of Woodley Park and Cleveland Park, separated by the bridge near the National Zoo. Immediately south of the bridge, at 3133 Connecticut Ave. in Woodley Park, are the **Kennedy-Warren Apartments.** The three structures of this block-long building were among the city's most prominent homes in the 1930s. The Egyptian roof adornments and mildly Art Deco exterior panels, as well as the gardens out front, still testify to the apartments' aristocratic stature. North of the bridge, Cleveland Park contains a collection of neighborhood restaurants and bars, some of which attract Washingtonians from other areas. **Grover Cleveland** planned to build a summer cottage in this area to which he could retreat incognito; in grateful recognition, the neighborhood immediately blew his cover and named itself in his honor. **Hillwood,** 4155 Linnaean Ave. (☎686-5807), just off Connecticut Ave., was the mansion of General Foods heiress Marjorie Meriweather Post. Now a museum (see p. 120), the house contains her extensive collection of Russian decorative arts and jewelry, including the largest collection of Fabergé eggs outside of Russia. Equally as beautiful, the adjacent gardens blossom with begonias.

Washington Dolls House & Toy Museum

Upper Northwest becomes more suburban the farther north on Connecticut Ave. one travels. At the corner of Van Ness and Connecticut, near the Van Ness-UDC Metro stop, stands the twisting, steel-and-glass headquarters of **Intelsat,** a cooperative satellite producer supported by 125 countries. A walk around **International Drive,** which forms a loop off of Van Ness, takes you past the entrance to Intelsat (3400 International Dr.) as well as the chunky concrete embassies of **Jordan** (3504), **Ghana** (3512), and **Israel** (3514). These buildings are closed to the public.

NATIONAL ZOO

🚩 *Location:* 3001 Connecticut Ave. NW. Drivers can park inside the Connecticut Ave. entrance. Parking $5 for the first 3hr., $2 per additional hr. *Metro:* A few blocks uphill from Calvert St. NW and the Woodley Park-Zoo Metro. A walk up Connecticut Ave. from the Cleveland Park Metro provides a more level (but longer) approach. *Contact:* ☎673-4800; www.si.edu/natzoo. *Hours:* Grounds open daily May 1-Sept. 15 6am-8pm, Sept. 16-Apr. 30 6am-6pm; buildings open daily May 1-Sept. 15 10am-6pm, Sept. 16-Apr. 30 10am-4:30pm. Closed Dec. 25. *Admission:* Free. *Events:* Summer concerts Th 6:30pm; call for details. Feeding schedules available at information desk; audio tours available. *Accessibility:* Wheelchair accessible. Free handicapped parking in lots B and D. Wheelchairs available.

National Zoo

The Washington National Zoological Park is one of the best and least crowded sights in D.C. The zoo began as a collection of North American mammals (bears, lynxes, and so on) penned on the Mall near the Smithsonian. It moved to its current location, a swath of land liberated from Rock Creek Park, in 1890. **Frederick Law Olmsted,** designer of Central Park in New York City, planned the zoo. Small animals like lizards live indoors, but most of the large animals are showcased in huge outdoor ranges replicating their native environments. Herd animals are kept on the fenced-off hillsides, and marsh dwellers have their own patches of wetland.

African American Civil War Memorial

Walking paths criss-cross the zoo. All are segments of either the blue-flagged **Valley Trail** or the red-flagged **Olmsted Walk.** The more level Olmsted Walk explores land-animal houses, and the Valley Trail winds among the bird and sea life exhibits. Ambitious visitors who don't want to miss a thing may follow one trail from the entrance to the far end of the zoo (near the lion-and-tiger hill), then pick up the other trail to return.

Visitors familiar with the zoo will be saddened to find that the beloved giant panda Hsing-Hsing no longer occupies the panda house along the Olmsted Walk. The 28-year-old bear, the last survivor of a pair donated by China as a gift from Mao to Nixon, died in November of 1999, and now the exhibit stands eerily empty. The Zoo is currently in negotiations with China in order to obtain another pair of pandas and expects to close the deal by spring 2001. Compensating for the tragic loss, the zoo has acquired a much larger collection of lions and tigers and beefed up the **Great Cats** exhibit where visitors can witness how these ferocious predators hunt in the wild.

Inhabitants of the **Elephant and Giraffe House** roam outdoors and are easy to spot. Also don't miss the **Great Ape House,** a ways down the Olmsted Walk, where chimps delight the crowd. Unfortunately, the reality of land constraints conflicts with the needs of many of the larger animals. The **Reptile Discovery Center** has soared in popularity now that the panda house has emptied. The lines to this display can sometimes slither out the door, so be prepared for a wait. Next door is the ambitious **Think Tank,** promoting the study of animal behavior. The conscientious visitor will wonder who is really on exhibit, as curious orangutans observe those passing by.

On the Valley Trail, the **Amazonia** building showcases the flora and fauna of the rainforest. Walk through a startlingly realistic rainforest replica filled with fish, monkeys, and birds. Further along the trail, at the **Seals and Sea Lion** exhibit, visitors can watch zookeepers brush the seals' and sea lions' teeth with tasty seafood-flavored toothpaste (11:30am daily). Near the main entrance, the **Cheetah Conservation Station** chronicles the cheetahs' disappearance from the wild—the result of over-hunting and low DNA variation. The station is part of a long-term project to protect the cheetahs from extinction.

WASHINGTON NATIONAL CATHEDRAL

🖪 *Location: Massachusetts and Wisconsin Aves. NW. Take Massachusetts Ave. north from downtown and turn right on Wisconsin Ave. Metro: From Tenleytown station, take a 30-series bus toward Georgetown; from Cleveland Park station, walk 15min. uphill on Ordway, turn left at 36th St., and walk south 5 blocks. Contact: ☎ 537-6200, recording ☎ 364-6616; www.cathedral.org/cathedral. Hours: May-Aug. M-F 10am-9pm, Sa 10am-4:30pm, Su 12:30-4:30pm; Sept.-Apr. M-Sa 10am-5pm, Su 12:30-4pm. Su 11am service takes place in the nave. Tours: Except for summer months, tours are offered every 15min. M-Sa 10-11:45am and 12:45 -3:15pm, Su 12:30-2:45pm; includes crypt and Observation Gallery. ☎ 537-6207 Admission: Suggested donation $3 for tour, $1 for children under 12. Accessibility: Call ahead. The wheelchair ramp is around the building's front facade on the left. Events: The Cathedral Choristers sing M and W at 4pm during the school year. The carillon plays Sa 12:30pm. Accommodations at the Cathedral: see p. 278.*

Construction of **The Cathedral Church of Saint Peter and Saint Paul,** commonly referred to as the Washington National Cathedral, has spanned three centuries. First proposed in 1791, the cathedral was not approved until 1893 when construction began. Today some of the stained glass windows still remain uncompleted. The cathedral, the world's sixth largest, is built entirely of stone in Gothic tradition in the shape of a Latin cross. All details on the walls were carved by hand. For the soaring ceiling slabs, artisans hovered on scaffolding more than 100 ft. above the floor while they sculpted.

The cathedral was built with two intentions: to attract dignitaries, and to serve as a burial ground for the nation's most important citizens. Successful on one count, the cathedral managed to attract **Rev. Martin Luther King, Jr.,** every US president since Theodore Roosevelt, and more recently, the Dalai Lama of Tibet. Unfortunately, as politicians flocked to the cathedral to speak, they did not approach the site to die. The only notable men buried on the property are **President Woodrow Wilson** and Secretary of State Cordell Hull, who both died during the brief moment when burial in the cathedral was in vogue. Wilson's tomb juts from the south aisle under the window commemorating him, halfway down the nave from the entrance to the cathedral. Immediately to Wilson's right is the cathedral's most unusual stained-glass window, a blue and red spacescape with an actual moon rock embedded in the center. Look closely, and you'll see that one gargoyle on the left tower is actually the head of **Darth Vader.** The crypt level harbors the **Bethlehem Chapel,** the **Chapel of St. Joseph of Arimathea,** and the **Resurrection Chapel.** Buried here are blind- and deaf-education pioneer Helen Keller and her teacher, Anne Sullivan Macy. To access the chapel at night, enter from the North Rd. side. An elevator, located near the main doors of the west entrance, takes you to the top floor of the **Pilgrim Observation Gallery,** which offers a spectacular view of Washington from one of its highest vantage points. The **Bishop's Garden,** near the South Transept and facing Wisconsin Ave., is filled with herbs and roses (open daily until dusk). Though the garden is technically closed at night, people have taken midnight strolls here for years.

SHAW / U DISTRICT

⚑ Highlights: *Nightlife, eateries.* **Food & Drink:** *p. 172.* **Nearby:** *Adams-Morgan, Northeast, Old Downtown.* **Metro:** *U Street-Cardozo, Shaw-Howard U.*

Shaw was once the address of choice for important African-American leaders (presidential advisor Mary McLeod), poets (Jean Toomer and Langston Hughes), musicians (Duke Ellington), journalists, and lawyers. In the early 20th century, these American legends developed the "Black Broadway" along U Street section as music lovers of every color and creed crowded into the **Howard Theater** while nearby **Lincoln Theater** showed movies to an integrated audience. Desegregation of the 50s lured much of the black middle class away from Shaw; with them, much of Shaw's artistic, business, and political influence left as well. The final blow came in 1968, when news of the assassination of Martin Luther King, Jr. started three days of looting and burning along 14th, 7th, and H St. NW, once the cultural arteries of black D.C.

U Street compresses all the excitement and possibilities of D.C. nightlife into a couple of blocks. Weekend nights reveal a U Street lit by the excited, electric glow of clubland and humming with the sweet sounds of hip-hop, techno, and live rock or jazz. U Street's daylight face and its branching avenues offer authentic Southern/country cooking with some tasty international options. Use Metro: Shaw-Howard University or U St.-Cardozo to access the neighborhood.

The "U" in U Street could stand for the *U*nderrated, *U*niquely inner-*U*rban aspect of the Shaw area. Give the neighborhood attention at mealtime or in the evenings, when a few establishments offer spectacular dining and entertainment options. Venerable neighborhood institutions like **Ben's Chili Bowl** and the **Florida Avenue Grill** (see **Restaurants,** p. 172) offer possibly the best country or Southern-style-cooking outside of the Deep South. Some of the city's best nightlife and music is in the U district (see **Nightlife,** p. 188 and **Entertainment,** p. 137).

AFRICAN-AMERICAN CIVIL WAR MEMORIAL

⚑ Location: *1000 U St. NW.* **Metro:** *U St.-Cardozo, Vermont St. exit.* **Contact:** *☎ 667-2667; fax 667-6771; www.afroamcivilwarmemorial.org.* **Hours:** *Visitor center open M-F 10am-5pm, Sa-Su 2-5pm.* **Tours:** *by appt.*

Dedicated on July 18, 1998, the monument honors the 209,000 black soldiers who fought for the Union Army during the Civil War. Its centerpiece is an 11-foot tall bronze statue entitled "The Spirit of Freedom," which depicts black troops bearing their rifles and the families left behind upon their heroic departure. The statue is set in a rose garden circled by plates of gray steel, which bear the names of all of the African-American soldiers who fought in the Civil War. Computers inside the adjoining Civil War Memorial Museum and Visitor Center link visitors to internet sites with information on the soldiers. Thematic exhibits in the museum showcase war medals, paintings, documents, and photographs.

HOWARD UNIVERSITY

⚑ Contact: *☎ 806-6100; www.howard.edu.* **Metro:** *Shaw-Howard Univ. From the Metro, walk north 20min. on 7th St., which changes into Georgia Ave.*

America's most historically important black university was founded in 1867 to educate newly freed slaves in the fields of religion, medicine, and law. Named for Gen. Oliver Otis Howard, head of the Freedmen's Bureau after the Civil War, the private university now has 12,000 students, most of whom are African-American. Late Supreme Court Justice Thurgood Marshall, ex-New York City Mayor David Dinkins, and novelist Toni Morrison are only a few of Howard's famous alums. The 89-acre campus stretches to the east along 7th and Georgia and has one of D.C.'s highest elevations and a great view of downtown. **Be very careful walking on 7th and Georgia St. at night, and do not walk alone.**

Two-hour campus tours include a videotape presentation and a question-and-answer session about admission to the university. *(M-F 9am-3pm by appt. only; call recruitment at ☎806-2900 or (800) 822-6363 for information.)* The main branch of the university library, **The Founders Library,** is open to the public. The library's **Moorland-Spingarn Research Center** maintains the largest collection of black literature in the US *(500 Howard Pl. ☎806-7250; www.founders.howard.edu. Open M-Th 8am-midnight, F 8am-5pm, Sa 9am-5pm, Su 12:30-9pm. Limited hours in summer; call for details.)*

DUKE ELLINGTON MURAL
🔲 *Location: 13th and U St. NW.*
The appealing, bright colors and inspiring subject of G. Byron Peck's impressive mural uplift the surrounding neighborhood. The mural of the famed musician greets those exiting the U St./African-American Civil War Memorial/Cardozo Metro Stop.

THE LINCOLN THEATER
🔲 *Location: 1215 U. St. NW. Contact: ☎328-6000. Tours: available by appointment.*
Opened in 1922, the Lincoln Theater provided illustrious entertainment (such as Duke Ellington) for the segregated black community. Recently renovated, the theater's stately and graceful accommodations currently host concerts, theater, and film productions.

BEYOND THE NW QUADRANT

SOUTHEAST CAPITOL HILL

🔲 *Highlights: Navy Yard, Nightlife. Museums: Navy Museum, Marine Corps Historical Museum. Nearby: Capitol Hill, Anacostia, South of the Mall, Waterfront.*

The Southeast quadrant isn't so much a neighborhood as a man-enforced geographical fact, a perfect right triangle bounded by East Capitol St., South Capitol St., and the District line. Washington's quadrants were designated with the Capitol building at their center, so naturally **Capitol Hill** straddles all four. The Hill is an odd companion for the run-down and crime-ridden portions of the neighborhood in the Southeast quadrant. Clubs and concerts in the Southeast are perhaps the rowdiest and most exciting in the District. Unfortunately, **the area can be dangerous: stay extremely cautious and do not walk alone in this area, especially at night**.

BARRACKS ROW
The Eastern Market Metro stop takes you close to the Navy Yard, a stretch sometimes known as "Barracks Row." The Metro escalator dumps visitors into a littered, unkempt grassy plot, and the walk down **8th Street SE** passes fast food restaurants, unglamorous and uninteresting shops and services, and boarded-up storefronts. The disorder and general disrepair on 8th St. is abruptly interrupted by the uniformity, nobility, and basic cleanliness of the **Marine Barracks** (☎433-2258), at 8th and I St. SE. The **Eighth and Eye Marines** live here. The **Commandant of the Marine Corps** dwells at one end of the parade ground in a house built in 1806. The barracks also house **The President's Own**, the Marine Corps marching band that John Philip Sousa (who hailed from D.C.) led from 1880 until 1892. No official tour exists, and the area is restricted to military personnel; however, you may be able to finagle a personal tour if you ask a Marine walking through the neighborhood. The only sure way to see the grounds is to attend one of the Friday

Evening Parades (see **Calendar of Events,** p. 10). Barracks Row is usually safe during the day (Marines keep watch over some of the blocks), but **don't walk alone here at night.**

NAVY YARD

⊠ Location: *Gate at 9th and M St. SE.* **Metro:** *Navy Yard or Eastern Market.* **Contact:** *Marine Corps Museum* ☎ *433-3840, Navy Art Gallery* ☎ *433-3815, Navy Museum* ☎ *433-4882; www.history.navy.mil.* **Hours:** *Apr.-Sept. Tu-Su 10am-4pm; Oct.-Mar. Tu-Su 10am-4pm.* **Tours:** *Call ahead for schedule; changes often.* **Note:** *Americans must show a photo ID; foreign tourists must show passports.* **Admission:** *Free.*

Three museums and a decommissioned destroyer give civilians reason to visit the Washington Navy Yard. Follow the main road 1½ blocks to find the white stucco **Building 58** on your right. Go past the building, make a right, and make another right on the other side of the building to enter the **Marine Corps Historical Museum.** For a description of the exhibits, see p. 121. From this entrance, go left and follow the road to find Building 67 on your right. The building houses the diminutive **Navy Art Gallery,** which shows two changing exhibits of naval art per year. The paintings are composed by talented sailors and "combat artists," who sailed on ships in wartime for the purpose of painting pictures of combat. Head for the **Anacostia River** from the Gallery to find the **Navy Museum** in Building 76, a large warehouse. The museum contains gargantuan model ships and Navy relics that visitors can climb all over (see p. 122).

Navy Yard

U.S.S. BARRY. The **U.S.S. Barry,** a decommissioned destroyer docked a few steps from the Navy Museum, offers an interesting glimpse of maritime life. Snappily dressed sailors lead tours through berths, control rooms, the bridge, and the combat center. Interesting aspects of the ship include the **AZROC Anti-submarine Rocket Launcher,** which shot parachuted torpedoes at enemy subs, and the **Anti-submarine Decoy,** which sailors threw overboard to distract heat-seeking torpedoes.

ANACOSTIA

YOU ARE HERE
SEE MAP P. 319

⊠ Highlights: *Douglass Home.* **Museums:** *Anacostia Museum.* **Nearby:** *Southeast Capitol Hill.*

Frederick Douglass House

Ironically enough, Anacostia began as Washington's first suburb when white developers founded the area know as **Uniontown** in the 1850s to escape the growing working-class presence on Capitol Hill. After the Civil War, the Freedmen's Bureau sold one-acre plots in the neighborhood for $200-300 to freed slaves, who founded the **Barry's Farm** community. Blue-collar African-Americans who took up residence in the neighborhood worked in the city by day and built their houses in Anacostia by firelight at night. While this kind of conscious self improvement built a strong sense of community for the neighborhood, its isolation from the rest of the city led to its virtual abandonment by city administration. Over the years, housing education and employment opportunities for area residents deteriorated, as drugs took over the neighborhood.

While community residents today struggle to overcome drug-related violence, progress is slow and costly, and **Anacostia remains extremely dangerous.** The neighborhood is domi-

Marine Barracks

nated by dilapidated low-rise apartment buildings, littered streets, and boarded up storefronts as a drive down **Martin Luther King, Jr. Avenue SE** will reveal. Bus rides provide a convenient and safe way to visit the neighborhood. **If you prefer exploring on foot, travel in groups.** Look north from the parking lot of **Our Lady of Perpetual Help Church,** 1600 Morris Rd. SE (☎ 678-4999), across the street from the Lucy Ellen Molten Elementary School, for a spectacular view of downtown, the Washington Monument, the Lincoln Memorial, and the Capitol. Although *The Washingtonian* called this lot the best vantage point for gazing at the monuments, it doesn't mean you should roam the area alone. Anacostia also houses the **Anacostia Museum,** 1901 Fort Place SE (☎ 357-2700), which focuses on African-American history and culture (see p. 115).

THE FREDERICK DOUGLASS HOME

⊠ Location: *1411 W St. SE. Take the Mt. Ranier B-2 bus from Howard Rd. near the Anacostia Metro station.* **Contact:** *☎ 426-5960, TDD 426-5961.* **Hours:** *Daily Apr.-Oct. 9am-5pm; Oct.-Mar. 9am-4pm.* **Tours:** *1½hr. tour daily 9, 10, 11am and 2, 3pm, with a 4pm tour in the summer; make early reservations.* **Admission:** *$3, seniors $1.50, kids free.*

Frederick Douglass taught himself to read and write while a slave, escaped from slavery in 1838, published the *North Star* newspaper and a best-selling autobiography in the 1840s, served as the US Marshall for D.C. from 1877 to 1881, and was the US Minister to Haiti from 1889 to 1891. No small work, eh? Over the course of his life, the great abolitionist and orator also spoke up as a champion for world peace, Irish home rule, women's rights, political activism, and human rights. The **Douglass Home** honors the great "Sage of Anacostia," who broke a whites-only covenant when he bought the building in 1877 and named it **Cedar Hill.** The house remains as Douglass furnished it. Tours begin with an informative movie in the Visitor's Center; sightseers then walk up 84 steps to the house where a park ranger points out interesting artifacts.

NORTHEAST

⊠ Highlights: *National Arboretum, Kenilworth Aquatic Gardens, Basilica of the National Shrine.* **Nearby:** *Capitol Hill, Shaw.*

Northeast Washington isn't so much a neighborhood as a geographic fact, a triangle formed by North Capitol St., East Capitol St., and Eastern Ave. that covers over a quarter of the District's land area, containing several distinct neighborhoods. Much of the area, however, has been overwhelmed by the crack epidemic, especially the areas near the Prince George's County line and east of the Anacostia River. **Catholic University** forms one safe enclave north of Michigan Ave. off N. Capitol St., while the **National Arboretum** and **Kenilworth Gardens** form another at the far eastern edge of D.C. Tourists should avoid walking through this quadrant, and should drive or take the Metro between sights. **Exercise extreme caution if you choose to visit this area.**

ORIENTATION. North Capitol Street bisects the area into its east and west quadrants and links the Capitol to the northern tip of the D.C. diamond. Four roads run roughly parallel through Northeast on a southwest-northeast diagonal: **Maryland Avenue,** which shoots out from the Capitol, eventually intersecting with the larger Bladensburg Rd. (which continues across the Maryland border); **New York Avenue,** which is Rte. 50 and links to points east in Maryland; **Rhode Island Avenue;** and meandering **Michigan Avenue,** which leads to the Catholic U. area. Maryland Ave. is the southernmost of the four roads. **Florida Ave.** runs from upper NW to lower NE, and is a way to avoid some of the congestion on other roads, but it tends to wander so drivers should watch road signs. **13th Street,** which becomes Brentwood Rd. south of Rhode Island Ave., slices through the middle-class Brookland neighborhood. **South Dakota Avenue** parallels the District line, while on-again, off-again **Eastern Ave.** follows the line itself. Northeast sights are spread out all over the quadrant; visitors should expect to spend a significant amount of time driving or riding the Metro to and from them. Use the Rhode Island Ave., Brookland-CUA, Ft. Totten, Minnesota Ave., or Deanwood Metro stops to access the area.

NATIONAL ARBORETUM

⁊ Location: *3501 New York Ave. NE. Main entrance at 24th and R St. NE. If possible, drive to the arboretum;* **the surrounding area is dangerous.** *Secure parking available inside R St. entrance. If walking, take the Metro to Stadium-Armory, take the B2 bus to the intersection of Bladensburg Rd. and R St., and walk down R St. approximately 300 yds. to the arboretum's gate on R St.* **Contact:** *☎ 245-2726; www.ars-grin.gov/ars/Beltsville/na/.* **Hours:** *Daily 8am-5pm, except Dec. 25. Bonsai collection open daily 10am-3:30pm.* **Tours:** *40min. narrated tram tour Sa-Su 10:30, 11:30am, 1, 2, and 3pm; additional 4pm tour in summer. Adults $3, seniors $2 ages 4-16 $1, under 4 free.* **Admission:** *Free.*

The National Arboretum is an expansive, peaceful collection of domestic and exotic flora. Nearly 10 mi. of roads criss-cross some 444 acres of land, which sprout plants and trees ranging from crabapples to crapemyrtles. Every month, new flowers and fruits come into season, from winter jasmine to summer waterlilies. The May azaleas are much beloved (ask at the visitor center about the 30min. **azalea walk**), as are the April cherry blossoms. The **historic roses,** located in the herb garden, are best seen in May.

From the enormous bonsai collection, visitors can see **columns** that once spanned the **East Portico** of the **Capitol.** Completed in 1826, the Portico was dismantled in 1958 to make room for an addition. The 22 columns were held in storage until 1984, when they were moved to the arboretum and set up in temple-like rows.

KENILWORTH AQUATIC GARDENS

⁊ Location: *Anacostia Ave. and Douglas St. NE. To reach the gardens from Deanwood Metro, take the Polk St. exit, walk west over the bridge and head straight down Douglas St. Entrance on Anacostia Ave. between Quarles and Douglas St. Drivers should take New York Ave. NE out of the city and take the first Kenilworth Ave. exit just after crossing the District line; continue straight and turn right on Quarles St., left on Anacostia Ave. and drive to the parking lot inside.* **Contact:** *☎ 426-6905.* **Hours:** *daily 7am-4pm; Visitors Center 8am-4pm.* **Tours:** *Sa-Su and holidays at 9, 11am, and 1pm; occasional evening and dawn walks, call for schedule.*

Across the Anacostia River from the National Arboretum, the Kenilworth Aquatic Gardens breed and raise aquatic plants and flowers. The gardens began as a Civil War veteran's hobby, but the gardens quickly turned into his and his daughter's exotic plant business. Now, the gardens sanctuary consists of thousands of lilies, lotuses, and hyacinths on 12 acres of marshy plots. The sticky D.C. summer is the best time to visit, when the lilies and tropical plants reach their luscious peak; morning is the best time to see most of the flowers. Of special note are the tall, white lotuses, which loom over others and catch fallen petals and pooled remnants of the last rainfall in their huge, bowl-like blossoms. The last patch of natural marsh on the Anacostia River lies next to the gardens. A ¾ mile river trail leads past the marsh to an outlook over the Anacostia. The patient and quiet can see turtles, frogs, waterfowl, muskrats, raccoons, opossums, and occasional flocks of migrating birds. The trails are a bit scraggly, but still pretty. The **Visitors Center** offers pamphlets and brochures, an exhibit on the history of the gardens, and an aquarium exhibit. If at all possible, come by car and **exercise caution: the gardens are located in an extremely dangerous area.**

CATHOLIC UNIVERSITY AND THE BASILICA OF THE NATIONAL SHRINE OF THE IMMACULATE CONCEPTION

⁊ Location: *at the corner of Michigan Ave. and Harewood NE.* **Metro:** *Brookland-CUA.* **Contact:** *University ☎ 319-5305; Shrine ☎ 526-8300, www.nationalshrine.com.* **Hours:** *daily Apr.-Oct. 7am-7pm; Nov.-Mar. 7am-6pm.* **Tours:** *1hr. tours M-Sa every hr. 9-11am and 1-3pm; Su 1-4pm. Great Upper Church masses held Sa 5:15pm, Su 9, 10:30am, noon, and 4:30pm; Crypt Church masses held M-F 7, 7:30, 8, 8:30am, 12:10 and 5:30pm, Latin Mass Su 7:30am, 1:30pm. Giftstore open 8:30am-7pm; cafeteria open 8:30am-2pm.* **Admission:** *Free.* **Accessibility:** *Wheelchair accessible.*

When touring CUA's campus (tours M, W, F 10:30am and 2pm), you can't possibly miss the Basilica. Completed in 1959 on the edge of the CUA campus, the Basilica is the eighth-largest church in the world and the largest Catholic church in the Western hemisphere. The shrine's striking architecture combines elements from all over Christendom and beyond. Romanesque arches support stark Byzantine facades and a blue-and-gold onion dome that seems straight from Kiev, while the bell tower beside the main entrance looks suspiciously like an Islamic minaret. The interior is covered with golden mosaics portraying highlights of the Christian scripture, from the Creation to the Last

Judgment. A huge mosaic Christ clad in fiery red robes presides over the sanctuary. Between the upper church and the lower crypt level, over 60 chapels dedicated to the Virgin Mary envelop worshippers in luxury and serenity.

GALLAUDET UNIVERSITY

Location: 800 Florida Ave. NE, at 8th St. NE. *Metro:* Union Station, then take a $6 cab ride to the university. *Contact:* ☎ 651-5000, TDD 651-5050; www.gallaudet.edu. *Hours:* Visitors Center open M-F 9am-5pm. *Tours:* 1hr. tours 10am and 1pm are conducted in American Sign Language (ASL); if an interpreter is needed, ☎ 651-5505.

Established in 1864, Gallaudet University is still the world's only university for the deaf. In 1988, Gallaudet students made national news by demanding—and subsequently getting—a deaf president, Dr. I. King Jordan. This 99-acre campus, with fine examples of Victorian Gothic and Queen Anne style architecture, has a student body of 2200 students. Of special note is the **Department of Drama,** which produces three shows annually in ASL; voice interpretation devices are available for the hearing.

TAKOMA PARK

Covering an area that includes both Northwestern D.C. and Montgomery County, Maryland, Takoma Park declared itself a nuclear-free zone during the mid-80s, joining Berkeley, CA, and Madison, WI, as the bastions of peace and love. Lately though, Takoma's rebellious counterculture has been compromised by increasing migration from Downtown into the suburbs. Luckily, a few offbeat shops and family restaurants remain (see **Food and Drink,** p. 174). Every Saturday from April to December, Takoma Park hosts a Farmer's Market at the corner of Laurel Ave. and Carroll Ave. from 10am-2pm. For Takoma Park's commercial heart, head up Carroll St. from Metro: Takoma to the point where Carroll St. becomes Carroll Ave. on the left and Laurel Ave. on the right.

ARLINGTON COUNTY   ☎ 703

Arlington County abandoned Washington in 1846 when Virginia snatched back its contribution to the Federal City; the only remaining links are four major bridges, Metro lines, and broad expanses of federally owned land. Arlington Cemetery, Ronald Reagan National Airport, and the Pentagon would be unthinkable in the capital on account of their sheer size. **Rosslyn,** a city in Arlington packed with skyscrapers, is just what D.C.'s designers were trying to avoid with the stringent limits they placed on the height of buildings. South or west of these behemoths, thousands of commuters find housing in modest suburbs.

If you try to drive in Arlington for any length of time, you'll probably get lost. The original, D.C.-esque street plan featured two- and three-syllable streets in alphabetical order running roughly north-south and crossed by east-west numbered streets. While these streets exist, they are often only a few blocks long; some end and pick up again miles from where they began. Add the network of non-parallel numbered routes, highways, and boulevards and you have total chaos. These disorienting major roads include **I-395** and the **Columbia Pike** (Rte. 244) in South Arlington, **Arlington Boulevard** (Rte. 50), **Wilson Boulevard,** and **Washington Boulevard** (Rte. 237). **I-66** runs through part of Arlington. Fortunately, the Metro and Metrobus can take you where you want to go. Check with the Metro (☎ 637-7000) before you make the trip. Use the Crystal City, National Airport, Rosslyn, Arlington Cemetery, Court House, Clarendon, or Ballston Metro stops. The Metro's Orange Line shuttles visitors to most of Arlington's hotspots for ethnic cuisine. The Blue Line will take you to sights like the Pentagon and the Cemetery. If you discover you're really lost, check streets signs for "N" (north of Rte. 50, or Arlington Blvd.) or "S" (south of it).

The **Arlington Visitors Center,** 735 18th St., will answer your questions, give you armloads of brochures and maps, and even give you directions to local sites. From Metro: Pentagon City, walk south on 18th St. (toward Crystal City); the entrance is at the back of the fire station. (☎ (703) 228-5720 or (800) 677-6267; www.co.arlington.va.us. Open daily 9am-5pm.)

THE REST OF ARLINGTON COUNTY

ARLINGTON NATIONAL CEMETERY

⚐ Location: *From downtown Washington, take Independence or Constitution Ave. and turn left onto 23rd St. to cross the Arlington Memorial Bridge. Stay in the left lane as you enter the circle and follow it into the cemetery directly in front. Police often pull drivers over for making last minute illegal lane changes.* **Metro:** *Arlington Cemetery.* **Contact:** *☎(703) 697-2131, Visitors Center ☎(703) 607-8052.* **Hours:** *Daily Apr.-Sept. 8am-7pm; Oct.-May 8am-5pm.* **Admission:** *Free. Parking $1.25 per hr. for first 3hr. and $2 each additional hr.* **Tours:** *Tourmobile (☎(202) 554-5100) drives the cemetery. Tours $4.75, ages 3-11 $2.25, seniors free.* **Information:** *Visitors Center dispenses guided maps of the grounds and will locate specific gravesites upon request. Temporary passes to drive into the cemetery can be obtained here, but only if visiting a family member's grave.*

Takoma Park

The largest military cemetery in the US, Arlington holds 260,000 veterans and their dependents within its 612 acres of rolling hills. Tombstones note the war in which each soldier fought, with a sunken shield representing service in either the Civil or Spanish-American Wars, and simple crosses denoting service in either world war. Each day, an average of 15 to 20 new burials take place. For some high-ranking officers, a caisson carrying the casket leads the funeral procession.

Robert E. Lee once owned an estate covering most of the cemetery grounds. The general abandoned his land when he moved to Richmond to join the Confederacy, and the Union government immediately seized the property. Major General Montgomery Meigs, who hated Lee for joining the Confederacy, began burying Union troops in places like Mrs. Lee's rose garden, ensuring that the family could never reclaim their estate. Lee's home, the pastel Arlington House, is still standing and open for visits.

Takoma Underground

Eventually **Pierre L'Enfant,** originally buried within the District, was reinterred at Arlington along with soldiers from the Revolutionary War and the War of 1812. His grave on the hillside in front of Arlington House overlooks the city he designed. Among the plain headstones of WWI soldiers lies General of the Armies John J. Pershing, commander of US forces during WWI, who asked to be buried among his men. Nearby is the grave of General Daniel "Chappie" James, the four-star Air Force general who was the highest-ranking African-American officer of his time. Arlington also holds the bodies of Joe Louis, history's longest-lasting world heavyweight boxing champion, Arctic explorers Robert E. Peary and Richard Byrd, and Supreme Court Justices Earl Warren and Oliver Wendell Holmes.

Nearby, the **Tomb of the Unknowns,** renamed after the original **Unknown Soldier** was identified and disinterred in 1998, honors servicemen who died fighting for the US Unidentified soldiers from both World Wars and the Korean War lie under the white marble sarcophagus overlooking the city. The famous inscription reads, "Here rests in honored glory an American soldier known but to God." The tomb is guarded 24 hours a day by delegations from the Army's Third Infantry. You can watch the ritualized changing of the guard every hour on the hour October to March and every half-hour from April through September. The towering sentinels take 21 steps and then turn to face the tomb for 21 seconds to symbolize the 21-gun salute, the highest military honor.

Tara Thai

The most visited gravesites, besides the Tomb of the Unknowns, are clearly the **Kennedy Gravesites. President John F. Kennedy** is buried next to his late wife, **Jacqueline Kennedy Onassis,** and two of their children who died shortly after birth are also buried here, Patrick Bouvier and an unnamed daughter. JFK supposedly once stood near Arlington House, and, seeing the spectacular view of Washington, declared, "I could stay here forever." The Purple Heart Kennedy won in WWII earned him the privilege. An **Eternal Flame,** lit by his widow at his funeral, flickers above his simple memorial stone. JFK's brother, **Senator Robert F. Kennedy's** modest grave lies a few feet away: the statesman wished for nothing more than a plain cross to mark his final resting place.

The newest addition to the cemetery is the impressive **Women in Military Service for America Memorial** (☎ (800) 222-2294). The nation's first major memorial honoring servicewomen, the Women in Military Service for America Memorial is set into the hill left of the 1932 Grand Entrance retaining wall. A skylit exhibit gallery traces the history of US servicewomen through photographs, artifacts, a computer database, and an informative video on the history of women in the US military.

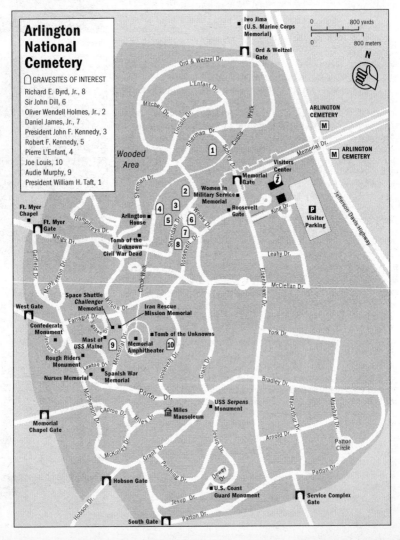

IWO JIMA MEMORIAL

◪ Location: *Walking from the cemetery continue down Custis Walk from Arlington House and exit through Weitzel gate. Follow the path for 20min. If driving, go to the junction between Arlington Blvd. and Ridge Rd. From Metro: Rosslyn, walk for 5min. east on Ft. Myer Dr. until you reach the memorial.*

Also known as the Marine Corps War Memorial, the Iwo Jima Memorial is a monumental sculpture based on Joe Rosenthal's Pulitzer Prize-winning photograph of six Marines straining to raise the US flag on Iwo Jima's Mount Suribachi. Iwo Jima saw 6321 US soldiers die in battle in February 1945, including three of the men the memorial depicts. The US flag is real, but the "flagpole" is a lead pipe—just as in the photo. The **Marine Corps Marathon** begins here each year, and the **Marine Corps Tuesday Evening Sunset Parades** (☎433-4073) are held at the memorial every Tuesday at 7pm. Parking is extremely limited, so consider parking at the Arlington Cemetery and taking the free shuttle from the Visitors Center to the memorial. The shuttle starts at 6pm.

Arlington National Cemetery

NETHERLANDS CARILLON

◪ Location: *near the Iwo Jima Memorial.* **Contact:** ☎*(703) 289-2530* **Hours:** *Bells play June-Aug. Sa 6-8pm; May and Sept. Sa 2-4pm. Briefing 30min. before each performance.*

A rectangular 127-foot tower houses the Netherlands Carillon, a set of 49 bells made in Dutch foundries to commemorate Holland's liberation from the Nazis on May 5, 1945. If the bells are ringing, you can climb the towers and watch the Carilloneurs do their stuff. Two bronze panthers guard the bells, and 15,000 tulips bloom nearby each spring.

CRYSTAL CITY

◪ Location: *2121 Crystal Dr., #0100, in the Crystal Plaza 2 Office Building. Exit the Crystal City Metro on S. 18th St. and walk to Crystal Dr. Turn right and walk down 1½ blocks.* **Contact:** ☎*(703) 305-8341.* **Hours:** *M-F 8:30am-4:30pm, and by appt.*

Past the Pentagon, on the other side of the cemetery, lies Crystal City, a half-underground community of offices and condos. The **Crystal Underground,** a massive underground mall, will continue to provide mediocre shopping opportunities during nuclear winter (open M-F 10am-7pm, Sa 10am-6pm). The best reason to visit Crystal City is to check out the small but interesting **Patent and Trademark Museum,** a tiny museum devoted to the history of intellectual property and the fruits thereof. Permanent exhibits include a look at the history of trademarks.

Iwo Jima War Memorial

THE PENTAGON

What would a visiting Martian make of the Pentagon?
—*The Economist, 1991*

◪ Location: *The Pentagon sits inside a triangle formed by 3 highways: Rte. 110, Rte. 27, and I-395. By car, take the 14th St. Bridge from D.C. to I-395. The Pentagon exit is about 15 seconds into Virginia. Visitor parking available but limited; enter through the South Parking Entrance, or try the parking lot next to Macy's in Pentagon Center and walk across the street and through the tunnel in the Visitor's Parking lot.* **Metro:** *Pentagon City; one of the Metro escalators leads directly to the tour office.* **Hours:** *By tour only.* **Tours:** *Every hour, on the hour. M-F 9am-3pm, except on federal holidays. Reservations accepted for special needs only; must be made two weeks in advance* ☎*(703) 695-1776. Tour slots are on a first-come first-served basis, starting at 8:45am. In the summer tours fill up for the day by 11am, so come early. No restrooms open to the public during the tour.*

Pentagon

the dopedc on

Blooms for Brahma and Buddha

Important in Hindu and Buddhist lore, lotuses thrive throughout the Asian continent. In 1951, seeds were found in a Manchurian lake bed, some of which later made their way to the **Kenilworth Aquatic Gardens.** Now the magnificent East Indian lotus bares its stunning pink blossoms in the gardens from seeds 640-960 years old, possibly the oldest seeds ever cultivated.

On July 17, 1941, the then War Department gave its planners one weekend to design a building that would hold all the capital's military offices. On Monday morning, the architects returned with the familiar five-sided behemoth, a testament to just how large a military bureaucracy can get. A work force of 13,000 toiled 24 hours a day for 16 months to create the steel-reinforced concrete edifice, which is still the world's largest office building. Franklin D. Roosevelt stipulated that no marble be used in the construction because he didn't want the Pentagon to look like a tourist attraction. The resulting polygon, therefore, cost "only" $50 million to build.

The statistics on the building are mind-boggling: five stories, five concentric hallways, a five-acre courtyard in the center, ten radial hallways, and four zip codes of its own. Two-and-a-half Washington Monuments would fit across it lengthwise. Twenty-three thousand civilians, soldiers, and sailors sprawl over 6.5 million square feet. They park their 9849 cars on 27 hectares of land. They climb 131 stairways and ride 19 escalators to walk through 17½ miles of corridors. Yet due to remarkable planning it takes no more than seven minutes to walk between any two points in the building. In 1946 the War Department took the more benign title of Defense Department, and today is comprised of the Army, the Navy, Marine Corps, and Air Force. Even with all of these military powers housed here, many of the Pentagon's offices and corridors are still empty—the building has more room, we hope, than the military will every need.

Tourists used to have free run of the place until 1972 when somebody bombed a bathroom. Now all visitors must sign in, walk through a metal detector, be X-rayed, show proper identification, and stick with the tour, which is an hour long and covers approximately 1½ miles. If nothing else tourists are left in awe at the sheer size of the United States defense establishment.

ROOSEVELT ISLAND

🚩 *Location: In the Potomac River between the Little River and the Georgetown Channel. Cross the Roosevelt Bridge, take a right onto the George Washington Parkway's northbound lanes, and exit into the Roosevelt Island lot; if you see Key Bridge, you've missed it.* **Metro:** *Rosslyn. From the station, walk towards Georgetown on N. Lynn St., cross Lee Hwy., and make a right onto the Mount Vernon Trail. Alternatively, cross Key Bridge from Georgetown and make a left onto the Mount Vernon Trail.* **Contact:** *☎(703) 426-6922.* **Hours:** *Dawn to dusk.* **Tours:** *Rangers give nature and history tours in summer if called 7 days in advance at ☎(703) 285-2600.* **Restrictions:** *Bicycles and camping prohibited.*

The Theodore Roosevelt Memorial Association felt that Teddy deserved better than the standard statue-and-pedestal memorial package. To commemorate the popular hunter, conservationist, and president, they purchased an entire 88-acre island that, with Congress's consent, was renamed Roosevelt Island in 1932. Now a wilderness preserve, the island sits in the Potomac River just west of Foggy Bottom, a mere 15 minutes from downtown. To transform the place from "swamp" to "memorial," Congress erected an impressive statue of Roosevelt and a parking lot, but not much else. Visitors are welcome to disappear into the thick forest on the island, but not to share Teddy's penchant for hunting.

The memorial is placed just west of the center of the island's northern half; look for signs directing visitors. The design by **Eric Gugler** includes a 17-foot bronze statue of Roosevelt in front of a slab of granite reminiscent of *2001: A Space Odyssey*. In front is an oval terrace surrounded by a moat spanned by a series of footbridges. Four 21 ft. granite "tablets" are inscribed with juicy Roosevelt soundbites, including "Keep your eyes on the stars, but remember to keep your feet on the ground."

The island bearing his name contains swamp, marsh, and forest habitats that host such critters as turtles, muskrats, cottontails, foxes, and redwing blackbirds (whose calls contrast strangely with the noise of cars rushing over Roosevelt Bridge). The island's 3 mi. of trails require an hour to hike; wide, flat paths make the long walks relaxing. Runners flock to the island for the cooler temperatures and soft paths (none are paved). Rocky beaches reward those who find them with views of the **Kennedy Center** and environs. On weekends, local fisherfolk cast off from here into the murky waters of the Potomac, where swimming is most emphatically for fish only. Even harder to find than the beaches are the restrooms, hidden in the delicately designated **comfort station,** a brown lodge at the southwest corner of the island near Theodore Roosevelt Bridge.

FAIRFAX COUNTY

Visitors to Fairfax County travel back in time to the 18th-century charm of porticoes, porches, and well-pruned presidential gardens. When Philadelphia was still the nation's capital, aristocratic planters like **President George Washington** and Bill of Rights supporter **George Mason** lived on lavish Fairfax County estates. Although the city touts itself as "The Gateway to History," Fairfax's most prevalent gates surround the rapidly growing housing developments. But, if you can grin and bear the endless barrage of fast food joints, Fairfax sights such as Mt. Vernon and Manassas Park are definitely worth a glimpse.

GETTING AROUND. In order to really explore Fairfax's dispersed attractions, a car may be the only resort. Only the areas of Fairfax immediately adjacent to the Potomac have efficient public transportation. While the Metro's Blue and Yellow Lines serve the southeastern portion of Fairfax and the Orange Line transports daily commuters from the northern stretch of the county, the central part of Fairfax remains inaccessible by rail. Metrobuses and Fairfax Connector Buses (☎ (703) 339-7200 for fare, route, and scheduling information) pick up some of the slack in the central areas of the county. Be forewarned that service is slow—it's a good idea to check departure times beforehand.

Providing some welcome scenery for bored commuters, the picturesque **George Washington Parkway** winds southward along gorgeous bluffs of the Potomac River from the northwest tip of the Capital Beltway towards Alexandria (where it becomes Mount Vernon Memorial Pkwy.). A 14-mile **bicycle trail** follows the road from D.C. to Mt. Vernon. The Parkway ends in southeastern Fairfax County at **Rte. 1** (Jefferson Davis Hwy.) which runs parallel to I-95 from Arlington to Richmond. Heading north, I-95 becomes I-395 inside the Beltway. Duke St. in Alexandria travels west to become the Little River Turnpike (Rte. 236). Lee Hwy. (Rte. 29) and Arlington Blvd. (Rte. 50) run east-west—from Arlington to Fairfax City and Falls Church—to the Manassas National Battlefield Park. In northern Fairfax County, the Georgetown Pike (Rte. 193) is a winding cross-river extension of the MacArthur Blvd. in NW Washington. The Dulles Access Rd. connects I-66 and the Capital Beltway to **Dulles International Airport.** Visitors to Fairfax should use the toll road for local traffic parallel to the Dulles Access Road or face a steep fine for traveling anywhere but the airport.

Old Town Alexandria

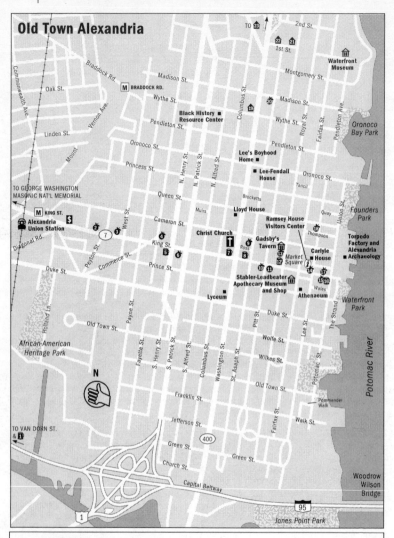

Old Town Alexandria

Though most roads are well marked, if you do plan to drive, remember to bring a map. Rush hour is hell in Fairfax, so avoid driving from 6 to 9am and 4 to 7pm if possible. Solo drivers should beware of the ticket-trap **HOV** ("High Occupancy Vehicle") lanes on almost every highway, including I-66 and Rte. 1.

OLD TOWN ALEXANDRIA ☎703

When George Washington's good friend, the Marquis De Lafayette, revisited Alexandria, VA in 1824, the whole town turned out for the festivities, which featured a Triumphal Arch complete with a live eagle and Liberty Cap. Legend has it that the eagle was made to bark a furious welcome as a little boy holding a pin on a stick acted as its cue, viciously poking the bird's bottom. Long before this comical scene unfolded, however, Alexandria's deep history was in the making. This American cultural center traces its origins over a century further back than Washington, D.C. Trading began in the area in 1669 when tobacco merchant John Alexander purchased the site from a Brit for "6000 pounds of Tobacco and Cask," foreshadowing Alexandria's rise as a tobacco trading center. In 1749, tobacco merchants bound together to turn Alexander's land into a city, changing the town's name from Hunting Creek Warehouse to Alexandria. Virginia ceded Alexandria to the federal government in 1789 as part of the land grants that created the District of Columbia. The ungrateful feds gave the city back in 1847.

Mount Vernon

Alexandria didn't become a tourist attraction until the 1980s, when Old Town reconstructed a twinge of tasteful colonialism and began capitalizing on its historical importance, notably all-star residents George Washington and Robert E. Lee. The town re-cobbled the streets, rebricked the sidewalks, installed gardens and patios, restored over 1000 original facades, and invited tall ships and contemporary shops. Today, the area is packed with tourists on weekends. Each Saturday the town hosts a **morning fair,** complete with waterfront activities, riverboat rides, and a **Farmer's Market,** 301 King St., in Market Square (☎(703) 370-8723; market open 5-9am). Fresh-baked goods, produce, crafts, and artwork are sold in brick arcades on the south plaza of the city hall. Free **lunchtime concerts** take place in Market Sq. at least once a week during the spring and summer, and **Waterfront Park Concerts** on Strand St. between Prince St. and King St. take place occasionally on Monday evenings in summer (call ☎(703) 883-4686 for an events schedule.)

Mount Vernon

ORIENTATION. Old Town Alexandria is about 20 minutes from downtown D.C. To reach the area by car, take the East King St. exit from the George Washington Pkwy. King St. and directly adjacent streets are lined with parking meters, and Old Town has plenty of parking garages. However, free parking for a few hours can be found a few blocks north in the more residential areas. The neighborhood is also accessible by Metro: Braddock or King St. To find Old Town from the King St. Metro, walk down King St. (to your left as you leave the Metro; walk away from the tracks, not under them). A DASH bus also runs from the Metro to Old Town; call (703) 370-3274 for a schedule. DASH also runs buses throughout the city (85¢).

Robet E. Lee's Boyhood Home

I-395 cuts Alexandria off from Arlington to the north of Old Town, and the Beltway rushes along to the south of Old Town. King St. (Rte. 7) connects I-395 to Old Town, and the George Washington Pkwy. runs nearly along the river until it reaches Old Town, where it becomes Washington St.

Forming a visitor-friendly grid, Old Town Alexandria lies in the square formed by Oronoco St. on the north, the Potomac River on the east, Gibbon St. on the south, and Alfred St. on the west. North-south streets switch from "North" to "South" at **King Street** (i.e., N. Washington St. becomes S. Washington St. as it crosses King St.). Block numbers (100, 200, etc.) indicate the number of blocks from the Potomac River (east-west) or from King St. (north-south). King St. divides Old Town Alexandria centrally from the Potomac River on the South and the George Washington Masonic National Memorial at its northernmost tip. Home of seafood restaurants, art galleries, and ships, the ever bustling King St. serves as Old Town's main thoroughfare for cars and pedestrians alike. The galleries huddle closer to the Metro, while the restaurants cluster closer and closer to the river. The **Ramsey House Visitors Center,** 221 King St. (☎ (703) 838-4200; www.Fun-Side.com), a 1724 building barged up river from Dumfries, VA to Alexandria, cordially offers free maps, literature, and directions to everything in town. The house went on to become a site for the manufacture of cigars after the Civil War. During Prohibition, the Ramsay House was briefly the location of "Ma's Place," where many an Alexandrian was introduced to the joys of beer under the proprietor's motherly influence.

GEORGE WASHINGTON MASONIC NATIONAL MEMORIAL

⏍ Location: 101 Callahan Dr., at the top of King St. **Contact:** ☎ (703) 683-2007. **Hours:** daily 9am-5pm. **Tours:** To go above the 2nd fl., you must take the free 1hr. tour. The tour can only be given to parties of 2 or more, so bring a friend or hope for company. 9:30, 10:30, and 11:30am, 1, 2, 3, and 4pm. Strollers and carriages not permitted. **Admission:** Free.

Rising 400 ft. over Alexandria, the lofty Greek-temple-style Masonic National Memorial is an imposing testament to the strength of masonry and the legacy of George Washington. The aged technology of the masonry exhibits, combined with the array of pamphlets on various masonic societies that you can join, will potentially be a bit disconcerting. The **Washington Room,** which displays artifacts such as Washington's Revolutionary War field trunk and a lock of his hair, is more successful. A 330 ft. observation deck above provides an amazing view of Old Town and the D.C. metropolitan area.

ROBERT E. LEE'S BOYHOOD HOME

⏍ Location: 607 Oronoco St., near Asaph St. **Contact:** ☎ (703) 548-8454. **Hours:** M-Sa 10am-4pm, Su 1-4pm. **Admission:** $4, ages 10-17 $2.

Currently undergoing indefinite renovations, Robert E. Lee's boyhood home has accommodated illustrious guests, including George Washington. The Revolutionary War hero "Light Horse" Harry Lee, was the first to lease the home in 1812; it was occupied by the famed family for many years. Confederate Robert E. Lee grew up here and attended the Quaker school next door. Candlelit tours are offered in December and on Robert's birthday (Jan. 18). The anniversaries of George Washington Parke Custis and Molly Fitzhugh's wedding (mid-July), and Lafayette's visit (mid-Oct.), are celebrated with period dress and clothing.

LEE-FENDALL HOUSE

⏍ Location: 614 Oronoco St. **Contact:** ☎ (703) 549-1789. **Hours:** Tu-Sa 10am-4pm, Su noon-4pm. Last tour 3pm. **Admission:** $4, ages 11-17 $2, 10 and under free.

Constructed by Phillip Fendall in 1785 on land once owned by man-about-Alexandria "Light Horse" Harry Lee, the Lee-Fendall House was inhabited by 37 different Lees. Among the Lee family documents on display is an original copy of a New York newspaper that printed Harry Lee's eulogy of George Washington in which he used the famous phrase "first in war, first in peace, first in the hearts of his country" to describe the President. On the third floor, an exhibit of antique doll houses is a miniature instruction in the history of American decoration and culture as much as it is a display of the ingenuity of doll technology. A 200-year-old magnolia tree is a fitting centerpiece of the large, well-maintained garden just outside the house.

LYCEUM

🏠 Location: *201 S. Washington St.* **Contact:** *☎(703) 838-4994.* **Hours:** *M-Sa 10am-5pm, Su 1-5pm.* **Admission:** *Free.*

This brick and stucco Greek Revival building has been a Civil War military hospital, a private home, and an office building. Originally a cultural center, the Lyceum has come full circle, offering historical exhibitions and audio-visual presentations detailing the history of Alexandria. The collection of period objects includes prized Alexandria silver and furniture.

BLACK HISTORY RESOURCE CENTER

🏠 Location: *638 N. Alfred St.; entrance on Wythe St.* **Contact:** *☎(703) 838-4356; http://ci.alexandria.va.us/oha/bhrc.html.* **Hours:** *Tu-Sa 10am-4pm, Su 1-5pm.* **Accessibility:** *Wheelchair accessible.*

Housed in the unassuming Robert H. Robinson Library, which was originally built in 1940 for African-Americans after a sit-in over the segregation of the Alexandrian library system, the **Black History Resource Center** showcases paintings, photographs, and other memorabilia that untangle African-American history in Alexandria. A printed walking tour, available at the information desk lists historical sites related to black history in Alexandria. Next door, the **Watson Reading Room** offers a small, non-circulating collection of research materials on African-American history.

Potomac Riverboat Company

ALEXANDRIA AFRICAN-AMERICAN HERITAGE PARK

🏠 Location: *Holland Lane, between Duke St. and Eisenhower Ave.* **Hours:** *daily from dawn to dusk.*

Walking distance from the King St. Metro, the park is an eight-acre memorial that includes a 19th-century cemetery where African-Americans were buried, a preserved wetland, and many memorial sculptures. More like a wildlife reservation than a memorial park, educational stone tablets inform the reader of the various species of plants and animals living in the park.

THE HEART OF KING STREET

GADSBY'S TAVERN

🏠 Location: *134 N. Royal St.* **Contact:** *☎(703) 838-4242.* **Hours:** *Apr.-Sept. Tu-Sa 10am-5pm, Su 1-5pm; Oct.-Mar. Tu-Sa 11am-4pm, Su 1-4pm. Last tour 4:15pm.* **Admission:** *$4, ages 11-17 $2.*

Lee Fendall House

Formerly a hotbed of political, business, and social life owned by Englishman John Gadsby in colonial times, the restored Gadsby's Tavern (see **Food & Drink,** p. 157) takes you back to the golden age of hospitality when as many as four hotel guests slept in one bed. Notable visitors in Gadsby's day included George and Martha Washington, Jefferson, John Adams, Madison, and Lafayette. Today, period food and paraphernalia represent historic dining.

STABLER-LEADBEATER APOTHECARY MUSEUM AND SHOP

🏠 Location: *105-107 S. Fairfax St.* **Contact:** *☎(703) 836-3713.* **Hours:** *M-Sa 10am-4pm, Su 1-5pm; closed W Nov.-Mar.* **Admission:** *$2.50, students $2, ages 10 and under free.*

A pharmacy open from 1792 to 1933, the Stabler-Leadbeater Apothecary closed during the Great Depression. With a little help from restorers, the oldest mercantile operation still

Pope-Leighey House

present in America has been preserved in its 1933 condition. In fact, shelves are lined with several hand-blown bottles, still resting in their original 1933 position. Martha Washington's letter to the pharmacy requesting castor oil hangs in a glass case. The gift shop sells antique apothecary bottles, antique books on medicine, and candy. Athenaeum.

Alexandria's oldest house is home to the **Alexandria Ballet** and holds occasional local and touring art shows. The peach-colored Greek Renaissance building stands out against the surrounding colonial architecture with its large, round columns and classical aura. Unless there is a ballet rehearsal, visitors can walk on the beautiful wood floors in the main hall and browse through the art exhibit. *(201 Prince St. ☎(703) 548-0035. Open W-Sa 11am-4pm, Su 1-4pm.)*

CARLYLE HOUSE

🔢 *Location: 121 N. Fairfax St. **Contact:** ☎(703) 549-2997. **Hours:** Tu-Sa 10am-4:30pm, Su noon-4:30pm. **Tours:** every 30min. **Admission:** $4, students 11-17 and seniors $2, under 11 free.*
Faithfully restored in 1976, the home of prosperous Scottish merchant John Carlyle is a unique showcase of Alexandria in the 18th century. Carlyle patterned his home after buildings in 18th-century Scotland and northern England, a design choice you won't find elsewhere in Old Town. Tours start in the basement, where the servants lived, and continue upstairs where visitors will be startled by the surprising vibrance of 18th century decor. Rumor has it that dungeons (now wine cellars) in Carlyle House once ran down the bluff to the edge of the river and housed captured Tauxenent Indians during the French and Indian War. Also during the French and Indian War, English General Edward Braddock convened a congress upstairs in the Carlyle House where the concept of taxing the colonists was first suggested, leading to the Alexandrian belief that the seeds of the Revolutionary War were actually planted at the Carlyle House. The "summer house" (a gazebo) and garden in the back serve as a public park, beckoning picnickers.

TORPEDO FACTORY

🔢 *Location: 105 N. Union St. **Contact:** ☎(703) 838-4565 for Torpedo Factory; ☎(703) 838-4399 for Alexandria Archaeology; www.torpedofactory.org. **Hours:** Torpedo Factory open daily 10am-5pm. Alexandria Archaeology open Tu-F 10am-3pm, Sa 10am-5pm, Su 1-5pm. Pavilion open daily 8am-midnight. **Admission:** Free.*
Exhibiting over 165 artists, the ex-factory houses 84 working studios on 3 floors. Visitors can observe works of nearly every artistic genre (painting, sculpting, jewelry design, ceramics, fiber and glass artistry, photography, and musical instruments) as they await completion or sale in workshops. The only relic of the building's role as a World War I munitions factory is a small exhibit with an inert torpedo. On the 3rd floor of the factory, **Alexandria Archaeology** welcomes visitors into the city's working urban archaeology lab and museum. The exhibits on 18th- and 19th-century artifacts are limited, but children and parents can become part of the action through Family Dig Days and other educational programs. A quick walk across the wharf behind the Torpedo Factory leads you to a **Food Pavilion** filled with cheap eats.

POTOMAC RIVERBOAT TOURS

🔢 *Location: Boats depart at the city pier. **Contact:** ☎(703) 548-9000. **Hours:** Apr.-Labor Day, Tu-F 11am-2pm, Sa noon-10pm, Su noon-7pm. **Admission:** $8, seniors $7, children ages 2-12 $4. Monuments' tour, $15, seniors $14, children 2-12 $7.*
40min. tours of the Alexandria Waterfront explain all of Old Town's legends including that of the Jones Point lighthouse keeper who managed to cram his small family of 17 into a telephone-booth sized home. A cruise up the Potomac departs from Old Town on a more erratic schedule; call ahead for hours, especially Sept.-Oct.

POTOMAC PLANTATIONS

MOUNT VERNON

🔢 *Address: P.O. Box 110, Mt. Vernon, VA 22121. **Driving Directions:** Take the George Washington Pkwy. south from D.C. (the Pkwy. becomes Washington St. in Alexandria) to the entrance. **Public Transportation:** From Metro: Huntington take the Fairfax Connector 101 bus. The Potomac Riverboat Company (☎(703) 548-9000 runs to and from Mount Vernon. **Contact:** ☎(703) 780-2000; www.mountver-*

non.org. ***Hours:*** *Daily Apr.-Aug. 8am-5pm, grounds close at 5:30pm; Sept.-Oct. and Mar. 9am-5pm, grounds close at 5:30pm; Nov.-Feb. 9am-4pm, grounds close at 4:30pm. Admission: $8, over 62 with ID $7.50, ages 5-11 $4, under 5 free. $14 annual admission.* ***Tour:*** *Mansion Tour, A Slave Life Tour, and other seasonal guided tours included in price of admission. Anecdote-filled 40min. audio tour of the grounds $2. 45min. round-trip cruises 11:15am Tu-Su ($7, seniors $5, ages 6-11 $4).* ***Accessibility:*** *Mostly wheelchair accessible. Shuttle to quay available for handicapped visitors.* ***Events:*** *Ceremonial wreath-laying at the Washington tomb daily 10am in summer. Free admission on George Washington's birthday. Call ahead for seasonal events. Gift shop and concessions undergoing 12.5 million dollar renovations. Grand reopening scheduled for Spring 2001.*

From 1754 to 1799, Mount Vernon served as George Washington's beloved abode. So close to the founding father's heart was this estate that he said, "I can truly say I had rather be at home at Mount Vernon with a friend or two about me, than to be attended at the seat of government by the officers of State and the representatives of every power in Europe." Even while completing his official duties as president, Washington found time to run the plantation and entertain up to 800 guests per year. A talented decorator and courteous host, Washington dedicated most of his leisure time to beautifying the mansion's interior and administering the corps of slaves that ran the farm. He died at Mount Vernon in 1799. The estate maintains 30-40% of GW's original furnishings, which are now on display in the house (the rest of the furnishings are period replicas).

THE MANSION. The stone-like exterior of the 1700s Georgian masterpiece is really a wooden illusion cleverly constructed by splattering sand on smooth wood before painting. Outside on the piazza, rocking chairs offer the ultimate Southern comfort: a cool breeze and the stunning Potomac. In the entrance hall, the key to the Bastille given to Washington in 1790 by the Marquis de Lafayette, a close friend of the family, is enclosed in a glass case. The Washingtons' second-floor bedroom may not have been known for steamy sessions between Martha and the big man himself (literally big—Washington stood at nearly 6'3"); instead, the room morbidly displays the horrible agony of his death in 1799 from an abscessed tonsil. Visitors will need to exercise some patience if they are to tour Mt. Vernon's main attraction; lines can be lengthy.

THE GROUNDS. Often overshadowed by the more renowned mansion, the sprawling grounds of Mt. Vernon encompass nearly 8000 acres of picturesque land. Behind the kitchen, a gravel path leads to the Washingtons' original graves in a small, hidden tomb marked with a rough, wooden door. Down the road, George and Martha Washington's new tomb, a marble mausoleum housing a pair of stone sarcophagi labeled "Washington" and "Martha, consort of Washington," contrasts sharply with the older, unpretentious tomb. Nearby is the unmarked area believed to have been the slave burial ground. In his time, Washington was the biggest slave owner in Northern Virginia, with over 400 slaves working at Mount Vernon. In his will, Washington freed his slaves. Tours of slave life at Mount Vernon (Apr.-Oct. daily at 10am, noon, 2, and 4pm) pay homage to Washington's slaves. The Mount Vernon Museum, located near the slave quarters in the upper garden, displays bizarre items such as the president's toothbrush and imported rum bottles from the Caribbean, which he issued to the slaves on special occasions.

WOODLAWN PLANTATION

🚩 *Address: 9000 Richmond Hwy., Alexandria, VA, at the intersection of Mt. Vernon Hwy. and Rte. 1 (Richmond Hwy.)* ***Public Transportation:*** *From the Metro: Huntington take the 9A or 9B Metrobus (marked "Pentagon") directly to the intersection.* ***Contact:*** *☎(703) 780-4000.* ***Hours:*** *Woodlawn Mansion open Mar.-Dec. M-Sa 10am-5pm. Pope-Leighey House open Mar.-Dec. daily 10am-4pm.* ***Admission:*** *Each house $6, students and seniors $5. Both houses $10, students and seniors $8.* ***Tours:*** *Every 30min. at each house, until 4:30pm.* ***Accessibility:*** *Wheelchair access limited to ground floor.*

Woodlawn Plantation was a wedding present from George Washington to Nelly Custis, his adopted daughter, and Lawrence Lewis, his nephew and personal secretary. The two startlingly different houses of the Woodlawn Plantation represent extremes of materialism and minimalism. The **Pope-Leighey House** was transported from Great Falls, VA, the final placement produces a design clash: Frank Lloyd Wright's simple and modern 1940 design forms little more than a glorified wooden box. A three-minute walk reveals the towering, 19th-century **Woodlawn Mansion,** completed in 1806 and still the anchor of the 125-acre lot. The view from the portico (plantation-speak for "back porch") includes miles of lazy green hills.

POPE-LEIGHEY HOUSE. A sign in the parking lot directs guests to the **Pope-Leighey House,** one of Wright's Usonian-style houses, designed for inhabitants of moderate means ("Usonia" was utopian author Samuel Butler's acronym for the United States of North America). Commissioned in 1939, the $7000 house first held the four-member family of Laurent Pope, a Washington newspaper writer. When Pope relocated to work for *The New York Times,* he sold the house to Robert Leighey, a Fairfax County attorney, which explains the name of the house. After devious highway planners sent Rte. 66 through the house's original location in Falls Church, VA, Mrs. Leighey rescued the house by donating it to the National Trust for Historic Preservation. The house was then moved to its present site on the grounds of Woodlawn Plantation. Strategic furniture arrangement (notice the kitchen cabinets open away from the window to prevent shadows on the shelves behind) reflects Wright's meticulous attention to detail.

WOODLAWN MANSION. Most obvious to visitors is the array of Washington portraits which hang as testaments to Nelly's benefactor. The 40-minute **tour** of the exquisitely preserved, five-part Georgian mansion begins in the master bedroom and proceeds to the back portico, where a view of five towering oaks marks the distant, beloved neighbor, Mt. Vernon. While descending the stairs, take note of the stitched image of two mourners in front of a grave hung on the wall. If you look at the reflection in the situated mirror, one of the mourners mysteriously disappears and an angel appears above the grave.

THE REST OF FAIRFAX

GREAT FALLS PARK

Directions: *Take the Beltway I-495 to Exit 13, then Georgetown Pike (Rte. 193) west. Turn right at Old Dominion and drive into the park (Rte. 738).* **Contact:** *☎(703) 285-2966.* **Hours:** *Daily 7am-dark. Visitors center open M-F 10am-5pm, Sa-Su 10am-6pm.* **Admission:** *$4 per vehicle, $2 per person without a vehicle. Under 16 and disabled persons free.* **Tours:** *Daily ranger walks. Call ahead for details. No swimming, wading, alcohol, unleashed pets, or fires allowed.*

Breathtaking views of the Potomac River abound across all 800 acres of Great Falls Park. The park's main attractions are the 16 miles of hiking trails along the river. Maps are available at the informative **Visitors Center** just inside the entrance gate. The falls' three overlook sites, including the most spectacular #2, are only a short walk from the center. Kayaking and whitewater rafting are available for experienced boaters on the Potomac. Serious rock climbers get vertical on Great Falls' bare granite (climbers must register first at the visitors center). No swimming is allowed in the Potomac, and for good reason—the churning river claims an average of seven lives a year in Great Falls alone. **Be careful when hiking near the river.** The park offers excellent catfish and carp fishing, but a Maryland or Virginia fishing license is required to cast your line at any of the three overlook points to the right of the visitors center.

RESTON ZOO

Location: *1228 Hunter Mill Rd., Vienna, VA. Take the Beltway (I-495) to Rte. 267W (parallel to Dulles Toll Rd.). Exit 14 is Hunter Mill Rd.* **Contact:** *☎(703) 757-6222.* **Hours:** *Apr.1-Dec.31 M-F 9am-5pm, Sa-Su 9am-6pm; June-Labor Day, daily 9am-6pm.* **Admission:** *W-Su $8.50, seniors and ages 3-12 $6.50. Season passes, adults $50 and children $40.*

Formerly Reston Animal Park, the recently renovated Reston Zoo will more than satisfy that inexplicable childhood desire to feed and play with creatures. Located in a wide field surrounded by housing developments, the zoo features a broad range of animals, including exotic giraffes and baby camels. The most popular human-animal modes of interaction are the lamb bottle feed and pony rides. "Intra-park transportation" includes elephant rides ($3) and pony rides (kids only, $1.50). Continuing plans to enhance the zoo include a Christmas extravaganza, scheduled to last the entire month of December.

MANASSAS NATIONAL BATTLEFIELD PARK

Location: *Along Rte. 234N. Take Rte. 495 to I-66W. Exit 47B is Rte. 234; the battlefield is on the right. No public transportation.* **Contact:** *☎(703) 361-1339.* **Hours:** *Daily 8:30am-5pm.* **Admission:** *$2, under 17 free. Tickets good for 3 days. Seniors 62+ eligible for Golden Age passport ($10), which gives* *lifetime access to all national parks. Golden Access with proof of disability gives lifetime access to all national parks free. **Tours:** 40min. Henry Hill self-guided walking tour in brochure. Call ahead for special and seasonal tours. **Accessibility:** Wheelchair access limited.*

Upon these undulating green hills, brother fought against brother not once but twice. Marking the battlefield of the First and Second Battles of Manassas, known to the Yankees as the **Battles of Bull Run,** this Virginia landscape witnessed the two-fold slaughter and defeat of the Yankees. On the morning of July 21, 1861, Northern General **Irvin McDowell** rallied his green—some only 16 years young—troops to march to the Confederate lines in the First Battle of Bull Run. The equally raw Southerners, led by **Stonewall Jackson,** sacked McDowell's untrained troops in a chaotic and disorganized fracas. Jackson would earn his nickname this day by stubbornly blockading McDowell's troops at Manassas Junction. Ironically, as the men battled ferociously in what was the first major battle of the Civil War, the event quickly became entertainment for civilians picnicking on the opposite side of Bull Run Creek. While sightseers sipped tea, the Union soldiers retreated with 1000 more casualties than the South. On August 29 of the following year, the forces gathered for a rematch. Once again, the Southerners prevailed.

The park's recently refurbished **Visitors Center,** located at the top of the hill when you enter the park, offers a variety of maps, exhibits, and historical information about the double battlefield. Relive the battles through an informative movie, prefaced by extremely well-versed rangers. The **Henry Hill Self-Guided Walking Tour** follows a one-mile trail, stopping at plaques explaining the area's significance to either or both battles. The endless expanse of greenery easily recalls the massive numbers of troops marching to their doom. A **driving tour** mapped in the brochure available at the Visitors Center covers a wider area of the park but loses the personal touch of treading upon the earth that decided the fate of thousands. **Ranger talks** are given eight times a day hourly. During the summer season, special tour sites, including the **Unfinished Railroad** where Confederate soldiers barricaded themselves during the Second Battle of Manassas, offer a creative alternative to the usual route. Call ahead for times and topics. Of special attraction are the modified reenactments held at the end of July and the end of August to commemorate the two battles. These simulated battles are tempered to prevent damage to the national park grounds.

Museums

ON THE MALL

SMITHSONIAN MUSEUMS

⛊ The following information applies to all of the Smithsonian Museums on the Mall, but excludes the National Gallery of Art. Contact: ☎ *357-2700 (TDD 357-1729) M-F 9am-5pm, Sa-Su 10am-4pm; 24hr. recorded information* ☎ *357-2020; www.si.edu.* **Hours:** *Museums open daily 10am-5:30pm. Castle open daily 9am-5:30pm. Visitors Center in the Castle open daily 10am-4pm. Special evening hours in the summer.* **Tours:** *Recorded audio tours available at some museums (usually less than $5).* **Admission:** *Free, except for the National Air and Space Museum.* **Accessibility:** *Wheelchair accessible. Constitution or Independence Ave. entrances are easier for wheelchairs.* **Events:** *Frequent lectures and music; call for details. See Entertainment, p. 138.* **Transportation:** *The Museum Bus offers transportation among museums on the Mall and throughout D.C. 1-day ticket for the 2hr. tour leaving every 15min. from outside the Castle ($16, children $7) can be bought on the bus.* **Metro:** *Use Smithsonian, L'Enfant Plaza, Federal Triangle, or Judiciary Square Metro stops.* **Parking:** *Difficult, but free 3-hour parking on Jefferson and Madison Dr. Metered parking on surrounding streets.*

Recalling memories from biology class to television milestones, the Smithsonian displays only a proportion of its holdings at any given time, but still offers more than anyone could see in a few days. The Institute was the brainchild of **James Smithson,** a British chemist who never visited the US but left 105 bags of gold sovereigns—the bulk of his estate—to "found at Washington, under the name of the Smithsonian Institution, an establishment for the increase and diffusion of knowledge among men." In all probability, Smithson probably didn't think his money would actually get to the New World: the first beneficiary of his estate was his nephew, and only if the nephew died without heirs would the estate go to America. Fortunately for the US, the nephew died heirless within

the dopedc on

Topless George

Outside the entrance to the **Field to Factory** exhibit is a statue of a strapping, shirtless George Washington. **Horatio Greenough** carved the figure at the request of Congress in 1832. The finished sculpture was so unwieldy that the Capitol's doors had to be removed to drag it inside, and so semi-naked that Congressmen openly snickered. When its weight caused the floor underneath to sink, Congress had an excuse to get rid of the monstrosity. After its reinstallation outside, snow collecting in George's lap and on his bare chest only worsened the jibes. The Smithsonian acquired **Topless George** in 1908.

a few years of Smithson's death, and the Institution was officially established in 1846. For the first few decades, the institute focused on research, concentrating on the "increase...of knowledge" more than its diffusion. The **Castle**—the large red brick Victorian Gothic building—was built to house both Smithson's collection of zinc and the bachelor scientists who monastically tended the growing collection of botanical and mineralogical specimens.

The Smithsonian is still a research institution, with facilities scattered from Boston to Nepal. The emphasis changed, however, after the **1876 Centennial Exposition in Philadelphia,** the first world's fair, when the exhibiting nations donated their displays to the US to save on shipping costs. Consequently, Congress built the **Arts and Industries Building** to house the displays. Since then, Smithsonian directors have been relentlessly collecting objects of historical importance, as when Smithsonian directors telegraphed Charles Lindbergh for his plane while he was still celebrating his famous transatlantic flight in France. Twenty million tourists visit every year to see Rodin sculptures, dinosaurs, Dorothy's ruby slippers, and the Apollo XI capsule.

NATIONAL MUSEUM OF AMERICAN HISTORY

↗ Tours: Interactive audio tours available ($4.25; students and seniors $3.75). On the Web: www.si.edu/nmah.

The National Museum of American History earned the entire institute the nickname "the nation's attic" because of the clutter of old goods from fiber-optic cable to harmonicas that reside here behind plexiglass and plaques. The most uncategorizable of American memorabilia is often the star attraction; the ruby slippers worn by Judy Garland in *The Wizard of Oz* have toured and charmed the nation, while others fall under the spell of a Babe Ruth-autographed baseball. When the Smithsonian inherits a quirky artifact of popular culture, like Irving Berlin's piano or the giant glass bucket used in the D.C. Vietnam draft, the article finds its home at the museum. Opened in 1964, the museum was named the **National Museum of History and Technology** until 1980, and a certain techno-focus remains evident in exhibits such as "Information Age" and "Power Machinery." Viewing itself as a walk-through history book, the museum is committed to ensuring that even unflattering aspects of American past are remembered.

On the ground floor, the Mall entrance brings you face to face with the swinging **Foucault's Pendulum,** which knocks over pegs set up in a circular pattern as the planet moves beneath it, demonstrating the rotation of the Earth. **The Star-Spangled Banner,** the enormous flag that inspired Francis Scott Key to pen the words to America's national anthem on September 14, 1814, usually hangs behind the pendulum. Extensive renovations began in June 1999 and will last approximately 3 years. Visitors can watch the preservation taking place on the 2nd floor (free timed passes available at the information kiosk on the second floor). Nearby, the **Hands on History** exhibit allows children to take part in craft demonstrations and other interactive historical mock-ups. *(Exhibit open Tu-Su noon-3pm; ages 5 and up.)* Down the escalator, **Hands on Science** allows children to play with science-related toys and games, and conduct experiments on DNA fingerprinting. *(Open Tu-Su 10am-5pm; free time passes distributed on busy days; ages 5 and up.)* An exhibit to the left of the rotunda entitled **Field to Factory** describes the experiences of African-Americans who migrated from southern farms to northern cities from 1915-1940, one of the largest population shifts in US history.

Scheduled exhibits for 2001 are a new permanent exhibit "The Presidency: an American Institution," and the temporary "Visualizing Time" and "Nobel: 100 Years of the Prize."

NATIONAL MUSEUM OF NATURAL HISTORY

1 *Location: 10th St. and Constitution Ave. Metro: Smithsonian or Federal Triangle. **Contact:** ☎ 357-1535. **Tours:** Interactive audio tours $4.75, students $4. Guided tours meet at info desk Tu-F 10:30am and 1:30pm. Open Tu-F noon-2:30pm, Sa-Su 10:30am-3:30pm. Obtain timed ticket at door. **IMAX Theater:** Screenings multiple times a day 10:10am-6:40pm. Tickets $5.50, seniors and children $4.50.*

The National Museum of Natural History contains three crowded floors of rocks, animals, people, and gift stores. When the museum was conceived, "natural history" meant geology and biology; the rarely seen tag "and National Museum of Man" licensed the curators to add anthropology exhibits. This museum exhibits the most variety of all of the Smithsonian buildings; its displays range from not-touched-in-decades to redone-last-year. The Hope Diamond and dinosaurs still attract crowds, regardless of their age.

The **History of Life** exhibit is just to the right of the Mall entrance, and holds some of the most popular displays on the Mall. A kind of fleshless *Jurassic Park*, the central pit can barely hold all the dino skeletons. A familiar favorite, the triceratops, will be receiving an extensive makeover which will be performed in front of museum-goers. Next door, **Life in the Ancient Seas** contains skeletons of our fishy predecessors and turtles the size of coffee tables. Rounding the corner at the northeast end of the exhibit brings you into the **Ice Age** rooms, where the giant ground sloth, the saber-toothed tiger, and the woolly mammoth await.

Kids can touch nearly everything in the **Discovery Room,** hidden beyond the Sea Life in between the Hall of North American Mammals and the Hall of Native Cultures of the Americas. Watching frustrated five-year-olds finally get their hands on a huge, fully touchable polar bear is a guaranteed parental amusement.

On the second floor, the breathtaking gem and jewelry exhibit sparkles with enough splendor to keep your eyes glittering for weeks. Visitors eagerly line up to see this exhibit and the allegedly cursed **Hope Diamond,** mailed to the Smithsonian in 1958 for $145.29 (insured up to $1 million). At 45.52 carats, this rare blue diamond is less than half its original size when first found in India in the 17th century; nonetheless, it could still choke a horse. The discreet brown wrapper in which it arrived is on display at the National Postal Museum (see p. 121). At the rotunda end of the exhibit, a display on **Moon Rocks and Meteorites** contains a fragment of rock older than the solar system that a meteorite brought to Earth. Also on the second floor, the **Orkin Insect Zoo** provides entertaining ways to give yourself the heebie-jeebies. The newest and most dramatic change to the museum is the recently-opened **IMAX Theater**.

Scheduled exhibits for 2001 include "Listening to the Prairie: the Forces of Change," collaborating with the National Geographic Society, and "Art of the Goldsmith: Master-works from Buccballati," which will feature Milanese goldsmith and jewelry designers.

NATIONAL AIR AND SPACE MUSEUM

▯ *Tours:* Free tours daily 10:15am and 1pm from the tour desk in the entrance gallery. Audio tours with touch screens can be rented at a station to the right of the Mall entrance. Tours $5, students, seniors and children $4. **IMAX:** Films every 40min. 10:10am-6:45pm. $5.50 adults, seniors and children $4.25. For IMAX info, call ☎357-1686. **Planetarium:** Shows 11am-5pm. $3.75. Tickets available at the box office on the 2nd fl., near the Spirit of St. Louis.

The National Air and Space Museum is colossal in its expanse and scope. The individual exhibits themselves soar stories from foundation to rooftop: DC-3s loom over visitors while 80 ft. rockets balance in a pit that reaches from basement to skylight. Because Air and Space captures those rare moments that have inspired humanity, all of humanity seems to appear on its doorstep every day. 7½ million visitors come here annually, exceeding the attendance of any other museum. Considering the human achievements it champions, this phenomenal head count is not surprising. Before 1903, human beings had never left the surface of the planet by mechanical means—the Wright brothers did so that year in a rickety biplane that now hangs in the museum's entrance gallery. But by 1969, just 66 years later, humans had the know-how to leave the Earth far behind—and on July 20, **Neil Armstrong** and **Buzz Aldrin** landed on the moon in a terrifyingly small lunar module, of which an experimental demo identical to the original, is on display.

Air and Space's best exhibits are, well, its biggest: the actual planes and crafts from all eras of flight. The **Wright brothers' biplane** in the entrance gallery looks fragile next to its younger kin, as it in fact is. Its wings are made of spruce and ash covered with cloth, making it flexible and strong compared to its predecessors. **Lindburgh's Spirit of St. Louis** hangs next to it, looking rickety. Planes and rockets congregate in the entrance, the **Space Race Hall** (Gallery 114), and **Milestones of Flight** (Gallery 100), which includes the shiny red Lockheed Vega **Amelia Earhart** used to set two records: first woman to fly solo across the US and the first solo woman to fly non-stop across the Atlantic. Check out exhibits **World War II Aviation** and **Legend, Memory, and the Great War in the Air** which explore the role of aviation in WWWII and WWI, respectively (Gallery 205-206). Some interactive options keep kids of all ages occupied.

Air and Space takes an odd interest in mass-market science fiction. In Gallery 209, a claymation Einstein hosts a lighthearted dissection of sci-fi staples from warp speed to light sabers. IMAX movies are shown on a five-story movie screen in the **Langley Theater.** Three rotating films are screened, including the perennially popular *To Fly,* an aerial tour of America from balloons to spaceships. The **Einstein Planetarium** houses a 70 ft. starry dome. Expect some exhibits to temporarily change locations, as the museum's five-year renovation project is scheduled to end in July 2001.

HIRSHHORN MUSEUM AND SCULPTURE GARDEN

▯ *Contact:* ☎357-3235 for tour info, ☎357-2700 for general info daily 10am-4pm, www.si.edu/hir-shorn/. **Hours:** Open daily 7:30am-dusk. **Tours:** Tours of the museum M-F noon, Sa-Su noon and 2pm, Su 12:30pm. Tours of the sculpture garden May-Oct. 10:30pm. Tours for disabled visitors also available.

If you're convinced that art ended with Picasso, stay away from the Hirshhorn Museum and Sculpture Garden—home to the modern, postmodern, and post-postmodern.

MUSEUM. Built around immigrant philanthropist Joseph Hirshhorn's gifts, the museum still carries the flavor of personal preference rather than institutional design. Each floor consists of two concentric circles: an outer ring of rooms and paintings, and an inner cor-ridor of sculptures. From the inner circle, windows face the courtyard and its fountain. The information desk distributes the *Family Guide,* which provides plenty of activities for kids visiting the museum. The ground floor holds temporary exhibits, an auditorium, and shows a film on the appreciation of modern art. The second and third floors show temporary exhibits and changing parts of the museum's permanent collection. The bulk of the collection is stored off-site, but as the collection rotates every six months or so, visitors can see a range of works over repeated visits.

The Hirshhorn's best shows feature tried-and-true art from 1960 and later. The halls are packed with the art of 20th-century artists from **Calder** to **Kelly** to **de Kooning** to **Stella.** More staid artists, like **Edward Hopper** and **Georgia O'Keefe,** are represented as well. The museum also claims one of the world's most comprehensive sets of 19th- and 20th-century Western sculpture, including small works by **Rodin** and **Giacometti.** The collection also includes pieces by **Renoir, Degas, Matisse, Gaugin,** and **Picasso,** which are not always on display.

SCULPTURE GARDEN. Outdoor sculpture shines in the courtyard of the museum, where aluminum, steel, bronze, and silver creations from the 1880s-1960s line the stony pavement. Across Jefferson Ave., the sculpture garden continues in a sunken display that exhibits impressive works by **Rodin, Aristide Maillol,** and **Matisse,** among others.

ARTS AND INDUSTRIES BUILDING

⚑ Events: Discovery Theater performances for children (see **Entertainment,** p. 142).

This large red-brick Victorian building opened in 1881 to celebrate Pres. James A. Garfield's inauguration and became the original home of the National Museum from which the Smithsonian sprang. Now the building has 4 main exhibition halls which host changing exhibits from various sources such as the Anacostia Museum of African American History and Culture, National Museum of the American Indian, and the Smithsonian Center for Latino Initiations. Exhibits included **Artifacts from the Paper Road/Tibet** which featured calligraphy, prints, papers, and photos of Tibetan artists and scholars. Finishing its run at the museum, **Speak to My Heart: Community of Faith and Contemporary African American Life** explored the role of black churches in major American cities.

AFRICAN ART AND SACKLER GALLERY COMPLEX

⚑ Contact: African Art, ☎ 356-4600, www.si.edu/nmafa, Asian art, ☎ 357-4880, TTY ☎ 786-2374, www.si.edu/asia. **Hours:** Open daily in summer 7am-8pm; in winter 7am-5:45pm. **Tours:** National Museum of African Art tours M-F 11am, Sa-Su 11am and 1pm. Sackler tours daily 11am.

Built in 1987, the National Museum of African Art and the Sackler Gallery hide their treasures underground, behind the castle and below the beautifully landscaped, four-acre **Enid A. Haupt Garden.** The garden's main entrance faces Independence Ave. and 10th St. SW. Both museums have two underground exhibit levels that connect, three stories down, to the **S. Dillon Ripley Center's International Gallery.** The museums access the outside world through paired postmodern pavilions in the Haupt Garden; facing the castle with Independence to your back, the Sackler entrance will be on your left, the African entrance on your right. Halls connect the Sackler, the African Art Museum, and the Freer Gallery.

NATIONAL MUSEUM OF AFRICAN ART. The National Museum of African Art collects, catalogues, and displays artifacts from Sub-Saharan Africa, offering insight into cultures where craftsmanship and artistic creativity go hand in hand, and where texture, color, form, and iconography are regularly incorporated into even the simplest of everyday objects. The museum is known in particular for its beautiful collection of metalwork from Benin, some of which is on permanent display in their exhibition entitled **The Ancient West African City of Benin, A.D. 1300-1897.** There are also pieces by contemporary African artists. The second floor houses temporary exhibits, such as **Audible Artworks: Selected African Musical Instruments.**

ARTHUR M. SACKLER GALLERY. Together with the Freer Gallery, the Arthur M. Sackler Gallery forms the national museum of Asian art. The Sackler Gallery showcases Sackler's extensive collection of art from China, Southeast Asia, and Persia. Illuminated manuscripts, Chinese and Japanese paintings from many centuries, carvings and friezes from the Middle East, Hindu gods, jade miniatures, and other works repose in low light and air-conditioned majesty. The Sackler's permanent displays are noteworthy in themselves, including **Puja: Expressions of Hindu Devotion,** which allows visitors a look at Indian worship rites, and the **Arts of China,** displaying exquisite objects ranging from ancient jade to Ming rosewood furniture. Sackler Gallery also featured **Music in the age of Confucius,** an extensive review and exhibit of music and instruments from ancient China. Exhibits occasionally have excellent self-guided tour materials for children under 12, as well as a monthly ImaginAsia program, where kids make their own works of art. The **Sackler Library** (☎357-2091), on the second level, is open to the public. The **Sackler Gallery Gift Shop** is also worth a peek (see **Shopping,** p. 133). The **Visitor Desk** at the entrance pavilion is open daily 10am to 4pm.

Scheduled exhibits for 2001 include: **Recording Persepolis 1923-1935** which will concentrate on an archaeological dig and is planned to run from Nov. 2000-May 6, 2001, and **Worshipping the Ancestors: Ritual and Commemorative Portraits in the Late Imperial China** (opens June 17, 2000 to Sept. 9, 2001).

FREER GALLERY

⑦ Contact: ☎357-4880, TTY 786-2374; www.si.edu/asia. **Hours:** Open daily 10am-4pm. **Tours:** Free tour daily at 11am.

Small compared to other Smithsonian buildings, the Freer Gallery displays both Asian and American art, the outgrowth of railway car manufacturer **Charles L. Freer's** personal holdings. Freer was **James McNeil Whistler's** main sponsor and donated his collection with the stipulation that the institution was not to add more American art, nor could any of the collection travel. The result is a museum whose Asian art exhibits change and grow, and whose static American art collection consists largely of Whistlers.

A sequence of connected galleries surrounds an elegant courtyard and leads visitors past the American art to the Japanese, Korean, Chinese, Buddhist, South Asian, and Islamic works. Connected to the Sackler via a shared underground exhibition gallery, the Freer's collection of over 26,000 objects contains works dating back to 1000 BC. Beautiful Japanese and Chinese screens and scrolls tell stories with pictures; look for the gorgeous 4th-century *Nymph of Two Rivers* scroll painting by **Gu Kaizhi. Thomas Wilmer Dewing's** *The Lute* is an interesting picture of four women, one playing a lute in a curious green miasma. Look for a new exhibit **Storage Jars of Asia,** which is scheduled from Oct. 29, 2000-March 10, 2002.

NATIONAL GALLERY OF ART

⑦ Contact: ☎737-4215, TDD 842-6176; www.nga.gov. **Hours:** M-Sa 10am-5pm, Su 11am-6pm. **Tours:** Self-guided, audiotaped Director's Tours $5; students, seniors, and groups $4. **Admission:** Free. **Events:** The museum offers guided tours, gallery talks, free classical music concerts, and other events. Schedules are available at the information desks, ☎842-6941. Concerts Oct.-June Su 7pm. Most events are free, but seating is limited.

The National Gallery was conceived, proposed, financed, and named by financier **Andrew Mellon,** who realized that other collectors would be more likely to donate to a gallery if it didn't bear his name. His plan succeeded, and the current collection is an impressively encyclopedic summary of the Western tradition. Walking from the West Building to the East sends you almost chronologically through European art. The West Wing, the gallery's original home, contains masterpieces by such famous folks as Fra Angelico, Leonardo da Vinci, El Greco, Raphael, Rembrandt, Vermeer, and Monet, among many, many, many others. The gallery's newer addition, the East Wing, is devoted to 20th-century art, with everyone from Magritte and Matisse to Man Ray and Miro, just to mention the "M"s. Together, the two wings make up North America's most popular art museum, with 6,000,000 visitors annually.

Rembrandt National Gallery of Art

WEST WING. The traditional bent of this wing was written into its charter: for its first few decades, the National Gallery only accepted works by artists who had been dead at least 20 years. At last they received an offer of Modernism too good to let go, and the policy was adjusted. The collection is still far from experimental, however. Both entrances to the West Wing lead to the domed rotunda, where black marble pillars and a fountain circle a 16th-century Italian sculpture of the god Mercury. Hallways decorated with sculptures lead right (east) and left (west) from the Mall entrance to the exhibition rooms. The West Wing will be undergoing roof and skylight replacement for the next year; exhibits temporarily relocate. Next to the rotunda information desk, the **Micro Gallery** invites museum-goers to look up words in the "talking dictionary" of fine arts terminology or design their own personal tour maps using touch-sensitive screens.

Dutch masters are another main attraction, though they have been moved to the basement level due to renovations. Three of the world's 30-odd **Vermeers** are here; Vermeer, who painted slowly and refused to sell his works, captures perfect moments of silence in his small canvases. Another room features *The Annunciation*, one of the few paintings by **Jan Van Eyck** in the US. Van Eyck is known for his gem-like use of color and for his ability to portray realistic interior space. **Rembrandt**, arguably the most well-known of the Dutch painters, is represented by a room full of self-portraits, as well as *The Mill*, a landscape that influenced later British artists. A good number of **Peter Paul Rubens** works are shown here, including paintings of his second wife and of the affluent and powerful in his day.

Corcoran Gallery

Salvador Dali's *Last Supper* bridges the ancient and modern, hung in the turn of the stairway between the first floor of the West Wing and the underground concourse leading to the East Wing. The West Wing's lower level holds relatively untrafficked collections of sculpture (including a room full of Rodins), prints and drawings, and temporary exhibits. At the lowest level is the concourse, which has a reasonable cafeteria, occasional temporary exhibits, and a moving sidewalk that takes you to the entrance hall of the East Wing.

New 2001 exhibits include "Art for the Nation: Collecting for a New Century," which will feature some of the best masterpieces obtained by the Gallery since 1991, and "Alfred Stieglitz and Modern Art in America," which will explore Stiezlitz's role in American modern art.

EAST WING. Completed in 1978, the East Wing contains much of the museum's plentiful 20th-century collection. **Alex-**

Rodin at Hirshorn Museum

ander Calder designed the 992-pound mobile *Untitled* expressly for this space, which explains why it comes so close to hitting the wall next to the info desk. In fact, Calder originally wanted his moving sculpture to strike the wall each time it completed a revolution, but the museum's designers rejected his plan.

At the 7th St. and Constitution Ave. NW end of the museum, the six-acre Ntional Gallery of Art **Sculpture Garden** was opened in the Spring of 1999. Sculptures are arranged around a large circular fountain. Featuring a Top 40-variety of the famous outdoor sculptors, few pieces stand out as particularly new and fresh, although **Lichtenstein's** wacky *House* and the looming *Typewriter Eraser* by husband and wife team **Claus Oldenburg** and **Coosje van Bruggen** are sure to please even jaded art viewers. Don't miss **Magdalena Abakanowicz's** disturbing army of limbs hidden in the cool shade of the trees.

Exhibits for 2001 include "Art Nouveau 1890-1914," which will exhibit approximately 350 works of Modern European and American art from 1890 until World War I; also, "Prints Abound: Paris in the 1890s" is scheduled to open with prints, drawings, periodicals, and illustrated books from Paris in the late 19th century.

OFF THE MALL

BETHUNE MUSEUM AND ARCHIVES

⬛ Location: *1318 Vermont Ave. NW, in Farragut. Metro: McPherson Square.* **Contact:** ☎ *673-2402; fax 673-2414; www.nps.gov/mamc.* **Hours:** *M-Sa 10am-4pm. Su call for appointments.* **Admission:** *Suggested donation $1. Tours for large groups must be arranged in advance.* **Events:** *On July 10, the museum throws a public birthday party for Mary McLeod Bethune.*

This testament to the participation of black women in American history commemorates the life of educator and pioneer civil rights activist **Mary McLeod Bethune.** One of 17 children in a family of slaves, Bethune grew up to become co-founder of the Bethune-Cookman College in Florida, head of the federal government's Division of Negro Affairs, and founder of the National Council of Negro Women. The museum, located in the NCNW's former headquarters and Bethune's former residence, chronicles her achievements with a 30-minute video and a series of exhibits. Also in residence is the extensive **National Archives for Black Women's History,** "the largest repository solely dedicated to the collection and preservation of materials relating to African-American women." The museum hosts occasional one-woman plays: call for information.

B'NAI B'RITH KLUTZNICK MUSEUM

⬛ Location: *1640 Rhode Island Ave. NW, in Farragut. Metro: Farragut North.* **Contact:** ☎ *857-6583.* **Hours:** *Su-F 10am-5pm, except Jewish holidays.* **Admission:** *Suggested donation $2; students, seniors, and children $1.*

A collection of Jewish cultural and ritual objects comprises the bulk of this museum dedicated to the exploration of Jewish life and tradition. Original copies of the correspondence between George Washington and Moses Seixas (the sexton of the Touro Synagogue in Newport, Rhode Island) contain the first written statement of America's commitment to religious and ethnic toleration. The Greenburg Sculpture Garden displays bronze cast into fluid stories from the Torah by Philip Ratner. Stars of David is a new room that offers tribute to Jews in the world of sports; exhibits rotate every few months. The museum continues to add to their collection by Jewish artists from the last 150 years, including Pissaro and Chagall. The bulletproof glass in the lobby isn't just evidence of paranoia; terrorists held over 100 people hostage in the building in 1977.

CAPITAL CHILDREN'S MUSEUM

⬛ Location: *800 3rd St. NE, directly behind the Union Station parking lot, in Capitol Hill. Metro: Union Station.* **Contact:** ☎ *675-4120; www.ccm.org.* **Hours:** *daily 10am-6pm Easter-Labor Day, 10am-5pm Labor Day-Easter.* **Admission:** *$6, seniors $4, children under 2 free. AAA $5. All children must be accompanied by an adult.* **Events:** *Craft activities every Sa-Su from noon to 3pm; call for details. "Scientific Sundays" hands-on experiments.* **Accessibility:** *Wheelchair accessible.* **Exercise caution in this area.**

This huge, hands-on, interactive experiment of a museum is the ultimate escape from glass-cased artifacts. Visitors can grind and brew their own hot chocolate, roll tortillas, and weave their own ponchos in a two-story mock-up of Mexico!, one of the museum's most popular exhibits. Demonstrations in the chemist-staffed laboratory teach science basics (what is carbonation, anyways?) and allow children to perform experiments of their own (under close supervision, of course). A high-tech animation exhibit on the third floor films kids against an animated background and teaches them how to draw animation cells and make kooky cartoon noises.

CORCORAN GALLERY OF ART

ꚊI Location: 500 17th St. NW, at the corner of 17th St. and New York Ave. NW, in Foggy Bottom. Metro: Farragut West. **Contact:** ☎639-1700; www.corcoran.org. **Hours:** M, W, and F-Su 10am-5pm, Th 10am-9pm. **Tours:** Free tours M, W-Su noon, Th 7:30pm. **Admission:** Suggested donation $3, families $5, students and seniors $1, under 12 free.

Originally housed in what is now the Renwick Gallery, Washington's oldest art museum now resides in a building that **Frank Lloyd Wright** somewhat inexplicably called "the best-designed building in Washington." The Corcoran specializes in American artists, with works from the extensive collection rotating through the exhibit halls. Highlights include impressive full-length portraits by **John Singer Sargent, Alfred Bierstadt's** powerful paintings *The Last of the Buffalo* and *Mount Corcoran*, and a meta-take on the House by **Samuel F. B. Morse.**

Renwick Gallery at Foggy Bottom

The Corcoran also houses a fine selection of modern and contemporary American art, displaying such greats as de Kooning and Kelly, as well as works from the affiliated Corcoran School of Art. Look for Andy Warhol's 1973 *Mao* as well as a number of Lichtenstein pieces. In 2001 the Corcoran will showcase the photo work of Arthur Tres and Robert Louis, as well as feature the exhibit *Painters in The American West.*

DUMBARTON OAKS

ꚊI Location: 1703 32nd St. NW, in Georgetown. **Contact:** Recorded info 339-6401, tour info 339-6409. **Hours:** Tu-Su 2-5pm. **Admission:** Adults $5, children $3. **Note:** no parking on site.

Hope Diamond at Museum of National Histo

Built by **Robert** and **Mildred Bliss** in the Dumbarton Oaks Mansion (see **Sights,** p. 78), this fine museum houses superbly documented exhibits focusing on Byzantine and pre-Colombian art. The **Byzantine Collection** contains floor mosaics, bronzes, and jewelry, mostly from the Byzantine Empire, but also including some interesting Coptic (Egyptian Christian) works. The collection is one of the greatest Byzantine collections in the world, but only a few of the pieces are on display at any one time. Examples of exquisite jewelry, ivories, and textiles are also on view. Icons depicting saints and Jesus show the increasing importance of the Christian church during the rule of Constantine.

Between the Byzantine and pre-Colombian galleries is the **Music Room,** whose Renaissance decoration would be passable but for El Greco's distinctively post-Renaissance painting **The Visitation.** Igor Stravinsky's **Dumbarton Oaks Concerto** premiered here for the Bliss's 30th wedding anniversary in 1934. Subscription concerts from the **Dumbarton Oaks Friends of Music** are held here every winter (call 339-6400 for information).

Gallery K at Dupont Circle

HILLWOOD

⚑ Location: *4155 Linnaean Ave. NW, in Upper Northwest, 10min. down Tilden St. off Connecticut Ave.; take the L2 or L4 bus. Metro: Van Ness.* **Contact:** *☎ 686-5807* **Hours:** *Reservation only, Tu-Sa 9am-5pm.*

Once the mansion of General Foods' heiress **Marjorie Meriweather Post,** Hillwood is now a museum displaying her collection of Russian art and French antique furnishings. She and her ambassador husband lived in Russia for a year in the late 1930s, just when the Communists were selling most of the treasures seized from the aristocracy during the Revolution. Inspired, Post amassed a collection, claimed to be the largest outside of Russia, featuring decorative arts and coins, as well as a number of Fabergé eggs (extremely ornate and bejeweled "eggs" exchanged as Easter presents among the Russian Imperial family). Outside, 25 acres of gardens replicate the landscaping styles of England, Japan, and imperial Russia.

US HOLOCAUST MEMORIAL MUSEUM

⚑ Location: *100 Raoul Wallenberg Pl. SW, south of the Mall. Metro: Smithsonian. Use the Holocaust Museum exit.* **Contact:** *☎ 488–0400, TDD 488-0406; www.ushmm.org.* **Hours:** *Daily in summer 10am-8pm; in winter 10am-5:30pm.* **Admission:** *Free, by timed ticket for the permanent exhibition. Get in line before 10am at the 14th and Independence Ave. entrance for timed tickets or buy tickets through Protix about 2 weeks in advance (☎ (800) 400-9373; $1.75 service charge).* **Accessibility:** *For accessibility requests call ☎ 488-6100.*

One of the darkest events of recent human history is addressed with historical and emotional frankness in the US Holocaust Museum. Visitors are sent over cobblestones from the Warsaw Ghetto, through a contemporary cattle car like those used to transport prisoners, and into part of an Auschwitz bunker.

The self-guided tour begins on the fourth floor with an exhibit entitled **Nazi Assault, 1933-39,** which depicts the Nazi's use of propaganda and the American and world response to the rise of the Third Reich. **The Final Solution, 1940-44** is brutal in its clarity: a black-and-white film shows barbaric medical experiments performed by Nazi doctors, as photos and dioramas depict the tortures inflicted on the Jews. **Aftermath, 1945 to the Present** recounts the last chapter of the Holocaust. Films show Soviet, British, and American troops entering the concentration camps, shocked by the mass graves and emaciated prisoners they encounter. A wall lists the names of those who heroically defied the Nazis to save Jewish lives, while more films and tapes bear the chilling testimony of Holocaust survivors. At the end of the permanent exhibit is the entrance to the free-standing **Hall of Remembrance,** with its eternal flame symbolically representing the central theme of the museum—never to forget. The **Wall of Remembrance,** composed of more than 3,000 tiles painted by American schoolchildren, memorializes the 1.5 million children murdered during the Holocaust.

While the main exhibit may be too intense for young children, the **Remember the Children** exhibit on the first floor (no ticket required) is recommended for children ages 8 to 11. The museum houses the **Wexner Learning Center,** equipped with computers and interactive films.

KREEGER MUSEUM OF ART

⚑ Location: *2401 Foxhall Rd. NW, in Upper Northwest. Minimally accessible by public transportation. The D2 bus runs to the corner of Reservoir and Foxhall Rd.; walk several blocks north on Foxhall.* **Contact:** *☎ 338-3552; www.kreegermuseum.com.* **Hours:** *By appointment only. Visitors permitted Tu-Sa 10:30am and 1:30pm. Call M-F 10am-1pm and 2-5pm to reserve a place.* **Admission:** *Suggested donation $5, children under 12 discouraged.*

David Lloyd Kreeger and his wife, Carmen, through their magnanimous gifts and tireless efforts, were instrumental in bringing the arts to D.C., and the Kreeger name is prominently displayed on buildings around the city as witness to their philanthropy. Their Museum of Art shows that size doesn't matter so much, as the limited but carefully selected collection allows for serious contemplation of paintings ranging from Monet and Miro to Moore. The Picassos on display span the Spaniard's entire career and include one painting that was in Gertrude Stein's personal collection. The African art collection is small but impressive, as is their sculpture garden which also features modern works by D.C. artists like Kendall Buster.

MARINE CORPS HISTORICAL MUSEUM

Location: Navy Yard, in Southeast Capitol Hill. Metro: Eastern Market or Navy Yard. *Contact:* ☎ 433-3534. *Hours:* M, W-Th, and Sa 10am-4pm; F 10am-8pm; Su noon-5pm. *Admission:* Free.

The Marine Corps Historical Museum, in **Building 58** at the Navy Yard, marches through Marine Corps time from the American Revolution to the present. Twenty exhibit cases give an awkwardly surreal replay of the actions, guns, uniforms, and swords of marines in a circular exhibition space. Highlights of the museum include the actual flags (complete with bullet holes) that were raised atop Mt. Suribachi in **Iwo Jima,** inspiring the memorial in Arlington. The austerity of the diorama-like displays of uniforms and artillery is shattered by an amazingly loud, interactive video kiosk with two short films.

NATIONAL BUILDING MUSEUM

Location: 401 F St. NW, in Old Downtown. Across the street from the National Law Enforcement Memorial. Metro: Judiciary Square. *Contact:* ☎ 272-2448; www.nbm.org. *Hours:* M-Sa 10am-4pm, Su noon-4pm; until 5pm in summer. *Tours:* M-W 11:30am-12:15pm and 12:30-1:15pm, Tu and Th-Su 11:30am-12:15pm, 12:30-1:15pm, and 1:30-2:15pm. *Admission:* Suggested donation $3, students and seniors $2. *Events:* Free lunchtime concerts in the Great Hall W-Th 12:15pm. *Accessibility:* Excellent disabled access, including assistance for the visually impaired.

National Air and Space Museum

Size isn't everything, but don't tell that to architect Montgomery Meigs: the center of his National Building Museum is the **Great Hall,** an ode to enormity at 316 ft. long, 116 ft. wide, and 159 ft. high—big enough to swallow a 15-story building. Its 75 ft. Corinthian columns are among the world's largest (and cheapest). They're made of brick painted with 4000 gallons of rose paint, giving the columns a marble appearance without marble's gargantuan cost. The museum's exhibits, tucked away under office space around the Great Hall, honor American achievements in urban planning, construction, and design. Permanent installations include *Washington: Symbol and City*, which offers a historical overview of the city's monuments and neighborhoods, and the larger *Building America*, celebrating American architectural and urban planning innovations.

National Portrait Gallery

NATIONAL MUSEUM OF AMERICAN ART AND NATIONAL PORTRAIT GALLERY

Both are closed until 2003 for major renovations. American crafts and decorative arts will be on special display at the **Renwick Gallery** (17th St. and Pennsylvania Ave, ☎ 357-1300). Information on re-opening can be obtained at ☎ 357-2700, or at www.si.edu.

NATIONAL POSTAL MUSEUM

Location: 1st St. and Massachusetts Ave. NW, in Capitol Hill. Located on the lower level of the City Post Office. Metro: Union Station. *Contact:* Information ☎ 357-2700, TDD 357-1729, library ☎ 633-9370; www.si.edu/postal. *Hours:* Daily 10am-5:30pm. *Tours:* 1hr. tours M-F 11am, 1, and 2pm, Sa-Su 11am and 1pm. *Admission:* Free. *Accessibility:* For tours for persons with visual or hearing impairments, call 786-2942 (TDD 786-2414).

Established in 1993, the National Postal Museum is the latest addition to the Smithsonian. Displays detail the history of the

Robert Brown's Gallery at Dupont Circle

postal system and showcase vehicles used to transport mail. In exchange for a photo and some personal information, a high-tech exhibit on mass mailings shows visitors why they get certain kinds of junk mail and gives free souvenirs. Excited philatelists crowd the Stamps and Stories exhibit, which displays the museum's collection of philatelic rarities (including the priceless "Inverted Jenny").

NAVY MUSEUM

🚩 *Location: Navy Yard, in Southeast Capitol Hill. Metro: Eastern Market or Navy Yard.* **Contact:** ☎ *433-4882; www.history.navy.mil.* **Hours:** *May-Sept. M-F 9am-5pm, Sa-Su 10am-5pm; Oct.-Apr. M-F 9am-4pm, Sa-Su 10am-5pm.* **Admission:** *Free.*

You can play Popeye at this refreshingly hands-on tribute to all things naval in **Building 76** at the **Navy Yard.** Visitors man huge ship guns (3 in., 50-caliber), squeeze into a bathysphere used to explore the sea floor, or roam the gun deck of a mock-up of the **U.S.S. Constitution,** the world's oldest commissioned warship. Exhibits focus on the Navy's involvement in US wars up to and including the Persian Gulf, as well as navy exploration across the globe. The most compelling artifacts are the surplus shells of **Little Boy** and **Fat Man,** the atomic bombs detonated over Japan at the close of WWII. The unused bombs flank a wall with information revisiting the controversial end of WWII. Next door, the **Museum Annex,** with its collection of old submarines (including the Intelligent Whale, a hand-propelled submarine from 1869), remains closed for renovations until 2003.

THE NEWSEUM

🚩 *Location: 1101 Wilson Blvd., in Arlington. Metro: Rosslyn.* **Contact:** *703-284-3544 or 888-639-7386; www.newseum.org.* **Hours:** *Tu-Su 10am-5pm.* **Admission:** *Free.*

Opened in 1997, the Newseum has Starship Enterprise decor and a video game feel. Kids love this place, parents love to see their kids love this place, and others just put up with the overwhelming noise (both audio and visual) that hits visitors like an irate Jerry Springer guest. Visitors sit through a short film about the glories of the press before entering the main exhibit area, which houses temporary exhibits as well as a chance to watch the production of a news program.

Just outside the Newseum, **Freedom Park** perches on an elevated concrete bridge over Wilson Blvd., displaying national and international symbols of freedom cast in bronze, such as Martin Luther King, Jr.'s Birmingham jail cell door, the Goddess of Democracy that reigned over the Tiananmen student uprising in 1989, ballot boxes from South Africa, and a replica of a tiny boat used by Cuban refugees.

PHILLIPS COLLECTION

🚩 *Location: 1600 21st St., at Q St. NW, in Farragut. Metro: Farragut North or Dupont Circle.* **Contact:** ☎ *387-2151.* **Hours:** *Tu-Sa 10am-5pm, Su noon-7pm.* **Admission:** *For weekends and suggested for weekdays, $7.50 to permanent collection, students and seniors $4, free to 18 and under, seniors over 62; audio tours free with admission; additional admission price to special exhibits.* **Events:** *"Artful Evenings," with music and gallery talks, Th 5-8:30pm ($5).*

The Phillips Collection houses the first and one of the finest modern art collections in the United States. This fantastic museum is less crowded and more intimate than the Smithsonian and houses a brand-name selection of relatively recent artistic legends. Its founder, **Duncan Phillips,** was heir to the family steel company and—lucky for us—had impeccable taste in art. Opened in 1921 in the family mansion, the museum is now home to 2500 pieces of art, only a fraction of which are shown at any given time.

Enter the museum through the annex at 1612 21st St., which was added when the collection grew too large for Phillips's original Victorian mansion at 1600 21st St. The most famous work in the museum is **Renoir's** *Luncheon of the Boating Party,* a painting of well-to-do socialites with varying degrees of facial hair (except for the women). This pastel-colored marvel contrasts vividly with the surrounding darker images of Francisco de Goya and El Greco. Georgia O'Keefe's display communicates her passion for natural beauty with depictions of fiery red hills and brilliant suns (*Red Hill, Lake George*). The stroll up the annex and through the original mansion reveals a parade of works by Delacroix, Matisse, Van Gogh, Mondrian, Degas, Miró, Gris, Kandinsky, Turner, Courbet, Daumier, Prendergast, Picasso, Klee, and Hopper—to name a few.

RENWICK GALLERY

Location: Across from the White House at 17th St. and Pennsylvania Ave. NW, in Farragut. Metro: Farragut West or Farragut North. *Contact:* ☎ 357-2700, tours ☎ 357-2531; www.nmaa.si.edu. *Hours:* Daily 10am-5:30pm. *Admission:* Free. *Events:* Workshops, lectures, receptions—they have it all. Ask for a schedule at the front desk. *Accessibility:* Wheelchair accessible via ramp at 17th St. *Note:* The Renwick Gallery is hosting a number of exhibits from the National Museum of American Art, which is undergoing extensive renovations.

William Corcoran originally commissioned **James Renwick** to design the Renwick Gallery in order to display Corcoran's mostly Renaissance art collection. The red-brick mansion is a beauty itself, and the interior's high archways, red velvet staircase, and eccentric design are equally intriguing. This Smithsonian-owned gallery now displays "American craft," with attractive contemporary pottery, blown glass, and silver, and many objects that defy categorization but ultimately fall under the term "craft." Larry Fuente's 1988 *Game Fish* is a huge sailfish trophy plastered with a rainbow of toys; how many of the action figures did you own?

THE TEXTILE MUSEUM

Location: 2320 S St. NW, in Dupont Circle. *Contact:* ☎ 667-0441, www.textilemuseum.org. *Hours:* M-Sa 10am-5pm, Su 1-5pm. Library open W-F 11am-2pm, Sa 10am-4pm. *Tours:* Sept.-May W and Sa-Su 2pm (one hour). *Admission:* Suggested donation $5.

The Textile Museum is the world's largest repository of rare and valuable textiles. The 15,000 holdings include strong collections of carpets from Asia, antique pieces, and contemporary work from the world over. Because it is impossible to show every article at one time, the holdings are rotated throughout the year. The **Textile Learning Center** has descriptive displays on the making and dyeing of different cloths. Several exhibits also allow visitors to try their hands at yarn-making. The **Arthur D. Jenkins Library** contains an immense collection of resources on textiles. Upcoming exhibitions for 2001 include "Village and Nomadic Weaving of Anatolia."

WASHINGTON DOLL'S HOUSE AND TOY MUSEUM

Location: 5236 44th St. NW, 1 block west of Wisconsin Ave. between Harrison and Jenifer St., in Upper Northwest. Metro: Friendship Heights. *Contact:* ☎ 244-0024. *Hours:* Tu-Sa 10am-5pm, Su noon-5pm. *Admission:* $4, students, seniors, and AAA $3, under 12 $2.

This museum is home to six rooms of antique dolls, doll houses, toys, and games. Some of the "doll houses" on display are probably construction models; others are documented Christmas gifts to (wealthy) little girls a century ago. The US Capitol and Mexican mansion (with chapel, radio tower, priest, and roost for homing pigeons) are among the miniature extravagances. The vignette of Noah's Ark is particularly interesting, as is the depiction of Teddy Roosevelt's African safari. Unfortunately, visitors must quelch their inner child; the museum is strictly touch-me-not.

Shopping

For guilt-free spending, try our shopping picks that will satiate even the most prodigal spending instincts without maxing out the plastic. After a day of hard-core monument-hopping, the siren song of consumer therapy calls. Let your inner materialistic glutton graze on the bazaar of spending treats D.C. offers. From hole-in-the-wall vintage stores to specialty boutiques to mammoth emporiums, stumble into a shopaholic's nirvana at Adams-Morgan, Alexandria, Dupont Circle, or Georgetown.

ANTIQUES

Millennium, 1528 U St. NW (☎483-1218). Metro: U St.-Cardozo. This co-op for vintage goods from the 1950s, 60s, and 70s, has a large and mellow collection of records, furniture, clothes, and even appliances in perfect condition. Glassware is sold in complete vintage sets (8 Uncola glasses run about $30). Wacky accessories that you won't find elsewhere include vintage pool balls ($3 each) and *Playboys* from the 1970s ($5). Open Th-Su noon-7pm.

Odds & Ends Antique Shoppe, 1325 King St. (☎(703) 836-6722), in Alexandria. Metro: King St. An old curiosity shop with a bizarre assortment of this and that. Scrounge around the front room and much larger space in the back for 1950s champagne stems ($5), swizzle sticks ($3), and postcards (around $1). Collection of LPs and 45s ($1) are user-friendly for those ready to rummage. Open daily 11am-5pm.

Takoma Underground, 7000B Carroll Ave. (☎(301) 270-6380). Metro: Takoma. You may feel like a long-tailed cat in a room full of rocking chairs, but the clutter underground hosts the best vintage action in Takoma. Rummage for sardine packed antiques in old suitcases, baskets, and baby carriages: the perfect gloves, scarves, and aprons lurk within. Old pipes are complemented by a horde of ancient matchbooks (50¢). Beautiful vintage bridal wear. Open Tu-F 11am-7pm, Sa 10am-6pm, Su 10am-5pm.

inside
SECRETS TO...

Thrift Shopping

America's gone retro. **Vintage envy** has made thrift stores ultra-trendy. Second hand shoppers, take note:

Secondi (see p. 129) reigns supreme with good-quality used clothing, as does **Christ Child Opportunity Shop** (1427 Wisconsin Ave.). All profits from the latter go towards funding inner-city school counseling and non-violence programs.

ARTS AND CRAFTS

Made By You, 3413 Connecticut Ave. (☎363-9590), in Cleveland Park; 4923 Elm St. (☎(301) 654-3206), in Bethesda; 2319 Wilson Blvd. (☎(703) 841-3533), in Arlington. Buy unfinished pottery, mugs, and sculptures made from terra cotta, glass, and ceramic ($10-50) and paint them yourself. Use of glazes, stencils, and final firing is included in the price of your purchase. Allow 5 days before picking up the finished piece. Cleveland Park store open M-Sa 10am-9pm, Su 11am-6pm; Bethesda M-F 10am-9pm, Sa 10am-7pm, Su 10am-6pm; Arlington M-F 10am-9pm, Sa 10am-8pm, Su 11am-6pm.

Plaza, 7825 Old Georgetown Rd. (☎(301) 718-8500), at the corner of Cordell Ave., in Bethesda. Metro: Bethesda. Two floors crammed full of art supplies and an expert staff. 20% student discount. Open M-F 9am-6:30pm, Sa 9am-6pm, Su noon-5pm.

S&A Beads, 6929 Laurel Ave. (☎(301) 891-2323), in Takoma Park. Metro: Takoma. Beads and buttons for every occasion. Pre-made jewelry includes chokers ($3.50-15) and anklets ($5). Indonesian and African clothes. Ethnic gifts like sarongs, Nepalese hanging lanterns, and wind chimes. Open M-F 11am-7pm, Sa 10am-6pm, Su 10am-5pm.

BOOKS

NEW

Barnes and Noble, 3040 M St. NW (☎965-9880), in Georgetown. The only branch of the beloved chain in town. All hardcovers 10% off. Huge selection, especially in children's literature, history, and travel. Open daily 9am-11pm.

Borders, 5333 Wisconsin Ave. NW (☎686-8270), at Chevy Chase Pavilion. Metro: Friendship Heights. Great assortment of books and music. Best-sellers and recent release discounts. Cafe serves up snacks and coffee. Open M-Th 10am-10pm, F-Sa 10am-11pm, Su 10am-9pm.

Chapters, 1512 K St. NW (☎347-5495), in Farragut. Metro: McPherson Square. D.C.'s premier literary bookstore. The collection is thoughtfully selected, with recommendations from the staff. Offers scheduled book readings, although you might need tickets to some of the high profile literary events. Open M-F 10am-6:30pm, Sa 11am-5pm.

Chuck and Dave's Books, Etc., 7001 Carroll Ave. (☎(301) 891-2665). Metro: Takoma Park. One of few bookstores where people use shopping baskets. Massive tables of bargain books in every category are a bit overshadowed by the toys, stationery, and other novelty items, including handcrafted Hebrew Alphabet puzzles ($15) and Czech handmade marionettes ($30). Open M-Sa 10am-8pm, Su 10am-5pm.

Kramerbooks, 1517 Connecticut Ave. NW (☎387-1400). Metro: Dupont Circle. Local favorite bookstore full of fiction and history, although the organization is confusing. Adjacent cafe tempts patrons to peruse instead of purchase. Open Su-Th 7:30am-1am, F-Sa 24hr.

Olsson's Books and Records, 1239 Wisconsin Ave. (☎338-9544), in Georgetown; 418 7th St. (☎638-7610), in Old Downtown; 1307 19th St. (☎785-1133), in Dupont Circle; 106 S. Union St. (☎(703) 684-0077), in Alexandria and elsewhere. Great selection of literature, travel, and history books at reasonable prices. Call for hrs. at specific location.

USED

Atticus Books, 1508 U St. NW. Metro: U St.-Cardoza. Stacks of books overflowing from the shelves make maneuvering around the store difficult, but the struggle is well worth it. In addition to a magnificent selection of used books in scholarly categories (i.e. American History, French History, The Kennedys), Atticus sells many obscure literary magazines. Open M and W-Sa 11am-7pm, Su noon-6pm.

Idle Time Books, 2410 18th St. NW (☎232-4774), near Columbia St. in Adams-Morgan. A smashing selection of used books in a house crammed to bursting. Double-stacked shelves of half-price fiction and collections of non-fiction in practically every genre. Also features some foreign-language titles and a very charming cat. Open daily 11am-10pm.

The Lantern Bryn Mawr Bookshop, 3241 P St. NW (☎333-3222), near the intersection with Wisconsin Ave., in Georgetown. Great prices on used books (hardcover from $3, paperbacks from $1). Packed, but well-organized inventory. Lots of dusty LPs ($1) and some CDs (starting at $2). All proceeds support the Bryn Mawr scholarship fund. Open M-F 11am-4pm, Sa 11am-5pm, Su noon-4pm.

Second Story Books, 4836 Bethesda Ave. (☎(301) 656-0170), in Bethesda; 2000 P St. NW (☎659-8884), in Dupont Circle; and 12160 Parklawn Dr. (☎(301) 770-0477), in Rockville, MD. Amazing collection of used books, including rare antiquities. Used LPs, CDs and posters. D.C. and Bethesda locations open daily 10am-10pm.; Rockville open Su-Th 10am-8pm, F-Sa 10am-9pm.

SPECIALTY

Backstage, Inc., 545 8th St. SE (☎544-5744). Metro: Eastern Market. Plays, performing art books, costumes, masks, fab wigs, and make-up. Rental costumes, too. Helpful staff is willing to field questions. Open M-Sa 11am-7pm.

Franz Bader Bookstore, 1911 I St. NW (☎337-5440), in Farragut. Metro: Farragut West. New and old books in the visual arts, including painting, sculpture, architecture, design, and photography. Some titles in French, German, and Italian. Open M-Sa 10am-6pm.

Lambda Rising, 1625 Connecticut Ave. NW (☎462-6969), between Q and R St. Metro: Dupont Circle. The largest selection of gay and lesbian literature in D.C., including travel guides, videos, CDs, t-shirts, and novelty items. Serves as an info center and ticket outlet for concerts and events. Helpful, friendly staff. Occasional book signings and live music. Wheelchair accessible. Open Su-Th 10am-10pm, F-Sa til midnight.

Lammas Women's Books & More, 1607 17th St. NW (☎775-8218), at Q St. Perhaps best known for their spirituality/new age books, videos, and erotica items, Lammas also has many books by and about women, including health books, travel books, books about childraising, and extensive feminist and lesbian literature. Weekly movie screenings. Open M-Th 11am-10pm, F-Sa 11am-11pm, Su 11am-8:30pm.

A Likely Story, 1555 King St. (☎(703) 836-2498), in Alexandria. Metro: King St. Children's bookstore with a wide selection of fiction, non-fiction, and audio books and incredibly knowledgeable staff. Leaf through some of the highlighted local author selections in the Winnie the Pooh decorated sitting area, or find gifts among the large assortment of games, puzzles, and crafts. Open M-Sa 10am-6pm, Su 1-5pm.

Luna Books, 1633 P St. NW (☎332-2543), on the 3rd fl. above Cafe Luna and Skewers. Metro: Dupont Circle. A tiny bookstore devoted to liberal and radical politics. Discount non-fiction and political texts. Discussion groups and poetry readings held periodically. Open M-F 11am-3pm, and whenever events are held.

Mystery Books, 1715 Connecticut Ave. NW (☎483-1600 or (800) 955-2279). Metro: Dupont Circle. Devoted solely to mysteries, with a special collection of signed first editions. The interior is appropriately creepy, resembling an old library with dusty leather chairs and paisley wallpaper. Open M-F 11am-7pm, Sa 10am-6pm, Su 1-5pm.

Newsroom, 1753 Connecticut Ave. NW (☎332-1489). Metro: Dupont Circle. Thousands of American and foreign newspapers and magazines. Upstairs language room is devoted to language education books and tapes. Open daily 7am-9pm.

Sisterspace and Books, 1515 U St. NW (☎332-3433). Metro: U St.-Cardoza. Independent bookstore specializing in books by and about African-American women. Also offers writing workshops, special presentations (often at the Martin Luther King Jr. Library) and an assortment of crafts and shirts. Open M-Sa 10am-7pm, Su noon-5pm.

Travel Books & Language Center, Inc., 4437 Wisconsin Ave. NW (☎237-1322). Metro: Tenleytown-AU. Large store with excellent selection of travel books, maps, phrasebooks, and foreign newspapers and magazines. Open M-Sa 10am-10pm, Su noon-7pm.

CLOTHING

INDEPENDENT STORES

Commander Salamander, 1420 Wisconsin Ave. NW (☎337-2265), near O St. in Georgetown. A Georgetown original featuring chic clothes and trendy accessories. Vinyl dresses ($55), various t-shirts sporting glam declarations like "smack-a-ho" and "porn star" ($16-20), and a glorious flame-job courier's bag ($32) are just some of their over-the-top inventory. Open M-Th 10am-9pm, F-Sa 10am-10pm, Su 10am-7pm.

Hats in the Belfry, 1237 Wisconsin Ave. NW (☎342-2006), a block north of M St. in Georgetown. The huge selection of hats, both men's and women's, adapts you to any season. Some novelty hats (with attached hair), a surplus of baseball caps, and many accessories, especially scarfs. Open Su-Th 10am-10pm, F-Sa 10am-midnight.

Kobos Afrikan Clothiers, 2444 18th St. NW (☎332-9580), in Adams-Morgan. Although they cost an arm and a leg, these amazingly beautiful traditional and contemporary clothes from Western Africa are well worth a look. Interesting selections of jewelry and greeting cards with African pictures. Open M-Sa 11am-8pm.

La Petite Classique, 7716 Woodmont Ave. (☎(301) 986-1990). Metro: Bethesda. Friendly fashion advice is *gratis* at this retail store for women's petite sizes and accessories. A stress on utilitarian chic characterizes the more casual attire; formal dresses are luxuriously indulgent. 50% off rack. Open M-W 10am-7pm, Th 10am-8pm, F-Sa 10am-6pm, Su noon-5pm.

CHAIN STORES

Preppie mallrats, rejoice! Valhalla is found in Georgetown! All the old standbys are either in the Georgetown Park Mall or in satellites a short walk away.

Banana Republic, 3200 M St. NW (☎333-2554), on the corner of M St. and Wisconsin. Pricey yuppie duds and home furnishings for any suburban adventure. Open M-Th 10am-9:30pm, F-Sa 10am-10pm, Su 11am-8pm.

Benetton, 1200 Wisconsin Ave. NW (☎625-0443) offers pricey women's, men's and children's high-quality clothing. Open M-Th 10am-9pm, F-Sa 10am-10pm, Su noon-8pm.

Diesel, 1249 Wisconsin Ave NW (☎625-2780) in Georgetown. Presenting the "luxury of dirt" or low-brow as high-brow: broken-in jeans, t-shirts, and other more quirky items that are part cowboy, part runway model. This small boutique's offerings will cost you a pretty penny; jeans seldom retail for under $100. Open M-F 10am-8pm, Sa 11am-9pm, Su 12pm-5pm.

The Gap, 1258 Wisconsin Ave. NW (☎333-2805). Banana Republic's androgynous kid sibling. Good for staples like t-shirts, jeans, and of course, khakis. Open M-Th 10am-10pm, F-Sa 10am-11pm, Su 11am-7pm.

J. Crew, 3222 M St. NW (☎965-4090), in the Georgetown Mall. Demographics somewhere between the Banana Republic and Gap crowds. Women's and men's urban/suburban wear. Open M-Sa 10am-9pm, Su noon-6pm.

Patagonia, 1048 Wisconsin Ave. NW (☎333-1776). For the chic outdoorsy person's clothing and camping needs. Open M-F 11am-8pm, Sa 10pm-7pm, Su 11am-5pm.

Urban Outfitters, 3111 M St. NW (☎342-1012). Chain-store alterna-wear for alterna-teens with alterna-attitudes. Dudewear, chickwear, and other accessories for the alterna-life. Open M-Th 10am-10pm, F-Sa 10pm-11pm, Su 11am-9pm.

VINTAGE AND CONSIGNMENT

Deja Blue, 3005 M St. NW (☎337-7100), in Georgetown. Jeans, jeans, jeans: flairs to slim-fits, all secondhand ($25-40). Cutoffs ($10-15) and Hawaiian shirts ($16). Open M-Sa 11am-9pm, Su 11am-7pm.

Washington Ave & M St. in Georgetown

Designer Resale, 4815 Rugby Ave. Bethesda, MD (☎(301) 656-3722). Only designer labels make their way into this small consignment store crammed with women's clothes. Furs, shoes, and formal dresses are priced down from thousands to hundreds of dollars, but a rack of $10 cocktail dresses makes for a steal in after-five attire. Open M-Sa 10am-6pm.

Funk & Junk, 106½ N. Columbus St. (☎(703) 836-0749), just north of King St., in Alexandria. Metro: King St. Whether you're looking for an embroidered Chinese robe or a red velvet smoking jacket, chances are you'll find it here among the meticulously catalogued wealth of vintage items. Dynamite stash of Hawaiian shirts $25 and up. Open M-F 11am-7 or 8pm, Sa 12:30pm-7 or 8pm (call to take advantage of later hours), Su noon-5pm.

Meeps Fashionette, 1520 U St. (☎265-6546). Metro: U St.-Cardoza. Well-stocked vintage store in a beautiful old townhouse. Clothes and accessories from the past century are marked with an ontological decade. Don't forget to check out the Bargain Bathroom, where all clothes are half price. Open M-F 3-7pm, Sa noon-7pm, and Sun 2-6pm.

Discovery Channel Store

Runes & Relix, 2412 18th St. (☎265-4460), in Adams-Morgan. An eclectic gathering of vintage clothing that scratches below the surface of trend setting accessories: delicate 40s dresses, stoles, canes, and hats have quite the twinge of authenticity ($15-30). Vintage men's shirts in original packaging $15. Open M, W-Th noon-9pm, F-Sa noon-late, Su noon-6pm.

Secondi Consignment Clothing, 1702 Connecticut Ave. NW (☎667-1122) between R St. and Florida Ave. Metro: Dupont Circle. Upstairs boutique filled with discount designer clothing, shoes and other accessories. Coveting Prada pumps? Buy on consignment and pay a fraction of the cost. Prices go down the longer the items sit on the shelf: 20% discount after 1 month, 40% after 2. Open M-Tu 11am-6pm, W-F 11am-7pm, Sa 11am-6pm, Su 1-5pm.

Vintage to Vogue, 8121 Woodmont Ave. (☎(301) 656-0889). Metro: Bethesda. Billie Holiday chic with peacock feathers, beaded gloves, and formal gowns for under $100. A split between contemporary designers and vintage garments means a variety of styles. The back room is accessory heaven, full of shoes and purses. Open M-Sa 10am-6pm.

Takoma Park

COMICS

Aftertime Comics, Inc., 1304 King St. (☎ (703) 548-5030), in Alexandria. Metro: King St. Tiny store unpretentiously dedicated to the art of comic book collecting; wrapped DC and Marvel comics at various ages and prices are layered in thumb-through archives. Back issues of *MAD* and *Eerie* Magazines. Some new comics. Open W 11:30am-7pm, Th-Sa 11am-7pm, Su noon-6pm.

DEPARTMENT STORES

Bloomingdale's, (☎ (301) 984-4600) at the White Flint Mall, Kensington, MD. Metro: White Flint. Expensive, designer garments and home furnishings. Open M-Sa 10am-9:30pm, Su noon-6pm.

Filene's Basement (☎ 966-0208) at Mazza Galleries; 1133 Connecticut Ave. NW (☎ 872-8430) in Farragut. Metro: Farragut North. Marked down designer brands. Galleries location open M-Sa 9:30am-9pm, Su noon-6pm; Farragut open M-Sa 9:30am-8pm, Su noon-5pm.

Hecht's (☎ 628-6661), 12th and G St. NW. Metro: Metro Center. Another location in Friendship Heights (☎ (301) 654-7600). Strictly middle-class department store with clothes and housewares at average prices. 12th and G St. open M-Th 10am-8pm, F-Sa 9am-10pm, Su noon-6pm. Friendship Heights open M-Th 10am-9:30pm, F 10am-11pm, Sa 9am-11pm, Su 11am-7pm.

Lord & Taylor, 5255 Western Ave. NW (☎ 362-9600), at Jenifer St. Metro: Friendship Heights. Also at White Flint Mall, Kensington MD, (☎ (301) 770-9000). Metro: White Flint. Expensive clothes for folks with hefty credit. Friendship Heights open M-F 10am-9:30pm, Sa 10am-8pm, Su 11am-7pm. White Flint Mall open M-Th and Sa 10am-9:30pm, F 10am-10pm, Su 11am-7pm.

Macy's, 1000 S. Hayes St. in Arlington (☎ (703) 418-4488). Metro: Pentagon City. If Macy's doesn't have it, Nordstrom will. Open M-Sa 10am-9:30pm, Su 11am-6pm.

Nordstrom, 1400 S. Hayes St. (☎ (703) 415-1121), in Arlington. Metro: Pentagon City. Also at the Montgomery Mall in Bethesda. Renowned for its service, Nordstrom is an excellent place for makeup counter pampering. Both locations open M-Sa 10am-9:30pm, Su 11am-6pm.

EROTICA

Dream Dresser Boutique, 1042 Wisconsin Ave. NW (☎ 625-0373), in Georgetown. Serious erotic clothing boutique, with leather, lace, and latex. Fantasy-wear French maid's uniform $150. If "healthcare" is a turn-on, the naughty nurse outfits come in vinyl ($150) or rubber ($400). Some S&M, a few sexual toys. Open M-Sa 11am-8pm.

Pleasure Place, 1063 Wisconsin Ave. NW (☎ 333-8570), in Georgetown; 1710 Connecticut Ave. NW (☎ 483-3297) in Dupont Circle. Mostly sex toys, instructional books, and videos. Some clothes including leather, shoes, and boots. Wide array of penis-shaped novelty items. 18 and over. Georgetown location open M-Tu 10am-10pm, W-Sa 10am-midnight, Su noon-7pm. Dupont location open M-Sa 10am-midnight, Su noon-7pm.

GIFT

Al's Magic Shop, 1012 Vermont Ave. NW (☎ 789-2800). Metro: McPherson Square. Real magic tricks for serious magic junkies. Don't expect to have all your sleight of hand befuddlement magically cleared, however; store policy reads, "to learn the secret you have to buy the trick." For those who want to terrorize enemies (or friends and family), annoying pranks are available ($2). Open M-F 9:30am-5:45pm, Sa 9:30am-4:30pm.

Another Universe, M St. NW (☎ 333-8651), in Georgetown. Sci-Fi toys, comic books, novelty gifts. Star Wars, Star Trek, and large Xena: Warrior Princess section (Xena doll, $20) with some Hercules paraphernalia, including a bronze bust of Kevin Sorbo as Hercules. Open M-Th 11am-9pm, F-Sa 11am-10pm, Su 11am-7pm.

Discovery Channel Destination Store, 601 F St. NW (☎ 783-5751), in the MCI Center. Metro: Gallery Place-Chinatown. Find anything from a Harley Davidson keychain ($12) to a small fountain for your bedroom ($195) or a *Feng Shui* handbook ($21) that explains how to arrange a keychain and fountain to maximize your *chi* (positive energy). Four stories of science- and nature- oriented fun.

Diversities, 821 King St. (☎(703) 548-1236), in Alexandria. Metro: King St. The expensive gifts here are well worth a once over for their off-the-wall sensibilities. In addition to *chi*-geared fountains and big papier-maché ornaments, check out the display vest, concocted from yarn and screen door wire mesh ($89). Quirky Talistones are magical rocks ($6). Open daily 11am-6pm.

dZi, The Tibet Collection, 117 Carroll St. NW. (☎882 0008) Metro: Takoma. The staff here is eager to explain Tibetan garments, handicrafts, music, and politics. Thai clay buddhas from Ayutthaya ($2-12), handmade paper cards from Kathmandu ($2), and all the Dalai Lama's books are on display. Open Tu-Sa 11am-7pm, Su 11am-5pm.

Finewares, 7042 Carroll Ave. (☎(301) 270-3138). Metro: Takoma. This craft gallery sells pottery, silk, jewelry, and more at less-than-museum-store prices. Folk art in the more eclectic genres includes handmade magnets ($2) and cookie cutters ($3.50). Open M-F 11am-7pm, Sa 11am-6pm, Su 11am-3pm.

Ginza, 1721 Connecticut Ave. NW (☎331-7991). Metro: Dupont Circle. Japanese ceramics, gifts, and clothing run from tacky to tasteful. Open M-Sa 11am-7pm, Su noon-6pm.

The Irish Walk, 415 King St. (☎(703) 548-0118), in Alexandria. Metro: King St. If it's not Irish, it's not here. Claddagh rings, Guinness polo shirts, knick-knacks emblazoned with shamrocks, and Irish CDs and cassettes. Open M-Sa 10am-6pm, Su noon-5pm.

Leatherrack, 1723 Connecticut Ave, NW. (☎797-7401). Metro: Farragut North or Dupont Circle. In addition to all the sublimely hip leather gear and fetish accessories you can think of, Leatherrack also sells t-shirts and teddy bears. Open daily 10am-11pm.

Little German World, 1512 King St. (☎(703) 684-5344), in Alexandria. Metro: King St. Beyond the unexpressive Deutschland t-shirts and hats, this crash course in all things German has hand-painted ceramics, Bavarian painted wooden nutcrackers, Christmas ornaments, and a selection of Germany's über-important exports: beer steins ($10-200) and chocolate (bars $1.30). Open Tu-Sa 11am-6pm.

Martial Arts World, 1105 F St. NW. (☎347-2455) Metro: Metro Center. Get all the nun chucks ($10-22), fancy fighting knives ($9 and up), and attire you need to star in a kung fu flick. Also offers discounts on the finest collection of Bruce Lee t-shirts and films this side of Taiwan. Open M-F 10am-7pm, Su 11am-5pm.

Moose Chocolates, 1800 M St. NW (☎463-0992). Metro: Farragut North. Bizarre boutique and sweet shop has crazy fetish for moose: t-shirts, cards, stuffed animals, and a wall papered with news clippings about the shy, reclusive animals. Also sells weird practical jokes, toys, jewelry, clothing, and of course, chocolate. Open M-Sa 10am-6pm.

Now & Then, 6939 Laurel Ave. (☎(301) 270-2210). Metro: Takoma. This new age gift shop cleans up in the scented candle department. Cheap toys from childhood resurface with more allure than ever (25¢-$2). Open M-F 11am-7pm, Sa 10am-6pm.

Outlook, 1706 Connecticut Ave. NW (☎745-1469). Metro: Dupont Circle. Gift and card shop catering to a gay and lesbian clientele. Lots of cool slogans on t-shirts, bumper stickers, magnets, and hats. Get your own Tinky-Winky Teletubby—you know, the purple one Jerry Falwell outed. Open Su-Th 10am-10pm, F-Sa 10am-11pm.

Paula's Imports, 2405 18th St. NW (☎328-2176), in Adams-Morgan. A quirky assortment of clothes, jewelry, shoes, bedspreads, and gifts imported from Pakistan, India, and Africa. Open M-F 12:30-7pm, Sa 12:30-9pm, Su 12:30-6pm.

The Pet Gallery, Inc., 3204 O St. NW (☎333-3172), in Georgetown. A small, cramped boutique for pet lovers. Wind chimes, vests, and hats with animals on them for pet owners; cutesy collars, sweaters, and gourmet food for pets, all at upscale boutique prices. Open M-Sa 10am-6pm, Su noon-5pm.

Rockville Arts Place, 100 East Middle Ln., Rockville, MD (☎(301) 309-6900). Metro: Rockville. Alternative arts space showing works of local artists who you probably won't find in mainstream galleries downtown. A place to see, and purchase, works by up-and-coming artists before they make it big. Open Tu-Sa 10am-5pm.

Transcendence-Perfection-Bliss of the Beyond, 3428 Connecticut Ave. NW (☎363-4797). Metro: Cleveland Park. Is it a greeting card shop? A toy shop? A gift shop? A new age paraphernalia shop? Yes! It's all this plus a transcendent, perfect, blissful shrine to Sri Chinmoy. Open M, W and Sa 10am-6pm, Tu and Th-F 10am-7pm.

Women's Work, 1201 King St. (☎(703) 684-7376), in Alexandria. Metro: King St. Discoveries in this calm, wicker-walled gallery might include charms made from the bones of water buffalo ($3-5), stone frogs from Bali that play musical instruments ($29), or Japanese puppets made in Java, Indonesia ($25-45). All of the traditional textiles, pottery, and wood carvings are recently made by women from the Western Pacific islands. Open Tu-Sa 11am-6pm, Su noon-5pm.

MALLS

Georgetown would like to think that it has mastered the art of mall-building; what other D.C. neighborhood could blend the occasional cherub and hanging garden with fine stores like Polo/Ralph Lauren, bebe, The Limited, and Pretzelmaker? Located at 3222 M St. NW (☎298-5577), near Wisconsin Ave., **Georgetown Park's** palatial Victorian architecture shines even underground with brass galore and 150 stores. Take the Orange Line to Foggy Bottom and walk 20 minutes west. Shopping hours are M-F 10am-9pm, Sa 10am-7pm, and Su noon-6pm. If Georgetown Park doesn't wear you out, consider taking a pilgrimage to more consumer meccas:

Ballston Common Mall, 4238 Wilson Blvd. (☎(703) 243-8088), between Stuart and Randolph St., 1 block from the Ballston Metro. Walk straight from Metro stop into the nearest building facing the Metro and follow the signs. This large, bright mall is frequented by locals and employees of nearby businesses. Open M-Sa 10am-9pm, Su noon-6pm.

Chevy Chase Pavilion, 5335 Wisconsin Ave. (☎237-7900). Metro: Friendship Heights. The Friendship Heights Metro connects with the Chevy Chase; look for the signs in Metro tunnel. Residents of the Embassy Suites Hotel (located within the mall) and locals shop in this more mature mall. Open M-F 10am-8pm, Sa 10am-6pm, Su noon-5pm.

Fashion Centre at Pentagon City, 1100 S. Hayes St. (☎(703) 415-2400), in Arlington. Metro: Pentagon City. Metro stop connects with Fashion Centre. This sunny and cheery mall invites locals and tourists to its 160+ stores. Open M-Sa 10am-9:30pm, Su 11am-6pm.

Mazza Gallerie, 5300 Wisconsin Ave. (☎966-6114). Metro: Friendship Heights. Exit Metro on the Jennifer St. exit and go left. For the budget traveler and shopper, Mazza Gallerie could be renamed Mazza Museum; with names like Prada and Armani gracing the shelves, one may choose to sit back and admire rather than buy. Open M-F 10am-8pm, Sa 10am-7pm, Su noon-5pm.

Montgomery Mall, 7101 Democracy Blvd. (☎(301) 469-6000; www.montgomerymall.shoppingtown.com), in Bethesda. Metro: Grosvenor. Take Montgomery County bus #47 (approx 15min. ride from Grosvenor Station). One of the more distant malls in the D.C. area, Montgomery Mall offers quality shopping for those willing to make the trek. Staple mall stores like Gap and Express sell alongside A/X and bebe. Open M-Sa 10am-9:30pm, Su 11am-6pm.

Tyson's Corner Center, 1961 Chain Bridge Rd. (☎(703) 893-9400), off the Beltway at Exit 10B in McLean, VA. Open M-Sa 10am-9:30pm, Su 11am-6pm. **Tyson's Galleria** (☎(703) 837-7730), off the Beltway at Exit 11B. Open M-Sa 10am-9pm, Su noon-6pm. For both, take Metro Orange Line to West Falls Church and then take bus #28A, 28B, 5S, or 3B to Tyson's Corner Center, or a shuttle (M-F 6:40am-8:40pm; 75¢) to the Galleria.

MARKETS

Eastern Market (☎546-2698), on 7th St. SE between C St. and North Carolina Ave. From the Eastern Market Metro, walk up Pennsylvania Ave. towards the Capitol; Eastern Market is on the right. Butchers and bakers hawk their wares all week long. On weekends, they are joined by farmers who line the walk outside with flowers and produce—even in December. Sa is the best day for produce; Su tends to be more of a flea market. Open Tu-Sa 8am-6pm, Su 8am-4pm.

Georgetown Flea Market, in a parking lot where 34th St. and Wisconsin Ave. NW meet in northern Georgetown. Tired of tiny boutiques and assembly-line chain stores? Fed-up with air-conditioning? Push the shopping envelope and head over to the Georgetown Flea Market. Lots of cool, pre-owned stuff including faux jewelry, vintage clothing, china, and furniture. Vendors ready to wheel and deal. Fresh fruit and vegetable stalls, along with Uptown Bakery vendors selling energy-reviving sweets and foccacia. Open Su 9am-4pm (although true diehards get there as early as 6am) year-round, weather permitting.

Marvelous Market, 1511 Connecticut Ave. NW (☎332-3690). Metro: Dupont Circle. Mah-velous market with multitude of mah-velous pastries, breads, fresh veggies, fruits, and some prepared foods. Open M-F 8am-9pm, Sa 8am-9pm, Su 8:30am-7pm.

MUSEUM STORES

B'nai B'rith Klutznick Museum Shop, 1640 Rhode Island Ave. NW (☎857-6608), in Farragut. Metro: Farragut North. Fine jewelry and gifts include Murano glass dreidels handmade in Israel ($12-20) and Russian lacquered boxes ($280-2400). Open Su-F 10am-5pm. Closed Jewish and National Holidays.

Renwick Gallery Museum Shop (☎357-1445), Pennsylvania at 17th St. NW. Metro: Farragut North or Farragut West. The gift store to this museum of crafts is laden with instructions and materials for everything from quilting and jewelry making to the art of writing children's books. Craft items include handpainted silk. Open 10am-5pm daily.

Sackler Gallery Gift Shop (☎357-4880), in the Smithsonian's Sackler Gallery. Metro: Smithsonian. Asian-focused gift store with a great selection of books on Asian art and culture, tempting reproduction pieces, and a sizeable children's toys and books section. Open M-W, F-Su 10am-5:30pm, Th 10am-8pm.

MUSIC

NEW

12" Dance Records, 2010 P St. NW (☎659-2010), above the Subway restaurant. Metro: Dupont Circle. The throbbing music will draw you in and the dim lights and disco ball will make you want to stay. House, club, techno, go-go, underground, and the like on CDs and lots 'n' lots of vinyl. Open M-Th, Sa noon-9pm, F noon-midnight, Su 1-6pm.

Melody Record Shop, Inc., 1623 Connecticut Ave. NW (☎232-4002). Metro: Dupont Circle. New CDs with an impressive international section, especially the Latino music category. Some audio equipment, including CD players and accessories. Open Su-Th 10am-10pm, F-Sa 10am-11pm.

Music Now Records, 3209 M St. (☎338-5638), in Georgetown. LP collections in dance, techno, house, and drum 'n' bass. Some CDs and DJ mix tapes. Industrial decor matched by industrial and alterna-teen clothing. You can listen to most of the music in the store. Open M-Th noon-10pm, F noon-10:30pm, Sa 11am-10:30, Su noon-8pm.

Olsson's Books and Records. Offers classical, blues, jazz, gospel, and pop. See p. 127.

The Record Mart, upstairs at 217 King St. (☎(703) 683-4583), between Lee and Fairfax St., in Alexandria. Metro: King St. Jam-packed with music aficionados, this dusty LP warehouse has a killer selection of everything from chicken-killing punk to acid jazz. Hard-to-find used records, CDs, and tapes are sold at predictably outlandish prices. Open Su-Th 10am-9pm, F-Sa 10am-10pm, Su 10am-7pm.

Tower Records, 2000 Pennsylvania Ave. NW (☎331-2400), in Foggy Bottom; 6200 Little River Turnpike (☎(703) 256-2500), in Alexandria. A music staple; 2 floors packed with CDs, LPs and tapes of every genre. Staff are especially knowledgeable, and telescreens help locate almost every recording ever made. Open daily 9am-midnight.

USED

CD Warehouse, 3001 M St. NW (☎625-7101), in Georgetown. If Goth ain't your thang, check out their good selection of used CDs. Mostly mainstream pop, rock, jazz, some classical and movie soundtracks. The place doubles as a hip garage music-lover's haven—a bulletin board just inside the door is crammed with requests for musicians of all kinds. Open M-Th 11am-9pm, F-Sa 11am-10pm, Su noon-7pm.

DC CD, 2432 18th St. NW (☎588-1810), near Columbia Rd., in Adams-Morgan. Mostly modern music—alternapunk, indy bands, etc.—with a standard smattering of jazz, classical, and world music. A few LPs, new and used CDs, and video games. Feel free to listen to any CD in the store, a great way to get a feel for D.C.'s underground punk scene. Open M-Th noon-midnight, F noon-1am, Sa 10am-1am, Su noon-10pm.

Flying Saucer Discs, 2318 18th St. NW (☎265-3472), in Adams-Morgan. A quick fix for the electro-styled music junkie or anyone in search of obscure titles. A variety of new and used CDs covering everything from rare white label imports to classics, technofunk, lounge, acid jazz, and alternative rock. Just ask to listen to any CD in the store. Open M-F noon-9pm, Sa noon-8pm, Su noon-6pm.

Smash!, 3285½ M St. NW (☎337-6274), in Georgetown. New and used CDs, some LPs. Specializing in punk, hardcore, Goth, and alternative. Buy/sell/trade LPs, CDs. Also sells clothing. Open M-Th 11am-9pm, F-Sa 11am-11pm, Su noon-6.

MUSICAL INSTRUMENTS

The Guitar Shop, 1216 Connecticut Ave. NW (☎331-7333), on the 2nd fl. Metro: Dupont Circle. Jammed-packed store buys, sells, and repairs new and used guitars, banjos, mandolins, and just about anything else you can strum or pluck out. Amplifiers and other accessories available, plus instructional books and sheet music. Lessons available. Open M-F noon-7pm, Sa 11am-6pm.

The House of Musical Traditions, 7040 Carroll Ave. (☎(301) 270-9090). Metro: Takoma. A folk music enterprise with a passport: beautifully carved wooden instruments from all over the world are on display with an immense collection of international music. To explore your talent a bit less expensively, try a hand at the $1 nose flutes, fruit and veggie shakers ($6), or a $12 hand-painted Indian cane whistle. Open Tu-Sa 11am-7pm, Su-M 11am-5pm.

OUTDOOR

Sunny's Affordable Outdoor Store, 917 F St. (☎737-2032), between 9th and 10th St. in Old Downtown. Metro: McPherson Square. Camping gear, outdoor clothing, and sports supplies (wet suits to rollerblades) at unnervingly low prices. Open daily 9am-6:30pm.

POSTERS/PRINTS

Movie Madness, 1083 Thomas Jefferson St. NW (☎337-7064), in Georgetown off M St. between 30th and 31st. Small but good selection of movie posters, including classics, foreign, children's, cult, and new releases. Black-and-white still photographs and posters. Open M and W-Th noon-8pm, F-Sa noon-9pm, Su noon-6pm.

The Old Print Gallery, 1220 31st St. NW (☎965-1818), in Georgetown. Specializes solely in antique prints, maps, and posters. Shopping here is like ransacking a museum. Prices $45-200. Framing on site. Open M-Sa 10am-5:30pm.

PSYCHICS

Psychic Readings by Tiffany, 1221 Connecticut Ave. NW (☎887-5039). Wondering when you'll meet Mr. Tall-dark-and-handsome? Tiffany tells all for a reasonable $25. Beware, you might not like what you hear. Best to schedule an appointment, but feel free to drop by during normal business hours (M-F 9am-5pm).

Mrs. Natalie of Georgetown, 1500 Wisconsin Ave. NW (☎333-1245), near the intersection with P St. NW in Georgetown. Mrs. Natalie does various readings (palm $10, tarot card $30, crystal ball $25, psychic life $40, and aura $50) on an appointment or walk-in basis. Open M-Sa noon-7pm, Su 1-6pm.

SHOES

Shake Your Booty Shoes, 2324 18th St. NW (☎518-8205), in Adams-Morgan. Metro: Woodley Park-Zoo or Dupont Circle. Platform tennies, patterned fishnet pumps, and extreme spike heels for less than designer prices sold at this friendly yet sophisticated fashion retreat. Accessories (scarves, handbags, jewelry) sold at boutique prices. Open M-Sa noon-8pm and Su noon-6pm.

SKATE

East Coast Board Company, 10358 Lee Hwy. Arlington VA (☎(703) 352-4600), in the Fairfax Shopping Center. Skateboards ($60-150), snowboards ($225-600), boogie boards (around $125) and coffee ($1-3). Skate, street, and snow clothes for men and women in the $25-50 range. Great summertime snowboard deals. Open M-F 11am-9pm, Sa 10am-9pm, Su noon-7pm.

SPY

Counter Spy Shop, 1027 Connecticut Ave. NW (☎887-1717), in Farragut. Metro: Farragut North. No novelty items here; just state of the art goodies for your average spy, private investigator, or corporate eavesdropper. Highlights include a pager that goes off when someone in the room is using a wireless microphone; cameras with lenses the size of the tip of a ball point pen; and the "truth phone," which picks up nervous tremors in liar's voices. To get more than a glimpse at the hardcore spy equipment, make an appointment. Open M-F 9am-6pm, Sa 10am-3pm.

TATTOOS AND PIERCINGS

Grafixx Tattoos, 1340 G St. NW (☎628-9556). Metro: Metro Center. Get the Chinese character for Ecstasy *(muchu)* tattooed on your arm for $60, or use the on-site internet access to choose from thousands of designs. Tattoos start at $40. Graffix also does body piercing ($35 plus cost of jewelry) and carries a line of "Expressive" t-shirts, stickers and posters that are sure to shock the family. Open M-Sa 11am-8pm, Su by appt.

TOYS AND GAMES

FAO Schwarz, 3222 M St. NW (☎965-7000), in the Georgetown Park Mall. This branch of the king of toy stores still has the piano from the Tom Hanks movie *Big* on display. Steer right and dive into the gigantic stuffed animal selection. Barbie reigns supreme in her own feifdom mid-store. Open M-Sa 10am-9pm, Su noon-6pm.

Sullivan's Toy Store, 3412 Wisconsin Ave. NW (☎362-1343) Provides a nice mix of mass produced Pokemon dolls and more unique wood-carved toys. The perfect place to bring the kids and browse. Open M-Tu 10am-6pm, W-F 10am-7pm, Sa 10am-6pm, Su noon-5pm.

Entertainment

Culture-wise, Washington has earned its nickname as the "Cinderella city." Once upon a time, D.C. was an unsophisticated country bumpkin as far as urban centers went. That all changed when the **Kennedy Center** (see p. 143) opened in 1971. This fairy godmother of a megaplex whipped up a makeover, transforming the provincial capital into a cosmopolitan arts center. Today, the Kennedy Center proudly houses the **Washington Opera,** the **Washington Ballet,** and the **National Symphony Orchestra.**

If highbrow ain't yo' thang, there's always **U St.** (p. 138), D.C.'s kickin' punk and alternative rock outpost. Jazz mavens sing the blues in any number of D.C.'s smoky lounges (p. 140), as experimental plays unfold nightly in black boxes along the **14th St. theater district** (p. 141). The beauty of the Washington arts scene is that you can enjoy much of it without forking over any precious dough. Just consult the *City Paper* or the *Washington Post's* Friday "Weekend" or "Style" sections for packed schedules of free performances.

MUSIC

ROCK AND POP

The D.C. punk scene is, or at least was, one of the nation's finest. The biggest events take place at the sports arenas: **RFK Stadium** in the summer and the **USAir Arena** year-round. Tickets for many shows are available from **Protix** (☎ (410) 481-6500, (703) 218-6500, or (800) 955-5566) or **TicketMaster** (☎ 432-SEAT/7328; www.ticketmaster.com).

the on
dopedc

free music

Carter Barron Amphitheater,
located at 16th St. and Colorado Ave. in Rock Creek Park.
This 4200 seat complex hosts
varied artists on summer Saturdays and Sundays. Located at
16th and Colorado Ave in Rock
Creek Park, TicketMaster
☎432-7328 for tickets (from
free-$25). Gates open at 7pm.

Millennium Stage, 2700 F St.,
at the Kennedy Center. Free
concerts start at 6pm daily in
the Grand Foyer. ☎416-8000.

The **Twilight Tattoo Series**
(☎685-2851), on the Ellipse
between the White House and
the Washington Monument,
offers free tattoos. Just kidding.
Actually, the series features
parades and free music from
the Army brass band, July-Aug.
W at 7pm.

The Phillips Collection, 1600-
1612 21st St. (☎387-2151), at
Q St. NW, has a small concert
room for chamber music and
classical piano concerts, along
with the occasional jazz show.
Performances are held each
Sunday from September to May
at 5pm and are free with
museum admission.

THE U STREET SCENE

The U District, D.C.'s ear-blasting epicenter, has sent
the D.C. punk and rock scene off the Richter scale
for decades. Unfortunately, the area is not the safest:
be careful in the area at night. Use Metro: U St.-Car-
dozo for all of the following.

9:30 Club, 815 V St. NW (concertline ☎393-0930,
tickets ☎265-0930; www.930.com). D.C.'s most established local and alternative rock venue. Noteworthy before-
they-were-big bands that played here include Nirvana,
Smashing Pumpkins, and R.E.M. Cover usually $3 to see
local bands or $5-20 for nationally known acts, which sell
out weeks in advance. The crowd's ages and styles vary
according to concert line-up (18+). 50¢ surcharge for
advance tickets from box office. Cash-only box office open
M-F noon-7pm, until 11pm on show days, Sa 6-11pm on
show days, Su 6-10:30pm. Door time Su-Th 7:30pm-mid-
night, F-Sa 9pm-2am.

2:K:9, 2009 8th St. (☎667-7750; www.2k9.com), at U
St. This club pulls out the red carpet to prove that size
really does matter. With a capacity of 2000, 2:K:9 scores
big name acts like Eminem, Lil' Kim, and Ricky Martin.
Martini lounge, 45ft. bar, two mega dance floors. Complimentary valet parking available. Happy Hour Th 5-10pm, F
5-8pm. Cover $5-10. Women must be 18+, men 21+.
Open M, W-Sa 9pm-3am.

The Black Cat, 1831 14th St. NW (concertline ☎667-
7960, bar ☎667-4490; www.blackcatdc.com), between S
and T St. One of Washington's best live music venues also
offers weekly poetry and indie-movie nights (check weekly
listings). Plays host to a variety of alternative rock bands
like Foo Fighters, Garbage, and Radiohead. The Club,
where the bands perform, includes a full bar. The mellower
Red Room next door offers pool, pinball, leather booths,
couches, and the most rocking jukebox in the area. Happy
Hour (F-Sa 7-9pm). All ages. Some shows free, most $5-
10, but no cover for the Red Room. Open Su-Th 8pm-2am,
F-Sa 7pm-3am.

Velvet Lounge, 915 U St. (☎462-3213 or 462-ROCK to
hear samples of upcoming acts). Glowing with all the
intrigue of a hidden, indie venue, the Velvet Lounge is actually well-known for its rocking acts. Live bands upstairs 6
nights a week on a small, vine-covered stage where you'll
feel like you're lounging in your best friend's rumpus room.
Small bar downstairs. Happy hour F 5-8pm. 21+. Cover F-
Sa $5, Su-Th $3. Open Su-Th 8pm-2am, F-Sa 8pm-3am.

OTHER VENUES

The Garage, 1214-B 18th St. NW. (☎331-7123;
www.garage-dc.com). Metro: Dupont Circle. Two blocks
from the Metro. at the intersection of 18th St. and Connecticut Ave. Attracting many acts spanning from rock to
hip-hop, the Garage maintains an intimate environment
between the artist and the audience. The decor resembles
a highly-stylized mechanic shop/garage. Fairly well-known
acts have parked it here at the Garage, including John

Popper Band and Amel Larrieux (the other half of Groove Theory). Tickets $5-10. Tickets available at the Garage box office and all TicketMaster outlets.

Birchmere Music Hall, 3701 Mount Vernon Ave. (☎(703) 549-7500; www.birchmere.com). Metro: King St. This gruesomely decorated ex-factory exhumes an eclectic mix of modern to light rock acts including Aimee Mann, Shawn Colvin, and the Bacon Brothers. Most shows start 7:30-8:30pm. Box office opens 5pm on showdates only; buy advance tickets from TicketMaster. Tickets $15-25.

DAR Constitution Hall (☎628-4780), 18th and D St. NW. Metro: Farragut West (18th and I exit). Located 5 blocks south of Metro. One of Washington's most beautiful theaters presents both classy and raunchy acts to sold out crowds. Box office operated on the day of the show by the show's promoter. Order tickets from TicketMaster.

Lisner Auditorium (☎994-6800), 21st and H St. NW, at George Washington University. Where David Letterman broadcasts his D.C. shows. Lisner hosts plays, ballets, operas, and rock concerts by "alternative" acts like Weird Al Yankovic and Milton Nascimento (the leading vocalist of contemporary Brazilian sounds). Most shows start at 8pm. Tickets are sometimes free and rarely more than $25. Order from TicketMaster. Call for prices and purchase locations.

Velvet Lounge

Merriweather Post Pavilion (☎(410) 730-2424/5/6, TDD (410) 730-2345; www.mppconcerts.com), at Rte. 29 Columbia Pike in Columbia, MD, less than an hour from D.C. or Baltimore. Hosts popular bands like Counting Crows, No Doubt, Red Hot Chili Peppers, the Cure, and their ilk. Lawn tickets run $12.50-25; seats inside run $25-100. For tickets, call Protix.

Nation, 1015 Half St. SE (☎554-1500; www.nation-dc.com), 1 block from the Navy Yard Metro. This mega-concert hall is a truly inspired attempt to recreate its former glory as the Capital Ballroom, D.C.'s hammer site for funkadelica. In addition to world concerts and techno dance parties, alternative and mainstream acts from the summer of 2000 include Cherry Poppin' Daddies, the Deftones, and Big Bad Voodoo Daddy. Nation also hosts weekly theme dance parties: Tu Destination (Industrial and Gothic), W Mango, Th Nation 2000, F Buzz, Sa Velvet. All shows all ages, unless otherwise specified. Doors open at 7pm. Tickets available from TicketMaster.

Chief Ike's Mambo Lounge

State Theater, 220 N. Washington St. (☎(703) 237-0300; www.thestatetheatre.com), ¾mi. from E. Falls Church Metro. Renovated 1935 movie theater brings in great emerging bands. Come early for dinner and choice of seats (first-come, first-served), although all seats are fantastic. Box office (open 7pm) sells tickets for same night shows only. Advanced sales for big name groups handled through TicketMaster. Tickets $5-50.

The Wolftrap Filene Center, 1551 Trap Rd., Vienna, VA (☎(703) 255-1900; www.wolftrap.org), about 45min. from D.C. Hosts acts ranging from Patti LaBelle to Mary J. Blige. Ticket prices vary according to the performance, though lawn seats are generally $10 cheaper than pavilion seats. Tickets available through Protix.

CLASSICAL MUSIC

ORCHESTRA AND CHAMBER MUSIC

Dumbarton Concert Series at Dumbarton Church, 3133 Dumbarton St. NW (☎965-2000), near Wisconsin Ave. in Georgetown.

Black Cat

▰ ▰ ▰ ▰ ▰ ▰ ♫ ▰ ▰ ▰ ▰ ▰ ▰ ▰

Sponsors chamber, choral, jazz, and other concerts in a historic, candlelit hall Oct.-May. Reserve tickets at least 1 week in advance. Tickets $18-24, students and seniors $3 off. Box office hours 9:30am-5:30pm.

Dumbarton Oaks Friends of Music Series, 1703 32nd St. NW (☎ 339-6436), at the Dumbarton Oaks Museum. Winter subscription concert series. See Museums, p. 119.

The Folger Consort, 201 E. Capitol St. (box office ☎ 544-7077), in the Elizabethan Theatre. The resident ensemble at the Folger Shakespeare Library brings 16th- and 17th-century music to the stage. Box office open daily 10am-5pm. Tickets $25-40; half-price tickets at the door with student ID, or in advance for any Su 5:30pm performance.

Kreeger Museum, 2401 Foxhall Rd. NW (☎ 338-3552), in Upper Northwest. Regular concerts by professionals and student performers are held in the Kreeger Museum's intimate concert hall. Ticket prices vary; call Protix to purchase tickets.

National Symphony Orchestra, (☎ 416-8000; www.kennedy-center.org). In its 69th season, the NSO continues to delight Washington all over town, but primarily in the Kennedy Center's Concert Hall. Look for the Beethoven Festival to follow up the succesful 2000 Mozart Festival. Box office hours M-Sa 10am-9pm, Su noon-9pm.

OPERA COMPANIES

Washington Opera (☎ 295-2400, TTY 416-8534; www.dc-opera.org). Under the awesome leadership of artistic director and opera superstar Placido Domingo, performances in the Kennedy Center's Eisenhower Theatre sell out at an amazing pace. The 2001 season includes *Don Quichotte*, *Il Trovatore*, and *Parsifal*. Tickets weekday shows $40-234, weekend $41-259.

Summer Opera Theatre Company, 3801 Harewood Rd. NE (☎ 319-4000), in the Hartke Theatre at Catholic University. Metro: Brookland-CUA. The second-largest opera company in D.C. performs classics like Puccini's *Madama Butterfly*. Performances June-July; call for schedule. Tickets $32-55.

Opera Theatre of Northern Virginia, 125 S. Old Glebe Rd. (☎ (703) 528-1433), at intersection of Rte. 50 and Glebe Rd. in Thomas Jefferson School. Performances for kids and adults. Season runs Sept.-Apr. Look for *Rocky and Bullwinkle* (for children) and *Lost in the Stars* (for adults) in 2000. Tickets $20-35.

JAZZ AND THE BLUES

Washington has a surprisingly diverse and thriving jazz and blues scene, with venues perfect for anyone's budget. A free lunchtime jazz series takes place downtown at the **Corcoran Gallery,** 17th St. between E St. and New York Ave. NW (☎ 638-3211), in the Hammer Auditorium every Wednesday at 12:30pm. (Metro: Farragut West or Farragut North.) The **Kennedy Center** and the **Smithsonian Museums** also sponsor free shows, especially in the summer.

Blues Alley, 1073 Rear Wisconsin Ave. NW (☎ 337-4141), in an alley below M St. running between Wisconsin and 31st St., in Georgetown. Cool jazz in an intimate, candlelit supper club. This is a listening club, not a place for conversation. Past performers include Eartha Kitt, Nicholas Payton, and Wynton Marsalis. The New Orleans atmosphere solidified by the bread pudding ($4) and other authentic Creole dishes served 6-10pm (entrees $15-20). Late fare, $4-9.50, during the 10pm show. Beer $5; mixed drinks from $7. Min. $7 food or drink per set. Ticket prices $14-40, plus $1.75 surcharge if bought in advance. Students recieve half off cover during 10pm shows Su-Th. Shows at 8 and 10pm, additional midnight show on Sa.

Madam's Organ, 2461 18th St. NW (☎ 667-5370), near Columbia Rd. in Adams-Morgan. Metro: Woodley Park. Voted one of the 25 best bars in the nation by *Playboy Magazine*. Neon signs above the door shout "Sorry, we're open" and advertise the party as "where the beautiful people go to get ugly." An eclectic crowd mingles among the pink walls, dark red lighting, and upside down deer heads, and listens to live blues, rock or bluegrass nearly every night. The 2nd fl. is **Big Daddy's Love Lounge and Pick Up Joint,** which pulls crowds in for pool. Others lounge on the hideaway roof deck with $1 off all beers and rail drinks til 10pm Su-Th. Cover $3-5. Drafts $3-4; mixed drinks $4. Open Su-Th 5pm-2am, F-Sa 5pm-3am.

One Step Down, 2517 Pennsylvania Ave. NW (☎955-7141), near M St. Metro: Foggy Bottom-GWU. Smaller, more casual, and less expensive than Blues Alley. Mellow tunes from the well-stocked jukebox soothe blues fans in this fave stone dig with stained glass windows. Daily Happy Hour (5:30-7:30pm) features $2 Bud. Local jazz M and W-Su, out-of-town talent F-Sa. Cover M-Tu $7, W-Th $5, F-Su $13. Open daily 5:30pm-2am.

Saloun, 3239 M St. (☎965-4900), in Georgetown. Local bar with live music nightly. Mostly local bands play jazz (Su-Tu and Th) and R&B (W and F-Sa). Shows start at 9pm. Cover Su-Th $2, F-Sa $3. Extensive beer menu ($5-9). 2-drink min. during performances, which they don't seem to enforce. Open M-Th 5pm-2am, F-Sa 5pm-3am, Su 4pm-3am.

Vegas Lounge, 1415 P St. NW (☎483-3971), 4 blocks east of Dupont Circle. Metro: Dupont Circle. Tiny tables, dim red lights, and clouds of smoke give this blues den a true Vegas air. Vocal-intensive jazz bordering on soul. Shows Tu-Th 8pm, F-Sa 9pm. Professional jam sessions Tu-W. Th night free for students with college ID. Cover $7-15, depending on the band. Wheelchair accessible. Open Tu-Th 8pm-1am, F-Sa 8pm-3am. **Be careful in this area at night.**

Whitlow's on Wilson, 2854 Wilson Blvd. Arlington, VA (☎(703) 276-9693). Metro: Clarendon. A strange combination of New Orleans jazz club and Mexican villa, this large airy joint features a rotating schedule of live blues, jazz and rock music. Call ahead for the weekly schedule. Half-price burgers M; 25¢ wings all day T; $6 pitchers of Sierra Nevada all day W. Happy Hour (M-F 4-7pm): $1 off drafts, rails, house wines. 21+ after 9:30pm. Cover Th-Sa $3, Tu $5. Open daily 11:30am-2am.

THEATER AND DANCE

D.C. enjoys a very active and experimental theater and dance scene, featuring everything from massive Broadway hits at the Kennedy Center to small, modern dance performances. Thespians particularly thrive in Washington's **14th Street theater district,** where tiny repertory companies explore and experiment with truly enjoyable results. However, Woolly Mammoth, Studio, the Source, and the Church Street Theaters dwell in a potentially dangerous neighborhood east of Dupont Circle, near or on 14th St. NW between P and Q St., so **don't go there alone at night.**

VENUES AND COMPANIES

THEATER

Arena Stage, 1101 6th St. (☎488-4377, TTY 484-0247; www.arenastage.org), at Maine Ave. SW. Metro: Waterfront. Often cited as the best regional (non-New York) theater company in America, the 45-year-old theater has its own company and 3 different stages: the **Kreeger** and **Fichandler** stages present new and classic plays, while the **Old Vat Theater** hosts more experimental productions. The 2001 50th Anniversary season features performances of *Coyote Bill's North America,* and Tennessee Williams' *A Streetcar Named Desire.* Arena's **It's an Alternative** series includes a reception for gay and lesbian audiences (F; $40 plus cost of ticket). Box office open M-Sa 10am-

ESSENTIAL
INFORMATION

TICKETS

Ticket Place (☎842-5387), in the Pavilion at the Old Post Office, 1100 Pennsylvania Ave. at Pennsylvania Ave. and 12th St. NW. Metro: Federal Triangle. Sells half-price (plus 10% surcharge) day-of-show tickets for theater, music, dance, and special events on a walk-up basis. Cash, travelers checks, Visa, Mastercard and some debit cards accepted (no credit cards for TicketMaster events). Some full-price advance sales available. Open Tu-Sa 11am-6pm (some discount tickets for shows Su-M sold on Sa). Call for available shows.

USHERING

If tickets are out of your price range, don't despair: usher. All of the regular companies need unpaid help in the aisles, and once the paying crowds are inside, ushers usually watch the play for free. Call as far in advance as you can.

▪ ▐ ▌ ▦ ▥ ▐ ♫ ▧ ▨ ▮ ▪ ▐ ▐ ▤

8pm, Su noon-8pm. In the Fichandler and Kreeger, tickets $25-45, students 35% off, seniors 20% off; half-price tickets usually available 1½hr. before start of show. In the Old Vat, tickets $25-32, including a pre-performance pint and sausage roll in the adjacent pub.

Church Street Theater, 1742 Church St. NW (☎265-3748; www.smart.net/~efm). Metro: Dupont Circle. This medium-sized theater houses productions ranging from Shakespeare to Mamet. Performances year-round W-Sa 8pm, Su 7pm. Box office opens 1hr. before showtime. Last-minute tickets sometimes available from Ticket Place. Tickets $15-25, with student and senior discounts decided on a show-by-show basis.

Discovery Theater, 900 Jefferson Dr. SW (☎357-1500), located in the Smithsonian Arts and Industry Building. This large theater features plays for children, such as *The Adventures of Leif Ericson* and *Pinocchio*. $5, groups of 10 or more $3.50 per person. Reserve by calling the box office, open M-F 10am-4pm. Summer performances Tu-F 10 and 11:30am, Sa 11:30am and 1pm. Call for schedule and winter performance hours.

Ford's Theatre, 511 10th St. NW (☎347-4833; www.fordstheatre.org). Metro: Metro Center, 11th St. exit. The theater where President Lincoln was assassinated now infrequently hosts new American musicals and big-budget shows. *A Christmas Carol* plays every year Nov.-Jan. Tickets $27-50 (Sa is most expensive). Rush tickets available for seniors (55+) and students 1hr. before showtime ($18). Box office open M-F 10am-6pm, Sa-Su noon-6pm, and 30min. before each performance.

GALA Hispanic Theatre, 1625 Park Rd. NW (☎234-7174; www.incacorp.com/gala), near Mt. Pleasant Rd. in the Sacred Heart School. Take the #42 bus up Columbia to 16th St. Turn left, and walk 3 blocks to Park Rd., then turn left again; GALA is behind the Sacred Heart School. The national award-winning *Grupo de Actores Latino Americanos* present 4 plays by modern or classical Latin American or Spanish authors each season (Sept.-June). Most plays are in Spanish (a simultaneous English translation is usually provided via headset). Productions Th-Sa 8pm, Su 4pm. Reservations recommended. Box office open M-F 10am-6pm. Tickets $20, students and seniors $15-18.

The Kennedy Center (☎416-8000), 2700 F St. NW, near 25th St. and New Hampshire Ave. The Kennedy Center contains 2 theaters, the **Terrace Theater** and the **Theater Lab** (see **Sights,** p. 66), and a larger stage for Broadway productions. *Shear Madness* still draws crowds after its 12th anniversary. Coming in 2001 are *It Ain't Nothin' But The Blues* and *Dinner Party*. Tickets $10-75 depending on the show, day, and time you desire, but reduced pricing is available (see p. 139). Half-price discounts for seniors and students. Box office open M-F 9am-5:30pm

Le Neon Theatre, 4350 N. Fairfax Drive, #127 (☎(703) 243-6366; www.leneon.org). Performance space is **The Rosslyn Spectrum,** 1601 N. Kent St. in Rosslyn. A multi-cultural French-American theater with performances in both English and French. New takes on Molière and Beckett are standard fare, as well as contemporary French plays. Box office open M-F 10am-5pm.

Lincoln Theater, 1215 U St. NW (☎328-6000), directly across from the U St.-Cardozo Metro; take the 13th St. exit from the station. Built in 1920, the Lincoln was the first theater in the area to show movies to an integrated audience. Now the small historic venue hosts plays, opera, jazz, movies, and comedy. Tickets $25-40. Box office open M-F 10am-6pm, Sa-Su noon-5pm (opens 2 hrs. before shows on show days). Tickets also available through TicketMaster.

National Theatre, 1321 Pennsylvania Ave. NW (☎628-6161; www.nationaltheatre.org). Metro: Metro Center or Federal Triangle. Big-name, big-budget, big-capacity theater often hosts visitors from Broadway such as *Miss Saigon* at big Broadway prices ($35-75, sometimes special $15 matinees). The fall-spring "Monday Night at the National" program puts on a free variety show in the lounge (info ☎783-3372), and free old movies play as part of the "Summer Cinema" program on M evenings. "Saturday Morning at the National" is a free kids' events. Half-price tickets available for students, seniors, military, and the disabled Tu-W (8pm) and Su matinees (2pm).

Open Theatre/T.U.T.A., 1725 17th St. NW #404 (☎234-9816; www.visuallink.net/optima). The Utopia Theatre Asylum breaks ground as one of D.C.'s most progressive performance groups, largely occupied with laboratory theatre research and kinetic art. T.U.T.A.'s prospective projects for 2001 include Rumi's *Mathnazi*.

Signature Theatre, 3806 Four Mile Run Dr. (☎(703) 820-9771). Metro: Pentagon and then take #7 bus. Five productions each season (Nov.-May). 2001 features *Rhythm Club,* In *The Absence of Spring, Gypsy,* and *In The Garden*. Tickets $21-30, available from ProTix or at the box office open M-F 10am-6pm.

Shakespeare Theatre at the Lansburgh, 450 7th St. NW at Pennsylvania Ave. (☎547-1122, TTY 638-3863; www.shakespearedc.org). Metro: Archives-Navy Memorial. The Bard-heavy repertoire for the 2001 season includes *Richard II, Timon of Athens, The Two Gentlemen of Verona,* and *Friedrich Schiller's Don Carlos.* Call months in advance for reservations, ticket prices ($14-56), performance times, and discounts for students and seniors. Standing-room tickets ($10) are available 1hr. before showtime. **"Free for All"** performance series in June (☎334-4790) presents free performances at the Carter Barron Amphitheater in Rock Creek Park. Obtain free tickets in advance from the box office.

The Source Theater, 1835 14th St. NW (☎462-1073), between S and T St. Metro: U St.-Cardozo. 14th St.'s oldest, most established "alternative" theater. Produces the Washington Theater Festival (30 brand new shows) every summer at various D.C. locations, in addition to its regular off-Broadway shows. The 2001 season features Mamet's *American Buffalo,* as well as *The Most Fabulous Story Ever Told.* Shows W-Su. Tickets sold through Box Office Tickets (☎884-0060; $25). Students and seniors $2 off. Ushers watch for free. Source box office open 30min. prior to show.

Stage Guild, Carroll Hall, 924 G St. NW (☎529-2084). Metro: Metro Center or Gallery Place. Specializing in new plays and lesser-known plays by well-known playwrights. 4 plays in the Sept.-May season. W-Th evening and Sa-Su matinees $20, F-Sa evenings $23. Call well in advance for group rates (10 or more qualify for half-price tickets). Box office open M-F 10am-6pm.

Studio Theater, 1333 P St. NW (☎332-3300), at 14th St. Metro: Dupont Circle. Contemporary theater on 2 Mainstages, with a Second Stage series for up-and-coming playwrights. (Mainstage plays W-Su, Second Stage F-Su). Shows for Jan.-May 2001 are as follows: *The Vigil, Trudy Blue, The Invention of Love,* and *Jitney.* Box office open M-Tu 10am-6pm, W-Su 10am-9pm. Tickets for Second Stage $15; for Mainstage $19.50-38.50. Students with ID, military personnel, and seniors $5 off Mainstage shows if purchased in advance; students can get half-price tickets 30min. before shows, depending on availability.

Theater of the First Amendment, at TheaterSpace Center for the Arts at George Mason University in Fairfax, VA (admin ☎(703) 993-2915, box office ☎(703) 993-8888; www.gmu.edu/cfa). Experimental theater company hosts a number of area premieres on contemporary issues of political, emotional, and social importance. Recent productions include *Much Ado About Nothing* and a revisionary take on Marlowe's *Dr. Faustus.* Box office open Tu-Sa 10am-6pm.

Warner Theatre (☎783-4000), 13th St. and Pennsylvania Ave. NW. Metro: Metro Center or Federal Triangle. Next door to the National Theatre, the Warner Theatre also hosts big names from Broadway such as *Descending the Caveman,* in addition to many music and ballet acts. Box office open M-F 10am-4pm, Sa noon-3pm, and 2hrs. before each performance. TicketMaster office located here as well. Tickets $21-76.

Washington Shakespeare Company, at the Clark St. Playhouse, 601 S. Clark St. (administration ☎(703) 418-4807, box office ☎(703) 418-4808), in Arlington. The fluency of this local based company stretches beyond the Bard to produce more experimental, cutting-edge existential dramas. Prospective projects for 2001 include *Bloodwedding.* Box office open M-F 10am-6pm.

ESSENTIAL INFORMATION

THE KENNEDY CENTER

The Kennedy Center (☎416-8000; see p. 142), 25th St. and New Hampshire Ave. NW, is home to the well-respected National Symphony Orchestra conducted by **Leonard Slatkin.** The orchestra usually performs at the Kennedy Center's Concert Hall, and tickets are normally on the expensive side ($18-47). However, the center has the largest discount program in the country, offering 50% off tickets to most shows for full-time students, seniors, disabled travelers, and military personnel. In addition, the center also has a sliding scale fee available to people of limited incomes; ask at the ticket office for further information. The NSO also gives free concerts each year on **Memorial Day,** the **Fourth of July,** and **Labor Day.** The **Millennium Stage** is a free concert series which takes place at the Kennedy Center every day at 6pm and by the Capitol on Tu and Th at noon; other free concerts depend on the season; call the Kennedy Center box office for details. **Chamber music** in the Kennedy Center is sometimes cheap or free, especially during December's events, which culminate in the pre-Christmas **Messiah** sing-along. The spectacular **Washington Opera** also performs in the Kennedy Center, as does the nationally recognized **Washington Ballet** (see p. 144).

Woolly Mammoth, 1401 Church St. NW (☎393-3939; www.woollymammoth.net). Metro: Dupont Circle. Take P St. east away from the Circle to 14th St. Make a left on 14th St. and another left on Church St. One of Washington's best-known alternative theaters welcomes aspiring play-wrights to send in manuscripts, which it then produces. Box office open M-F noon-6pm and 1hr. before showtime. Purchase tickets through **Protix** (☎(703) 218-6500; open M-F 10am-9pm). Tickets $16-29, 25 and under $10, $3 discounts for seniors and groups of 8 or more.

DANCE

Dance Place, 3225 8th St. NE (☎269-1600). Metro: Brookland-CUA. A dance school that focuses on modern movement and African dance. Professional or student performances every weekend throughout the year. **Dance Africa D.C. Festival** held here every June. Tickets $15, students $12. Call for schedule of events. Office open M-F 10am-5pm.

Washington Ballet, 3515 Wisconsin Ave. NW (☎362-3606). Nationally recognized company performs a full season annually at the Kennedy Center (see p. 142), as well as performing *The Nutcracker* every Dec. at the Warner Theatre. Under new Artistic Director Septime Webre, the 2001 program will feature *Peter Pan: Feel Like A Child Again*, as well as *Romeo and Juliet*.

COMEDY

Chelsea's, 1055 Thomas Jefferson St. NW (☎298-8222), below M St. in Georgetown. Home of the Capitol Steps, a renowned political satire troupe composed of Congressional staffers, whose proximity to the antics of the federal government means never running out of material for their hilarious musical parodies. Caters to a 30- and 40-something crowd. Performances most F at 8pm, Sa at 7:30pm; doors open 2hr. early. Tickets $33.50 with $10 credit towards drinks, $50 with dinner and parking. Live bands Su-Th 10pm-2am, F-Sa 10pm-4am. M Ethiopian; W Arabic; Th-Sa Latin, Su Iranian. No jeans. $5-10 cover.

The Improv, 1140 Connecticut Ave. (☎296-7008; www.dcimprov.com), between L and M St. in Farragut. Metro: Farragut North. Cheap, wacky comedy for a young crowd. Features 3 different comic acts at each show with occasional guests from Def Comedy Jam and Comedy Central. The Improv doubles as a restaurant at all shows before 10pm (preference seating given to dining patrons) and generally sells out on weekends; you may want to buy tickets in advance. Tu-Th shows $12, F-Sa $15. Shows Su-Th at 8:30pm, F-Sa at 8 and 10pm.

The Fun Factory, 3112 Mt. Vernon Ave. (☎684-5212), in Shops at the Calvert, in Alexandria. Lodged within a shabby strip mall, the flaming blue facade battles air-brushed t-shirts for tacki-ness and Hollywood for expertly manufactured laughs. The attack at improvisational comedy drags in compulsory audience participation and jokes with a strict PG rating. Be prepared for anything. Shows F-S 8 and 10:30pm. Tickets $10.

POOL

Atomic Billiards, 3427 Connecticut Ave. (☎363-7665), close to the Metro. Take the east exit of the Cleveland Park Metro and walk straight down Connecticut. Metro: Cleveland Park. A crowd of 20-30-something locals fills Atomic Billiards, along with 2 Jetsonian murals behind the bar and 50s vintage furniture along the walls. Over 30 board games pass the long wait for 6 tables ($5 per person per hr. before 9pm, $12 per doubles per hr. after 9pm). Beer, selections of scotch and bourbon, and abundant coffee drinks. Free darts. Happy Hour daily until 8pm; nightly beer spe-cials. Open M-Th 4pm-1am, F 4pm-2am, Sa noon-2am, Su noon-midnight.

Babe's Billiards Cafe, 4600 Wisconsin Ave. NW (☎966-0082), in Tenleytown, exit the west side exit of Tenleytown-AU metro, go left on Wisconsin for 2 blocks. Metro: Tenleytown-AU. A bright pool hall/restaurant with a crowd ranging from mid 20s-40s. Happy Hour (M-F 3-7pm) means $2 domestic beers, rail drinks $3.15. Pool starts at $7 per person per hr. Late-night breakfast served from midnight on. 19+; after 9:30pm 21+. Open M-Th 3pm-3am, F-Sa 1pm-4am, Su 1pm-3am.

Buffalo Billiards, 1330 19th St. NW (☎331-7665), across from the 19th St. Metro exit. Metro: Dupont Circle. Wild Wild West theme in a not-so-wild saloon-wannabe scene, but 29 tables keep billiard cowboys happy. On weekends be prepared for the haze of cigar smoke. Regular rates per person: $5 per hr., $10 for 2hr., $12 for 3hr., $14 for 4hr.; $2-4 more Th-Sa 8pm-close. Free les-sons with Gus the Pool Shark (M and W 6-9:30pm). Happy Hour M-F 4-8pm, Sa-Su 1-7pm: $2.50 domestic pints and $3 rails. Open M-Th 4pm-2am, F 4pm-3am, Sa 1pm-3am, Su 1pm-1am.

Georgetown Billiards, 3251 Prospect St. NW (☎965-7665), in Georgetown. Definite college hangout, with a nouveau-pub feel. 18+. 13 pool tables $7-14 per hr., $1-2 more on weekends. Also features a ping-pong table and 4 dart boards for the tablesport-challenged. Happy Hour (daily 6-8pm) is 50% off. Pub fare ($4-7) served from 10pm to closing. Open M-Th 6pm-2am, F 6pm-3am, Sa 4pm-3am, Su 4pm-1am. Winter hrs. prone to change: call ahead.

LITERARY LIFE

With one of the biggest populations of working writers in the country, D.C. has a fine appreciation for the written word. For cafe-hoppers interested in a mellow nightlife scene, there are a number of cafes and other venues around the city hosting readings and workshops for literary-charged crowds.

Brooklands Cup of Dreams Coffee House, 3629 12th St. NE (☎526-6562). Metro: Brookland. Enjoy the relaxed evening entertainment in this community hangout spot far removed from the self-conscious bohemia of city coffeehouses. Each fabulous espresso drink is $1.25. Open poetry readings W 8pm (poets arrive at 7pm). Other evening entertainment includes open-mic M, and local live jazz Th-F. Open M-Tu 6am-9pm, W-F 6am-midnight, Sa 8am-11pm, Su 8am-3pm.

Iota Poetry Series, 2832 Wilson Blvd. (☎(703) 522-8340), in Arlington. Metro: Clarendon. At the Iota Bar and Restaurant, featuring local poets and open-mic nights every W (signups at 8pm). Poetry series occurs 2nd Su of each month at 6pm. Free.

St. Elmo's Coffee Pub, 2300 Mt. Vernon Ave. (☎(703) 739-9268), at the corner of Del Ray Ave. Metro: King St. This laid-back neighborhood coffee bar is as close to barefoot as Alexandria gets. Two rooms piled with old couches and community artwork create an atmosphere part Chicago beat scene, part Mexican commune. Cosmic crusaders contemplate verse at weekly poetry readings (weekly schedule varies; call ahead). Live acts at least 4 days a week also include folk, jazz, blues, and acoustic rock (W, F-Sa 8pm-10pm, Th 7:30pm-9:30pm, Su 3-5pm; no cover, donations appreciated). Open M-Sa 6am-10pm; Su 7am-6pm.

The Writer's Center, 4508 Walsh St. (☎(301) 654-8664; www.writer.org), off Wisconsin Ave. The heart of literary life in the D.C. area, The Writer's Center has workshops, calls for submissions, and poetry and play readings by nationally known authors. The center's staff is eager to discuss every novel, poem, and play on sale in the very select offerings of **The Book Gallery** just inside the doors. Some evenings feature open poetry readings (or open-mic for songwriters) at the center's **New Words Coffeehouse,** although don't show up looking for a good cuppa joe. Other nights highlight special guest readers ($5). Open Tu-Th 10am-10pm, F 10am-6pm, Sa 9am-5pm.

MOVIES

D.C. is awash in movie theaters, although for those unfamiliar with urban theaters, you should expect incredibly small screens. The alternative is found at **The Uptown** in Cleveland Park, which with its gigantic screen and booming sound sytem is the perfect place to catch a special effects-laden film. Check *The Washington Post*'s "Style" or "Weekend" sections ("Weekend" published Fridays) or *City Paper* for complete listings of movies showing in the District, or call ☎333-3456 for a $1.50 surcharge, and use the automated movie info line to find a film anywhere in the city. Find reviews and showtimes online at **www.washingtoncitypaper.com.** The **Hirshhorn Museum** (☎357-3091), on the Mall at Independence Ave. and 7th St. SW, runs three separate weekly film series featuring foreign/independent films, documentaries about modern art, and animated movies for kids; call for a schedule. **The Museum of American History** also hosts classic films, as does the **National Gallery of Art.** The excellent **American Film Institute** (☎785-4600), at the Kennedy Center, shows classic foreign and avant-garde films, usually two per night. American University film classes show movies most nights on a varying schedule, free and open to the public; for a schedule, call ☎885-2042 (8:30am-5pm). **The National Theatre,** 1321 Pennsylvania Ave. NW (☎783-3372), runs canonical American films.

AMC Union Station 9, 50 Massachusetts Ave. NE (☎(703) 998-4262), on the lower level of Union Station. Shows the largest lineup of 1st-run hits on decent-sized screens. Before 4pm $5.50, between 4-6pm $4.50, after 6pm $8. Students, seniors, and ages 2-13 $5.50. Wheelchair accessible.

Cineplex Odeon cinemas have identical pricing schemes: before 6pm $5.50, after 6pm $8 (seniors and under 11 $5). Call ☎333-FILM and dial the extension number for showtimes: 5612 Connecticut Ave. (#787), in Upper Northwest; 5100 Wisconsin Ave. (#788), in Friendship Heights; 1350 19th St. NW (#792), in Dupont Circle.

The Foundry, 1055 Thomas Jefferson St. (☎333-8613), half-block south of M St. in Georgetown. This 2nd-run movie house shows all those flicks you thought you missed for only $3, with some first-runs up to $7.50.

Outer Circle, 4849 Wisconsin Ave. NW (☎244-3116), across from Safeway. Metro: Tenleytown-AU. First-run foreign films, some exclusive engagements. Admission $8, seniors and children under 11 $5.50. All shows before 6pm $5.50.

Uptown Theater, 3426 Connecticut Ave. NW (☎966-5400). Metro: Cleveland Park. Big blockbusters in a vintage theater with a mongo-big screen. Admission $7.75, seniors and children under 11 $5. All shows before 6pm $5.25.

SPORTS AND RECREATION

PARTICIPATORY SPORTS

HIKING, JOGGING, ROLLERBLADING AND BIKING TRAILS AROUND D.C	
THE MALL	Cool runnings near the museums. The Reflecting Pool, Constitution Gardens, and West Potomac Park are better suited for other recreation. See p. 54.
TIDAL BASIN	D.C.'s joggers' mecca. See p. 58.
WATERFRONT	Quiet, scenic, conveniently located pedestrian pathway runs from Water St. to Ft. McNair. See p. 60.
EAST POTOMAC PARK	Pleasant run to Hains Point along Ohio Dr. See p. 59.
ROCK CREEK PARK	Huge, scenic, and full of places for woodsy R&R. Beech Dr., through the heart of the park, is closed to traffic Su for rollerblading and biking. See p. 85.
GLOVER ARCHIBALD PARK	In Upper Northwest just off of Tenley Circle. Very joggable park directed by the National Park Service.
C&O CANAL	Towpath packed on weekends. If you want, you can jog all 184mi. from D.C. to Cumberland, VA. See p. 77.
CAPITOL CRESCENT TRAIL	A new, paved 11mi. trail along the Potomac on an old railroad right-of-way from Georgetown to Silver Spring, MD. Public parking on K St. in Georgetown (near Key Bridge), at the boat house, and in Bethesda. ☎234-4874 for info.
MOUNT VERNON TRAIL	18mi. trail starts on Roosevelt Island and follows the Potomac to Mt. Vernon.
WASHINGTON AND OLD DOMINION BIKE TRAIL (W&OD)	Starts in Arlington and runs 45mi. west to Purcellville. To reach the W&OD heading south from D.C., take the Shirlington exit from I-395, bear right onto Shirlington Rd. (north), and go a block to South Four Mile Run Dr.

The **Department of Recreation and Parks** (☎673-7660) is an excellent source of information for the athletically inclined.

JOGGING

Joggers flock to the **Tidal Basin,** the **Mall,** the **Mt. Vernon Trail,** and the **Washington and Old Dominion Bike Trail.** April's 10-mile **Cherry Blossom Festival** race is a celebrated event.

ROLLERBLADING

The hotspots are basically the same for rollerbladers and joggers, but steer clear of the monuments, where rollerbladers are unwelcome.

Washington Area Rollerskaters (☎466-5005). This group meets weekly on Pennsylvania Ave., in front of the White House, for a city skate. Beginners Su 11am, F 7pm; advanced Su 1pm; social W 7pm. If you're in a competitive mood, there are also pick-up street hockey games on Pennsylvania Ave., in front of the White House, on weekends.

Ski Center, corner of Mass Ave and 49th St. NW (☎966-4474). Rents skates. Rollerblades $15 per day, $25 for two days. Open M-F 11am-5:30pm, Sa 10am-5:30pm, Su noon-5pm.

BIKING

Some of the most popular bike paths are the C&O Canal Towpath, the Capital Crescent Trail, and the Washington and Old Dominion Bike Trail. ADC's Washington Area Bike Map on the Greater Washington Area Bike Map, available from the publisher (☎(703) 750-0510) or at area sporting goods stores; both list a number of good routes. Here are some of the many bike rental options:

Better Bikes (☎293-2080). Delivers bikes anywhere in the D.C. area. 10-speeds $25 per day, $95 per week; mountain bikes $38 per day, $135 per week. Helmet, map, backpack, locks, and breakdown service included. $25 deposit; driver's license, credit card, or passport required for collateral. Cash only. Open 24hr, although additional fees charged for deliveries before 8am.

Bike the Sites, Inc., 3417 Quesada St. NW (☎966-8662). Metro: Friendship Heights. Bicycle tours of the Capitol and 55 landmarks, $35. Reservations required.

BOATING

For tours, see **Sights,** p. 60. To be captain of your own ship, grab an oar and rent a boat:

Fletcher's Boat House, 4940 Canal Rd. NW (☎244-0461), in Rock Creek Park. Canoes $18 per day, rowboats $16 per day. Single speed bike $8 for 2hr. No rentals after 6pm. Open M-F 9am-7pm, Sa-Su 7:30am-7pm. See **Sights,** p. 150.

Thompson Boat House, at Rock Creek Pkwy. and Virginia Ave. NW. Canoes $8 per hr., $24 per day. Ocean kayaks $8 per hr., $24 per day. Double kayaks $10 per hr., $30 per day. Bicycles from $4 per hr., $15 per day. No rentals after 5pm. Open M-F 9am-5pm, Sa-Su 9am-6pm. See **Sights,** p.150.

Tidal Basin Boat House, 1100 Maine Ave. SW (☎479-2426). Metro: Smithsonian. Rents paddleboats for use in the Tidal Basin. 2-seaters $7 per hr.; 4-seaters $14 per hr. Open Mar.-Oct. M-F 10am-5:30pm, F-Sa 10am-8pm. Boats must be returned no later than one hour past closing.

BOWLING

Bowl America, 8616 Cameron St. (☎(301) 585-6990), in Silver Spring, MD. Metro: Silver Springs. Closest bowling alley to D.C. M-F $1.79 per game before 5pm, $3.50 afterward; Sa-Su $2 and $3, respectively. Shoes $2. Open M-F 4pm-midnight, Sa noon-1am, Su noon-6pm.

Shirley Park Bowl, 2945 S. Glebe Rd. (☎(703) 684-5800), in Arlington. Take I-395S and get off at Exit 7. M-F $1.75 per game until 5pm, $3.50 afterward; Sa $2.50 and $3.50, respectively. Shoes $2.50. Su-M games are $1. Open M-F noon-11pm, Sa-Su 9am-2am.

DANCE

Joy of Motion Dance Center, 1643 Connecticut Ave. NW (☎387-0911), 1 block up from Dupont Circle Metro. Also at 5207 Wisconsin Ave. NW (☎362-3042), 1 block south of Friendship Heights Metro. A dance studio that offers everything from ballet to yoga, flamenco to swing, belly dance to kick-boxing. $11-12 for most single classes, students $10.

GAY SPORTS AND RECREATION

Crew Club, 1321 14th St. NW (☎319-1333; www.crew-club.com), between N St. and Rhode Island Ave. Metro: McPherson. Social/recreational facility, health club, and gym for gay males. Weight gym, showers, free tanning, and game room. M and W free masseur. Admission $6 plus $10 for a personal locker, photo ID required. Open 24hr.

GOLF

Langston Golf Course (☎397-8638), across from RFK Stadium. Metro: Stadium-Armory. M-F 9 holes $9, 18 holes $15. Sa-Su, 9 holes $12.25, 18 holes $19. Club rentals $5.75-8.50. Pull carts $2.64-3.70. Riding carts $12-19. Open daily dawn-dusk.

Rock Creek Park Golf Course (☎882-7332), in Rock Creek Park at 16th St. and Rittenhouse. M-F 9 holes $9, 18 holes $15. Sa-Su 9 holes $12.25, 18 holes $19. Club Rentals $6-8.75. Open from dawn until dusk. See **Sights,** p. 85.

inside

SECRETS TO...

stealing a kiss

The rambling rolling hills of the **National Zoo** (see p. 89) make it the perfect place to slowly stroll, hold hands, and steal a smooch. Careful though, the mating sounds of monkeys and elephants can easily excite both parties and hasten the voyage back to the hotel. Remember, "you and me baby ain't nothing but mammals."

HIKING

Closed at night, all of the following offer tame hiking adventures. Within the district, the small but scenic **Roosevelt Island** (☎ (703) 285-2598) offers about 2 miles of trails (see p. 100). **Rock Creek Park** (☎ 282-1063 or ☎ 426-6829) contains a network of hiking trails. The **George Washington Carver Nature Trail** at the Anacostia Museum, 1901 Fort Pl. SE (☎ 357-2700), provides a 1¾ mile urban walk. Virginia's **Great Falls Park** (☎ (703) 285-2965) offers 15 miles of footpaths (open daily in summer 8am-7pm; Visitors Center open daily in summer 10am-5pm; see p. 108).

HORSEBACK RIDING

Rock Creek Park Horse Center (☎ 362-0117), in Rock Creek Park. Offers a slow-paced guided trail ride on one of the Center's fine horses ($25). See **Sights,** p. 85.

ICE SKATING

When winter hits hard, there's **free ice skating** on the **Reflecting Pool** in front of the **Lincoln Memorial** and on the **C&O Canal.** If these options aren't available, try the **National Sculpture Garden Rink,** 7th and Madison Ave. NW, (☎ 737-6938), near the Smithsonian Metro. Open Oct.-Mar. Admission is free; call for rental prices.

PAINTBALL

Adventurous gunmen must trek out to Maryland or Virginia to enjoy a good game. Try **Outdoor Adventures,** fields near Bethesda (☎ (800) 456-6636, $25 per player; call for seasonal hours; make reservations well in advance).

SWIMMING

Public pools can be found in most neighborhoods outside the center city. The facilities themselves are generally clean and safe; many of the surrounding areas, particularly those within the city itself, are not. (Indoor and outdoor pool times vary by location.) Call 673-7660 or 576-6436 to find the pool nearest you. Coolspots include the pools at **Fort Lincoln** (31st St. and Ft. Lincoln Dr. NE. ☎ 576-6135, call for weekly hours) and in **Anacostia** (Pennsylvania Ave. Bridge and 11th St. SE ☎ 645-5043, call for weekly hours). Many hotels will let you use their swimming facilities for a small fee.

SKYDIVING

Learn to pull off aerial feats from **Skydive Virginia,** an instruction school in Louisa, VA. (Rte. 208, Louisa County Airport, 540, ☎ 967-3997; www.skydive-virginia.com). Prices depend on size of group, season, and experience. Call to make reservations.

TENNIS

Rock Creek Park (☎ 722-5949), at 16th and Kennedy NW, and **East Potomac Park,** 1090 Ohio Dr. SW (☎ 554-5962), offer courts ($3-$8 per hour for hardcourt, $10-14 per hour for clay). See **Sights,** p. 150. Free neighborhood courts are also sprinkled around D.C. Try 18th St. and Florida Ave. NW.

SPECTATOR SPORTS

The Washington sports scene proves that politicians can't buy victories. In recent years, D.C.'s pro teams have struggled to achieve mediocrity.

BASKETBALL

When it comes to roundball, the loyalty of D.C. fans has been tested year after year. The **Washington Wizards,** the city's professional male team, constantly serves as the league's laughingstock for both its poor play and lame mascot. Behold the Wizardry between November and April at the **MCI Center** (☎ 628-3200, tickets $19-85). The **WNBA's Washington Mystics,** led by superstar Chamique Holdsclaw, have been bottom-dwellers each of the last four years. Mystics also play at the MCI Center (☎ 628-3200, tickets $8-25). Once a perennial collegiate powerhouse, the lately mediocre **Georgetown University Hoyas** hoop it up in the ever-competitive **Big East Conference** (☎ 628-3200, tickets $5-35).

HOCKEY

The poorly supported **Washington Capitals** haven't exactly dominated the high-speed game of **hockey,** but managed to make it to the **Stanley Cup** finals in 1998 before suffering an annhilating defeat at the hands of the Detroit Red Wings. Games Oct.-Apr. at the **MCI Center** (☎ 628-3200, tickets $20-75).

FOOTBALL

Despite a politically incorrect name, the **Washington Redskins** are a source of pride and joy for residents. With recent addition of superstar **Deion Sanders,** the team is poised to continue its winning ways. The three-time Super Bowl champions ('82, '87, '92) draw crowds to **Fed-Ex Field,** 1600 Raljon Rd., Landover, MD (☎ (301) 276-6050). Tickets $40-60, season Sept.-Dec. Regular season tickets always sell out so try for pre-season ones.

SOCCER

Buoyed by swelling interest and US victory at the 1999 Women's World Cup, **soccer** has undergone a meteoric rise in popularity. The **D.C. United** have had a promising beginning, drawing record crowds and winning the first two MLS Championships. From mid-Apr.-Sept., the United play at **RFK Stadium,** 2400 E. Capitol St. (☎ 547-9077). Metro: Stadium-Armory. Tickets $12-40. Box office ☎ 608-1119 or TicketMaster ☎ (800) 551-7328.

BASEBALL

Although D.C. packs in hard-hitters with national politics, it fouls up the national pasttime. The city hasn't had a **major league baseball** team since 1971, when the **Washington Senators** (best known for their role in *Damn Yankees*) left to become the **Texas Rangers.** Although Washington has been content to play godparent to the **Baltimore Orioles** for almost 30 years, there has been a recent movement to bring an expansion team to the greater D.C. area. **Mayor Anthony Williams** is behind a proposed $330 million baseball stadium adjoining the **Mt. Vernon Square/UDC Metro station,** but a number of critical oversights have postponed the project. Furthermore, D.C.'s proposed venture is at the whim of the money holders. Major league owners may not allow a new team only 40 miles south of where the Orioles play. For the time being, thousands of Washingtonians will continue to commute to Baltimore's beautiful **Camden Yards** (☎ (410) 685-9800; see **Daytripping,** p. 193). Tickets for **Orioles** games $7-$35.

Food & Drink

How does one feast like a senator on an intern's slim budget? Savvy natives go grubbing at Happy Hours. Bars often leave out free appetizer platters to bait early-evening clients (see **Nightlife,** p. 179). Or, frugal do-it-yourselfers pack their own lunches to dine al fresco. Choice picnic places include Rock Creek Park, the Tidal Basin, and the Mall.

We list restaurants by neighborhood. **Dollar signs ($)** after a restaurant's name label its price bracket. A plus **(+)** sign means that a restaurant's menu prices cluster near the upper end of a range. (Note: prices may have changed since *Let's Go: Washington, D.C. 2001* went to print). The index lists eateries by cuisine and by theme and marks them with a neighborhood abbreviation. We recommend venues marked by a **Let's Go Pick** (◆) as the District's cream-of-the-crop in taste and price.

PRICE SYMBOL	AVERAGE ENTREE PRICE
$	entrees average under $5
$$	entrees average $5-10
$$$	entrees average $10-15
$$$$	entrees average $15-20

NEIGHBORHOOD KEY

AL Alexandria **AM** Adams-Morgan **AR** Arlington **CH** Capitol Hill **DP** Dupont Circle **FB** Foggy Bottom **G** Georgetown **NE** Northeast **OD** Old Downtown **SH** Shaw/U District **UN** Upper Northwest

CUISINE BY TYPE

AFGHANI

Kabul Caravan	AR

AFRICAN

▨ Meskerem	AM
Red Sea	AM
Entotto	UN
Zed's Ethiopian Cuisine	G

AMERICAN

Gadsby's Tavern	AL
Steak Around	AR
The Market Lunch	CH
The Baja Grill	F
Sizzling Express	F
Furini's	G
Houston's	G
Ebbitt Express/Old Ebbitt Grill	OD
a.k.a. Frisco's	UN

BAGEL

Whatsa Bagel	F

BAKERY

Bread and Chocolat	CH
China Doll	CHT
Palais du Chocolat	F, UN
Patisserie Poupon	G
Reeves	OD
Negril the Jamaican Bakery	SM
Firehook Bakery & Coffeehouse	UN

BAR AND GRILL

Chatter's	B
The Dubliner	CH
Hawk 'n' Dove	CH
Mr. Henry's Victorian Pub	CH
Harry's	G
Cafe Amadeus	OD
▨ Polly's Restaurant	SH

BARBECUE AND RIBS

▨ Rocklands	AR, UN
Red Hot and Blue	AR
Kenny's Smoke House	CH
Wingmaster's	UN

BURMESE

Burma Restaurant	CHT

CAFES

Tryst	AM
La Madeleine	AL
The Java Shack	AR
Thyme Square Cafe	B
Le Bon Cafe	CH
Roasters on the Hill	CH
Afterwords Cafe	DP
Jolt 'n' Bolt Coffeehouse	DP
Soho Tea and Coffee	DP
Teaism	DP

CAFES, CONT.

Xando	DP
Cup A' Cup A'	FB
The Little Cafe	G

CYBERCAFES

Atomic Grounds	AR
The Cyberstop Cafe	DP
Myth.com Cybercafe	G

CARIBBEAN

Mobay Cafe	AM
Banana Cafe and Piano Bar	CH
Hibiscus Cafe	G
The Islander	OD
Zanzibar on the Waterfront	SM
Spicy Delight	TP

CHINESE

See also anywhere in Chinatown, p. 163.

Hunan Dynasty	CH
City Lights of China	DP
Yenching Palace	UN

CREOLE AND CAJUN

The Bayou Room	AL
Louisiana Express	B
Tropicana	OD

CHILI

▨ Hard Times Cafe	AL, AR
Ben's Chili Bowl	SH

DELI

So's Your Mom	AM
Jack's Place	AL
Philadelphia Mike's	B
Misha's Deli	CH
2nd St. Deli	CH
Lindy's Bon Appetit	FB
Irene's Deli	SM
Everyday Gourmet	TP

DINER

▨ Five Guys Famous Burgers and Fries	AL
Royal Restaurant	AL
Bob & Edith's Diner	AR
Silver Diner	AR
American City Diner	B
Tastee Diner	B
Capitol Hill Jimmy T's	CH
Luna Grill & Diner	DP
Trio Restaurant	DP
The Art Gallery Grille	F
Booeymonger	G,UN
Georgetown Cafe	G
Furini's	G
Stoney's Restaurant	OD
▨ Wilson's	OD
Mark's Kitchen	TP

AL Alexandria **AM** Adams-Morgan **AR** Arlington **CH** Capitol Hill **DP** Dupont Circle **FB** Foggy Bottom
G Georgetown **NE** Northeast **OD** Old Downtown **SH** Shaw/U District **UN** Upper Northwest

FRENCH

Grapeseed	B
Vie de France	F
☙ Cafe la Ruche	G
Au Pied du Cochon	G

GERMAN

German Deli	OD

GREEK

Crystal Pallas Cafe & Grill	AR
Taverna the Greek Islands	CH
Zorba's Cafe	DP
☙ Yanni's	UN

HEALTH FOOD/ORGANIC

Thymes Square Cafe	B
Cafe Luna	DP
Juice Joint Cafe	F
Dean and Deluca	G
Wrap Works	G
☙ Savory	TP

ICE CREAM

The Scoop Grill and Homemade Ice Cream	AL
Lazy Sundae	AR
Bob's Famous Homemade Ice Cream	B
Cone E. Island	FB
Thomas Sweet	G
Summer Delights	TP
Uptown Scoop	UN

INDIAN

Delhi Dhaba	AR
Aditi	G
Amma Vegetarian Kitchen	G
Mayur Kabab House	OD

ITALIAN

Pasta Mia Trattoria	AM
Aldo Cafe	B
Il Radiccho	CH
Mediterranean Blue	DP
Dupont Italian Kitchen	DP
Il Pranzo	F
Famous Luigi's	F
Via Cucina	F

JAPANESE AND KOREAN

☙ Perry's	AM
Fresco, Italian Gourmet at Watergate	FB
☙ Il Radiccho	G
Luciano's Cafe	G
San Marzano	G
☙ Mama Maria and Enzio's	UN
Maggiano's Little Italy	UN
☙ Tako Grill	B
Sakana	DP

MEXICAN

☙ Mixtec	AM
El Tamarindo	AM
El Charro Caruso	AR
Rio Grande Cafe	B

MEXICAN, CONT.

Tia Queta	B
☙ Lauriol Plaza	DP
Casa Blanca	F
Burrito Brothers	CH, G
Enriqueta's	G
Austin Grill	UN
Cactus Cantina	UN

MICROBREW

Capitol City Brewing Company	OD
John Harvard's Brew House	OD

MIDDLE EASTERN

Mama Ayesha's Calvert Cafe	AM
Food Factory	AR
Paradise Restaurant	B
Anatolia	CH
Skewers	DP
Fettoosh Express	G
Moby Dick House of Kabob	G
Bistro Med	G
Quick Pita	G
Shiney's Kabab and Curry House	OD
☙ Cafe Ole	UN
The Lebanese Taverna	UN
Medaterra	UN
Mediterranean Deli	UN

MOROCCAN

Casablanca	AL

PAN-ASIAN, ASIAN FUSION

Pan Asian Noodles & Grill	DP
Peppers	DP
☙ Raku	DP
☙ Spices Asian Restaurant	UN

PIZZA

Bertucci's Brick Oven Pizzeria	DP
Pizzeria Paradiso	DP
Dove and Rainbow	FB
Julio's	OD
Taliano's	TP
☙ Faccia Luna	UN

SEAFOOD

The Fish Market	AL
☙ Lite 'n' Fair	AL
Bethesda Crab House	B
Steamer's Seafood House	B

SOUL FOOD

King Street Blues	AL
☙ Florida Avenue Grill	SH
Outlaw's	SH

SPANISH

Julia's Empanadas	AM, F
El Caribe	G
☙ Jaleo	OD

THAI

Star of Siam	AM

AL Alexandria **AM** Adams-Morgan **AR** Arlington **CH** Capitol Hill **DP** Dupont Circle **FB** Foggy Bottom
G Georgetown **NE** Northeast **OD** Old Downtown **SH** Shaw/U District **UN** Upper Northwest

THAI, CONT.		VIETNAMESE	
Tara Thai	B	Saigonnais	AM
Bua	DP	Cafe Saigon	AR
Sala Thai	DP	Cafe Dalat	AR
Thai Kingdom	F	Queen Bee	AR
Haad Thai	OD	Little Viet Garden	AR
Ivy's Place	UN	Saigon Inn	G
Thai Town	UN	Vietnam-Georgetown Restaurant	G
Jandara	UN	Nam Viet Pho 79	UN
		Saigon Gourmet Restaurant	UN

BY NEIGHBORHOOD

ADAMS-MORGAN

Adams-Morgan's cultural melting pot dishes up ethnic cuisine—from Latin American to Ethiopian to Caribbean—to a young, international crowd into ungodly hours. As this neighborhood grows ever hipper, pricey yuppie joints rub shoulders with old reliables. Establishments cluster along 18th St. and Columbia Rd. NW. Although the area is generally safe, **areas off of the main streets become dangerous at night.** Adams-Morgan is a 15-minute walk or short cab ride from the Dupont Circle or Woodley Park-Zoo Metro.

Mixtec ($$), 1792 Columbia Rd. NW (☎332-1011), near 18th St. A familial, friendly staff serves some of the area's tastiest Mexican food to locals and travelers. Paper lanterns and colorfully hand-painted chairs add flair to rooms with an otherwise fast-food atmosphere. Mexican specialties and favorites include *tacos al carbon* (two small tortillas filled with beef $7), tacos and Mexican submarines $4-6, and nachos $6. Try the various fruit drinks for a refreshing treat ($1.75). Some vegetarian options. Appetizers $2.95-6.50. Entrees $7-11; sangria $2.50 per glass. Su-Th 11am-10pm, Fri-Sa 11am-11pm.

Perry's ($$$+), 1811 Columbia Rd. NW (☎234-6218), near 18th St. Progressives line up in front of the hieroglyphics-covered awning for an evening of nouvelle Japanese-American cuisine. A typical entree: phyllo-wrapped salmon stuffed with crab on a bed of spicy beans, mango salsa, and grilled asparagus ($17). Entrees $9-18; sushi 50¢-$5 per piece. The coveted rooftop patio offers superb views of the surrounding area. Open M-Sa 5:30pm-1:30am, Su 5:30-11:30pm; kitchen closes daily 10:15pm, sushi closes daily 11:15pm; drag brunch Su 11am-2:30pm.

So's Your Mom ($), 1831 Columbia Rd. NW (☎462-3666). This busy sandwich shop offers an assortment of meat, cheese, and bread as eye-popping as your mom. First-rate sandwich ingredients (such as imported meats and cheeses), portions as big as your mom, and unexpected sandwich choices (sliced beef tongue $5.95) keep So's Your Mom a spankin' takeout option. Sandwiches $3.25-5.95. Fresh baked goods include cinnamon rolls, muffins, other sweet pastries, and your mom ($1.75). Takeout only. Open M-F 7am-8pm, Sa 8am-7pm, Su 8am-3pm.

Tryst, 2459 18th St. NW (☎232-5500) Coffee bar with an atmosphere that splendidly combines an art gallery and a rec room; huge sofas, pastiche paintings, board games, books, and caffeine addicts. International jetsetters and Americans mingle in a pretentious haze of cigarette smoke while sipping java. The unique menu includes sandwiches named after employees: try Sal (black forest ham, smoked gouda, lettuce, spicy mustard with ricotto with rustico $4.95) or Mary (oven roasted turkey breast, avocado spread, white cheddar with rustico $4.95). Waffles $3.50 and up. Night turns the place into a mind-blowing, Bohemian smoke fest. 21+ F-Sa after 9pm. Open M-Th 7am-last call (around 12:30am), F-Sa 7am-3am, Su 8am-midnight.

Saigonnais ($$), 2307 18th St. NW (☎232-5300). Vietnamese straw hats dangle from this intimate restaurant's ceiling while cheery framed-photos of famous past visitors line the wall. Savory dishes include rolling your own sugarcane spring rolls using fresh shrimp ($7) or other Saigon specialties like Five Spice Chicken (chicken marinated in five spice powders and grilled) $7.50-8.25. The friendly and experienced staff are helpful. Few vegetarian options. Lunch specials $5.50-7; dinner entrees $7.50-14.50. Free delivery. Open daily 11:30am-3pm and 5-11pm.

Pasta Mia Trattoria ($$), 1790 Columbia Rd. NW (☎328-9114), near 18th St. Red-and-white checked tablecloths in an airy room complete dusky evenings devoted to Disney-worthy romance. Standard Italian fare features large pasta entrees ($7-10), some appetizers, and a few desserts. Open M-Sa 6:30pm-late.

El Tamarindo ($$), 1785 Florida Ave. NW (☎328-3660), just off of 18th St. Salvadoran food served into the early morning in this casual joint off the beaten track. Appetizer combination plate includes cheese quesadillas, nachos, chicken wings, a taquito, and guacamole and sour cream ($8.15). Pupusas and tamales ($1.35-5.25) keep the customers happily returning. Entrees $7.25-12.95. Bar options. **Be careful in this area at night.** Open M-Sa 11am-3am, Su 10am-3am.

Julia's Empanadas ($), 2452 18th St. NW (☎328-6232), near Columbia Rd. Other locations at 1000 Vermont Ave. NW (☎(202) 789-1878) and 2452 18th St. NW (☎(202) 328-6232). Having a fast-food atmosphere, Julia's serves empanadas "Made by Hand, Baked with Love." The delicious meat/vegetable filled pastries attest to the "love" spent in their making. Empanada options include Chorizo, spinach, vegetarian and more ($2.89-3.00). Seasonal soups include gazpacho ($1.50-2.59). Open Su-W 10:30am-10:30pm, Th 10:30am-midnight, F-Sa 10:30am-3:30am.

Red Sea ($$), 2463 18th St. NW (☎483-5000), near Columbia Rd. The first neighborhood Ethiopian restaurant is still among the best, serving a clientele of neighborhood regulars and visitors. Red decor dominates in a potentially romantic atmosphere. *Doro Wat* (chicken marinated in lemon, sauteed in seasoned butter with other spices) $8.45; *Michet Abesh* (beef cubes simmered in butter sauce with spices) $8.95. Entrees $8-11.50 and served over thin *injera* bread. Vegetarian options. All orders come with choice of 2 vegetable sides. Open daily 11:30am-11pm.

Mama Ayesha's Calvert Cafe ($$), 1967 Calvert St. NW (☎232-5431), next to the Calvert St. bridge. Mama Ayesha's earthy-colored restaurant has a small patio for outdoor dining and two large, colorful rooms. Options range from stuffed grape leaves to *shish taouk* (marinated chicken breast kebab with tomatoes and onions; $9.50) or *mujadrah* (rice with lentils, fried onions, and yogurt; $8.50). Feeling indulgent? Try the richly sweet Baklava $2.00. Appetizers $2.50-5.50; entrees $8.50-12.50. Open daily 11am-midnight.

Mobay Cafe ($$), 2437 18th St. (☎745-1002), near Columbia Rd. Rollicking restaurant and bar serves Jamaican food with an American twist in a crowded dining room and patio. Busting at the seams on F-S nights, Mobay offers a good selection of Jamaican drinks ($4.95-5.50) and a happy hour (4pm-7pm M-F). Choices include appetizers ($2.95-$7.95), salads, soups, wraps and subs ($4.95-8.95), and various entrees (curry goat $8.25, jerk chicken $8.95). Breakfast served all day. Open Su-Th 10am-2am, F-Sa 10am-5am.

Star of Siam ($$), 2446 18th St. NW (☎986-4133), near Columbia Rd. Acclaimed Thai cuisine is served on a rooftop deck or in a 2nd-floor dining room with traditional, low Thai tables. The food is light and flavorful. Local favorites include the *pad thai* (rice noodle with chicken, shrimp, bean sprout, and egg; lunch $6.50, dinner $8.25) and curry dishes (lunch $7.50-8.25, dinner $8.50-10.95). Lunch entrees $6.25-8.50; dinner $8-11. Free delivery daily 5-10:30pm. Open M-Th 5-11pm, F 5pm-midnight, Sa noon-midnight, Su noon-11pm.

Meskerem ($$), 2434 18th St. NW (☎462-4100), near Columbia Rd. An ecstatic, sun-themed decor lights up this three-floor restaurant named after the Ethiopian month marking spring. Appetizers include *sambussas* (vegetable or meat filled pastries) $2.25-5.25. For an intro to Ethiopian cuisine, split the *Meskerem Messob*, a popular combination platter with various meats and vegetables served over paper-thin *injera* bread. Like the sun-beamed decor, F and Sa burst with energy as a live band plays in the downstairs lounge. Lunch entrees $5-10.50, dinner entrees $7-12.95. Free delivery. Open daily noon-midnight.

ALEXANDRIA

SEE MAP P. 320

The dining scene in Old Town capitalizes on a large assortment of historic re-creations, multicultural additions, and sizzling burger joints. The waterfront's city specialties are seafood and cheap BBQ. Use Metro: King St. unless otherwise noted.

Lite 'n' Fair ($$), 1018 King St. (☎(703) 549-3717). Ki Choi, former executive chef of the ritzy Watergate Restaurant, runs this gem disguised by a modest facade, a few small tables, and the convenience of carryout. Exquisite seafood sandwiches and burgers $4-8.

inside
SECRETS TO...

late-night eats

Creatures of the night with the munchies flock to **Afterwords Cafe** (see p. 166), serving a wide array of breakfast and sandwich dishes as well as dessert 'round-the-clock on Friday and Saturday nights. Similar offerings can be found in Georgetown at **Au Pied De Cochon** (see p. 170) and **Georgetown Cafe** (see p. 171), which *never close*. In Adams Morgan, one can run for the border well into the wee hours of the morning at **El Padrino** (1742 Columbia Rd.).

Specials occasionally include smoked salmon ($3.95), calamari tempura ($3.95), or seafood paella with shrimp, mussels, calamari, and saffron rice ($9). Dessert such as Baked Alaska $2.95 and up. Open M 11am-3pm, Tu-Th 11am-9pm, F-Sa 11am-10pm.

Hard Times Cafe ($$), 1404 King St. (☎(703) 683-5340; www.hardtimes.com), near West St. This country cafe blends the tastes of the Midwest, West, and South to satisfy nearly all chili lovers. Your basics include Cincinnati, Texas, Terlingua, and vegetarian chili ($5, kids $4). Chili invades conventional American fare on hot dogs ($5.50-5.95), burgers ($5.75-6.95), or spaghetti ($5.65-6.50). If your stomach can't handle the beans, go for the beer-battered onion rings ($4.95). Open Su-Th 11am-10pm, F-Sa 11am-11pm.

Five Guys Famous Burgers and Fries ($), 107 N. Fayette St. (☎(703) 549-7991). A 50s diner straight out of Grease. Fantastic service makes for great burgers in this large diner plastered with customers' praise and peanut shells. Basic burger $3-3.40, bacon cheeseburger $3.99; you pick all the toppings as they prepare it fresh in front of your eyes. Fries (boardwalk or Cajun) $1-3. Munch on free peanuts while you wait. Open daily 11am-10pm.

King Street Blues ($$+), 112 N. S. Asaph St. (☎(703) 836-8800; fax 836-9541), near King St. The flamboyant decor boasts with neon confidence "Cheap Thrills, Cool Blues, Good Eats," and they ain't lying. Southern traditions like slow-smoked ribs (1 lb. rack $9.95), BBQ chicken ($9.95), and pulled pork "sammiches" ($6.95). Blueplate special ($5.95; served until 6pm) changes daily. Low-fat, low-calorie options as well. Live blues Su 9pm-midnight. Kitchen open M-Th and Su 11:30am-10pm, F-Sa 10:30am-midnight. Bar open daily until 1:45am.

Casablanca ($$$), 1504 King St. (☎(703) 549-6464). You can sample the delights of Moroccan cuisine during the all-you-can-eat lunch buffet ($6), but there's true magic in the nightly Moroccan feast served over the course of a few hours. **Reservations** are usually necessary to enjoy soup, salad, couscous, delicately spiced meat, pastries, mint tea, and fruit amidst cushion-ladened luxury (1 entree $18, 2 for $20, 3 for $22). Starting at 8pm, belly dancers gyrate tums in each alcove of the restaurant. Open M-F 11:30am-2:30pm and 6-11pm, Sa 6-11pm.

Royal Restaurant ($$), 734 N. Asaph St. (☎(703) 548-1616). Metro: Braddock. Family friendly and ready to serve up some of the best homestyle cooking this side of momma's kitchen. The king of the sandwich selection ($3.25-6.25) is the Charles Royal Club (wheat toast, turkey, cheese, bacon, lettuce, and tomato; $6 with fries). Omelettes $3.30-5 for breakfast, $5.50-5.75 for lunch or dinner. Burger with fries $4.50, crab-cake sandwich with fries $6.25. All-you-can-eat Su brunch buffet $6.50. Open M-Sa 6am-9:30pm, Su 7am-2:30pm.

The Bayou Room ($+), downstairs at 219 King St. (☎(703) 549-1141). Downstairs from its more expensive brother, this Cajun pub has delicious Creole specials, including red beans and rice ($5.95), jambalaya ($6.50), and shrimp creole ($6.50). Happy Hour M-F 4-6pm offers $1.75 drafts. Open daily at 11:30am, closes anywhere from 11:30pm to 2am.

The Fish Market ($$), 105 King St. (☎(703) 836-5676), near Union St. This rollicking seafood restaurant seats 450 and features live ragtime piano, Broadway tunes, and jazz with enthusiastic audience participation (W-Sa 8pm; cover $2-3). Try to sit on the balcony for a bird's eye view of the happy commotion of King St. 3 bars and rustic decor make the baby-blue building a happening 20-something hangout. Clam chowder $2, salads $4-9, seafood sandwiches $4-7, platters $8-16. Open M-Sa 11:15am-2am, Su 11:15am-midnight. Kitchen closes daily at midnight.

Gadsby's Tavern ($$$), 134 N. Royal St. (☎(703) 548-1288), near King St. Part of the Gadsby's Tavern Museum. Waiters in costume deliver pricey 18th-century cooking in a restaurant once frequented by George Washington. While the menu definitely doesn't deliver 18th century prices, entrees such as dinner stews and colonial pies simmer down to $6.50-8.50 at lunch. Traditional tea, bread, and English trifle for dessert ($5.50). Nightly "colonial" entertainment often features a violinist in period costume. Open daily 11:30am-3pm and 5:30-10:30pm. Tours Tu-Sa 10am-4pm, Su 1-5pm. Reservations recommended.

La Madeleine ($+), 500 King St. (☎(703) 739-2854). Food served cafeteria-style, but the warm country decor—replete with bright wood furnishings and hanging cooking utensils—eliminates any institutional feel. French bakery and cafe serves great breakfast omelettes ($5), sandwiches and pasta ($3-11), and an extensive selection of desserts ($1-3). The *sacher torte* (chocolate cake with raspberry filling; $2.69) is decadent. Open Su-Th 7am-10pm, F-Sa 7am-11pm.

Jack's Place ($+), 222 N. Lee St. (☎(703) 684-0372), at Queen St. Tiny deli whose specialty is Jack's Own Reuben Sandwich (corned beef, turkey breast, pastrami, or roast beef with Swiss cheese, Russian dressing, and sauerkraut on rye; $6). Hearty breakfasts ($1.75-7.50) and deli sandwiches ($4.50-7) are specialties. Breakfast served M-F until 11am, Sa until noon, Su until 2:30pm. Open M-F 6am-4pm, Sa-Su 8am-3pm.

The Scoop Grill and Homemade Ice Cream ($), 110 King St. (☎(703) 549-4527). Old ice cream parlor charm and funky flavors like Orange Chocolate Chip, Blueberry Marble, and Jack Daniels ($2.50-3.95). The Breakfast Special includes 2 eggs, bacon or sausage, home fries, toast, and jelly ($3.35). Burgers and sandwiches $2-5. Freshly baked goods $1-2. Hours fluctuate; call ahead. Generally open M-Th 8am-11pm, F-Sa 8:30am-midnight, Su 9am-11pm.

ARLINGTON

Arlington gives Adams-Morgan a run for its money by offering up an equally impressive assortment of ethnic eateries. The Clarendon area, nicknamed **Little Saigon,** is home to some excellent and reasonably-priced Vietnamese restaurants. Nearby, all-American places dish out chili and ribs. If for some unfortunate reason you are stuck in the Crystal City area, the eateries along **23rd Street South** are notable for their worldly offerings.

Cafe Dalat ($$), 3143 Wilson Blvd. (☎(703) 276-0935). Metro: Clarendon. The first Vietnamese restaurant in the area continues to serve up premiere *pho* (Vietnamese noodle soup) $4. Specialties include *chao tom* (shrimp grilled on sugar cane and assembled into delicate rolls with rice paper, clear vermicelli noodles, cucumber, lettuce, and peanut sauce; $10). All-you-can-eat lunch buffet M-F 11am-2pm $5. Dinner entrees $7-10. Large vegetarian menu. Open Su-Th 11am-9:30pm, F-Sa 11am-10:30pm.

▨**Rocklands ($$),** 4000 Fairfax Dr. (☎(703) 528-9663). Metro: Ballston. Branch in Glover Park. Great BBQ ribs ($5 half rack; $17 whole rack) and sandwiches ($7-9.50) guaranteed to be served within 8min. of your order. Limited seating in a trendy spot attached to the **Carpool Bar** (see p. 182). Heat seekers can sample from over 120 hot sauces on the "Wall of Fire." Open Su-W noon-10pm, Th-Sa noon-11pm, appetizers served until Carpool's last call.

Crystal Pallas Cafe & Grill ($$), 556 22nd St. S. (☎(703) 521-3870). Metro: Crystal City. Slow relaxed pace befits largely elderly clientele. Everything from a traditional hummus appetizer ($4) to more unusual selections like their delicious roasted red peppers mixed with feta and oregano ($4.25). The Greek salad is a large affair with chunks of feta and *dolma* (stuffed grape leaves) combined with a smooth homemade dressing ($6). Open M-F 11am-10pm, Sa 5-11pm.

Bob & Edith's Diner ($), 2310 Columbia Pike (☎ (703) 920-6103). Not easily Metro accessible, but a great place to get breakfast at 3am. The extra-loud rock music makes you feel like you never left the party. Authentic diner with most dishes under $5. Blueberry pancakes $4; grilled cheese $1.90; subs around $5. Open 24hr.

Food Factory ($), 4221 N. Fairfax Dr. (☎ (703) 527-2279, delivery ☎ (703) 527-4433), across from Metro: Ballston. Enter in the rear until renovations are completed. Served over the counter, the Middle-Eastern charbroiled kebabs still shame American "shish kebab" imitations. *Nan* (tandoori bread) and skewers of chicken, beef, or lamb ($4-7) are excellent. For vegetarians, the rows of *samosas* ($1) are tempting. Open M-F 11am-10pm, Sa-Su noon-10pm.

Cafe Saigon ($+), 1135 N. Highland St. (☎ (703) 243-6522 or (703) 276-7110, delivery (703) 820-1000), across from Clarendon Metro. Yet another Vietnamese place with great food and "French" decor (Pepto Bismol pink walls, cheesy Christmas lights, and floral table cloths). Excellent entrees include *cha gio* (grilled pork and crispy rolls, served on noodles; $8) and the "special squid" deep-fried with ginger and onions ($11). Open Su-Th 11am-10pm, F-Sa until midnight.

Delhi Dhaba ($), 2424 Wilson Blvd. (☎ (703) 524-0008). Not visible from the street; enter through the parking lot behind the deli. Metro: Clarendon or Courthouse. Solid Indian fare at great prices is ordered at the counter and brought to your table. *Saag* lamb ($6.25) as well as lots of vegetarian specialties (all around $5.50). Open Su-Th 11am-10pm, F-Sa 11am-11pm.

The Java Shack ($), 2507 North Franklin Rd. (☎ (703) 527-9556), off Wilson Blvd. Metro: Clarendon or Courthouse. Eavesdrop on e-commerce jockeys or Feng Sui fanatics at this small hidden coffeehouse. Hand-painted tabletops with crazy magazine cut-outs. Pastries $1.75. The Java Blizzard (coffee, espresso, chocolate, caramel, and milk blended with ice and topped with whipped creme; $3.25) is outrageously delicious. Quiche and sandwiches $3.25-4.25. Open M-Th 7am-10pm, F 7am-11pm, Sa 8am-11pm, Su 8am-10pm.

Little Viet Garden ($$), 3012 Wilson Blvd. (☎ (703) 522-9686), 1 block from the Clarendon Metro. Upscale Vietnamese restaurant with sleek black chairs, a padded bar, and live palm trees. The beautifully landscaped patio is a lovely reprieve from Wilson Blvd. Most entrees under $9. Lunch specials (M-F 11am-2:30pm; $5-7) like skewered shrimp and scallops come with rice and a salad. Open M-F 11am-2:30pm and 5-10pm, Sa-Su noon-10pm.

Lazy Sundae ($), 2925 Wilson Blvd. (☎ (703) 525-4960), at the intersection with Garfield. Metro: Clarendon. Those dining elsewhere won't regret skipping dessert in order to sample Lazy Sundae's delicious homemade ice cream. Super-friendly family service will recommend specialties like Adam's Apple (apple crisp folded into cinnamon ice cream). Single scoop $2.25. Sells hard to find candies like Pop Rocks and Teaberry gum. Open Su-Th 11am-10:30pm, F-Sa 11am-11pm.

Hard Times Cafe ($), 3028 Wilson Blvd. (☎ (703) 528-2233), across from Clarendon Metro. Identical to Alexandria location (See p. 156). Open Su-Th 11:30am-10pm, F-Sa 11:30am-11pm.

Kabul Caravan ($$), 1725 Wilson Blvd. (☎ (703) 522-8394). Metro: Court House. With numerous Afghani artifacts and decorations, this restaurant feels more like a museum. Authentic entrees include *Aushak* (scallion-filled dumplings with yogurt and meat sauce; $10). Entrees $11-17; lunch entrees $8-15. Open M-F 11:30am-2:30pm and 5:30-11pm, Sa-Su 5:30-11pm.

Silver Diner ($+), 3200 Wilson Blvd. (☎ (703) 812-8667), at the corner of N. Irving St., Washington Blvd., and Fairfax Dr. Metro: Clarendon. A local chain that serves up good American fare in a 50s-style diner. A great place to bring kids. Huge stack of 3 buttermilk pancakes $4, chicken tenders $5.50, half-pound burger $6. Look for daily lunch specials ($6-7). Open Su-Th 7am-midnight, F-Sa 7am-3am.

Steak Around ($$), 2317 Wilson Blvd. (☎ (703) 526-9300). Metro: Courthouse. This unique joint delivers tender juicy steaks to local fanatics but also has limited seating for dining in. Carnivorous patrons chose from NY strip steaks, rib eye steaks, and steak tips as well as grilled salmon and chicken ($10-15). The sandwiches are equally delicious and more affordable ($5-8). Open M-F 11am-11pm, Sa-Su noon-1pm.

Atomic Grounds ($), 1555 Wilson Blvd. #105 (☎ (703) 524-2157). A small IBM-only cybercafe concentrating more on providing a high number of terminals than a high number of coffee and food options. Online rates: $2 for 15 min., $7 per hr. Printing 25¢ per page. Open M-T 6:30am-6:30pm, W-F 6:30am-9:30pm, Sa 8:30am-9:30pm, Su 9am-5pm.

Red Hot and Blue ($$+), 1600 Wilson Blvd. (☎(703) 276-7427, delivery (703) 578-3663), under an office building near Pierce St. Metro: Court House or Rosslyn. One of many area locations offering run-of-the-mill BBQ ribs. Regular order $10, full rack $18 (feeds 2) available basted with sauce or rubbed with traditional Memphis spices. Fabulous pulled-pig sandwich ($5). Key lime pie $3.50. Lines often long on weekends. Open Su-Th 11am-10pm, F-Sa 11am-11pm.

Queen Bee ($$), 3181 Wilson Blvd. (☎(703) 527-3444). Metro: Clarendon. No affiliation with rapper Lil' Kim, although the Vietnamese dishes offered will blow your socks off. Spring rolls for appetizers are a good choice, as are the lighter summer rolls (both $3). Entrees ($7-11) include visually delightful crispy noodles, a vegetable and seafood stir-fry nestled on a bed of fried noodles ($9). Rotating lunch specials come with a spring roll and fried rice (M-F 11am-3pm; $3.50). Open daily 11am-10pm

BETHESDA

Purportedly the highest concentration of restaurants in the US, Bethesda's 150 eateries cluster between **Wisconsin Avenue** to the east, **Bethesda Avenue** to the south, **Rugby Avenue** to the north, and **Arlington Road** and **Old Georgetown Road** to the west. There are dining options for almost any cuisine, ambience, or price. Use Metro: Bethesda for all of the following.

▨ Tara Thai ($$+), 4828 Bethesda Ave. (☎(301) 657-0488). Excellent Thai dishes served within a cool, aqua-themed dining room which makes you feel like you're eating at the bottom of the sea, chitty-chitty-bang-bang-style. Delicately spiced *goong phuket* (grilled black tiger shrimp topped with crabmeat and chicken sauce; lunch $8, dinner $13) and classic *pad thai* (lunch $6, dinner $8) are among the house specialties. Open M-Th 11:30am-3pm and 5-10pm, F 11:30am-3pm and 5-11pm, Sa noon-3:30pm and 5-11pm, and Su noon-3:30pm and 5-10pm.

▨ Aldo Cafe ($$), 4940-8 Fairmont Ave. (☎(301) 986-0042), near Old Georgetown Rd., enter through Positano's next door. *Very* Italian; even the tablecloths are red, white, and green. *Agnolotti all panna* (half moon pasta stuffed with spinach and cheese; $10), pizza and pasta dishes $5-10. Open daily 11:30am-10:30pm.

▨Tako Grill ($$), 7756 Wisconsin Ave. (☎(301) 652-7030). Modern Japanese grill ornamented with glazed wood, frequented by a young professional clientele. The $6 lunch special, including miso soup, sprout salad, 6 pieces of sushi, rice, and an entree, is an impeccable dining experience (M-F 11:30am-2pm). Fresh sushi $5.50-17. Mouth watering *nabeyaki* (noodle soup served with chicken, egg, and seafood; $10.50). Free delivery M-Th 5:30-9pm. Open M-Th 11:30am-2pm and 5:30-10pm, F 11:30am-2pm and 5:30-10:30pm, Sa 5:30-10:30pm, Su 5-9:30pm.

Rio Grande Cafe ($$+), 4919 Fairmont Ave. (☎(301) 656-2981), near Old Georgetown Rd. Louder and more crowded than Mexico City, Rio packs them in for the Mexican fare and party atmosphere. $9 buys 3 delicious tacos. *Plato gordo* includes beef and chicken *fajitas*, ribs, and shrimp (serves 2 for $36). Sunday brunch features *huevos manchacado* (3 eggs scrambled with chicken or beef *fajitas* rolled in a flour tortilla; $7.75). Open M-Th 11:30am-10:30pm, F-Sa 11:30am-11:30pm, Su 11:30am-10:30pm.

Tia Queta ($$+), 4839 Del Ray Ave. (☎(301) 654-4443). Go north on Old Georgetown Rd. and turn right onto Del Ray Ave. Leather-bound menus and rustic decorations (*sombreros*, cacti, old barn equipment, and lots of pottery) make a vain attempt to whisk patrons away to the streets of Mexico. Classics like *fajitas* ($7) and *enchiladas verdes* ($7) compete with divine abstract creations like *mole bueno* (chicken doused in a chocolate, banana, peanut, and pumpkin seed sauce; $12). Second floor outdoor patio open in summer. Open M-Th 11:30am-10pm, F-Sa 11:30am-11pm, Su 1-10pm.

Bethesda Crab House ($$$), 4958 Bethesda Ave. (☎(301) 652-3382), a block from Arlington Rd. Following 39 years of tradition, patrons flock to long picnic tables lined with brown paper to protect them from the piles of shells accumulated during serious hard shell crab eating. All-you-can-eat crab for $20 including coleslaw and corn. Crab also available by the dozen or bushel (call to reserve the biggest crabs). Shrimp, corn on the cob, and cole slaw are the only other menu items ($3-7). Open daily noon-midnight.

inside
SECRETS TO...

indigenous food

Imported from nearby Maryland, **hard shell crabs** are an area favorite with a plethora of crab-houses in Maryland, Virginia, and the District. These hard shell crabs are often cooked in a special **Old Bay Spice Seasoning,** the indigenous D.C. flavor. Many of these restaurants tantalize patrons with **all-you-can-eat** specials. Don't worry, they'll give you a bib, too!

Crab fetish aside, D.C. is an undeniably meat and potatoes town, as menus overflow with beef dishes and steakhouses such as Ruth's Chris (1801 Connecticut Ave.) pack them in nightly. D.C. is also infamous for its sweet tooth, with succulent late-night dessert spots like Thomas Sweet (see p. 170) and Afterwords Cafe (see p. 166).

Thyme Square Cafe ($$+), 4735 Bethesda Ave. (☎(301) 657-9077). The friendly service, colorful decorations, and healthy vegetarian salads, sandwiches, pasta dishes, and entrees all lend to an aura of good karma. Vegan dishes are available. Steamed Beijing vegetable pot stickers ($8), chickpea polenta (lunch $10, dinner $12.50), and avocado "PLT" (grilled portobello, lettuce, tomato, avocado, and eggless mayo on toasted multigrain bread; $7.50) radiate wholesomeness. Open M-Th 11:30am-9:30pm, F-Sa 11:30am-10:30pm, Su 11am-9:30pm.

Steamer's Seafood House ($$$), 4820 Auburn Ave. (☎(301) 718-0661), near Norfolk Ave. Fresh fish, crab cakes, shrimp, and mussels served on patio tables in a summery atmosphere that feels like a backyard picnic. The main attraction: all-you-can-eat hard shell crab ($22 with corn, cole slaw, and fries). M-F 4-7pm bar specials include sandwiches with side dish ($2-3.50). Appetizers like Buffalo Shrimp ($7) and entrees like Alaskan King Crab ($20) are pricier. Outdoor patio seating available. Open Su-Th noon-11pm, F-Sa until midnight.

Philadelphia Mike's ($), 7732 Wisconsin Ave. (☎(301) 656-0103), near Middleton Ave. Mike's successfully replicates the gooey taste of an authentic Philly cheesesteak ($4-7) served over the counter in a modest, pizza shop atmosphere. Also serves burgers and deli sandwiches $3-6, breakfast subs under $2. Delivery min. $12. Open M-F 8am-10pm, Sa 9am-10pm, Su 9am-4pm.

Louisiana Express ($$), 4921 Bethesda Ave. (☎(301) 652-6945), near Arlington Rd. Authentic Cajun cuisine in a bright, white-lattice dining room. Crawfish bisque ($3.50) and chicken *jambalaya* ($6.25) are loaded with Cajun spices, as is the half-chicken platter with vegetable jambalaya and soft biscuits ($5.75). Sunday brunch (9am-2:30pm) offers a concoction of scrambled eggs with ham, bacon, and sausage on French bread with cheese. Delivery available ($15 min.). Open Su-Th 7:30am-9:30pm, F-Sa 7:30am-10:30pm.

Tastee Diner ($+), 7731 Woodmont Ave. (☎(301) 652-3970), at Cheltenham Dr. A classic Dick Tracy-esque diner: the aged wooden booths, long counter, and table jukeboxes look like they've been here since the place opened in 1935. The prices haven't changed much either; breakfast served around-the-clock for a few bucks. Deliciously greasy hamburgers $2.25-3.50. Fries $1.25, with gravy $1.75. Daily dinner specials (M-F 11am-9:30pm, Sa-Su noon-10pm) take up home-cooking with a vengeance. Open 24hr.

Paradise Restaurant ($$$), 7141 Wisconsin Ave. (☎(301) 907-7500), near Bethesda Ave. Pictures on the menu of the various Persian and Afghan dishes make ordering a little less risky for the timid newcomer. Lunch ($10) and dinner ($15-16) all-you-can-eat buffets cover soup, 6 entrees, salad, and fruit (daily 11:45am-2:30pm and 6-9pm). Try the *sambosa* (deep-fried pastry filled with spiced beef; 4 for $6). Entrees $9-14; baklava $2.50. Open Su-Th 11:45am-10pm, F-Sa 11:45am-11pm.

Bob's Famous Homemade Ice Cream ($), 4706 Bethesda Ave. (☎(301) 657-2963). Bob's daily rotating selection of gourmet ice cream and frozen yogurt flavors ($2-3) includes orange chocolate chip, Mozambique (cinnamon, nutmeg, and clove), and rum raisin (with real, face-flushing rum). Can't choose? Get three different flavors on the banana split ($5.30) Open M-Th 7:30am-10:30pm, F 7:30am-midnight, Sa 10am-midnight, Su noon-10:30pm; call for winter hrs.

Grapeseed ($$$), 4865 Cordell Ave. (☎(301) 986-9592; www.grapeseedbistro.com). Aimed at making connoisseurs of us all, Grapeseed provides an unpretentious environment for adventurous experimentation in the intimidating field of wine tasting. Serves dishes in both *tapas*-sized ($4-6) and full entree-sized portions ($15-19) with accompanying wine recommendations. Wine can be ordered by the bottle, by the glass, or by the taste. The cornmeal fried oysters ($4) and recommended Domaine Merlin-Cherrier Sancerre wine make a perfect combination. Open for lunch M-F 11:30am-2pm; dinner M-Th 5-10pm, F-Sa 5-11pm.

Chatter's, 8400 Wisconsin Ave. (☎(301) 654-1000). Located on the ground floor of the Bethesda Ramada. Calling itself the "Rock'n Sports Bar," this bar and grille gets rowdy come dinnertime as loud, boisterous families and a collection of area professionals gather to chow on the extra large "stadium" sandwiches served with french fries ($5-11). The wide walk-around bar is packed three deep during Chatter's Happy Hour M-F 4-7pm when patrons score rail drinks, domestic bottles, and drafts all for $1.50, as well as half-priced appetizers. Open Su-Th 6:30am-1am, F-Sa til 2am, kitchen closes at 10pm.

CAPITOL HILL

The secret to fine dining on "the Hill" is venturing away from all the white marble; peripheral areas harbor reasonably priced establishments free from congressional bigwigs and government flunkies. **Pennsylvania Ave.** dominates the restaurant scene, but Massachusetts Ave. NE and the surrounding residential areas offers some attractive, unique alternatives. Over 50 eateries inhabit **Union Station**. In the glitzy food court on the lower level and on the concourse between the shops and the trains, cheap takeout counters ring the walls, offering international fast food for under $5. Outside, street vendors offer even better deals: a hot dog, chips, and soft drink run $2. Do-it-yourselfers should brave the bustle of block-long **Eastern Market**, where butchers, bakers and farmers hawk their wares (see **Shopping**, p. 132). **At night, the areas northeast of Union Station or southeast of Seward Square warrant caution.**

🄳 **Armands Chicago Pizzeria ($)**, 226 Massachusetts Ave. NE (☎547-6600). Metro: Union Station. Armands' masterful New York and Chicago style pizzas continue to keep Armands a Capitol Hill hotspot. The lunch buffet (11:30am-2:30pm, $5.99) with all-you-can-eat pizza and salad lures nearby Hill staffers for a feeding frenzy. Pizza ($6.50-14.95), pasta ($3.95-5.25), salads ($3.50-4.75), and subs/sandwiches ($3.75-4.75). M-Sa 11:30am-11pm, Su 4pm-10pm.

Banana Cafe and Piano Bar ($$$), 500 8th St. SE (☎543-5906). Metro: Eastern Market. Fake banana trees and tropical portraits painted by the owner accompanied by a garish yellow interior and Cuban music make for a crazy fiesta. Marvelous Tex-Mex, Puerto Rican, and Cuban entrees ($6.95-15.95) include various tapas ($3.25-9), plantain soup ($4.50), shrimp fajitas ($15), and stuffed plantains with beef, chicken, or seafood ($15.95). Lunch entrees $6.25-9. Su brunch 11am-3pm ($13). Live music (every night) and outdoor seating available. Open M-Th 11:30am-10:30pm, F 11:30am-11pm, Sa noon-11pm, Su 11am-10pm.

Bread and Chocolate, 666 Pennsylvania Ave., (☎547-2875). Metro: Eastern Market. This gourmet pastry/coffee shop meticulously creates and displays delicious cakes (French Chocolate Raspberry Truffle Cake, Tiramisu $3.25 a slice), French pastries (Strawberry Chantilly $2.95, Caramel Triangle $2.20), and an assorted selection of appetizing sandwiches ($3.95-5.45). The inside seating and patio are perfect places to unwind from the hectic museum and monument crowd. M-Sa 7am-7pm, Su 8am-6pm.

Il Radiccho ($$), 223 Pennsylvania Ave. (☎547-5114). A pleasnt place to dine with an impressive painted backdrop of a small Italian farm and countyside. The food and service recreates the feel of an Italian countryside restaurant. All-you-can-eat spaghetti starts at $6.50 per person; add 1 or more sauces ($1.50-4) to the huge bowls and go crazy. Sauces range from a standard *pomodoro* ($1.50) to *cozze* (mussels with tomato and basil; $3.25). 25 varieties of pizza ($8-18). Open M-Th 11:30am-10pm, F-Sa 11:30am-11pm, Su 5-10pm.

The Market Lunch ($$), 225 7th St. SE (☎547-8444), in the Eastern Market complex. Metro: Eastern Market. The hallowed craft- and bargain-hunting halls and patios open on the weekdays for some of the freshest meals at relatively good prices. Crab cakes ($6-10) and soft shell crab (sandwich $7, platter $12) are the local specialties, but the Blue Bucks (buckwheat blueberry pancakes $3.50) have people lined up around the corner Sa mornings (breakfast served Sa until 11am). Open Tu-Sa 7:30am-3pm.

Misha's Deli ($), 210 7th St. SE (☎547-5858), north of Pennsylvania Ave. on 7th St., across from the Eastern Market complex. Metro: Eastern Market. Inexpensively scrumptious Russian and Eastern European food served in a comfortable Russian cafe. Sandwiches are named for famous Russian celebrities: try the Dostoevsky (veggie burger with hummus, lettuce, tomato, onions, and mustard on a pita; $4) or the Stalin (veggie cutlet on Russian black bread with cheese, spicy *ajvar*, lettuce, and tomato; $4). A great bakery and lots of vegetarian and non-fat options; very limited indoor seating with some outdoor seating available. *Let's Go* readers 10% discount. Open M-F 8am-7:30pm, Sa 7:30am-6pm, Su 9am-5pm.

Burrito Brothers ($), 205 Pennsylvania Ave. SE (☎543-6835). Metro: Capital South. Local chain is the takeout haven for busy interns and Hill-staffers. The cheapest hard taco around goes for only $1.70 with combos available ($3.15-3.55). Burritos ($3.95-4.95) and quesadillas ($2.95-3.15) round out the cheap Mexican dishes. Limited counter seating only. Open M-Sa 11am-9pm.

Le Bon Cafe ($), 210 2nd St. SE (☎547-7200), a stone's throw from the Capitol. Metro: Capitol South. Tastefully sparse and cheery coffee shop makes excellent food from scratch with all-natural ingredients. Espresso ($1.25), *café au lait* ($1.75) and pastries ($1.10-3.50) make for a light breakfast until 11am. Sandwiches (after 11am, $5-6) and elegant salads ($3.75-6.95) complete the repertoire. Outdoor seating. Open M-F 7:30am-5pm, Sa-Su 8:30am-3:30pm.

Anatolia ($$+), 633 Pennsylvania Ave. SE (☎544-4753). Metro: Eastern Market. This casual but refined restaurant serves traditional Turkish cuisine in a room with *kilim* (hanging quilts) and copper pots. Chicken shish kebab ($6.95-9.95) and *baba ghanoush* are the specialties at lunch. Lots of lamb dishes and house specialties ($6.95-7.95). Doner kebab served only F nights (ground beef and lamb marinated for 48 hr. on a skewer; $14). Open M-Sa 11:30am-3pm and 5-10pm.

Capitol Hill Jimmy T's ($), 501 E. Capitol St. (☎546-3646), at 5th St. under the brick octagonal turret. Metro: Eastern Market. Red vinyl benches and classic phone booths throw this ancient neighborhood joint a fantazmo touchdown to the 50s. Friendly service, fabulous fare, and unbeatable prices: sandwiches $1.50-3.55, burgers around $3. Nothing over $6. Open Tu-F 6:30am-3pm, Sa-Su 8am-3pm.

Roasters on the Hill ($), 666 Pennsylvania Ave. SE (☎543-8355), on the 7th St. side of the building. Metro: Eastern Market. Murals of coffee bean pickers, bright yellow walls, and a red tile counter color Roasters an adrenaline-rush fantasy. Cappuccino ($2), and iced mocha ($3) are among the hot or cold beverages; biscotti ($1), scones ($1.75), and muffins ($1.75) buffer the caffeine. The aroma of fresh waffles is breathtaking ($2.75, add $1.25 for whipped cream and strawberries). Inside and outside seating. Open M-Sa 7am-7pm, Su 8am-5:30pm.

The Dubliner ($$), 520 N. Capitol St. (☎737-3773), look for the Phoenix Park Hotel awning. Metro: Union Station. Relaxed professionals collect here after the working day is done for pub grub like fish and chips ($9.50) and Beef O'Flaherty (hot roast beef in a casserole with melted bleu cheese and fries; $8.50). Guinness ($4 a pint) flows freely. Live Irish music nightly (M-Sa 9pm, Su 7:30pm). Open Su-Th 7-10am and 11am-2am, F-Sa 7-10am and 11am-3am.

Hawk 'n' Dove ($+), 329 Pennsylvania Ave. SE (☎543-3300). Metro: Capitol South. Popular watering hole with the feel of an old English pub has served the neigborhood since 1967. Functional bar food includes sandwiches ($4.50-8), 12 bottled beers ($2.75 and up), and 13 drafts ($1.75 and up). Open Su-Th 10am-2am, F-Sa 10am-3am.

Hunan Dynasty ($$), 215 Pennsylvania Ave. SE (☎546-6161/2). Metro: Capitol South. Ultra-modern, pale pink surroundings include an aquarium full of goldfish, a huge mural of the Great Wall, and Hill staff power-lunching. Standard Chinese cuisine comes in generous portions (entrees $5-12); a sushi bar complements the selection (60¢-$1.35 per piece). Takeout available. Weekday lunch specials (11:30am-3pm; $6). Open M-Th 11:30am-10pm, F 11:30am-11pm, Sa 5:30-11pm, Su 5:30-10pm.

Kenny's Smoke House ($+), 732 Maryland Ave. NE (☎547-4561), at 8th St. Metro: Union Station. A short hike away from the Hill, hearty grilled meat and picnic benches create an atmosphere like a neighborhood barbecue. Lunchtime specials like pork chops ($6) come with cornbread and 2 sides. Sandwiches $2.50-5, entrees $4-9. Large parties can order ribs by the slab ($15). Open M-Th 11am-9:30pm, F-Sa 11am-10:30pm.

Taverna the Greek Islands ($$), 307 Pennsylvania Ave. SE (☎547-8360). Metro: Capitol South. White stucco walls and shady outdoor tables host a happy clientele feasting on *moussaka alla Greek islands* (tomato and besamala sauce over layers of eggplant, ground beef, and parmesan cheese; $8) and other Greek sandwiches and entrees ($7-14). The *Saganaki alla Paros* ($6) conjures 8ft. flames shooting from your plate; cool down with a fresh piña colada or margarita ($4). A downstairs deli has provisions as well. Open M-Sa 11am-midnight, Su 3:30-11pm.

Mr. Henry's Victorian Pub ($$), 601 Pennsylvania Ave. SE (☎546-8412). Metro: Eastern Market. Victorian decor and meatloaf-esque meals bring new meaning to the concept of comfort food, while an outdoor patio on the 6th-St. side is a popular lounge spot. Big burgers and sandwiches ($3.50-7) and entrees ($6-8) are enjoyed by a mostly gay and lesbian crowd. Live jazz Su during brunch (10am-3pm). Open daily 11:30am-1:30am.

2nd St. Deli ($), 209½ Pennsylvania Ave. SE (☎544-3049). Metro: Capitol South. Standard D.C. deli handles business clientele during the lunch rush. Hot Chinese food bar ($3.89 per lb.), cold salad bar ($3.89 per lb.), ready-made salads ($3-5), and made-to-order sandwiches ($3.50-4.50). Changing lunch special (after 11am) features a sandwich with free fries and soda. Open M-F 7am-6:30pm, Sa 8am-4pm.

CHINATOWN

SEE
MAP
P. 308

Most of D.C.'s best Chinese, Burmese, and Mongolian restaurants cling to tiny **H Street NW** and its adjacent blocks. Many restaurants serve dim sum (Chinese a la carte brunch), arguably the best and undeniably the most popular meal in Chinatown. Don't be turned off by the decrepit exterior of many of these restaurants; they all serve wonderful food, and all have extensive takeout options. The area is fairly safe, but exercise caution at night. Use Metro: Gallery Place-Chinatown for all of the following.

Szechuan Gallery ($$), 617 H St. NW (☎898-1180). Recognize this place? A scene from the movie *True Lies* was filmed here, and they've got autographed pictures to prove it. Locally renowned for its unusual dishes such as congee, a delicious Chinese gruel ($5). Lunch specials $5-8. Open Su-Th 11am-10pm, F-Sa 11am-11pm.

Burma Restaurant ($$), upstairs at 740 6th St. NW (☎638-1280), between H and G St. Mild Burmese curries, unique spices, and a plethora of garnishes replace typical Chinese soy sauce. Fried golden prawns with sweet and sour chili sauce ($6) are a delicious starter, while the squid, sauteed in garlic, ginger, and scallions is a tasty main dish ($8). Entrees $6-8. Open M-F 11am-3pm and 6-10:30pm daily.

Hunan Chinatown ($$$), 624 H St. NW (☎783-5858). Upscale restaurant with two levels serving standard Chinese food. Kung Pao chicken (diced and sauteed in brown sauce with red peppers and peanuts; lunch $6.75), tea smoked duck (dinner $15), and local favorite Hunan lamb (thin slices of lamb sauteed over broccoli; dinner $11).

Mr. Yung's Restaurant ($$), 740 6th St. NW (☎628-1098), between H and G St. This sparsely decorated dive serves typical Cantonese fare ($5-12) with specials like mushrooms with crab ($14). Dim sum $2.30-4 (daily 11am-3pm). 10% discount on takeout orders over $30. Open M-F 11am-10:30pm, Sa-Su 11am-midnight.

Tony Cheng's Seafood Restaurant ($$+), 619 H St. NW (☎371-8669), on the 2nd floor of a garishly decorated building. Reminiscent of scenes from the great gangster movies, the restaurant consists of a large room with wide chandeliers and lobster tanks. Full *dim sum* menu (daily 11am-3pm). In **Tony Cheng's Mongolian Restaurant** a floor below, patrons chose from a buffet of beef, leeks, mushrooms, and sprouts, which are then stir-fried by the cooks (lunch: 1 serving $8.50, all-you-can-eat $15). Open Su-Th 11am-11pm, F-Sa 11am-midnight.

Go-Lo's ($$), 604 H St. NW (☎347-4656). The assassins conspiring to kill President Lincoln met in the Surrat Boardinghouse, which is now the site of Go-Lo's. Lavishly decorated and divided into smaller rooms, the restaurant provides greater intimacy than its H St counterparts. Lunch specials ($5-6) vary daily. Entrees ($8-18). Open Su-Th 11am-10:30pm, F-Sa 11am-11:30am.

New Big Wong Restaurant ($+), 610 H St. NW (☎628-0491). Friendly but cluttered, basement Cantonese restaurant. Pint and quart-sized take-out entrees ($5-8) are family friendly. Feel free to have spicy dishes altered to your taste. Free delivery ($10 min.). Open Su-Th 10:30am-3am, F-Sa til 4am.

Tai Shan Restaurant ($$), 622 H St. NW (☎639-0266) Slightly unkempt, but nevertheless, a busy tourist lunch spot providing a quick sit down meal, offering dim sum platters and noodle soups ($5-8). Lunch specials $5. Open Su-Th 11am-midnight, F-Sa 11am-3am.

China Doll ($$), 627 St. NW (☎289-4755). Standard Chinese dishes with dinner include combination meals with soup, spring roll, and steamed rice (lunch $6-7, dinner $8-9). Also doubles as a bakery, serving Chinese and French pastries. *Dim sum* M-F 11am-3pm, all day Su. Open Su-Th 11am-10pm, F-Sa 11am-midnight.

DUPONT CIRCLE

SEE MAP P. 318 *Rock Creek Park* YOU ARE HERE

With eye candy everywhere, dining in Dupont is as much about people-watching as grabbing a good meal. The restaurants on 17th St., 18th St., and Connecticut Ave. all spill out onto the street in an endless series of patios which get packed daily with young professionals. Many restaurants are more upscale than those in bohemian Adams-Morgan, but there are still some delectable bargains to be had. The neighborhood is a lot of fun, but east of 17th St. it becomes rapidly less safe. Park as far west as possible to avoid break-ins. Use Metro: Dupont Circle for all of the following.

🌋 **Raku ($$)**, 1900 Q St. NW (☎265-7258, delivery ☎232-8646), off Connecticut Ave. Taking its name from the Japanese word for "pleasure," this upscale restaurant serves pan-Asian noodles ($9-13), salads ($5-11), sushi ($4-13), and "pan-Asian *tapas*" (a variety of dumplings, rolls, and skewers; $3-8). Skylights illuminate the warm wooden tones of the comfortable dining room filled with picnic table like booths. In summer, the patio is the perfect place to sample specialty cocktails. Open Su-Th 11:30am-10pm, F-Sa 11:30am-11pm.

🌋 **Lauriol Plaza ($$)**, 1865 18th St. NW (☎387-0035), Recently moved to the corner of 18th & T St. NW. Dupont's hottest spot serves Latino food served in copious quantities. Patio and winding maze of dining rooms continuously host large crowds. The complimentary chips and salsa are addictive. Appetizers like fried plantains and guacamole $2.50-7; entrees $6.50-16. Su brunch entrees $6-9 (11am-3pm). Free parking. Open Su-Th 11:30am-11pm, F-Sa and holidays 11:30am-midnight.

🌋 **Mediterranean Blue ($$)**, 1910 18th St. NW (☎483-2583), near the corner of T and 18th St. Avoid the crowds at nearby Lauriol Plaza and enjoy a delicious Italian meal in the romantic, dimly-lit dining room. Locals prefer the *penne estivi*, penne pasta tossed w/ fresh mozzarella, fresh basil, and sun-ripened tomatoes ($10). Also serves lamb, chicken, and shrimp kabobs ($9-16). Open daily 5pm-midnight, Su brunch 11am-3pm.

Sakana ($$+), 2026 P St. NW (☎887-0900). The enticing smell of fresh Japanese food welcomes guests to this small, dimly-lit, primarily sushi restaurant. Well-prepared tempura and teriyaki dishes also. Takeout available. Entrees $8.50-13, sushi rolls $2-10. Open M-F 11:30am-2:30pm and 5-10:30pm, Sa 11:30am-2:30pm and 5-11pm.

Luna Grill & Diner ($$), 1301 Connecticut Ave. NW (☎835-2280), south of Dupont Circle. Friendly and slightly eccentric waitstaff serving diner fare in a moon-themed dining room. Salads, pastas, sandwiches ($6-10), and entrees ($10-16), all great in taste, generous in proportion, and modest in price. Lunch during the week is always crowded, so call ahead to get on the waiting list. No reservations otherwise. Open M-F 8am-11pm, Sa 10am-midnight, Su 10am-10pm.

Pizzeria Paradiso ($$), 2029 P St. NW (☎223-1245), near 21st St. A modest awning hides the surprisingly airy, light-filled restaurant. Their brick oven bakes up some of the most genuinely Italian thin-crust pizza in town. 8 in. $7-10; 12 in. $12-16. Toppings 75¢-$1.75. Also offering an array of panini sandwiches ($5-7) and salads ($3-5). Open daily 11:30am-11pm.

Skewers ($$), 1633 P St. NW (☎387-7400), near 17th St. Above Cafe Luna. Excellent Middle Eastern served in a stylish restaurant with mosaic surfaces, tapestries, and shimmery drapes. Lunch sandwiches include filet mignon pita ($8), grilled eggplant with yogurt ($5.25), and grilled vegetable sandwich ($5.25). The appetizer platter for 2 ($11.50) is a meal in itself. Appetizers $3-6, full-sized entrees $11-15. Open Su-Th 11am-11pm, F-Sa 11am-midnight.

Pan Asian Noodles & Grill ($$), 2020 P St. NW (☎872-8889), near 20th St. Truly pan-Asian, offering Thai, Chinese, Japanese, Filipino, and Vietnamese delicacies in an informal dining room. A local favorite is the Borneo fried rice, an Indonesian style of fried rice cooked with your choice of meat ($8). Lunch specials $6-8. Entrees $8-17. Open M-Th 11:30am-2:30pm and 5-10pm, F 11:30am-2:30pm and 5-11pm, Sa noon-2:30pm and 5-11pm, Su 5-10pm.

Ben's Chili Bowl

Zorba's Cafe ($$), 1612 20th St. NW (☎387-8555), at Connecticut Ave. by the Q St. entrance to the Dupont Circle Metro. Named after the title character from the movie "Zorba the Greek" this joint offers homemade Greek food served up quickly in a relaxed atmosphere. Specialties like *spanakopita* ($4), creamy hummus, and moist, cinnamony *baklava* ($2). Also serves pizza (12 in. $10-15). Sandwiches $5-7. Entrees $7-10. Open M-Sa 11am-11:30pm, Su 11:30am-10:30pm, last orders 30min. before closing.

City Lights of China ($$+), 1731 Connecticut Ave. NW (☎265-6688), between R and S St. *Washingtonian Magazine* award-winning restaurant from 1992-99 serves delicious Chinese food in an intimate dining room. Special steamed dishes for the calorie-conscious. Entrees $8-14. Open M-Th 11:30am-10:30pm, F 11:30am-11pm, Sa noon-11pm, Su noon-10:30pm. Reservations suggested.

Bua ($$), 1635 P St. NW (☎265-0828, delivery ☎232-8646), near 17th St. Cool, brick dining room and breezy patio with delicious Thai cuisine. Nice array of vegetarian entrees for $7.50. Tasty cashew chicken ($8.25). Lunch entrees $6-8. Dinner entrees $6-13. Open lunch M-F 11:30am-2:30pm; dinner M-Th 5-10:30pm, F 5-11pm, Open all day Sa noon-11pm, Su noon-10:30pm.

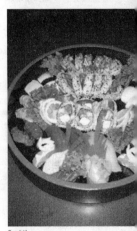
Sushi!

Peppers ($$), 1527 17th St. NW (☎328-8193). People-watch from the patio of this pepper-themed restaurant serving everything from fajitas and pastas to excellent Oriental vegetarian dumplings. Regulars give rave reviews of the "No Ordinary Calamari" (breaded squid stir-fried in soy sauce; $7). Happy Hour M-W nights. Open Su-Th 11:30am-2am, F-Sa 11:30am-3am; kitchen closes 11pm.

Sala Thai ($$), 2016 P St. NW (☎872-1144). A *Washingtonian Magazine* award-winning restaurant for 1999 for both its delicious Thai cuisine and romantic, dark blue and purple dining room. Large servings of traditional dishes like *pad thai* ($8) and harder to find *pu-nim* (spicy soft shell crab; $13). Open M 11:30am-3pm and 5-10:30pm, Tu-Th 11:30am-3pm and 5-11pm, F 11:30am-3pm and 5-11:30pm, Sa noon-11:30pm, Su noon-10:30pm.

Dupont Italian Kitchen ($$), 1637 17th St. NW (☎328-3222), at R St. Delicious, no-frills Italian food at excellent prices. Meat entrees served with spaghetti and tomato sauce ($8-10). Daily specials offer large portions ($10). Pasta $5-8. Sandwiches $5-6. Free delivery (min. $10). Open Tu-Sa noon-midnight, Su-M noon-11pm.

Meskerem at Adams-Morgan

Cafe Luna ($$), 1633 P St. NW (☎387-4005), near 17th St. Not to be mistaken for the Luna Grill and Diner. Popular basement cafe/restaurant, with well-prepared veggie and lowfat fare. Efficient waitstaff handles large lunch and dinner crowds with ease. Breakfast served all day ($1-5). Huge sandwiches satisfy almost any appetite ($4-6). Pasta $6-9. Salads and pizza $5-7. Brunch served Sa-Su 10am-3pm ($5-7). Takeout available. Open M-Th 8am-11:30pm, F 8am-midnight, Sa 10am-midnight, Su 10am-11pm.

Trio Restaurant ($$), 1537 17th St. NW (☎232-6305), at Q St. The organizers of the 1963 March on Washington met at this historic diner to strategize. Classic American meals including BLTs, turkey pot pie, steaks, and huge chocolate malts. Hearty breakfasts served until 5pm ($2-5). Burgers and sandwiches $3-7. Entrees $7-14. Lunch specials M-F $7.50. Some vegetarian items. Locals frequent the adjacent bar and late-night pizza joint. Open daily 7:30am-midnight.

CAFES

▧ **Xando ($),** 1350 Connecticut Ave. NW (☎296-9341), south of the Dupont Metro; 1647 Connecticut Ave. NW (☎332-6364), north of the Dupont Metro. Two great locations for this trendy see-'n'-be-seen coffee bar. Large outdoor patio makes Xando's Dupont North location the perfect place to relax and watch the crowds go by. Reminisce about days as a Boy or Girl Scout by making s'mores around the portable campfire ($6 for 2 and $11 for 4). Also serves wraps and grilled "xandwiches" ($5-6). They kindly provide telephone cords if you want to bring your laptop in and work online. Open M-Th 6:30am-midnight, F 6:30am-2am, Sa 7am-2am, Su 7am-midnight.

Teaism ($$), 2009 R St. NW (☎667-3827) just west of Connecticut Ave. Elevating their love of tea to idolatry, this quiet tea house offers a huge selection of green, black, and oolong teas, as well as tisanes (fruit infusions). Sedate, would-be intellectual crowds muse over the meaning of life and the scrumptious ginger scones (90¢). Pots of tea $1.75-5. Breakfast ($2.75-7.25) served M-F until 11:30am; Sa-Su until 2:30pm. "Bento Boxes," Japanese lunches with salad, entree, and fruit $8. Open M-Th 8am-10pm, F 8am-11pm, Sa 9am-11pm, Su 9am-10pm.

Jolt 'n' Bolt Coffee and Tea House ($), 1918 18th St. NW (☎232-0077), 5 blocks from the center of Adams-Morgan, 6 blocks from Dupont Circle. Pleasant neighborhood lingering spot where students, readers, and writers relax. The brick patio is charmingly decorated with ivies and a small fountain, and populated by over-friendly sparrows. Espresso drinks $1.30-3; fruit smoothies $3.50; impressive selection of desserts $1.50-3.50. Open daily 7am-1:30am.

The Cyberstop Cafe ($), 1513 17th St. NW (☎234-2470), just north of P St. The comfortable upstairs lounge feels more like a living room than a cafe. Internet rates are reasonable: 30min. $5, $8 per hr., as are the food prices: coffee $1-3, cookies $1. Open Su-Th 7:30am-midnight, F-Sa 7:30am-2am.

Afterwords Cafe ($$), 1517 Connecticut Ave. NW (☎387-1462), near Q St. Enter through Kramerbooks (see p. 126) or behind on 19th St. Overcrowded and overpriced, but one of the few places to indulge a late-night sweet tooth. The cakes, pies, and mousse ($4.25-6.25) are delicious; unfortunately serving size is sacrificed for cute presentation. Free email access at the bar. Espresso and huge lattes $1.50-3.50. Live music W-Sa. Open Su-Th 7:30am-1am, F-Sa 24hr.

FARRAGUT

Suits and fannypack-donning tourists alike surge through Farragut's tasty and inexpensive lunchtime delis, quick ethnic eateries, and street vendors. Health-conscious yuppies have also generated an array of low-fat dining options throughout the Farragut area. Establishments hawking frozen yogurt, salads, and espresso compete for attention with bars offering free Happy Hour buffets.

SEE MAP P. 309 — YOU ARE HERE

The Art Gallery Grille ($$), 1712 I St. NW (☎298-6658; www.artgallerygrille.com), near 17th St. Metro: Farragut West. This Art Deco flashback doesn't skimp on the neon lighting, jukebox, and a DJ spinning rock hits every Thursday and Friday night. The schizo combination of old-style diner charm and sophisticated, healthy, Middle Eastern specialties draws in the corporate lunchers. Falafel trays $9.95. The White Pizza (mozzarella, parmesan, and havarti cheese pizza) $8, Caesar salad $8.25, and specialty sandwiches $8.25-10.95 are favorites. Happy Hour 4-8pm with specials varying each night. Outdoor seating available. Open M-W 6:30am-11pm, Th-F 6:30am-2am.

Casa Blanca ($), 1014 Vermont Ave. NW (☎393-4430), between K and L St. Metro: McPherson Square. The modest decor is deceiving: Casa Blanca has mastered homemade Peruvian, Salvadoran, and Mexican cuisine, and they have the crowd to prove it. Basic tacos are 2 for $3.50. The Peruvian specialty *pollo a la braza* (roasted chicken with salad and fried potatoes or rice and beans) is a steal at $5.50. Carry-out 50¢ less at lunch, $1 at dinner. Daily specials $4. Free delivery. Open M-Sa 9:30am-10pm, Su noon-5pm.

Il Pranzo ($), 1800 M St. NW (☎659-6464). Metro: Farragut North. Lively and authentic Italian restaurant expertly bakes some of the neighborhood's finer Napoletona (thin-slice) and Sicilian (thick-slice) pizza. The menu doesn't end with pizza though ($1.65-2.15 slice); salads ($2.75-4.50), pasta ($5.65-6.35), subs ($4-5), daily specials, and an espresso bar also please the hungry crowd. Open M-F 7am-7pm, Sa 10am-3pm.

Juice Joint Cafe ($+), 1025 Vermont Ave. NW (☎347-6783). Metro: McPherson Square. Health-nuts, vegans, and people simply craving cool smoothies and good food frequent this peppy juice joint. Customize your own juice ($2.75-4.25) or smoothie ($3.75-4.25) from a long list of vegetable and fruit juices, power additions, and minerals. Vegan and non-vegan (turkey burger, fresh seared yellow-fish tuna) sandwiches and wraps ($3.50-7.25) mix up a variety of creative flavors such as spinach and sweet potato. Multigrain breakfasts served until 10:30am. Open M-F 7:30am-5pm, Sa 7:30am-3pm.

The Baja Grille ($$), 1133 20th St. NW (☎659-4136). Metro: Farragut North or Dupont Circle. Cuisine from Baja California served in a chill dining area with a southwestern motif. Tasty soft *cabos* (pizzas made on flour tortillas; $3.29-6.49) and *brochettas* (kebabs with marinated and grilled shrimp, steak, mahi mahi, or chicken with onions, tomatoes, and peppers; $6.19-7.25) are the specialties, along with an impressive Caesar salad (a dish they claim was invented in Baja; $4.25). Open M-F 7am-4pm.

Sizzling Express ($), 1445 K St. NW (☎408-1234). Metro: McPherson Square. Denizens of the political and corporate worlds ransack the scrumptious hot and cold food bars of this popular take-out restaurant. For $4.59 per lb., combine piping hot food (featuring Chinese noodle dishes) and cold salad bars (including sushi, fresh fruit, and creative salads). Breakfast favorites include egg and cheese sandwiches, omelettes, and more ($1.65-3.95). Ice cream and frozen yogurt $1.60-3. A host of deli sandwiches and subs $4-7. Very limited outdoor seating. Open M-F 6am-4pm.

Thai Kingdom ($$), 2021 K St. NW (☎835-1700), near 21st St. Metro: Farragut West or Foggy Bottom-GWU. Overflowing with gilt decorations, pink satin, and photos of Thai celebrities, gaudy Thai Kingdom features ingenuously named specialties like "Famous Wings" (chicken wings stuffed with crabmeat, mushrooms, and bean thread noodles; $5) and "Anna and the King" (scallops wrapped in minced chicken fried with basil sauce; $7.25). Open M-Th 11:30am-2:30pm and 5-10:30pm, F 11:30am-2:30pm and 5-10:30pm, Sa noon-11pm, Su noon-10pm.

Famous Luigi's ($$+), 1132 19th St. NW (☎331-7574). Metro: Farragut North or Dupont Circle. The red-and-white checkered tableclothes, soft candlelight, and fine cuisine blend to create a classic Italian ambiance with a hint of amore. Good selection of *I Panini* (sandwiches $4.25-7.25) and pastas ($6.25-12.50). More complicated dishes like *calamari alla griglia* climb the price ladder (grilled squid with vegetables and pasta; $11.25). Pizza $6.50-17.95. Open Su-Th 11am-midnight, F-Sa 11am-2am.

Julia's Empanadas ($), 1000 Vermont Ave. NW (☎789-1878). Metro: McPherson Square. Also located at 1221 Connecticut Ave. NW (☎861-8828) and 2452 18th St. NW (☎328-6232). Julia's sells a variety of *empanadas* (calzone-like pockets of dough filled with various ingredients; $3) in a relaxed take-out/eat-in atmosphere. *Empanada* options include *chorizo* (Spanish sausage with rice and black bean), Chilean-style beef (beef ground and served with raisins, hard-boiled egg, onion, and ripe olive), and *saltenas* (chicken with potato, green peas, hard boiled egg, green olives, and onion). Lunch combos $4.95. Seasonal soup menu often includes gazpacho ($1.39-3). Open M-F 10:30am-7pm.

Via Cucina ($), 1120 20th St. NW (☎463-4221), in the courtyard at Lafayette Ctr. Metro: Farragut North. Friendly Italian cafe caters to the lunchtime and late afternoon crowd. Pick from pasta specials, pizza slices ($1.70-2.50, thin or thick crust), American deli sandwich favorites, or salads ($6-7). Leftover pizza slices and sandwiches are 50% off after 3pm. Open M-F 7am-4pm.

Vie de France ($), 1723 K St. NW (☎775-9193). Metro: Farragut North. A clear example of cultural exchange, Vie de France mixes American fast-food decor, uniforms, and service with the appetitizing dishes of France. Combos featuring soups, salads, and sandwiches are the special-ties ($5.99). The ham and cheese sandwich and Californian sandwich (turkey, swiss, avocado, and sprouts) are also great ($5.29-5.35). The bakery also sells various sweet cakes and pastries (99¢-$1.69). M-F 6:30am-6pm, Sa 8am-3pm.

FOGGY BOTTOM

With the exception of a few popular local spots and restaurant chains, Foggy Bottom is a culinary wasteland. A short walk to Farragut or Dupont Circle may provide more interesting dining options. Use Metro: Foggy Bottom-GWU.

Lindy's Bon Apetit ($), 2040 I St. NW (☎452-0055), at the corner of 21st St. and I St. Famous for its selection of over 23 humongous burgers ($3-6), including veggie and turkey. Serves breakfast until 11am, 1pm on weekends. Outdoor seating. Open M-F 8am-9pm, Sa-Su 11am-8pm.

Cup A' Cup A' at the Watergate ($), at the intersection of New Hampshire and F St. in the Water-gate Complex. Large, indoor dining area in shades of apricot and sea-green. Reenact the infa-maous crime with The Break-In Sandwich (turkey breast and avocado on a baguette; $5.49) Standard wraps and sandwiches, coffee drinks ($1.25-3.50), and great pies and cookies ($1.50-5). Open M-Th 7:30am-8pm, F-Sa 7:30am-8pm, Su 10am-6pm.

Cone E. Island ($) (☎822-8460), in the mall at 2000 Pennsylvania Ave. A modern ice cream parlor with Ionic columns ringed in neon lights and seven tables cramped into a small second level. Soft-serve frozen yogurt vies with many flavors of divine hard ice cream. Generous cones $2-3, plus 40¢ for homemade cones. Fat-free bakery treats $1-3, including delicious blondie brownies ($1.45). Open daily noon-midnight.

Fresco, Italian Gourmet at Watergate ($), 2554 Virginia Ave. NW (☎337-6432), in the Water-gate Compound; go down the stairs where Virginian Ave exits west of the rotary. While the white stucco, aqua awnings and pink neon sign might recall a cheap strip in Florida, the generous por-tions and outdoor seating make this a lunchtime hotspot. Spaghetti and sauce is the specialty ($3.50). Also offers fruit and salad bar, frozen yogurt ($1.50-3), and subs ($3.50-5). Whole piz-zas start at $10. Jumbo slice of pizza $1.70. Open M-F 7:30am-7pm, Sa 10:30am-5pm.

Thai Kitchen ($$), 2311 M St. NW (☎452-6090), at the corner of M St. and 23rd St. Stepping down off of M St., patrons are greeted by the soothing sounds of a fountain waterfall setting the mood for a relaxed meal in this upscale Thai restaurant. Beautiful varnished wood decor is matched by presentations of *som tum* (papaya blended with peanuts and shrimp; $6.95) and scallops and snow peas ($12.95). Open M-Th 11am-11pm, F 11am-11:30pm, Sa noon-11:30pm, Su noon-10:30pm.

GEORGETOWN

Among the many quality attractions in Georgetown (shopping, shop-ping, and more shopping) are also fab eats. Georgetown's dining options mostly line M Street and Wisconsin Avenue, vying for the attention of college kids, tourists, and power-lunching execs. Eateries range from expensive wood-and-brass establishments to more afford-able Italian, Indian, Middle Eastern, Thai, and Vietnamese restaurants. Use Metro: Foggy Bottom-GWU or Dupont Circle to access the area. It's a 20-minute walk from either station to Georgetown's restaurants; the 30-series buses run down M St. and Wisconsin Ave. between Downtown and Tenleytown or Friendship Heights.

🔲 **Cafe La Ruche ($$)**, 1039 31st St. NW (☎965-2684, takeout 965-2591), 2 blocks south of M St. "La Ruche" means "the beehive," and this place gets buzzin' late at night when romantics move in for dessert and coffee. La Ruche serves up French fare, including soups ($4), salads ($4-9), quiche ($8), and sandwiches ($7-16). Enjoy the full meal or skip right to the the delicious chocolate mousse ($5) or kiwi tart ($5). Open M-Th 11:30am-11:30pm, F 11:30am-1am, Sa 10am-1am, Su 10am-10:30pm.

Dean and Deluca ($$), 3276 M St. NW (☎ 342-2500), next to Georgetown Park Mall, near the corner of 33rd and M St. This glitzy gourmet market blends right in with the chi-chi atmosphere of the Mall next door, but don't let the pretension stop you from trying out the adjacent espresso bar's offerings. In the summer, sip latte and watch the beautiful people enter and exit the mall from the garden seating. Featuring an assortment of salads ($5-7), gourmet soup and sandwich combos ($9), coffee drinks, and sweets. Espresso Bar open Tu-Th 8am-8pm, F-Sa 8am-9pm.

Furini ($+), 2805 M St. NW (☎ 965-1000), at M and 28th St. The potted plants, bookshelves, floral theme, old-fashioned hospitality, and good home cooking attract the masses at lunch. Businesspeople, students, tourists, and local shopkeepers flock for Furini's made-with-love sandwiches, salads, and sweets. Breakfast served M-F until 11:30am, Sa 1:30pm. $1.50-4 per item, specials $8, desserts $4. Open M-F 7:30am-7pm, Sa 8am-5pm.

Bistro Med ($$) 3288 M St. (☎ 333-0955), at the corner of M and 33rd St. Inviting smells waft from the open air storefront of this brand new restaurant specializing in Levantine cuisine from the eastern Mediterranean. Offering Turkish style pizzas such as the *Lahmacun*, a turkish favorite with ground beef ($11) as well as entrees($11-17) including the *Merquez de Maroccaire:* lamb sausage with eggplant and couscous ($11). Special late-night brunch served Th-Sa 11pm-5am. Open daily 11:30am-10:30pm.

Adams-Morgan dining

Patisserie Poupon ($+), 1645 Wisconsin Ave. NW (☎ 342-3248), near the corner or Wisconsin and Q St. A new upscale branch of the award-winning Baltimore bakery known for its intense French pastries. Start the day off with the real breakfast of champions: butterful brioche, pear danishes, and croissants ($1-2). Fruit tarts, raspberry mousse cakes, and mocha cream cakes available from individual to party portions ($4-34). Sandwiches, quiches, and salads ($4-7). Open Tu-Sa 8am-6:30pm, Su 8am-4pm.

Amma Vegetarian Kitchen ($), 3291 M St. NW (☎ 625-6025), at the corner of M and 33rd St. Traditional south Indian cuisine in a spare, spotless dining room. Regional specialities like *idli sambar* (light, steamed rice flour cakes served with a dazzling vegetable sauce, $3) initiate the newcomer to the fine flavors of Indian cuisine. Very affordable—the most expensive dish will set you back only $5. Open M-Th 11:30am-2:30pm and 5:30-9:30pm; F-Su 11:30am-3pm and 5:30-10pm.

Gadsby's Tavern

Saigon Inn ($$), 2928 M St. NW (☎ 337-5588), at 30th St. Less costly than Vietnam-Georgetown, its next-door rival. The presidents of Haiti and Peru have eaten in its ornate dining room. The lunch special, a generous 4-dish sampler, wins raves from locals ($4.50, daily 11am-3pm). The Saigon pancake, a crispy crepe filled with tender meat and seafood, is the house specialty ($8). Delicately spiced "fresh" rolls with or without the shrimp and pork ($4 for 2). Entrees $6-9. Free delivery ($12 minimum). Open M-F 11am-11pm, Su noon-11pm.

Vietnam-Georgetown Restaurant ($$), 2934 M St. NW (☎ 337-4536), at 30th St. Diners can choose to eat in the intimate dining room decorated with ornate Asian lamps or enjoy a meal under the stars on the patio. Menu includes traditional Vietnamese noodle soups ($4-7), crispy spring rolls ($4.75), grilled chicken ($9.50), and crepe entrees ($7-9). Open daily 11am-11pm.

Tako Grill

Houston's ($$$), 1065 Wisconsin Ave. NW (☎338-7760), a block south of M St. The staid, wood-paneled dining room dimly lit with fire lanters attracts both tourists and locals looking for a hearty meal. The enormous appetizers ($4-6) as well as hickory-grilled burgers and fries ($8) will fill any appetite. The steaks and prime ribs ($11-24) can be costly, but are especially tender and juicy. Few vegetarian options are served; the Veggie Burger ($8) and Vegetable Platter ($9) are the only concessions in this meat den. Frequent lines and no reservations, but worth the wait. Open M-Th 11:30am-11pm, F 11:30am-midnight, Sa noon-midnight, Su noon-10pm.

Burrito Brothers ($), 3273 M St. NW (☎965-3963, delivery 232-8646), at the corner of M and Potomac St. Nothin' fancy, just good, cheap eats. Basically takeout, though there's a line of benches and a counter in this bright storefront. Features tacos with beans for under $4 and enormous burritos ($4-6). Open M-Th 11am-9:30pm, F-Sa 11am-3am, Su 11-8pm.

Booeymonger ($), 3265 Prospect St. NW (☎333-4810), at the corner of Prospect and Potomac St. Tucked amidst townhouses this non-descript restaurant gets packed with locals at lunchtime. Don't be deterred by long lines—they move fast. Hot grilled sandwiches and cold cuts run $4-5. Veggie and black bean burgers ($4). The breakfast special ($3.50 for 2 eggs, bacon, toast, and homefries) and dinner special ($7 after 5pm for a sandwich, drink, and soup or salad) are bargains. Open M-F 7:30am-midnight, Sa-Su 8am-midnight.

Aditi ($$), 3299 M St. NW (☎625-6825), at the corner of M and 33rd St. The Washingtonian magazine awarded this restaurant as "Best of Georgetown" in 1999 for its delicious and skillfully prepared Indian food. The dining room is understated and elegant with a carved wooden ceiling. Weekday lunch specials $5.95, appetizers $2-6, entrees $8-13. Open M-Th 11:30am-2:30pm and 5:30-10pm, F-Sa 11:30am-2:30pm and 5:30-10:30pm, Su noon-2:30pm and 5:30-10pm.

Myth.com Cybercafe ($+), 3241-3 M St. NW (☎625-6984). With twenty different workstations, Myth.com can easily provide for the large number of netphiles who come to surf the web and check email. Access is expensive at $8 per hour, however, students with an ID can break up the hour into 15 minute increments ($2). The variety of coffee drinks, juices, and smoothies hydrate the most exhausted cyber-hiker. If you don't crave cyberspace, the Nutella crepes ($4 for 2) are reason enough to stop by. Open Su-Th 11am-1am, F-Sa 11am-3am.

Fettoosh Express ($$), 3277 M St. NW (☎342-1199). This small and clean, mostly take-out restaurant with limited seating offers an extensive menu of Middle Eastern food at cheap prices. Enjoy lip-smacking pita sandwiches ($3-4), entrees ($7-15), and lots of traditional Middle Eastern desserts ($1-4). Open Su-Th 11am-2am, F-Sa 11am-5am.

Quick Pita ($), 1210 Potomac St. NW (☎338-7482), just north of M St. Grab one of the few seats and enjoy a quiet lunch at this Lebanese restaurant set back from the bustle of M St. Lunch special (11am-4pm) includes sandwich, fries, and soda ($5). The falafel ($3.65) is a local favorite. Sandwiches $2.75-4. Small meat and vegetable savory pies $1.25. Free delivery in the Georgetown area after 6pm ($10 min.). Open Su-W 11:30am-3:30am, Th-Sa 11:30am-4:30am.

Zed's Ethiopian Cuisine ($$), 1201 28th St. NW (☎333-4710), at the corner of 28th and M St. Recently moved, the new dining room offers a much more elegant and intimate meal than its earlier incarnation. Serving traditional Ethiopian dishes such as *kitfo*, steak prepared with a special bitter sauce. Apps $4-5. Entrees $9-14 at dinner, $1-2 cheaper at lunch. Open daily 11am-10:30pm.

Au Pied du Cochon ($$+), 1335 Wisconsin Ave. NW (☎337-6400). At the corner of Wisconsin and Dumbarton St. This French bistro, whose name means "at the foot of the pig," features a disturbing mural of two cooks slaughtering a dirty pig. The food, however, is delicious. French specialties like *coq au vin* ($10) and *bouillabaisse* ($16) along with all-American sandwiches and burgers ($6-7). "Early bird special" 3-8pm includes appetizer, entree, dessert, and coffee or tea for $10. Open 24hr.

Thomas Sweet ($), 3214 P St. NW (☎337-0616), at the intersection with Wisconsin Ave. A local ice cream parlor that serves cheap bagel sandwich breakfasts ($1-2), sandwiches ($4-5) and over 30 flavors of homemade ice cream and frozen yogurt (single scoop cone $2). Open M-Th 8am-midnight, F-Sa 8am-1am, Su 9am-midnight.

San Marzano ($$) 3282 M St. (☎965-7007). Near the corner of M and 33rd St. This trendy hotspot opening in April 2000 claims to specialize in "pizza, vino, y birra" or pizza, wine, and beer for the non-Italian. Rightly so, the pizza is delicious, the beer and wine list extensive. The salads are also incredible; especially the *Salade Nicoise*, a mix of tuna, eggs, anchovies olives, and baked dough balls ($8). Pizza ($7-10). Beer ($3-5). Glass of wine ($3-8). Open daily 11am-11pm.

Georgetown Cafe ($) 1623 Wisconsin Ave. (☎333-0215). At the intersection with Q St. This 24hr cafe is the perfect place to grab a slice of pizza or a sub after a night out and as a result is often packed come 3am. Offering breakfast 24 hours as well as serving your typical sandwiches ($4-6) and pizzas ($7-12), the cafe also dishes up some Middle Eastern specialties like *babaghanouj*, a tasty eggplant dish ($4.25). Happy Hour M-F 4pm-8:30pm. Open daily 24 hours.

Luciano's Cafe ($$) 1219 Wisconsin Ave. (☎342-1888). Just north of the intersection with M St. Limited seating is offered in this takeout restaurant's storefront, however for those lucky enough to grab a seat, the second floor window offers a great view of those shopping Wisconsin Ave.'s many fine stores. Serving traditional Italian pasta and chicken dishes ($5-7), but no pizza. Open M-F 11am-8:30pm, Sa 11am-5:30pm.

Wrap Works ($), 1079 Wisconsin Ave. directly south of M St. (☎333-0220). The wooden walls and rusted counter give this joint a unique log cabin feel that contrasts with the usual selection of wraps and smoothies. The medium wrap and salad lunch combo is a deal at $5. Fruit smoothies ($2.50-4) spiked with vitamins or protein powders keep your motor running all day long (50¢ and up per spike). Open Su-M 11am-9pm, Tu-Th 11am-10pm, F-Sa 11am-11pm.

OLD DOWNTOWN (PENN QUARTER)

Discover the best food in Old Downtown in **Chinatown** (see p. 163). A surprising number of good non-Chinese options also lurk among the neighborhood's delis. If food courts float your boat, your best bet is the glistening new collection of 20 fast-food eateries on the lower level of the recently built **Ronald Reagan Building**, at 1300 Pennsylvania Ave. (Metro: Federal Triangle. Open M-Sa 7am-7pm, Su noon-5pm). With government workers home for the weekend this location becomes hauntingly empty as do the **Shops at National Place and Press**, 1331 Pennsylvania Ave. NW (Metro: Metro Center. Open M-Sa 10am-7pm, Su noon-5pm). A slightly more upscale food court mixed in with various memorabilia shops can be found at the **Pavilion at the Old Post Office** (Pennsylvania Ave. and 12th St. NW. Metro: Federal Triangle. Open Mar. 1-Labor Day M-Sa 10am-9pm, Su noon-7pm; Labor Day-Mar. 1 M-Sa 10am-7pm, Su noon-6pm.) Area can be dangerous at night. Use Metro: Metro Center, unless otherwise noted, for all of the following.

▧ **Haad Thai ($$),** 1100 New York Ave. NW (☎682-1111), entrance on 11th St. between H and I St. The descriptive menu makes Haad Thai sweet for newcomers to Thai cuisine, while its extra spicy options satiate aficionados. Popular *pad thai* (lunch $6.25, dinner $9) and *panang gai* (chicken sautéed with fresh basil leaves in curry peanut sauce; lunch $7.25, dinner $10) are offered alongside their vegetarian counterparts. Open M-F 11:30am-2:30pm and 5-10:30pm, Sa noon-10:30pm, Su 5-10:30pm.

▧ **Harry's ($+),** 436 11th St. (☎624-0053), on the corner of E and 11th, directly across from the ESPNZone. Metro: Metro Center or Federal Triangle. Spilling out onto the street during the summer, Harry's draws tourists and locals alike with its large 8oz. burgers and fries ($6.25). Come to cool the night off and watch the Orioles game with with a beer or daiquiri ($3-5.25). Open Su-Th 11am-2am, F-Sa 11am-3am.

▧ **Stoney's Restaurant ($+),** 1307 L St. NW (☎347-9163), near 13th St. Metro: Farragut North. Despite a recent move of headquarters, Secret Service employees still frequent this favorite bar and grille. Half price pizza on W and the longest Happy Hour in D.C. (M-F 4pm-midnight) attract loyal locals. Outdoor seating in the summer. Open Su-Th 10am-2am, F-Sa 10am-3am; kitchen closes at 1:30am.

Jaleo ($$$), 480 7th St. NW (☎628-7949), 2 blocks from the Gallery Place-Chinatown Metro stop at 7th and E St. The cheesy Spanish decorations expose the fabricated authenticity of this commercial knock-off. Genuine or not, the Spanish cuisine *is* undeniably tasty. Choose from over 34 different tapas (appetizer-sized dishes of various meats and vegetables, $3-7). The local favorite is the *paella*, a large traditonal rice dish that serves up to four people ($39.50). Full bar includes a Sangria and Sherry Sampler ($8). Sevillana (similar to Flamenco) dancers on W nights at 8:45pm. Su brunch 11:30am-3pm. Open Su-M 11:30am-10pm, Tu-Th 11:30am-11:30pm, F-Sa 11:30am-midnight.

Reeve's ($+), 1306 G St. NW (☎628-6350), between 13th and 14th St. Established in 1886, Reeves has a little bit of everything, from an all-you-can-eat breakfast and fruit bar ($5.75-6.75) and a variety of sandwiches ($3.50-6.25) to amazing cake doughnuts (60¢) and eclairs ($1.75). This bakery cafe is most famous though for its mouth-watering strawberry pie ($15.50). Everything on the menu is available for takeout. Open M-Sa 7am-6pm.

Mayur Kabab House ($+), 1108 K St. NW (☎637-9770), near the Washington International Hostel in the same building as the HI-AYH Travel Center. An all-you-can-eat lunch ($5) buffet runs the gamut of Pakistani, Indian, Afghan, Arab, and Iranian favorites in this busy lunch spot. **The Traveler's Circle** (www.killyourtv.com/travelcircle/), an open travel discussion group, meets W 6:30-10:30pm. Open M-Th 11am-10pm; F-Sa 11am-11pm.

Cafe Amadeus ($$), 1300 I St. NW (☎962-8686), entrance on 13th St. Metro: McPherson Square. Don't let the name fool you—this is a hearty American grill offering healthy "Hunter-Style" dishes of bite-sized meat (lamb, chicken, beef, or shrimp) sautéed with onion, tomato, and a special no-fat seasoning ($5-8 takeout, $10-15 eat in). Happy Hour (M-F 4-8pm) brings free appetizers with any drink. Open M-F 11am-9pm.

Capitol City Brewing Company ($$), 1100 New York Ave. NW (☎628-2222), entrance at the corner of 11th and H St. Other locations at 2 Massachusetts Ave. NE (☎842-2337) and 2700 South Quincy St. (☎(703) 578-3888), in Arlington. Opened in 1992, the first brewery in D.C. since Prohibition, this poor imitation of an industrial warehouse is known for its home-brewed beer and hearty grub. Luckily the Filibuster Burger ($7) and "Pork Barrel" Pork Chops ($14) taste good enough to forgive their cheesy names. Restaurant open Su-Th 11am-11pm, F-Sa 11am-midnight.

John Harvard's Brew House ($$), 1299 Pennsylvania Ave. NW (☎783-2739), below the Warner Theatre on the corner of E and 13th. This import from Cambridge, MA bears the marquee facade of an adjoining theatre, so watch carefully for it. Don't miss the rotating laundry list of beers brewed on the premises (pints $3-$4, sampler of 5 beers $5) and massive grill portions. Favorites include The Brew House Burger ($7) and Chicken Pot Pie ($9). M-Th 11:30am-11pm, F 11:30am-midnight, Sa noon-midnight, Su 3-10pm. Takeout available until one hour before closing.

Ebbitt Express ($$), 675 15th St. NW (☎347-8881), across from the Treasury Building, in the atrium of Metropolitan Square Plaza. The Express offers better-than-average breakfast sandwiches, deli soups, sandwiches, and salads at reasonable prices to local government workers. Daily specials may include vegetable or sausage ziti ($4) or chicken quesadilla with feta cheese and cucumber dill dressing ($7). The daily pasta specials (half-order $3.50, whole $7.25) always have a vegetarian option. The fountains and foliage of the Metropolitan Square Atrium offer pleasant scenery for feasting on takeout. Open M-Th 7:30am-8pm, F 7:30am-6pm.

Old Ebbitt Grill ($$$), next door to **Ebbitt Express**, reincarnates William Ebbit's boarding house (est. 1856), which catered to Presidents McKinley, Cleveland, Harding, and Grant. The restaurant retains the parlor room feel of the original and feeds the modern Old Boy's Club of Senators and Representatives. Hit up the Oyster Bar (half dozen $9.95). Grill open M-F 7:30am-1am, Sa 8am-1am, Su 9:30am-1am (light fare only after midnight M-Su).

SHAW/U DISTRICT

SEE MAP P. 314
YOU ARE HERE
U.S. Capitol Building

Shaw's edge near the U St.-Cardozo Metro stop, in the immediate vicinity of **14th and U St. NW,** is a source for supreme soul food, chic clubs and bars, and some of the best live music in the city (see **Rock and Pop,** p. 188). Fast food options abound at 14th and U St., but nearby home-cooked options are better and almost as inexpensive as the nearby fast food joint. Use Metro: U St.-Cardozo unless otherwise noted. This area may be dangerous at night.

🞰 **Polly's Cafe ($$)**, 1342 U St. NW (☎265-8385), near 14th St. Popular neighborhood restaurant with a cozy wood, jukebox-playing interior divides its menu and clientele into vegetarians and carnivores. Grilled veggie sandwich ($5) and portabello mushroom steak with bean salad ($9) are veggie faves. Hamburger $4.95, ham and cheese sandwich $4. Hearty American Sunday brunch serves mixed drink pitchers ($5-9) and heaps of meat, potatoes, and eggs ($7-8). Live acoustic music W after 10pm. Happy Hour M-Th 11pm-midnight knocks $1 off drafts. Open M-F 6pm-midnight, Sa-Su 10am-midnight.

Wilson's ($$), 700 V St. NW (☎462-3700 or 462-2992). Corner of V. St. and Georgia Ave. Sports memorabilia decks the walls of this cheery and spacious diner. Locals, nearby Howard students, and visitors comfortably sit in the two dining areas for quality lunch and dinner options. Choose from a great selection of hot/cold sandwiches (hot sandwiches $3.95-6.49, cold sandwiches $3.05), salads ($1.60 tossed), or various dinner entrees (ribs $10.05, pork chops $8.05). Open M-Sa 7am-8pm, Su 8am-7pm.

Ben's Chili Bowl ($), 1213 U St. NW (☎667-0909), at 13th St. across from the Metro. The bulging yellow awning of this venerable neighborhood hangout beckons all to a chili-drenching good time. Chili seems to find its way on most things at Ben's with chili dogs ($2.25), chili burgers ($2.95), chili or cheese fries ($2.50). and plain chili (small $2.25, large $3). Veggie chili (small $2.75, large $3.50) and veggie subs ($4.95). Photos of Bill Cosby and Denzel Washington (a scene from the movie *The Pelican Brief* was filmed here) pay homage to Ben's food and the friendly diner atmosphere. The jukebox spins everything from Motown to hip/hop. Open M-Th 6am-2am, F 6am-4am, Sa 7am-4am, Su noon-8pm. Breakfast M-Sa until 11am.

Florida Avenue Grill ($$), 1100 Florida Ave. NW (☎265-1586), at 11th St. From the Metro, walk east on U St. to 11th St., then north up 11th St. to Florida Ave. Small, enduring diner opened in 1944 and has since fed many famous leaders and entertainers such as Denzel Washingon, Wesley Snipes, and Janet Reno. Authentic country cooking and Southern food. Breakfast (served until 1pm) with salmon cakes or spicy half-smoked sausage and grits, apples, or biscuits ($2-7). Lunch specials $4 (Tu-F 11am-4pm). Sandwiches $1.75-5.50. Entrees served with choice of 2 veggies ($6.50-10). Open Tu-Sa 6am-9pm.

Outlaw's ($+), 917 U St. NW (☎387-3978), between Vermont Ave. and 9th St. Family-run establishment crowds in regulars for meat-laden home cooking. Cramped, no-frills quarters open onto the kitchen, where daily specials like meat loaf, baked chicken, and Salisbury steak disappear like so much magic ($6-8). Dinners $5.55-8.25, sandwiches $3.85-5.50, fresh cobbler $2. Takeout available. Open M-F 11am-6pm.

The Islander ($$), 1201 U St. (☎234-4955), at 12th St. Metro: U St.-Cardozo. Tropical pinks and turquoise color this culinary Caribbean getaway. Excellent cuisine from Trinidad and Tobago served with the sweet lullings of calypso music in the background. Favorites include goat ($9.50), chicken curry ($8.95), calypso chicken ($9.25), and *roti* (similar to a burrito, but stuffed with curried meats or vegetables and potatoes; $3.50-7). Fabulous ginger beer $2. Happy Hour Tu-F 5-8pm: 2-for-1 Caribbean mixed drinks, F free appetizers. Outdoor seating available. Open M-Th noon-11pm, F-Sa noon-1am; kitchen closes 1hr. before bar.

Tropicana ($$), 725 Florida Ave. NW (☎588-5470), between 8th and Georgia St. NW. Painted green palm trees designate an oasis of Jamaican takeout, complete with generous servings of fried plantains ($2), jerk chicken ($5.50), and fricaseed chicken ($5.50). Oxtail ($6.50) and ginger beer ($1.25). Most people can't wait to take it home; a crowd usually scarfs down food in the parking lot. Open M-Sa 11am-9pm.

Adams-Morgan dining

Wharf Seafood Market

Thyme Square Café

Julio's ($$), 1604 U St. (☎483-8500; fax 463-5553), at 16th St. An upscale pizza parlor and bar with pool tables, carryout window, dining room, and 2 popular bars. Pizzas $7-16, sandwiches $6-7.25. Chicken fajitas ($12) and fried calamari ($7) are specialties. All-you-can-eat brunch (Su 10am-3pm) $13, with champagne and mimosas $15; before 10:30am $10, with drinks $12. Happy Hour M-F 5-7pm: $2 rails and drafts. Open M-F 5pm-midnight, Sa 11am-midnight, Su 10am-midnight.

SOUTH OF THE MALL

Water Street restaurants lie heavy on prices and tourists. However, find a bite of fresh seafood just short of the high seas at these tempting locales:

Zanzibar on the Waterfront ($$+), 700 Water St. SW (☎544-1900; www.zanzibar-otw.com). Metro: Waterfront. Ultra-classy restaurant filled with tropical trees and large windows providing romantic waterfront vistas. The lunch menu combines exotic African/Caribbean/Latin American spices in dishes like the Waterfront Burger (grilled seasoned seafood, with crab fritters, cracked conch, and herbed pickle mayonnaise served on a spinach roll, $9) and has a sizeable vegetarian menu. Dinner entrees $12-25. Open M-Sa 11am-3pm and 5-9:30pm, Su 11am-3pm (buffet) and 5-9:30pm. Live jazz, blues, R/B for dinner hours, and free admission to club/bar upstairs with meal.

Wharf Street Seafood Market ($), between 9th and 11th St. SW and Maine Ave. NW, next to Memorial Bridge. Metro: L'Enfant Plaza. Floating booths steeped with the pungent smell of raw fish attract die-hard seafood grubbers. Specialties include seafood sandwiches ($6-10), clams ($7), and shrimp ($7), cooked while you wait. Raw seafood available for takeout. Open daily 8am-9pm.

Negril the Jamaican Bakery ($), 401 M St. SW (☎488-3636), in the Waterside Mall right off the Metro. Metro: Waterfront. Jamaican spices and cheap prices make this tasty takeout spot a local favorite. Specialties at this takeout place include chicken loaves (similar to a calzone stuffed with chicken; $1.85), vegetable patties ($1.75), and amazing chicken noodle soup ($2.25). Baked goods include bagels (55¢) and killer jumbo cookies ($6.45 per lb.) Open M-F 6:30am-7pm, Sa 8:30am-4pm.

Irene's Deli ($), 300 7th St. SW (☎488-5555), between C and D St., in the Reporter's Building. Metro: L'Enfant Plaza. Frenzied takeout deli ideal for those craving a good sandwich and home cooking. Standard breakfast items include grits (75¢) or a Western omelette sandwich ($1.79). Lunch sandwiches $2-4. No indoor seating; occasional outdoor seating. Open M-F 6:30am-4pm.

TAKOMA PARK

Takoma, Maryland, is no tourist trap. There are no glitzy, gimmicky restaurants or overpriced chains to draw credit-carded travelers. In fact, Takoma's earth-consciousness means you can get coffee discounts almost everywhere if you bring your own mug. And when hunger strikes, you won't have to reach far into your wallet—meals rarely exceed $10. Use Metro: Takoma for all of the following.

🔲 **Savory ($+),** 7071 Carroll Ave. (☎(301) 270-2233). Bright, airy cafe has a veggie-art sense of humor and a predominantly vegetarian lunch/dinner menu ($4-9) that changes daily. Quiet relaxed coffeehouse atmosphere without the pretension that plagues D.C. competitors. Offers espresso drinks ($1.50-3) and homemade desserts like lemon shaker pie ($3.50 per slice). Leather couches line the lower level, a relaxed venue for art receptions and author readings. Open M-Th 7am-9pm, F 7am-10pm, Sa 8am-9pm, Su 9am-4pm.

Mark's Kitchen ($$), 7006 Carroll Ave. (☎(301) 270-1884). Mark himself often greets patrons deciding among the diverse range of both American classics and Korean specialties. Korean offerings include seaweed soup ($2.25), Korean steak ($6), and the ever-changing Royal Sampler Surprise Box ($8). Deli sandwiches $3-6, selections from the juice bar $2.75-4. Open M-Sa 8am-9pm, Su 8am-8pm.

Spicy Delight ($+), 308 Carroll St. NW (☎(202) 829-9783), right up the street from the Metro. This small takeout spot lined with various posters of Jamaica offers large tasty portions of traditional Caribbean food. Jerk chicken wings are deliciously spicy ($4.75 for 10). Curried goat ($6.30) and Curry Chicken Roti (dough wrap with chick peas; $6.10) are other specialties.

Jamaican Style Breakfast ($7.25) includes dumplings, yams, boiled bananas, and fried plantains. Open M-Th 10am-9pm, F 10am-10pm.

Taliano's ($$), 7001B Carroll Ave. (☎(301) 270-5515). Slow, reluctant service takes away from excellent Italian dishes. Specialties include pasta ($5.25-7.25), calzones ($7.75), and pizza ($7-17). 8-topping, 12 in. Taliano's special $14; cheese slice $1.75. Half-price pizza 1st M of each month 5-9pm. A small stage hosts blues M and F nights, jazz Th nights, Latin Sa night. Kitchen open Su-Th 11:30am-11pm, F-Sa til midnight.

Everyday Gourmet ($), 6923 Laurel Ave. (☎(301) 270-2270). Potted plants, a checkered linoleum floor, an antique fountain, and ceiling fans single out this half gourmet-supply, half bakery/ deli from big city coffee chains. Baked goods like muffins, croissants, and cinnamon buns $1-2. Soup and sandwich combo $6.45. "High Rollers" tortilla wraps with meat and veggies ($4-5), are a specialty. Open M-F 7am-8pm, Sa 8am-6pm, Su 8am-3pm.

Summer Delights ($), 6939 Laurel Ave. (☎(301) 891-2880) Inviting patrons in with the sounds of Motown, this icecream joint makes customers want to shout out "I Feel Good!" Look for posters of Elvis and Monroe. Soft-serve ice cream $1-3.50, old fashioned bottled Coca-Cola $1, hot dogs $2, and pastries $1-3. Open Tu-Th 1-8:30pm. F-Sa noon-10pm, Su noon-7:30pm.

UPPER NORTHWEST

WOODLEY PARK

Exiting from the Metro, travelers are greeted by a mural of Marilyn Monroe, Woodley Park's effort to associate with the fabulosity of Dupont to the south. The small neighborhood has a surprising number of ethnic eateries clustered around the Woodley Park-Zoo Metro stop on Connecticut Ave. and also houses busy local pubs, especially **Murphy's of D.C.** and the **Oxford Tavern "Zoo Bar"** (see **Nightlife,** p. 190). Use Metro: Woodley Park-Zoo:

🔳 **Jandara ($$)**, 2606 Connecticut Ave. NW (☎387-8876). Celestial decorations and heavenly blues and purples create an out-of-this-world atmosphere. The food is equally stunning with Thai standards and specialty dishes like *gaeng ped yang* (slices of roasted duck simmered in a red curry sauce with pineapple, $8.95). Lunch menu features reduced price entrees ($5-10). Open Su-Th 11:30am-10:30pm, F-Sa 11:30am-11pm.

The Lebanese Taverna ($$$), 2641 Connecticut Ave. NW (☎265-8681). This refined restaurant has a beautiful dining room and serves mezza platters which let you sample many different appetizers and entrees ($13.50 and up). Grilled meat plates ($10-15) are delectable, but sandwiches ($7.75) are cheaper. Many vegetarian options available. Open M-Th 11:30am-2:30pm and 5:30-10:30pm, F 11:30am-2:30pm and 5:30-11pm, Sa 11:30am-3pm and 5:30-11pm, Su 5-10pm.

Medaterra ($$+), 2614 Connecticut Ave. NW (☎797-0400). Beautiful dining room filled with Mediterranean shades of yellow, orange, and deep blue. The food is mostly North African, with standards like hummus and *baba ghanoush* ($4-5). The Sea Fusion is a special broth served over couscous ($15). Entrees, including vegetarian dishes, with couscous ($10-21). Lunch is cheaper ($5-10). Open Su-Th 11:30am-2:30pm and 5-10pm, F-Sa 11:30am-3pm and 5-10:30pm.

Thai Town ($$), 2655 Connecticut Ave. NW (☎667-5115). Beautiful, romantic dining room decorated with many shades of pink. One of the first Thai restaurants in the city, Thai Town compensates for slow service with delicious standards from *pad thai* to basil chicken. All entrees $7-10. Open daily lunch 11am-3pm; dinner 5-11pm.

Saigon Gourmet Restaurant ($$), 2635 Connecticut Ave. NW (☎265-1360). Grilled pork and rice crepe specialties served amidst a jungle-like atmosphere overflowing with potted plants and flowers. Options include vermicelli with spring rolls or grilled meat. Appetizers $4-5; meat entrees $9-12; vegetarian entrees $9; and noodles $13. Lunch features the same items for almost half price. Outdoor seating available. Open daily 11am-3pm and 5-10:30pm.

GLOVER PARK

The restaurants lined along Wisconsin Ave. between W. Place and Calvert St. feature some of the best bargains in the city, and are often much less crowded than those in Georgetown, which lies a few blocks to the south.

▧ **Mama Maria and Enzio's ($$)**, 2313 Wisconsin Ave. NW (☎965-1337), near Calvert St. Amazing southern Italian cuisine served in a tiny dining room (9 tables), with a casual, family atmosphere. The owner is likely to serve you, and it's best to go with whatever they recommend. Perfectly cooked large shrimp in lemon sauce ($16) is cause enough to endure any wait. Begin with an appetizer like *caprese* (tomato, fresh mozzarella with olive oil) or prosciutto and melon ($6.25-11.75) and move on to pastas cooked al dente with fresh sauces ($9-13). Canelloni $5. Lunch entrees $7-11. Open lunch M-F 11:30am-3pm; dinner M-Sa 5-10:30pm.

▧ **Faccia Luna ($$)**, 2400 Wisconsin Ave. NW (☎337-3132). A wood-fired oven bakes up thin, crisp-yet-tender crusts. The dining room is welcoming with intimate brick alcoves and booths. Steps lead down into beautiful outdoor patio. Basic pie $6.50-12; toppings $1.25-2 each. There are pasta dishes and sandwiches too, and an appealing lunch special ($5-6) which includes entree and drink. Open M-Th 11:30am-11pm, F-Sa 11:30am-midnight, Su 11am-midnight.

▧ **Rocklands ($)**, 2418 Wisconsin Ave. NW (☎333-2558). The sweet smell of barbecue emanating from Rocklands attracts long lines at lunch and dinner; snack on free peanuts while you wait. No gas or electricity in the BBQ pit—just red oak, hickory, and charcoal. Very limited seating at the weathered mahogany counters, but you can take out a quarter-rack of pork ribs ($5) or a half chicken ($5). Sandwiches $4-6.25, salads $1.39. Open M-Sa 11:30am-10pm, Su 11am-9pm.

Entotto ($$+), 1609 Foxhall Rd. NW (☎333-1200), at the corner of Foxhall and Reservoir Rd. Take the D4 bus directly to the restaurant or the D5 to Foxhall Village and walk east (with traffic) on Q St. Stunning Ethiopian food served in a quiet, classy room with 5 tables. Be prepared for a leisurely dinner: your orders are cooked from scratch by one chef, who moved to D.C. after years running a restaurant in Paris. Appetizers $6.50-7.50, entrees $7-12, combo platters $12. Take-out available. Open M-Sa 11:30am-2:30pm and 5:30-10pm (closes at 9pm in winter).

CLEVELAND PARK

Located just north of the Cathedral between Wisconsin and Connecticut Aves., Cleveland Park reveals its suburban tendencies in the form of strip malls and chain restaurants. Look close though, dining jewels can be found within the quiet neighborhood's conformist blah. Use Metro: Cleveland Park for all of the following.

Spices Asian Restaurant & Sushi Bar ($$), 3333A Connecticut Ave. NW (☎686-3833). Popular upscale restaurant with limited seating—be prepared for a wait on weekends. Pan-Asian delights including sushi (entrees $9-21), hot pots ($9-13), and a large assortment of vegetarian dishes ($7-9). Open M-Sa 11:30am-3pm and 5-11pm, Su 5-10:30pm.

▧ **Yanni's ($$)**, 3500 Connecticut Ave. NW (☎362-8871). Bright, airy neighborhood restaurant with extra-friendly service and homestyle Greek cooking (e.g. fresh herbs and a whole lot of olive oil). Appetizers like *tzatziki* (cool yogurt and cucumber dip, $4.25, pave the way for traditional treats like charbroiled octopus, crunchy on the outside and delicately tender within, served with rice and vegetables ($11). Appetizers $4, entrees $8-16. Open daily 11:30am-11pm.

Nam Viet Pho 79 ($$), 3419 Connecticut Ave. NW (☎237-1015). Budget Vietnamese food with trad entrees like curried chicken in coconut juice as well as special veggie dishes ($8-13). Listed in *Washingtonian Magazine* as one of the 100 best restaurants in D.C., this small dining room is packed on weekends. Open M-Th 11am-3pm and 5-10pm, F-Sa 11am-11pm, Su 11am-10pm.

Ivy's Place ($$), 3520 Connecticut Ave. NW (☎363-7802). Indonesian and Thai dishes. Creative entrees allow you to choose meats and veggies, made as spicy as you like ($8-13). Free delivery (min. $12). Open Su-Th 4:30-10:30pm, F-Sa 11:30am-10:30pm.

Firehook Bakery & Coffeehouse ($), 3411 Connecticut Ave. NW (☎362-2253). A local upscale branch serving the main Alexandria bakery's fresh breads and sinfully rich cookies, as well as a variety of coffee drinks. Open 7am-9pm.

Yenching Palace ($$), 3524 Connecticut Ave. NW (☎362-8200). The 1961 Cuban Missile Crisis was secretly devised in this dining room, and Nixon's rapprochement with China was planned here a decade later. The aged decor strangely augments the pink tones and intimate circular booths. Standard Chinese fare like chicken in garlic sauce ($9). Dinner entrees $7-13; lunch specials $6 (rice, eggroll, entree, and soup; M-F noon-2:30pm). Free delivery. Open M-Th 11:30am-11pm, F-Sa 11:30am-11:30pm, Su noon-11pm.

TENLEY CIRCLE AND FRIENDSHIP HEIGHTS

If you just can't bear to spend one more minute in Nieman Marcus, venture south along Wisconsin Ave. from the Friendship Heights malls and grab a bite to eat at one of many cheap and unpretentious restaurants.

Maggiano's Little Italy ($+), 5333 Wisconsin Ave. NW (☎966-2593). Metro: Friendship Heights. Main restaurant is pricier and more formal, so stick with the more affordable front room. Salads, pastas, and incredibly thick pan pizza ($16.95). Outdoor seating perfect for people-watching. Takeout available. Open M-Th 11:30am-10pm, F-Sa 11:30am-11pm, Su noon-9pm.

a.k.a Frisco's ($), 4115 Wisconsin Ave. NW (☎244-7847), between Van Ness and Upton St. Metro: Tenleytown-AU. A casual sandwich shop divided into several small rooms imitating San Francisco with their wooden floors, white walls, and light blue trim. Generous sandwiches ($3.75-4.75) and large baked potatoes ($1.25-3.75) with West Coast names like the Berkeley or the Alcatraz. Nice assortment of vegetarian dishes. Open M-Th 11am-4pm, F-Sa 11am-3pm.

Cafe Ole ($$), 4000 Wisconsin Ave. NW (☎244-1330), across from the Post Office. Metro: Tenleytown-AU. This upscale, colorful Middle Eastern joint serves mezze dishes (small appetizers; 3 make a good sized meal; $2.25-4.50 each). Try the *shankleesh,* a sharp and seasoned sheep's cheese, or the warm vegetable tart. Lunch menu focuses on panini sandwiches (around $6) and rollups ($6-7). Open Su-Th 11am-10pm, F-Sa 11am-11pm.

Cactus Cantina ($$), 3300 Wisconsin Ave. NW (☎686-7222; fax 362-5649), at Macomb St. near the Cathedral. Metro: Tenleytown-AU and any 30-series bus towards Georgetown. Dodge cheese-o-rama Xmas lights by lounging on the breezy outdoor patio, perfect for sipping on some sirop. Great Tex-Mex, from fajitas ($12-15) to lunch specials like enchilada platters ($6-7, M-F until 3pm). Salsa made on the spot. Open Su-Th 11:30am-11pm, F-Sa 11:30am-midnight.

INSIDE

Nightlife

The White House of future poems, of dreams, of dramas, there
in the soft and copious moon—
      —Walt Whitman, *Specimen Days*

Talk about leading a double life. When darkness falls, Washington swaps the flesh-toned nylons for the fishnet stockings. D.C. denizens who crawl through red tape by day paint the town red by night. If you accidentally find yourself taking Jell-O bodyshots off a beautiful stranger at an all-you-can-drink-fest, just don't say we didn't warn you.

Here's our advice on tripping the light fantastic: If you ache for a pint of amber ale, swing by the Irish pub-laden **Capitol Hill.** If you like girls (or boys) who wear Abercrombie & Fitch, hit up **Georgetown,** where youthful prepsters go to get happy. Gay and lesbian travelers traipse nightly through the glam **Dupont Circle,** while **Adams-Morgan** seethes with Eurotrash scuzziness. And to party *with* rock stars, head to none other than Shaw / U for the best live rock 'n' roll in all of Dixieland. To party *like* a rock star, find high times in the **Southeast** wasteland.

D.C.'s nightclub turnover rate is obscenely high. Establishments open, fold, and change hands before you can say "bottoms up." Count on flyers and posters in Georgetown and Dupont Circle to keep you up-to-date on the scene.

The following index organizes bars and clubs by type. **Let's Go Picks** (■) mark the dopest places to hang out until the sun comes up over Pennsylvania Avenue.

BY VENUE TYPE

AL Alexandria **AM** Adams-Morgan **AR** Arlington **CH** Capitol Hill **DP** Dupont Circle **FB** Foggy Bottom
G Georgetown **NE** Northeast **OD** Old Downtown **SH** Shaw/U District **UN** Upper Northwest

BARS

Brass Monkey	AM
Millie & Al's	AM
Rhino	G
Carpool	AR
Capitol Lounge	CH
Politiki	CH
Tune Inn	CH
The Big Hunt	DP
The Fox and Hounds	DP
The Madhatter	F
Odds	F
Rumors	F
Sign of the Whale	F
Lindy's Red Lion	FB
Garrett's	G
Island Jim's Crab Shack Tiki Bar	NE
Johnny K's	NE
Sky Terrace	OD
Cafe Nema	SH
Kaffa House	SH
Utopia/The Bar	SH
Taliano's	TP

BAR AND GRILL

The Alamo	AL
Red River Grill	CH
Tequila Grill	F

COCKTAIL LOUNGES

Toledo Lounge	AM
Xando	CH
Ozio	F
The Aroma Company	UN

DANCE CLUBS

Chief Ike's Mambo Room	AM
Club Heaven and Club Hell	AM
Prive	AM
Blue Room	AM
Nick's	AL
Dragonfly	DP
Lewie's	B
Red	DP
Lulu's New Orleans Cafe	FB
DC Live	OD
The Ritz	OD
Tuscana West	OD
Zei	OD
Bar Nun/Club 2000	SH
Republic Gardens	SH
State of the Union	SH
Southeast Tracks	SE
Zanzibar on the Waterfront	SM

GAY AND LESBIAN

See **Gay Bars and Clubs,** p. 190.

HOOKAH LOUNGES

Chi Cha Lounge	SH

IRISH PUBS

Ireland's Own	AL
Murphy's Pub	AL
Ireland's Four Courts	AR
Kelley's "The Irish Times"	CH
The Dubliner	CH
Fado	OD
Kelly's Ellis Island	NE
Ireland's Four Provinces	UN
Murphy's of D.C.	UN
Nanny O'Brien's	UN

LATIN DANCE CLUBS

Tom Brazil	AM
Coco Loco	OD

LIVE MUSIC

Iota	AR
Whitlow's on Wilson	AR
Bukom Cafe	AM
Mr. Henry's	AM

also see **Jazz and Blues,** p. 140,
and **Rock and Pop,** p. 137.

MICROBREWERIES

Virginia Brewing Company	AL
Bethesda Rock Bottom Brewery	B
J. Paul's	G
Capitol City Brewing Co.	OD

MOVIES 'N' BOOZE

Arlington Cinema 'n' Drafthouse	AR
Bethesda Theater Cafe	B

PIANO BARS

Mr. Smith's	G

PUBS/TAVERNS

The Bayou Room	AL
Tiffany Tavern	AL
Galaxy Hut	AR
Hawk 'n' Dove	CH
Brickskeller	DP
The Childe Harold	DP
Timberlake's	DP
Townhouse Tavern	DP
Old Glory	G
The Tombs	G
Colonel Brooks Tavern	NE
Stoney's Restaurant	OD
Takoma Station Tavern	TP
Oxford Tavern "Zoo Bar"	UN

SPORTS BARS

Parker's	B
Froggy Bottom Pub	FB
Champions	G

BY NEIGHBORHOOD

ADAMS-MORGAN

Dance-party chaos unravels at the speed of light in Adams-Morgan nightly. Weekends explode with a diverse crowd of twenty- and thirty-somethings hungry for frenzied late-night mischief and mayhem. Some of D.C.'s trendiest nightclubs and swankiest lounges unveil themselves on the main strip near 18th and Columbia St. Although the area is generally safe, **areas off of the main streets become dangerous at night.**
It's a 15-minute walk or a short cab ride from Dupont Circle or Woodley Park-Zoo Metro.

Club Heaven and Club Hell, 2327 18th St. NW (☎667-4355), near Columbia Rd. The devoted reveler makes a pilgrimage to Club Heaven and Club Hell where everyone is a believer in Dionysian tenets. Hell is a hip, smoky bar greasily ornamented with pimpish gold tables and loud alterna-music. Heaven looks more like an old townhouse with scuffed wood, comfy couches, a small bar, and 3 TVs, but the dance floor throbs to pounding beats of techno that spill out onto the back patio. 80s dance party in Heaven is crammed (Th, cover $5). No cover F-W. Mixed techno and progressive F-Sa. Domestic beer $3, imports $4-5. Happy Hour in Hell M-Th until 10pm and F-Su until 8:30pm. Dancing at 10pm. Heaven open Su, Tu-Th 9:30pm-2am; F-Sa 9:30pm-3am. Hell open Su-Th 7pm-2am; F-Sa 7pm-3am.

Prive, 2424 18th St. NW (☎328-7194), between Belmont and Columbia Rd. The posh and crowded restaurant and bar, **Cities,** opens its stairwell to connoisseurs of pounding international music and the Euro-club scene F-Sa nights. The tragically hip lounge and dance in the Armani threads until the music dies (around 2:30am). The upstairs club offers a great view of the plebes below on 18th St. Opens at 9pm but doesn't really get lively until 11:30pm. Proper attire required. No cover. 21+. International music F-Sa.

Blue Room, 2123 18th St. (☎332-0800). *I'm blue, da-ba-dee-da-ba-die...*A chic tapas restaurant by day, an alluring lounge and dance club at night. Trendy mid-twenties to early-thirties clientele gravitate to this stylish, blue world with polished chrome. Beer $4-9, cocktails $5-8. Downtempo/deephouse/techno Th-Sa. The club starts jumping at around 11:30pm, closes at 3am. Proper attire required (no jeans, athletic gear, sneakers).

Bukom Cafe, 2442 18th St. NW (☎265-4600), near Columbia Rd. A fabulous West African bar and restaurant with live music from West African bands, starting at 9pm weekdays, 10pm weekends. Filled to capacity with a 30-something crowd. Also specializes in West African cuisine: appetizers $3-4, entrees $6-10. 12oz. beer $4, 22oz. $8. Open M-Tu 4-10pm, W 4pm-2am, Th-Sa 4pm-3am, Su 4pm-2am.

Tom Brazil, 1821 Columbia Rd. NW (☎232-4668). This steamy venue has all the sexiness, spice, and heat of a Miami nightclub. Stylish internationals and other party-people shake their bon-bons to DJ-spun salsa and Brazilian music (F-Sa) and super Samba (Su). Large bar downstairs and a dance floor upstairs. Cover varies. Open M-Th 5-11:30pm, F-Su 8pm-late.

Chief Ike's Mambo Room, Chaos, and Pandemonium, 1725 Columbia Rd. (☎332-2211 or 797-4637), near Ontario Rd., 1 block from 18th St. Its aqua and red innards worthy of a pulp novel cover, Chief Ike's serves pub-style American fare (nachos $5). DJ spins dance classics, hip-hop, funk, and disco for a late 20s crowd. Up a long red staircase are Chaos and Pandemonium, two tumultuous rooms featuring alternative tunes, pseudo-Japanese decor, and pool tables. M "Cosmopolitan Art Night"; Tu open mic; Th live music. $1 off drinks during Happy Hour (M-Tu 6-8pm, W-F 4-8pm). Beer $3; rails $4. Higher drink prices and occasional cover when a band plays. 21+. Casual dress. Chief Ike's open M-Th 4pm-2am, F-Sa 4pm-3am. Chaos and Pandemonium open Su-Th 8pm-2am, F-Sa 8pm-3am.

Mr. Henry's, 1836 Columbia Rd. (☎797-8882), near 18th St. Mr. Henry's dark-wood interior and summer patio host those interested in the sounds and stylings of Ethiopia. Mr. Henry discovered Roberta Flack here, and the live-music tradition continues F-M with Ethiopian bands. W open mic; Tu comedy. Drafts $2.25. Appetizers $4-5. Sandwiches $5-7. Cover $5-7.50. Happy Hour (M-Sa 4-8pm) features changing specials and 75¢ off drinks. 21+. Open M-Th 4pm-2am, F-Sa 4pm-3am, Su 4pm-2am.

Toledo Lounge, 2435 18th St. (☎986-5416). Like a suburban garage sale gone awry (note the shrunken head above the bar, the large Texaco oil sign, and the sporadic jack-a-lope), Toldedo Lounge makes a chill spot for pre- or post-clubbing. Cocktails $4+, beer $3+. Mega-packed on the weekends, the lounge also serves burgers (basic burger with fries or onion rings $5.95), salads, and sandwiches ($4.95). Open F-Sa 8pm-3am, Su-Th 6pm-2am.

Millie & Al's, 2440 18th St. (☎387-8131). Jukebox bar draws an ultra-casual crowd into its dark booths with pizza, subs, and jello-shooter specials. Happy Hour (M-F 4-7pm) features 50¢ off drinks and daily specials. Open M-Th 4pm-2am, F-Sa 4pm-3am.

Brass Monkey, 2317 18th St. (☎667-7800). The inside's long wooden floor and outdoor patio fill with a fashionably preppy crowd partying to international music and rock from Bob Dylan to the Beastie Boys. Funky Hour M-F 4-7pm has $2 Rolling Rocks and rails. Drafts always $3, bottles $3.50, rail drinks $4-5. No cover. Open daily Su-Th 6pm-2am, F-Sa 6pm-3am.

ARLINGTON

Featuring great Happy Hours, fantastic live music, and safe streets, the bars in Arlington provide fun alternatives for those don't want to venture into the city.

Iota, 2832 Wilson Blvd. (☎(703) 522-8340). Metro: Clarendon. Famous for showcasing breakthrough bands of every musical style with performances nightly. The exposed rafters, hanging Christmas lights and wooden tables give this place a ski-lodge feel. Microbrews $3.75-4.25, 35 bottled beers from $3. Happy Hour (M-F 5-8pm): $1 off rails and drafts. Cover $3-15 during shows. Call for show times. New extended hours for lunch and dinner; brunch on Sa and Su 9am-2pm. Open M-F 11am-2am, Sa-Su 9am-2am.

Whitlow's on Wilson, 2854 Wilson Blvd. (☎(703) 276-9693). Metro: Clarendon. Live blues, jazz, and rock fill this large space Tu-Sa around 10pm. Half-price burgers M; 25¢ wings all day T; $6 pitchers of Sierra Nevada all day W. Happy Hour (M-F 4-7pm): $1 off drafts, rails, house wines. 21+ after 9:30pm. Cover Th-Sa $3, Tu $5. Open daily 11:30am-2am.

Ireland's Four Courts, 2051 Wilson Blvd. (☎(703) 525-3600). Metro: Court House. Classic Irish pub with a gimmick: for $55 they'll personalize an oversized pewter mug for you which can be refilled with an extra 2 oz. of beer every time you revisit. The promotion has been so popular the bar now has no more room to hang the mugs along the wall. Enjoy Guinness ($4.75 a pint) and live traditional Irish music (Tu-Sa 9pm; no cover). Also serves lunch and dinner. Happy Hour (M-F 4-7pm): $1 off all beers. 21+ after 8pm. Open M-Sa 11am-2am, Su 10am-2am.

Carpool, 4000 Fairfax Dr. (☎(703) 532-7665). Metro: Ballston. Wash down a rack of ribs from adjoining Rockland's with a nice cold one. The festive atmosphere and testosterone-driven pool games lead to some heavy drinking, so carpool. Depending on time, pool $5-12 for 1 player, $10-12 for 2. Happy Hour (M-F 4-7pm) features $1.75 Miller Lite specials. Open Su-Th 4pm-1am, F-Sa 4pm-2am.

Galaxy Hut, 2711 Wilson Blvd. (☎(703) 525-8646; www.galaxyhut.com). Metro: Clarendon. Mellow, though slightly grungy, pub with exotic beers: 15 taps and over 50 bottles to choose from. Limited liquor. Happy Hour M-F 5-8pm: $1 Bud, $1 off pints, $3 off pitchers, and reduced-price appetizers. Sa-M live music. Open M-F 5pm-2am, Sa-Su 7pm-2am.

Arlington Cinema 'N' Drafthouse, 2903 Columbia Pike (☎(703) 486-2345). Now this is entertainment: food and beer served while the movie is rolling. Smoking and non-smoking sections available. Shows mostly second-run movies, making the evening even more affordable (ticket $3.99). 21+ or with a parent. Call for showtimes.

CAPITOL HILL

While the nightlife in other parts of Washington is in constant flux, Capitol Hill stands by its steadfast neighborhood institutions. Political aides don't do much heated dancing, but visitors can capitalize on Happy Hours and bar specials all around the area.

█ Kelley's "The Irish Times," 14 F St. NW (☎543-5433). Metro: Union Station. Irish street signs, the *Irish Times*, and Joyce on the wall give the pub an authentic feel, but late-night disco differentiates Kelley's from most other Irish bars. Happy Hour (M-F 4-7:30pm): domestic drafts $2. Live music (Th-Sa 9pm) can be any genre that fits with an acoustic guitar. Open Su-Th 9:30am-2am, F-Sa 9:30am-3am.

█ The Dubliner, 520 N. Capitol St. (☎737-3773). Metro: Union Station. A more subdued crowd than Kelly's enjoys Guinness and the house brew, Auld Dubliner Amber Ale ($4 a pint). Traditional live Irish music often includes familiar pop melodies injected with an Irish twist (M-Sa 9pm, Su 7:30pm). A large patio turns lounge-style as the night ticks on. Open Su-Th 7-10am and 11am-2am, F-Sa 7-10am and 11am-3am.

Politiki, 319 Pennsylvania Ave. SE (☎546-1001). Metro: Capitol South. A dark wood paneled, mostly subterranean bar goes Hawaiian with tiki-style drinks and food with bamboo. M free pool, W salsa night (free lessons start at 8pm); F-Su swing in the 2nd fl. "War Room." Jumbo piña coladas and $1 drinks during Happy Hour (M-F 4-7pm). Open M-Sa 4pm-last call.

Xando, 301 Pennsylvania Ave. SE (☎546-3345). Metro: Capitol South. Dupont Circle import makes a Capitol Hill debut. The ultra-chic coffeehouse by day morphs into a smoky liquor bar at night. Drafts $3, Guiness $3.50, and coffee drinks like a Mocha Kiss Cocktail $4. Open Su-Th 7am-midnight, F-Sa 7am-1am.

Capitol Lounge, 224-231 Pennsylvania Ave. SE (☎547-2098). Metro: Capitol South. Laid- back local bar has front and back patios and every NFL game on Sunday. A pool room and casual seating for staple drinking in this, the closest bar to the Capitol. Happy Hour (M-F 4-7pm): food specials, rails $2.75, and pints of Bud $2. Occasional live music. Open Su-Th 11am-2am, F-Sa 11am-3am.

Tune Inn, 331½ Pennsylvania Ave. SE (☎543-2725). Metro: Capitol South. Mounted fish, game heads, and sports trophies decorate the walls in this place for unpretentious fun since 1933. Clients range from Congressional staffers to construction workers to students. Sandwiches under $5, breakfast all day, and a well-stocked jukebox. Drafts $1.50, bottles $2.25, mixed drinks $2.75. Pitchers $4 (Sa 4-11pm, Su 5pm-2am). Open Su-Th 8am-2am, F-Sa 8am-3am.

Blue Room

Hawk 'n' Dove, 329 Pennsylvania Ave. SE (☎543-3300). Metro: Capitol South. The 3 buildings, all over 100 years old, have served as a blacksmith shop, a saltwater taffy plant, and D.C.'s 1st gas station. 12 kinds of bottled beer and 13 drafts available. Sandwiches $4-6.50. Happy Hour (M-Th 4-9pm) features $2 Bud and Miller Lite, sometimes free munchies and pool. M night is "Intern Night" with $1 drafts. Midnight breakfast served M-Th 11pm-1am, F-Sa 11pm-2am ($7, with steak $9). Sa-Su brunch (10am-3:30pm) offers Screwdrivers, Mimosas, or Bloody Marys for $2. Open Su-Th 10am-2am, F-Sa 10am-3am.

Red River Grill, 201 Massachusetts Ave. NE (☎546-7200). Metro: Union Station. Tex-Mex bar and grill stuffs Capitol Hill interns and staffers into a series of rooms or lets them overflow onto an outdoor patio. Happy Hour (M-F 4-7pm) includes W $1 Bud, Th $10 margarita pitchers, and $2 drafts everyday. All-you-can-drink Miller Lite $5 (F 5pm-3am). Open M-Th 11:30am-2am, F 10:30am-3am, Sa noon-3am, Su noon-2am.

Chief Ike's Mambo Room

DUPONT CIRCLE

YOU ARE HERE

U.S. Capitol Building

SEE MAP P. 306

While many clubs have recently closed down in Dupont Circle, the neighborhood retains a hopping bar scene and remains the prime area for gay and lesbian nightlife (see **Gay Bars and Clubs,** p. 190). Use Metro: Dupont Circle for all of the following.

Dragonfly, 1215 Connecticut Ave.* NW (☎331-1775). Beauty may be fleeting, but there is no better place to revel in the now than amidst the ultra-hot clientele of Dragonfly, *the* club in town to see and be seen. Ice-white interior, pod-like chairs, techno music, and video projections. Drinks are expensive but sushi is served all night for reasonable prices. DJs every night. No cover. Open M-Th 5:30pm-1am, F 5:30pm-2am, Sa 6pm-2am, Su 6pm-1am.

Brickskeller, 1523 22nd St. NW (☎293-1885), between P and Q St. With a list of over 850 bottled brews, the Brickskeller claims to have the largest selection in the world. Basement bar "where everybody knows your name" embodies the typical neighborhood tavern atmosphere.

Club Chaos

inside
SECRETS TO...

Raves

British breakbeat first broke D.C. in 1992, when the first-documented rave took place. Among the raverkids was a DJ named **Ian Christopher** who under the name **Bezerker** would come to develop a new flavor called **happy hardcore**. As Christopher's sound blossomed in popularity, so did the all-night dance parties he would spin at. In varied venues, ranging from D.C. clubs (such as **Evolve**, **Urban Space**, and **Buzz**) to warehouses in Maryland and Virginia; young ravers would dance the night away to local DJs spinning **house** and **trance** music. Notorious for high levels of drug use, especially **ecstasy**, **ghb**, and **special k**, raves have recently come under the watchful eye of law enforcement officials.

Although the scene is slightly more subdued than that of New York or Boston, today's ravers can still grab their glowsticks and pacifiers and head to Buzz (Friday nights at **Nation**) or check online at **DCNites.com** for a list of warehouse parties in the surrounding metropolitan area.

"Beer-tails" are mixed drinks made with beer: a favorite is the classic Black Velvet (stout and champagne; $4.50). Monthly tastings hosted by brewers (call ahead for prices and schedule). Pub menu available. Open M-Th 11:30am-2am, F 11:30am-3am, Sa 6pm-3am, Su 6pm-2am.

Red, 1802 Jefferson Place NW (☎466-3475), at Connecticut Ave. NW. This subterranean club doesn't even get hopping until 1am on weeknights and 3am on weekends, so don't bother rolling in here early. Follow the pack of ravers or look for the dark, red velvet curtains across the windows and door—the sign is almost impossible to see. Dress code: no shorts for men. No cover before midnight, $5-10 after midnight. Open W-Th 10pm-3am, F-Sa 10pm-6am.

The Childe Harold, 1610 20th St. NW (☎483-6700), near Connecticut Ave. A pub-type restaurant and bar that just misses living up to its rebellious, Byronic namesake. A mixed crowd revels downstairs and on the patio, especially at Happy Hour (M-F 5-7pm), where rails are only $2.75. Open Su-Th 11:30am-2am, F-Sa 11:30am-3am.

The Fox and Hounds, 1537 17th St. NW (☎232-6307). Early-20s crowd fills the patio while older, mellower patrons make conversation along the small bar inside. All ages and orientations keep coming back for the strong mixed drinks and the relaxed atmosphere. Food supplied by **Trio** (see p. 166). Happy Hour M-F 4:30-6:30pm includes $2.25 rail drinks and $2.25 domestic beers. Regular prices won't break any banks at $2.75-4 for beer and rails. Open M-Th 11:30am-2am, F 11:30am-3am, Sa 10:30am-3am, Su 10:30am-2am. Patio closes at midnight.

Timberlake's, 1726 Connecticut Ave. NW (☎483-2266). Neighborhood pub serves sandwiches and entrees throughout the week. Su brunch. Bar in front is a great place to catch a brew and the game. Happy Hour (M-F 3-7pm) $1 off all drinks. Open M-Th 11am-2am, F 11am-3am, Sa-Su 9:30am-3:30am.

The Big Hunt, 1345 Connecticut Ave. NW (☎785-2333). On the prowl? Play prey or predator in this local hangout, a notorious pick-up spot full of hunting and wilderness memorabilia. 27 brews on tap, mostly microbrews, pretty good pubfare, and pool tables. Don't miss the intriguing **rib room,** which is literally in the shape of a monstrous rib cage. Happy Hour M-F 4-7pm: $2.25 Buds and $1 off all other beers. Open Su-Th 4pm-2am, F-Sa 4pm-3am.

Townhouse Tavern, 1637 R St. NW (☎234-5747). Three floors on which to hang out and get to know the locals. In summer, tables spill out onto the sidewalks. Nothing fancy or pretentious, just good beer. Open Su-Th noon-2am, F-Sa noon-3am.

FARRAGUT

A number of bars in Farragut transition into casual quasi-clubs as the evening grows late, making Farragut a busy place to shake your booty.

Rumors, 1900 M St. NW (☎466-7378). Metro: Farragut North or Dupont Circle. The anchor of the bar-heavy M St. block between

19th and 20th St. NW. The DJ spins Top 40 and some 80s faves for a 20-something crowd on a small dance floor. Happy Hour M-F 4-7pm: $2.75 domestic beers, wines, rails. 21+ after 8pm. F-Sa $2-3 cover. Open Su-Th 11am-2am, F-Sa 11am-3am.

Sign of the Whale, 1825 M St. NW (☎ 785-1110). Metro: Farragut North or Dupont Circle. A laid-back and comfortable bar during the week gets hopping with a DJ on the weekends. Varnished dark wood and the usual bar decor sets the scene for Happy Hour relaxation and fun. Varied crowd ranging from mid-20s to early 40s. DJ plays Top 40 and 80s favorites. Happy Hours 4-7pm M-Thurs, 4-9pm Fri. Th-Sa 21+. No cover. Open Su-Th 11:30am-1:30am, F-Sa 11:30am-2:30am.

The Madhatter, 1831 M St. NW (☎ 833-1495), near 19th St. Metro: Farragut North or Farragut West. Much more arm-jostling than the Whale next door, with a younger party-hard clientele. Starts hopping during Happy Hour (M-F 4-7pm; $2 rails and a free buffet) and stays packed until closing. DJ spins Top 40 and mainstream dance hits Tu-Sa from 9pm. Live acoustic music M. Open Su-Th 11am-1:30am, F-Sa 11am-2:30am.

Tequila Grill, 1990 K St. NW (☎ 833-3640), entrance on corner of 20th St. Southwestern food and decor mixes with a Top 40, dance, and hip-hop DJ on Tu and weekends. Inexpensive domestic beers and mixed drinks are complemented by tasty margaritas (M-F 3:30-7:30pm $2.50-2.95). Droves of 20-somethings visit for the free beer on Tu (9pm-1am, no cover before 10pm). Sunday night football on a 52" screen. 18+. Open M-Th 11am-1am, F-Sa 11am-3am.

Ozio, 1813 M St. NW (☎ 822-6000). Metro: Farragut North or Farragut West. The très exclusive Ozio packs in a pretty crowd that sizzles with techno and international music. Real and wannabe internationals fill the club with style and pomp until the late night. Tables available for reservation. International techno. 21+. Th-Sa $10 cover. Open M-Th 11am-2am, F-Sa 6pm-3am.

Odds, 1160 20th St. NW (☎ 296-8644). Metro: Farragut West, Farragut North, or Foggy Bottom-GWU. For a good dose of alcohol and pre-1990s pop culture, look no further. The bar and walls are lined with remnants of pop-culture past, paying homage to people from John Wayne to the Ninja Turtles. Tourist blood breaks up the college crowd during the summer. Cover: Th $12 with open bar, F $12 for all-you-can-drink draft beer and rail drinks 9pm-2am, Saturday $10. 25¢ pitcher night Tu. Happy Hour 4-8pm with various specials. Open M-Th 11am-2am, F-Sa 9pm-3am.

Relish, 1800 M. St. NW (☎ 785-1177; www.relish1800.com). Metro: Farragut North. Entrance on 18th St. between L and M St. This classy martini lounge, restaurant, and bar by day turns into a pulsing international dance-craze when the sun goes down. Besides trying to look unbearably hip, the crowd knows how to boogie, especially on Saturday's salsa night. House & hip-hop music Th; international, Latin, and club music F; salsa, merengue, international Sa. Happy hours M-F, 5-7:30pm, rail $3.50 and half off second martini. No cover before 10pm, otherwise $10.

FOGGY BOTTOM

YOU ARE HERE — SEE MAP P. 310

U.S. Capitol Building

Nightlife in the Foggy Bottom area is geared towards a relaxed crowd and devoted sports fans. A few favorite neighborhood bars fill up early in the evening and pin until last call. Use Metro: Foggy Bottom-GWU for all of the following.

Froggy Bottom Pub, 2142 Pennsylvania Ave. (☎ 388-3000). The beer-stained floors and smoky air in this popular dive manage simultaneously to appeal to the Homer Simpson in all of us while disgusting the Martha Stewart. Poor service is compensated for by changing drink specials every night starting at 6pm, with anything from 32oz. domestic schooners for $3 to 16oz. margaritas for $3 to $1.50 Bud Ice. Open M-Th 11:30am-1am, F-Su 11:30am-2am.

Lindy's Red Lion, 2040 I St. (☎ 785-2766), at the corner of 21st St. Table service upstairs with awesome burgers and a friendly crowd. Old-reliable neighborhood bar with reasonably priced drinks; 10 beers on tap and $1.50 shooter specials every night. Happy Hour M-F 4-7pm features $1 off everything. Open Su-Th 11am-2am, F-Sa til 3am.

Lulu's New Orleans Cafe, 2119 M St. NW (☎ 861-5858), at M St. Features 2 bars, one posing as a cybercafe, the other a dance club, where DJs generally play progressive and rock music to a crowd chock full of Mardi Gras madness. Happy Hour (M-F 4-7pm) and nightly cheap drink specials make Lulu's a popular spot with the intern crowd. Tu salsa night, with dancing and lessons. Live jazz Su 9pm. Cybercafe open M-F 4pm-1:30am and Sa-Su 4pm-2:30am. Club open M-Th 7pm-1:30am, F-Sa 7pm-2:30am.

GEORGETOWN

YOU ARE HERE

U.S. Capitol Building●

SEE MAP P. 312

Georgetown rocks at night in more ways than one, with a variety of bars for every taste. Unfortunately, it's hard to take advantage of Georgetown nights without a car or a hefty amount of cab fare. To get to Georgetown nightlife from the Metro, take the Foggy Bottom-GWU stop on the Orange line and walk up to Pennsylvania Ave. Take a left on Pennsylvania Ave. which becomes M St. Follow that into Georgetown. For red-line users, get off at Dupont Circle and follow P St. west (away from the Circle) to Wisconsin Ave. Hang a left and walk down Wisconsin to the intersection with M St. Since the Metro has limited hours, plan on taking a cab ride back.

Garrett's, 3003 M St. NW (☎333-1033), near 30th St. Georgetown's most popular bar is a body-to-body, all-night frat party. Avoid the late night frenzy by grabbing lunch and experience the charm of Garrett's relaxed atmosphere and friendly staff. The "Hemingway" rhino was reportedly shot by one of Ernest's wives, but is disappointingly a fiberglass model. Beer and mixed drinks $3.50. Half-priced drinks, beer, and house wine during Happy Hour (M-F 5-7pm). The glass enclosed terrace upstairs is open for lunch M-F 11:30am-2:30pm, Sa-Su noon-2:20pm; dinner Su-Th 6-10pm, F-Sa 6-11pm; bar open M-F 11:30am-2am, Sa noon-3am, Su noon-2am.

Rhino, 3295 M St. (☎333 3150), at the corner of M and 33rd St. The black facade and shaded windows might be intimidating, but have no fear, only good times await inside. The attractive twentysomething crowd gathers to watch the game on the first floor's big screen TV, while upstairs patrons shoot the breeze while they shoot pool ($10 per hr.). Happy Hour F 5-9pm features ½ price drafts. Open T-Th 9pm-1:30am, F 5pm-2:30am, Sa 9pm-2:30am.

J. Paul's, 3218 M St. NW (☎333-3450), near Wisconsin Ave. Attracting yuppies of all colors, shapes and sizes, this spacious saloon gets packed most nights around dinner. Typical pub fare and prices (sandwiches $8-13, entrees $11-21), but it boasts its famous brand of amber lager, a recent National Beer-Tasting award winner (pint $4.25). Open M-Th 11:30am-11:30pm, F-Sa 11:30am-1am, Su 10:30am-11:30pm.

Champions, 1206 Wisconsin Ave. NW (☎965-4005), at the end of an alley in the 1st block up from M St. This sports bar features signed photos of sports stars on the wall, some of whom occasionally stop by. Early on, the crowd gathers to watch the "big game" on the bar's two big screen TVs. Later, young career singles replace armchair quarterbacks. Feast on various platters of wings ($7-17). Happy Hour M-F 6pm-10pm, Sa 6pm-midnight. Dancing Th-Sa nights. No cover, but a 1 drink min. F-Sa. Drafts $3.25, domestic bottled beers $3.25. Open M-Th 6pm-2am, F 6pm-3am, Sa noon-3am, Su noon-midnight.

The Tombs, 1226 36th St. NW (☎337-6668), at Prospect St. Very close to G.U., and a favorite with students, interns, locals, and occasionally more high profile clientele (Clinton, Chris O'Donnell). Despite the rather forboding name, this basement restaurant is cozy, with a nautical-theme decor. Drop in for burgers ($6), dinner ($8-13), and pitchers of beer ($6-13, mugs $1.50). Open M-F 11:30am-2am, Sa 11am-3am, Su 9:30am-1am (Su brunch til 3pm).

Mr. Smith's, 3104 M St. NW (☎333-3104), near 31st St. Self-proclaimed "Friendliest Saloon in Town" tends to be a pick-up joint for Georgetown thirtysomethings. Welcomes bands of all types F-Sa nights upstairs. If the bar gets too raucous slip out to the garden seating in the enclosed Greenhouse out back. Drafts $2 and appetizers half-price M-F 5-7pm. Mixed drinks $3.25-6. Sandwiches $6-9, entrees up to $15. Open Su-Th 11:30am-2am, F-Sa 11:30am-3am.

Old Glory, 3139 M St. NW (☎337-3406). A diverse, late 20s crowd gathers here every night for unparalleled ribs featuring region-specific barbecue sauces and cooking techniques (dry vs. wet, Memphis vs. Texas). Some also take a crack at joining Old Glory's Bourbon Club by sampling each of Old Glory's 80 varieties (usually in more than one sitting). Drafts $3-4.50, bottled beer $3-6. Mixed drinks $4-6. Bar open Su-Th 11:30am-2am, F-Sa 11:30am-2:30am; dinner served Su-Th until 11pm, F-Sa til midnight.

YOU ARE HERE

SEE MAP P. 316

NORTHEAST

Many bars in the Northeast are either hard-to-reach or appear in highly dangerous neighborhoods. The following restaurants/bars are notable exceptions, all located near Metro: Brookland-CUA. Regardless, **always be careful in the area and never walk alone at night.**

Island Jim's Crab Shack & Tiki Bar ($+), 901 Monroe St. NE (☎635-8454). Next door to Colonel Brooks Tavern. This tropical hideaway provides everything an islander could want except for the actual ocean. Indulge in a great dish (chicken sandwich with fries $7.99, steak salad $8.99) or drink while sitting in the festive patio or the fun, sand-filled back area. Frequented by locals and students for good food and fun. Drafts $2.50-3.95; margaritas $4.50-6.50. Live music W 6-9pm and F 8pm. Open Tu-Sa 11:30am-midnight. Casual dress.

Kelly's Ellis Island, 3908 12th St. NE (☎832-6117). Nice dining room with exposed bricks and skylights make this Irish pub a refreshing departure from similar establishments. Well-prepared, large dishes served by attentive waitstaff. The house brew is a refreshing Irish ale ($2.75 pint). Su brunch 7-11am. Kitchen open Su-Th 11:30am-10pm, F-Sa 11:30am-11pm; bar open nightly until around 2am. Casual dress.

Johnny K's, 3514 12th St. (☎832-3945). Catholic University students and locals make this the popular Brookland hangout. Live music or DJ keeps the weekend crowd happy along with great drink specials: Sa 8pm-midnight. All you can drink $10, pitcher of beer with lbs. of wings or plate of nachos $9.95. Also a favorite for TV football games. M-F 3-8pm $1.50 pint and Fri with a complimentary buffet. Open M-F 3pm-3am, Sa-Su 11am-3am.

Club Hell

Colonel Brooks Tavern ($$), 901 Monroe St. NE (☎529-4002). A wood interior gives this establishment a relaxed, welcoming feel. Fine food draws crowds by day; fine beer draws crowds by night. A handful of microbrews tops the list (mug $3, pitcher $12.50). Live Dixieland band Tu 8-11pm. Open Su-Th 11am-2am, F-Sa 11am-3am. Casual dress.

OLD DOWNTOWN (PENN QUARTER)

YOU ARE HERE
U.S. Capitol Building

Clubs in Old Downtown are concentrated in two main areas: near the McPherson Square Metro and just shy of Chinatown. The close proximity of many clubs makes club-hopping very tempting, despite the steep expenses. Drinks in Old Downtown tend to be pricey, but there are happy hours almost everywhere—just keep your eyes open.

Zei, 1415 Zei Alley (☎842-2445; www.zeiclub.com), between 14th and 15th and H and I St. NW. Metro: McPherson Square. The streets of D.C. are abuzz about Club Zei's mix of hot hip-hop and hi-nrg house music. The crowd is a mix of D.C. college students. No sneakers or athletic gear, jeans ok. 18+. Cover $10. Open Th-Sa 10pm-3am.

Millie and Al's Bar

Fado, 808 7th St. NW (☎789-0066). Metro: Gallery Place-Chinatown. On 7th in between H and I St. Boasting itself as an authentic Irish pub, Fado transports local patrons to the city streets of Dublin with is traditional Irish folk music, walls lined with soccer jerseys, cobblestone floor, and intricately carved tables and booths. The bar gets packed most nights with a crowd ranging from grad students to retired government workers. Here's the place to get Red Bull, a popular energy drink used as a mixer for vodka or rum (Red Bull and vodka, $8.25). Open Su-Th 11:30am-1:30am, F-Sa til 2:30am.

DC Live, 932 F St. NW (☎347-7200). Metro: Metro Center (11th St.) or Gallery Place-Chinatown (9th St.). 4 floors (3 for dancing) decorated with blacklights and funky ethnic artwork. Bars and free pool tables flank large dance floors. 21+ except Su. Reggae-HipHop Jam W 10pm-2:30am; $7; no athletic gear, jeans allowed. Closed Th. Hip-hop, R&B or live jazz F 5pm-3am, $10, free before 8pm. Sa 10pm-4am, $10 cover, no jeans or khakis. Su (18+) is the biggest college night in D.C. from 10pm-3am; $10, $7 before 11pm; jeans allowed, but no T-shirts, sneakers, or work boots.

Diners

inside
SECRETS TO...

senator spotting

Dying to hob-nob with political bigwigs? Want a whiff of the original old boys' clubs? Find senators and congressmen galore at the **Capital Grille** or the **Old Ebbitt Grill** (see p. 172). Spot top policymakers and lawyers dining and drinking between filibusters at **The Palm** (1225 19th St.).

the singles' scene

Violins and hearts and poetry-spouting nobles might be in short supply at D.C. clubs (read: meat markets). However, singles in heat often make a beeline for **Lulu's New Orleans Cafe** (see p. 185) or **Sequoia** (3000 K St. NW) in Georgetown.

If you're gay...

The oft-asked question "What's your type?" rings true in D.C.'s segregated gay scene. Chocolate queens looking for action can head to **The Fireplace** (see p. 191), A&F boys find good company at **JR's** (see p. 190), and Latin lovers frequent **Chaos** (see p. 191) on Thursdays. **Omega** (see p. 191) hosts a good mix. Ladies might bounce on over to **Hung Jury** (see p. 191) for friendly fun.

Coco Loco, 810 7th St. NW (☎289-2626), between H and I St. Metro: Gallery Place-Chinatown. This chic Brazilian restaurant lends its bright, mosaic-tiled floor to DJ-driven salsa, merengue, and samba dancing every Th-Sa beginning at 10pm. Free salsa dance lessons are given every Th 9-10pm. No food during nightclub hours; the kitchen has to close to make room for the traditional Brazilian dance show (F-Sa, 11:30pm). No sportswear, no sneakers. 21+. Cover $10. Nightclub open Th 10pm-2am, F-Sa 10:30pm-2:30am.

The Ritz, 919 E St. NW (☎638-2582), near 9th St., across from the FBI Building. Metro: Gallery Place-Chinatown. A mega-club with all genres of music; different floors open up as the crowd gets bigger. Sweet talk that intern over candlelight in a moody-blues jazz atmosphere downstairs, then head upstairs to the packed and sweaty reggae dancefloor to show off that thong-thong-thong-thong-thong. On Fr the club becomes **The Spot** (10pm-4am), while Saturdays are touted as "Big Saturday." Cover $7. F-Su 9pm-5am.

Diva at the restaurant **Tuscana West,** 1350 I St. NW (☎289-7300). Metro: McPherson Square. Face glitter and tinted sunglasses are typical acessories worn by the beautiful and young international crowd which dances the night away to hot Middle Eastern, Persian, and European dance hits at this upscale bar and club. Plenty of seating and large dance area all on one floor. 21+. Cover $10. Open F-Sa 11pm-3am.

Capitol City Brewing Company, 1100 New York Ave. NW (☎628-2222), enter on the corner of 11th and H St. Metro: Metro Center. Locations also in Arlington and Union Station, where Tiger Woods drank during the U.S. Open. Sit around, watch the game, and get sloshed the yuppie way: microbrew. Happy Hour features $3.25 pints (M-Th 5-7pm). All other times, pints $4-4.50. Open M-Sa 11am-1:30am, Su 11am-11pm.

Sky Terrace, 515 15th St. NW (☎638-5900), on the roof of the Hotel Washington. Metro: Metro Center or McPherson Square. Located right next door to the ritzy Willard Hotel, this canopied rooftop bar tends to get crowded with the very well-to-do. Patrons perched 11 stories up enjoy great views of the White House complex, the Lincoln Memorial, and, from an angle, the Washington Monument. Get here early. Open daily 11:30am-1am; kitchen closes at 11:30 pm.

Stoney's Restaurant, 1307 L St. NW (☎(202) 347-9163), near 13th St. Metro: Farragut North. Greasy spoon meets the Godfather in this neighborhood tavern with the longest Happy Hour around (4pm-midnight). Kick back and relax in the homey atmosphere for the Thursday beer specials (pitcher $7), and Friday Margarita and Corona specials. Open Su-Th 10am-2am, F-Sa 10am-3am; kitchen closes at 1:30am.

SHAW/U DISTRICT

Artsier-than-thou nightspots cluster around **U St.** Most clubs sport a distinct style, from highbrow Marxist to Rastafarian chic. Regulars maintain an unspoken dress code; conform accordingly. For live music venues, see **Rock and Pop,** p. 137. The area can be dangerous at night: **exercise caution and always travel in groups.** Use Metro: U St.-Cardozo.

State of the Union, 1357 U St. NW (☎588-8810, www.stateoftheu.com), near 14th St. Partying and shaking some booty under Marx and Lenin's watchful eyes (murals and busts abound) might seem an unlikely combo, but this cozy club's throbbing hip-hop, techno, and other jazzy genres keep the crowd dancing on a small floor. Stylishly casual. Happy Hour (daily until 8:30pm) means half-off beer and rails, with twists on Russian faves—Starburst vodka, anyone? The back room has a movable wall for summer patio action. 21+. Occasional $7 drink min. Open M-Th 5pm-2am, F-Sa 5pm-3am, Su 7pm-3am.

Republic Gardens, 1355 U St. NW (☎232-2710). This large, 2 floor club pumps the latest hip-hop and rap in sexy lounge areas and heated dance floors. The clientele's choice in fashion varies from hip urban wear to the standard club wear of dark pants and black shoes. Poshly decorated rooms flaunt the club's good fashion sense. 21+. Cover $10.

Chi Cha Lounge, 1624 U St., NW (☎234-8400). Metro: U St.-Cardozo. A swanky crowd dresses to impress in this mellow, 2 room lounge. The coffeehouse crowd sips liquor instead of java here, lounging at the various couches, chairs, and tables. Andean food and Arabic tobacco are also served in this hip-even-for-U-St. lounge. Fruit-flavored water pipes available Su-Tu. Live Latin music spices up the chill comfort Su-W 9pm. Open Su-Th 5:30pm-1:30am, F-Sa 5:30pm-3am.

Bar Nun/Club 2000, 1326 U St. (☎667-6680). This smaller, hipper version of the mega-clubs in Old Downtown gets frenzied faster than any other club on U St. 2 floors, 3 bars, and a danceable mix of hip-hop, jungle, and reggae music. Ethiopian night F. 18+ on Tu, otherwise 21+. Cover can be up to $5, depending on the crowd. Open M 7:30pm-1am, Tu 9pm-2:30am, W-Th 9pm-2am, F 5pm-3am, Sa 8pm-3am.

Cafe Nema, 1334 U St. (☎667-3215). Showcasing a lot of local talent, the small downstairs bar combines avant-garde art with the toe-tapping vibes of live jazz Th-Sa (10pm-1am). Kitchen open 10am-11pm. All ages, but crowd tends to be 25+. Frequented by internationals. No cover but occasional 2 drink min. Happy Hour offers 2 for $5 bottled beers and $1 off top shelf (M-F 4-8pm). Open Su-Tu 9am-midnight, W-Sa 9am-2am.

Kaffa House, 1212 U St. (☎462-1212). Live reggae music grooves in this small cafe/bar, which also serves cheap Jamaican and Ethiopian cuisine. The dancing area is small, but blinking colored lights and murals of mellow rastafarians keep the crowd smiling. Sunday Jam is Clash of the Oldies. 18+. Cover Sa-Th $5, F $7. Open daily 8pm-3am.

Utopia/The Bar, 1418 U St. NW (☎483-7669), near 14th St. This upscale "bar and grill, art and eat" hosts exhibits by local artists every month in the back room. With glam-farmhouse decor highlighted by mood lighting, this low key venue satiates any jazz aficionado. Lunch, brunch, dinner. Live Brazilian music Th, live jazz Sa (11:30pm-2:30am), live blues and jazz Su. Open Su-Th 11am-2am, F-Sa 11am-3am.

SOUTH OF THE MALL

Zanzibar on the Waterfront, 700 Water St. SW (☎544-1900). Metro: Waterfront. Neon abstract elegance, shimmering waterfront views, and international clientele meet at this "avante-garde entertainment centre." Five bars, 2 large dance floors, VIP lounge, and a stage. M sports night; Tu International jazz and blues; W salsa and merengue; Th reggae, top 40, or swing; F-Sa International music; Su International classics. $10 cover most nights or get free admission with dinner. Arrive early or purchase tickets in advance for live acts (around $30). Open Su-Tu 5pm-midnight, W-Th 5pm-2am, F 5pm-3am, Sa 9pm-3am.

TAKOMA PARK

Takoma Station Tavern, 6914 4th St. NW (☎829-1999). Just steps west of the Metro. Patrons from VA, MD, and D.C. pack this popular club nightly to see jazz, R&B, and comedy acts. Offers sandwiches and bar food ($7-9). Daily specials during Happy Hour M-F 4-8pm. 18+. Live acts nightly; $6-20 cover for performances. Open daily 4pm-2am.

Taliano's, 7001B Carroll Ave. (☎(301) 270-5515). The only bar on Takoma's main drag that features live folk, blues, acoustic, and rock music. The first M of the month draws a diverse crowd for its family-friendly half-price pizza 5-9pm; blues after 8pm. W swing, Th jazz, F rock, Sa Latin. $5-8 cover. Bar open Su-Th 11:30am-midnight, F-Sa til 1am. Kitchen stops 1hr. before closing.

UPPER NORTHWEST

With so many alternatives downtown, Upper Northwest's bars rarely draw anyone besides local residents. However, the neighborhood feel of these places can be a relief to those sick of posing in Dupont's or Foggy Bottom's wholesale singles' markets.

Marilyn and the Mermaids

For the past 14 years, local drag queens dressed as everyone and everything from Marilyn Monroe to mermaids have flocked to the Halloween High Heel Race in Dupont Circle. The stilletoed sashay used to be held on the weekend of Halloween, but crowds have gotten so large recently that the race has been moved to the Tuesday prior to Halloween. The race begins at **J.R.'s**, the sponsors of the event, at 1519 17th St. NW and goes to 17th and R St. Drag beauties start jockeying for prime position around 9pm, but come early to get the best view of Washington's loveliest ladies.

Ireland's Four Provinces, 3412 Connecticut Ave. NW (☎244-0860). Metro: Cleveland Park. Large open space is a refreshing deviant from long narrow bars. Nightly live Irish folk music at 8:30pm. Indoor and outdoor seating available during the summer. Happy Hour (5-7pm) discounts domestics ($2), imports ($3.50), rails ($3.50), and, of course, Guinness ($3.50). Open Su-Th 5pm-2am, F-Sa 4pm-3am.

The Aroma Company, 3417 Connecticut Ave. NW (☎244-7995). Metro: Cleveland Park. Despite the name, the Aroma Company really isn't a cigar bar—it's actually more of a funky martini lounge for neighborhood elites. With lots of small tables and 50s-motif couches in the front window, locals come to just hang out and discourse into the wee hours of the morning. Call for a list of special events including theme nights and live music. Happy Hour M-F 6-8pm with $2.75 Jack Daniels and Bombay Sapphire drinks. Open Su-Th 6pm-2am, F-Sa 6pm-3am.

Murphy's of D.C., 2609 24th St. NW (☎462-7171), one block west of Connecticut Ave. Metro: Woodley Park-Zoo. An old neighborhood Irish pub with live Irish music Th-Su nights; stay late enough in the evening and you might see the occasional impromptu jig. Guinness ($4.50), microbrews ($4), and lots more on tap. Menu has salads, burgers, and bar food. Brunch is served on Su. Open Su-Th 11am-1am, F-Sa til 2am. Kitchen open daily until midnight.

Nanny O'Brien's, 3319 Connecticut Ave. NW (☎686-9189). Metro: Cleveland Park. A mix of locals, college students, and cast of regulars. Cheap drinks at Happy Hour (M-F 4-8pm): $1.75 domestic bottles and drafts, $2.50 import bottles and drafts, $1.75 mixed drinks. Nightly Irish music starting around 9pm, both trad and contemporary folk; Irish countryside dances in winter. Open M-Th 4pm-2am, F 4pm-3am, Sa-Su noon-3am.

Oxford Tavern "Zoo Bar," 3000 Connecticut Ave. NW (☎232-4225), across the street from the zoo. Metro: Woodley Park-Zoo. One of Washington's oldest saloons and it shows. Tourists and regulars mingle at Happy Hour (M-F 5-7pm) and chug $2.50 pints. Live blues bands play F-Su nights. Seniors 10% off food. Open Su-Th 11am-2am, F-Sa 11am-3am.

GAY BARS AND CLUBS

J.R.'s, 1519 17th St. NW (☎328-0090). Metro: Dupont Circle. D.C.'s busiest bar for good reason: beautiful bartenders, beautiful barhoppers, beautiful interior. Don't be intimidated by the "guppies" (gay urban professionals); D.C. men can be *very* friendly. M Show-tune Sing-a-Long; W South Park. Happy Hour (M-F 5-8pm) specials throughout the week including $7 all-you-can-drink (Th 5:30-8pm). Open M-Th 11:30am-2am, F-Sa 11:30am-3am, Su noon-2am.

Badlands, 1415 22nd St. NW (☎296-0505), near P St. Metro: Dupont Circle. Ditch the inhibition, approach that hottie you've been eyeing, and invite him to bump and grind on Badlands' wild dance floor. The Annex upstairs hosts a mellower video bar with pool table, but most come for the drag queen karaoke F-Sa. Tu, Th under 21 nights. Th no cover with a college ID. Cover $4 F-Sa 9-10pm, $8 after 10pm. Open Th-Sa 9pm-close (usually very late, whenever the crowd dies down).

☒ Hung Jury, 1819 H St. NW (☎785-8181). Metro: Farragut West. Lesbians from all over D.C., from older couples to young singles scoping the scene, spend their weekend nights bopping to Top 40. Shooters $1. Cover $5. Open F-Sa 9pm-3:30am.

Club Chaos, 1603 17th St. NW (☎232-4141), at Q St. Metro: Dupont Circle. Different nights cater to different crowds, though all nights are usually cool, crowded, and completely gender and orientation mixed. Happy Hour Tu-F 5-8pm. W lesbian night. Th Latin night. The best drag show in town Sa 10pm. Open Tu-Th 4pm-1am, F-Sa 4pm-2am, Su 11am-1am.

Club de Sade, 1824 Half St. SW (☎331-4455). Metro: Navy Yard. A friendly pervert family welcomes all races, genders, and sexual orientations to giant special gatherings throughout the year. Fetish, leather, or imaginative wear suggested (coat check available). Call for events.

DC Eagle, 639 New York Ave. NW (☎347-6025), in Old Downtown. Metro: Gallery Place/Chinatown. Busy, mostly male, all-leather bar. 2 pool tables, 2 floors. Happy Hour M-Sa 6-9pm; the Su Beerblast (6-10pm) $1 drafts. Open M-Th 6pm-2am, F-Sa noon-3am, Su noon-2am.

The Edge, 56 L St. SE (☎488-1200). Metro: Navy Yard. Seductively dark and secluded, this male entertainment warehouse features 6 bars, 4 dance floors, a snack bar, and a game room. Th Ladies Night 10pm with strip show (women $6, men $15); M Afro-dizica dance party 10pm ($6). F-Sa mixed productions range from raves to dungeon dances; call ahead. Secure parking in nearby lots. **This area is very unsafe: take a cab home.** Open Su-Th 8pm-3am, F-Sa 9pm-4am.

The Fireplace, 2161 P St. NW (☎293-1293). Metro: Dupont Circle. Two floor video bar catering to mostly African-American males and the men who love them. Look for the eternal flame in their "outdoor" fireplace, blazing throughout the day and night. Happy Hour M-F 1-8pm. Weekends and evenings can get pretty packed. Open Su-Th 1pm-2am, F-Sa til 3am, no cover.

La Cage Aux Follies, 18 O St. SE (☎554-3615), at S. Capitol St. Metro: Navy Yard. The self proclaimed "friendliest gay bar in D.C." Male go-go dancers hit the stage and mingle with the crowd nightly (10pm). Amateurs Night W 11:30pm—contestants receive a $25 tab. Th draws a sophisticated crowd for Martini night. Open Su 5pm-2am, Tu-Th 8pm-2am, F-Sa 8pm-3am, no cover.

Lizard Lounge, held at the Eleventh Hour Club, 1520 14th St. NW (☎331-4422). Sunday can be your fun day too as this upscale club allows D.C. boys to prolong the weekend by hosting a gay night. Food available. Reduced drink specials 8-10pm. No cover. Open Su 8pm-2am.

Mr. P's, 2147 P St. NW (☎293-1064), near 22nd St. Metro: Dupont Circle. Oldest gay bar in the Circle attracts the oldest crowd, as 40-somethings flock for $2 beers and $2.50 mixed drinks during Happy Hour (M-F 2-9pm). In the evenings, mostly male patrons spill out onto the patio and head upstairs to the video bar (open 9pm-close). Look for drag shows where locals lip-sync to popular songs Su, Tu, and Th 10:30pm. Open Su-Th 2pm-2am, F-Sa 2pm-3am, no cover.

Omega, 2122 P St. NW (☎223-4917), at the rear of P St. in the alley between 21st and 22nd St. Metro: Dupont Circle. Attracts an ethnically mixed crowd of young gay men. More of a bar than dance place, but it still boasts 2 floors of techno music videos and arcades with 4 bars. Happy Hour (Su-F 4-9pm) features $2 domestics. Specials every weeknight; Su, Tu, and Th $2.25 vodkas. Open Su-Th 4pm-2am, F 4pm-3am, Sa 8pm-3am.

Phase One, 525 8th St. SE (☎544-6831). Metro: Eastern Market. Lesbian club with casual atmosphere draws slightly older women of all styles for dancing. Pool tables, video bar, darts, and DJ spinning typical house music (F-Sa). Occasional live music. Beer $2.50. No cover Su-Th, F-Sa $5. Open W-Th and Su 7pm-2am, F-Sa 7pm-3am.

Remington's, 639 Pennsylvania Ave. SE (☎543-3113). Metro: Eastern Market. A gay country-western nightclub where "the men make their moves on and off the dance floor." Country music on the large 1st fl. dance floor, Hi-NRG upstairs in the "Sante Fe Lounge," which features posters of James Dean, a pool room, and bar. Happy Hour (M-F 4-8pm) features $2 domestic rails. Country-western dance lessons M and W-Th $5 including 1 free rail or domestic (8:30pm). Cover $4 includes half off any drink F-Sa after 9pm. Open Su-Th 4pm-2am, F-Sa 4pm-3am.

Ziegfeld's, 1345 Half St. SE (☎554-5141). Metro: Navy Yard, take the Half St. exit. Young and older gays and lesbians take turns attending Ziegfeld's nightly dance shows; subtle to electric drag shows liven up the business on Th and Su. Male strippers every night in the adjacent club Secrets. Cover $5-10. Open Th and Su 9pm-2am, F-Sa 9pm-3am.

Daytripping

BALTIMORE   ☎ 410

Birthplace of *The Star-Spangled Banner*, Baltimore lies just north of the nation's capital—an urban mecca with a historic flair. Even before Baltimore exploded into the nation's fourth largest seaport in 1825, **Francis Scott Key** was already penning the national anthem from Baltimore's shores, and Napoleon's brother was divorcing his first wife within the city limits. Today's Baltimore still retains its famed forts and waterfront, as well as enough seafood delicacies to feed the Army of the Potomac.

    The Native American name for Baltimore, *Patipasco*, means backwater, and nothing breeds crabs better than Baltimore's mucky waters. But while crab cakes, Orioles games, Inner Harbor, and the fabulous National Aquarium are all fine reasons to visit Baltimore, the true pulse of the city lies beyond the glimmering Inner Harbor, in its overstuffed markets, coffee shops, and diverse cityfolk. Baltimore's Southern heritage is visible in its many neighborhoods. In Roland Park, for instance, every house has a front porch and everyone greets you in a friendly "Bawlmer" accent. Certain natives have gained notoriety for digging beneath this genial Southern complacency: **John Waters' films** capture the city's twisted side, while **Edgar Allan Poe's writing** evokes its gloominess.

ORIENTATION

Baltimore lies 35 mi. north of D.C. and about 150 mi. from the Atlantic Ocean. To get to Baltimore from D.C., take the **Capital Beltway (I-495)** to **I-95** at **Exit 27** or to the **Baltimore-Washington Parkway** at **Exit 22**. The two highways run roughly parallel. **Exit 53** for **Rte. 395** leads right into **Inner Harbor.** Without traffic, the trip takes less than an hour.

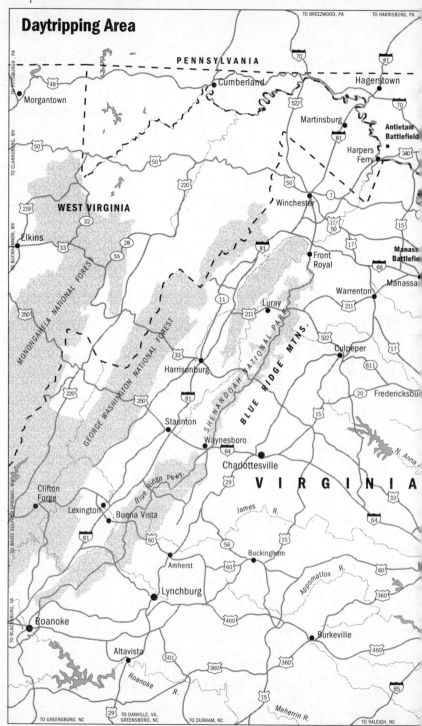

Daytripping Area

TO BREEZWOOD, PA

TO HARRISBURG, PA

PENNSYLVANIA

TO PITTSBURGH, PA

48

Morgantown

Cumberland

70

81

Hagerstown

70

522

Martinsburg

81

Antietam Battlefield

50

TO CLARKSBURG, WV

219

WEST VIRGINIA

32

Elkins

33

TO BUCKHANNON, WV

28

55

Harpers Ferry

340

50

Winchester

7

17/
50

15

17

Manass Battlefie

66

Manassa

250

50

220

81

Front Royal

11

211

Luray

211

Warrenton

522

Culpeper

17

611

MONONGAHELA NATIONAL FORES

GEORGE WASHINGTON NATIONAL FOREST

33

Harrisonburg

SHENANDOAH NATIONAL PARK

BLUE RIDGE MTNS.

20

Fredericksbu

250

81

Staunton

15

N. Anna

Waynesboro

64

Charlottesville

220

Blue Ridge Pkwy.

29

V I R G I N I A

33

Clifton Forge

Lexington

Buena Vista

James   R.

64

TO WHITE SULPHUR SPRINGS, WV

81

60

56

Buckingham

15

60

Amherst

60

Appomattox   R.

360

Lynchburg

460

Burkeville

460

TO BLACKSBURG, VA

Roanoke

Altavista

501

360

15

85

Roanoke   R.

29

TO GREENSBORO, NC

TO DANVILLE, VA,
GREENSBORO, NC

TO DURHAM, NC

Meherrin R.

TO RALEIGH, NC

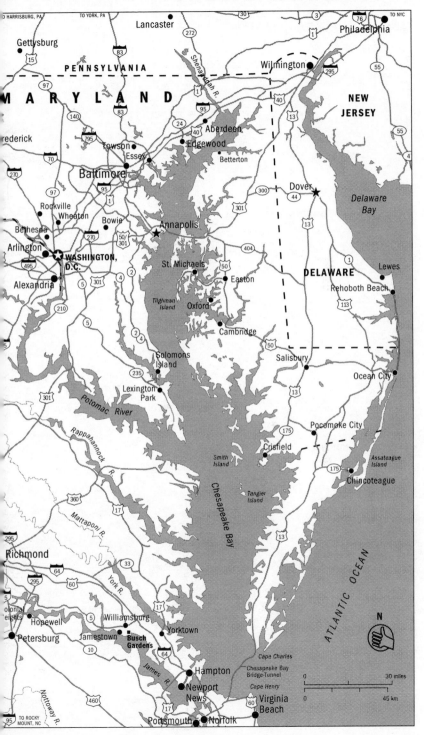

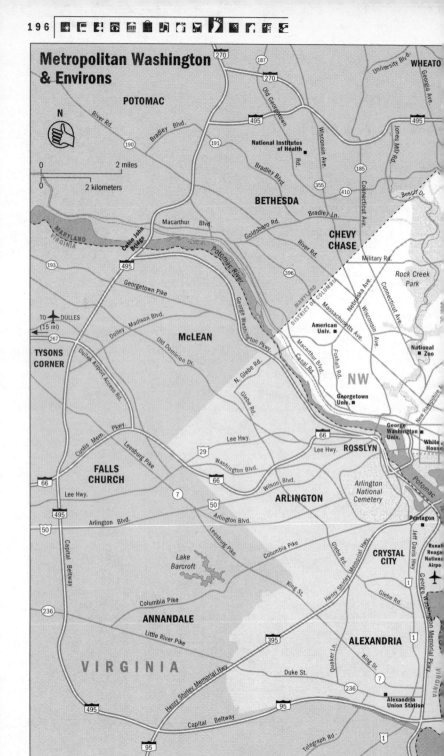

Metropolitan Washington & Environs

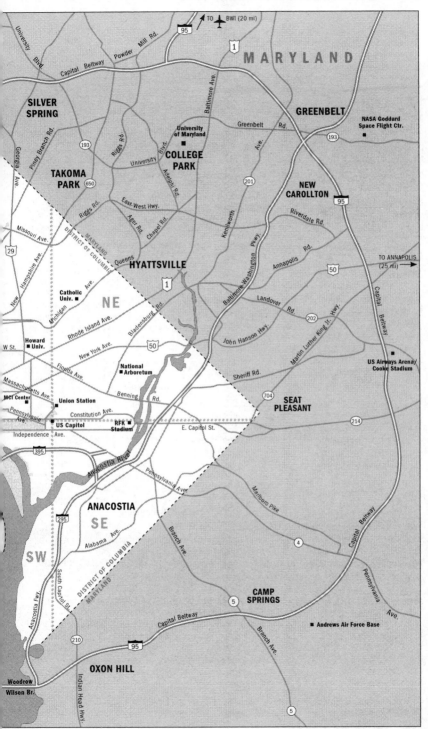

REGIONAL HIGHLIGHTS

Loud, boisterous, and colorful, Baltimore's 17th-century **markets** (see p. 205) transform dining and shopping into a sweet, cheap adventure.

In Virginia Beach, bikini-clad revelers on **"Beach Street USA"** (see p. 231) prove that beach parties only get better when the sun goes down.

At **Fredericksburg and Spotsylvania National Battlefield Park** (see p. 245), visitors march in the footsteps of thousands of slain Confederate and Union soldiers.

The city is divided into quarters by **Baltimore Street** (east-west) and **Charles Street** (north-south). Directional prefixes indicate every other street's relation to these main streets.

Inner Harbor, near the corner of Pratt and Charles St., is a scenic tourist trap and home to historic ships, a shopping mall, and an aquarium. The museum-laden **Mount Vernon** neighborhood—served by city buses #3, 9, and 11—occupies **N. Charles St.,** north of **Baltimore St.,** around **Monument St.** and **Centre Ave.** Ethnic **Little Italy** sits a few blocks east of the Inner Harbor, past the **Jones Falls Expressway.** Continuing past Little Italy, a short walk to the southeast brings you past Broadway to bar-happy **Fells Point.** Old-fashioned **Federal Hill** preserves Baltimore history, while the area east of **Camden Yards** has recently been re-urbanized.

The southern end of the **Jones Falls Expressway (I-83)** halves the city near the Inner Harbor, and the **Baltimore Beltway (I-695)** circles the city. I-95 cuts across the southwest corner of the city as a shortcut to the wide arc of the Beltway. During rush hour, these roads slow to a crawl. Baltimore, like any other major US city, lacks free parking. So either come fisting shiny quarters or expect to pay garages about $7 per day. Meters and garages away from the harbor are less expensive.

PRACTICAL INFORMATION

Airport: Baltimore-Washington International (BWI),

(☎859-7111; www.bwiairport.com), on I-195 off the Baltimore-Washington Parkway (I-295), about 10 mi. south of the city center. Take MTA bus #17 to the Nursery Rd. light-rail station. Airport shuttles to hotels (☎859-0800; www.supershuttle.com) run daily every 30min. 5:45am-11:30pm ($11 to downtown Baltimore, $17 round-trip). For D.C., shuttles leave hourly 5:45am-11:30pm ($21-31). Amtrak trains from BWI run to Baltimore ($5) and D.C. ($12). MARC commuter trains are cheaper but slower, and only run M-F (Baltimore $3.25, D.C. $5).

Trains: Penn Station, 1500 N. Charles St. (☎(800) 872-7245), at Mt. Royal Ave. Easily accessible by bus #3 or 11 from Charles Station downtown. Amtrak trains run every 30min.-1hr. to: **New York** ($62-71); **Washington, D.C.** ($19+), and **Philadelphia** ($35+). On weekdays, 2 **MARC commuter lines** (☎(800) 325-7245 in MD) connect Baltimore to D.C.'s Union Station (☎859-7400 or 291-4268) via Penn Station (with stops at BWI Airport) or **Camden Station** (☎613-5342), at the corner of Howard and Camden St. near Oriole Park. Both are $5.75, round-trip $10.25. Open daily 5:30am-9:30pm, self-serve open 24hr. (credit card only).

Buses: Greyhound (☎(800) 231-2222) has 2 locations: downtown at 210 W. Fayette St. (☎752-7682), near N. Howard St.; and at 5625 O'Donnell St. (☎752-0908), 3mi. east of downtown near I-95. Connections to **New**

York ($24, round-trip $43); **Washington, D.C.** ($6, round-trip $10); and **Philadelphia** ($15, round-trip $24).

Public Transport: Mass Transit Administration (MTA), 300 W. Lexington St. (bus and Metro schedule info ☎539-5000 or (800) 543-9809), near N. Howard St. Operator available M-F 6am-9pm. Bus, Metro, and light-rail service to most major sights in the city and outlying areas. Some buses run 24hr. Metro operates M-F 5am-midnight, Sa 6am-midnight. Light rail operates M-F 6am-11pm, Sa 8am-11pm, Su 11am-7pm. One way fare for all is $1.35, but may be higher depending on distance traveled. Bus #17 runs from the Nursery Rd. light-rail to BWI Airport.

Water Taxi: Main stop at Inner Harbor (☎563-3901 or ☎(800) 658-8947). Stops every 8-18min. (Nov.-Mar. every 40min.) at the harbor museums, Harborplace, Fells Point, Little Italy, and more. An easy way to travel to 40 of Baltimore's main sights, especially in summer when service continues until midnight. Service daily May-Aug. 9am-midnight, Apr. and Sept.-Oct. 9am-9pm, Nov.-Mar. 9am-6pm. 1 day unlimited rides $4.50, ages 10 and under $2. Ticket includes coupons for Baltimore attractions. Run by **Harbor Boating, Inc.,** 1615 Thames St.

Taxis: Checker Cab, ☎685-1212. **Royal Cab,** ☎327-0330.

Car Rental: Thrifty Car Rental, BWI Airport (☎859-1136), and 2042 N. Howard St. (☎783-0300), 9 blocks from Penn Station. Economy cars from $35 per day and $185 per week. Unlimited miles in MD and bordering states. Under 25 $15 extra per day. Must be 21 and have credit card. Airport branch open daily 6am-11pm.

Visitor Information: Baltimore Area Visitors Center, 451 Light St. (☎837-7024). Located in a red-trimmed, white trailer, the user-friendly center provides dozens of maps, brochures offering discounts to sights and restaurants, and the city's helpful *Quickguide*. Knowledgeable volunteers will also happily point weary travelers in the right direction. Open in summer M-Sa 9am-7pm, Su 10am-5pm; in winter daily 9am-5pm.

Traveler's Aid: ☎685-3569 (M-F 8:30am-3:30pm) or ☎685-5874, voice-mail only. Two desks at BWI Airport (☎859-7209; open M-F 9am-9pm, Su 1-9pm). Direct-line telephones at Penn Station and Greyhound terminal.

Emergency: 911.

Help Lines: Suicide: ☎531-6677. Open 24hr. **Sexual Assault and Domestic Violence:** ☎828-6390. Open 24hr. **Gay and Lesbian:** ☎837-8888. Operators daily 7pm-midnight, recording all other times.

Post Office: 900 E. Fayette St. (☎347-4425). Open M-F 7:30am-9pm, Sa 7:30am-5pm.

ZIP Code: 21233.

ACCOMMODATIONS AND CAMPING

Expensive chain hotels dominate the Inner Harbor, and reputable inexpensive hotels elsewhere are hard to find. For a convenient way to reserve bed and breakfasts call Amanda's Bed and Breakfast Reservation Service, 1428 Park Ave. (☎225-0001 or (800) 899-7533). Rates begin at $50 a night. Reservations are recommended. M-F 8:30am-5:30pm, Sa 8:30am-noon.

Baltimore International Youth Hostel (HI-AYH), 17 W. Mulberry St. (☎576-8880), centrally located at Cathedral St. in the historic Mount Vernon neighborhood. Near bus and Amtrak terminals. Take MTA buses #3 or 11 along Charles St. **Note: The hostel is temporarily closed for renovations with plans to reopen in the summer of 2001. Prices quoted are from 1998. Call for new rates.** Elegantly shabby 19th-century brownstone harbors 35 beds in spacious dorm rooms. Full kitchen and laundry service. Lounge with marble fireplaces and a TV. Friendly manager is great source of information about Baltimore. A/C in bedrooms and fans in common areas. Free baggage storage ($5 deposit) and linen ($10 deposit). Curfew 11pm, but house keys available with $10 deposit. 3-night max. stay (may be extended with manager's approval). Reservations recommended, especially in summer. HI members $14, non-members $17. **BE CAREFUL AT NIGHT.**

Duke's Motel, 7905 Pulaski Hwy. (☎686-0400), in Rosedale off the Beltway. The bulletproof glass in the front office is nothing to worry about—all the neighborhood motels have it. Nevertheless, the area is actually safer than most parts of downtown Baltimore. Clean and efficiently run.

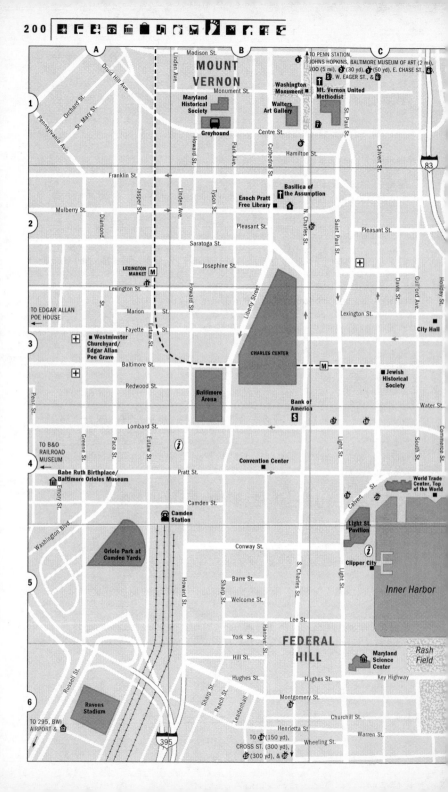

MOUNT VERNON

Madison St.

Monument St.

Washington
Monument ■

Maryland
Historical
Society

Walters
Art Gallery

Mt. Vernon United
Methodist

Greyhound

Centre St.

Hamilton St.

TO PENN STATION,
JOHNS HOPKINS, BALTIMORE MUSEUM OF ART (2 mi),
ZOO (5 mi), (30 yd), (50 yd), E. CHASE ST.,
W. EAGER ST., &

Druid Hill Ave.

Orchard St.

St. Mary St.

Pennsylvania Ave

Linden Ave.

Howard St.

Park Ave.

Cathedral St.

St. Paul St.

Calvert St.

83

Franklin St.

Mulberry St.

Jasper St.

Diamond

Linden Ave.

Tyson St.

Enoch Pratt
Free Library ■

Basilica of
the Assumption

N. Charles St.

Saint Paul St.

Pleasant St.

Pleasant St.

Saratoga St.

Josephine St.

LEXINGTON
MARKET

Lexington St.

Marion   St.

Liberty Street

Lexington St.

Guilford Ave.

Davis St.

Holliday St.

TO EDGAR ALLAN
POE HOUSE

St.

Howard St.

Eutaw St.

Fayette   St.

City Hall

Westminster
Churchyard/
Edgar Allan
Poe Grave

Baltimore St.

CHARLES CENTER

Jewish
Historical
Society

Redwood St.

Baltimore
Arena

Bank of
America

Water St.

Penn St.

Lombard St.

TO B&O
RAILROAD
MUSEUM

Babe Ruth Birthplace/
Baltimore Orioles Museum

Greene St.

Paca St.

Eutaw St.

Emory St.

Pratt St.

Convention Center

Camden St.

Calvert   St.

World Trade
Center, Top
of the World

Camden
Station

Washington Blvd

Oriole Park at
Camden Yards

Russell St.

Howard St.

Conway St.

Barre St.

Welcome St.

Lee St.

York   St.

Hanover St.

S. Charles St.

Sharp St.

Light St.

Light St.

South St.

Commerce St.

Light St.
Pavilion

Clipper City

Inner Harbor

FEDERAL
HILL

Hill St.

Hughes St.

Montgomery St.

Peach St.

Leadenhall

Sharp St.

Hughes St.

Maryland
Science
Center

Key Highway

Rash
Field

Ravens
Stadium

TO 295, BWI
AIRPORT &

395

Churchill St.

Henrietta St

TO (150 yd),
CROSS ST. (300 yd),
(300 yd), &

Wheeling St.

Warren St.

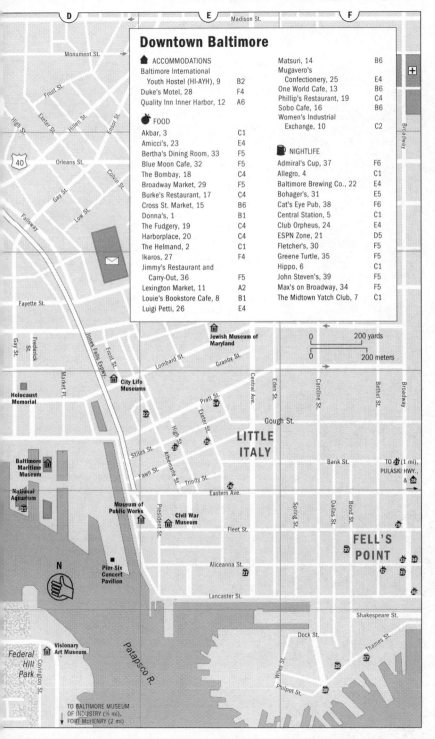

Downtown Baltimore

🏠 **ACCOMMODATIONS**

Baltimore International Youth Hostel (HI-AYH), 9	B2
Duke's Motel, 28	F4
Quality Inn Inner Harbor, 12	A6

🍴 **FOOD**

Akbar, 3	C1
Amicci's, 23	E4
Bertha's Dining Room, 33	F5
Blue Moon Cafe, 32	F5
The Bombay, 18	C4
Broadway Market, 29	F5
Burke's Restaurant, 17	C4
Cross St. Market, 15	B6
Donna's, 1	B1
The Fudgery, 19	C4
Harborplace, 20	C4
The Helmand, 2	C1
Ikaros, 27	F4
Jimmy's Restaurant and Carry-Out, 36	F5
Lexington Market, 11	A2
Louie's Bookstore Cafe, 8	B1
Luigi Petti, 26	E4

Matsuri, 14	B6
Mugavero's Confectionery, 25	E4
One World Cafe, 13	B6
Phillip's Restaurant, 19	C4
Sobo Cafe, 16	B6
Women's Industrial Exchange, 10	C2

🍸 **NIGHTLIFE**

Admiral's Cup, 37	F6
Allegro, 4	C1
Baltimore Brewing Co., 22	E4
Bohager's, 31	E5
Cat's Eye Pub, 38	F6
Central Station, 5	C1
Club Orpheus, 24	E4
ESPN Zone, 21	D5
Fletcher's, 30	F5
Greene Turtle, 35	F5
Hippo, 6	C1
John Steven's, 39	F5
Max's on Broadway, 34	F5
The Midtown Yatch Club, 7	C1

Welcome to Baltimore, Hon

As *The Baltimore Sun* puts it, **hon** is a "provincial term of affection" in Baltimore. Got that, hon? If you stay in the city long enough, someone is likely to call you by this unusual but interesting appellation. In 1994, the **"Hon Man,"** a mysterious vandal whose real name has never been revealed, led a campaign to add "Hon" to the "Welcome to Baltimore" sign on the Baltimore-Washington Parkway. For two years, he repeatedly stuck placards saying "Hon" to the sign only to have highway workers remove them. His antics inspired state senators to add an amendment to the state budget that would have withheld $1 million in highway funds until "Hon" was permanently added to the sign. The mayor, fascinated by his pranks, even invited him to City Hall. But Hon Man's campaign ended in failure, with state troopers catching him in the act and extracting a promise never to hang a "Hon" sign again. Despite one relapse (troopers found one of the distinctive signs up again in January of 1998), he's kept his word ever since.

Simple, dark rooms have A/C and cable TV. Best for people with cars. $5 key deposit and ID required. King-sized beds optional. Singles from $47; doubles $48 and up. Rates increase in summer and weekends.

Quality Inn Inner Harbor, 1701 Russell St. (☎ 727-3400 or (800) 221-2222), near the Beltway in South Baltimore, about 1mi. from Inner Harbor. Standard rooms, cable TV, pool, and complimentary continental breakfast. Most suitable for those with cars. **Be careful at night.** Weekdays: singles $72; doubles $77. Weekends: singles $85; doubles $90. AARP/AAA and military 10% discount.

Capitol KOA, 768 Cecil Ave. (☎923-2771 or (800) 562-0248, from Baltimore ☎987-7477), in Millersville, between D.C. and Baltimore. From D.C., take **Rte. 50E** (John Hanson Hwy.) to **Rte. 3N** (Robert Crain Hwy.). Bear right after 8 mi. onto Veterans Hwy.; after a short distance turn left under the highway onto Hog Farm Rd.; follow blue camping signs. Mostly RVs, some cabins, and a small wooded area for tents. Pool, volleyball courts, and bathroom/shower facilities centrally located. Movies and crafts for kids nightly; occasional evening events for adults like slide shows and wine and cheese parties. Free weekday shuttle to MARC commuter train ($7.25 round trip to Union Station, ages 65+ $4, as many as 2 children ages 6 and under may travel free with each adult). Weekend shuttle to New Carollton Metro Stop. Standard maximum stay 2 weeks but can vary based upon availability. Open Mar. 25-Nov. 1. Tent site for 2 $27; RV complete hookup $35, water and electricity $32; 1-room cabin $46, 2 rooms $55. Each additional adult $5, child $3.

FOOD

Maryland blue crab, fresh from the Chesapeake Bay, appears on the menu at nearly every restaurant in Baltimore. The crab craze is so contagious that even ethnic restaurants serve up the crustacean delight. But a person can't live on crab alone. Luckily, Baltimore rushes to the rescue with a wide variety of culinary choices.

INNER HARBOR

The neon lights of the Hard Rock Cafe and Planet Hollywood brand Inner Harbor as a fat-walleted tourist's haven. Avoid pricey chains and opt for less hyped fare. The **Pavilions** at **Harborplace** (☎332-4191), on Pratt and Light St., have enough food stalls and restaurants to please any palate, though growing prices reflect tourism's influence.

The Fudgery, 301 Light St. (☎(401) 539-5260), on the 1st fl. in the Light St. Pavilion. Nirvana for chocolate cravers. Vocal employees musically create and promote fudge while snagging some free samples. Products are pricey ($6 per ½lb. slice) but worth the sacrifice for a delectable treat. Open M-Th 9am-10pm, F-Sa 9am-11:30pm, Su 9am-9pm.

Phillip's Restaurant, 301 Light St. (☎(800) 782-2722), on the 1st fl. of the Light St. Pavilion. Loyal fans flock to the Inner

Harbor's seafood hot-spot for magnificent marine dishes. Indoor and outdoor seating. Sandwiches ($6-13) are just as delicious as the expensive entrees ($12 and up). Tykes under 5 years old eat for free. Or try **Phillip's Seafood Market** right next door for inexpensive takeout (crab cakes $7). Both open M-F 9am-10pm, Sa 9am-11pm, Su 9am-8pm.

Burke's Restaurant, 36 Light St. (☎752-4189), across from the Convention Ctr. on Pratt St. Dimmed lighting has created European tavern aura in this Baltimore fixture since 1934. Just about everything from fish to spaghetti to steak is cheap, tasty, and delivered with speedy service. Sizable sandwiches hit the spot at lunch hour for only $3-6. Entrees run $4-11 and satisfy late into the night. If you're not bogged down by your meal, trek upstairs for a sidesplitting comedy show ($5 cover, F-Sa 8:30pm and 10:30pm). Open daily 7am-2am.

The Bombay, 114 E. Lombard St. (☎539-2233). Help yourself to a comprehensive selection of authentic Indian cuisine while listening to the soothing sounds of native music. Not feeling creative? Just order a mouth-watering Shrimp Pakoda ($6.50) or an entree ($9-$12) from helpful waitresses clad in traditional garb. South Indian Buffet Sa-Su 11:30am-3pm.

FEDERAL HILL

Baltimore's most historic district, Federal Hill caters primarily towards an upscale crowd. Spread throughout S. Charles St. and Light St., many of the restaurants will strain bank accounts, but the cafes provide affordable meals and a welcome break from tourist arenas. For more casual dining, check out the chaotically fun **Cross Street Market** for cheap, international fare.

One World Cafe, 904 S. Charles St. (☎234-0235). The appeal of sitting amidst local art while sipping one of multiple creative coffee blends draws all types to this chic cafe. A vegetarian's delight, the bean burrito ($5.25) is a hit with regulars. Pay special attention to the apt quotations that accompany each piece of artwork. Open M 7am-10pm, Tu-F 7am-11pm, Sa 8am-11pm, Su 8am-10pm.

Sobo Cafe, 6-8 W. Cross St. (☎752-1518). Quiet cafe distinguishes itself by changing its dinner and dessert menus daily. The turkey melt ($5), a fixture on the lunch menu brings stability to a constantly varying array of wild choices, including a vegetable stir fry in Chinese black bean sauce ($9). Bright, pastel colored walls gives the cafe a cheery feel. Open daily 11:30am-10pm.

Matsuri, 1105 S. Charles St. (☎752-8561). The combination of an outgoing staff and tight quarters creates a friendly environment for patrons to chopstick to their heart's content in this popular Japanese restaurant. Locals line up on weekends for Bento box lunches ($7.50-8) and sushi dinners. Open M-Th 11:30am-2:30pm and 5-10pm, F 11:30am-2:30pm and 5-11pm, Sa 5-11pm, Su 4:30-9:30pm.

MOUNT VERNON

Mount Vernon manages to squeeze a tremendous number of restaurants in between its art galleries and conservatories. Virtually all are on **North Charles Street,** within the blocks on either side of the Washington Monument. **Use caution in the areas around Cathedral St., Saratoga St., and Mulberry St. at night.**

🖾 **Louie's Bookstore Cafe,** 518 N. Charles St. (☎962-1224). Louie's appetizing menu attracts all types to dine in the shadows of the Washington Monument. In the front, an upscale, intellectual bookstore flaunts extensive sections on music and literature. In the back, a lively restaurant and bar mixes well-tailored concert-goers with scruffy indy-rockers. Sandwiches, salads, and burgers $5-10, entrees $9-17. Lunch is cheap, but the dinner scene is groovier. Live classical music nightly (Su-W 8-10:30pm, Th-Sa 8-10pm). Live jazz Th-Sa 10pm. Open Su-Tu 11am-10pm, W-Th 11am-11pm, F-Sa 11am-1:30am, Sa-Su brunch 11am-3pm. Hours vary; call ahead.

Donna's, 2 W. Madison St. (☎385-0180), just north of the Walters Gallery. Baltimore goes for ultrachic with this hip and healthy cafe. If a salad ($5-9) doesn't hit the spot, try the veggie rotolo ($6) and add some roasted potatoes ($1.50) for good measure. If your mouth is left dry after a dainty meal, quench your thirst with a beverage from Donna's gaudy list of beers (Heineken $2.50, Sapporo $4.50). Open M-Th 7:30am-11pm, F 7:30am-midnight, Sa 9am-midnight, Su 9am-8pm.

Women's Industrial Exchange, 333 N. Charles St. (☎685-4388). Baby-blue-uniformed waitresses serve food of the 50s for less than $7, including wonderful chicken salad ($5.50, with deviled eggs and tomato aspic $6.50). Founded by a group of socially active Quaker women in the

1880s, the Exchange is still a predominantly female-operated establishment. Open for breakfast M-F 7-11am, hot lunch 11am-1:45pm, and cold lunch 1:45-3pm. Gift Shop open 7am-3pm.

Akbar, 823 N. Charles St. (☎539-0944). Excellent Indian food served at prices almost as steep as the stairs leading to the basement level restaurant (entrees $10-15). All-you-can-eat lunch buffet (M-F 11:30am-2:30pm; $7), all-you-can-eat weekend brunch buffet (Sa-Su noon-3pm; $9), and the large appetizers ($2.50-5.50) are the steals. Try the pricey but tasty Chicken Malai Kabab ($11.95), served straight out of the oven. Open M-Th 11:30am-2:30pm and 5-11pm, F 11:30am-2:30pm and 5-11:30pm, Sa noon-3pm and 5-11:30pm, Su noon-3pm and 5-11pm.

The Helmand, 806 N. Charles St. (☎752-0311). Rug-strewn Afghan restaurant serves authentic cuisine like *kaddo borani* (pan-fried and baked baby pumpkin appetizer in a yogurt-garlic sauce; $3). Walls heavily adorned with authentic garb create a genuine Afghan aura as you dine. Entrees rarely exceed $10. Vegetarians will find a variety of options. Wheelchair accessible. Open Su-Th 5-10pm, F-Sa 5-11pm.

LITTLE ITALY AND FELLS POINT

Little Italy hosts an incredible number of (surprise, surprise) Italian restaurants among its row houses. Residents sit out on their stoops on summer evenings, gossiping and watching diners stroll past. If the timing is right, you'll even walk into a frenzied bocce tournament pitting two local families in a traditional Italian contest. In contrast to the homey neighborhood atmosphere, the cobblestoned streets of nearby **Fells Point** swarm with visitors wandering between shops, restaurants, and bars. If you're lucky, you'll bump into neighborhood free-style rapper, "Mr. RealiT" who will eagerly bust a spontaneous rhyme on the spot for your listening pleasure. In Fells Point, **Broadway Market** (see p. 205) sits square in the middle of S. Broadway St., about three blocks from the dock. To reach **Little Italy** from central Baltimore, take bus #7 or 10 from Pratt St. to Albemarle St. Continue on bus #7 or 10 to Broadway, and walk four blocks to **Fells Point.**

Mugavero's Confectionery, 300 S. Exeter St. (☎539-9798). This menu-less deli has been a fixture at the cozy corner of Fawn St. for 54 years thanks to the unwavering service of the friendly proprietor. Patrons can invent their own sandwiches or entrust their sandwich to the owner-operator's creative imagination ($4). Cash only. Open daily 10am-9pm or 10pm.

Amicci's, 231 S. High St. (☎528-1096). Movie posters line the walls of Amicci's, paying homage to such Italian film classics as *The Godfather* and *La Vita e Bella*. Mediterranean zest is apparent on the menu as well as the walls; *ziti la rosa* (ziti in tomato pesto served with shrimp in marsala sauce; $13) is a standout. Live large with the renowned *Pane Rotunde*, jumbo shrimp stuffed into a round loaf of soft Italian bread ($6). Loosen your belt to accommodate one of the 11 immense pasta dishes under $10. Open M-Th 11:30am-10pm, F-Sa 11:30am-11pm, Su 11:30am-9pm. Shorter off-season hrs.; call ahead.

Blue Moon Cafe, 1621 Aliceanna St. (☎522-3940), between Bond St. and Broadway. Breakfast all day and all Saturday night draws munchers from the Fells Point festivities to this hip diner. Meet your daily egg quotient with *chorizo* and eggs ($6.25) or one of the eccentric special omelettes. Open M-Sa 7am-3pm, reopens Sa night 7pm-Su 3pm.

Bertha's Dining Room, 734 S. Broadway (☎327-5795), at Lancaster. The nautical-themed (read bare wooden tables) decor would satisfy the appetite of even the pickiest mariner. Test the hype with the black-shelled mussels ($8.50-10) or the vegetable mussel chowder (cup $2.50). High tea offers scones and pastries (M-Sa 3-4:30pm; call 1 day in advance for reservations). Live jazz Th and live blues F-Sa evenings. 20 beers on tap (half-pint $2.50). Kitchen open Su-Th 11:30am-11pm, F-Sa 11:30am-midnight; bar open daily until 2am.

Jimmy's Restaurant and Carry-Out, 801 S. Broadway (☎327-3273). This 77-year-old diner offers a quick bite on the way to the pier. Calms cravings for fresh crab cakes ($11) and burgers $2.50. Pancakes with 2 eggs and coffee $3.75. Spinach pie with Greek salad ($6.50) is popular among Jimmy's regulars. Open daily 5am-10pm.

Luigi Petti, 1002 Eastern Ave. (☎685-0055), near S. Exeter. Restaurant, bar, and garden offer the true romance of Italy. Indoor and outdoor seating. Hearty weekday lunch buffet $9. If the wallet can spare it, delectable homemade pastas run $14-15, including the homemade *Mama Maria Gnocchi*. Pianist Sa evening. Open M-Th 11:30am-midnight, F 11:30am-1am, Sa 12:30pm-1am, Su 10:30am-10pm; bar open daily until 2am.

EAST OF LITTLE ITALY

Ikaros, 4805 Eastern Ave. (☎633-3750), 2mi. east of downtown. Take bus #10. With its romantic, Mediterranean atmosphere, this Baltimore standby has served scrumptious *souvlaki* ($5) for 28 years. Greek salads ($3.50-7), *moussaka* ($8.50), and calamari ($11). Few vegetarian entrees. Open Su-M and W-Th 11am-10pm, F-Sa 11am-11pm.

MARKETS

In 1763, Baltimore instituted a unique way to bring together independent food vendors under one roof: the market system. Today, a few markets still remain and offer an endless variety of cheap eats that will excite the pickiest eaters.

◨ **Cross St. Market,** 1065 S. Charles St., at the intersection of S. Charles St. and Cross St. in Federal Hill. Offers a less chaotic and more sophisticated version of the Lexington Market without losing the exciting market experience. Lunch hour brings locals and business professionals to the extravagant (and cheap) sushi bars and fish fries. Grab a pretzel dog ($1.50) while shopping for baked goods, flowers, and candy. Many of the businesses are family owned and run; the oldest establishment in the market, Nunnally Bros. Poultry has occupied its space for 125 years. Open M-Sa 7am-6pm.

Lexington Market, 400 W. Lexington St., spanning Eutaw through Greene St. Take the subway to Lexington Station or the #7 bus. Established in 1782, Lexington is Baltimore's oldest and most populous market. With all the attractions of a three-ring circus, Lexington Market is home to a wide assortment of inexpensive eats. The locals flock here during the lunch and dinner hours for hearty, and often greasy international and American fare. Fried chicken is a down-home draw. Be alert to avoid head-on collisions with low-flying pigeons. Open M-Sa 8:30am-6pm.

Broadway Market, at the intersection of Fleet St. and Broadway, near Fells Point. Smaller and more subdued than other markets in town, mainly attracts senior citizens. Broadway offers few ready to eat options, selling primarily uncooked prepared foods, fresh fruit, and raw fish. The fishy smell could wake the dead, but all food is extremely fresh, sanitary, and delicious. Open M-Sa 6am-6pm. **Use caution north of the market at night.**

SIGHTS

INNER HARBOR

Baltimore's generally gray and functional harbor ends with a colorful bang in Inner Harbor, a five-square-block body of water surrounded by a bevy of eateries, museums, and boardable ships.

THE NATIONAL AQUARIUM

🔢 *Location: Pier 3, 501 E. Pratt St.* ***Contact:*** *☎576-3800; www.aqua.org* ***Hours:*** *July-Aug. daily 9am-8pm; Mar.-June and Sept.-Oct. Sa-Th 9am-5pm, F 9am-8pm; Nov.-Feb. Sa-Th 10am-5pm, F 10am-8pm. Remains open 2hr. after last entrance time. Tickets can be purchased from TicketMaster ☎481-7328 before 3pm in Baltimore, ☎(202) 432-7328 in Washington, D.C.). Budget 3hr. for aquarium.* ***Admission:*** *$14, seniors $10.50, ages 3-11 $7.50, under 3 free. $5 discount price offered on winter F after 5pm.* ***Accessibility:*** *Excellent disabled access.* ***Events:*** *Lobby lists slide shows and feeding times.*

The National Aquarium makes the whole Inner Harbor worthwhile. The museum's intelligent layout funnels visitors past each of the aquatic wonders in an ascent to a glass-enclosed tropical rainforest. Visitors can remain outdoors to watch the slaphappy seals splash around their pool. The eerie **Wings in the Water** exhibit at the bottom of the spiral showcases 50 species of stingrays in an immense, backlit pool. Levels two through four spiral over central tanks and through Atlantic sea cliffs inhabited by cheeky puffins and a lush kelp forest. The **Children's Cove** was recently moved to Pier 4 and is scheduled to reopen in March 2000 with a newly-expanded **Touching Pool.** At the top of the spiral is the steamy **Tropical Rainforest,** where piranhas, parrots, and a pair of two-toed sloths peer through the dense foliage in a 157 ft. glass pyramid. From the rainforest, visitors descend a remarkable four-story ramp around a 13 ft. deep, doughnut-shaped tank containing a mock coral reef. Back on ground level, an enclosed bridge leads to the **Marine**

Mammal Pavilion, which contains dolphins and whales, with an amphitheater featuring dolphin performances à la Sea World every hour on the half-hour. A visit to the aquarium's outdoor seal pool is free to the general public. Special events slated for 2001 include exhibits on seahorses and the ecosystems of the Amazon.

BALTIMORE MARITIME MUSEUM

fl Location: *Piers 3 and 4.* **Contact:** ☎ *396-3453.* **Hours:** *Ticket stand open daily 10:30am-5:30pm; in winter F-Su 10am-6:30pm. Boats stay open 1hr. later than ticket stand.* **Admission:** *$6, seniors $5, ages 5-13 $3.* **Accessibility:** *All boats are wheelchair accessible.*

Several ships bob in the harbor by the aquarium, most of which belong to the Baltimore Maritime Museum. Visitors may clamber through the interior of the *U.S.S. Torsk,* a gray submarine painted with a red, toothy grin that sank the last WWII Japanese combatant ships. Covered under the same entrance fee are the lightship *Chesapeake* and one of the final survivors of the Pearl Harbor attack, the Coast Guard cutter *Roger B. Taney.* The fee also allows access to the octagonal lighthouse mounted on Pier 5. Historic boats belonging to the Living Classrooms Foundation tie up behind the lighthouse and include the *Lady Maryland,* a replica 18th-century pungy schooner, and the *Mildred Belle,* a 20th-century motor buyboat.

OTHER SHIPS

fl Location: *Inner Harbor.*

The Clipper City, a beautiful 19th-century topsail schooner, provides a scenic, two-hour jaunt around the Inner Harbor and a full open bar. Sunset cruises provide breathtaking views and depart daily at 6pm from just outside the Baltimore Visitors Center on Light St. *(☎539-6277; www.sailingship.com. Cruise departs M-Sa noon and 3pm. Tickets $12, children $2. F-Sa nights calypso and reggae and Su brunch sails also offered.)* On weekends, the **Minnie V.,** a replica of the skipjacks traditionally used to harvest oysters from the Chesapeake, offers two-hour history sails *(tickets $12, children $3).* **Harbor Boating** rents out paddle boats during the summer. *(1615 Thames St., next to the World Trade Ctr. Open 10:30am-4:30pm. 2-person boats $7 per 30min.)*

NEAR FEDERAL HILL

MARYLAND SCIENCE CENTER

fl Location: *601 Light St.* **Contact:** ☎ *685-5225; www.mdsci.org.* **Hours:** *June-Aug. M-Th 9:30am-6pm, F-Su 10am-8pm; Sept.-May M-F 10am-5pm, Sa-Su 10am-6pm.* **Admission:** *$11, seniors $10, ages 4-12 $8.50, under 4 free. Admission to the IMAX and the planetarium included.*

South of Harborplace at Inner Harbor's far edge lurks the kid-oriented Maryland Science Center. The waving astronaut balloon on the roof welcomes guests and appeals to children, but the electric shock-dispensing Van de Graaff generator, the five-story IMAX Theater, and the impressive 50-foot-tall Davis Planetarium draw mobs and awe adults. Those interested in astronomy can attend both nighttime and daytime observing sessions on the restored 1927 observatory telescope (stargazing every Th, sneezing every Su.; call ahead for events). Enigmatic features two IMAX films for the price of one (F 7:30pm). Don't fret if the exhibit visiting leaves you hungry, the front lobby is equipped with a Friendly's Restaurant.

FEDERAL HILL PARK

fl Location: *Behind the Science Center.* **Hours:** *8am-dusk.*

Federal Hill Park offers unparalleled views of Baltimore Harbor for those willing to climb Federal Hill. A stately Star Spangled Banner flies atop the hill where children can frolic in a playground by day and couples can enjoy the romantic scenery of the city skyline by night. Also perched on the hill is a statue honoring Major General Satin Smith, who thwarted a British land and sea attack on Baltimore in the War of 1812.

VISIONARY ART MUSEUM

fl Location: *800 Key Hwy.* **Contact:** ☎ *244-1900.* **Hours:** *Tu-Su 10am-6pm.* **Admission:** *$6, students and seniors $4, under 4 free.*

On the east side of Federal Hill, the Visionary Art Museum specializes in 20th-century works by untrained, independent artists. The art is colorful, individual, captivating and often troubling. Many of the works exhibited were produced in psychiatric wards. The three-story museum changes its collection frequently, with exhibits revolving around a central theme like "Love" or "Apocalypse." The museum store sells folk art on consignment. 2000 exhibit focused on "Angels and Aliens." Who knows what is next at this non-conformist museum?

BALTIMORE MUSEUM OF INDUSTRY

🔏 *Location:* 1415 Key Hwy. *Contact:* ☎ 727-4808. Take bus #1 or the Water Taxi. *Hours:* Tu-Sa 10am-5pm, W evenings 6-9pm, Su noon-5pm. *Admission:* $6; students, children, and seniors $4.50; families $20; under 6 free. *Accessibility:* All of museum is wheelchair accessible.

A former oyster cannery holds the Baltimore Museum of Industry, a land of magic and make-believe for grownups. After paying at a late 19th-century replica bank teller, guests explore different stores and learn about the history of each industry through captivating paraphernalia and the museum's innovative design. Guides will lead you through a functional belt-driven machine shop, let you print a handbill on an 1880 press, and pass around a weighty pair of shears once used in Baltimore's flourishing clothing trade. The museum sits on the harbor and houses the only operative steam tugboat on the east coast. A comparative *Turning the Century* exhibit is scheduled for 2001.

FORT McHENRY NATIONAL MONUMENT

🔏 *Location:* At the foot of E. Fort Ave., off Rte. 2 (Hanover St.) and Lawrence Ave. *Contact:* ☎ 962-4290; for cruise: ☎ 685-4288. *Hours:* daily June-Aug. 8am-8pm; Sept.-May 8am-5pm. $5, seniors and under 16 free. Film shown 9am-7pm. *Tours:* Take bus #1 or a narrated cruise from Finger Pier in the Inner Harbor. Cruises depart every 30min., 11am-5:30pm. Round-trip $5, ages 2-11 $3.75. *Accessibility:* Wheelchair accessible.

The Fort McHenry National Monument marks the site of the Union victory against British forces in the War of 1812. Visitors can see the ruins of Fort McHenry and the site where Francis Scott Key wrote **"The Star-Spangled Banner."** The flag that flew when Key wrote the anthem is now in the collection of the Smithsonian Museum of American History in Washington. On weekends, the Fort McHenry Guard performs a living history program in which daily activities of 1812 garrison life are simulated. Seasonal events include an elaborate fireworks celebration on Flag Day (June 14) and military activities celebrating Defender's Day (early Sept.). Knowledgeable rangers conduct focused discussions on such aspects of military life as pioneering.

WEST BALTIMORE

BABE RUTH BIRTHPLACE AND BALTIMORE ORIOLES MUSEUM

🔏 *Location:* 216 Emory St., off the 600 block of W. Pratt. Take bus #31. *Contact:* ☎ 727-1539; www.baberuthmuseum.com. *Hours:* daily Apr.-Oct. 10am-5pm, on game nights until 7pm; Nov.-Mar. 10am-4pm. *Admission:* $6, seniors $4, ages 5-16 $3, under 5 free. AAA 20% discount.

The Babe Ruth Birthplace and Baltimore Orioles Museum remembers the greatest player known to America's national pastime. Revelatory exhibits divulge obscure childhood facts of the "hopeless incorrigible" who would grow up to be the "Sultan of Swat". Ruth's illustrious career is chronicled beginning with his ephemeral stint with the hometown Orioles. Some exhibits pitch to die-hards only, like the display recalling each of his 714 home runs. Others take a swing at a wider audience, honoring Baltimore's beloved baseball team, the Orioles and their "Mr. Durable," Cal Ripken Jr.

ORIOLE PARK AT CAMDEN YARDS

🔏 *Location:* Just west of the Inner Harbor at Eutaw and Camden St. Take lightrail to Camden Yards. *Contact:* ☎ 547-6234; for game tickets ☎ 685-9800. *Hours:* Tours M-F 11am-2pm every hr., Sa 10:30am-2pm every 30min., Su 12:30-2pm. *Admission:* $5, seniors and under 12 $4.

In response to the 1970s trend to build large, impersonal stadiums on the outskirts of cities, in 1992 Baltimore constructed an intimate, vintage-style stadium on an old industrial yard in the heart of downtown. The result: an absolute jewel of a ballpark that the

the dope on dc

Roses and Cognac For Poe

Since 1949, on the eve of Edgar Allen Poe's birthday, a dark stranger creeps to Poe's grave and performs a silent memorial service, leaving three roses and a half-empty bottle of cognac for the master of horror's spirit. In 1993, a note accompanied the eerie gifts with only the words "The torch will be passed" scrawled on the paper. Three different visitors have taken up that torch since 1993. The Poe House handpicks a group of onlookers from masses of requests to observe the mysterious man in action, never daring to question the identity of Poe's earthly friend.

Babe would have been proud to call home. Camden Yards, as it is most popularly known, proved to be a pioneer, triggering the most recent Major League trend of new, retro ballparks. If the Orioles aren't playing in the afternoon, visitors can follow energetic tour guides, taking a behind-the-scenes tour of the stadium, including the clubhouses, dugouts, press box, and scoreboard.

EDGAR ALLAN POE HOUSE

🛈 Location: 203 N. Amity St., near Saratoga St. Take bus #15 or 23. **Contact:** ☎ 396-7932. **Hours:** Oct.-July W-Sa noon-3:45pm; Aug.-Sept. Sa noon-3:45pm. **Admission:** $3, under 13 $1.

Horror pioneer Edgar Allan Poe was born in 1809 in what is now a preserved historical landmark in the heart of a rundown neighborhood. In between doses of opium, Poe penned famous stories like "The Tell-Tale Heart" and "The Pit and the Pendulum", as well as macabre, rhyming poems like "The Raven" and "Annabelle Lee". He wrote for money and considered his stories trash, never imagining they would be lauded as innovative and captivating. The house contains period furniture and exhibits relating to Poe, all impeccably maintained. Almost as spooky as echoes of "Quoth the Raven, Nevermore" is this neighborhood at night, so **be careful.**

WESTMINSTER CHURCHYARD

🛈 Location: Fayette and Greene St. **Contact:** ☎ 706-7228. **Tours:** Apr.-Nov. 1st and 3rd F of each month at 6:30pm, Sa 10am. Reservations required. **Admission:** $4, seniors and under 12 $2.

After dying of alcoholism (or rabies or syphilis, as many argue) in 1849, Poe was buried in someone else's clothes at the tiny Westminster Churchyard where he lays alongside other notable local citizens, such as Revolutionary War heroes. For over 100 years, his grave has remained a popular pilgrimage for horror fans. Be persistent in your search; Poe's grave can be found in the back left portion of the yard. **Use caution in this area at night.**

B&O RAILROAD MUSEUM

🛈 Location: 901 W. Pratt St. Take bus #31. **Contact:** ☎ 752-2490. **Hours:** daily 10am-5pm. **Tours:** Call in advance for tours. **Admission:** $7, seniors $6, ages 3-12 $5, under 3 free. **Parking:** Free parking.

Once a station for the busy Baltimore & Ohio Railroad, the B&O Railroad Museum now looks out on train tracks where dining cars, Pullman sleepers, and mail cars park themselves permanently for curious tourists. In fact, visitors park their cars in a converted railroad station lot. Inside the museum, three films chug through the history of railroads, and numerous interactive exhibits entertain grownups and kids. The enormous **Roundhouse** contains replicas of historic trains, including a full scale model of the 1829 *Tom Thumb*, America's first steam-driven locomotive, and an authentic red caboose from

1907. The upstairs hall houses an extensive model-train display. The museum sits on the site where the first telegraph message was received in 1844. Visitors can attempt to imitate the dots and dashes on a replica telegraph machine. Train rides are currently unavailable while tracks undergo renovation.

EAST BALTIMORE

CIVIL WAR MUSEUM

⌑ Location: *601 President St.* **Contact:** ☎ *385-5188.* **Hours:** *daily 10am-5pm.* **Admission:** *$2, ages 4-17 $1, under 4 free.*

Beyond Pier 7 on the edge of Little Italy, the new Civil War Museum, on the site of the old President St. railroad station, offers exhibits explaining the role of Baltimore railroads in the Civil War. Highlights include a display on the first bloodshed of the Civil War, which occurred on Pratt St. in 1861 when pro-Southern mobs attacked Federal troops marching between the President St. and Camden train stations. Gift shop offers affordable Civil War and Baltimore paraphernalia.

JEWISH MUSEUM OF MARYLAND

⌑ Location: *15 Lloyd St.* **Contact:** ☎ *732-6400; www.jhsm.org.* **Hours:** *Tu-Th and Su noon-4pm, and by appointment.* **Admission:** *$4, students $2, under 12 free.* **Parking:** *Free parking for visitors at Lloyd and Lombard St.*

In the historically Jewish heart of East Baltimore, the Jewish Museum of Maryland occupies a large, three-building complex. The lefthand building, the **Lloyd Street Synagogue,** built in 1845, was Maryland's first synagogue; the **B'nai Israel Synagogue,** the building on the far right, was founded in 1876 to preserve Orthodox religious practices. Between the two synagogues, the **Jewish Historical Society of Maryland** houses documents and photographs reflecting on the history of Maryland's Jewish community.

HOLOCAUST MEMORIAL

⌑ Location: *Hillside at Gay and Water St.*

Back towards Inner Harbor, the concrete Holocaust Memorial powerfully and graphically remembers the six million Jews who died in concentration camps during World War II. On the other side of the hill, facing Lombard St., a statue depicts the anguished faces of the Nazis' victims as their bodies are engulfed in flames. In the background, six columns of Venetian blinds represent endless train tracks.

MOUNT VERNON

WALTERS ART GALLERY

⌑ Location: *600 N. Charles St. Take Bus #3, 9, or 11.* **Contact:** ☎ *547-9000.* **Hours:** *Tu-W and F 10am-4pm, Th 10am-4pm, Sa-Su 11am-5pm.* **Tours:** *W noon and Su 1:30pm.* **Admission:** *$5, students with ID and seniors $3, ages 6-17 $1, under 6 free, under 18 free Sa before noon.* **Accessibility:** *Wheelchair access through the Hackerman House.* **Note:** *The museum will be undergoing extensive renovations until 2001 that will include a revamped patron-friendly "1974" building and a newly installed atrium.*

Spanning 50 centuries through three buildings, Baltimore's premiere art museum, the Walters Art Gallery, houses one of the largest private art collections in the world. The Ancient Art collection on the second level, featuring sculpture, jewelry, and metalwork from Egypt, Greece, and Rome, is the museum's pride and joy. The medieval art on the third floor from the Byzantine, Romanesque, and Gothic periods displays primarily jewelry and metalwork. Paintings on the third and fourth floors give a nod to every European style between the 12th and 19th centuries, highlighting the later periods. The 2001 exhibit will feature the impressionist paintings of Monet. At the **Hackerman House,** in an exquisite third-floor townhouse/mansion attached to the Walters, rooms filled with dark wood furniture, patterned rugs, and plush velvet curtains display art from China, Korea, Japan, and India. Ample reading and research space available. Museum manuscripts curator Will Noll is a former *Let's Go* guide user and avid fan of our books, so be sure to tell him we sent you.

WASHINGTON MONUMENT

⚑ Location: Take bus #3 or 31 up N. Charles St. to reach the sights in this area. **Hours:** W-Su 10am-4pm. **Admission:** Suggested donation $1.

Splitting N. Charles St. in two at its intersection with Monument St. stands the nation's inaugural memorial to the first president. Designed by Robert Mills, who later would blueprint the more famously phallic memorial in D.C., the monument curiously displays a very ancient Roman founding father. Washington presides over N. Charles St., at 16ft. tall and toga-clad, while resigning his commission as commander of the Continental Army atop a 160ft. column. The 228-step climb to the top yields a splendid view of the Mt. Vernon area, not to mention a day's worth of exercise.

BASILICA OF THE ASSUMPTION

⚑ Location: 408 N. Charles St. **Contact:** ☎ 727-3564; www.baltimorebasilica.org. **Hours:** First mass M-F 7:30am, last mass 12:10pm; Sa first mass 7:30am, last mass 5:30pm. **Tours:** Su at noon. **Admission:** Free.

A few blocks south of the Washington Monument sits the Basilica of the Assumption, at Cathedral and Mulberry St. (no sign is posted, just go through the gates). Benjamin Latrobe, who helped design the US Capitol, planned the Basilica in 1806. The first Roman Catholic Cathedral in the US, the church has twin onion domes reminiscent of a Russian Orthodox Church. The Archdiocese of Baltimore Catholic Center is located across the street at 320 Cathedral St.

MT. VERNON UNITED METHODIST CHURCH

⚑ Location: 10 E. Mt. Vernon Pl. **Contact:** ☎ 685-5290. **Hours:** daily 9am-3pm. **Tours:** M-F 9:30-2:30. **Admission:** Free. Ring the bell at Asbury House, 10 East St.

Across the cobblestone street from the Washington Monument looms the 1872 lime-green Gothic Mt. Vernon United Methodist Church, which owes its striking color to rare serpentine stone block. The straw fans in every pew bring a striking touch of the South to the city.

NORTH BALTIMORE

BALTIMORE MUSEUM OF ART

⚑ Location: 10 Art Museum Dr., at N. Charles and 31st St. **Contact:** ☎ 396-7100. **Hours:** W-F 11am-5pm, Sa-Su 11am-6pm; www.artbma.com **Admission:** $6, students and seniors $4, under 18 free; Th free. **Parking:** Metered parking. **Accessibility:** Handicapped accessible. Wheelchairs available. **Events:** Jazz series; tickets $6, students and seniors $4. Call for dates.

To the west of Johns Hopkins University, the Baltimore Museum of Art displays a fine collection of Americana and modern art, including several pieces by Warhol, Picasso, Renoir, and Van Gogh, and a large collection of works by Matisse. The museum hosts live jazz on select summer Saturdays in the two sculpture gardens. In spring 2001, the Modern and Post-impressionist art gallery will reopen, entirely refurbished.

BALTIMORE ZOO

⚑ Location: Off I-83 at Exit 7; bear right off ramp onto Druid Hill Park. **Contact:** ☎ 396-7175. **Public Transportation:** Shuttle bus from Woodberry light rail stop Memorial Day-Labor Day Sa-Su. **Hours:** M-F 10am-4pm, Sa 10am-8pm, Su 10am-5:30pm; in winter daily 10am-4pm. **Admission:** $9, over 62 and ages 2-15 $5.50, under 2 free. **Accessibility:** Handicapped accessible. Wheelchairs available at Raven's Roost kiosk. **Events:** Live jazz, country, and oldies June-Aug. Sa 4-8pm.

The Baltimore Zoo occupies a corner of the rolling hills of **Druid Hill Park,** the nation's second largest city park after New York's Central Park. The park features a spectacular palm tree **Conservatory** (Th-Su 10am-4pm; free), housed in a soaring Victorian greenhouse, and a lake surrounded by lush greenery. In the zoo, small enclosures typical of older zoos bring visitors almost within touching distance of some of the animals. Signs in front of the Siberian tigers warn all to get out of the way to avoid being sprayed by tiger urine when Frasier (the mascot of nearby Towson University) moves to mark the boundaries of his territory. Other features include the **African Watering Hole** (a simulated savannah with elephants and giraffes), a **chimpanzee house** with a seven-member troupe of chimpanzees and a waterfall, and a **reptile house** outside the zoo gates (additional charge $1, closed Tu). The award-winning **Children's Zoo** imports animals like otters and crafty woodchucks from nearby farms and the Maryland wilds. Children can also ride a carousel and a "zoo choo" train (rides $1.25), or mount a camel ($2.50).

JOHNS HOPKINS UNIVERSITY

⛪ Location: 3400 N. Charles St. Take Bus #3, 9, or 11. **Contact:** ☎516-8171. **Tours:** Sept.-May M-F 10am, noon, and 3pm; call for summer hrs. **Admission:** Free. **Office of Admissions:** ☎516-5589. Open Tu-Sa 11am-4pm, Su noon-4pm. Tours hourly 11am-3pm. **Homewood:** ☎516-5589. Open Tu-Sa 11am-4pm, Sun noon-4pm. $6, students $3, seniors $5. Tours hourly 11am-3pm. **Evergreen House:** 4545 N. Charles St. Take Bus #11. ☎516-0341. Open M-F 10am-4pm, Sa-Su 1-4pm. $6, students $3, seniors $5. Tours hourly 10am-3pm. **Lacrosse Foundation:** 113 West University Pkwy. ☎235-6882. Open June-Jan. M-F 10am-3pm; Feb.-May Tu-Sa 10am-3pm, $3, students $2.

Approximately 3 mi. north of the harbor, prestigious Johns Hopkins University spreads out from 33rd St. The beautiful campus lies on a 140-acre wooded lot that was originally the Homewood estate of Charles Carroll, Jr., the son of the longest-lived signer of the Declaration of Independence. A breeding ground for doctors, one-third of JHU students declare pre-med as a major. Although not an athletic powerhouse, the "Johnnies" do perennially field one of the nation's premiere college lacrosse teams. One-hour campus tours begin in Garland Hall at the **Office of Admissions.**

Homewood, Carroll's Georgian brick mansion, displays a fine collection of 18th- and 19th-century furnishings, some original to the house. Next to Loyola College and 1 mi. north of the main campus, **Evergreen House** is an exercise in excess. Even the bathroom of this elegant mansion is plated in 23-carat gold. The hour-long tour displays the mansion, private theater, carriage house, and gardens. Gracefully displayed collections feature Chinese pottery, an early Picasso, two full folios of Audubon's bird sketches, and a 16th-century treatise on the New World.

The **Lacrosse Foundation and Hall of Fame Museum,** at the end of the Johns Hopkins lacrosse fields, houses uniforms, trophies, and equipment from the past 350 years. Recommended only for die-hard fans of the sport, the museum may prove tedious for lacrosse unenthusiasts.

NIGHTLIFE AND ENTERTAINMENT

MUSIC, DANCE, AND THEATER

Vacationing in the city can be expensive, but fortunately for the budget traveler, much of Baltimore's finest entertainment can be enjoyed free of charge. At **Harborplace,** performers are constantly entertaining tourists with magic acts, juggling, and clowning around during the day. At night, dance, dip, and dream to the sounds of anything from country to calypso to oldies at the Harborplace (occasional Th-Sa nights). The **Baltimore Museum of Art** offers free summer jazz concerts in its sculpture garden (see p. 210). **Jazzline** (☎466-0600) lists jazz shows from Sept. to May; call for schedules and information.

When the music isn't free in Baltimore, it's still just as good. Big-name musicians perform several times a week from May to October at **Pier 6 Concert Pavilion** (☎625-3100). Tickets ($15-30) are available at the pavilion or through Ticketmaster (☎625-1400 or 481-7328). With local artists and some big names, **Fletcher's** (see **Bars and Clubs,** below) features everything from indy rock to rap to blues. Purchase tickets ($6-15) through the box office (☎880-8124) or TicketMaster (all shows 18+). Zydeco enthusiasts gather to dance to bands from Louisiana at **Harry's,** 1200 N. Charles, a Las Vegas-type bar and performance space. (☎685-2828. Shows F-Sa; cover $3-10. Open F 11am-2am, Sa 2pm-2am.)

The **Baltimore Symphony Orchestra** plays at Meyerhoff Symphony Hall, 1212 Cathedral St., from September to May and during their month-long Summerfest. (☎783-8000. Tickets $15-52. Box office open M-F 10am-6pm, Sa-Su noon-5pm, and 1hr. before performances. Call for dates of Summerfest.) The **Lyric Opera House,** down the street at 110 W. Mt. Royal Ave., near Maryland Ave., hosts the **Baltimore Opera Company** from late October to April. (☎727-6000. Tickets $24-109; box office open M-F 10am-5pm.)

Broadway shows are performed all year at the **Morris Mechanic Theater,** 25 Hopkins Plaza (☎(800) 638-2444; tickets at TicketMaster or the box office open 9am-5pm), at Baltimore and N. Charles St. The **Theater Project,** 45 W. Preston St., near Maryland St., experiments with theater, poetry, music, and dance. (☎752-8558. Shows W-Sa 8pm, Su 3pm. $8-14. Box office open 1hr. before showtime; call to charge tickets.)

The **Arena Players** (☎728-6500), a black theater group, perform comedies, drama, and dance at 801 McCullough St. at Martin Luther King, Jr. Blvd. (tickets start at $15) Box office open M-F 9am-5pm. The **Showcase of Nations Ethnic Festivals** celebrate Baltimore's ethnic neighborhoods with a different culture featured each week (June-Sept.). The festivals take place all over the city; call the Baltimore Visitors Bureau (☎(800) 282-6632) for info.

BARS AND CLUBS

Baltimore law requires that bars close at 2am, and the police are cracking down on violators. Hearty partiers should plan to start their evenings early. After 2am, check out Fells Point to meet consoling throngs of fellow revellers.

Cat's Eye Pub, 1730 Thames St. (☎276-9866), in Fells Point. An older crowd of regulars packs it in every weeknight for live blues, jazz, folk, or traditional Irish music (M-Th 9pm, F-Sa 4pm). Live blues Su 4-8pm. Occasional cover for national musical acts. Over 25 different drafts and 60 bottled beers. Numerous flags drape the walls, generating international flavor to the bar. Happy Hour M-F 4-7pm. Open daily noon-2am.

Fletcher's, 701 S. Bond St. (☎558-1889), at the intersection of Bond and Aliceanna St. Hidden from the tourist and collegiate hype, this laid-back, mostly-locals scene thrives on a jukebox, pool and foosball (50¢), and friendly bartenders. Beer specials vary nightly. 18+ concert venue upstairs (cover $5-$20). Open M-Th 4pm-2am, F-Su 11am-2am. Happy Hour M-F 4:30-7pm.

Admiral's Cup, 1645 Thames St. (☎522-6731), on the corner of Thames and Broadway in Fells Point. Bartenders call you "hon" when they offer you the $1 per crab special. Recent college grads spontaneously bust-a-move alongside local 30-somethings in this intimate, no frills bar. Dancing is especially festive after chowing on 50¢ summertime mussels. Open daily 11am-2am.

Bohager's, 701 S. Eden St. (☎563-7220), in Fells Point. After undergoing extensive renovations, Bohager's has transformed into an enclosed tropical paradise for college students and locals. Under a 29,000sq.ft. retractable dome, patrons rage to the sounds of live island music until the wee hours of the morning. Tickets available at the club or through TicketMaster (☎481-7328). Happy Hour Th-F 5-8pm. Open M-F 11:30am-2am, Sa-Su 3pm-2am.

Greene Turtle, 720 Broadway (☎342-4222). With foosball, pool (50¢), and an extensive CD jukebox, this relaxed bar is popular with the Baltimore college crowd, the Ravens, and anyone else interested in tanking up for next to nothing. $2.50 drafts are a dollar cheaper during Happy Hour (M-F 4-7pm), which also offers half-price apps (M 7-close, Tu-F 4-7pm). Sandwiches $5-7.50. Sa-Su special yields ½lb. spicy steamed shrimp for $4.50. Open daily 11:30am-2am.

John Steven's, 1800 Thames St. (☎327-5561), near the Water Taxi stop on the corner of Ann St. in Fells Point. Acclaimed wood and brass restaurant and bar caters to a mature, sophisticated crowd. In addition to standard barfare, John Steven's has a sushi bar with offerings like the "Bawlmer roll" (backfin crab with avocado and scallions; $7.75). Shaded patio in back. Open daily 11am-2am; kitchen closes at 11pm M-Th, midnight F-Su.

Max's on Broadway, 737 S. Broadway (☎675-6297), at Lancaster St. in Fells Point. Max's offers a relaxed haven for genuine beer-lovers. Tu night beer socials offer connoisseurs an opportunity to discuss their beloved barley and hops. 62 taps and over 200 different bottled brews. Cigars and cognac offered upstairs. Happy Hour (M-F noon-8pm) brings $1 discounts on drafts. Downstairs open Th-Su 11am-2am; upstairs open 6pm-2am.

Baltimore Brewing Co., 104 Albemarle St. (☎837-5000), just west of the Inner Harbor on the outskirts of Little Italy. Use back entrance at Granby St. Brewmaster Theo de Groen has captured the hearts and livers of Baltimoreans with his original and distinctive lagers brewed right on the premises of this spacious restaurant and bar. Call in advance for friendly tours (1:30pm daily). Happy Hour (daily 4-7pm) offers $2.50 half-liters. Open M-Th 4pm-midnight, F-Sa 11:30am-1am, Su 2-10pm.

The Midtown Yacht Club, 15 E. Centre St. (☎837-1300), just off N. Charles St. Serves a lively mix of tourists, students, and locals. Pub offers both full American and Mexican specialties. 14 beers on tap. Happy Hour (M-F 4-7pm) yields $4.75 pitchers. Game room on 2nd fl. Elegant Su brunch 11am-3pm. Live blues Su nights. Open daily 11am-2am.

Club Orpheus, 1003 E. Pratt St. (☎276-5599), in Little Italy. Don't come here without dancing shoes. This Art Deco establishment is a serious dance club attracting a diverse crowd. Bar offers

Evian, margaritas, and Jolt, all $3. Each night has a different theme; call ahead. Sa always fetish industrial dance ($5 before 11:30pm, $7 after, $10 if not in fetish attire). Open M-Sa 9pm-2am.

ESPNZone, 601 E. Pratt St. (☎685-3776). Ever wanted try your hand at downhill skiing, snowboarding, white-water kayaking, horse racing, or auto racing without all the risk? This sports junkie's paradise offers 3 floors of virtual games, over 200 TVs broadcasting live sports, and a stadium-shaped bar. Patrons feast on huge portions of standard bar fare (burgers, nachos, wings) as updates from around the sporting world constantly flash before their eyes. The NFL-themed 2 minute drill steak ($10) is a hit with those in a hurry. Open Su-Th 11am-11pm, F-Sa 11am-midnight. 18+ unless accompanied by an adult.

GAY AND LESBIAN BARS AND CLUBS

Baltimore's staunch gay population concentrates its social scene in the northern portion of Mt. Vernon in an area known as the "gayborhood." Snag a free copy of *Baltimore Alternative* for complete club listings. *Baltimore Gaypaper* contains news and club advertisements for the gay population. Or check out the *Citypaper*, Baltimore's indy paper, for other weekly happenings.

Allegro, 1101 Cathedral St. (☎837-3906). A single pink door marks the entrance on a dead end block off Chase St. in Mount Vernon. This popular and friendly gay nightspot welcomes everyone to join in crazy partying. Drag show 1st M of each month; Men's Night Tu; "alternative" music W; "Baywatch" F; various theme nights Sa. Cover F and Su $3. Half-price domestics and rails at Happy Hour (daily 6-10pm). Open daily 6pm-2am.

Central Station, 1001 N. Charles St. (☎752-7133), on the corner of Eager St., across from Hippo. Chill under lights bought off the set of *A Few Good Men* or play some pre-partying pool with a mellow crowd. Newly installed dance floor is the scene for bumping and grinding W-Su. Happy Hour 4-8pm daily. Karaoke M-Tu. Open 3pm-2am daily.

Hippo, 1 W. Eager St. (☎547-0069), across the street from Central Station. Baltimore's largest gay bar provides pool tables, videos, and a packed dance floor in an industrial setting. First Su of every month is Ladies' Tea, one of the largest lesbian events this side of the Mississippi (6-10pm). Men's Night Th. Cover Th-F $3, Sa $6. On Th, cover buys "drink chips" redeemable for $3 worth of drinks. Happy Hour 4-8pm daily. Interior overflows with rainbows, the color pink, and gay pride. Saloon open daily 4pm-2am; dance bar open Th-Sa 10pm-2am.

SPECTATOR SPORTS

The beloved **Baltimore Orioles** play ball at **Camden Yards** (see p. 207), just a few blocks from the Inner Harbor at the corner of Russell and Camden St. Tickets for Orioles games range from $7 (standing room) to $35 (reserved boxes). Call ☎547-6234 to order tickets. The three-year-old **Ravens** represent Baltimore's second chance at professional football. The Ravens, formerly the Cleveland Browns, play in **Raven Stadium,** adjacent to Camden Yards. To order individual game tickets, call ☎481-7328. Just outside of Baltimore, head off to the races at **Laurel** (☎792-7775; on MD-216 off I-95) and **Pimlico Race Tracks** (☎542-9400; on MD-129). The two tracks alternately hold thoroughbred horse races for much of the spring, summer, and fall. **The Preakness Stakes** (☎542-9400, ext. 4484 for tickets), leg two of the Triple Crown, is run annually at Pimlico on the third Saturday in May.

ON CHESAPEAKE BAY

Once upon a time, on Maryland's rural eastern shore, inhabitants captured crabs, raised tobacco, and ruled the Maryland economy. BOOM! Bye-bye Miss American pie with one road: the Baltimore-Washington Parkway. Enter suburban mania. Yet even with commercial invasion, the bay area still offers great times and intriguing sights and stories. Annapolis fills its seaside streets with the largest tourist mecca Maryland has to offer (not to mention everything you ever wanted to know about the Navy). Escape from the throngs of tourists and fast-food chains can be found on the Eastern Shore and among the rural southern islands. One tourist staple has refused to wash away with the eroding shoreline—the popular Chesapeake Bay crab, marketing tool and delicacy extraordinaire. Almost every restaurant boasts "The world's best crab cakes" and T-shirts in the souvenir shops proclaim "Don't bother me, I'm *crabby.*"

ANNAPOLIS   ☎410

Annapolis walks the tightrope between a heartwarming, nostalgic port town and a
dockside cliché. With its brick-paved sidewalks and narrow streets, the historic waterfront district retains its 18th-century appeal despite the presence of ritzy boutiques and
pricey retail stores. Crew-cut "middies" (a nickname for Naval Academy students, or
"midshipmen") mingle with longer-haired students from St. John's and couples on
weekend getaways amid the highest concentration of historic homes in America.

Settled in 1649, Annapolis became the capital of Maryland in 1694. The fine Georgian
houses once packed in colonial aristocrats and their slaves. Annapolis made history
when the Continental Congress ratified the Treaty of Paris here in 1784, marking the
official end of the American Revolution. After its 1783 stint as temporary capital of the
US (hot on the heels of Philadelphia, New York, and Trenton, NJ), Annapolis relin-
quished the national limelight in favor of a more tranquil existence. Now, guests are
treated to a surprisingly accurate taste of what costal America once was: squished, pastel row houses with gorgeous gardens, friendly strollers, and an endless array of boats.

ORIENTATION AND PRACTICAL INFORMATION

Annapolis lies southeast of US 50 (also known as US 301), 30 mi. east of D.C. and 30 mi.
south of Baltimore. From D.C. take US 50E, which begins at New York Ave. and can
also be accessed from the Beltway, I-495. From Baltimore, follow Rte. 2S to US 50W,
cross the Severn River Bridge, and then take Rowe Blvd. into the city.

The city extends south and east from two landmarks: **Church Circle** and **State Circle.
School Street,** in a blatantly unconstitutional move, connects Church and State. **East
Street** runs from the State House to the Naval Academy. **Main Street** (where food and
entertainment congregate) starts at Church Circle and ends at the docks. Those who
lose their bearings (it's easy to do this on the diagonal streets) can reorient themselves
by looking for the State House dome or St. Anne's spire in Church Circle. The latter is
also home to many banks and ATMs. The downtown area of Annapolis, besides being a
vibrant town center, is also very safe. As West St. winds into western Annapolis, the
area becomes a bit run-down, but even this area is safe to explore. Downtown Annapolis is compact and easily walkable, but finding a parking space—unless in an expensive
lot or in the public garage ($5-9 per day)—can be tricky. Parking at the **Visitors Center**
($1 per hr., $8 max. weekdays, $4 max. for the weekend) is the best bet. There is also
free weekend parking in State Lots A and B at the corner of Rowe Blvd. and Calvert St.

Buses: Greyhound (☎(800) 231-2222) buses stop at the local Mass Transit Administration bus
stop in the football field parking lot at Rowe Blvd. and Taylor St. Tickets are available from the
bus driver; cash only. To and from: **Washington, D.C.** (1hr.; 1 per day; $10.50); **Philadelphia** (5-
6hr.; 2 per day; $42, students $34); **Baltimore** (3hr.; 1 per day; $10, $7.50 students).

Mass Transit Administration: (☎539-5000 or (800) 543-9809). Express #210 runs to Baltimore M-F (1hr., $2.85); local #14 runs daily (1½hr., $1.35). M-Sa you must take the light rail
downtown once you reach Baltimore; Su the bus goes downtown. Buses leave from St. John's
and College Ave. and St. John's and Calvert St.

Public Transportation: Annapolis Dept. of Public Transportation (☎263-7964) operates a web
of city buses connecting the historic district with the rest of town. Buses run M-Sa 5:30am-10pm,
Su 8am-7pm. Base fare 75¢, over 60 or disabled 35¢.

Car Rental: Budget, 2001 West St. (☎266-5030). **Discount,** 1032 West St. (☎269-6645).
Thrifty, 252 West St. (☎267-0900), rents to ages 21-24 for $20 extra per day.

Taxis: Annapolis Cab Co. (☎268-0022). **Checker Cab** (☎268-3737).

Visitor Information: Annapolis and Anne Arundel County Conference & Visitors Bureau, 26
West St. (☎280-0445; www.visit-annapolis.org). Free maps and brochures. Open daily 9am-
5pm. On-the-spot questions answered at the information desk at the **State House** (☎841-3810).
Desk open daily 10am-4pm. A second visitor information center is located at the bottom of Dock
St. at the city dock.

EMERGENCY: 911 (NON-EMERGENCY POLICE LINE ☎268-9000).

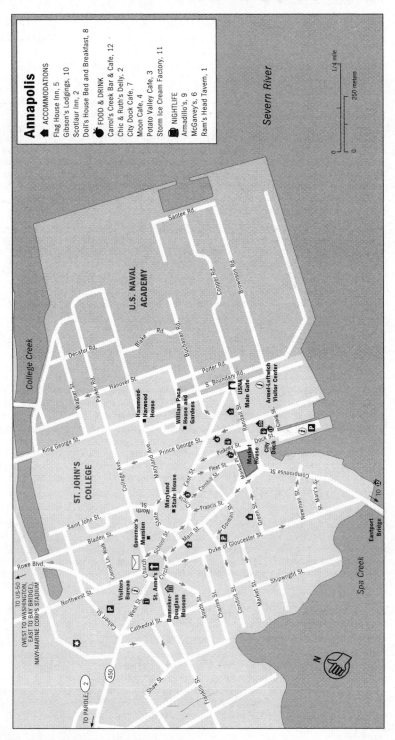

Annapolis

🏠 ACCOMMODATIONS
Flag House Inn, 5
Gibson's Lodgings, 10
Scotlaur Inn, 2
Doll's House Bed and Breakfast, 8

🍴 FOOD & DRINK
Carrol's Creek Bar & Cafe, 12
Chic & Ruth's Delly, 2
City Dock Cafe, 7
Moon Cafe, 4
Potato Valley Cafe, 3
Storm Ice Cream Factory, 11

🎭 NIGHTLIFE
Armadillo's, 9
McGarvey's, 6
Ram's Head Tavern, 1

Severn River

U.S. NAVAL ACADEMY

College Creek

ST. JOHN'S COLLEGE

Santee Rd.

Cooper Rd.

Brownson Rd.

Blake Rd.

Buchanan Rd.

Decatur Rd.

Hanover St.

Porter Rd.

Parker Rd.

Wagner St.

S. Boundary Rd.

USNA Main Gate

Armel-Leftwich Visitor Center

King George St.

College Ave.

Maryland Ave.

Prince George St.

Hammond-Harwood House

William Paca House and Gardens

Randall St.

Craig St.

Pinkney St.

East St.

Fleet St.

Cornhill St.

City Dock

Dock St.

Market House

Maryland State House

North St.

State Cir.

Francis St.

Compromise St.

Newman St.

St. Mary's St.

Saint John St.

Governor's Mansion

School St.

Main St.

Green St.

Duke of Gloucester St.

Eastport Bridge

TO 10

Spa Creek

Bladen St.

Carroll Ln. Walk

Church Cir.

St. Anne's Church

Banneker-Douglass Museum

Shipwright St.

Rowe Blvd.

(WEST TO WASHINGTON, EAST TO BAY BRIDGE), NAVY-MARINE CORPS STADIUM

TO US-50

Visitors Bureau

Northwest St.

Calvert St.

West St.

Cathedral St.

South St.

Charles St.

Conduit St.

Market St.

Shaw St.

Franklin St.

TO PAROLE (2)

(450)

N

1/4 mile

250 meters

Hot Lines: Rape and Sexual Assault Crisis Center: 1419 Forest Dr. Suite 100, ☎222-7273. **Youth Crisis Hotline:** ☎(800) 422-0009. **Poison Control Center:** ☎(800) 492-2414. **Drug Abuse Hotline:** ☎(800) 492-8477. All lines 24hr.

Post Office: 1 Church Circle (☎263-9292). Open M-F 8:30am-5pm. **ZIP Code:** 21401.

ACCOMMODATIONS

The heart of Annapolis lacks cheap motels in favor of elegant, homey (and pricey) bed and breakfasts. In general, these B&Bs prove a better choice than the hotels scattered about western Annapolis, which aren't actually cheaper and are far from central attractions. Rooms should be reserved in advance, especially for weekends and the busy summer months, when accommodations frequently sell out. **Bed and Breakfasts of Maryland** aids in arranging accommodations in Annapolis (☎ (800) 736-4667, ext. 15; open M-F 9am-5pm, Sa 10am-3pm). **Amanda's** offers a similar service (☎225-0001; open M-F 8:30am-5:30pm, Sa 8:30am-noon). All lodgings listed are near the dock and within walking distance of major attractions.

Scotlaur Inn, 165 Main St. (☎268-5665), atop Chick and Ruth's Delly. Ten tiny guest rooms with A/C, TVs, and private baths grace this homey "bed & bagel," which is less fancy than the other B&Bs and far more affordable. Huge complimentary breakfasts, including a stack of pancakes or eggs, are available from Chick & Ruth's and more than compensate for the rooms' lack of luxury. (see **Food**, below). Check-in 2pm. Check-out 11am. Rooms range from $75-$95.

Gibson's Lodgings, 110 Prince George St. (☎268-5555). 1 block from City Dock on Randall St. Gibson's offers a patio and spacious common parlors among its 3 ivy covered buildings and 18 total rooms. The 200-year-old Patterson House is cheaper than the Berman or Lauer Houses but has no private bathrooms. Free continental breakfast and courtyard parking. One handicap accessible room available. Single rooms start at $79, most inexpensive doubles $109 (all with A/C). Rollaway $20 extra. $10 discount in off season.

Flag House Inn, 26 Randall St. (☎280-2721 or (800) 437-4825). A prime location next to the visitors entrance to the Naval Academy and true to its name, six flags wave from the porch of this comfortable B&B. TV, A/C, and free off-street parking. King-sized beds and private baths in each of the 5 rooms. Complimentary full cooked breakfast. Try to reserve 2-4 weeks in advance. Most affordable rooms begin at $95; 2-person suites $140; 4-person suites $220.

Dolls' House Bed and Breakfast, 161 Green St. (☎626-2028). Defined by its soft, pink appearance, this cozy B&B resembles an inflated version of something your little sister plays with. Each of its 3 rooms is outfitted with a theme and its own doll collection. The wicker-furnished front porch partners with a beautiful back deck and rose-draped garden. Reserve at least a month ahead. Check or cash only. Charming Victoria and Sun rooms with private hall baths sleep 1 or 2 for $85; the Nutcracker Suite sleeps up to 6 for $140 ($110 as a double).

FOOD

Most restaurants in the area cluster around **City Dock,** an area packed with people in summertime (especially Tu nights at 7:30pm when the spinnaker races finish at City Dock). The best place to find cheap eats is the **Market House** food court at the center of City Dock, where a hearty meal costs under $5.

Chick & Ruth's Delly, 165 Main St. (☎269-6737), about a block from City Dock towards the State House. Numerous newspaper clippings adorn the walls, paying homage to this Annapolis insitution of over 30 years. Dishes named for local and national politicians like the "Al Gore" Chicken Salad ($5). Omelettes ($3-7), corned beef sandwiches ($5), and malted milkshakes ($2.75) highlight an inexpensive menu. Delivery available. Open M-Tu 6:30am-4pm, W-Th, and Su 6:30am-10pm, F-Sa 6:30am-11pm.

Moon Cafe, 137 Prince George St. (☎280-1956), a block up East St. from the Naval Academy. Full of Middle Eastern choices. Vegetarians flock here to sample creamy hummus ($4) and other "light fare" options. Lyrical Tu nights offer poetry slams at 9pm ($3 cover). Extensive tea and coffee selection $1-3. Live music Th-Sa. Weekend brunch until 2pm. If you have money to spend but aren't hungry, handmade oriental rugs are on sale inside. Open M-F 11am-midnight, Sa-Su 9am-midnight.

Potato Valley Cafe, 47 State Circle (☎267-0902), across from the State House. Swedish coffee-house with an Idaho twist. Specializes in oven-roasted baked potatoes ($2.75-6.50); 3 make a filling meal. Open M-F 9am-6pm, Sa-Su 11:30am-5pm.

City Dock Cafe, 18 Market Space (☎269-0969), at Pinkney St. Cool, calm coffeehouse adds sophistication to Annapolis with its Frank Lloyd Wright-esque appearance and great espresso drinks ($1-3). Cheery oil paintings liven an otherwise drab interior. The quiche ($5) and fresh fruit salads ($3) are light and delicious. Open Su-Th 6:30am-10pm, F-Sa 6:30am-midnight.

Storm Brothers Ice Cream Factory, 130 Dock St. (☎263-3376). Lick up tasty and creatively named homemade ice cream like muddy sneakers (white chocolate ice cream with caramel, pea-nuts, and chocolate chips) or moose tracks (vanilla ice cream with a fudge swirl and peanut butter cups) while enjoying an equally great view of the docked ships. Smily and enthusiastic teenage staff delights the throngs with their swift scooping abilities. 45 ice cream flavors, 3 yogurt flavors. $1.45 for 1 scoop, $2.40 for 2, $3 for 3. Handpacked pints, quarts, and half-gallons also available. Open M-F 10:30am-11pm, Sa-Su 10:30am-midnight.

Carrol's Creek Bar & Cafe, 410 Severn Ave. (☎263-8102), in the Annapolis City Marina Com-plex, across the Eastport Bridge. Homecooked food overlooking the Annapolis waterfront. A favor-ite for Texas BBQ shrimp ($8) and Maryland crab soup ($5.25). Happy Hour (M-F 4-7pm) features 95¢ 10-oz. beers, $2 pints and rails, and a complimentary buffet. Open M-Sa 11:30am-10pm, Su 11:30am-9:30pm.

SIGHTS

THE US NAVAL ACADEMY

⛴ Location: *52 King George St.* **Contact:** *☎263-6933; www.nadn.navy.mil.; www.usna.com.* **Tours:** *Every half hr. M-Sa 9:30am-3:30pm, Su 12:15pm-3:30pm.* **Admission:** *$5.50, seniors $4.50, students $3.50.*

The US Naval Academy is the single institution whose name most typifies Annapolis. At the academy, harried, short-haired "plebes" (first-year students) in official, intentionally silly-looking sailor dress try desperately to remember and flawlessly recite the words of Navy fight songs while the rest of the undergraduates, "middies" (midshipmen), scream orders. By graduation rite, the outgoing 1st class leaps into the placid waters of the Sev-ern River. President Jimmy Carter and billionaire H. Ross Perot number among the academy's celebrity alumni; more recently, the school produced NBA superstar David Robinson. The first stop should be the **Armel-Leftwich Visitors Center,** in the Halsey Field House. Tours include historic Bancroft Hall, the crypt, a dorm room, and the athletic facilities where the middies test their seafaring prowess on land. Visitors also view the original **Tecumseh,** a shiphead carving on the third ship in the United States Navy named after an Indian chief by joking midshipmen. The name stuck, and the icon is now one of the academy's mascots.

Named for George Bancroft, founder of the 1st Naval school, the **Bancroft Hall** dormi-tory houses the entire brigade of 4000 midshipmen in an imposing stone structure about three blocks long. In the yard outside Bancroft Hall, visitors can witness the middies' noon lineup and formations. A statue of Tecumseh stands out front; Navy legend has it that landing a penny into his slightly recessed quiver garners good luck. The rest of Ban-croft Hall is closed to tourists.

King Hall, the academy's gargantuan mess hall, turns into a madhouse at lunchtime, serving an entire brigade in under 20 frenzied minutes. On summer Saturdays, alumni's weddings (sometimes one per hour) take place in the academy's **chapel.** Underneath the chapel is the final resting place of **John Paul Jones,** father of the United States Navy, who uttered the famous words, "I have not yet begun to fight!" as he rammed his sinking ship into a British warship. *(Chapel open to visitors M-Sa 9am-4pm, Su 1-4pm. Often closed Sa in sum-mer for weddings.)* The **Naval Museum** in Preble Hall houses two rooms of naval artifacts. Antique swords, model ships, and the personal belongings of American prisoners of war are among the exhibits. *(Open M-Sa 9am-5pm, Su 11am-5pm. Free.)* Throughout the summer, the academy provides entertainment for the public, from parades and sporting events to movies and concerts. A schedule is published in the **Trident,** the academy's newspa-per, obtainable at the Visitors Center.

the dope on dc

Freudian Slipping

Like a pubescent rite of passage, first-year "plebes" at the Naval Academy must shimmy on up **Herndon Monument,** a large, imposing obelisk in front of the chapel. At the starting gun's shot, the mob of inexperienced plebes thrusts towards the shaft. The hilariously humiliating event ends only when a plebe hat is popped off the top of the structure. Sounds easy, right? But it's not just wham, bam, thank you ma'am: the midshipmen lubricate the massive shaft with over 200 lb. of lard to prolong the event and frustrate the participants. Grunting, sweating plebes attempt to scale the slippery obelisk again and again, growing more passionately intent on their goal with each try. The climactic grasping of the hat is never a quickie: last year, the spectacle lasted over three hours.

STATE HOUSE

Location: *90 State Circle* **Contact:** ☎ *974-3400.* **Hours:** *daily 9am-5pm.* **Tours:** *11am and 3pm.* **Admission:** *Free.*

Built from 1772 to 1779, the Corinthian-columned State House, in the center of State Circle, is the oldest working capitol building in the nation. It was the US Capitol building from 1783 to 1784, and the Treaty of Paris was signed inside on January 14, 1784. Great for a romp through Maryland's history, visitors can explore the historical exhibits and silver collection, or watch the state legislature bicker in two exquisitely adorned marble halls from the second Wednesday in January until mid-April. Cordial State House guide, clad in authentic colonial garb, gladly fields guests' questions.

HAMMOND-HARWOOD HOUSE

Location: *19 Maryland Ave., at King George St.* **Contact:** ☎ *263-4683.* **Hours:** *M-Sa 10am-4pm, Su noon-4pm.* **Tours:** *On the hr.; last tour 1hr. before closing.* **Admission:** *$5, ages 6-18 $3, uniformed armed service personnel free. $10 joint tickets available for both the Hammond-Harwood and William Paca houses.* **Accessibility:** *Not handicapped accessible; video available for handicapped visitors.*

Historic Hammond-Harwood House, an elegant 1774 building designed by Colonial architect **William Buckland,** retains period decor right down to the candlesticks. The house is most renowned for its impeccably preserved colonial doorway.

WILLIAM PACA HOUSE

Location: *186 Prince George St.* **Contact:** ☎ *263-5553.* **Hours:** *M-Sa 10am-4pm, Su noon-4pm; Jan.-Feb. F-Sa 10am-4pm, Su noon-4pm.* **Tours:** *Given every hr. on the half-hour; arrive at least 1hr. before closing.* **Admission:** *House $5, garden $4, both $7. $10 joint tickets available for both the Hammond-Harwood and William Paca houses.* **Accessibility:** *The garden and the Shiplap Building are handicap accessible.*

The William Paca House is the first Georgian-style home built in Annapolis. Paca, an early governor of Maryland, was one of the original signers of the Declaration of Independence. The elegant house overlooks two acres of lush vegetation, and the garden hides shaded benches that gaze upon trellises, water lilies, and gazebos.

CITY DOCK

Contact: ☎ *268-7600.* **Hours:** *Boats depart M-F every hr. 11am-4pm, Sa-Su every hr. 11am-7pm.* **Admission:** *$6, under 12 $3.*

It's difficult to escape the eats and greets at Annapolis' spirited City Dock which is easily accessed by following Main St. to its aquatic dead end. The city's main hub of activity, restaurants, and touristy shops line the waterfront, and Naval Academy ships (skippered by fresh-faced "plebes" in the summertime) ply the waters. The civilian yachtsmen congregate at bars to flex their alcohol tolerance and biceps simultaneously, earning the street its nickname, **"Ego Alley."** Smaller cruise boats leave on tours Apr.-Oct.

BANNEKER-DOUGLASS MUSEUM

7 **Location:** 84 Franklin St., adjacent to Church Circle. **Contact:** ☎ 974-2893. **Hours:** Tu-F 10am-3pm, Sa noon-4pm. **Admission:** Free.

Preserving Maryland's African-American heritage, the Banneker-Douglass Museum is named after two eminent black Marylanders: Benjamin Banneker and Frederick Douglass. The ecclesiastical stained glass windows remind visitors the museum is housed in the Victorian-Gothic **Mount Moriah African Methodist Episcopal Church.** The museum highlights the history of African-Americans in Annapolis from slavery to the present, including an extensive exhibit on the life and works of Frederick Douglass.

ST. JOHN'S COLLEGE

7 **Location:** 60 College Ave. **Contact:** ☎ 263-2371. **Tours:** Call ahead for tours.

This small, liberal arts college, founded in 1696 as King William's School, is the third-oldest in the nation (after Harvard and William and Mary). It graduates every one of its 450 students from the same rigorous Great Books academic program. This small institution, which once served as headquarters for the Union forces in the Civil War, also schooled star-spangled alumnus, Francis Scott Key.

NIGHTLIFE AND ENTERTAINMENT

Locals and tourists generally engage in one of two activities: wandering along City Dock or schmoozing 'n' boozing at upscale pubs. Bars and taverns line downtown Annapolis, drawing crowds every night. If you want a little more culture than drink can provide, Annapolis also has limited performance options.

MUSIC AND THEATER

Theater-goers can check out **The Colonial Players, Inc.,** 108 East St., for innovative and often unknown works. (☎ 268-7373. Performances Th-Su at 8pm, additional Su show at 2:30pm. Tickets Th and Su $7, students and seniors $5, F-Sa $10.) During the summer, the **Annapolis Summer Garden Theater,** 143 Compromise St., offers musical "theater under the stars" in an open courtyard theater near the **City Dock.** (Tickets $10, students and seniors $8.) The **Ram's Head Tavern** (see below), 33 West St., marks the city's only big name performance venue, drawing crowds for bands like 10,000 Maniacs and comedy performances. (☎ 268-4545 or call Ticketmaster for tickets. Prices vary.)

BARS AND CLUBS

McGarvey's, 8 Market Space (☎ 263-5700). A variety of locals pack in among naval pilot-donated helmets and a candle-lit mezzanine level in this Irish bar. Happy Hour (M,W 10pm-2am) features buffalo wings for $3-10, 32oz. drafts for $2.75, and 10oz. mugs for $1. 6pm-2am Th the house beer is only $1.50. Open M-Sa 11:30am-2am, Su 10am-2am.

Armadillo's, 132 Dock St. (☎ 280-0028). Spend the end of the day south of the border with an ageless, casual crowd. After undergoing renovations and a change of ownership, this reborn bar sports a homey brick interior and a cordial, talkative staff. Happy Hour (M-F 4-7pm) offers buffalo wings ($2), frozen margaritas ($2.50), and discounted beer ($2). Live music W-M 9:30pm. 21+ upstairs. Open daily 9am-1:30am.

Ram's Head Tavern, 33 West St. (☎ 268-4545). Beer connoisseurs, midshipmen, and tourists enjoy 135 different beers, including international microbrews amongst the beer history decor. Happy Hour (M-F 4-7pm and midnight daily) provides free food and reduced prices on drafts ($2). Thick steaks ($16-22) are a popular form of sustenance. Dinner and Show combination yields a 10% discount on your meal and a complementary drink after showing ticket. Open M-Sa 11am-2am, Su 10am-2am.

SOLOMONS ISLAND, MD   ☎410 OR 443

Solomons Island, a tiny land mass sitting between the Patuxent River to the west and Back Creek to the east, has transformed itself since its early days as Bourne's Island. The coastal community, first inhabited in 1680, did not blossom into prominence until the late 19th century, when Isaac Solomon, the island's namesake, founded his booming oyster processing facilities. The **Patuxent,** America's deepest river at 130 ft., also served as a crossroads for vessels traveling between the American naval bases of Annapolis and Norfolk. Although the renowned crabcakes, countless docks, and ubiquitous rivers and creeks hark back to the island's origins, most local residents have succumbed to the demands of an ever-industrializing economy and rely on neighboring Calvert County town factories and power plants for employment.

Although the island was formerly separated from the mainland by 550 ft., nowadays with a running start and a lot of faith, you can almost leap across the shrunken divide. If, however, you prefer to span the 23 ft. inlet more conventionally, a bridge does connect mainland to island.

ORIENTATION AND PRACTICAL INFORMATION. Highway 2, which is synonymous with **Highway 4** at Solomons, conveniently leads directly into the island. Drivers from points north should access Highway 4 from the Capital Beltway just east of the Woodrow Wilson Bridge. From points south, follow I-95 north to the Beltway (I-495/95) and continue east before catching Highway 4 and heading south to Solomons. Driving is the only practical way to reach Solomons. But if you have no car, public buses (☎535-1600, ext. 381) run M-Sa throughout Calvert County. **Calvert Taxi** (☎535-6272) and **Smart Ride** (☎535-6932) faithfully serve the terranean parts of the County, while Solomons Water Taxi (☎535-7022) carries passengers to aquatic destinations. Navigating through the town itself is simple as all major sites are within walking distance of each other and revolve around Solomons Island Rd. The **Island's Visitors Information Center,** at the corner of Solomons Island Rd. and Lore Rd., gladly volunteers information, maps, brochures, and coupon-filled guides. **Post Office:** 13046 Solomons Island Rd.

ACCOMMODATIONS. Call in advance to reserve one of the seven homey rooms at **The Back Creek Inn Bed & Breakfast** (cable TV and phone in every room, garden teas W 3-5pm, www.bbonline.com/md/backcreek/,$95+). The Inn is filled with several pieces of artwork painted by one of the two extremely friendly owners. Comfortable lodging unparalleled on Solomons also includes a hot tub in the shaded, peaceful backyard of Back Creek. Two doors down on quiet Calvert St. is more cozy lodging at **By the Bay Bed & Breakfast** (2 night min. stay required, reservations recommended (☎326-3428; www.chesapeake.net/~bythebaybandb, $85-$110). For a more commercial visit, shack up in one of the clean but bland rooms at the **Solomons Comfort Inn** on Lore St. (☎326-6303. $64+ weekdays and $99+ weekends, waterview rooms available.)

FOOD. Conveniently located behind the Comfort Inn on the Lore St. docks, the **Captain's Table,** 275 Lore Rd., and its diverse array of seafood and meats offers the island's heartiest portions and most eclectic menu. Polish off a locally caught soft-shell crab sandwich ($7.45) or, if you can spare the penny, the $16.95 house specialty, baked jumbo stuffed shrimp. (☎326-2772. Open year-round Su-Th 7am-9pm, F-Sa 7am-10pm.) If you're in search of some barley and hops to accompany the local seafood, try **Catamaran's,** 14470 Solomons Island Rd., and their renowned Crab 'N Beer All You Can Eat Fest. (☎326-8399. Happy Hour everyday 4-8pm. All You Can Eat Fest F-Su 10am-10pm.) For more sedate eating visit **Solomon's Pier,** 144575 Solomons Island Rd., (☎326-2424); and indulge in a Captain Pert's Sidebite ($4-$11), named in honor of the pier's builder.

SIGHTS AND ENTERTAINMENT. Solomons' **Tiki Bar,** Charles St. off Solomons Island Rd., single-handedly keeps the otherwise sleepy nightlife of the island from lapsing into a full-fledged coma. Beer-thirsty and party-hungry patrons infiltrate the island to rock and rollick on the waterfront amidst enough Polynesian decor to create a luau atmosphere. (Open M-F 4pm-2am, Sa-Su 2pm-2am.) For those who prefer kicking up their heels to tipping their elbows, the previously listed **Catamaran's** also features an upstairs dance club ($5 cover). To pass the daytime, acquaint yourself with the surrounding waters at **Solomons Boat Rental,** Rte. 2 and Alex St., (☎326-4060. Boat rentals $17+ per hr.;

kayak rentals $15+ per hr.). For a landlocked education of the marine origins of the island, the **Calvert Marine Museum** (right at the corner of Solomons Island Rd. and Lore Rd.) offers multiple nautical displays. Highlights include a Sharkfest exhibit and a scenic, informative 1 hour cruise around the Back Creek and Patuxent River environs. ($5, seniors 55+ $4, children 5-12 $2, under 5 free. Open daily 10am-5pm.)

THE EASTERN SHORE   ☎ 410 OR 413

Although travel brochures claim that combining Delaware, Maryland, and Virginia into one peninsula results in the aptly-named "Delmarva Peninsula," don't be fooled: anyone who has ever been here knows the peninsula as the Eastern Shore. Until recently, the Eastern Shore's distinct niches were held secret from inland citizens. One colorful crab house conversation with a local will tell you, though, proper English accents have long since drowned in the Chesapeake. Disappearing with the Colonial speak have been the gaps that formerly separated Maryland and Virginia from the Shore. In the 1950s and 60s, both states built bridges to the summer resort outpost, connecting it to the mainland. Today, residents still work the Bay, but not without flocks of tourists watching.

The area around **Easton** abounds in good seafood, charming places to stay, and some mellow points of interest. Mainly uneventful, however, Easton is best used as a base for exploring the waterside towns of **Oxford, St. Michaels,** and **Tilghman Island.** The Eastern Shore, with its beautiful shoreline and relaxed lifestyle, is the perfect balance for those looking to escape tourist madness without completely forgoing the luxury of a vacation. The colonial village of St. Michaels is the most touristy and therefore pricey. Oxford and Tilghman, two sleepy towns defined by working watermen and weekend tourists, offer a quieter pace and excellent alternatives for lodging and food. On the whole, few locations or accommodations are handicapped accessible. The **Talbot County Chamber of Commerce** (☎822-4606) will mail brochures, maps, and discounts to those who call ahead of their trip.

ORIENTATION AND PRACTICAL INFORMATION. To get to Easton, take Rte. 50E from either Washington, D.C. or Baltimore. There is no easy public transportation to this area. **Trailways buses** (☎(800) 231-2000) will drop passengers from **Baltimore** ($28.75) or **Washington, D.C.** ($32.75) at a Texaco station a few miles north of Easton, but from the station the only way into town is by foot. **Enterprise Rent-a-Car** (☎(800) 736-8227) on Rte. 50 in Easton rents to those 25 and older. For a small fortune, **1876 Travel** (☎226-5496) sends vans for one or two people from BWI Airport or the Amtrak station ($65), the New Carrollton Amtrak station ($70), or Penn Station in Baltimore ($75) to Easton. From Easton, St. Michaels is an eight-mile drive down west MD-33, and Tilghman is 15 mi. past St. Michaels. Oxford can be reached either entirely by car (US 50 south of Easton to MD-33W) or by a combination of car (MD-33W, turn off on Bellevue Rd. toward Royal Oak) and the 20- minute **Oxford-Bellevue Ferry** (☎745-9023) across the Tred Avon River (runs June-Labor Day M-F 7am-9pm, Sa-Su 9am-9pm; Labor Day-June 1 M-F 7am-sunset, Sa-Su 9am-sunset, closed mid-Dec. to Feb.; car and driver $5, bicycle $2, passengers 50¢, walk-on $1). Flat terrain makes the area perfect for biking. **Sexual Assault and Crisis Help Centers:** 6 Dover St. (☎820-5600). **Easton Post Office:** 116 E. Dover St. **Postal Zip Code:** 21601.

ACCOMMODATIONS. St. Michaels abounds with Bed and Baths, though it lacks budget motels. The least expensive accommodations are in Easton. The **Talbot County Chamber of Commerce,** in the Tred Avon shopping mall off Rte. 322 at Marlboro Rd. in Easton, provides lodging suggestions, maps, and coupons (☎822-4606; open M-F 9am-5pm). The **Atlantic Budget Inn,** 8058 Ocean Gateway, on Rte. 50, offers clean but bland standard motel rooms (phone, TV, A/C) and an outdoor pool. (☎822-2200. Singles $55-85; doubles $65-99; under 11 free; $10-20 weekend surcharge.)

For a more homestyle atmosphere, three St. Michaels' bed and baths (no breakfast) at the intersection of E. Chew St. and New Ln. each feature two beautiful rooms and the friendliness of an afternoon porch chat with the elderly residents. **Captain's Quarters,** 115 E. Chew St. (☎745-9152), has two double suites (both $85). Across the street, and extremely similar in appearance and price, are the **Chew Inn,** 114 E. Chew St. (☎745-9678), and **Fleet's Inn,** 200 E. Chew (☎(888) 859-2147), where homey doubles are $85.

In Tilghman, the rustic **Sinclair House,** 5718 Black Walnut Hill Pt. Rd. (☎886-8147), right off Rte. 33, provides comfy beds with private baths and sumptuous breakfasts ($75-$100; in winter $60). The most affordable of Oxford's simple but attractive inns is the **Oxford Inn,** 504 S. Morris St. (☎226-5220), where air-conditioned doubles start at $75.

FOOD. The area's best dining is in St. Michaels which, incidentally is the only one of the three towns that doesn't require sleuth skills to find restaurants. The **Carpenter Street Saloon,** 113 Talbot St., serves filling breakfasts (omelettes with toast $3-6), substantial lunches and dinners (catch-of-the-day $9), and is the most popular bar in town ((☎745-5111; restaurant open daily 7am-9pm; lounge open 11am-2am). The spicy-smelling **Crab Claw,** on Navy Pier near the museum, ships barrel-loads of fresh seafood in daily. The restaurant's namesake crab claw appetizer ($3.50) and the backfin crab cake ($10) have loyal followings. (☎745-2900 or 745-9366. Open Mar.-Nov. daily 11am-10pm.) **Higgins' Crab House,** at Rte. 33 and Pea Neck Rd., serves large portions of fresh seafood in a nautical-theme interior, lined with model boats and a life-size replica of a Maine lobster. All-you-can-eat specials are available at market prices and broiled crab cakes (entree $14, sandwich $7) turn the normally fried food into a healthy alternative. After hours, the bar draws locals, including watermen who work the bay ($2.50 drafts). (☎745-5151. Happy Hour daily 4-7pm. Open M-Th 3pm, F-Sa 11am, Su 1pm; closing hrs. vary.)

Eating options are minimal in Tilghman, so unless you're willing to starve, be ready to break the bank at **Harrison's Chesapeake House,** at the end of Chesapeake House Dr. This borderline elegant restaurant gets raves for soft crabs ($16) and oyster stew ($3.75). Entrees are $11-20. (☎886-2121. Open daily 6am-10pm.)

Good food in Easton is hard to come by, but the **Washington Street Pub,** 20 N. Washington St., around since the War of 1812, serves up good, plain burgers and sandwiches ($6-7.25) and brews ($3) in the brass and brick pub. (☎822-9011. Happy Hour M-F 4pm-6pm; open daily 11am-10pm, bar open until midnight.) For some ethnic zest, try **Cafe 25,** 25 Goldsborough St., (☎822-9360) where predominantly Italian entrees ($10-$13) please after a kitchen sink bread basket ($4) whets appetites.

In Oxford, fuel your body and your car simultaneously at **Oxford Spirits and Gas,** on Rte. 333 leading into Oxford. While the pump flows, overfill your own tank with an overstuffed deli sandwich ($5). (☎226-0002. Open Tu-Sa 8am-8pm, Su 8am-6pm; winter hrs. vary.) For finer dining and fresh seafood, bear left at the end of Rte. 333 and take your first right to the **Pier Street Restaurant and Marina,** at the end of W. Pier St. Seasonal fish dinner specials are affordable, but standard entrees are not cheap ($9-18). The friendly staff and dockside restaurant attract a motley crew of locals, including legendary "Wayne the Waterman" who has frequented the "claw" for 40 years. (☎226-5411. Open daily 11:30am-9:30pm.)

SIGHTS. The Eastern Shore is known for its lack of tourist destinations: the area's only real sight is what Eastern Shorers know and love best—the Bay. The **Chesapeake Bay Maritime Museum,** 1257 Mill St. (☎745-2916) spreads along the waterfront and contains everything anyone could ever want to know about the Bay, its inhabitants, and its history. Admission is steep but the museum's multi-building set-up is worth the extra money, filled with intricate boating replicas and originals, a vacationing section that teaches guests how to foxtrot, and a hands-on crabbing lesson. Avoid the admission fee and meander among the relocated historic buildings, including an authentic lighthouse with a spectacular view of the Bay. For those with a marine biological thirst for knowledge, the visitors center offers an educational exhibit, detailing several of the species that call the Bay home. Several of the more important maritime festivals in the region are held at the museum, notably the **Mid-Atlantic Maritime Arts Festival** in May, **Crab Days** in August, and the **Mid-Atlantic Small Craft Festival** in October. *(Open daily in summer 9am-6pm; in spring and fall 9am-5pm; in winter 9am-4pm. Guided tours free with admission; call ahead. Audio tours $1. Admission $7.50; students, seniors, AARP, AAA, and military $6.50; ages 6-17 $3; under 6 free. All buildings save for the lighthouse and the Boat Shop are handicapped accessible.)* **Patriot Cruises** offer hour-long harbor trips that depart daily at 11am, 12:30pm, 2:30pm, and 4pm. Evening cruises depart at 5:30pm and 7pm F-Sa.

Early birds can watch as the half dozen members of America's last fleet of skipjacks (sailing work boats) sets out at dawn on Mondays and Tuesdays from **Dogwood Harbor,** located on Rte. 33, ½ mile after entering Tilghman Island. A fit man might be able to volunteer on one such boat for the day, but because the area is, well, rather old-fashioned, ladies are not allowed on the boats. Captain Wade Murphy, a rare third-generation skipjack waterman, and his 1886 sailboat, **Rebecca T. Ruark,** bring tourists on fishing expeditions (☎886-2176, www.skipjack.org. $30 per person for 2hrs).

ON THE ATLANTIC

LEWES, DE   ☎302

Founded in 1613 by the Zwaanendael colony from Hoorn, Holland, Lewes was Delaware's first town and for a brief stint of three years, a Dutch West India Company colony. Lewes (pronounced Lewis) hasn't changed much with the times. Featuring Victorian gingerbread houses, quiet streets, and a genuine lack of tourist culture, this ferry town has remained old-fashioned for ages. The town's main draw, Lewes' beautiful beach draws vacationers in and away from the chaos of nearby Rehoboth Beach.

ORIENTATION AND PRACTICAL INFORMATION. Unless you own a private chopper, automobile is the only sensible way to reach Lewes. From points North, Rte. 1 South brings you directly to Lewes before simply accessing Savannah Rd. which dissects Lewes. From the West, begin traveling East on Rte. 404, then take Rte. 9 East at Georgetown. This will land you at Rte. 1 where you continue South until Savannah Rd. Greyhound/Trailways (☎(800) 231-2222) serves Lewes with **buses** to and from **Washington, D.C.** (3½hr., $32.75), **Baltimore** (3½hr., $28.75), and **Philadelphia** (4hr., $30.75). The buses stop in front of the Ace Hardware Store on Rte. 1. In Lewes and Rehoboth, the **Delaware Resort Transit** (☎(800) 553-3278) shuttle bus runs from the ferry terminal through Lewes to Rehoboth and Dewey Beach (every 30min.; operates late May to early Sept. daily 7am-3am; $1 per ride, seniors and disabled 40¢, day pass $2). **Seaport Taxis** (☎645-6800) will take you door to door anywhere in Lewes for a small fee. Note that the beach is not in town—a bridge separates the two and it's a long walk to the beach without a car. Thankfully, the beach does offer abundant parking. **Post Office:** 116 Front St.

ACCOMMODATIONS. A charming, kid-friendly seven-room B&B with a lavish vegetarian breakfast, the **Savannah Inn,** 330 Savannah Rd., tops other Lewes accommodations in price and earth-friendly philosophy. Don't be fooled by the hints of peeling paint, this building is well-maintained and clean. (☎645-5592. No A/C. Double rooms with shared bath $50, with largest rooms sleeping 3-4 and running $75-$80. Oct.-May no breakfast and $10 off room rates.) **Captain's Quarters,** 406 Savannah Rd. (☎645-7924), a small motel on the beach side of the town drawbridge offers comfy but less personal lodgings. All rooms are doubles (rooms on summer weekends $85), each additional person $5, check-in 3pm, check-out 11am). Sandy campsites are available in **Cape Henlopen State Park**, off Rte. 1 (from the North bypass Savannah Rd. and continue on Rte. 1 for ½mi. before signs direct you to take a left, leading to the park), around the clock on a first come-first served basis. (☎645-2103. Campground open Apr.-Oct. Park open year-round 8am-sunset. Sites $18. No RV hook-ups.)

FOOD. The few restaurants in Lewes cluster primarily on 2nd St. **Rosa Negra,** 128 2nd St., offers filling Italian fare in a rather bare dining room. Be an anxious early bird, though, because the post 6pm menu is pricey (early bird special daily 4-6pm; choice of 8 pastas, 9 sauces for $7, seniors $6). (☎645-1980. Open daily 4-11pm. Sniff the rich aroma of brews like "linzer torte" and "coconut kiss" at **Oby Lee Coffee Roasters,** 124 2nd St. Tiptoe around the several bags of coffee bean imports decorating the floor to order sandwiches ($2-4) and the "opposite of Hot Cocoa" Vanilla Dream ($1.50). (☎645-0733. Open daily 7am-5:15pm.) Locals jam to live music (Tu-Sa), including blues, rock, and karaoke at the wood-paneled **Rose and Crown Restaurant and Pub,** 108 2nd St. (☎645-2373. Happy hour daily 4-6pm yields 75¢ discounts. Open daily 11am-1am.)

the on dopedc

Crabs, Start Your Engines

Every Labor Day weekend, thousands descend on the hamlet of Crisfield for the legendary **Annual Crab Derby and Fair.** Approximately 300 crabs are entered by their owners and trainers (yes, their trainers). Usually, 6 heats of 50 crabs are conducted. The magnitude grows for the famous **Governor's Cup,** for which neighboring states airmail crabs to Crisfield to compete alongside the local crustaceans. Winning crabs and owners are awarded trophies. Sorry dice-rollers, no gambling is permitted; races are strictly recreational.

SIGHTS. While the towns on the Eastern Shore pride themselves on their independence from the tourism industry, Lewes is struggling to turn itself into a vacationer's historical playground. Unfortunately, Lewes has few notable historical sites—the real draw of the city is and always will be the beautiful **beach** (see below). The **Lewes Chamber of Commerce,** 20 King's Hwy., operates out of the Fisher-Martin House (c. 1730) and offers useful Lewes info and a free walking tour. (☎645-8078. Open in summer M-F 10am-4pm, Sa 9am-3pm, Su 10am-2pm; off-season closed Sa-Su.) The modest hub of Lewes lies along 2nd St. The town has gathered some historic buildings into the **Historical Society Complex,** located on Shipcarpenter St. near 2nd St. Amongst these preserved relics stands the town's oldest surviving home, the Bunton House, built in 1690. (☎645-7670. Open June-Labor Day Tu-F 11am-4pm, Sa 10am-12:30pm. Admission $5). Secluded among sand dunes and scrub pines 1 mi. east of Lewes on the Atlantic Ocean is the 4000-acre **Cape Henlopen State Park.** A family-oriented beach, youngsters frolic in the waves while their ever watchful parents soak up some rays in their lawnchairs. The park is home to a seabird nesting colony, sparkling white "walking dunes," a two-mile paved trail perfect for in-line skating (but bring your own blades because they can't be rented), and an expansive, beautiful beach with a bathhouse. (Open daily 8am-sunset. Admission $5 per car; bikes and walkers free.)

REHOBOTH BEACH, DE ☎302

The cotton candy, mini-golf, fast-food, beach volleyball, and discount t-shirt shops clustered on Rehoboth's boardwalk strip contrast sharply with the serenity of seaside Lewes. On the surface, Rehoboth appears to be little more than a commercial beach attraction, but if you venture inland past the hoopla of the beach, you'll find a well-heeled resort community with numerous Washington families and a burgeoning gay population.

ORIENTATION AND PRACTICAL INFORMATION. Rehoboth is located about 6 miles south of Lewes. To reach the town from Rte. 1, take Rte. 1B to Rehoboth Ave. and follow it to the water. Don't become discouraged too quickly; you'll drive through some pasture off the exit before reaching the main strip. The vibrant section of town is very concentrated within the beachside boardwalk, so walking is the preferred mode of transportation. Greyhound/Trailways, 251 Rehoboth Ave. (☎227-7223 or (800) 231-2222), stops next to the Rehoboth Beach Chamber of Commerce. **Buses** go to and from **Washington, D.C.** (3½hr., 1 per day, $32.75), **Baltimore** (3½hr., 1 per day, $28.75), and **Philadelphia** (4hr., 2 per day, $30.75). **The Rehoboth Beach Chamber of Commerce,**

501 Rehoboth Ave. (☎227-2233 or (800) 441-1329), a recycled railroad depot next to an imitation lighthouse, doles out Delaware info, free maps, and coupons (open M-F 9am-5pm, Sa-Su 9am-noon). **Internet Access:** Avenue Video and Internet, 71 Rehoboth Ave. **Post Office:** Rehoboth Ave. and 2nd St.

ACCOMMODATIONS. Inexpensive lodgings, mostly charming bed and breakfasts, abound in Rehoboth. **Mr. and Mrs. Downs of the Lord Baltimore,** 16 Baltimore Ave., half a block from the boardwalk, have rented out clean, antiquated rooms with TVs, refrigerators, and A/C for over 25 years. Mr. and Mrs. Downs, the warm elderly couple at the helm of the motel, are very approachable sources of information. (☎227-2855. Singles and doubles $40-70; in winter $25-50; each additional person $5, check-in 2pm, check-out 11am). **The Abbey Inn,** 31 Maryland Ave., is just a street away from the noise of Rehoboth Ave and always has a conversation waiting on the porch. (☎227-7023. 2-day min. stay; open late May to early Sept.; singles from $40; doubles from $50; 15% surcharge on weekends.) The wooded **Big Oaks Family Campground,** 1 mi. off Rte. 1 on Rd. 270, offers a rugged alternative to town lodging. There's never a dull moment on the grounds as game rooms, a playground, and planned activities such as shuffleboard and art contests pass the time. Shaded sites, a bathhouse, and a pool are all available. (☎645-6838. Sites $28.50, with hookup $33.)

FOOD. Rehoboth is known for its deluxe beach cuisine and its many bars. **Cafe Papillion,** 42 Rehoboth Ave., in the Penny Lane Mall offers an authentic European twist to a very American town. French cooks speaking the international language of good food serve up fresh crepes ($2.50-5), croissants ($1.75-3), and stuffed baguette sandwiches ($5-7). (☎227-7568. Open May-Oct. daily 8am-11pm.) Heavenly is the best word for the delicacies and the decor at **Dream Cafe,** 26 Baltimore St., a few doors down from the Lord Baltimore. The friendly help and outgoing customers will happily engage you in conversation amidst the starry wallpaper while devouring the quiche of the day ($4.25). (☎226-2233. Open Su-Tu and Th 7am-4pm, F 7am-5pm, Sa 7am-10pm.) At **Nicola's Pizza,** 8 1st St. (☎227-6211) tempt your appetite with the enticing aroma of an Italian kitchen and then indulge with a satisfying and economical pasta dish ($3-6). For filling breakfasts like mom used to make, saunter over to the **Royal Treat,** 4 Wilmington Ave., where a stack of pancakes and bacon is $5.25. The restaurant doubles as an ice-cream parlor in the afternoon and evening, catering to traditionalists with an old-fashioned ice cream soda ($3.50) and authentic Hershey's syrup on hot fudge sundaes ($3.50). (☎227-6277. Breakfast served 8-11:30am; ice cream 1-11:30pm.)

ENTERTAINMENT. The congestion on the sparkling **beach** thins to the north of the boardwalk. Early risers will find even the boardwalk beach deserted and may witness the daily southward commute of the dolphins. **The Blue Moon,** 35 Baltimore Ave., rocks to the sounds of techno music for a predominantly gay crowd until 1am. (☎227-6515. Happy Hour M-F 4-6pm. Open daily 4pm-1am.) A new addition to the Rehoboth bar scene, the **Full Moon Saloon** uses the universal appeal of live classic rock 'n roll to attract young and old. (Open M-Sa 10am-1am, Su 11am-1am; Happy Hour M-Th 5-8pm offers $1 drafts.) **Arena's Deli,** 149 Rehoboth Ave., offers drinks and relaxation on a newly installed deck for its predominantly local crowd. Indoors or out, the beer ($3) and sandwiches ($5) will still draw a crowd. Happy Hour (M-F 4-7pm) yields $1.50 beer. (☎227-1272. Open daily 11am-1am.) **The Frogg Pond,** 3 S. 1st St., welcomes young, old, gay, and straight to jam Tuesday through Sunday to live alternative music. The photo collage on the wall is a colorful chronicle of the patrons' exploits. (☎227-2254; occasional weekend cover $2; open M-F 10-1am, Sa-Su 9-1am.) The town's gay dance club, **Cloud 9,** 234 Rehoboth Ave., spins club rock in its celestial interior. (☎226-1999. Happy Hour daily 4-7pm. DJ F-M. Open Apr.-Oct. daily 4pm-1am; closed Nov.-Mar. Tu-W.)

OCEAN CITY, MD   ☎410

Ocean City is a lot like a kiddie pool—it's shallow and plastic, but can be a lot of fun if you're the right age. This ten-mile strip of land packs endless bars, all-you-can-eat buffets, hotels, mini-golf courses, boardwalks, flashing lights, and sweaty tourists into a

the on dopedc

Misty's Got an Attitude

From a car window, the beautiful ponies grazing on the grass of the Chincoteague marshes seem the most serene creatures nature could imagine. Sometimes the truth can hurt – literally. Each year, numerous overly eager visitors approach the sweet ponies for a closer look and end up with multiple injuries due to pony bites and kicks. Signs all over the park warn to stay away from these feisty foals. They don't call them wild for nothing.

thin region between the Atlantic Ocean and the Assawoman Bay. Tourism is the town's only industry; in season the population swells from 5000 to 300,000, with a large migratory population of "June bugs," high school seniors that descend in swarms after graduation to celebrate (read: to drink beer). Proceed with caution if you're driving; the scantily clad grads tend to prance the Ocean City streets recklessly. July and August cater more to families and singles looking for fun in the sun.

ORIENTATION AND PRACTICAL INFORMATION.
Driving is the most sensible mode of transportation to reach the ocean resort. From the north, simply follow Rte. 1 which becomes Coastal Highway (also synonymous with Philadelphia Ave.). From the west, Rte. 50 also leads directly to Ocean City. If you're trekking to Ocean City from points south, take Rte. 113 to Rte. 50 and follow that to town. Ocean City runs north-south, with numbered streets linking the ocean to the bay. Most hotels are in the lower numbered streets toward the ocean; most clubs and bars are uptown toward the bay. Trailways (☎ 289-9307), at 2nd St. and Philadelphia Ave., sends **buses to Baltimore** (3½ hr., 7 per day, $25) and **Washington, D.C.** (4-6hr.; $39-44; June-Aug. daily 7-8am and 10am-5pm, Sept.-May 10am-3pm). In town, **public buses** (☎ 723-1607) run the length of the strip and are the best way to get around town 24 hours a day ($1 per day for unlimited rides). **The Ocean City Visitors Center,** 4001 Coastal Hwy. (☎ (800) 626-2326), at 40th St. in the Convention Center, gives out discount coupons (open June-Aug. M-W 8:30am-5pm, Th-Sa 8:30am-8pm; Sept.-May daily 8:30am-5pm). Byte Size, 4100 Coastal Hwy. (☎ 723-2702), offers **internet access** to electronically deprived beachgoers ($5 per 30min.; open M-Sa 9am-8pm). **Post Office:** 11805 Coastal Hwy. **Zip Code:** 21842. **Area code:** 410.

ACCOMMODATIONS. The **Whispering Sands,** 15 45th St., rents out eleven spacious rooms with kitchen access. Lodging available on a daily or a full-summer basis tends to draw a mostly European crowd in a location convenient to nightlife. Personable inn operator gladly provides visiting advice and conversation. (☎ 723-1874; Nov.-Apr. ☎ (202) 362-3453 or (954) 761-9008. A/C in all rooms but one. Open May-Oct.; rooms $20-25.) For a wilder experience with an impersonal flair, **Ocean City International Student Services,** 9 Somerset St., in the south end of town, provides a cheap summer boarding house for predominantly international college students. Private rooms and dorm rooms, both without A/C, have access to kitchen, TV, living room, deck, hammock, and grill. (☎ 289-4542. Open Apr.-Oct.; cost averages $87 per week; reservations necessary.) The **Cabana Motel,** 1900 Coastal Hwy. (a.k.a. Philadelphia Ave.), caters to families with small, comfortable rooms outfitted with A/C and TV, and an outdoor pool. (☎289-9131. Open May-Oct., singles and doubles $80-85, prices decrease in May and fall seasons.) The serene **Atlantic House Bed and Breakfast,** 501 N. Baltimore Ave., only a few bucks more, offers free breakfast and a wholesome change of pace from the Ocean City motel trend. (☎289-2333. A/C, cable TV, parking, shared baths start at $50, private baths $125). **Ocean City Travel Park,** 105 70th St., runs the only in-town campground (☎524-7601; tents $25-38; RVs $25-53).

FOOD. Besides the beach, food is Ocean City's prime attraction. With freshly caught food and a friendly atmosphere, **The Embers,** 24th St. and Coastal Hwy., flaunts the biggest seafood buffet and most potent fish stench in town. Smell, then eat clams, oysters, shrimp, crab, prime rib, and more ($23, $2 off before 5pm). (☎289-3322 or (888) 436-2377. Open daily July-Aug. 2-10pm; Sept.-June 3-9pm). When filling your belly matters more than aesthetics, **Fat Daddy's Sub Shop,** 216 S. Baltimore Ave., a grimy but economical dive around the corner from the hostel, offers satisfying deli sandwiches ($2-4.50) and subs ($4-6) on the beach until the early morning (☎289-4040; free delivery; open daily 11am-4am). For a slightly healthier eating experience, dodge the fried frenzy and join a young, alternative crowd on the soft blue couches of **Common Grounds Cafe,** 5 S. Baltimore St., near the hostel. Sandwiches on hearth baked bread ($4-6.50) like the Avocado Melt ($4.75) can be accompanied with a "smart drink" fortified with amino acids ($4). (☎289-5252. Open M-F 10am, Sa-Su 7am; closing hrs. vary daily, also offers internet access.) Breakfast is the best meal of the day at the seaside **Brass Balls Saloon,** between 11th and 12th St. on the boardwalk. Enjoy oreo waffles ($4.75) or light, fluffy omelettes ($4.25-5.25) amidst a mural of smiling celebrities. (☎289-0069. Open daily 8:30am-2am May-October.)

ENTERTAINMENT. Ocean City's star attraction is its beautiful **beach.** The wide stretch of surf and sand runs the entire 10 mi. length of town and can be accessed by taking a left onto any of the numerous side streets off of Philadelphia and Baltimore Ave. The breaking waves know no time constraints but beach-goers are technically limited to 6am-10pm hours. When the sun goes down, hard-earned tans glow under the glaring lights of Ocean City's bars and nightclubs. An amusement park for adults, the island oasis **Seacrets,** on 49th St., features 11 bars, including two floating bars on the bay. Barefoot barflies wander from bar to bar, sipping the signature frozen rum runner mixed with piña colada ($5.25) to the strains of three live bands nightly. A magnificent sunset view ushers in the early revelers. (☎524-4900. Cover $3-5. Open M-Sa 11am-2am, Su noon-2am.) After finishing your feast at Common Grounds Cafe (see above), venture upstairs to the **Skylab,** 5 S. Baltimore St., to burn off those calories on the dance floor. DJs spin house trance music for all strictly on Saturday nights. The elder statesman of the bayside clubs, **Fager's Island,** 60th St. in the bay, attracts hordes across a plank walkway to its island location. Music plays nightly. No one seems to know the source of the classical music tradition but the 1812 Overture rings aloud daily with the sunset. Start the week with a festive bang at the Monday night deck party ($7 cover). (☎524-5500. Happy hour Su-Th 4-7pm. Open daily 11am-2am.)

VIRGINIA BEACH ☎ 757

After decades as the capital of the cruising collegiate crowd, Virginia Beach is gradually shedding its playground image and maturing into a family-oriented vacation spot. The town has grown into Virginia's largest city, and along with its nearby neighbors, Norfolk, Newport News, and Hampton, the city is attempting to make the entire Hampton Roads region an attractive place to visit. Although increasingly popular among families, balmy summer temperatures continue to draw party-craving students in droves. For the time being, tipsy twenty-somethings share the streets with parents and their baby carriages. Even the most dogged clean-up campaigns cannot conceal the omnipresence of fast-food joints, motels, and discount shops that characterize every beach town. But beyond all the slurpees and suntan oil, Virginia Beach's beautiful ocean sunrises, substantial dolphin population, and frequent military jet flyovers distinguish it from its East Coast counterparts.

ORIENTATION AND PRACTICAL INFORMATION

Virginia Beach is easy to get to and easy to get around. The shortest route from D.C. follows I-64 east from Richmond through the perpetually congested Hampton Roads Bridge Tunnel into Norfolk. At Norfolk turn onto I-264 (the Virginia Beach-Norfolk Expwy.), which leads straight to 22nd St. and the beach. Alternately, avoid the Hampton Roads Bridge-Tunnel and get off I-64E at I-664. Take I-664 to I-64W via the Monitor-Merrimac Bridge-Tunnel. From I-64W, get off on Rte. 44 and follow it to the beach. From the northern coast (near Ocean City, MD), take Rte. 13S across the 20-mile Chesapeake Bay Bridge-Tunnel (toll $10). Follow Rte. 60E into the Virginia Beach resort community.

In Virginia Beach, east-west streets are numbered and the north-south avenues, running parallel to the beach, have ocean names. Prepare to feel like a thimble on a Monopoly board: **Atlantic** and **Pacific Avenue** comprise the main drag. **Arctic, Baltic,** and **Mediterranean Avenues** are farther inland.

Trains: Amtrak (☎245-3589 or ☎(800) 872-7245). The nearest train station, in Newport News, runs 45min. bus service to and from the corner of 19th and Pacific St. When leaving, you must call to reserve your train ticket. To Newport News from: **Washington, D.C.** (6hr., $44); **New York City** (10hr., $73); **Philadelphia** (8½hr., $81); **Baltimore** (7hr., $58); **Richmond** (4hr., $19); and **Williamsburg** (2hr., $15).

Buses: Greyhound, 1017 Laskin Rd. (☎422-2998 or ☎(800) 231-2222). Connects with Maryland via the Bridge Tunnel. Station located ½ mile from the oceanfront area. From: **Washington, D.C.** (6½hr., $31); **Richmond** (3½hr., $24); and **Williamsburg** (2½hr., $15).

Public Transportation: Virginia Beach Transit/Trolley Information Center (☎640-6300), Atlantic Ave. and 24th St. Info on area transportation and tours, including trolleys, buses, and ferries. Trolleys transport riders to most major points in Virginia Beach. The Atlantic Avenue Trolley runs from Rudee Inlet to 42nd St. (May-Sept. daily noon-midnight; 50¢, seniors and disabled 25¢, day passes $1.50). Other trolleys run along the boardwalk, the North Seashore, and to Lynnhaven Mall. **Hampton Roads Regional Transit (HRT)** (☎222-6100), in the Silverleaf Commuter Center at Holland Rd. and Independence St., buses connect Virginia Beach with Norfolk, Portsmouth, and Newport News (fare $1.50, seniors and disabled 75¢, children under 38 in. free).

Car Rental: All the national companies have offices in Virginia Beach, and some, like **Enterprise Rent-A-Car** (☎486-7700), will make hotel deliveries.

Bike Rental: RK's Surf Shop, 305 16th St. (☎428-7363), in addition to aquatic entertainment, rents bikes for $4/hr. or $16/day.

Taxi: Yellow Cab ☎460-0605, 24 hr. service.

Tourist Office: Virginia Beach Visitors Center, 2100 Parks Ave. (☎437-4888 or (800) 446-8038), at 22nd St. Info on budget accommodations and area sights. Helpful, knowledgeable docents. Open daily 9am-8pm; Labor Day to Memorial Day 9am-5pm.

Emergency: 911.

Post Office: 2400 Atlantic Ave. (☎428-2821), at 24th St. and Atlantic Ave. Open M-F 8am-4:30pm. **ZIP Code:** 23458.

Internet Access: WebCity Cybercafe, 1307 Atlantic Avenue, Suite 112, on the boardwalk. Minimum charge: $5 for 30 min.

ACCOMMODATIONS AND CAMPING

As could be expected with an ocean resort, a string of endless motels lines the waterfront in Virginia Beach. Oceanside, Atlantic and Pacific Aves. buzz with activity during the summer and boast the most desirable hotels. If you reserve in advance, rates are as low as $45 in winter and $65 on weekdays in summer. If you're traveling in a group, look for "efficiency" apartments, which are rented cheaply by the week. As with any beach town, the further from the shore, the lower the price of lodging.

🖾 **Angie's Guest Cottage, Bed and Breakfast, and HI-AYH Hostel,** 302 24th St. (☎428-4690; www.bbinternet.com/angies). Filled with friendly staff, sparklingly clean rooms, and plenty of

Here's your ticket to freedom, baby!

*Airline Tickets | Hotel Rooms | Rental Cars
New Cars | Long Distance*

Wherever you want to go, priceline.com can get you there for less. Our customers regularly save up to 40% or more off the lowest published airfares. But we're more than just airline tickets. At priceline.com, you can Name Your Own Price℠ and save big on brand-name hotels nationwide. Get great rates on all your long distance calls — without changing your long distance carrier. Even get the car of your dreams, at the price *you* want to pay. If you haven't tried priceline.com, you're missing out on the best way to save. **Visit us online today at www.priceline.com.**

boogie boards in a prime area of town—only one block from the oceanfront. Barbara "Angie" Yates and her personable staff welcome predominantly young international and domestic guests with exceptional warmth, free trolley tokens, and great advice about the beach scene. Co-ed dorm rooms offer added perks. Kitchen, lockers available. Linen $2. No lockout. No A/C. Open Apr. 1-Oct. 1. Reservations helpful, but not required. Check-in 10am-9pm. Two-day min. stay for private rooms. Private hostel rooms with A/C $35.10, 2 people $26.90 per person, 3 people $23.40 per person; substantially less in off-season. Eight-guest capacity in each dorm room, HI-AYH members $14.50; off-season $14.50, HI-AYH members $11.

Ocean Palms Motel, 2907 Arctic Ave. (☎428-8362), at 30th St. Two-person efficiencies with non-descript decor. Exchange a longer walk from beach locations for the chance to cook your own meal. Not likely to be mistaken for a five-star hotel, the brick building skimps on aesthetics but offers close to the cheapest rates in the immediate resort area. TV, A/C, kitchen. $30-50 per night.

First Landings, 2500 Shore Dr. (☎412-2300, reservations (800) 933-7275), about 8 mi. north of town on Rte. 60. Take the North Seashore Trolley. Located in the State Park bearing the same

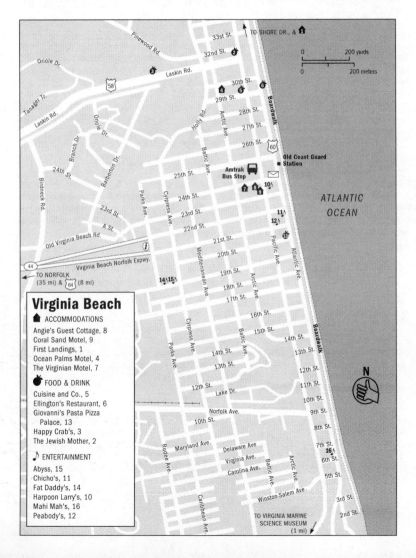

Virginia Beach

♦ ACCOMMODATIONS

Angie's Guest Cottage, 8
Coral Sand Motel, 9
First Landings, 1
Ocean Palms Motel, 4
The Virginian Motel, 7

🍎 FOOD & DRINK

Cuisine and Co., 5
Ellington's Restaurant, 6
Giovanni's Pasta Pizza
  Palace, 13
Happy Crab's, 3
The Jewish Mother, 2

♪ ENTERTAINMENT

Abyss, 15
Chicho's, 11
Fat Daddy's, 14
Harpoon Larry's, 10
Mahi Mah's, 16
Peabody's, 12

name, beachfront sites thrive on the natural beauty of Virginia's shore. Because of its desirable location amid sand dunes and cypress trees, the park is very popular; call 2-3 weeks ahead (during business hrs.) for reservations. The park features picnic areas, a private swimming area on a sprawling beach, a bathhouse and boat launching areas.

Coral Sand Motel, 2307 Pacific Ave. (☎425-0872), only two blocks from the ocean front, offers bland standard doubles starting at $49 on weekdays. Weekend prices around $109. Cable TV, A/C, 11am check-out.

The Virginian Motel, 310 24th St. (☎428-5333), a couple doors down from Angie's hostel, lacks the glamor of an oceanfront motel but does feature an outdoor pool and reasonable rates. $69-79 weekdays, $79-99 weekends. Cable TV, A/C, kitchenettes.

FOOD

Prepare for more $5 all-you-can-eat breakfast specials than you have ever previously encountered. Alternatively, fish for a restaurant on **Atlantic Avenue** where each block is a virtual buffet of fried, fatty, sweet or creamy dining options.

⬛ The Jewish Mother, 3108 Pacific Ave. (☎422-5430). Let Mama fill your belly with deli in this popular VA chain restaurant where kids-at-heart can color on the walls with free crayons. Mama doesn't want no skin 'n' bones in her home, so unfold a newspaper format menu to find humongous sandwiches with a scoop of potato salad ($4-6.25), followed up by overwhelming desserts ($3.50-4.50). Live music nightly with popular Blues Jam W. Happy Hour (daily 3-7pm) features $2 domestic drafts and $1.50 for a cooling mixed drink. Cover normally $3-5. Open M-F 8:30am-2am, Sa 8am-3am, Su 7am-2am.

⬛ Giovanni's Pasta Pizza Palace, 2006 Atlantic Ave. (☎425-1575). In a land of pizzerias, young, outgoing waiters serve with gusto and speed in this affordable and plentiful pasta restaurant. But don't overstuff yourself before the main course when tasty, inexpensive Italian pastas, pizzas, hot strombolis ($5-9), and a fabulous veggiboli ($6) satiate the appetite. If you're cutting back on the calories, spinach ravioli ($7.25) is a delicious healthy option. Open daily noon-11pm.

Ellington's Restaurant, 2901 Atlantic Ave. (☎428-4585), located inside the Oceanfront Inn, on the boardwalk. Patrons gaze at the undulating Atlantic in a relaxing atmosphere. Beach souvenir hunters can help themselves to a handful of seashells at the entrance. Grilled portabello burgers ($6), a huge lunch salad ($5), and affordable dinner entrees ($9-15) like the blackened tuna steak with pineapple salsa ($13). Open Su-Th 7am-10pm, F-Sa 7am-11pm.

Happy Crab's, 550 Laskin Rd. (☎437-9200). Don't be intimidated by the massive crab carving on the wall or get entangled in the plentiful fishnets hanging from the walls. Park your beach-weary body on a bench and get ready to fill buckets with crab shells galore. Early-bird specials (daily 5-6:30pm) offer unbeatable 2-person size seafood platters ($13) or huge 1-person servings big enough to split, like sumptuous ribs ($11). Open M-Th 11am-10pm, F-Su 11am-11pm.

SIGHTS

The **beach and boardwalk,** jam-packed with college revelers, bikini-clad sunbathers, and an increasing number of families, is the *raison d'être* at Virginia Beach. Unlike similar surf-wise coastal destinations in Maryland, however, Virginia Beach provides more than a commercial, splashy boardwalk. If you're willing to drive, the environs surrounding the oceanfront offer an enticing diversion.

VIRGINIA MARINE SCIENCE MUSEUM

🏛 Location: 717 General Booth Blvd. **Contact:** ☎425-FISH, excursion trips ☎437-2628; www.vmsm.com. **Hours:** Daily 9am-9pm; off-season 9am-5pm. **Admission:** $9, seniors $8, ages 4-11 $6. IMAX tickets $7, seniors $6.50, ages 4-11 $6. Combined museum and IMAX admission $13, ages 4-11 $10, seniors $12. Excursion trips $12, ages 4-11 $10. **Accessibility:** Handicapped accessible.

A 30-minute walk from the oceanfront or a 10-minute drive down Pacific Avenue lands visitors at Virginia Beach's most enthralling attraction: the **Virginia Marine Science Museum.** When driving to the museum, follow Pacific Avenue south as it becomes General Booth Blvd. until you encounter the sprawling museum a mile down on the right. Home to hundreds of species of fish, including crowd-pleasing sharks and stingrays. Two touch pools let kids and adults get friendly with the fish, and the **Owls Creek Marsh Pavilion** is dedicated completely to salt marsh life. For more marsh fun, a ride on the pontoon boat (40min., $3) is relaxing and informative. The museum also houses a six-story IMAX theater (8 screenings daily) and offers excursion trips for dolphin sighting in summer and whale watching in winter. Be on the lookout for the reptile exhibit in the spring of 2001.

OLD COAST GUARD STATION

¶ Location: *24th St. and oceanfront.* **Contact:** *☎ 422-1587.* **Hours:** *M-Sa 10am-5pm, Su noon-5pm; closed M Oct. 2-Memorial Day.* **Admission:** *$3, seniors and military with ID $2.50, ages 6-18 $1, under 6 free. Last tour leaves at 4pm.*

The newly installed high-tech *Touch 24* video system allows visitors to view an array of sea screenings, including a tear-jerking German U-boat movie. Pay no mind to the nostalgic pictures of the "surfman" ready to save shipwreck survivors pay homage to what the beach once was—the **Tower Cam** is the brightest attraction at the Old Coast Guard Station. Designed as an interactive way to view ships from a camera atop the museum, most guests hone their secret voyeur fantasies, focusing instead on sunbunnies strolling near the beach.

BACK BAY NATIONAL WILDLIFE REFUGE

¶ Location: *Take General Booth Ave. to turn left onto Princess Anne Dr. From Princess Anne Dr. turn left onto Sandbridge Rd. Follow Sandbridge Rd. for approximately six miles until turning right onto Sandpiper Rd. Sandpiper leads directly to the Visitors Center.* **Be careful driving** *as Sandbridge and Sandpiper Rds. are narrow and sinuous.* **Contact:** *☎ 721-2412.* **Hours:** *Visitors Center open daily 9am-4pm.* **Admission:** *$4 per car, $2 on foot, under 16 free.* **Tours:** *Tram daily 9am; $6, seniors and under 12 $4; disabled visitors must reserve 48 hr. in advance; cash only.*

Bathing suits are swapped for hiking boots at the Back Bay National Wildlife Refuge, a remote but pristine sanctuary for an array of endangered species and other wildlife. With nesting bald eagles and peregrine falcons, the natural wonderland is open to the public and features a four-hour tram tour departing daily at 9am from **Little Island City Park** up the road. The visitors center offers a taste of the wild with captivating stuffed bird exhibits.

NAVY JET OBSERVATION AREAS

¶ Contact: *☎ 433-3131 for information on visiting the base.*

The frequent roar of F-14 and Tomcat engines will remind you of the Navy bases nearby. For those who want a closer view of the air dynamics, the city maintains two observation areas where the base can be viewed, both of which are about 10 mi. from town. One is off Oceana Blvd., south of Southern Blvd. and right before the turn-off to the base, and the other, a better view—300ft. from a runway—is off London Bridge Rd.

ENTERTAINMENT

On summer nights, the Virginia beach boardwalk becomes a haunt for lovers and teenagers, and **Atlantic Avenue,** a.k.a. "Beach Street, USA.," burgeons with minstrel shows and street performers. Rousing jazz and classic rock performances can be heard every other block. Larger outdoor venues at 7th, 17th, and 24th draw bigger names and bigger crowds. (Free. Schedules for the main events are posted along the street. ☎ 440-6628 for more info.) Gay and lesbian bars can be found away from Virginia Beach in the chi chi Ghent neighborhood of nearby Norfolk.

Harpoon Larry's, 216 24th St. (☎ 422-6000), at Pacific Ave., 1 block from the HI-AYH hostel, serves tasty fish ($6) in an everyone-knows-your-name atmosphere. The amicable bartender and manager welcome twenty- and thirty-somethings to escape the sweat and raging hormones of "The Block." Specials include amazing seafood deals ($8-12) and rum runners (Tu, Th $2). Shout "Arriba!" W with 25¢ jalapeño poppers. Happy Hour M-F 7-9 pm. Open daily noon-2am.

Peabody's, 209 21st St. (☎ 422-6212; www.peabodysvirginiabeach.com). Boogie your body not your board at the biggest dance floor on the beach. A young, scantily-clad crowd bops to Top 40 hits, especially during Peabody's "Hammertime" when drinks are only $1.50 (daily 7-9pm). All-you-can-eat fresh crab legs and shrimp ($15). Aside from the intense dance scene, Peabody's scores big with the fresh-faced crowd on its theme nights: College Night on Friday (free admission with college ID) and Saturday's Summer Saturdaze (discount with tropical attire). Cover $5; pool $1. Open Th-Sa 7pm-2am.

Chicho's, 2112 Atlantic Ave. (☎422-6011), on "The Block" of closet-sized, college bars clustered between 21st and 22nd St. One of the hottest spots on the hot-spot strip features gooey pizza dished out from the front window (all-you-can-eat daily noon-5pm $6), tropical mixed drinks ($3.25), and live rock 'n roll music. Bring your Hawaiian shirt for the Tropical Fiesta Night Th, a fitting theme for the surfer decor. Open M-F noon-2am, Sa-Su 1pm-2am.

Abyss, 1065 19th St. (☎422-0486), while yuppies inhale martinis at Fat Daddy's, next door the Abyss fuels randy 18+ clubbers with pop and alternative dance music F-Sa, and W concerts. Cover $3-6. Open W and F-Sa 7pm-4am.

NORFOLK   ☎ 757

Just west of the popular summer resort of Virginia Beach lies its less glamorous cousin, Norfolk. Most notable for housing the United States' largest Navy Base, the city of Norfolk used to rely on the ocean for sustenance. Until the 1970s, the waterfront, now the city's most celebrated region, featured an eyesore of decaying industrial facilities and warehouses. If the city was to lure any tourists, this area direly needed a facelift. The building of the public esplanade in 1974 triggered a string of installations that has most recently resulted in the opening of the mammoth anchor of the waterfront: the National Maritime Center. Despite the modernization, Norfolk balances the new with the old, paying homage to its marine history with captivating museums.

ORIENTATION AND PRACTICAL INFORMATION. Thanks to the invention of the bridge, Norfolk is easily accessed from points north. From the Maryland Eastern Shore area, take the scenic Chesapeake Bay Bridge tunnel (Rte.13) to I-64 south. After entering Norfolk, connect to I-264 west. Then, take the Waterside Dr. exit and follow to the waterfront. From northern Virginia, follow I-64 south over the Hampton Roads Bridge-Tunnel which leads to I-264 west and the Waterside Dr. exit. If travelling from Virginia Beach, use 22nd St. which becomes I-264 west. I-264 leads to the Waterfront Dr. exit. From points south and west, use I-64 and I-264, respectively to reach the Waterside Dr. exit. Within the downtown area, Waterside Dr. runs along the waterfront and the Elizabeth River. Flanked by Monticello Ave. to the west and St. Paul's Blvd. to the east, the enormous MacArthur Center marks the middle of the city. Around the MacArthur Center, running from east to west is Freemason St. to the north and City Hall Ave. to the south.

Greyhound Buses, at the corner of Granby St. and Brambleton St. (☎(800) 231-2222), serves downtown Norfolk. (Buses from Washington D.C. to Norfolk, $32.00, $60.50 round trip; Philadelphia to Norfolk, $59.50, $119.00 round trip.) For public transportation the **Hampton Roads Transit System,** (☎222-6000), sells tokens for $1.50, $.75 seniors. Talkative desk attendants man Norfolk's two **Visitor Information Centers,** located in the Nauticus Maritime Center and the MacArthur Center (☎441-1852). **Taxi: Norfolk Checker Taxi** (☎855-3333), **Yellow Cab, Inc.** (☎622-3232). **Post Office:** 126 Atlantic St. (☎622-4751). **Zip Code:** 23510.

ACCOMODATIONS. The city of Norfolk severely lacks budget lodgings. More affordable accommodations should be sought in nearby Virginia Beach. Norfolk does feature a **Motel 6,** 853 Military Hwy. (☎461-2380). Standard, and clean, but impersonal rooms range from $50-70. (A/C, Cable TV, Check-out noon.)

FOOD. The Waterside Festival Marketplace, 333 Waterside Dr., is home to the bulk of Norfolk's culinary options. Infiltrated by businesspeople on lunch break and vacationing families, the Marketplace offers an eclectic range of choices:

Pastaria, 333 Waterside Dr., located inside the Waterside Festival Marketplace, adds Italian zest at affordable prices to the Waterfront. Stick to the basics with a plateful of spaghetti and meatballs for a paltry $4 or dare to mix land and sea with the bestselling nautical fettucine, shrimp, scallops, and fish served over fettucine alfredo ($7). Open daily 10:30am-9pm.

Skinney's Fresh Fare, 333 Waterside Dr. at the Marketplace (☎ 624-5774), keeps its customers stringbean-thin with a super healthy menu. Wash down a chicken caesar wrap ($4.25) or turkey wrap ($4) with a refreshing fruit smoothie ($2.50). Open daily 10:30am-9pm.

Famous Uncle Al's, 216 Granby St. (☎ 625-1135), has been a downtown Norfolk lunch staple for 15 years. Everyone feels like family amidst the classic sports photography and homey presence of owner Brian "Uncle Al" Calabrito. Cheap eats include a juicy hot dog ($1.60) and the always mouth-watering New York sausage ($2.25). Open M-Sa 7:30am-4pm, closed Su.

SIGHTS. Nauticus, located on the second and third floors of the National Maritime Center, promotes itself as a maritime science center with an educational twist. Its visitors can learn all about marine biology by viewing *The Living Sea*, the museum's permanent movie that airs periodically throughout the day. More audio-visual fun can be had with Nauticus' several computer interactive games, one of which, the *Aegis*, lets its users simulate sea combat. Highly anticipated for the year 2001 is the arrival of the USS Wisconsin. The massive battleship will be available to the public beginning with a grand opening, April 16, 2001. *(1 Waterside Dr. ☎ 664-1000. Open Tu-Sa 10am-5pm, Su noon-5pm. $7.50, children $5. Handicapped accessible.)*

At the heart of the town square looms the **MacArthur Memorial,** a gripping tribute to former Commander General of the United States Armed Forces. Converted from Norfolk City Hall to memorial, the impeccably maintained four building complex dazzles its guests with intriguing displays and galleries characterizing the General's legendary career. Signs recommend visiting the Memorial theater initially to view an orientation film but the stately rotunda, designed by MacArthur two years before his death, is most galvanizing to guests. Here rest the tombs of General MacArthur and his wife, surrounded by inscriptions of his most memorable and poignant words. Worthy of a 21-gun salute, the historic memorial welcomes guests free of charge. *(MacArthur Square. ☎ 441-2965. Open M-Sa 10am-5pm, Su 11am-5pm. Handicapped accessible.)*

Contrary to popular belief, Norfolk's history contains more than marine and military laurels. The Georgian style apparent in the symmetry of the **Willoughby-Baylor and Moses Myers Homes** reflects colonial Norfolk's architecture. Recently revamped gardens vivify the landscape of both houses and starkly contrast the pale coloring of the buildings. Myers, one of the only standing historic Jewish museum houses, provides guests with an opportunity to explore the oddity of Jewish colonial living. *(Willoughby-Baylor Home at 601 E. Freemason St.; Moses Myers Home at 323 East Freemason St. ☎ 627-2737 connects to both houses. Tours hourly; last one 4pm. $4; students, seniors, military, and teachers $2.50; children under 12 free.)*

NIGHTLIFE AND ENTERTAINMENT. Norfolk's flourishing waterfront rules the city's bar scene. Night owls flock to the **Waterside Festival Marketplace** which houses several bars all within convenient access to each other. Aside from this concentration of nightlife, party-seekers can opt for less scenic revelry a few blocks inland at a Granby St. bar:

Dixie's Tavern, 333 Waterside Dr. (☎ 624-9427), welcomes a diverse crowd for a temporary Big Easy bayou escape on the Norfolk waterfront. Festive patrons sport Mardis Gras signature beads alongside dreadlocked rastafarians at the weekly Sunday night "Reggae on the River" Wave. Happy Hour M-F 5-8pm. Open 11am-2am daily.

Jillian's, 333 Waterside Dr. (☎ 624-9100), on the second floor of the Marketplace, excites adults who revisit their childhood while simultaneously testing their hand-eye coordination in the enormous game room. If you can detach yourself from the pinball machine, continue to satisfy your longings for yesteryear and pretend it's the high school dance at the **Groove Shack** where a mix of the best 70's, 80's, and 90's dance music beats all night long. Open 11am-2am daily.

Open Wide, 124 Granby St. (☎ 533-9153), will indeed leave your mouth agape at the appetizing sight of their best-selling shepherd's pie ($8.50). Serving a wide range of microbrews, this American bar is a local favorite. Familiarity with the bar's layout is key lest the presiding swordfish, an emblem of the bar, gouge out your eye. Open M-F 11:30am-2am, Sa 5:30pm-2am, closed Su.

The Garage, 731 Granby St. (☎ 623-0303), an immensely popular Levi/leather cruise bar welcomes a gay crowd to rock to Top 40 dance hits. Happy Hour 3-8pm daily. Turn out your pockets for loose change to feast on 10¢ shrimp Mondays. Open 9am-2am daily.

the dopedc on

William & Mary Bridge o' Love

A jaunt across the **Crim Dell Bridge** at William and Mary College is risky business. If student lore holds truth, then the fate of many a lovelife has been sealed in a single crossing, or shall we say in crossing singly. Superstition dictates that those who tread the bridge's path alone will never marry. On the opposite extreme, if passions lead a couple to engage in a kiss with the bridge underfoot, destiny has eternally bound them together. Scared of commitment? Don't panic. Simply break the bind by throwing your fellow kisser over the side. Maybe this chance to escape "I do" has something to do with Playboy naming the bridge the "second most romantic spot on a college campus." The view is great while tossing your mate!

THE HISTORIC TRIANGLE

If Virginia seems obsessed with its past, it has good reason: many of America's formative experiences—the white settlement of North America, the shameful legacy of the slave trade, the final establishment of American independence, and much of the Civil War—all took place here. English colonists founded Jamestown in 1607, and the New World's first black slaves joined them unwillingly 12 years later. What began as a humble colony with Jamestown exploded into revolution in ensuing years and ultimately the nascence of a new nation with George Washington's decisive victory over the British at Yorktown. While home to much of America's Revolutionary War glory, Virginia also witnessed the anguish and bloodshed of the devastating Civil War, mercifully settled at Appomattox, VA.

WILLIAMSBURG ☎757

Economically floundering after colonial prosperity, Williamsburg was rescued in the late 1920s by philanthropist John D. Rockefeller, Jr., who showered the troubled spots with money and restored a large chunk of the historic district, now known as **Colonial Williamsburg.** Nowadays a fife-and-drum corps marches down the streets, and costumed wheelwrights, bookbinders, and blacksmiths go about their tasks using 200-year-old methods on old gas station sites. Travelers who visit in late fall or early spring will avoid the crowds, heat, and humidity of summer. However, they will also miss the extensive array of special summer programs. December visitors will find an array of charming Colonial Christmas activities.

ORIENTATION AND PRACTICAL INFORMATION

Williamsburg lies some 50 mi. southeast of Richmond between Jamestown (10 mi. away) and Yorktown (14 mi. away). **The Colonial Parkway,** which connects the three towns, has no commercial buildings and is a beautiful route between historic destinations. The general Colonial Williamsburg area is accessed by I-64 and the Colonial Parkway exit.

Airport: Newport News/Williamsburg International Airport, 20min. away in Newport News with frequent connections to Dulles by United Express and USAir. Take state road 199W to I-64S.

Transportation Center, 408 N. Boundary St., behind the fire station. Houses offices for Amtrak, Greyhound, and taxi service.

Trains: Amtrak (☎229-8750 or ☎(800) 872-7245). From: **New York** (7½-8hr., 2 per day, $72); **Washington, D.C.** (3½hr., 2 per day, $33); **Philadelphia** (6hr., 2 per day, $56); **Baltimore** (5hr., 2 per day, $41); and **Richmond** (1hr., 2 per day, $14). Station open Tu-Th 7:30am-5pm, Su-M and F-Sa 7:30am-10:30pm.

Buses: Greyhound (☎229-1460 or ☎(800) 231-2222). From: **Richmond** (1hr., 8 per day, $10); **Norfolk** (1-2hr., 9 per day, $10); **Washington, D.C.** (3-4hr., 8 per day, $29); **Baltimore** (via D.C.; 6-7hr., 8 per day, $45); and **Virginia Beach** (2½hr., 4 per day, $14). Ticket office open M-F 8am-5pm, Sa 8am-2pm, Su 8am-noon.

Public Transportation: James City County Transit (JCCT) (☎220-1621). Bus service along Rte. 60, from Merchants Sq. in the historic district west to Williamsburg Pottery or east past Busch Gardens. Operates M-Sa 6:30am-5:15pm. Fare $1 plus 25¢ per zone-change. **Williamsburg Shuttle** (R&R; ☎220-1621), provides service between Colonial Williamsburg and Busch Gardens every 30min. Operates May-Sept. daily 9am-9pm. $1 for an all day pass.

Taxi: Yellow Cab (☎245-7777). 24hr. **Williamsburg Limousine Service** (☎877-0279). To Busch Gardens or Carter's Grove $6-10 one-way. To Jamestown and Yorktown $20 round-trip. Call between 8:30am-midnight.

Car Rental: Colonial Rent-a-Car, (☎220-3399) in the transportation center. $36-51 per day. Min. age 21. Open M-F 8am-5:30pm, Sa-Su 8am-2pm. Required to present credit card with $250 available balance.

Bike Rental: Bikes Unlimited, 759 Scotland St. (☎229-4620), rents 21-speed bikes for $15 per day. $5 deposit required (includes lock). Open M-F 9am-7pm, Sa 9am-5pm, Su noon-5pm.

Visitor Information: Williamsburg Area Convention & Visitors Bureau, 201 Penniman Rd. (☎253-0192), ½ mi. northwest of the transportation center. Provides a free Visitor's Guide to Virginia's Historic Triangle. Open M-F 8:30am-5pm. **Colonial Williamsburg Visitors Center,** 102 Information Dr. (☎(800) 447-8679), 1 mi. northeast of the transport center. Tickets and transportation to Colonial Williamsburg. Maps and guides to historic district, including a guide for the disabled. Info on prices and discounts for Virginia sights. Open daily 8:30am-8pm; winter hrs. vary.

EMERGENCY: ☎911.

Post Office: 425 N. Boundary St. (☎229-4668). Open M-F 8am-5pm, Sa 10am-2pm. **ZIP Codes:** 23185 (Williamsburg), 23690 (Yorktown), and 23081 (Jamestown).

ACCOMMODATIONS AND CAMPING

The hotels operated by the **Colonial Williamsburg Foundation** are generally more expensive than other lodgings in the area. **Route 60W** and **Route 31S** are packed with budget motels, which grow cheaper the farther they are from the historic district. At the various bed and breakfasts around William and Mary, guests pay more for gorgeous colonial decors. Guest houses don't serve breakfast, but still offer the bed, a reasonable price, abounding warmth, and "like-home" feelings.

🛇 **Lewis Guest House,** 809 Lafayette St. (☎229-6116), a 10min. walk from the historic district, rents three comfortable rooms, including an upstairs unit with private entrance, kitchen, partial A/C and shared bath. Undoubtedly offering the most homey lodging in the area, the ageless proprietor, Mrs. Lewis, eagerly reminisces about 1930s Williamsburg while her adorable dog, Brandy, clips at your heels. Rooms $25-35.

Carter Guest House, 903 Lafayette St. (☎229-1117). Two doors down from Mrs. Lewis, are 2 lovely, spacious rooms with 2 beds and a shared bath. Be forewarned: no bed till wed! the God-fearing Mrs. Carter—a woman of very traditional Southern values—will not let unmarried men and women sleep in the same room. Singles $25; doubles $30.

Bryant Guest House, 702 College Terr. (☎229-3320). Offers rooms with private baths, TV and limited kitchen facilities in a stately, exquisitely landscaped brick home. Singles $35; doubles $45; 5-person suite $55.

Carrot Tree Kitchens and Lodging, 1782 Jamestown Rd. (☎229-0957), more convenient to Jamestown than Williamsburg, features two snug rooms geared towards couples and outfitted with Native American decor. Guests enjoy free breakfast from the superb in-house bakery/deli. Cable TV, A/C. Bakery open Tu-F 7am-6pm, Sa-Su 8am-4pm. Rooms $50.

the on dopedc

Electric Lady

Even Lady Liberty is no match for Mother Nature. The **Yorktown Victory Monument,** the first war monument commissioned in the newly formed United States, perches Liberty 98 ft. above the land she commemorates. Though the British couldn't stop American liberty, a bolt of lightening beheaded the stone maiden with a single strike in 1942. She remained decapitated for 14 years until, in 1956, the statue was fixed with one addition—a lightning rod in her head.

Jamestown Beach Campsites, 2217 Jamestown Rd. (☎229-7609), immediately adjacent to the Jamestown Settlement. One of the largest campgrounds in the area. Frolic by the pool and waterslide or splash around in the more natural James River. Don't disturb the peace; quiet hours (11pm-8am) are strictly enforced. Sites $18, with water and electricity $23, full hookup $25. Six person maximum at each campsite.

FOOD

Instead of rowdy farmers and proper colonists, most of the authentic-looking "taverns" in Colonial Williamsburg are packed with sweaty tourists and are subsequently overpriced (lunch $5-10, dinner $18 and up). Jumping back into the 21st century for food proves the most price-savvy option.

🍴 **Chowning's Tavern** (☎220-7012), on Duke of Gloucester St. within the grounds of Colonial Williamsburg. Don your tri-cornered hat and let the wenches fulfill your every need. Odd dishes like "Bubble and Squeak" (cabbage and potatoes $5) and "Welsh Rarebit" (bread in beer sauce with ham, $7) will have you chowing like George Washington. After 9pm, peanuts are at stake as patrons roll the dice against their servers. The merriment continues as costumed waiters sing 18th-century ballads and challenge guests to card games over light meals ($3-7). Cover $3. Open daily 8am-midnight.

🍴 **Giuseppe's,** 5601 Richmond Rd. (☎565-1977), in Ewell Station shopping center on Rte. 60, about 2½ mi. from the historic district. Personable owner Joseph (that's Giuseppe in Italian) welcomes diners with a sterling sense of humor and a wine list that would impress the most refined connoisseur. 8 pasta dishes for under $6 and an untraditional menu with fusion entrees like the Fettucine New Mexico (pasta with black beans and Monterey jack cheese; $5.25). Open M-Sa 11:30am-2pm and 5-9pm.

Green Leafe Cafe, 765 Scotland St. (☎220-3405). Resembling a church with a wooden interior and stained glass windows, this classy restaurant spins a modern twist on pub food and great beer. William and Mary students and locals attest that the substantial sandwiches ($5-6) like the pan-fried pumpernickel make a great light supper. Thirty brews on tap ($2.75-4), including savory Virginia micros. Su "Mug Night" brings half-price beer. Open daily 11am-2am.

The Cheese Shop, 424 Prince George St. (☎220-0298 or (800) 468-4049). On weekdays, tourists overflow out the doors at this gourmet shop and deli. The local Virginia ham sandwich ($4) is balanced with the international flavor of the Braunschweiger ($3.75). Desserts like the asparagus tart ($2.75) are worth the wait. Outdoor seating only. Open M-Sa 10am-6pm, Su 11am-5pm.

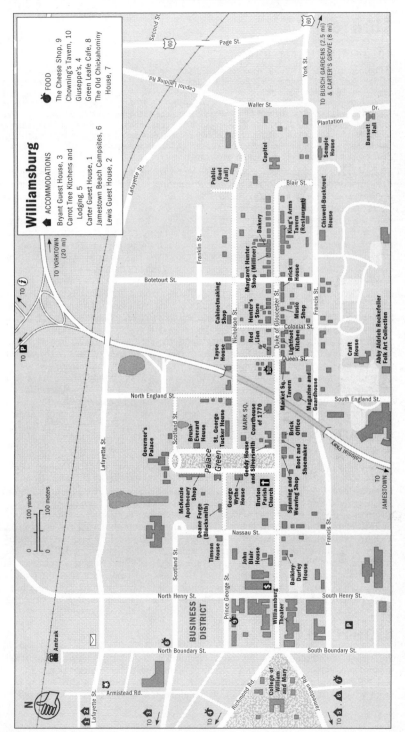

Williamsburg

ACCOMMODATIONS

Bryant Guest House, 3
Carrot Tree Kitchens and
  Lodging, 5
Carter Guest House, 1
Jamestown Beach Campsites, 6
Lewis Guest House, 2

FOOD

The Cheese Shop, 9
Chowning's Tavern, 10
Giuseppe's, 4
Green Leafe Cafe, 8
The Old Chickahominy
  House, 7

0   100 yards
0   100 meters

N

TO YORKTOWN
(20 mi)

TO BUSCH GARDENS (2.5 mi)
& CARTER'S GROVE (8 mi)

Second St.

Page St.

Capitol Landing Rd.

York St.

Waller St.

Plantation Dr.

Bassett Hall

Lafayette St.

Public Gaol (Jail)

Capitol

Semple House

Blair St.

Bakery

King's Arms Tavern (Restaurant)

Chiswell-Bucktrout House

Franklin St.

Botetourt St.

Margaret Hunter Shop (Milliner)

Hunter's Store

Brick House

Francis St.

Cabinetmaking Shop

Red Lion

Duke of Gloucester St.

Music Shop

Colonial St.

Nicholson St.

Tayoe House

Lightfoot Kitchen

Craft House

Queen St.

Abby Aldrich Rockefeller Folk Art Collection

North England St.

Market Sq. Tavern

South England St.

Magazine and Guardhouse

Governor's Palace

Scotland St.

Brush-Everard House

St. George Tucker House

MARK SQ.

Colonial Pkwy.

Courthouse of 1770

Brick Office

Palace Green

Geddy House and Silversmith

Boot and Shoemaker

TO JAMESTOWN

McKenzie Apothecary Shop

George Wythe House

Bruton Parish Church

Spinning and Weaving Shop

Lafayette St.

Deane Forge (Blacksmith)

Nassau St.

Francis St.

Timson House

John Blair House

Scotland St.

Balkley Durfey House

Prince George St.

Williamsburg Theater

North Henry St.

South Henry St.

BUSINESS DISTRICT

Amtrak

North Boundary St.

South Boundary St.

Armistead Rd.

College of William and Mary

Richmond Rd.

Jamestown Rd.

TO 3

TO 4

TO 5, 6

SIGHTS

COLONIAL WILLIAMSBURG

🛈 *Contact:* ☎ *(800) 447-8679; www.colonialwilliamsburg.org.* **Hours:** *Visitors Center open daily 8:30am-8pm. Most sights open 9:30am-5pm; for complete hours see the Visitor's Companion newsletter.* **Admission:** *Basic admission ticket includes all exhibition buildings and trade sites plus the Orientation Walk and 2 museums; day pass $30, ages 6-12 $18, under 6 free; 2 consecutive days $35, ages 6-12 $18, under 6 free. Individual museums $10, ages 6-12 $6.50. Governor's Palace only $18, ages 6-12 $11. Disability discount 50%.* **Accessibility:** *The grounds are handicapped accessible. Tickets available at any of the visitors centers.* **Events:** *A free "Grand Illumination" festival in early Dec. signals the start of the season and draws thousands. The 4th of July festival includes fireworks, parades, and special programs.*

Every day is a historical reenactment at Colonial Williamsburg—you will be spending 1774 treasury notes and singing "my hat, it has three corners" while you dodge horse droppings all the way to the milliner's. Though the sight's administration prides itself on its authenticity, the pristine paint on the houses and dirtless garb on the "natives" gives the place more of an amusement park feeling. The sneaky but hardly revolutionary way to immerse in the colonists' world doesn't require a ticket—visitors can enjoy the gorgeous gardens, march behind the fife-and-drum corps, lock themselves in the stocks, use the rest room, and laugh at everyone wearing an admission tag without ever duking over a shilling. No ticket is necessary for interacting with the locals, the most entertaining way to learn at Williamsburg. Also open to the public is a colonial flea market where you can test your haggling skills or just peaceably buy a tri-cornered hat for $9. Two of the historic buildings—the **Wren Building** and the **Bruton Parish Church**—are free. The Visitor's Companion newsletter, printed on Mondays, lists free events and evening programs.

The real fun of Colonial Williamsburg is interacting hands-on with history. Trade shops afford a wonderful opportunity to learn from skilled artisans such as the carpenter, and slightly less-skilled workmen like the brickmaster, who may invite you to take off your shoes and join him in stomping on wet clay. Though only paying guests can enter the shops, passersby are welcome to watch from outside. Colonial denizens are quick to play up their antiquated world view (admitted Floridians are likely to be greeted with startled cries of "Spanish territory!").

COLLEGE OF WILLIAM & MARY

🛈 *Tours: M-F 10am and 2:30pm.* **Admission:** *Free.*

Spreading west from the corner of Richmond and Jamestown Rd., the College of William & Mary, founded in 1693, is the second-oldest college in the US (after Harvard) and has educated luminaries such as actress Glenn Close and Presidents Jefferson, Monroe, and Tyler. The Office of Admissions, located in Blow Hall, offers free tours throughout the year. The free self-guided walking tour contains a bit more history. On the campus, the gorgeous lawns and wildflowers encircling brick buildings clash with the concrete roads that cut everywhere. Old Campus dispels these paved nuisances as the lawn opens up and beckons romance with a delicate picket fence. The Sir Christopher Wren Building, a beautiful example of Wren's unique architectural style (though not designed by Wren himself) was built two years after the college received its charter and is the nation's oldest classroom building. Nearby, shops sprawl a hair's breadth from the historic district in **Merchant Square,** an overflow from Colonial Williamsburg filled with souvenirs and 18th-century trinkets.

NIGHTLIFE

Following true colonial tradition, most activity in Williamsburg comes to a halt when the sun goes down. Shell out more than a few shillings to be treated to one of Colonial Williamsburg's early evening programs, like "Spellbound," a storytelling program where young audiences listen with amazement to the recounted legends of

Colonial Williamsburg ($10, under 6 $7; daily 7pm and 8:30pm). Or, party with the colonists at **Chowning's Tavern** (see p. 236) as they dole out card tricks and witty retorts to the wenches flying around the rustic tables. More interesting than chilling, the **Haunted Williamsburg Ghost-watching Tour** (☎565-4821) recounts the lost souls of the town, including the final steps of Blackbeard and his crew (tours daily 8 and 8:45pm; $8, under 6 free; call before 5pm for reservations). The **Library Tavern,** 1330 Richmond Rd. (☎229-1012), turns literary greats into great subs. If you're feeling belligerent, rather than accosting the hospitable bartender, wrestle the Hemingway sandwich ($5.25) or, if you just can't seem to pinpoint the right order cite the Thesaurus ($5.25). After eating your academic calories, enjoy free pool, pizza ($3.25), and DJ-fueled dance (F-Sa; open daily 11am-2am). Away from the city, the **Music Theatre of Williamsburg,** 7575 Richmond Rd. (☎564-0200 or (888) 687-4220, box office open M-Sa 9am-10pm), offers summer performances of folksy music in the southern 'opry' style. Call for performance schedules.

NEAR WILLIAMSBURG

The **"Historic Triangle"** is a tri-cornered hat brimming with United States history. More authentic and less crowded than the Colonial Williamsburg empire, Jamestown and Yorktown show visitors where it all *really* began. **Jamestown,** founded in 1607 as the first permanent English settlement in the New World, eventually failed as a settlement but left a democratic legacy after the election of the first representative legislature in 1619. Twenty miles to the east, **Yorktown** sprang up in 1691. Ninety years later, George Washington and his persistent rebels officially defeated the British in Yorktown. Williamsburg's central location allows easy access to its counterparts on the James River by way of the shaded, rock-paved, and richly green **Colonial Parkway,** which runs from Williamsburg to both Jamestown and Yorktown. Further down the **James River,** Southern culture dominates at 19th-century plantations. If history is beginning to wear on you, forget the forefathers for a day in lieu of beer, water slides, and loopy roller coasters at Anheuser-Busch's two theme parks, **Busch Gardens** and **Water Country, USA.** (Unless otherwise noted, all of the attractions have area code 757.)

BUSCH GARDENS AND ENVIRONS

BUSCH GARDENS

🚩 *Location: 3 mi. southeast of Williamsburg on Rte. 60. From Colonial Williamsburg, travel east on Francis St. which becomes Rte. 60. Continue for 3 mi. Busch Garden exit leads into park from the highway.* **Contact:** *☎253-3350; www.buschgardens.com.* **Hours:** *Late June-Aug. Su-F 10am-10pm, Sa 10am-11pm; Sept.-Oct. F-Su 10am-6pm, Sa-Su 10am-7pm; call for winter hrs.* **Admission:** *$37, seniors (55+ with ID) $34, ages 3-6 $26. After 5pm, admission $31, ages 3-6 $26. Parking $6. Rental strollers ($7) and wheelchairs ($9) available at entrance. 3-day ticket for both Busch Gardens and Water Country USA $60. Five-day Revolutionary Fun pass includes Busch Gardens, Water Country, Colonial Williamsburg, Yorktown, and Jamestown $120, ages 3-5 $104. Add a day before exiting park for $12. Min. 54 in. on some rides.*

Proceed with caution; an arduous journey fraught with dangerous dragons, monsters, and angry gods awaits the innocent tourist in "17th-Century Europe." Ward off rubber rats and magicians' spells in England by seeking refuge in the Globe theater. Run away to Italy only to be swept up in the Roman Rapids. Even the New World ravages the brave soul, for the Alps have been transplanted onto New France's (a.k.a. Canada's) soil and there's a blizzard a-brewing. All this, and a lot of lines, too. Espionage? Nope, just all in a day's work, or, rather, play at Busch Gardens. Naturally the bulk of amusements are geared towards children. For the 21+ crowd, indulge in a home-brewed Anheuser-Busch beer, but consume in moderation lest your stomach churn after a pulsating 70 mph scream on the **Apollo's Chariot** rollercoaster.

WATER COUNTRY, USA

🚩 *Location: 2mi. northeast of Busch Gardens. From Colonial Williamsburg take Rte. 60 east to the Rte. 199 east exit. and follow for a mile. The Water Country highway exit leads directly to the parking lot.* **Con-**

tact: ☎ 253-3350 or (800) 243-7946; www.watercountryusa.com. **Hours:** Late May to mid-June daily 10am-6pm; mid-June to late Aug. daily 10am-8pm; Sept. Sa-Su 10am-7pm. Hours vary; call ahead. **Admission:** $28, ages 3-6 $20.50. After 3pm $19 for all. 3-day ticket for both Busch Gardens and Water Country USA $60. **Parking:** $6. **Accessibility:** Limited handicapped access.

The wet companion to Busch Gardens, this 40-acre water park will soak you in waves of refreshing fun. Thirty-five water rides, slides, and attractions laced with a 1950s surfing theme keep barefooted waterbabies splashing with delight. Cram the gang onto a high-octane toboggan for **Meltdown,** the newest, fastest, and steepest water adventure in the park. The fiercer rides require a 42 in. height minimum, but for kiddies still waiting for their growth spurt, **H20 UFO** contains child-geared excitement.

JAMESTOWN

In 1607, the crew of 104 proper Englishmen chartered by the Virginia Company finally found their foothold on land that was supposedly golden. Chosen for settlement because of its deep river and naturally defensive position against the Spaniards, Jamestown was the first permanent English settlement in the American colonies and home to Capt. John Smith, the Englishman supposedly rescued by the Native American heroine **Pocahontas.** Any semblance of financial prosperity perished, along with many settlers, as disease and starvation crippled the new world forerunners. Neither silk farming nor glass-blowing proved profitable, and the town remained destitute until John Rolfe pioneered tobacco production. Jamestown thrived for 92 years as the state capital and home of the first representative assembly, but attacks by Native Americans, Bacon's Rebellion, and resource exhaustion led to the town's downfall. Today, visitors must make do with imagining Jamestown in its heyday, so, close your eyes, wander off into the wonderful world of make believe, and picture a pipe dream turned sour before being salvaged to jumpstart a nation.

JAMESTOWN SETTLEMENT

⚑ Location: Off Rte. 31, outside Colonial National Park. From Williamsburg, follow Jamestown Rd., which becomes Rte. 31 south. The settlement is approximately 3 mi. down on the left. **Contact:** ☎ 229-1607. **Hours:** Daily 9am-5pm. **Tours:** 1hr. tours 10am-3:30pm. **Admission:** $10.25, ages 6-12 $5. Combination ticket, including Yorktown Victory Center $14, ages 6-12 $6.75, under 6 free. Seniors 62+ discount 10%, AAA cardholders 10% discount. **Accessibility:** Ships are not wheelchair accessible.

Let the fifty proudly flying flags of each United State escort you into the Visitors Center, which springboards guests into a profoundly fascinating, diverse museum and numerous living-history displays. Exhibiting the influence of many peoples in the shaping of colonial America, the Jamestown Settlement incorporates Native Americans, Spaniards, Dutch, French, Irish, and English into a comprehensive and fun look at cultural history. The **Powhatan Indian Village** outside interactively teaches visitors the age old art of basket-weaving and explains why rubbing brains on animal skins kept them soft. By the dock, three boardable **ships,** replicas of the first vessels to land at Jamestown, are manned by enthusiastic Englishmen. In **James Fort,** visitors try on armor and marvel at the fort's minimalist approach to lodging and clothing. Equally captivating to kids and adults, the settlement is more extensive and authentic than Colonial Park or the Yorktown attractions.

COLONIAL NATIONAL PARK

⚑ Location: Southwest of Williamsburg on Rte. 31. Follow Jamestown Rd. and take a left at the Jamestown Settlement. The National Park is a mile beyond the settlement on the right. **Contact:** ☎ 229-1733. **Hours:** Park entrance open daily year round 9am-5pm; once you enter you are allowed to remain until dusk. Visitors Center closes 30min. before park entrance. Glasshouse open daily 9am-5pm. **Tours:** Two 35min. walking tours (free with site admission) describe life in Jamestown. **Admission:** $5, under 17 free; $7 joint pass includes other Jamestown and Yorktown sites. Both passes good for 7 days.

While waiting for a tour, pass the time by browsing through the Visitors Center of colonial artifacts, including armored suits and housewares. The movie is extremely outdated, so politically correct activists should take it with a grain of salt when the Native Americans are referred to as "redmen." For healthy portions of natural and historical beauty, a 45-minute audio tape ($2) narrates the 3- or 5-mile **Island Loop Route** through woodlands and marsh. If time doesn't allow for the jaunt, the drive over the isthmus to the island reveals excellent photo opportunities. In the remains of the settlement itself, archaeologists have uncovered the original site of the triangular **Jamestown Fort.** This ongoing dig has already unearthed over 300,000 artifacts, the pride and joy of which is the skeleton of an original settler who died of a gunshot wound to the leg. For those most intrigued by living history events, a spirited Bacon's Rebellion reenactment causes an uprising in September.

YORKTOWN

British troops led by General Charles Lord Cornwallis seized Yorktown for use as a port during the Revolutionary War in 1781. The British were left stranded, however, when 17,000 American and French infantry surrounded them while the French fleet blocked the British Navy's rescue attempt. The British surrender at Yorktown was a shock to the world and marked the end of the Revolutionary War.

COLONIAL NATIONAL PARK

🏴 *Location: From Williamsburg, simply follow the Colonial Parkway east, leading directly to Yorktown. Contact:* ☎ *898-3400. Hours: Visitors Center open daily 8:30am-5:30pm; in winter 9am-5pm; last tape rented at 3:30pm. Tours: 45min. walking tours every hour. Admission: $4, under 17 free, includes Nelson and Moore Houses. $7 joint pass to Jamestown and Yorktown Colonial National Park sites. Both passes good for 7 days. Accessibility: Handicapped accessible.*

The Yorktown branch of Colonial National Park vividly re-creates the battle of Yorktown with an engaging film, dioramas, and an electronic map diagramming the advances during the war. Pass through a British ship, check out George Washington's tents, or watch a 15-minute film before journeying into the historic siege site. While envisioning the decisive Revolutionary battle of yesteryear, be careful not to damage any historic relics; the sturdy fortifications and trenches that protected Washington have aged into fragile relics. Knowledgeable rangers entertain and educate visitors with non-firing artillery demonstrations every 2 hours. For those driving the 7 mi. Battlefield and 9 mi. Encampment Tour routes, the **Visitors Center** loans tape cassettes and players ($2).

YORKTOWN VICTORY CENTER

🏴 *Location: One block from Rte. 17 on Rte. 238. Follow the Colonial Parkway east; the Victory Center is right off the Parkway and very well marked. Contact:* ☎ *887-1776. Hours: Daily 9am-5pm. Admission: $7.75, seniors $6.50, ages 6-12 $3.75. Accessibility: Wheelchair accessible.*

Brush up on your high school history as you listen to the rallying cries of revolutionary figures like Benjamin Franklin and Patrick Henry foretelling the independence won at Yorktown. Audio narratives focus on the often overlooked perspectives of women, slaves, and Native Americans towards the war. Less interactive than Jamestown Settlement, the **Continental Encampment** and the **1780s Farm** are rather small and less informative than the other living history attractions.

JAMES RIVER PLANTATIONS

Built along the James River, America's first Main Street, the James River Plantations housed Virginia's slaveholding aristocracy. Exhibits focus on plantation life, tobacco farming, and slavery, and include beautiful, expansive grounds perfect for picnicking. The majority are widely dispersed off of Rte. 5 so plan accordingly.

CARTER'S GROVE PLANTATION

🏴 *Location: 6 mi. east of Williamsburg on Rte. 60. Contact:* ☎ *229-1000, ext. 2973. Hours: Plantation open May-Oct. Tu-Su 9am-5pm; Nov.-Dec. 9am-4pm. Museum and slave quarters open Mar.-Dec. Tu-Su 9am-5pm. Admission: $18, ages 6-12 $11.*

Exhibits on the grounds and in the outbuildings of the Carter's Grove Plantation emphasize the estate's 18th-century origins, while the main house itself focuses on the era of its last owners (before the Colonial Williamsburg Foundation bought them out in the 1940s). In true colonial Williamsburg fashion, costumed enthusiasts encourage guests to partake in plantation life on this 18th-century estate. The opulence of the plantation

the on dopedc

Wrapped in a Rabbitskin

The **Powhatan Indians,** the tribe Captain John Smith encountered first in the New World, held their oral traditions sacred. According to Powhatan legend, the **Great Hare Spirit** created the world. This swift rabbit allegedly created men and women and stored them in a bag until he could create nourishment for them. After crafting the water and the land and defeating the evil "Caniball [sic] Spirits," the Great Hare released the Powhatan people gently onto the earth, without the thundering noise of any Big Bang.

contrasts starkly with the poverty portrayed in the slave quarters, where costumed staff members lead eye-opening, interactive discussions and impromptu singing sessions. The little known **Winthrop Rockefeller Archaeological Museum,** built into a hillside, provides a fascinating look at household remains from **Wolstenholme Towne,** a British settlement and the first planned town in America.

BERKELEY PLANTATION

⋔ Location: Halfway between Richmond and Williamsburg on Rte. 5. From Colonial Williamsburg take Jamestown Rd. and follow signs west to Rte. 5 for approximately 40 mi. **Contact:** ☎(804) 829-6018. **Hours:** Daily 8am-5pm. **Admission:** $8.50, seniors $6.65, ages 13-16 $6.50, ages 6-12 $4, under 6 free. Grounds only $5, seniors $3.60, ages 6-16 $2.50, under 6 free. AAA and military 10% discount.

Touted as the most historical plantation on the James River, Berkeley Plantation witnessed the birth of short-term president **William Henry Harrison,** whose father, Benjamin, had repatented the plantation after it was abandoned in 1669. Historians trace the first "official" Thanksgiving dinner in 1619 and the first distilling of Bourbon whiskey in 1726 back to the gorgeous grounds of this still-occupied plantation. When Union soldiers camped on the plantation grounds in 1862, a somber youth composed the funereal bugle tune **"Taps,"** now military mourning mainstay. Yet, like the Shirley Plantation, the house is still occupied, and public access is restricted to the first floor.

SHIRLEY PLANTATION

⋔ Location: West of Berkeley on Rte. 5. **Contact:** ☎(800) 232-1613; www.shirleyplantation.com. **Hours:** House open daily 9am-5pm, grounds 9am-6pm; closed Jan.-Feb. M-F. **Admission:** $8.50, over 60 $7.50, ages 13-21 $5.50, ages 6-12 $4.50, under 6 free. AAA discount.

Surviving war after war in colonial times, this 1613 plantation has a gorgeous Queen Anne-style mansion unrivaled in beauty by other area estates. Unless you feel comfortable as an imposition on aristocrats, don't plan on penetrating the lavish walls of the brick mansion occupied by the 10th and 11th generations of the Hill-Carter family.

FREDERICKSBURG ☎540

Sometimes popularity really hurts. Smack dab between the Union Capital at Washington, D.C., and the Confederate capital at Richmond, a foothold in Fredericksburg during the Civil War meant control of the road between the capitals and, thus, a distinct military advantage. As a result, Fredericksburg experienced merciless amounts of bloodshed as men battled for control of the city. Years before the battle of Fredericksburg shattered the silent landscape with gunshots, the colonial post was already established as an important tobacco port on the banks of the Rappahanock River. George Washington so loved his Fredericksburg childhood that he erected a retirement mansion for his mother among the tree-lined, cobblestone streets. After the Civil War dust cleared in 1865, Fredericksburg lay stained with carnage. The town has recovered, mixing gorgeous city plantations and somber battlefields with cafes and elegant boutiques.

ORIENTATION AND PRACTICAL INFORMATION

Fredericksburg's position on I-95 directly between Washington and Richmond makes it an easily accessible and pleasant destination en route to either capital. Exit 130A off I-95 and onto Rte. 3 accesses the city, which is divided into two parts by **Lafayette Boulevard.** South of Lafayette lie personal residences, while the **Historic Downtown** crams museums, historical sites, and chic cafes into a network of one-ways that is easily traversed by foot. **William Street** (Rte. 3) runs northeast over the Rappahanock River into Falmouth. One-way **Caroline Street** is the main historic and commercial route.

Trains: Amtrak, 200 Lafayette Blvd. (☎872-7245 or ☎(800) 872-7245), near Caroline St. Trains run twice daily as a stop on the long line from Maine to Florida. No ticket office. Must call for reservations. Virginia Railway Express (VRE), (☎(703) 684-1001 or (800) 743-3873) in the same building, makes several trips daily to Union Station in D.C. ($6.70) Station open M-F 7am-7pm.

Bus: Greyhound/Trailways, 1400 Jefferson Davis Hwy. (☎373-2103 or (800) 231-2222). Buses from: Washington, D.C. ($9.50, 70 min.), Baltimore ($22, 65min.), and Richmond ($12.50, 1hr).

Public Transportation: Fredericksburg Regional Transit, 1400 Jefferson Davis Hwy (☎372-1222). Extended bus service around the city with Caroline St. and Princess Anne St. as main thoroughfares. 25¢ per ride.

Car Rental: U-Save Auto Rental, 4724 Harrison Rd. (☎898-1569), rents to 21+. Open M-F 9am-6pm, Sa 9am-noon.

Taxi: Yellow Cab (☎371-7075), Virginia Cab Service (☎373-5111).

Visitor Information: Fredericksburg Visitor Center, 706 Caroline St. (☎373-1776 or ☎(800) 678-4748) at the corner of Charlotte St. Offers extensive free info on Historic Fredericksburg, including a walking tour, 3, 9, and 20 mi. bike tours, maps, and a 14min. orientation video about the town. Free parking pass and *Fredericksburg, Spotsylvania & Stafford Visitor Guide* available upon request. Assists in discount accommodation reservations. The center also sells a Hospitality Pass into 7 of the major sites ($19.75, ages 6-18 $7) and a Pick Four Pass for admission to 4 sites ($13.75, ages 6-18 $5.50). Open daily 9am-7pm; in winter 9am-5pm.

Emergency: 911.

Help Lines: HIV/AIDS: ☎371-7532. Rape Crisis: ☎371-1212. Open 24hr.

Post Office: (☎373-8860) Princess Anne St. between Charlotte St. and Lafayette Blvd.

ZIP Code: 22401.

ACCOMMODATIONS AND CAMPING

Chain motels rule the areas around Fredericksburg's Exits 118, 126, 130, and 133 off I-95, while historic B&Bs scattered near the Rappahannock River cost more than a few pence, colonially speaking. Snag a copy of the *Traveler Discount Guide* in fast-food chains such as **Denny's** for discount coupons, or get the coupons off the web at www.exitguide.com.

Econo Lodge, 7802 Plank Rd. (☎786-8374). Exit 130B off I-95 then left at 1st light. Forfeit colonial romance for the cheapest rates in Williamsburg. Desks, A/C, cable TV and rosy interiors. Free doughnuts, coffee, and juice. Singles $37, doubles $50; off-season singles $35, doubles $48.

Fredericksburg Colonial Inn, 1707 Princess Anne St. (☎371-5666). Ascend the grand staircase to encounter walls exquisitely decorated with Civil War nostalgia. TV, refrigerators, A/C, and antiques. Complimentary breakfast and papers. Singles and doubles $65, suites $90.

Selby House, 226 Princess Anne St. (☎373-7037), 4 blocks from the historic district. Fragrant Victorian bed and breakfast operated by a certified Civil War battlefield tour guide. Private bathrooms, A/C, and a lounge with cable TV. Complimentary full breakfast served on fine china daily in the sunlight-washed dining room and patio. Singles $75; double with canopy bed $85.

FOOD

Nearly every fast food and restaurant chain known to man accompanies the motel mania off Exits 130A and 130B. Supermarkets thrive along the same strip, including **Ukrops,** 4250 Plank Rd. (☎785-2626). The locals head to **Caroline Street** for a barrage of healthy options and less congested dining.

☒ **Sammy T's,** 801 Caroline St. (☎371-2008), a block from the Visitors Center. Formerly the Fredericksburg post office, Sammy T's delivers a comprehensive menu (chicken parmesan $8.50; vegan sandwich $7). Those of age can wash down their meal with a bottle from an impressive selection of imports. Open M-Sa 11am-10pm, Su 11am-9pm.

☒ **La Familia Castiglia's,** 324 William St. (☎373-6650). The effervescent staff of family greet customers with wide grins. Indulge in veal marsala ($10) but not before a seafood start with *zuppa di cozze antipasti* (fresh mussels in wine sauce $6.50). Open M-Sa 11am-10pm, Su 11am-9pm.

Goolrick's Pharmacy, 901 Caroline St. (☎373-3411). While prescriptions are being filled in the back, patrons climb baby blue barstools to chow on cheap chicken salad ($2.50) in this time warp to the '50s. Thick milkshakes ($3) and freshly squeezed lemonade ($1) refresh on steamy summer days. Open M-F 8:30am-7pm, Sa 8:30am-6pm.

SIGHTS

Mansions, medicine, and Monroe (James, not Marilyn) take center stage in Fredericksburg's **Historic District.** Restored in a miraculously untacky manner, the town relishes its revolutionary and antebellum history without banning modern influence. Pick up a **walking tour** guide at the Visitors Center for routes to the sights.

KENMORE PLANTATION

🛈 Location: 1201 Washington Ave. **Contact:** ☎373-4255. **Hours:** Mar.-Dec. M-Sa 10am-5pm, Su noon-4pm. **Admission:** $6, children 6-17 $3, AAA and military $5. Grounds free. **Tours:** All day.

If beauty truly lies within, then the Kenmore Plantation radiates like golden sunlight. Built in 1775 for Fielding Lewis and his wife, George Washington's sister Betty, the mansion quietly resides four blocks to the north of town among 20th-century homes and paved streets. Tea and gingerbread await guests in the gift shop.

MARY WASHINGTON HOUSE

🛈 Location: 1200 Charles St. **Contact:** ☎373-1569. **Hours:** Mar.-Nov. daily 9am-5pm, Dec.-Feb. 10am-4pm. **Admission:** $4, ages 6-18 $1.50, AAA $3. **Tours:** All day.

Since George was a bit busy founding a nation, he wanted his aging mother to be nearby the care of sister Betty. The result is the Mary Washington House, which George ordered built for dear old Ma. Tours are packed with trinkets from 18th-century life.

HUGH MERCER APOTHECARY SHOP

🛈 Location: 1020 Caroline St. **Contact:** ☎373-3362. **Hours:** daily Mar.-Nov. 9am-5pm; Dec.-Feb. 10am-4pm. **Admission:** $4, ages 6-18 $1.50 **Tours:** All day.

As live leeches squirm in a bottle, listen to the doctor's graphic presentation on colonial medicine. Take special care to keep your lunch down during the primitive and painful descriptions of amputations and tooth pullings. Cringe at the sights and sounds of archaic operations while you thank the heavens for modern medicine.

JAMES MONROE MUSEUM

🛈 Location: 908 Charles St. **Contact:** ☎654-1043. **Hours:** daily Mar.-Oct. 9am-5pm; Nov.-Feb. 10am-4pm. **Admission:** $4, seniors and AAA $3.20, children $1. **Accessibility:** Handicapped accessible.

Personal letters uncovered 100 years after his death inspired the Monroe family to found the museum. Originally James' law office, this repository of memorabilia filled with Parisian-purchased, Louis XVI-influenced furniture includes the desk at which Monroe drafted his famous doctrine.

ENTERTAINMENT AND NIGHTLIFE

In the olden times, sundown meant bedtime. Well, not much has changed in Fredericksburg. Though flanked by **Mary Washington College** on the north, the town and its students usually quiet down when the tourists retire to their lodgings. The town does have a few postprandial pleasures. The **Colonial Theatre,** 907 Caroline St. (contact visitor's center at ☎(800) 678-4748), showcases symphonic performances and the occasional play. At the **Klein Theater** (☎654-1124), College Ave. and Thornton Ave., the **Fredericksburg Theatre Co.** performs in the summer ($13-15; performances W-Sa 8pm, Su 2pm).

Orbits, 406 Lafayette Blvd. (☎371-2003). Predominantly folk music attracts a local crowd among trendy, purple walls. Roaming rastafarians jam to a monthly reggae performance. Intercontinental alliance of pesto nachos ($5.50). Drafts $3. Cover $5 weekends. Open M-Th 11:30am-10pm, F-Sa 11:30am-2am, Su 11:30am-4pm.

The Underground, 106 George St. (☎371-9500), in the basement of George St. Grill. This club takes its name literally with its dark basement location and alternative rock players. Brews ($2.75). Open F-Sa. Opening hrs. vary with shows; call ahead.

Santa Fe Grille and Saloon, 216 William St. (☎371-0500). The theme screams salsa for the time being but will soon be transformed into a New Orleans Cajun fest. Graffiti is encouraged as patrons tag the walls with their drunken wisdoms. Open Su-Th 11am-2pm, F-Sa 11:30am-2pm.

NEAR FREDERICKSBURG

FREDERICKSBURG AND SPOTSYLVANIA NATIONAL BATTLEFIELD PARKS

🆘 *Location: Visitors Center at 1013 Lafayette Blvd. Contact: ☎373-6122. Hours: Daily 8:30am-6:30pm; in winter 9am-5pm. Tours: Six rotating tours offered by rangers highlight different features of the battlefield. Admission: $3, under 17 free; tickets valid for 7 days at all 4 parks including Chatham.*

What today is a vast and serene green expanses, witnessed bloody decimation between December 1862 and May 1864. Under the leadership of Confederate generals Robert E. Lee and "Stonewall" Jackson and Union Generals Ambrose E. Burnside, Joseph Hooker, and Ulysses S. Grant, four devastating Civil War battles were contested in the 20 mi. that surround the town. Today, a 76 mi. driving tour winds through the battlefields of **Fredericksburg, Chancellorsville** (from Fredericksburg use Rte. 3 West), the **Wilderness** (from Chancellorsville continue on Rte. 3 West to Wilderness), and **Spotsylvania** (accessed by Rte. 613 South from Wilderness), paying homage to the many soldiers who risked their lives for the Confederate stripes.

An essential first stop is the **Visitors Center,** which offers maps, walking tours, a 12 minute orientation film, and some artistic soldiers' portrayals of Civil War bloodshed. A similar Visitors Center at Chancellorsville, about 15mi. west of the historic district, offers summertime guided tours at varying hours. Both Wilderness and Spotsylvania lack a Visitors Center but maintain history shelters where park rangers are available for questions daily 9am to 5pm. Pull over to find several historical and scenic walking trails to the heart of the battlefields. Two walking tours, the **Sunken Road Walking Tour** following the entrenchment line at Fredericksburg, the **Chancellorsville History Trail,** and the **Spotsylvania History Trail,** encircle the battlefields and provide strategic viewpoints of all major sights of battle, including the Bloody Angle at Spotsylvania. A captivating and comprehensive journey into the Civil War, the battlefields inspire everyone to be a history buff for at least a day.

Planning Your Trip

Make no little plans, for they have no power to stir men's minds.
—Daniel Burnham, designer of Union Station (1899)

DOCUMENTS AND FORMALITIES

US CONSULAR SERVICES ABROAD

Contact your nearest embassy or consulate to obtain info regarding visas and passports to the United States. If your country is not listed here, try visiting **www.embassyworld.com** for a complete, updated list of consulates.

AUSTRALIA
Embassy: Moonah Pl., **Canberra,** ACT 2600 (☎(02) 6214 5600; fax 6214 5970,www.usis-australia.gov/embassy/). **Consulates:** MLC Centre, 19-29 Martin Pl., 59th fl., **Sydney** NSW 2000 (☎(02) 9373 9200; fax 9373 9125); 553 St. Kilda Rd., P.O. Box 6722, **Melbourne,** VIC 3004 (☎(03) 9625 1583; fax 9510 4646); 16 St. George's Terr., 13th fl., **Perth,** WA 6000 (☎(08) 9231 9400; fax 9231 9444).

CANADA
Embassy: 100 Wellington St., **Ottawa,** ON K1P 5T1 (☎(613) 238-5335 or ☎(238) 4470; fax 238-5720, www.usembassycanada.gov). **Consulates:** 615 Macleod Trail #1050, S.E., **Calgary,** AB T2G 4T8, (☎(403) 266-8962; fax 264-6630); Cogswell Tower #910, Scotia Sq., **Halifax,** NS, B3J 3K1, (☎(902) 429-2480; fax 423-6861); P.O. Box 65, Postal Station Desjardins, **Montréal,** QC H5B 1G1 (☎(514) 398-9695; fax 398-0973); 2 Place Terrasse Dufferin, C.P. 939, **Québec,**

QC, G1R 4T9 (☎(418) 692-2095; fax 692-4640); 360 University Ave., **Toronto,** ON, M5G 1S4 (☎(416) 595-1700; fax 595-0051); 1095 West Pender St., **Vancouver,** BC V6E 2M6 (☎(604) 685-4311; fax 685-5285).

IRELAND

Embassy: 42 Elgin Rd., Ballsbridge, **Dublin** 4 (☎(01) 668 8777; fax 668 9946, www.usembassy.ie). **Consulate:** Queen's House, 14 Queen St., **Belfast,** N. Ireland BT1 6EQ, PSC 801, Box 40, APO AE 09498-4040 (☎(01232) 328239; fax 224 8482)

NEW ZEALAND

Embassy: 29 Fitzherbert Terr., Thorndon, **Wellington** (☎(04) 472 2068; fax 472 3537, http://usembassy.state.gov/wellington). **Consulates:** Yorkshire General Bldg., 4th fl., 29 Shortland St., **Auckland** (☎(09) 303 2724; fax 366 0870); Price Waterhouse Ctr., 109 Armagh St., 11th fl., **Christchurch** (☎(03) 379 0040; fax 379 5677).

SOUTH AFRICA

Embassy: 877 Pretorius St., Arcadia 0083, P.O. Box 9536 Pretoria 0001 (☎(012) 342 1048; fax 342 2244, http://usembassy.state.gov/pretoria). **Consulates:** Broadway Industries Centre, P.O. Box 6773, Heerengracht, Foreshore, **Cape Town** (☎(021) 214 280; fax 211 130); Durban Bay House, 333 Smith St., 29th fl., **Durban** (☎(031) 304 4737; fax 301 8206); 1 River St. c/o Riviera, Killarney, **Johannesburg** (☎(011) 646 6900; fax 646 6913).

UNITED KINGDOM

Embassy: 24/31 Grosvenor Sq., **London** W1A 1AE (☎(020) 499 9000; fax 495 5012, www.usembassy.org.uk). **Consulate:** 3 Regent Terr., **Edinburgh,** Scotland EH7 5BW, PSC 801 Box 40, FPO AE 90498-4040 (☎(0131) 556 8315; fax 557 6023).

FOREIGN EMBASSIES IN D.C.

Australia, 1601 Massachusetts Ave., 20036; (☎797-3000; fax 797-3168). **Canada,** 501 Pennsylvania Ave., 20001; (☎682-1740; fax 682-7726). **Ireland,** 2234 Mass. Ave., 20008, (☎462-3939; fax 232-5993). **New Zealand,** 37 Observatory Circle, 20008; (☎328-4800; fax 667-5227). **South Africa,** 3051 Mass. Ave., 20008; (☎232-4400; fax 265-1607). **UK,** 3100 Mass. Ave., 20008, (☎588-6500; fax 588-7870).

PASSPORTS

REQUIREMENTS

All foreign visitors except Canadians need valid passports to enter the United States, and to re-enter their own country. Returning home with an expired passport is illegal, and may result in a fine. Canadians need to demonstrate proof of Canadian citizenship, such as a citizenship card with photo ID. The US does not allow entrance if the holder's passport expires in under six months; returning home with an expired passport is often illegal, and may result in a fine.

PHOTOCOPIES

Be sure to photocopy the page of your passport with your photo, passport number, and other identifying information, as well as any visas, travel insurance policies, plane tickets, or traveler's check serial numbers. Carry one set of copies in a safe place, apart from the originals, and leave another set at home. Consulates also recommend that you carry an expired passport or an official copy of your birth certificate in a part of your baggage separate from other documents.

LOST PASSPORTS

If you lose your passport, immediately notify the local police and the nearest embassy or consulate of your home government. To expedite its replacement, you will need to know all information previously recorded and show ID and proof of citizenship. In some cases, a replacement may take weeks to process, and it may be valid only for a limited time. Any visas stamped in your old passport will be irretrievably lost. In an emergency, ask for immediate temporary traveling papers that will permit you to re-enter your home country. Your passport is a public document belonging to your nation's government. You may have to surrender it to a US government official, but if you don't get it back in a reasonable amount of time, inform the nearest mission of your home country.

NEW PASSPORTS

File any new passport or renewal applications well in advance of your departure date. Most passport offices offer rush services for a steep fee. Citizens living abroad who need a passport or renewal should contact the nearest consular service of their home country.

Australia Citizens must apply for a passport in person at a post office, a passport office, or an Australian diplomatic mission overseas. Passport offices are located in Adelaide, Brisbane, Canberra, Darwin, Hobart, Melbourne, Newcastle, Perth, and Sydney. New adult passports cost A$128 (for a 32-page passport) or A$192 (64-page), and a child's is A$64 (32-page) or A$96 (64-page). Adult passports are valid for 10 years and child passports for 5 years. For more info, call toll-free (in Australia) 13 12 32, or visit www.dfat.gov.au/passports.

Canada Citizens may cross the US border with proof of citizenship.

Ireland Citizens can apply for a passport by mail to either the Department of Foreign Affairs, Passport Office, Setanta Centre, Molesworth St., Dublin 2 (☎(01) 671 16 33; fax 671 1092; www.irlgov.ie/iveagh), or the Passport Office, Irish Life Building, 1A South Mall, Cork (☎(021) 27 25 25). Obtain an application at a local Garda station or post office, or request one from a passport office. 32-page passports cost IR£45 and are valid for 10 years. 48-page passports cost IR£55. Citizens under 18 or over 65 can request a 3-year passport (IR£10).

New Zealand Application forms for passports are available in New Zealand from most travel agents. Applications may be forwarded to the Passport Office, P.O. Box 10526, Wellington, New Zealand (☎0800 22 50 50 or 4 474 8100; fax 4 474 8010; www.passport.govt.nz). Standard processing time in New Zealand is 10 working days for correct applications. The fees are adult NZ$80, and child NZ$40. Children's names can no longer be endorsed on a parent's passport—they must apply for their own, which are valid for up to 5 years. An adult's passport is valid for up to 10 years.

South Africa South African passports are issued only in Pretoria. However, all applications must still be submitted or forwarded to the applicable office of a South African consulate. Tourist passports, valid for 10 years, cost around ZAR165. Children under 16 must be issued their own passports, valid for 5 years, which cost around ZAR120. Time for the completion of an application is normally 3 months or more from the time of submission. For further information, contact the nearest Department of Home Affairs Office (http://usaembassy.southafrica.net/VisaForms/Passport/Passport2000.html).

ESSENTIAL INFORMATION

ENTRANCE REQUIREMENTS

Passport (see p. 248). Required for all visitors to the US.

Visa In general a visa is required for visiting the US, but it can be waived. (See p. 250 for more specific information.)

Work Permit (see p. 250). Required for all foreigners planning to work in the US.

Driving Permit (see p. 250) Required for all those planning to drive.

United Kingdom Full passports are valid for 10 years (5 years if under 16). Application forms are available at passport offices, main post offices, travel agents, and online (www.ukpa.gov.uk/ forms/f_app_pack.htm). Apply by mail or in person to one of the passport offices, located in London, Liverpool, Newport, Peterborough, Glasgow, or Belfast. The fee is UK£28, UK£14.80 for children under 16. The process takes about four weeks, but the London office offers a five-day, walk-in rush service; arrive early. The UK Passport Agency can be reached at ☎(0870) 521 04 10.

VISAS AND WORK PERMITS

As of August 2000, citizens of **South Africa** and most other countries need a visa—a stamp, sticker, or insert in your passport specifying the purpose of your travel and the permitted duration of your stay—in addition to a valid passport for entrance to the US. To obtain a visa, contact a US embassy or consulate.

VISITS OF UNDER 90 DAYS

Citizens of Andorra, Argentina, Australia, Austria, Belgium, Brunei, Denmark, Finland, France, Germany, Iceland, Ireland, Italy, Japan, Liechtenstein, Luxembourg, Monaco, the Netherlands, New Zealand, Norway, Portugal, San Marino, Singapore, Slovenia, Spain, Sweden, Switzerland, the United Kingdom and Uruguay can waive US visas through the **Visa Waiver Pilot Program.** Visitors qualify if they are traveling only for business or pleasure (*not* work or study), are staying for fewer than 90 days, have proof of intent to leave (e.g., a return plane ticket), an I-94W form (arrival/ departure certificate attached to your visa upon arrival), and are traveling on particular air or sea carriers.

VISITS OF OVER 90 DAYS

All travelers planning a stay of more than 90 days (180 days for Canadians) also need to obtain a visa. The **Center for International Business and Travel (CIBT),** 23201 New Mexico Ave. NW #210, Washington, D.C. 20016 (☎244-9500 or (800) 925-2428), secures travel "pleasure tourist," or **B-2** visas to and from all possible countries for a variable service charge (6-month visa around $45). If you lose your I-94 form, you can replace it at the nearest **Immigration and Naturalization Service (INS)** office (☎(800) 375-5283; www.ins.usdoj.gov), although it's unlikely that it will be replaced during your stay. **Visa extensions** are sometimes attainable with a completed I-539 form; call the forms request line (☎(800) 870-3676). HIV-positive individuals are not permitted to enter the US.

Be sure to double-check on entrance requirements at the nearest US embassy or consulate, or consult the **Bureau of Consular Affairs** Web Page (http://travel.state.gov/ visa;visitors.html).

IDENTIFICATION

When you travel, always carry two or more forms of identification on your person, including at least one photo ID. A passport combined with a driver's license or birth certificate usually serves as adequate proof of your identity and citizenship. Many establishments, especially banks, require several IDs before cashing traveler's checks. Never carry all your forms of ID together. It is useful to carry extra passport-size photos to affix to the various IDs or railpasses you may acquire.

DRIVER'S LICENSE

A foreign driver's license is usually acceptable for driving in the United States and Canada for a temporary period. To rent a car and to avoid the incredulousness of a disgruntled Southern sheriff, purchase an **International Driving Permit** from a certified agent, such as the AA in the UK (☎0990 500 600; www.theaa.com). A driver's license without an attached photo will seldom be accepted.

STUDENT AND TEACHER IDENTIFICATION

While less widely recognized in the US than in Europe, the **International Student Identity Card (ISIC)** is still the most widely accepted form of student identification. Flashing this card can often procure you discounts for sights, theaters, museums, transportation, and other services. You must present an ISIC card to purchase reduced-rate student fare airplane tickets. Cardholders have access to a toll-free 24hr. ISIC helpline whose multilingual staff can provide assistance in medical, legal, and financial emergencies overseas (☎877-370-ISIC in the US and Canada; elsewhere call collect ☎715-345-0505).

Many student travel agencies around the world issue ISICs, including STA Travel in Australia and New Zealand; Travel CUTS in Canada; USIT in Ireland and Northern Ireland; SASTS in South Africa; Campus Travel and STA Travel in the UK; Council Travel, STA Travel, and via the web (www.counciltravel.com/idcards/default.asp) in the US (see p.32). When you apply for the card, request a copy of the *International Student Identity Card Handbook*, which lists some of the available discounts in the US and Canada. You can also write to Council for a copy. The card is valid from September of one year to December of the following year and costs AU$15, CDN$15, or $22. Applicants must be at least 12 years old and degree-seeking students of a secondary or post-secondary school. Because of the proliferation of phony ISICs, many airlines and some other services require additional proof of student identity, such as a signed letter from the registrar attesting to your student status that is stamped with the school seal or your school ID card. The **International Teacher Identity Card (ITIC)** offers similar but limited discounts. The fee is A$13, UK£5, or $22. For more info on these cards, contact the **International Student Travel Confederation (ISTC),** Herengracht 479, 1017 BS Amsterdam, Netherlands (from abroad call 31 20 421 28 00; fax 421 28 10; email istcinfo@istc.org; www.istc.org).

YOUTH IDENTIFICATION

The International Student Travel Confederation also issues a discount card to travelers who are 26 years old or younger, but not students. This one-year card, known as the International Youth Travel Card (IYTC) and formerly as the GO25, offers many of the same benefits as the ISIC, and most organizations that sell the ISIC also sell the IYTC. To apply, you will need either a passport, valid driver's license, or copy of a birth certificate, and a passport-sized photo with your name printed on the back. The fee is $22.

CUSTOMS

Upon entering the United States, you must declare certain items from abroad and pay a duty on the value of those articles that exceed the allowance established by the US customs service. Keeping receipts for purchases made abroad will help establish values when you return. It is wise to make a list,

ESSENTIAL INFORMATION

CUSTOMS RESOURCES

Australia

Australian Customs National Information Line (in Australia call (01) 30 03 63, from elsewhere call +61 (2) 6275 6666; www.customs.gov.au).

Canada

Canadian Customs, 2265 St. Laurent Blvd., Ottawa, ON K1G 4K3 (☎(800) 461-9999 (24hr.) or (613) 993-0534; www.revcan.ca).

Ireland

Customs Information Office, Irish Life Centre, Lower Abbey St., Dublin 1 (☎(01) 878 8811; fax 878 0836; taxes@revenue.iol.ie; www.revenue.ie/customs.htm).

New Zealand

New Zealand Customhouse, 17-21 Whitmore St., Box 2218, Wellington (☎(04) 473 6099; fax 473 7370; www.customs.govt.nz).

South Africa

Commissioner for Customs and Excise, Privat Bag X47, Pretoria 0001 (☎(012) 314 9911; fax 328 6478; www.gov.za).

United Kingdom

Her Majesty's Customs and Excise, Passenger Enquiry Team, Wayfarer House, Great South West Road, Feltham, Middlesex TW14 8NP (☎(020) 8910 3744; www.hmce.gov.uk).

including serial numbers, of any valuables that you carry with you from home; if you register this list with customs before your departure and have an official stamp it, you will avoid import duty charges and ensure an easy passage upon your return. Be especially careful to document items manufactured abroad, and don't try to bring perishable food over the border.

Upon returning home, you must declare all articles acquired abroad and pay a **duty** on the value of articles that exceed the allowance established by your country's customs service. Goods and gifts purchased at **duty-free** shops abroad are not exempt from duty or sales tax at your point of return; you must declare these items as well. "Duty-free" merely means that you need not pay a tax in the country of purchase.

MONEY

Accommodations in D.C. start at about $22 per night in a hostel bed, while a basic sit-down meal costs about $10 and up. If you stay in hostels and prepare your own food, you can spend anywhere from $32-60 per person per day. Transportation will increase these figures. Carrying cash around with you, even in a money belt, is risky (D.C. is the playground of many hungry pickpockets) and personal checks from another country, or even another state, will probably not be accepted no matter how many forms of identification you have (some banks even shy away from accepting checks).

CURRENCY AND EXCHANGE

The main unit of currency in the US is the **dollar,** which is divided into 100 **cents.** Paper money is green in the US; bills come in denominations of $1, $5, $10, $20, $50, and $100. Coins are 1¢ (penny), 5¢ (nickel), 10¢ (dime), and 25¢ (quarter). The currency chart below is based on published exchange rates from August 2000.

THE GREENBACK (THE US DOLLAR)

CDN$1=US$0.67	US$1=CDN$1.49
UK£1=US$1.62	US$1=UK£0.62
IR£1=US$1.37	US$1=IR£0.73
AUS$1=US$0.66	US$1=AUS$1.52
NZ$1=US$0.54	US$1=NZ$1.86
SAR1=US$0.16	US$1=SAR6.15

Watch out for commission rates and check newspapers for the standard rate of exchange. Up-to-date currency info can be found at websites such as http://finance.yahoo.com. Banks generally have the best rates. A good rule of thumb is only to go to banks or money-exchanging centers/bureaux de change that have at most a 5% margin between their buy and sell prices. Since you lose money with each transaction, convert in large sums. Also, using an ATM card or a credit card will often get you the best possible rates.

FINANCIAL SERVICES

BANKS

Many times, the best exchange rates for foreign currency are obtainable at the many banks scattered around D.C. If you are planning on staying in Washington for more than a month to study or work, you may wish to open a checking account in D.C. Many banks have different interest rates, service charges, and ATM policies; when shopping for a bank, don't forget to ask about their policies on traveler's checks, bank credit cards, and cash advances. For more info on banks in D.C., see **Living in D.C.,** p. 288.

AMERICAN EXPRESS

In D.C., American Express offices are located downtown at 1730 M St. NW Suite 206 (☎835-0603), and at 1150 Connecticut Ave. NW (☎457-1300). Call ☎(800) 528-4800 for locations in Virginia and Maryland suburbs.

TRAVELER'S CHECKS

Traveler's checks are one of the safest and least troublesome means of carrying funds, since they can be refunded if stolen. In the United States, traveler's checks are widely accepted in both rural and urban areas. Several agencies and banks sell them, usually for face value plus a small percentage commission. **American Express** and **Visa** are the most widely recognized. If you're ordering checks, do so well in advance, especially if you are requesting large sums.

In order to collect a **refund for lost or stolen checks,** keep your check receipts separate from your checks and store them in a safe place or with a traveling companion. Record check numbers when you cash them, leave a list of check numbers with someone at home, and ask for a list of refund centers when you buy your checks. Never countersign your checks until you are ready to cash them, and always bring your passport with you when you plan to use the checks.

American Express: ☎(800) 251 902 in Australia; in New Zealand ☎(0800) 441 068; in the UK ☎(0800) 52 13 13; in the US and Canada ☎(800) 221-7282. Elsewhere, call US collect +1 (801) 964-6665; www.aexp.com. American Express traveler's checks are available in US (but not Canadian) dollars. Checks can be purchased for a small fee (1-4%) at American Express Travel Service Offices, banks, and American Automobile Association offices. AAA members can buy the checks commission-free. American Express offices cash their checks commission-free (except where prohibited by national governments), but often at slightly worse rates than banks. *Cheques for Two* can be signed by either of two people traveling together.

Citicorp: Call (800) 645-6556 in the US and Canada; in Europe, the Middle East, or Africa, call the UK office at 44 020 7508 7007; from elsewhere, call US collect +1 (813) 623-1709. Traveler's checks in 7 currencies. Commission 1-2%. Guaranteed hand-delivery of traveler's checks when a refund location is not convenient. Call 24hr.

Thomas Cook MasterCard: From the US, Canada, or Caribbean call (800) 223-7373; from the UK call (0800) 622 101; from elsewhere, call (44) 1733 318 950 collect. Available in 13 currencies. Commission 2%. Offices cash checks commission-free.

Visa: Call (800) 227-6811 in the US; in the UK (0800) 895 078; from elsewhere, call 44 1733 318 949 and reverse the charges. Any of the above numbers can tell you the location of their nearest office.

CREDIT CARDS

Credit cards are generally accepted in all but the smallest businesses in D.C., and are sometimes expected or required at places like car-rental agencies. Major credit cards such as **MasterCard** and **Visa** can be used to extract cash advances in dollars from associated banks and teller machines throughout D.C. for wholesale (e.g. very good) exchange rates. **American Express** cards also work in some ATMs, as well as at AmEx offices and major airports. All such machines require a **Personal Identification Number (PIN).** You must ask your credit card company for a PIN before you leave; without it, you will be unable to withdraw cash with your credit card outside your home country. If you already have a PIN, make sure it will work in the US Credit cards often offer an array of other services, from insurance to emergency assistance; check with your company. **Visa** (☎(800) 336-8472), **MasterCard** (☎(800) 307-7309), **American Express** (☎(800) 843-2273), the **Discover Card** (☎(800) 347-2683; outside US, call +1 (801) 902-3100) are all popular and widely recognized cards in the US.

CASH CARDS

Cash cards—popularly called ATM (Automated Teller Machine) cards—are widespread throughout D.C. Depending on the system that your home bank uses, you can probably access your own personal bank account whenever you need money. ATMs get the same wholesale exchange rate as credit cards. Despite these perks, do some research before relying too heavily on automation. There is often a limit on the amount of money you can withdraw per day (usually about $200-500, depending on the type of card and account), and computer networks sometimes fail.

The two major international money networks are **Cirrus** (☎ (800) 424-7787) and **PLUS** (☎ (800) 843-7587). To locate ATMs around the world, use www.visa.com/pd/atm or www.mastercard.com/atm. A typical ATM transaction fee is $1 in the US

GETTING MONEY FROM HOME

AMERICAN EXPRESS

Cardholders can withdraw cash from their checking accounts at any of AmEx's major offices and many of its representatives' offices, up to $1000 every 21 days (no service charge, no interest). AmEx also offers Express Cash at any of their ATMs in the US Green card holders may withdraw up to $1000 in a seven day period. There is a 2% transaction fee for each cash withdrawal, with a $2.50 minimum/$20 maximum. To enroll in Express Cash, Card members may call (800) 227-4669 in the US; outside the US call collect +1 (336) 668-5041. The AmEx national number in the US is (800) 221-7282.

WESTERN UNION

Travelers from the US, Canada, and the UK can wire money abroad through Western Union's international money transfer services. In the US, call ☎ (800) 325-6000; in Canada, ☎ (800) 235-0000; in the UK, ☎ (0800) 833 833). To cable money within the US using a credit card (Visa, MasterCard, Discover), call ☎ (800) CALL-CASH (225-5227). The rates for sending cash are generally $10-11 cheaper than with a credit card, and the money is usually available at the place you're sending it to within an hour. To find the nearest Western Union location online, consult www.westernunion.com.

INSURANCE

Travel insurance generally covers four basic areas: medical/health problems, property loss, trip cancellation/interruption, and emergency evacuation. Although your regular insurance policies may well extend to travel-related accidents, you may consider purchasing travel insurance if the cost of potential trip cancellation/interruption is greater than you can absorb. Prices for travel insurance purchased separately generally run about $50 per week for full coverage, while trip cancellation/interruption may be purchased separately at a rate of about $5.50 per $100 of coverage.

Medical insurance (especially university policies) often covers costs incurred abroad. **Homeowners' insurance** (or your family's coverage) often covers theft during travel and loss of travel documents (passport, plane ticket, railpass, etc.) up to $500.

ISIC and **ITIC** provide basic insurance benefits, including $100 per day of in-hospital sickness for a maximum of 60 days, $3000 of accident-related medical reimbursement, and $25,000 for emergency medical transport (see **Identification**, p. 250). Cardholders have access to a toll-free 24-hour helpline whose multilingual staff can provide assistance in medical, legal, and financial emergencies overseas (☎ (877) 370-4742 in the US and Canada; elsewhere call the US collect +1 (713) 342-4104. **American Express** (☎ (800) 528-4800) grants most cardholders automatic car rental insurance (collision and theft, but not liability) and ground travel accident coverage of $100,000 on flight purchases made with the card.

INSURANCE PROVIDERS

Council and **STA** (see p. 258 for complete listings) offer plans that can supplement your basic insurance coverage. Other private insurance providers in the **US** include: **Access America** (☎(800) 284-8300); **Berkely Group/Carefree Travel Insurance** (☎(800) 323-3149 or ☎(516) 294-0220; email info@berkely.com); **Globalcare Travel Insurance** (☎(800) 821-2488); and **Travel Assistance International** (☎(800) 821-2828 or ☎(202) 828-5894; email wassist@aol.com). Providers in the **UK** include **Campus Travel** (☎(018) 6525 8000) and **Columbus Travel Insurance** (☎(020) 7375 0011). In **Australia** try **CIC Insurance** (☎(02) 9202 8000).

PACKING

Pack light: a good rule is to lay out only what you absolutely need, then take half the clothes and twice the money. The less you have, the less you have to lose (or store, or carry on your back). Don't forget the obvious things: no matter when you're traveling, it's always a good idea to bring a rain jacket (Gore-Tex is a miracle fabric that's both waterproof and breathable), a warm jacket or wool sweater, and sturdy shoes and thick socks. You may also want to add one outfit beyond the jeans and t-shirt uniform, a collared shirt and a nice pair of shoes if you have the room. Remember that wool will keep you warm even when soaked through; wet cotton is colder than wearing nothing at all.

BACKPACK. See p. 46 for information about different types of backpacks. Before you leave, pack your bag, strap it on, and imagine yourself walking uphill on hot asphalt for three hours; this should give you a sense of how important it is to pack lightly.

SUITCASE OR TRUNK. Hard-sided luggage is more durable but more weighty and cumbersome. Soft-sided luggage should have a PVC frame, a strong lining to resist bad weather and rough handling, and its seams should be triple-stitched for durability.

DAYPACK. In addition to your main vessel, a small backpack may be useful as a daypack for sight-seeing expeditions; it doubles as an airplane **carry-on.** An empty, lightweight **duffel bag** packed in your luggage may also be useful for dirty clothes or purchases.

SLEEPSACKS. Some youth hostels require that you have your own sleepsack or rent one of theirs. If you plan to stay in hostels you can avoid linen charges by making the requisite sleepsack yourself: fold a full size sheet in half the long way, then sew it closed along the open long side and one of the short sides. Sleepsacks can also be bought at any Hostelling International store.

WASHING CLOTHES. Laundromats are common in D.C., but it may be cheaper and easier to use a sink. Bring a small bar or tube of detergent soap, a small rubber ball to stop up the sink, and a travel clothesline.

CONVERTERS AND ADAPTERS. In the US, electricity is 110V. 220V electrical appliances don't like 110V current. Visit a hardware store for an adapter (which changes the shape of the plug) and a converter (which changes the voltage). Don't make the mistake of using only an adapter (unless appliance instructions explicitly state otherwise).

TOILETRIES. Toothbrushes, towels, cold-water soap, talcum powder (to keep feet dry), deodorant, razors, tampons, and condoms are readily available. **Contact lenses,** on the other hand, can be expensive, so bring enough extra pairs and solution. Machines which heat-disinfect contact lenses will require a small converter (about $20) to 110V; consider switching temporarily to a chemical disinfection system. Also bring your glasses and a copy of your prescription in case you need emergency replacements.

FILM. If you're not a serious photographer, you might want to consider bringing a **disposable camera** or two rather than an expensive permanent one. Despite disclaimers, airport security X-rays *can* fog film, so either buy a lead-lined pouch, sold at camera stores, or ask the security to hand inspect it. Always pack it in your carry-on luggage, since higher-intensity X-rays are used on checked luggage.

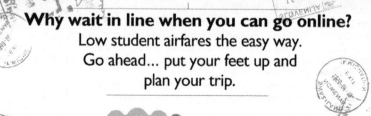

FIRST-AID KIT. No matter how you're traveling, it's always a good idea to carry a first-aid kit including bandages, aspirin or another pain killer, antibiotic cream, a thermometer, a Swiss army knife with tweezers, moleskin, decongestant for colds, motion sickness remedy, medicine for diarrhea or stomach problems (Pepto Bismol tablets or liquid and Immodium), sunscreen, insect repellent (you might want to get an extra-strength repellent if you plan on camping), burn ointment, and a syringe for emergency medical purposes (get a letter of explanation from your doctor).

OTHER USEFUL ITEMS. Other useful items include: an umbrella; sealable plastic bags (for damp clothes, soap, food, shampoo, and other spillables); alarm clock; waterproof matches; sun hat; needle and thread; safety pins; sunglasses; pocketknife; plastic water bottle; compass; rope (makeshift clothesline and lashing material); padlock; whistle; rubber bands; flashlight; earplugs; electrical tape (for patching tears); tweezers; garbage bags; a small calculator for currency conversion; a pair of flip-flops for the shower; a money-belt for carrying valuables; deodorant; and razors.

IMPORTANT DOCUMENTS. Don't forget your passport, traveler's checks, ATM and/or credit cards, and adequate ID (see p. 250). If you think you'll need it, bring along a hostelling membership card and driver's license.

GETTING THERE

BY PLANE

When it comes to airfare, a little effort can save you a bundle. If your plans are flexible enough to deal with the restrictions, courier fares are the cheapest. Tickets bought from consolidators and standby seating are also good deals, but last-minute specials, airfare wars, and charter flights often beat these fares. The key is to hunt around, to be flexible, and to persistently ask about discounts. Students, seniors, and those under 26 should never pay full price for a ticket. For information on Washington airports, see **Washington's Airports,** below.

DETAILS AND TIPS

Timing: Airfares to D.C. peak between mid-June and early September, and holidays are also expensive periods to travel. Midweek (M-Th morning) round-trip flights run $40-50 cheaper than weekend flights, but bargain weekend fares to D.C. can be had from many US cities. Return-date flexibility is usually not an option for the budget traveler; traveling with an "open return" ticket can be pricier than fixing a return date when buying the ticket and paying later to change it.

Fares: Round-trip fares from Western Europe to D.C. range from $100-400 (during the off-season) to $200-550 (during the summer); from Australia the cost ranges from $700-1000.

Commuter Shuttles from New York: If you are flying to Washington from New York's **La Guardia Airport,** the **Delta Shuttle,** and the **US Airways Shuttle** are a relatively inexpensive mode of transportation.

ESSENTIAL
INFORMATION

BUYING TICKETS BY INTERNET

The **Web** is a great place to look for **travel bargains**—it's fast, it's convenient, and you can spend as long as you like exploring options without driving your travel agent insane.

Many airline sites offer special last-minute deals on the Web. Other sites do the legwork and compile the deals for you—try **www.bestfares.com, www.onetravel.com, www.lowestfare.com,** and **www.travelzoo.com.**

STA
(www.sta-travel.com) and **Council**
(www.counciltravel.com) provide quotes on student tickets.

Expedia
(msn.expedia.com) and **Travelocity**
(www.travelocity.com) offer full travel services.

Priceline
(www.priceline.com) allows you to specify a price, and obligates you to buy any ticket that meets or beats it; be prepared for antisocial hours and odd routes.

Skyauction
(www.skyauction.com) allows you to bid on both last-minute and advance-purchase tickets.

Just one last note—to protect yourself, make sure that the site uses a secure server before handing over any credit card details. Happy hunting!

The USAir Shuttle, which leaves every hour on the hour, is slightly cheaper than the Delta Shuttle under most circumstances. The cheapest fare offered by USAirways is a $85 one-way weekend fare, available from 12:01 a.m. Sat. to 3 p.m. Sun.

WASHINGTON'S AIRPORTS

From within the US, it's most convenient (and scenic) to fly into **Ronald Reagan National Airport** (☎(703) 417-8000; www.netwashairports.com), located in Arlington County, VA. National is close to Washington and on the Metro. Though National is more convenient, **Dulles International Airport** (☎(703) 369-1600; www.netwashairports.com), in rural Chantilly, VA, is Washington's major international airport and a number of (often cheaper) domestic flights touch down here. The drive from downtown takes about 40 minutes (more during rush hour). Cheaper flights generally jet into **Baltimore-Washington International (BWI) Airport** (☎(800) 435-9294), which lies 10 mi. south of Baltimore.

BUDGET AND STUDENT TRAVEL AGENCIES

A knowledgeable agent specializing in flights to the US and Canada can make your life easy and help you save, too, but agents may not spend the time to find you the lowest possible fare—they get paid on commission. Those holding **ISIC and IYTC cards** (see **Identification**, p. 250), respectively, qualify for big discounts from student travel agencies. Most flights from budget agencies are on major airlines, but in peak season some may sell seats on less reliable chartered aircraft.

usit world (www.usitworld.com). Over 50 **usit campus** branches in the UK (www.usitcampus.co.uk), including 52 Grosvenor Gardens, **London** SW1W 0AG (☎(0870) 240 1010); **Manchester** (☎(0161) 273 1721); and **Edinburgh** (☎(0131) 668 3303). Nearly 20 **usit now** offices in Ireland, including 19-21 Aston Quay, O'Connell Bridge, **Dublin** 2 (☎(01) 602 1600; www.usitnow.ie), and **Belfast** (☎(02890) 327 111; www.usitnow.com). Offices also in Athens, Auckland, Brussels, Frankfurt, Johannesburg, Lisbon, Luxembourg, Madrid, Paris, Sofia, and Warsaw.

Council Travel (www.counciltravel.com). US offices include: Emory Village, 1561 N. Decatur Rd., **Atlanta,** GA 30307 (☎(404) 377-9997); 273 Newbury St., **Boston,** MA 02116 (☎(617) 266-1926); 1160 N. State St., **Chicago,** IL 60610 (☎(312) 951-0585); 931 Westwood Blvd., Westwood, **Los Angeles,** CA 90024 (☎(310) 208-3551); 254 Greene St., **New York,** NY 10003 (☎(212) 254-2525); 530 Bush St., **San Francisco,** CA 94108 (☎(415) 566-6222); 424 Broadway Ave E., **Seattle,** WA 98102 (☎(206) 329-4567); 3301 M St. NW, **Washington, D.C.** 20007 (☎(202) 337-6464). **For US cities not listed,** call (800) 2-COUNCIL (226-8624). In the UK, 28A Poland St. (Oxford Circus), **London,** W1V 3DB (☎(020) 7437 7767).

CTS Travel, 44 Goodge St., **London** W1 (☎(020) 7636 0031; fax 7637 5328; email ctsinfo@ctstravel.com.uk).

STA Travel, 6560 Scottsdale Rd. #F100, Scottsdale, AZ 85253 (☎(800) 777-0112; fax (602) 922-0793; www.sta-travel.com). A student and youth travel organization with over 150 offices worldwide. Ticket booking, travel insurance, railpasses, and more. US offices include: 297 Newbury St., **Boston,** MA 02115 (☎(617) 266-6014); 429 S. Dearborn St., **Chicago,** IL 60605 (☎(312) 786-9050); 7202 Melrose Ave., **Los Angeles,** CA 90046 (☎(323) 934-8722); 10 Downing St., **New York,** NY 10014 (☎(212) 627-3111); 4341 University Way NE, **Seattle,** WA 98105 (☎(206) 633-5000); 2401 Pennsylvania Ave., Ste. G, **Washington, D.C.** 20037 (☎(202) 887-0912); 51 Grant Ave., **San Francisco,** CA 94108 (☎(415) 391-8407). In the UK, 11 Goodge St., **London** WIP 1FE (☎(020) 7436 7779 for North American travel). In New Zealand, 10 High St., **Auckland** (☎(09) 309 0458). In Australia, 366 Lygon St., **Melbourne** Vic 3053 (☎(03) 9349 4344).

Travel CUTS (Canadian Universities Travel Services Limited), 187 College St., **Toronto,** ON M5T 1P7 (☎(416) 979-2406; fax 979-8167; www.travelcuts.com). 40 offices across Canada. Also in the UK, 295-A Regent St., **London** W1R 7YA (☎(020) 7255 1944).

Cheap Tickets (☎(800) 377-1000; www.cheaptickets.com) offers cheap flights around the US.

Travel Avenue (☎(800) 333-3335; www.travelavenue.com) rebates commercial fares to or from the US and offers low fares for flights anywhere in the world. They also offer package deals, which include car rental and hotel reservations, to many destinations.

COMMERCIAL AIRLINES

The commercial airlines' lowest regular offer is the **APEX** (Advance Purchase Excursion) fare, which provides confirmed reservations and allows "open-jaw" tickets. Generally, reservations must be made 7 to 21 days in advance, with 7- to 14-day minimum and up to 90-day maximum-stay limits, and hefty cancellation and change penalties (fees rise in summer). Book peak-season APEX fares early, since by May you will have a hard time getting the departure date you want. Although APEX fares are probably not the cheapest possible fares, they will give you a sense of the average commercial price, from which to measure other bargains. Specials advertised in newspapers may be cheaper but have more restrictions and fewer available seats.

OTHER CHEAP ALTERNATIVES

AIR COURIER FLIGHTS. Couriers help transport cargo on international flights by guaranteeing delivery of the baggage claim slips from the company to a representative overseas. Generally, couriers must travel light (carry-ons only) and deal with complex restrictions on their flight. Most flights are round-trip only with short fixed-length stays (usually one week) and a limit of a single ticket per issue. Most of these flights also operate only out of the biggest cities. Generally, you must be over 21 (in some cases 18), have a valid passport, and procure your own visa, if necessary. Groups such as the **Air Courier Association** (☎(800) 282-1202; www.aircourier.org) and the **International Association of Air Travel Couriers**, 220 South Dixie Hwy., P.O. Box 1349, Lake Worth, FL 33460 (☎(561) 582-8320; email iaatc@courier.org; www.courier.org) provide their members with lists of opportunities and courier brokers worldwide for an annual fee.

CHARTER FLIGHTS. Charters are flights a tour operator contracts with an airline to fly extra loads of passengers during peak season. Charters can sometimes be cheaper than flights on scheduled airlines, some operate nonstop, and restrictions on minimum advance-purchase and minimum stay are more lenient. However, charter flights fly less often than major airlines, make refunds particularly difficult, and are almost always fully booked. Schedules and itineraries may also change or be cancelled at the last moment (as late as 48 hours before the trip, and without a full refund), and check-in, boarding, and baggage claim are often much slower. As always, pay with a credit card if you can, and consider traveler's insurance against trip interruption. **Discount clubs** and **fare brokers** offer members savings on last-minute charter and tour deals. Study their contracts closely; you don't want to end up with an unwanted overnight layover.

STANDBY FLIGHTS. To travel standby, you will need considerable flexibility in the dates and cities of your arrival and departure. Companies that specialize in standby flights don't sell tickets, but rather the promise that you will get to your destination (or near your destination) within a certain window of time (anywhere from 1-5 days). You may only receive a monetary refund if all available flights that depart within your date-range from the specified region are full, but future

ESSENTIAL
INFORMATION

COMMERCIAL AIRLINES

Southwest Airlines (☎(800) 435-9792) offers outrageously low fares, but only flies to Baltimore-Washington International Airport. If you live in a domestic city serviced by Southwest, the slight inconvenience is probably worth it for the tremendous discounts. Southwest also offers occasional dirt-cheap 24-hour advance fares, and always offers student and senior discounts. Other popular carriers to D.C. include:

American, ☎(800) 433-7300; www.americanair.com.

Continental, ☎(800) 525-0280; www.flycontinental.com.

Delta, ☎(800) 241-4141; www.delta-airlines.com.

Northwest, ☎(800) 225-2525; www.nwa.com.

TWA, ☎(800) 221-2000; www.twa.com.

United, ☎(800) 241-6522; www.ual.com.

US Airways, ☎(800) 428-4322; www.usairways.com.

travel credit is always available. Carefully read agreements with any company offering standby flights, as fine print can leave you in the lurch. To check on a company's service record, call the Better Business Bureau of New York City (☎(212) 533-6200). It is difficult to receive refunds, and clients' vouchers will not be honored when an airline fails to receive payment in time.

Airhitch, 2641 Broadway, 3rd fl., New York, NY 10025 (☎(800) 326-2009 or ☎(212) 864-2000; www.airhitch.org) and Los Angeles, CA (☎(888) 247-4482). The flagship offices are in Paris (☎+33 01 47 00 16 30), and Amsterdam (☎+31 (20) 626 32 20). Offers one-way flights to and from Europe to the Northeast ($159).

AirTech.Com, 588 Broadway #204, New York, NY 10012 (☎(212) 219-7000; email fly@airtech.com; www.airtech.com). AirTech.Com also arranges courier flights and regular confirmed-reserved flights at discount rates.

TICKET CONSOLIDATORS

Ticket consolidators, or **"bucket shops,"** buy unsold tickets in bulk from commercial airlines and sell them at discounted rates. The best place to look is in the Sunday travel section of any major newspaper, where many bucket shops place tiny ads. Call quickly, as availability is typically extremely limited. Not all bucket shops are reliable establishments, so insist on a receipt that gives full details of restrictions, refunds, and tickets, and pay by credit card. For more information, check the website **Consolidators FAQ** (www.travel-library.com/air-travel/consolidators.html).

TRAVELING WITHIN THE US AND CANADA

Travel Avenue (☎(800) 333-3335; www.travelavenue.com) tries to beat best available published fares using several consolidators. **NOW Voyager,** 74 Varick St., #307, New York, NY

10013 (☎(212) 431-1616; fax 219-1793; www.nowvoyagertravel.com) arranges discounted flights, within the US and to the world. Other consolidators worth trying are **Interworld** (☎(305) 443-4929; fax 443-0351); **Pennsylvania Travel** (☎(800) 331-0947); **Rebel** (☎(800) 227-3235; email travel@rebeltours.com; www.rebeltours.com); **Cheap Tickets** (☎(800) 377-1000; www.cheaptickets.com); and **Travac** (☎(800) 872-8800; fax (212) 714-9063; www.travac.com). Yet more consolidators on the web include the **Internet Travel Network** (www.itn.com); **SurplusTravel.com** (www.surplustravel.com); **Travel Information Services** (www.tiss.com); **TravelHUB** (www.travelhub.com); and **The Travel Site** (www.thetravelsite.com). Keep in mind that these are just suggestions to get you started in your research; *Let's Go* does not endorse any of these agencies. As always, be cautious, and research companies before you hand over your credit card number.

TRAVELING FROM THE UK, AUSTRALIA, & NEW ZEALAND

In London, the **Air Travel Advisory Bureau** (☎(020) 7636 5000; www.atab.co.uk) can provide names of reliable consolidators and discount flight specialists. From Australia and New Zealand, look for consolidator ads in the travel section of the *Sydney Morning Herald* and other papers.

BY TRAIN

The locomotive is still one of the cheapest ways to travel in the US. You can save money by purchasing your tickets as far in advance as possible, so plan ahead. It is essential to travel light on trains; not all stations will check your baggage. **Amtrak** (☎(800) USA-RAIL/872-7245; www.amtrak.com) is the only provider of intercity passenger train service in the US. The informative web page lists up-to-date schedules, fares, and arrival and departure info. You can reserve tickets on the web page. Many qualify for discounts: senior citizens (10% off); students (15% off) with a Student Advantage Card (call ☎(800) 96-AMTRAK/962-6872 to purchase the $20 card); travelers with disabilities (15% off); children 2-15 accompanied by a parent (50% off); children under age two (free); current members of the US armed forces, active-duty veterans, and their dependents (25% off). "Rail SALE" offers online discounts of up to 90%; visit the Amtrak web site for details and reservations.

Amtrak's trains connect Washington to most other parts of the country through **Union Station,** 50 Massachusetts Ave. NE (☎484-7540). Amtrak offers service to D.C. from New York. Trains (3½hrs.) leave New York about once every hour between 6am and 10:45pm. Fares are: around $67 reserved; $118 metroliner. Amtrak also leaves for D.C. from **Baltimore** (40min., around $21), **Philadelphia** (2hr., around $50), and **Boston** (8½hr., around $68). Additional routes to Washington start in **Richmond** (2hr., $33); **Williamsburg** (3½hr., $42); and **Virginia Beach** (6hr., $55). Maryland's commuter train, **MARC** (☎(410) 539-5000, 24hr.), also departs from Union. It offers weekday service to **Baltimore** ($5.75) and elsewhere.

BY BUS

If you're coming from rural America or have a tight budget, you might want to consider traveling to D.C. by bus. **Greyhound** (☎(800) 231-2222, TDD (800) 345-3109; www.greyhound.com) operates the largest number of lines, departing for D.C. daily from **Philadelphia** ($20), **New York City** ($39), **Baltimore** ($10), and **Richmond** ($17.50). Washington's Greyhound station, 1005 1st St. NE (☎289-5154) at L St., is rather decrepit. A number of **discounts** are available on Greyhound's standard-fare tickets (restrictions apply): senior citizens (10% off); children ages two to 11 (50% off); Travelers with disabilities and special needs and their companions ride together for the price of one. Active and retired US military personnel and National Guard Reserves (10% off) and their spouses and dependents may take a round-trip between any two points in the US for $169. If you purchase your ticket 3 days in advance in the off-season or 7 days in advance in the summer, a second ticket is half off.

BY CAR

Most drivers arrive from the north or south, on or parallel to I-95. To go downtown from the Baltimore-Washington Pkwy., follow signs for **New York Avenue**. From **I-95,** get onto the **Capital Beltway (I-495)** and get off the merry-go-round at whichever exit you choose. Three of the easiest and most useful exits are **Wisconsin Ave.** (to upper NW and Georgetown), **Connecticut Ave.** (Chevy Chase, Upper NW, Adams-Morgan, Dupont Circle, and downtown), and **New Hampshire Ave.** (through Takoma to downtown). From the south, take I-95 to I-395 directly to the 14th St. Bridge or Memorial Bridge (both lead downtown). From the west, take I-66E over the Roosevelt Bridge and follow signs for Constitution Ave. I-66 is simpler and faster than I-495. Due to outrageously congested rush hours (M-F 5:30-9:30am on I-66E and 3-7pm on I-66W), the extreme left lane is reserved for those vehicles with at least two passengers ("High Occupancy Vehicles," or HOV-2). An extra lane is open to rush-hour traffic, but try to steer clear of I-66, I-495, I-270, and I-95 during these hours. The **speed limit** in and around D.C. is 55 miles per hour.

SPECIFIC CONCERNS

WOMEN TRAVELERS

American women visiting D.C. will quickly come to notice that it is in many ways a Southern city and consequently has a certain gentility and "friendliness." Women traveling alone may be surprised by the number of pick-up attempts that they encounter. A polite, "No, I'm sorry, I can't," almost invariably results in gracious good-byes and being left alone again. For persistent, rude, or frightening propositions, the best answer is no answer and a swift retreat to a safe, populated area.

In general, women on their own may wish to avoid cheap accommodations in peripheral and risky areas; Georgetown and Upper Northwest are generally very safe, though a little remote and a bit expensive. Youth hostels, university housing, bed and breakfasts, and organizations offering rooms to women only may give more of an opportunity to meet people with whom you can explore places at night.

When walking around, look as if you know where you're going, even when you don't, and try to maintain an assertive, confident posture. Be careful about unfamiliar territory and avoid dark or isolated areas, especially at night. If you do get lost and feel uncomfortable asking strangers for information or directions, consider approaching other women, couples, or a storekeeper. Always carry enough money for a Metrobus, Metrorail, or taxi ride, and carry enough change for a phone call. Remember that 911 is free from pay phones; stay aware of where you are at all times so that you can tell the emergency staff your location. If you're scared, don't hesitate to yell (conventional wisdom says that screaming "Fire" attracts more help than something like "Rape"). Most importantly, trust your instincts: if you feel nervous or uncomfortable, get out of the area and ask for help.

Don't hesitate to seek out a police officer or a passerby if you are being harassed. An **IMPACT Model Mugging** self-defense course will not only prepare you for a potential attack, but will also raise your level of awareness of your surroundings as well as your confidence (see **Self Defense,** p. 33). Women also face some specific health concerns when traveling (see **Women's Health,** p. 266). For general information, contact the National Organization for Women (NOW), 733 15th St. NW, 2nd floor, Washington D.C. 20005 (☎(202) 331-0066; email now@now.org, website www.now.org).

FURTHER READING

A Journey of One's Own: Uncommon Advice for the Independent Woman Traveler, by Thalia Zepatos (Eighth Mountain Press, $17); or *Handbook for Women Travelers,* by Gemma Moss (Piatkus, $15).

OLDER TRAVELERS

Discounts abound for travelers over 62 (and sometimes, over 60). All you need is ID proving your age. Pick up the free **Golden Washingtonian Club Gold Mine** directory—which lists establishments offering 10-20% discounts to seniors on goods and services—at local hotel desks or at the **D.C. Office on Aging** at 441 4th St. NW, #900 (☎724-5626). The Office on Aging also offers an information and referral service to those 60 and over. (Hours M-F 8:30am-5pm.) For **further information,** consult *No Problem! Worldwise Tips for Mature Adventurers*, by Janice Kenyon (Orca Book Publishers, $16), or *A Senior's Guide to Healthy Travel*, by Donald L. Sullivan (Career Press, $15).

BISEXUAL, GAY, AND LESBIAN TRAVELERS

Washington's bisexual, gay, and lesbian communities are exceptional for their diversity and visibility, and for the comfortable geographic and legal positions they occupy within the city. A number of gay neighborhoods have developed in the Washington area. **Dupont Circle** is the hub of gay activity in D.C. Easily accessible by Metro, the neighborhood offers whole blocks of gay and gay-friendly establishments. Most bars and Restaurants cluster around 17th and P St. between 21st and 22nd St. **Southeast** Washington contains upwards of 10 gay and gay-friendly bars and clubs. Exercise caution if you choose to explore Southeast. Don't visit here alone at night and try to drive or take a cab home after dark.

There are a handful of gay publications in D.C. Most are free and widely circulated. **The Washington Blade** (www.washblade.com) is an indispensable source of news, reviews, and club listings; published every Friday, it's available in virtually every storefront and many restaurants in Dupont Circle. **MW,** a newer arts and entertainment weekly published on Thursdays, contains brief public interest items, short fiction, extensive nightlife coverage, and is almost as easy to find as *The Blade*. **The Lambda Rising bookstore,** (see p. 127) is a source for these periodicals. **Women In The Life,** a lesbian periodical, may be more difficult to find. It is available at the **Lammas bookstore** (see p. 127). For the most comprehensive listing of businesses serving Washington's gay community, try **The Other Pages,** a free gay and lesbian telephone directory available at Dupont Circle restaurants or online at www.otherpages.com. For gay and lesbian nightlife in D.C., see **Gay Bars and Clubs,** p. 190.

TRAVELERS WITH DISABILITIES

Parts of Washington, especially those administered by the federal government, do their best to accommodate disabled travelers. At any Smithsonian information desk, visitors can pick up a free copy of **Smithsonian Access,** which gives details regarding the accessibility of each Smithsonian museum (to receive a copy through the mail, call 357-2700). The **Metro System Guide** (☎637-7000) provides information on Metro's bus and rail provisions for the disabled. The Washington Convention and Visitor's Association (☎789-7000) publishes a fact sheet for the disabled that gives details on the accessibility of area hotels, restaurants, malls, and attractions. Guide dogs are allowed almost everywhere in Washington, but call ahead to be sure. Both Amtrak and major airlines will accommodate disabled passengers if notified at least 72 hours in advance. Hearing-impaired travelers may contact Amtrak using teletype printers (☎(800) 872-7245). **Greyhound** (☎(800) 752-4841) buses will provide free travel for a companion; if you are without a fellow traveler, call at least 48 hours before you plan to leave and they will make arrangements to help. For more information on getting to or around D.C., see p. 296.

inside
SECRETS TO...

vegging out

Granola kids feast at Dupont Circle and Adams-Morgan restaurants, which offer extensive vegetarian and vegan dining options. Restaurants offering an entirely-vegetarian menu include the **Juice Joint Cafe** (see p. 167) and the Indianfood **Amma Vegetarian Kitchen** (see p. 169) in Georgetown. For unique takes on vegetarian fare, try **Honest to Goodness Burritos** (15th and K St. NW) which offers veggie burritos, or **Taj Mahal** (1327 Connecticut Ave.) which features vegetarian Indian cuisine. Wash these healthy options down with a cup of specialty leaves at **Teaism** (see p. 166).

TRAVELERS WITH CHILDREN

Washington is a great place for kids. Just about every big thing that fascinates children—animals, dinosaurs, railroad trains, crime fighters, presidents—is represented in the D.C. area. Consult the list of kid-friendly current events which appears every Friday in the *Post*'s Weekend section for more great ideas on what to do with the kiddies in D.C. The sculpture garden outside the Hirshhorn Museum offers a contained stroll.

D.C. is full of museums, a number of which particularly draw children. Family vacations often require that you slow your pace, and always require that you plan ahead. When deciding where to stay, remember the special needs of young children; if you pick a B&B or a small hotel, call ahead and make sure it's child-friendly. If you rent a car, make sure the rental company provides a car seat for younger children. Consider using a papoose-style device to carry a baby on walking trips. Be sure that your child carries ID in case he or she gets lost, and arrange a reunion spot in case of separation.

Restaurants often have children's menus and discounts. *Let's Go: Washington D.C.* makes note of restaurants that are particularly kid-friendly (see **Cuisine by Type**, p. 152). Virtually all museums and tourist attractions also have a children's rate. Children under two generally fly for 10% of the adult airfare on international flights (not necessarily including a seat). International fares are usually 25% off for children from two to 11.

FURTHER READING

Going Places with Children in Washington, D.C., 15th Edition (published by the staff of Green Acres School, ☎(301) 881-4100; $19, including postage); or *Kidding Around Washington D.C.*, by Debbie Levy (John Muir Publications, $8).

DIETARY CONCERNS

Travelers who keep kosher should call the **Jewish Information Line** (☎(301) 770-4848), which provides listings for kosher restaurants in D.C. Vegetarians shouldn't have any trouble in D.C. *Let's Go* lists many establishments that serve vegetarian options. For information about vegetarian travel, contact the **North American Vegetarian Society**, P.O. Box 72, Dolgeville, NY 13329 (☎(518) 568-7970), which publishes the *Vegetarian Journal's Guide to Natural Food Restaurants in the US and Canada* ($12).

HEALTH

Travelers to a destination as prosaic as Washington D.C. need not worry overly about health issues. D.C. is relatively disease free and has some of the best medical care in the US—as long as you keep your clothes on you are unlikely to catch anything serious.

BEFORE YOU GO

In your passport, write the names of any people to be contacted in case of a medical emergency and list allergies or medical conditions that doctors should be aware of. Bring any medication you regularly take and a statement of preexisting medical conditions, especially if you will be bringing insulin, syringes, or any narcotics into the US.

MEDICAL CONDITIONS

Those with medical conditions (e.g., diabetes, allergies to antibiotics, epilepsy, heart conditions) may want to obtain a stainless steel **Medic Alert** identification tag ($35 the 1st year, and $15 annually thereafter), which identifies the condition and gives a 24-hour collect-call information number. Contact the Medic Alert Foundation, 2323 Colorado Ave., Turlock, CA 95382 (☎(800) 825-3785; www.medicalert.org). Diabetics can contact the **American Diabetes Association,** 1660 Duke St., Alexandria, VA 22314 (☎(800) 232-3472), to receive copies of the article "Travel and Diabetes" and a diabetic ID card, which carries messages in 18 languages explaining the carrier's diabetic status. If you are **HIV** positive, contact the **Bureau of Consular Affairs,** #4811, Department of State, Washington, D.C. 20520 (☎(202) 647-1488; http://travel.state.gov). According to US law, HIV positive persons are not permitted to enter the US. However, HIV testing is conducted only for those who are planning to immigrate permanently. Travelers from areas with particularly high concentrations of HIV positive persons or persons with AIDS may be required to provide more information when applying.

AIDS, HIV, STDS

Acquired Immune Deficiency Syndrome (AIDS) is a growing problem around the world. The World Health Organization estimates that there are around 30 million people infected with the HIV virus, and women now represent 40% of all new HIV infections. The easiest mode of HIV transmission is through direct blood-to-blood contact with an HIV-positive person; *never* share intravenous drug, tattooing, or other needles. The most common mode of transmission is sexual intercourse. Health professionals recommend the use of latex condoms. For more information on AIDS, you may contact the **US Center for Disease Control's** 24-hour hotline at ☎(800) 342-2437. In Europe, contact the **World Health Organization,** Attn: Global Program on AIDS, Avenue Appia 20, 1211 Geneva 27, Switzerland (☎44 22 791 21 11, fax 791 31 11), for statistical material on AIDS internationally. Council's brochure, *Travel Safe: AIDS and International Travel*, is available at all Council Travel offices and at their web site (www.ciee.org/study/safety/travelsafe.htm). In D.C., the **Whitman-Walker clinic** is synonymous with AIDS treatment. The D.C. area has the highest rate of new HIV infections per capita of any metropolitan area in the United States. There is an estimated number of 50,000 people infected with HIV in the D.C. area. Whitman offers a variety of resources, such as: counseling, medical care, legal service, housing, HIV/AIDS education, day treatment centers, lesbian and gay services, and mental health or addiction treatment services. (1407 S. Street, NW Washington, D.C. 20009, ☎797-3500.)

WOMEN'S HEALTH

Women on the pill should bring enough to allow for possible loss or extended stays. Bring a prescription, since forms of the pill vary a lot. In D.C., the **National Abortion Federation Hotline,** 1755 Massachusetts Ave. NW, Washington, D.C. 20036 (☎(800) 772-9100, M-F 9am-7pm) provides referrals to area physicians. **Planned Parenthood,** 1108 16th St. NW, Washington, D.C. 20032 provides birth control, emergency contraception, and abortions (☎347-8500; www.ppmw.org; metro: Farragut North).

OTHER RESOURCES

TOURISM BUREAUS

Washington, D.C. Convention and Visitors Association (WCVA), 1212 New York Ave., #600 NW (☎789-7000; www.washington.org). Call for copies of *The D.C. Visitor's Guide* and a calendar of events. Hours M-F 9am-5pm.

D.C. Committee to Promote Washington, 1212 New York Ave. NW, #200 (☎347-2873 or ☎(800) 422-8644). Hours M-F 9am-5pm. Call or write for a tourist package.

Meridian International Center, 1630 Crescent Pl. NW (☎667-6800). Metro: Dupont Circle. Call for brochures in a variety of languages. Office Hours M-F 8:30am-5pm.

The following offices may also be helpful: **Conference and Visitors Bureau of Montgomery,** 12900 Middlebrook Rd., #1400, Germantown, MD 20874 (☎(800) 925-0880 or ☎(301) 428-9702; www.cvnmontco.com); **Prince Georges County Maryland Conference and Visitors Bureau,** 9200 Basil Ct., #101, Largo, MD 20774 (☎(301) 925-8300 or ☎(888) 925-8300); **Delaware Tourism Office,** 99 King's Highway, Dover, DE 19901 (☎(800) 441-8846; www.state.de.us); **Maryland Division of Tourism,** 217 E. Redwood St., 9th Floor, Baltimore, MD 21202 (☎(410) 767-3400; www.mdisfun.com); **Virginia Department of Tourism,** 901 E. Byrd St., Richmond, VA 23219 (☎(804) 786-4484 or ☎(800) 847-4882; www.virginia.org), which also offers a **Virginia Bed and Breakfast Information and Reservation Service** (☎(800) 934-9184); and the **West Virginia Travel Office,** 2101 Washington St. E., Charleston, WV 25305-0312 (☎(800) 225-5982; www.state.wv.us).

USEFUL PUBLICATIONS

Foreign visitors may find the publications of the **US Customs Service** useful. The service publishes 35 books, booklets, leaflets, and flyers on various aspects of customs (P.O. Box 7407, Washington, D.C., 20044; ☎927-6724; www.customs.ustreas.gov). *Let's Go: Washington, D.C.*, provides comprehensive map coverage of D.C. Additional maps of the city can be purchased at newsstands throughout the city. The best map available is the **Washington D.C. Visitor's Map** ($3) produced by ADC, The Map People, 6640 General Green Way, Alexandria, VA, 22312 (☎(703) 750-0510). *Let's Go* offers travelers detailed, fold-out maps and pocket-sized coverage in *Let's Go Map Guide: Washington, D.C.* ($8). If you plan on taking daytrips, purchase an accurate road map or atlas. The ADC map has a good general map of the city's immediate environs. **Rand McNally,** 150 S. Wacker Dr., Chicago, IL 60606 (☎(800) 234-0679 or ☎(312) 332-2009; fax 443-9540; www.randmcnally.com) publishes one of the most comprehensive road atlases of the US ($10).

THE WORLD WIDE WEB

Using the wonders of the World Wide Web, a veritable cornucopia of Washingtonia is accessible from your easy chair. *Let's Go: Washington, D.C.* lists specific web sites throughout the book for businesses and tourist attractions. For information on travel planning on the web, consult *How to Plan Your Dream Vacation Using the Web*, by Elizabeth Dempsey (Coriolis Group, $25), or *Travel Planning Online for Dummies*, by Noah Vadnai (IDG Books, $25). Here are some general travel and Washington links:

GENERAL TRAVEL

Microsoft Expedia (http://expedia.msn.com) has everything you'd ever need to make travel plans on the web.

The CIA World Factbook (www.odci.gov/cia/publications/factbook/index.html) has tons of vital statistics on D.C.

Shoestring Travel (www.stratpub.com), an alternative to Microsoft's monolithic site, is a budget travel e-zine listing home exchanges, links, and accommodations information.

Let's Go (www.letsgo.com). Our newsletter, up-to-the-minute travel links.

Yahoo (www.yahoo.com/Recreation/Travel). An excellent compilation of travel links.

TravelHUB (www.travelhub.com). A great site for cheap travel deals.

INSIDE WASHINGTON

Yahoo Washington D.C. (http://dc.yahoo.com). The best Washington page; links to travel, maps, real estate, transportation, employment, and community resources.

Discover Washington D.C. (www.washington.org). The "official tourism web site of Washington D.C." Info on attractions, special events, accommodations, dining and nightlife.

D.C. Pages (http://dcpages.com). A great list of links to hot D.C. web sites, especially for the newcomer.

Washington Post (www.washingtonpost.com). A fantastic amount of information on everything D.C., from news and reviews to daytrips and dancin' gear.

Fedworld (www.fedworld.gov). Oodles of government information.

Smithsonian (www.si.edu). Everything about the museums.

White House (www.whitehouse.gov). Info on Presidents, current political information, press releases, links to federal services, and pictures of the building.

White House for Kids (www.whitehouse.gov/WH/kids/html/home.html). Cute tour for children.

Washington Weather (www.intellicast.com/weather/dca).

Curtain Up (www.curtainup.com/dcmain.html). News on the Washington theater scene and reviews of current D.C. productions.

MusicDC (www.musicdc.com). Check out the D.C. scene and keep up on D.C. concerts.

Accommodations

On one soft spring day we glided down the Potomac in a painted boat, and jumped upon the shore.
  —Emily Dickinson, commenting on her visit to the Willard Hotel (1855).

Come nightfall, you're seeking sanctuary from the tourist dregs. But wherever should one squat in the District? Don't trip unwittingly into some chandeliered lobby. The capital's fancy hotels will surely get medieval on your wallet. But you can trick these gold-digging taverns; just shack up with them on weekends or in summer months when discount rates crop up. Also, hostels, guest houses, and university dormitories are drop-dead cheap. For information on long-term housing, see **Living in the City,** p. 285.

HOSTELS

If you plan to stay in D.C. for less than a month, you might consider the time-honored institution of budget travel: the hostel. Students, backpackers, and other down-market *Let's Go* types fill these top-quality D.C. hostels. All offer unbeatable rates and the chance to mingle with other travelers from around the globe. Hosteling International-American Youth Hosteling (HI-AYH) membership is $25 yearly for adults, $15 for those over 54, free for those under 18, $35 for families. Non-members who wish to stay at an HI-AYH hostel usually pay approximately $3 extra, which can be applied toward membership. Contact HI-AYH, 108 K St., Washington, D.C. 20001 (☎ 737-2333), or inquire at any HI-affiliated hostel.

Washington International Hostel (HI-AYH), 1009 11 St. NW (☎ 783-3262; fax 737-1508; email dchostel@erols.com; www.hiayh.org), 3 blocks north of Metro on 11th St. Metro: Metro Center (11 St. exit). The prime location, friendly staff, and reasonable rates make Washington Interna-

tional Hostel an appealing choice for the D.C. hosteler. Located in the heart of D.C. (5 blocks from the White House, 20min. walk from the National Mall), the D.C. Hostel welcomes American and international travelers alike. Clean A/C rooms hold 4-12 beds and are elevator accessible. The dormitory-style accommodations also include a common room, kitchen, game room, lockers, internet access, laundry facilities (open daily 4pm-2am), and luggage and bicycle storage. Alcohol, smoking, and sleeping bags prohibited. After 6 nights' stay, foreigners automatically become HI-AYH members. Reception 24hr. Check-in after noon. Check-out 11am. Telephone reservations recommended and accepted up to 24hr. prior to arrival; email reservations 1 week in advance; written reservations must be received 2 weeks in advance (include self-addressed, stamped envelope for confirmation). Wheelchair accessible (give advance notice). Use caution in this area at night. $25 for non-HI-AYH members, $22 for members.

Washington International Student Center, 2451 18th St. NW (☎(800) 567-4150 or 667-7681), in Adams-Morgan. Metro: Woodley Park-Zoo. Exiting metro stop, go right (southeast) on Connecticut Ave. until Calvert; then go right (east) across Duke Ellington Bridge. Continue on Calvert until 18th St. Look for the address number on the door as there is no other visible sign or marker. This hidden hostel barely squeezes itself into the fun-packed and lively Adams-Morgan area. A friendly and experienced staff manage the clean and cozy establishment, consisting of 5 A/C bedrooms, each with 3-4 sets of bunk beds. Two kitchens and three shared bathrooms. Internet access $2 per 10min. No lockout; keys are issued to each guest with a $5 deposit. Breakfast included. Lockers available. Free parking first two nights. Check-in 8:30am-10:30pm. Reimbursement given for cab fare from bus and train station (no more than $5-6). Reserve at least a week in advance, especially in summer. Beds $16 per night.

India House Too, 300 Carroll St. (☎291-1195), on the border of D.C. and Takoma Park. Metro: Takoma. Walk straight from metro stop on Carroll St. towards the hill on the right. India House Too may be too run-down, too distant from the rest of D.C., and too akin to to the local frat-house; but for travelers merely needing a place to sleep, India House Too will do. Though shabby outside, the inside is palatable, with colorful murals and fun photos from past travelers, but the tattered furniture begs for the curb and the pigeon-frequented porches desperately need cleaning. The relatively clean bathrooms and bedrooms serve the none-too-picky traveler. Frequented by international travelers. Free linens and use of kitchen. No A/C. Laid back atmosphere: alcohol and smoking allowed. Reservations preferred. 4-6 bed dorm rooms $14; private rooms $34 (no private bath).

GUEST HOUSES AND HOTELS

Downtown **hotels and guest houses** range from moderately to crazily expensive; if you stay on a weekend, however, you can live like a king for half the regular price or less. The *New York Times* Sunday Travel section lists the latest deals, though a little bargaining can sometimes procure a room for even less. D.C. adds an automatic **14.5% occupancy tax** to your bill. Hotels usually charge per room, not per guest; thus, even a $100 room becomes reasonable when you split it four ways. Some hotels will even give a third or fifth occupant a free cot. Suite hotels offer sweet deals for groups of three or more.

ADAMS -MORGAN

SEE MAP P. 313
YOU ARE HERE
U.S. Capitol Building

Adams-Morgan's charming guest houses and small hotels lie in safe, peaceful neighborhoods. Find accommodations near Woodley Park or Dupont Circle Metro stops, or take the #42 bus through the heart of Adams-Morgan to stops on Columbia Road.

Taft Bridge Inn ($$), 2007 Wyoming Ave. (☎387-2007; email tbi@pressroom.com; www.pressroom.com\~taftbridge), at the intersection of 20th and Wyoming. Quiet hotel with beautifully decorated antique-filled rooms in a stately 19th-century Georgian building. Various rooms have claw-legged bathtubs, fancy marble floors, canopy wood or big brass beds, window seats, and fireplaces. All rooms have modem hookup, phones, voicemail, and A/C; cable TV in all rooms with private bath. Laundry facilities available. Full breakfast included. Parking $8 per day. Handicapped accessible. Singles $59-74, with private bath $110-125; off-season singles $99-114. Each additional person $15.

Kalorama Guest House at Kalorama Park ($+), 1854 Mintwood Pl. NW (☎ 667-6369), off Columbia Rd. a block south of 18th St. This quiet, Victorian guest house offers 19th-century appeal with 20th-century convenience. Some suites with TV and phone. One internet hookup. Continental breakfast included. Limited parking behind guest house by reservation only, $7 per night. Reception M-Tu 8am-8pm, W-Su 8am-10pm. Reservations with credit card required, payment due upon arrival. Singles $55, with bath $75; off-season singles $45-50, with bath $85. Each additional person $5. Two-room suite (3-6 people) with private bath $115-125; off-season $95.

Adams Inn ($+), 1744 Lanier Pl. NW (☎ 745-3600 or (800) 578-6807; www.adamsinn.com; email adamsinn@adamsinn.com), behind the Columbia Rd. Safeway supermarket, 2 blocks north of the center of Adams-Morgan. From Columbia, turn left on Ontario Rd. and then left again on Lanier Pl. Three elegant Victorian townhouses and a carriage house with garden. Free doughnuts, cable TV, 2 pay phones, and coin laundry facilities. Rooms vary in size, but all have A/C, private sinks and unique furnishings reflecting the styles of 1913, the year the houses were erected. Friendly, helpful staff. Continental breakfast included. Limited parking $7 per night. Internet access in office. Reception M-Sa 8am-9pm, Su 1-9pm. Reservations require first night deposit. Singles $55, with private bath $70. Each additional person $10. ISIC 10% discount. Limited special weekly rates.

Windsor Park Hotel ($$+), 2116 Kalorama Rd. NW (☎ 483-7700 or (800) 247-3064; www.windsorparkhotel.com; email windsorparkhotel@erols.com), 3 blocks west of Columbia Rd. on Kalorama. Clean, plain rooms have cable TV, phone, refrigerator, private bath, hair dryer, phone-jack for modem access, and A/C. Wheelchair accessible. Continental breakfast included. Singles $108; doubles $120. ISIC and seniors 10% discount.

Normandy Inn ($$-$$$$), 2118 Wyoming Ave. NW (☎ 483-1350 or (800) 424-3729), 2 blocks off Columbia Rd. at the corner of Connecticut and Wyoming Ave. Stylish, spacious rooms with refrigerators, coffeemakers, hair dryers, safes, irons/ironing boards, phones with voicemail and modem port, and cable TV. Free wine and cheese Tu. Exquisitely furnished conservatory and outdoor patio add guest house charm. Nearby Marriott's fitness room and seasonal pool available for guest use. One smoking floor. Underground parking $10 per night. Two handicapped-accessible rooms. Singles $79-160; F-Sa singles $79, doubles $89. Each additional person $10.

ALEXANDRIA

While reasonably priced hotels in Alexandria are all a 10-to 20-minute walk from King St., the main thoroughfare in Old Town, most provide shuttles to nearby Metro stations and Old Town. The **Alexandria Hotel Association** (☎(800) 296-1000) can help you find a room and make a reservation; check the rates in the upscale restaurants just off King St. for Christmas-in-July and other specials. Use Metro: Braddock for all of the following.

Best Western Old Colony Inn ($$), 615 1st St. (☎(703) 739-2222 or (800) 528-1234) www.bestwestern.com, near N. Washington St. Lobby at S. Asaph St. (about 9 blocks from King St. in Old Town Alexandria). Pleasant, large rooms. Outdoor pool on premises. Sauna, indoor/outdoor pool, and large fitness center at the Holiday Inn next door are free for guests. Coffeemakers, A/C, cable TV, and complimentary continental breakfast. Frequented by tourists and government workers. Free shuttle to National Airport and Metro. Rooms $105 for up to 4 people; each additional person $10. AAA and AARP $83.99.

The Alexandria Lodge ($$), 700 N. Washington St. (☎(703) 836-5100 or (800) 237-2243), at Wythe St. Neat, standard motel rooms with cable TV, A/C, and no-frills service. Convenient to bus stop and Metro; close to King St. Complimentary shuttle to National Airport (M-F 7-11am and 6-11pm, Sa 9-11am and 6-11pm, Su no service). $10 cash key deposit required. Singles $55-70, doubles $65-85; in winter singles $45-55, doubles $49-59. Each additional person $5.

Executive Club Suites ($$$), 610 Bashford Ln. (☎(703) 739-2582 or (800) 535-2582; www.dcexeclub.com), take Washington St. north (away from King St.) past 2nd St. and make a right on Bashford Ln. Renovated apartment building offers very large, apartment-style suites with full kitchens, living rooms (with queen-size sofa bed), bedrooms, A/C, iron/ironing boards, datajacks, and 2 cable TVs. Outdoor pool, health club with sauna, and computer room. Frequented by people on government business. Complimentary continental breakfast (M-F 6-9:30am, Sa-Su 8-10am) and "Guest Reception" (soft drinks, appetizers) daily 5:30-7pm. Free shuttle to Metro, National Airport, and occasionally to King St. 1-bedroom suites starting at $130; 2-bedroom $160. Special weekend rates based on availability (2 night weekend at $100 per night). AAA and AARP discounts approximately $110. Government worker discount starting at approximately $118. Discounts for longer stays.

Holiday Inn Hotel and Suites ($$$), 625 1st St. (☎(703) 548-6300). Elegant and spacious rooms (some overlooking a beautiful courtyard) come with coffeemakers, iron/ironing boards, datajacks, cable TV, A/C, and hair dryers by request. Heated indoor/outdoor pool. Excellent fitness center with free weights, nautilus and cardiovascular machines, and saunas. Free shuttle to Metro and National Airport with occasional service to the center of Old Town. Singles $129, doubles $149. AAA and AARP discounts available. Prices subject to change upon availability so call ahead for the most accurate prices.

ARLINGTON

Although not as quaint as accommodations in other areas of D.C., the hotels in Arlington are functional, less expensive, and often only a short walk from Georgetown.

Highlander Motor Inn ($+), 3336 Wilson Blvd. (☎(703) 524-4300 or (800) 786-4301). Metro: Virginia Square/GMU. Simple, sparsely decorated motel with clean, spacious rooms each with 2 double beds. Refrigerators upon request. Free coffee and doughnuts. A/C and cable TV with HBO. Parking included. Weekly and monthly rates available. Singles and doubles $65-75. Each additional adult $5, children free. *Let's Go* readers $5 off.

Quality Inn Iwo Jima ($$), 1501 Arlington Blvd. (☎(703) 524-5000 or (800) 221-2222). Take the N. Fort Myer Dr. exit from the Rosslyn Metro and make a left onto N Fort Myer Dr. (toward Iwo Jima), then turn right onto Fairfax Dr.; the inn is on the right. Dependable hotel with modern rooms, laundry facilities, hair dryers, coffeemakers, cable TV, dataports, and free parking.

Enclosed heated pool open all year. Wheelchair accessible. Singles $99; doubles $109; off-season rates drop to $75. Each additional adult $7, children free. AAA/AARP 10% discount.

Holiday Inn Westpark Hotel ($$$), 1900 North Fort Myer Dr. (☎(703) 807-2000 or (800) 465-4329). Take the N. Fort Myer Dr. exit of the Rosslyn Metro, make a right, and walk 1½ blocks. Comfortable, spacious rooms with small balconies (some with great views), cable TV, A/C, dataports, iron/ironing board, safes, and coffeemakers. Heated indoor pool and fitness center. View D.C. from the **Vantage Point** rooftop restaurant. Parking included. Wheelchair accessible. Weekdays start at $150; weekends $90. AAA/AARP 10% discount.

Best Western Key Bridge ($$+), 1850 North Fort Myer Dr. (☎(703) 522-0400 or (800) 528-1234), next to the Holiday Inn Westpark. Metro: Rosslyn. A 10min. walk to Georgetown. A/C and dataports. Outdoor pool. Fitness room and video game room. Free parking. Singles and doubles $139-159; weekend rates $89-109. Under 18 free with parents. AAA/AARP 10% discount.

Quality Hotel ($$), 1200 North Courthouse Rd. (☎(703) 524-4000 or (888) 987-2555), at the corner of 13th St., a steep 10min. walk downhill from the Courthouse Metro. Price and room quality vary between buildings, from basic motel-style to luxurious full-kitchen suites. Seasonal pool and fitness facilities. Wheelchair accessible. Rates begin at $129 on weeknights, weekends $99. AAA/AARP 10-30% discount. Ask about extended stay rates.

CAPITOL HILL

Accommodations on Capitol Hill plunk the B&B scene in great locations near the center of D.C., but the added expense may not always be worth the attractive location. **Be careful in the area at night.**

BullMoose ($$), 101 5th St NE (☎547-1050 or (800) 261-2768; email reserve@BullMoose-B-and-B.com; www.BullMoose-B-and-B.com.) Metro: Capitol South. Fans of comfort, taste, and Teddy Roosevelt (pics of him dot the walls) should love this place. Formally the Capitol Hill Guest House, the Bullmoose pampers their guests with a great contintental breakfast, baked goods, and a rustic, early-20th century elegance. 10 rooms, 4 with private bath. A/C, no smoking, contintental breakfast, kitchen, phones and data jacks, business center with fax, phone, printer, and PC with internet. Reservations recommended. Twin beds approximately $89; doubles $129-149; queen beds $149-169.

Maison Orleans ($$), 414 5th St. SE (☎544-3694; email maisonorln@aol.com). Metro: Eastern Market. 3 comfortable rooms with 1930s-style furniture, all with private bath. The comfy rooms truly feel like guest rooms in someone's home. TV (no cable), A/C, and complimentary continental breakfast. Backyard/patio is small but pretty with lots of plants and small fountains stocked with large Japanese goldfish. No smoking. Check-out 11am. Singles $90-95; doubles $95-115. Rollaway $10. Furnished apartment $115-125, also available by the month.

Hereford House ($$), 604 South Carolina Ave. SE (☎543-0102; email herefordhs@aol.com; www.bbonline.com/dc/hereford), at 6th St., 1 block from the Eastern Market Metro. No sign marks this British-style B&B in a townhouse run by a friendly English hostess. Shared baths, laundry facilities, A/C, refrigerator, living room, homecooked breakfast, and garden patio. No smoking. No credit cards. 50% due for reservation, balance due on arrival. Singles $54-68; doubles $70-78.

William Penn House ($), 515 E. Capitol St. (☎543-5560), 5 blocks from the Capitol. Metro: Eastern Market. Dorm-style guest house financed and supported by the Quakers of the United States. Shared rooms board 3-10 people. Complimentary continental breakfast. Optional Quaker worship in the mornings. No TV, limited A/C. Alcohol and tobacco prohibited. Only groups and Quakers will be allowed to stay here. Reception 9am-9pm. $5 key deposit required. Beds $35.

Holiday Inn on the Hill ($$$), 415 New Jersey Ave. NW (☎638-1616 or (800) 638-1116), across from the Hyatt Regency. Metro: Union Station. Walk 2 blocks northwest on New Jersey Ave. from the Capitol. Standard, clean rooms, data jacks, irons/ironing boards, hair dryers, coffeemakers, and 24hr. reception. Rooftop swimming pool, fitness room. Parking $15. Singles and doubles $99-$184. AAA/AARP 10% discount.

DUPONT CIRCLE

The good news: Dupont's got a wide choice of lovely bed and breakfast inns, all near the Dupont Circle Metro. The bad news: Dupont's prime location equals $$$. The accommodations listed below are the best deals in the area. Beware: parking can only be found in one of the Circle's expensive garages or on D.C.'s crowded streets.

Tabard Inn ($$), 1739 N St. NW (☎785-1277), between 17th and 18th St., just south of the Circle. 3 townhouses connected by a maze of passages, stairways, and lounges. Features large rooms beautifully decorated with ornate and elegant furniture. Offers a patio, bar, and lounges. Rooms have A/C and phone. Breakfast included. Reception 24hr. Singles $65-95, with private bath $99-155; doubles $90-110, with private bath $114-170. $15 per additional person.

The Brenton ($$), 1708 16th St. NW (☎332-5550 or (800) 673-9042), across from the Masonic Temple. From the Metro, walk up New Hampshire Ave., take a right on R St. and a left on 16th St. Beautiful, well-kept B&B in a Victorian townhouse with 8 spacious rooms and one suite catering primarily to gay travelers. All rooms with A/C, phones, and shared bathrooms. Continental breakfast included. 18+. Singles or doubles $79. $10 per additional person.

Embassy Inn ($$), 1627 16th St. NW (☎234-7800 or (800) 423-9111), near R St. Small Nouveau Victorian rooms in flowery paisley. Tea and coffee, evening sherry, daily newspaper, and continental breakfast included. All rooms have private bath, cable TV, hair dryers, phones, and A/C. Not handicapped accessible. Singles $79-109; doubles $89-139. Additional adults $10, children free. AAA and AARP 10% discount.

Carlyle Suites Hotel ($$$), 1731 New Hampshire Ave. NW (☎234-3200 or (800) 964-5377), between R and S St. The official Art Deco hotel of D.C., offering huge rooms with standard hotel furniture and kitchenettes, A/C, cable TV, and private baths. Very Glenn Close, very late 80s feel. Free access to local gyms. Laundry facilities available. Very limited free parking. Singles and doubles $79-159 based on availability. Call far in advance. $10 each additional adult.

The Windsor Inn ($$$), 1842 16th St. NW (☎667-0300 or (800) 423-9111), between Swann and T St. Same management and amenities as the Embassy Inn. More personal service than the corporate hotel, without the shared baths and lounges of B&Bs. Decorated with bona fide antiques and 19th-century prints. Rooms vary from teeny-tiny singles to expansive suites. Reception 24hr. Singles $79-110; doubles $89-130; suites $109-159. AAA and AARP 10% discount.

The Columbia Guest House ($), 2005 Columbia Rd. NW (☎265-4006), just off Connecticut Ave. Eccentric, patrician townhouse with dark wood paneling, polished hardwood floors, ornate fireplaces, and neatly furnished rooms (some with A/C and private bath). Most clientele are students or other budget travelers. Affordability definitely makes this joint appealing. Singles $29-33; doubles $36-59; triples $46-69. $10 per additional occupant. Students 10-15% discount.

Brickskeller Inn ($$), 1523 22nd St. NW (☎293-1885), between P and Q St. Under renovation to be completed in 2001, the Brickskeller aims to offer clean, reasonably priced rooms with simple furnishings. Pricier rooms have A/C, TV, private sinks, and/or private baths. Laundry facilities. The bar downstairs is a local fave. Singles $49-69; doubles $69-89.

FARRAGUT

Hotel accommodations in Farragut are outrageously pricey across the board; however, they offer high quality rooms in a safe neighborhood. Towards the end of the summer, ostensibly upscale hotels may actually offer rates comparable to cheaper tourist chains.

Farragut Lincoln Suites ($$+), 1823 L St. NW (☎223-4320 or (800) 424-2970), near 18th St. Metro: Farragut North or Farragut West. 99 spacious studio suites, all with wet bars or kitchens, refrigerators, modem jacks, hair dryers, and coffee/tea makers. Electric locks, free passes to nearby Bally's Holiday Spa, laundry service, A/C, and room service from Luigi's (see p. 167). Continental breakfast Sa-Su 7-10am. Milk and freshly baked cookies daily 6-8pm. Reservations recommended. All suites $119-169 for 1-2 people. Extended-stay rates available.

Quality Hotel and Suites Downtown ($$), 1315 16th St. NW (☎232-8000 or (800) 368-5689). Metro: Farragut North. The rooms are large, most with 2 double beds, some with a sofabed and kitchenette ($9 rental fee for kitchen utensils). Safes in every room. Laundry machines and dishwasher in basement. Small fitness room. Use of swimming pool at the Howard Johnson's 2 blocks away. If available, parking $11.50 per day. Summer room rates $79-160 for 1-2 people; in fall and winter from $69. $15 each additional adult (under 12 free). Seniors and AAA 10% discount.

Holiday Inn Downtown ($$$), 1155 14th St. NW (☎737-1200), at Thomas Circle. Metro: McPherson Square. Recently renovated rooms are clean and spacious, some with great views. Cable TV, modem hookups, and rooftop pool. Newly added full-service restaurant in the lobby. Hair dryers, irons, and coffeemakers available on request (subject to availability). Underground parking $15 per day. Singles and doubles $99-199. Seniors, AARP/AAA members 10% discount.

Center City Hotel ($$), 1201 13th St. NW (☎682-5300; fax 371-9624; www.centercityhotel.com), 2 blocks from Thomas Circle. Metro: McPherson Square. Small, recently renovated rooms with cable TV, A/C, and coffeemakers. Laundry service available. Complimentary continental breakfast. Free apples and friendly service. Wheelchair accessible. Parking $10 per day. Rates for 1-2 people approximately $89, with lowest rates in winter; $10 each additional person. Seniors, students, and AAA members 10% discount.

Governor's House Hotel ($$$), 1615 Rhode Island Ave. NW (☎296-2100 or (800) 821-4367; fax 331-0227; www.governorshousewdc.com). Metro: Farragut North or Dupont Circle. Newly renovated hotel features large, luxurious rooms, each with desk and table, cable TV, A/C, iron, hair dryer, and modem jacks. Coffeemakers on request. Beautiful fitness room with TV and remotes. Outdoor swimming pool. $99-235 for 1-2 people, but call ahead for day-specific pricing; each additional person $20. AAA and AARP discount; special summer rates sometimes available.

Marriot Residence Inn ($$$), 1199 Vermont Ave. NW at Thomas Circle, (☎(800) 331-3131; email ri.wasdc.gm@marriott.com; www.residenceinn.com). Metro: McPherson Square. Nice rooms and a good location create an environment great for business types and families. Cable TV, kitchen, refrigerator, irons, full cooking set and dinette, exercise facility. Complimentary breakfast, free grocery shopping service, and small weekly socials for guests. Studio or 1 bedroom approximately $165-190. Reservations recommended, especially in the summer.

FOGGY BOTTOM

Expensive hotels in the Foggy Bottom area cater to a business community; when politicians desert town on weekends, tourists can snag classsy comfort at fathomable rates.

One Washington Circle Hotel ($$), 1 Washington Circle NW, (☎872-1680, reservations ☎(800) 424-9671), between 23rd and New Hampshire. Metro: Foggy Bottom-GWU. Huge suites with beautiful, modern design, full kitchens, and excessive closet space attract a largely business clientele. First-class service; fitness center and outdoor pool, complimentary USA Today (M-Sa). Laundry and dry cleaning available. Valet parking $16. Rooms $119-230; summer weekend rates may go as low as $89-99; in winter $69. Each additional person $15.

Hotel Lombardy ($$$), 2019 I St. NW (☎828-2600, ☎(800) 424-5486), near 21st St. Two blocks from the Farragut West Metro. This beautiful, up-scale, hotel was an apartment building 30 years ago. It still has its original dormer windows and enormous rooms with wet bars, refrigerators, coffeemakers, irons/ironing boards, and hair dryers. Chinese and European antiques create a very international atmosphere. Parking $17 a night. Singles $120-210; doubles $140-235. Each additional person $20. Off-season rates as low as $99.

GEORGETOWN

Georgetown has no metro stop so the area's accomodations are less convenient than others. For directions to Georgetown from Foggy Bottom-GWU or Dupont Circle Metro Stops, see **Orientation,** p. 76.

Georgetown Suites ($$$), 1111 30th St. NW and 1000 29th St. NW (☎298-7800 or (800) 348-7203), 1 block south of M St. bus stop. Large, sunny suites in pastel colors. The 1-bedroom suite easily fits 2-3. Every room has a fully-equipped kitchen including a microwave, coffeemaker, and tea kettle. Wheelchair accessible rooms available. Parking $15 per day. Even the studio suites are impressive in size ($130-200). Convenience has its price, though: 1-bedroom suites $145-225, 2-bedrooms $275. $15 extra for a rollaway. Lowest rates in summer and on weekends. Get lower prices with earlier reservations, so plan ahead.

Holiday Inn ($$$), 2101 Wisconsin Ave. NW (☎ 338-4600), in northern Georgetown. Comfortable, simply decorated rooms that include hair dryers, modem hookups, ironing boards, and irons in every room. Fitness center and outdoor pool for guest use. All rooms accommodate 4 people, with either a king-size bed and a fold-out couch or 2 double beds. Wheelchair accessible rooms available. $10 extra for a rollaway. Parking $15 per day. Rooms around $159, suites with mini-kitchen $189. AAA and AARP discounts. Summer promos can drop rates to $109.

NORTHEAST

Although the accommodations in the area are generally inexpensive, many parts of the Northeast are dangerous: **always be careful in the area.**

Days Inn ($$), 2700 New York Ave. NE (☎ 832-5800 or (800) 325-2525). Standard, clean hotel rooms 15-20min. away from Capitol Hill. Pool, TV with HBO, Showtime, and cable. Free shuttle service runs to and from Union Station; call ahead to get the schedule. Singles $85; doubles with 2 double beds $89. Extra rollaway $5.75. AAA/AARP 10% discount.

OLD DOWNTOWN

Old Downtown is loaded with ultra-expensive hotels serving everyone except the budget traveler. Call far in advance for reservations at one of these rare budget steals:

Hotel Harrington ($$), 11th St. and E St. (☎ 628-8140 or (800) 424-8532). Metro: Metro Center or Federal Triangle. On the verge of turning ninety, the hotel shows its age but offers clean rooms and a great location. Next door to the newly built ESPNZone and 3 blocks from the Smithsonian, the hotel features a Deluxe Family Room (2 adjoining rooms $125). Cable TV, A/C, and laundromat. Singles $85-89, doubles $95-99. Discounts for students, AAA.

Swiss Inn ($$), 1204 Massachusetts Ave. NW (☎ 371-1816 or (800) 955-7947; www.theswissinn.com), 4 blocks from Metro Center. More like a guest house than a hotel. 7 clean, quiet studio apartments with private baths, high ceilings, kitchenettes, A/C, and TV (no cable). International crowd welcomed by French- and German-speaking managers. Complimentary parking on weekends, weekdays $8. All rooms $78-108; off-season $53-75. 40% discounts for seniors and students.

Red Roof Inn ($$), 500 H St. NW (☎ 289-5959; www.redroofinn.com), 2 blocks from Metro. Metro: Gallery Place-Chinatown. Moderately priced hotel resides in the midst of Chinatown one block from the MCI Center. Clean comfortable rooms with A/C, cable TV, in-room video games. Small fitness center. The neighborhood is fairly safe, but exercise caution at night. Parking $9.50. 24hr. check-in with reservation. Singles $90-110, doubles $100-120; each additional adult $10. Discounts for AAA, over 60, and internet reservations.

SOUTH OF THE MALL

The waterfront suffers a lack of variety in accomodations, but the subdued atmosphere is worlds away from the crowded tourist arenas nearby.

Waterfront Channel Inn Hotel ($$+), 650 Water St. (☎ 554-2400). Metro: L'Enfant Plaza or Waterfront. Crushed between upscale seafood restaurants, the hotel has spacious rooms with queen beds or 2 double beds, a small sitting area, desks, A/C, cable TV, modem hookups, and balconies. Half the rooms overlook the marina and Washington Channel (waterfront rooms can be requested). Outdoor pool open in summer. Free underground parking. Free passes to fitness center with indoor pool across the street and same-day dry-cleaning. No student groups. Su-Th singles $120, doubles (up to 4 people) $135; F-Sa $98 for up to 4 people. AAA discounts available.

UPPER NORTHWEST

Kalorama Guest House at Woodley Park ($$), 2700 Cathedral Ave. NW (☎328-0860). Metro: Woodley Park-Zoo. Walk 2 blocks up Connecticut Ave. toward the zoo and take a left on Cathedral; it's 1 block up on the left. A very bare guest house with aspirations toward Victorian charm. Rooms are clean, quiet, and all have A/C. Laundry facilities. Breakfast included. No children under 6 years old. No pets. No smoking. Limited parking by reservation only ($7). Reception M-F 8am-8pm, Sa-Su 9am-7pm. Reservations with credit card required (or full payment by check at least 2 weeks in advance); cancellations at least 1 week in advance for a full refund. Rooms with shared bath $45-65 for 1; for 2 $50-70. Rooms with private baths $60-100 for 1; $65-105 for 2.

College of Preachers at the Washington National Cathedral ($$), 3510 Woodley Rd. NW (☎537-6383). Metro: equidistant to Woodley Park-Zoo, Cleveland Park, and Tenleytown-AU (approx. 1 mi.). Bus: 90 & 92 from Woodley Park-Zoo, 30-series buses from Tenleytown, N2 & N4 from Dupont Circle metro. Retreat-like housing for the public and clergy on the grounds of the National Cathedral. Quiet, immaculate rooms have sinks but share bathrooms; suites have private baths. No locks on individual doors. Telephones in suites. Chapel and garden open to guests for quiet contemplation. Credit card to reserve. Singles $70; doubles $110; suites $145.

Savoy Hotel ($$+), 2505 Wisconsin Ave. NW (☎337-9700, reservations 800-964-5377), near Calvert St. in Glover Park, north of Georgetown. Take any 30-series bus from Metro: Tenleytown, Foggy Bottom, or Friendship Heights. Free shuttle service to and from Metro: Woodley Park-Zoo; call for schedule. Great views of the monuments from the top floors. Free passes to local gym. Non-smoking floors available. Some rooms have kitchenettes or jacuzzis, and all have either 1 king-size or 2 queen-size beds. Singles $79-169; doubles $89-179. Discounts for affiliates of local universities, depending on availability. AAA and AARP discounts also.

Woodley Park Guest House ($+), 2647 Woodley Rd. NW (☎667-0218). Metro: Woodley Park-Zoo; walk 1 block up Connecticut Ave. toward the zoo, take a left on Woodley Rd. The guest house is across the street from the Marriott. Under renovations to be completed in Spring 2001. Parking $5 per night. Reception open daily 8am-8pm. No televisions; no smoking. 48hr. cancellation policy. Singles with semi-private bath $60; singles and doubles with full private bath $75-88.

CAMPGROUNDS

Greenbelt Park, 6565 Greenbelt Rd. (☎(301) 344-3948, (800) 365-2267 for reservations Apr.-Nov.). 12 mi. from D.C. Take I-95N to Exit 23 Kenilworth Ave. (Rte. 201S); after the exit, take the left lane to Greenbelt Rd. (Rte. 193E); the park entrance is on the right further down the road. Alternatively, take the Baltimore-Washington Pkwy. to Greenbelt Rd. and follow the signs. A few miles walk or a short drive to the College Park/UMd or Greenbelt Metro Stations. The cheapest and nicest place to camp in the D.C. area, courtesy of the National Park Service. 174 very quiet, wooded sites for tents, trailers, and campers. Nature and bike trails. Electricity only in sites 60-69 (including wheelchair accessible site). Bathrooms and showers. Alcoholic beverages prohibited. Checkout noon. Max. stay 2 weeks; max. 2 tents, 2 vehicles, and 6 people per site. Sites $13. 50% discount for seniors with Golden Age Pass.

Cherry Hill Park, 9800 Cherry Hill Rd. (☎(301) 937-7116 or (800) 801-6449). From D.C., follow route I-95N or 495E toward Baltimore for approx. 30min.; take Exit 25 (Rte. 1S, College Park); make the first right onto Cherry Hill Road and go 1 mi. to park entrance on left. From Baltimore take Exit 29B (Rte 212-Calverton) off I-95S; Follow Rte 212(Powder Mill Rd.) for 1 mi., then turn left onto Cherry Hill Rd. Park entrance 1 mi. on right. This Las Vegas of campgrounds operates with an agenda described by owner Norman as "traditional values and modern luxuries." Most of the 400 sites are for RVs and include utilities. Cable hookup available. Coin-operated laundry. 2 outdoor swimming pools (1 heated with whirlpool), sauna, playground, and cafe. Metrobus stop located on the grounds leads to Metro stations every 30min. Tent site for 2 $27; RV site with electricity, water, and sewer $35; each additional person $3. $25 deposit with reservation. AAA, military, AARP, and KOA 10% discount. Call for weekly rates.

Capitol KOA, 768 Cecil Ave. (☎(410) 923-2771 or (800) 562-0248, from Baltimore (410) 987-7477), in Millersville. From D.C., take Rte. 50E (John Hanson Hwy.) to Rte. 3N (Robert Crain Hwy.); bear right after 8 mi. onto Veterans Hwy.; after a short distance turn left under the highway onto Hog Farm Rd.; follow blue camping signs. Mostly RVs, some cabins, and a small wooded area for tents. Pool, volleyball courts, and bathroom/shower facilities centrally located. Movies and crafts for kids nightly; occasional evening events for adults like slide shows and wine and cheese parties. Free weekday shuttle to MARC commuter train ($7.25 round-trip to Union Station, ages 65 and up $4, up to 2 children 6 and under may travel free with each adult). Weekend shuttle to New Carrollton Metro stop. Max. stay 2 weeks. Open Mar. 25-Nov. 1. Tent site for 2 $26; RV complete hookup $34, water and electricity $31; 1-room cabin $44, 2 rooms $53. Each additional adult $5, child $2.

Living in D.C.

Even the Bostonian became simple, good-natured, almost genial, in the softness of a
Washington spring...One could not stay there a month without loving the shabby town.
—Henry Adams, *The Education of Henry Adams* (1902)

VISAS AND WORK PERMITS

LONG-TERM VISAS

All travelers planning to stay more than 90 days (180 days for Canadians) need to obtain
either a non-immigrant (for temporary stay) or immigrant (for permanent stay) visa.
Most travelers need a **B-2**, or "pleasure tourist," visa. Those planning to travel to the US
for a different purpose—such as for study or temporary work—must apply for a different visa in the appropriate category (see **Study and Work Visas,** below). Be sure to double-
check on entrance requirements at the nearest US embassy or consulate, or consult the
Bureau of Consular Affairs web page (http://travel.state.gov/visa_services.html#niv).

SIX-MONTH TOURIST VISAS. Visa applications should generally be processed through
the American embassy or consulate in their country of residence (see **Planning Your Trip,**
p. 247). Or, the **Center for International Business and Travel (CIBT),** 23201 New Mexico Ave.
NW #210, Washington, D.C. 20016 (☎244-9500 or (800) 925-2428), can secure B-2 visas
to and from all possible countries for a variable service charge (6-month visa around
$45). If you lose your I-94 form, you can replace it at the nearest **Immigration and Natural-
ization Service (INS)** office (☎(800) 375-5283; www.ins.usdoj.gov), although it's unlikely
that the form will be replaced during your stay. **Visa extensions** are sometimes attainable
with a completed I-539 form; call the forms request line (☎(800) 870-3676). HIV-positive

inside
SECRETS TO...

alternasports

D.C. citizens wishing to risk their lives purely for the **adrenaline rush** have two major options: walk the streets of Southeast, or head to one of many **adventure sports** locations in surrounding Maryland and Virginia. **Paintball** is very popular with those in D.C. However, hardcore paintballers migrate towards Maryland to wreak mischief and mayhem upon the **Anne Arundel Paintball Park** (7600 Race Rd., Jessup, MD). Daredevils, also try **windsurfing** at the **Washington Sailing Marina** (near National Airport) which also rents equipment. Tempt gravity and fate by joining the **Capitol Hang Glider Association** (www.mhga.com), which coordinates monthly hang-gliding diversions.

individuals cannot get a visa to enter the US. B-2 applicants must prove that they do not intend to immigrate by demonstrating that the purpose of their trip is for business, pleasure, or medical treatment; they plan to remain for a limited period; and they have a residence outside the US.

STUDY AND WORK VISAS

Working and studying are the only means of staying in the US for longer than six months. Unfortunately, separate visas are required for each. Holders of B-2 visas and those who have entered the US visa-free under the Visa Waiver Pilot Program cannot enter into full-time study or paid employment.

STUDY VISAS. Two types of study visas are available: the **F-1**, for **academic studies** (including language school), and the **M-1**, for **non-academic and vocational studies.** In order to secure a study visa, you must already be accepted to a full course of study by an educational institution approved by the Immigration and Naturalization Services (INS). F-1 applicants must also prove they have enough readily-available funds to meet all expenses for the first year of study; M-1 applicants must have evidence that sufficient funds are immediately available to pay all tuition and living costs for the entire period of intended stay. Applications should be processed through the American embassy or consulate in your country of residence (see **Planning Your Trip,** p. 247).

WORK PERMITS. In typical bureaucratic style, there are dozens of employment visas, most of which are nearly impossible to get. There are three general categories of work visas/permits: **employment-based visas,** generally issued to skilled or highly educated workers that already have a job offer in the US; **temporary worker visas,** which have fixed time limits and very specific classifications (for instance, "artists or entertainers who perform under a program that is culturally unique" or "persons who have practical training in the education of handicapped children"); and **cultural exchange visas,** which allow for employment by participants in either fellowships or reciprocal work programs with the aim of promoting cultural and historical exchange. For more on the requirements for each type of visa, visit http://travel.state.gov/visa_services.html#niv. While the chances of getting a work visa may seem next to impossible, there is hope: the **Council on International Educational Exchange (CIEE)** facilitates a **work/study/intern exchange** program between the US and citizens of Australia, China, France, Germany, Italy, Japan, Spain, Taiwan, and the UK. For a fee, CIEE guides university students and recent graduates through the visa application process; once in the US, they can help you find employment (see **Finding Work,** below). For more information, contact your local Council Travel office (see p. 258) or visit the CIEE web site (www.ciee.org).

FINDING WORK

Although the District's job market is still competitive, its economy is cresting, and D.C.'s unemployment rate has hit an impressively low 2.5%. Do your job-hunting homework, keep a resume handy, and you'll swiftly start raking in greenbacks.

Minimum wage is a meager $5.15/hr., considering the high cost of living in D.C. When you are hired you will have to fill out **W-2 and I-9 tax forms** that authorize the government to take out state, federal, and Social Security taxes from your paycheck. Income taxes in D.C. can get up to from 20-50%, but generally expect to it to fall in the 25% range. Paycheck withholdings do not include government **health insurance;** only full-time, year-round jobs provide insurance, and then through a private provider. The standard work week is 40 hours; if you work more than this, you are entitled to **overtime pay,** usually 150% of your hourly wage. In an eight-hour workday, most jobs allow you to take a lunch break, although whether it is paid or unpaid varies.

RESOURCES

As Washington is one of the most tech-savvy cities in the world, the **internet** is a priceless resource when looking for a job here (see **Job Hunting on the Internet,** below). But for technophobes and neo-luddites, highlighting listings in D.C.'s newspapers, and old-fashioned legwork will prove fruitful as well. Be sure to check out the **classifieds** in **The Washington Post** and **The Washington Times.**

In addition, many of D.C.'s colleges and universities have **career and employment offices;** even if you can't get into the office itself (some may require a school ID to enter), most have bulletin boards outside (for a list of colleges and universities in D.C., see **Studying in D.C.,** p. 285) for you to peruse.

OPTIONS FOR WORK

INTERNSHIPS

Every summer, when sensible year-round Washington politicos escape from their sweltering city, their ranks are fortified by an influx of collegiate go-getters with bigshot dreams. Internships give students a glimpse of the Washington political scene, and perhaps even a chance to become intimate with power—just ask, ahem, Monica Lewinsky.

Congress is the main employer of summer interns. Senators stuff their office with anywhere from five to 15 interns, and the typical representative's office snags two or three. House interns usually hail from their boss's own district, whereas Senate internships are less geographically correlated. Many interns work for a committee or a subcommittee, meaning that they work for the committee chair. Other prime intern-havens are **think tanks** and **lobbying groups.**

If you're interested in an internship, start looking early—by January, it may be too late. Connections help, of course—this is politics. To inquire about interning for a congress person, contact his or her home state office (Senate ☎ (202) 224-3121; House ☎ (202) 225-3121). Send many, many, many cover letters and

inside

SECRETS TO...

buzzwords

D.C. has lately been abuzz over the perennial issues of health care, social security, and education.

With health care, the debate storms over **elder care**, as both parties propose solutions for dealing with the rapidly rising expense of care for increasing numbers of elderly citizens. Many of these solutions attack the current social security. Here the main argument is over the recent **budget surplus**, which has been amassed by the government through careful financial planning. Some say that the surplus should be protected from use by Congress, invested, and used to finance care for the elderly of the future. Others present different plans for reinvigorating the social security system and propose using the surplus towards education instead.

Within the broad field of education, current buzz hovers over **school choice**. Many anti-school choice parties propose using the surplus to build better schools, attract better teachers with higher pay, and spend more on books and computers. Those arguing for school choice, however, do not believe an infusion of money will enliven the long-stagnant system. Instead they propose more open competition, almost a form of natural selection.

resumes to congressional offices, the White House, government departments, museums, lobbying groups, and any other organizations that interest you. If you're lucky, you'll get an invitation to answer phones for a summer amid a pile of curt rejection letters.

Here are few of the best current resources for finding internships in Washington:

Peterson's Internships, Princeton, New Jersey: Peterson's (☎(800) 338-3282; fax (609) 243-9150; http://www.petersons.com).

The National Directory of Internships, by Gita Gulati and Nancy Baley, Raleigh, NC: National Center for Experiential Education (☎(919) 767-3263).

The Internship Bible, by Mark Oldman and Samer Hamadeh, Princeton Review (☎(800) 733-3000; www.review.com/tools/books/).

The vast majority of the summer opportunities for college students are non-paying. Fortunately, there are ways to finagle some cash out of the deal. Some universities and foundations award grants to students to cover the summer expenses of working at an unpaid public-sector job. Some government branch might have some intern funds at its disposal; the House of Representatives, for instance, retains an endowment known as **The Lyndon Baines Johnson (LBJ) Fund,** which gives each member $2000 to split among any number of interns from his home district.

Despite its cachet, **interning** in D.C. is rarely profitable and may require either a supplementary night job or magical source of disposable funds. Interning for half the summer is a viable and common option that allows time for some gainful employment.

The intern social scene can be remarkably homogeneous. Most collegiate interns live in the dorms of **George Washington, American,** or **Georgetown Universities** (all of which are usually booked by April), in Georgetown townhouse **sublets,** or in **apartments** near Capitol Hill. Foreigners who have already secured internships in Washington can contact **Council Travel** (see p. 258), which will arrange all necessary paperwork.

TEMPORARY WORK

Temp work—a far cry from titillating, but still a way to score cash fast with minimal effort. Offices often hire employees for short periods (anywhere from a few days to several months) through temp agencies, massive clearinghouses of skilled workers. Most jobs are secretarial in nature: data entry, filing, answering phones, etc. Often, agencies can place you in full-time work after only a few weeks; if they do, health insurance is often included. See p. 293 for agencies.

STUDYING IN D.C.

If you are a foreigner interested in college or university study in the United States, you are likely to be required to take the **Test of English as a Foreign Language (TOEFL)**. Requirements are set by each school. A TOEFL bulletin, with information on how to apply to take the test, can be obtained at most universities in the U.S. and abroad, or from the **Educational Testing Service** (ETS). In the U.S. contact TOEFL/ETS Registration, P.O. Box 6151, Princeton, NJ 08541-6151. ETS can be reached by telephone at ☎ (609) 771-7100 (M-F 8am-9:45pm, Sa 9am-4:45pm) or on the web at http://www.toefl.org. In Europe, write to CITO/Sylvan Learning Systems, BV P.O. Box 1109, 6801 BC Arnhem, Netherlands; call 31 26 352 15 77; fax 31 26 35 21 278; or email registration@cito.nl. Colleges accept foreign applicants directly.

For those interested in a briefer stay, see p. 294 for **language school** listings.For general info on language study in America, consult *English Language and Orientation Programs in the U.S.* (IIE Books, $43), *Funding for U.S. Study* ($40), or *Study Abroad* (Peterson's, $27), which all provide info on study programs for foreigners.

UNIVERSITIES IN THE AREA

SCHOOL	LOCATION	CONTACT	AFFILIATION/SPECIALTY
American University	4400 Massachussetts Ave., around Ward Circle in the **Upper Northwest**	☎ (202) 885-6000 www.american.edu	Private, national and international student body.
The Catholic University of America	main entrance at Michigan Ave. and 4th St. in the **Northeast**	☎ (800) 673-2772 www.cua.edu	Private, Catholic, liberal arts and theology, philosophy, and canon law.
Gallaudet University	800 Florida Ave. and 8th St. in the **Northeast**	☎ (202) 651-5000 TDD (20) 651-5050 www.gallaudet.edu	University for the deaf, with an excellent drama department.
George Mason University	4400 University Drive in **Fairfax, VA**	☎ (703) 993-1000 www.gmu.edu	Private, liberal arts college.
Georgetown University	main gate at 37th and O St. in **Georgetown**	☎ (202) 687-1457	Private, Catholic and Jesuit, coed. Hosts many international programs.
George Washington University	north of F St. in **Foggy Bottom,** visitors center at 801 22nd St. NW	☎ 994-4949 http://gwis.circ.gwu.edu	Private, liberal arts college.
Howard University	2400 6th St. NW in **Shaw / U**	☎ (202) 806-6100 www.howard.edu	historically black university
Marymount University	2807 Glebe Rd. in **Arlington, VA**	☎ (800) 548-7638 www.marymount.edu	Private, Catholic, coed.
Southeastern University	501 I Street SW	☎ (202) 265-5343 www.seu.edu	Private, coed. Has international campuses.
Trinity College	125 Michigan Ave. NE	☎ (202) 884-9000 www.trinitydc.edu	Private, Catholic, women's college. Has a weekend college program.
University of the District of Columbia	4200 Connecticut Ave. NW	☎ (202) 274-5000 www.udc.edu	Public, with open admissions for District residents.

LONG-TERM HOUSING

The secret to D.C. house-hunting is to **act early** and to **act fast.** Prospective landlords generally pick tenants at the start of the month *before* the lease begins (signing at the start of May for a June lease). If you're migrating to D.C. for the summer, get your act together and start making contacts in February or early March. Early planning will give you that needed extra edge, because you'll be competing for space with the intern influx, which descends like a locust plague on the nation's capital come summertime. No worries, though. With a bit of luck and a concentrated search, you'll be unpacking cardboard boxes and souping up your new player's castle in no time.

APARTMENTS

Unless you are planning on permanently relocating to D.C., **subletting** an apartment in the District is a smart idea. See **Apartment Hunting**, p. 291, to get started. **Newspaper listings** often include apartments for rent or sublet, as well as requests for roommates and housesitters. Check **The Washington Post** (especially F-Su) and **City Paper** (Th). Roommate services are also helpful as are flyer-laden kiosks on college campuses and areas such as Adams-Morgan and Dupont. **Bulletin boards** and **newsletters** can help you find rentals and sublets; some are for everybody, others are "special interest." **Georgetown University** offers a wealth of info on sublets throughout D.C., Maryland, and Virginia via an on-line database at **http://data.georgetown.edu/admin/auxiliarysrv/och/**. Other university housing offices and web sites often provide similar help. Gay and lesbian visitors should check the resource centers at **Lammas** and **Lambda Rising** bookstores, also in Dupont Circle (see p. 126). For professional help, try an **Accommodations Agency** (see p. 291).

OTHER OPTIONS

DORMS

Interns and similar summer guests tend to stay in **university dorms,** where rates are cheap and students abound. Most university housing programs won't admit self-declared tourists, and even students must have a job or an official excuse to visit D.C.

The following is a list of good university housing programs in the District. Most are completely full by early spring; all require applications:

Georgetown University Summer Housing, G.U. Office of Housing and Conference Services, 100 Harbin Hall, Washington, D.C. 20057 (☎687-4560; fax 687-4590; www.georgetown.edu/housing/summer), on the Georgetown University campus in Georgetown. Metro: Rosslyn. Exit Rosslyn stop, go north on Lynn St., and cross Francis Scott Key Bridge. Much of Georgetown's residential charm lies in its uniquely located hilltop campus and the hip happenings of nearby M St. The stylishly terraced campus welcomes D.C.-bound student interns and those involved in summer programs or other educational pursuits (housing is available for non-students with an additional occupancy tax). The Georgetown University Transportation Shuttle (GUTS) eases the commute for summer residents between the Dupont and Rosslyn Metro stops. The rooms (half apartment-style, half dorm-like) fill up quickly, usually before mid-May, so mail in the application early. A 20% non-refundable deposit is required, and the balance must be fully paid 30 days before move-in. Single-sex rooms available June-Aug. 15, but usually fill by May 1. 3-week min. stay for residence hall rooms, 8-week min. stay for apartments. Double occupancy rooms with A/C and communal bath $21 per night. Apartments with carpet, kitchens, and bathrooms accommodate 4-6: $24 per night, regardless of occupancy.

Georgetown Law School Summer Housing, in the recently constructed Gewirz Student Center, 120 F St. NW in Capitol Hill. Write to: Office of Residence Life, 600 New Jersey Ave. NW, Washington, D.C. 20001-2075 (☎662-9290; fax 662-9248; email housing@law.georgetown.edu; www.law.georgetown.edu/reslife). Metro: Union Station or Judiciary Sq. Excellent apartments in a not-so-excellent neighborhood. Carpeted 1-3 bedroom and 2-bedroom apartments with living rooms are spacious, well-furnished, and come equipped with kitchens, A/C, private phone lines, and bathrooms. Fitness center $45 for the summer or $25 per month; small outdoor basketball court free. $250 security deposit required with application. 3, 5, 7, and 9 week rentals available June-Aug. approx. $25-34 per person per day.

George Washington University Housing, 2121 I St. NW, #402, Washington, D.C. 20052 (☎994-9193; email sumhouse@gwu.edu). Metro: Foggy Bottom. For interns or students in academic programs only. The very air of GW seems to be politically charged as the conveniently located campus (right off the Metro and near the National Mall) abounds with interns. Average dorm rooms with hardwood floors and clean bathrooms. Laundry in dorms; restaurants close by. Some dorms have kitchens, carpeting, sunroofs, free cable hookup, and exercise facilities. Pillow and blanket provided upon request. All rooms A/C. Available late May to early/mid-Aug. 30-night min. stay. $720 deposit (applied toward rent) must be submitted with application. Singles $24-35 per person per day; doubles, triples, and quads with kitchen $24-30. Payments may be made in increments.

Catholic University Housing, Office of Conferences and Summer Programs, 106 St. Bonaventure Hall, Catholic U., Washington, D.C. 20064 (☎319-5277; email cua-summer@cua.edu; http://conferences.cua.edu/summer/). Metro: Brookland-CUA. The inspiring, if not intimidating, dome of the Basilica greets students and tourists alike to CU's pleasant campus. The safe and generally laid-back campus houses many national and international interns, but is open to all visitors with an "educational purpose," including tourists. The nearby Metro quickly transports summer residents to downtown DC or nearby areas. A variety of rooms available but are issued on a first-come, first-serve basis. Housing available mid-May to early Aug. Wheelchair accessible. Use caution in this area at night. Application must be received at least three business days prior to arrival. $50 refundable key deposit. 20% deposit required in advance. 3-day min. stay. Stays of 30-74 days discounted 5%. Non-CU student rates: singles $23 per day, with A/C $25; doubles $21, with A/C $23 per person. Payments may be made in increments.

Howard University Housing. Requests for applications should be directed to Rev. James Coleman, Office of Student Development: Residential Life, Office of the Asst. Dean, 2401 4th St. NW, Washington, D.C. 20059 (☎806-5661 or 806-9539). Metro: Shaw-Howard U. Walk down Georgia Ave., in the direction behind the Metro stop; go right on Bryant and then left on 4th St. Summer housing available for interns and students in the D.C. area. Most rooms are in the Bethune Residential Complex, and consist of spacious, bright suites for 3-5 people. Suites include small study area and full bath. Internet access. Not the best neighborhood, but full campus security present. Full payment required in advance. Rooms available June-July. Singles or doubles $14 per person per day, with A/C $18.

Interns

COMMUNAL LIVING

Community living is a quirky—and considerably more expensive—alternative to regular housing options:

International Student House, 1825 R St. NW, Washington, D.C. 20009 (☎387-6445 or 232-4007), near 18th St. Metro: Dupont Circle. Contact ISH for an application. Primarily long-term international students in a romantic Tudor townhouse with a mammoth dining hall, library, patio, and garden. All dorm-style rooms in the townhouse and adjoining annex are fully furnished, single-sex, and have A/C. Parking (when you can get it) $75 per month. 18+, over 21 preferred. Office open M-Tu and Th-F 9am-5pm, W 9am-8pm, Sa 11am-1pm. 10% additional fee for 1st 2 months if stay is under 3½ months. 1st month's fee due on arrival. Inclusion of daily breakfast and dinner mitigates hefty prices. Singles $935-980 per month; doubles, triples, and quads $680-860 per person per month.

Farmer's Market at Takoma Park

Thompson-Markward Hall, 235 2nd St. NE (☎546-3255), 4 blocks from Union Station near C St., across from the Hart Senate office building. Metro: Union Station or Capitol South. Women ages 18-34 only. 112 dorm-like singles and 4 doubles line the old but clean hallways. Small bedrooms have A/C and phones (personal extensions); communal baths are large and clean. Laundry room. Weekly maid service provided. Bring your own sheets. Breakfast and dinner served cafeteria-style in a pleasant dining hall. First floor common areas are elegant and spacious, including a piano, library, and garden. TV lounge in the basement has cable, VCR, and couches. Indoor bike storage. Men are not allowed beyond the lobby. No alcohol, cooking appliances, or smoking inside building. Make summer

Newscast for Live T.V.

inside
SECRETS TO...

chi chi salons

Ritzy **Salon Christophe**, the kingpin of D.C. beauty care, does the 'dos for the best of them. Former first lady **Hillary Clinton** prepared for press conferences, public appearances, and marital affirmations by stopping at Christophe's for frequent touch ups.

reservations by early Mar. Non-refundable $50 deposit (credited to rent from Sept. 1-Apr. 30) required with reservation. 2-week min. stay, 2-year max. stay. $147 per week, $625 per month.

HOME EXCHANGE AND RENTAL

For shorter stays, home exchange and rental can be cost-effective options, particularly for families with children. Home rentals, as opposed to exchanges, are much more expensive, although they are remarkably cheaper than an extended stay at a comparably serviced hotel. Unfortunately, it can be difficult to arrange an exchange or rental for more than one month. See p. 293 for home exchange agencies.

HOSTELS

Although many of D.C.'s hostels have maximum stay limits, some allow long-term stays. Hostel with limits on the length of stays usually hover between 25 and 30 days. Otherwise, it's always possible to stay at two or three different hostels for your trip. For a list of hostels, see **Accommodations,** p. 269.

MONEY MATTERS

BANKING

If you don't have an account at one of the city's banks, it'll pay off to open a checking account. That way you can avoid the extra ATM fees. Popular large D.C. banks are **Citibank** (☎(800) 926-1067); **SunTrust** (☎(301) 206-6000); **Allfirst** (☎(800) 441-8455); and **First Union Bank** (☎(800) 398-3862).

To open a checking account, you'll need a social security number, local address, and minimum deposit (for the cheapest accounts, it's usually around $100-200). Foreign visitors will find it near impossible to open a checking account; consider opening a savings account instead. Call your bank of choice about their requirements for foreign account holders; usually, you will need to register for a social security number first.

CUTTING CORNERS

Think scrimping in the nation's capital would be more painful than cutting off all ten toes? Think again. A few simple steps will ameliorate living on the cheap: **Step one:** buy a budget travel book to Washington D.C. with comprehensive and deliciously inexpensive listings. Done. You're already ahead of the game, smartie pants. **Step two:** live in an apartment in a lower-income neighborhood or suburb, and you'll save big bucks on rent. For instance, try Mt. Pleasant, the neighborhood up north along 16th St. NW. If you can split an apartment with a roommate, all the better. **Step three:** Avoid taxis and cars altogether. Plus, the state-of-the-art Metro will get you pretty much anywhere you need to go in District. Buy the **28-day Metro farecard** or a **SmarTrip** card. **Step four:** get your entertainment for free. There are frequent free concerts at the Kennedy Center and public spaces, especially during the summer. If you can't afford to pay tickets to a performance or play, call ahead and find out if ushers are needed, and you'll be able to watch the show for free.

MEDICAL CARE

Should you require medical attention while in D.C., clinics and emergency rooms are the best places to be treated. Both accept walk-ins and spare you the hassle of having to choose a doctor and go through an initial screening. For foreign visitors, arrange health insurance before you arrive in the US, as it is notoriously impossible to procure. Both clinics and emergency rooms in public hospitals will treat the non-insured. For a list of hospitals and pharmacies, see **Service Directory,** p. 291.

HEALTH INSURANCE

The United States is the only industrialized nation that lacks national health insurance, so **private-sector insurance** is the only option. Everyone should have health insurance, as health care costs are just too high to take a risk. The easiest way to get insurance is through your **employer** or if you are a student at a **university.** If you don't have a job and are not in school, you will need to find independent insurance.

There are four main types of coverage plans: Traditional, HMO, PPO, and Point of Service. **Traditional** plans have high premiums and fairly high deductibles, but you can go to any doctor, any time, anywhere. **HMOs** offer the "managed care" you've probably heard about in the media. HMOs have the lowest monthly premiums of all types of health insurance, but you must see doctors who participate in the HMO plan, and you must have all test and X-rays done at participating facilities. **PPO** plans have little or no deductible, but they do have co-payments similar to those of HMOs. **Point of Service** plans are the newest type of health insurance; they are another option between HMOs and traditional health insurance.

INSURANCE TERMS

Deductable. A fixed amount of money you must pay before your insurance kicks in.

Co-Payment. A fixed amount of money you must pay for doctor or hospital visits or for certain treatments

Premium. The regular monthly amount you pay for your insurance.

Dental Plan. A plan, often for an additional fee, that will cover dental expenses (usually including a certain number of routine visits excluding orthodontics).

First-Dollar Coverage. Coverage from the first dollar you spend on coverage without a deductible. HMOs and PPOs usually offer first-dollar coverage while traditional health insurance does not.

Last-Dollar Coverage. A plan that increases its coverage as expenses rise, eventually covering all major costs, up to and including the last dollar.

Services

ACCOMMODATIONS SERVICES

Bed & Breakfast Accommodations, Ltd., P.O. Box 12011, Washington, D.C. 20005 (☎328-3510; www.bedandbreakfastdc.com).
The Bed & Breakfast League, P.O. Box 9490, Washington, D.C., 20016 (☎363-7767). Call for reservations M-Th 9am-5pm, F 9am-1pm.

APARTMENT HUNTING

The Apartment Connection (☎(800) 916-2787; www.theApartmentConnection.com) will hunt down an apartment for you or set you up with a roommate. Open M-Th 9am-7pm, F 9am-6pm, Sa 9am-5pm, Su 11am-4pm.
Roommates Preferred, 2262 Hall Pl. NW, #202 (☎965-4004). Matches the supply of potential roomies with the demand thereof. Fee $75. Open M-F 11am-7pm, Sa 11am-3pm.
The Registry (☎(800) 999-0350; www.theregistry.com) lists apartments on-line for D.C., Maryland, and Virginia, with color photos.
Urban Apartments, 410 Kennedy St. Ste. #2 NW (☎(202) 723-6122; www.urbanapartments.com)

deals with both real estate sales and rentals. Open M-F 9:30am-5pm.

BUDGET TRAVEL AGENCIES

Cheap Tickets (☎(800) 377-1000; www.cheaptickets.com).
Council Travel, 3301 M St. NW (☎337-6464; www.counciltravel.com).
STA Travel, 2401 Pennsylvania Ave., Ste. G, (☎887-0912).
Travel Avenue (☎(800) 333-3335; www.travelavenue.com).

CAR RENTAL

Also see **Once in D.C.: Getting Around by Car,** p. 26.
Alamo (☎(800) 327-9633), with branches at National and Dulles Airports.
Avis (☎(800) 331-1212), with branches at National and Dulles Airports.
Bargain Buggies Rent-a-Car, 3140 N. Washington Blvd. (☎(703) 841-0000), in Arlington. Open M-F 8am-7pm, Sa 9am-3pm, Su 9am-noon.

Budget (☎(800) 527-0700), with branches at Union Station and Downtown.
Dollar (☎(800) 800-4000), with branches at National and Dulles Airports.
Hertz (☎(800) 654-3131), with branches at National and Dulles airports and Downtown.
Rent-A-Wreck (☎(800) 421-7253), with branches at 5455 Butler Rd. (☎(800) 664-2526), in Bethesda, and at 2415 Lincoln Dr. (☎(310) 589-4700), in Silver Spring. Open M-F 8am-6pm, Sa 9am-2pm.

COMPUTER SERVICES

Computer Service Association (☎388-6855).
Computer Supplies & Services, 955 L'Enfant Plaza SW (☎651-8005).
Magician Computer Service, 6230 Georgia Ave. NW (☎829-3160).

CONSULATES AND EMBASSIES

Australia, 1601 Massachusetts Ave., 20036 (☎797-3000; fax 797-3040).
Canada, 501 Pennsylvania Ave., 20001 (☎682-1740; fax 682-7726).
Ireland, 2234 Massachusetts Ave., 20008 (☎462-3939; fax 232-5993).
New Zealand, 37 Observatory Circle, 20008 (☎328-4800; fax 667-5227).

South Africa, 3051 Massachusetts Ave., 20008 (☎966-1650; fax 244-9417).
UK, 3100 Massachusetts Ave., 20008 (☎588-6500; fax 588-6500).

CURRENCY EXCHANGE

Thomas Cook Currency Services Incorporated, 5335 Wisconsin Ave. NW (☎237-2229).

DENTISTS & DOCTORS

Also see **Emergency, Hospitals, Pharmacies.**
24 Hours Dental Clinic, 908 New Hampshire Ave. NW (☎457-0070).
Advanced Dental Treatment Centers, 1800 I St. NW (☎296-6515).
Capitol Womens Clinic, 1339 22nd St. NW (☎338-2772).
Planned Parenthood, 1108 16th St. NW (☎347-8500).
Zacchaeus Medical Clinic, 1525 7th St. NW (☎265-2400).

DRY CLEANING

Dry Clean Express, 6450 Georgia Ave. NW (☎829-8578).
Lees Custom Tailoring and Dry Cleaning, 529 14th St. NW (☎639-8590).

Snow White Dry Cleaning, 333 Hawaii Ave. NE (☎636-3700).

EMERGENCY

Emergency Assistance (☎911).
Park Police (☎619-7300). Emergencies in Rock Creek Park or on federal parklands.
Poison Center (☎625-3333). Open 24hr.

GROOMING SERVICES

Big Head Unisex Salon, 4660 Martin Luther King Jr. Ave. (☎574-2811).
Bonnie's Dog & Cat Grooming Service, 1364 E St. SE (☎548-0044).
Casa Del Sol Tanning Club, 4906 Wisconsin Ave. NW (☎363-2401).
Styles International Incorporated Hairstylists, 611 K St. NW (☎638-1751).
Supercuts, 3416 Connecticut Ave. NW. (☎244-6800).

GYMS

City Fitness, 3525 Connecticut Ave. NW (☎537-0539).
Golds' Gym & Aerobics Center, 4310 Connecticut Ave. NW (☎364-4653).
Waterside Fitness & Swim Club, 901 6th St. (☎488-3701).

HOME EXCHANGE

HomeExchange.com, P.O. Box 30085, Santa Barbara, CA 93130 (☎(805) 898-9660; email admin@HomeExchange.com; www.homeexchange.com).
The Invented City: International Home Exchange, 41 Sutter St., Ste. 1090, San Fransisco, CA 94104 (☎(800) 788-2489 in the US, ☎(415) 252-1141 elsewhere; email invented@aol.com; www.invented-city.com). For $75, your offer is listed in 1 catalog and you have access to a database of thousands of homes for exchange.

HOSPITALS

Children's National Medical Center, 111 Michigan Ave. NW (☎884-5000).
Georgetown University Medical Center, 3800 Reservoir Rd. NW (☎687-2000).
George Washington University Medical Center, 901 23rd St. NW (☎994-1000).
Howard University Hospital, 2041 Georgia Ave. NW (☎865-6100).
Sibley Memorial Hospital, 5255 Loughboro Rd. NW (☎537-4000).
Whitman-Walker Clinic (☎797-3500). Provides AIDS and sexually transmitted disease counseling and a variety of other services.

HOTLINES & SUPPORT CENTERS

Also see Emergency, Hospitals, Pharmacies, Dentists & Doctors.
AIDS Hotline (☎(800) 342-AIDS/2437 or TDD (800) 243-7889). Open 24hr.
Addiction Prevention Hotline (☎727-1765). Open M-F 8:15am-4:45pm.
Department of Human Services Crisis Line (☎561-7000). Open 24hr.
Gay and Lesbian Hotline (☎833-3234). Open daily 7-11pm.
Gay Men and Lesbians Opposing Violence, 1511 K St. NW, #821, 20005 (☎737-GLOV/4568). Crisis counseling.
National Abortion Federation Hotline (☎(800) 772-9100). M-F 9am-7pm.
National Organization for Victim Assistance (☎232-6682). Open 24hr.
Medical Referral, George Washington University Hospital (☎994-4112). Open 24hr.
Rape Crisis Hotline (☎333-7273). 24hr.
Sexual Minority Youth Assistance League, 410 7th St. SE, 20003 (☎546-5940, TTY 546-7796). Metro: Eastern Market. Counseling for bisexuals, gays, and lesbians ages 13-21. Hotline staffed M-F 7-10pm; drop-in hours most weeknights; call for hours. Support groups and social programs.
Traveler's Aid Society, 512 C St. NE (☎546-3120). Open M-F 9am-5pm. Other desks at Union Station (☎371-1937; open M-F 9:30am-5:30pm), National Airport (☎(703) 417-3972; open M-Sa 9am-9pm, Su 9am-6pm) and Dulles International Airport (☎(703) 572-8296; open M-F 10am-9pm, Sa-Su. 10am-6pm).

INFORMATION LINES

Dial-a-Museum (☎357-2020).
Dial-a-Park (☎619-7275).
News (☎334-9000).
Time (☎844-1212).
Weather (☎936-1212).

INTERNET ACCESS

See also Computer Services.
Atomic Grounds, 1555 Wilson Blvd., #105 (☎(703) 524-2157), in Arlington. Open M-F 6:30am-6:30pm, Sa-Su 8am-6:30pm.
The Cyberstop Cafe, 1513 17th St. NW (☎234-2470), near P St. Open Su-Th 7:30am-midnight, F-Sa 7:30am-2am.
Myth.com Cybercafe, 3241-3 M St. NW (☎625-6984). Open Su-Th 11am-1am.

JOB HUNTING (TEMP)

Career Blazers, 1025 Connecticut Ave. NW, #210 (☎467-4222).

Manpower Temporary Services, 1130 Connecticut Ave., #530 (☎331-8300).
Temps & Co., 3325 M St. NW (☎337-7922 or ☎(800) 836-7726).
NRI Staffing Resources, 1899 L St. NW #300 (☎659-8282).

LANGUAGE SCHOOLS

Berlitz Language Center, 1050 Connecticut Ave. NW (☎331-1160).
Inlingua, 1901 N. Moore St., #ML-02 (☎(703) 527-7787).

LAUNDROMATS

Capital Laundry Mat, 1653 Benning Rd. NE (☎398-4312).
Capitol Hill Cleaners & Laundry, 661 C St. SE (☎544-7934.)
Hamilton Laundromat, 5201 Georgia Ave. NW (☎829-2262).
The Laundry Basket, 5007 New Hampshire Ave. NW (☎291-3450) and 5567 S. Dakota Ave. NE (☎529-1511).

LIBRARIES

Folger Shakespeare Library, 201 E. Capitol (☎544-7077).
Library of Congress, 100 1st St. NE (☎863-0120).
Public Television Library, 475 L'Enfant Plaza SW (☎488-5000).

PHARMACIES

Berkshire Food & Druggists, 4201 Massachusetts Ave. NW (☎363-6546).
Cathedral Pharmacy, 3000 Connecticut Ave. NW (☎265-1300).
D.C. General Hospital Pharmacy Core Building (☎675-5250).

POST OFFICES

Main Office, 900 Brentwood Rd. NE, 20066 (☎636-1532). Indescribably inconvenient. Mail sent "General Delivery" always comes here. Open M-F 8am-8pm, Sa 8am-6pm, Su noon-6pm
Farragut Station, 1145 19th St. NW, 20033 (☎523-2506). Open M-F 8am-6pm.
Friendship Station, 4005 Wisconsin Ave. NW 20016 (☎635-5305). Open M-F 8am-6pm, Sa-Su 8:30am-4pm, Su 10am-2pm.

Georgetown Station, 1215 31st St. NW 20007 (☎ 523-2405). Open M-F 8am-5:30pm, Sa 8:30am-2pm.

Martin Luther King Jr. Station, 1400 L St. NW. 20043 (☎ 523-2001). Open M-F 8:30am-7pm, Sa 10am-2pm.

National Capitol Station, 2 Massachusetts Ave. NW, 20013 (☎ 523-2628). At Union Station Metro. Open M-F 7am-midnight, Sa-Su 7am-8pm.

Temple Heights Station, 1921 Florida Ave. NW, 20009 (☎ 232-7613), near Connecticut Ave. between Dupont Circle and Adams-Morgan. Open M-F 8:30am-5:30pm.

RELIGIOUS SERVICES

Islamic Center, 2551 Massachusetts Ave. NW (☎ 332-8343), north of Dupont Circle, on the L2 and L4 bus routes. Sunni and Shi'ite.

Kesher Israel, 2801 N St. NW (☎ 333-4808), in Georgetown. Orthodox. Time of services depends on the season; call to find out weekly schedules.

Religious Society of Friends, Wisconsin Ave. 3900 block, across from Rodman St. on the 30-series bus line. Quaker. Worship Su 11am.

St. Matthews Cathedral, 1725 Rhode Island Ave. NW (☎ 347-3215). Metro: Farragut North. Catholic. Mass held M-F 7, 8am, 12:10, and 5:30pm, Sa 8am and 12:10pm, and Su 7, 8:30, 10 (in Latin), 11:30am, 1 (in Spanish), and 5:30pm.

St. Nicholas, 3500 Massachusetts Ave. NW (☎ 333-5060), on L2 and L4 bus lines. Russian Orthodox. Liturgies are Su at 9am (English) and 10:45am

St. Sophia (☎ 333-4730), Massachusetts Ave. NW, at the corner of 36th and Massachusetts, on the L2 and L4 bus lines. Greek Orthodox. Liturgy is Su at 10am.

Temple Micah, 2829 Wisconsin Ave. NW (☎ 342-9175), near Garfield St. on the 30-series bus route. Reform. Services F 8:15pm and Sa 10:15am during the summers.

SHOE REPAIR

Blue Flame Shoe Repairing and Tailoring Service, 940 F St. NW (☎ 638-7420).

Cobblers Bench Shoe Repair, 1050 Connecticut Ave. NW (☎ 776-0515).

Dupont Shoe Repair, 1 Dupont Circle NW (☎ 293-2159).

TAXIS

City Cab, 1420 Rhode Island Ave. NE (☎ 269-0990).

Diamond Cab D.C., 110 Q St. NW (☎ 387-6200).

Mayflower Cab, 920 1st St. SE (☎ 783-1111).

Yellow Cab, 1636 Bladensburg Rd. NE (☎ 544-1212).

TICKET SERVICES

TicketMaster (☎ 432-7328).

Ticket Place (☎ 842-5387) for recorded information. In the Pavilion at the Old Post Office at Pennsylvania Ave. and 12th St. Open Tu-Sa 11am-6pm.

TOURIST OFFICES

Washington, D.C. Convention and Visitors Association (WCVA), 1212 New York Ave. NW, #600 (☎ 789-7000; www.washington.org). Open M-F 9am-5pm.

D.C. Committee to Promote Washington, 1212 New York Ave. NW, #200 (☎ 347-2873 or ☎ (800) 422-8644). Call or write for a tourist package. Open M-F 9am-5pm.

Meridian International Center, 1630 Crescent Pl. NW (☎ 667-6800). Metro: Dupont Circle. Open M-F 8:30am-5pm.

TOURS

Also see Once in D.C.: By Tour, p. 27.

Anthony S. Pitch (☎ (301) 294-9514; www.dcsightseeing.com). Group tours $200, individuals $10.

Capitol Entertainment Services (☎ 636-9203). $22, children 3-11 $15.

D.C. Ducks, 1323 Pennsylvania Ave. NW (☎ 832-9800). Tours Apr.-Oct. daily every hr. 10am-3pm. $24, children 4-12 $12.

Grayline (☎ 289-1995 or ☎ (800) 862-1400). Bus tour. $19, children 3-11 $9.

Old Town Trolley, 2640 Reed St. NE (☎ 832-9800). Bus tour. June-Aug, ticket sales daily 9am-4pm, last reboarding at 4:30pm; Sept.-May ticket sales 9am-3:30pm, last reboarding at 4pm. $24, children 4-12 $12.

Scandal Tours (☎ (800) 758-8687). Tours Apr.-Sept. Sa at 1pm. Reservations required.

Tour D.C. (☎ (301) 588-8999). Tours Sa, Th, 10:30am. $12, group rates available.

Tourmobile Sight-seeing, 1000 Ohio Dr. SW (☎ 554-7950, ☎ 554-5100, or ☎ (888) 868-7707). Bus tour. Mid-Apr. through mid-Sept. 9:30am-6:30pm; off-season 8:30am-4:30pm. $14, children 3-11 $7.

TRANSPORTATION

Also see **Car Rental, Taxis.**

Amtrak (☎ (800) USA-RAIL/872-7245).

Baltimore-Washington International (BWI) Airport (☎ (800) 435-9294).

Dulles International Aiport (☎ (703) 369-1600).

Greyhound (☎(800) 231-2222).
Metro (☎636-3425).
Ronald Reagan National Airport (☎(703) 417-8000).
Union Station (☎484-7540).

TRAVELERS WITH DISABILITIES

Mobility International USA (MIUSA), P.O. Box 10767, Eugene, OR 97440 (☎(541) 343-1284 voice and TDD; fax 343-6812; email info@miusa.org; www.miusa.org). Sells *A World of Options: A Guide to International Educational Exchange, Community Service, and Travel for Persons with Disabilities* ($35).

Moss Rehab Hospital Travel Information Service (☎(215) 456-9600; www.mossresourcenet.org). A telephone and internet information resource center on international travel accessibility and other travel-related concerns for those with disabilities.

Volunteers for the Visually Handicapped, 8720 Georgia Ave., #210, Silver Spring, MD 20910 (☎(301) 589-0894; fax 589-7281). Provides readers for the blind.

Washington Ear, Inc., 35 University Blvd. E., Silver Spring, MD 20901 (☎(301) 681-6636; fax 681-5227; email information@washear.org; www.his.com/~washear/). For visually impaired travelers. Sells large-print and tactile atlases of the D.C. area. The organization also reads the *Washington Post* and *Washingtonian* magazine aloud to the blind; call for details.

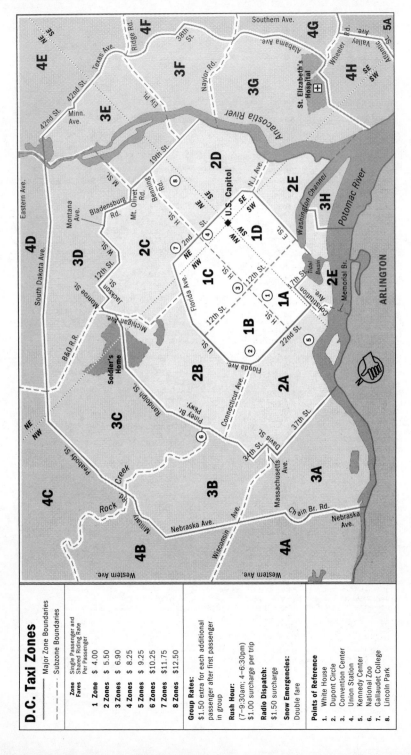

D.C. Taxi Zones

— — — Major Zone Boundaries
· — · — · Subzone Boundaries

Zone Fares	Single Passenger and Shared Riding Rate Per Passenger
1 Zone	$ 4.00
2 Zones	$ 5.50
3 Zones	$ 6.90
4 Zones	$ 8.25
5 Zones	$ 9.25
6 Zones	$10.25
7 Zones	$11.75
8 Zones	$12.50

Group Rates:
$1.50 extra for each additional passenger after first passenger in group

Rush Hour:
(7–9:30am; 4–6:30pm)
$1.00 surcharge per trip

Radio Dispatch:
$1.50 surcharge

Snow Emergencies:
Double fare

Points of Reference
1. White House
2. Dupont Circle
3. Convention Center
4. Union Station
5. Kennedy Center
6. National Zoo
7. Gallaudet College
8. Lincoln Park

Index

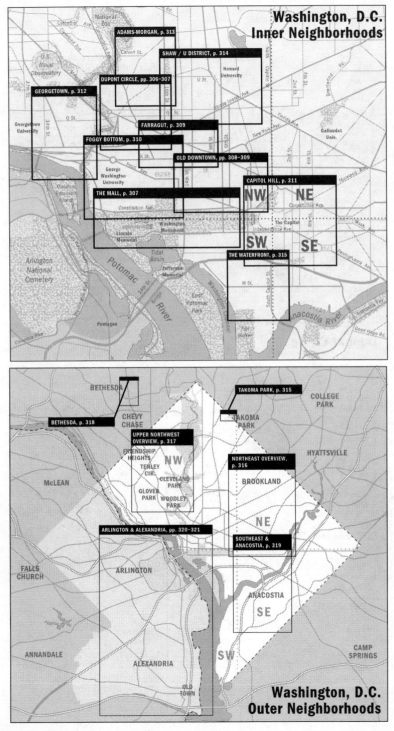

**Washington, D.C.
Inner Neighborhoods**

NW   NE

SW   SE

**Washington, D.C.
Outer Neighborhoods**

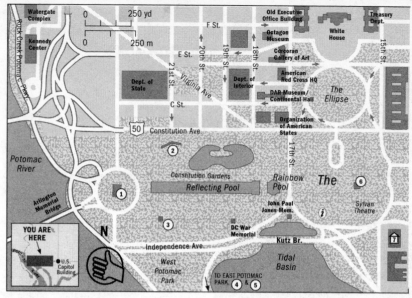

Dupont Circle

ACCOMMODATIONS
The Columbia Guest House, 19
Carlyle Suites Hotel, 28
The Brenton, 26
The Brickskeller Inn, 34
Embassy Inn, 25
Tabard Inn, 50
The Windsor Inn, 24

FOOD & DRINK
Afterwords Café, 29
Bua, 17
Café Luna, 18
City Lights of China, 8
The Cyberstop Café, 15
Dupont Italian Kitchen, 27
Jolt 'n' Bolt Coffee and Tea
    House, 21
Lauriol Plaza, 23
Luna Grill & Diner, 47
Mediterranean Blue, 22
Pan Asian Noodles & Grill, 42
Peppers, 13
Pizzeria Paradiso, 41
Raku, 30
Sakana, 40
Sala Thai, 43
Skewers, 18
Teaism, 6
Trio Restaurant, 12
Xando (north), 31
Xando (south), 45
Zorba's Café, 32

NIGHTLIFE
Badlands, 37
The Big Hunt, 46
Brickskeller, 35
The Childe Harold, 33
Club Chaos, 11
Dragonfly, 49
The Fireplace, 36
The Fox and Hounds, 12
J.R.'s, 14
Lizard Lounge, 51
Mr. P's, 38
Omega, 39
Red, 48
Timberlake's, 9

GALLERIES
Anton Gallery, 2
Fondo del Sol Visual Arts
    Center, 1
Foundry Gallery, 3
Gallery K, 4
Marsha Mateyka Gallery, 5
Robert Brown Gallery, 10
Studio Gallery, 2
Washington Printmakers
    Gallery, 7

SERVICES
Laundromat, 16
Pharmacy: CVS, 44
Pharmacy: Rite Aid, 20

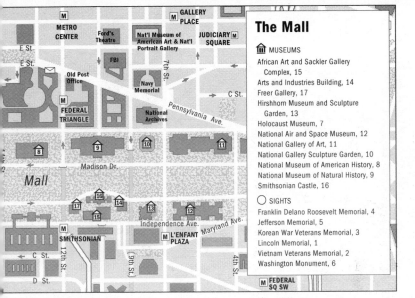

METRO CENTER

Ford's Theatre

GALLERY PLACE

Nat'l Museum of American Art & Nat'l Portrait Gallery

JUDICIARY SQUARE

E St.

E St.

FBI

7th St.

Old Post Office

Navy Memorial

C St.

FEDERAL TRIANGLE

Pennsylvania Ave.

National Archives

8

9

10

11

Madison Dr.

Mall

17

16

14

15

13

12

Independence Ave.

Maryland Ave.

SMITHSONIAN

L'ENFANT PLAZA

12th St.

9th St.

4th St.

C St.

D St.

FEDERAL SQ SW

The Mall

🏛 MUSEUMS

African Art and Sackler Gallery Complex, 15

Arts and Industries Building, 14

Freer Gallery, 17

Hirshhorn Museum and Sculpture Garden, 13

Holocaust Museum, 7

National Air and Space Museum, 12

National Gallery of Art, 11

National Gallery Sculpture Garden, 10

National Museum of American History, 8

National Museum of Natural History, 9

Smithsonian Castle, 16

○ SIGHTS

Franklin Delano Roosevelt Memorial, 4

Jefferson Memorial, 5

Korean War Veterans Memorial, 3

Lincoln Memorial, 1

Vietnam Veterans Memorial, 2

Washington Monument, 6

Dupont Circle

TO ADAMS-MORGAN

TO SHAW/ U DISTRICT

Connecticut Rd.

Columbia Rd.

19

20

U St.

Willard Pl.

23rd St.

California

Phelps Pl.

Leroy Pl.

T St.

21

T St.

Swann St.

24

Swann St.

Bancroft Pl.

Bancroft Pl.

Woodrow Wilson House

S St.

S St.

Scottish Rite Freemasonry Temple

Textile Museum

Decatur Pl.

Florida

Open Theatre/ T.U.T.A

28

Riggs Pl.

Riggs Pl.

26

TO ISLAMIC CENTER

R St.

GALLERY DISTRICT

31

21st St.

20th St.

Nat'l Museum of American Jewish Military History

R St.

27

25

SHERIDAN CIRCLE

Massachusetts Ave.

Phillips Collection

32

33

Corcoran St.

SEE INSET, BOTTOM LEFT

Q St.

16th St.

18th St.

17th St.

TO GEORGETOWN

Embassy Row

Anderson House

34

35

36

Indonesia

30

29

Riggs Bank

DUPONT CIRCLE

Church St.

TO 51 (250 yd)

Carnegie Institute

22nd St.

38

40 42 43

Hopkins St.

44

DUPONT CIRCLE

P St.

Brookings Institute

O St.

39

37

O St.

SEE INSET, TOP LEFT

Christian Heurich Mansion

46

45

50

SCOTT CIRCLE

N

Newport Pl.

N St.

Sunderland Pl.

Connecticut Ave.

N St.

B'nai B'rith Klutznick Museum

YOU ARE HERE

U.S. Capitol Building

TO FOGGY BOTTOM

New Hampshire Ave.

19th St.

M St.

Jefferson Pl.

48

The Garage

49

Rhode Island Ave.

National Geographic Society

De Sales St.

TO FARRAGUT NORTH METRO

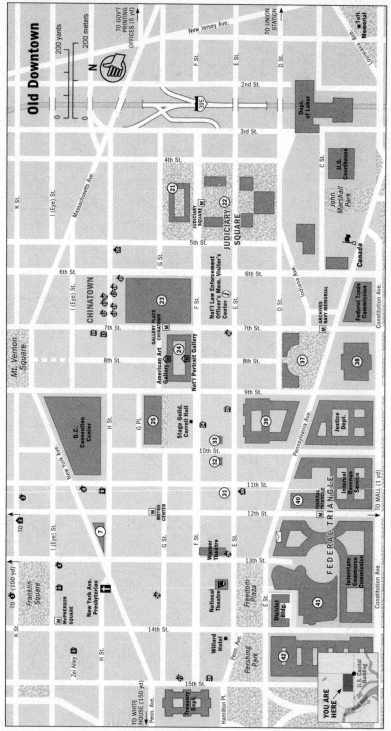

Old Downtown

N

200 yards
200 meters

TO GOVT PRINTING OFFICES (.5 yd)

New Jersey Ave.

TO UNION STATION

Louisiana Ave. ▲ 1st Memorial

F St.
E St.
D St.

2nd St.

395

Dept. of Labor

3rd St.

K St.
I (Eye) St.
Massachusetts Ave.

4th St.

21

JUDICIARY SQUARE M

22

JUDICIARY SQUARE

C St.

U.S. Courthouse

John. Marshall Park

Canada

5th St.

6th St.

Mt. Vernon Square

CHINATOWN

I (Eye) St.

6th St.

Indiana Ave.

23

GALLERY PLACE CHINATOWN M

F St.

Nat'l Law Enforcement Officer's Mem. Visitor's Center i

E St.

D St.

ARCHIVES NAVY MEMORIAL M

Federal Trade Commission

7th St.

American Art Gallery

24

Nat'l Portrait Gallery

7th St.

8th St.

37

8th St.

D.C. Convention Center

H St.

New York Ave.

9th St.

25

G Pl.

Stage Guild, Carroll Hall

33

32

10th St.

39

Pennsylvania Ave.

Justice Dept.

38

TO 2

I (Eye) St.

9

7

31

11th St.

METRO CENTER M

12th St.

40

FEDERAL TRIANGLE M

Internal Revenue Service

Constitution Ave.

TO MALL (1 yd)

TO (100 yd)

Franklin Square

McPHERSON SQUARE M

New York Ave. Presbyterian

G St.
F St.
E St.

Warner Theatre

13th St.

FEDERAL TRIANGLE

Interstate Commerce Commission

Zei Alley

H St.

National Theatre

Freedom Plaza

E St.

District Bldg.

41

TO WHITE HOUSE (150 yd)

14th St.

Willard Hotel

Penn. Ave.

Pershing Park

42

15th St.

Penn. Ave.

Treasury Dept.

Hamilton Pl.

YOU ARE HERE

U.S. Capitol Building

Old Downtown

⚑ ACCOMMODATIONS
Hotel Harrington, 30
Red Roof Inn, 20
Swiss Inn, 2

🍴 FOOD & DRINK
Burma Restaurant, 19
Café Amadeus, 4
Capitol City Brewing Co., 9
China Doll, 12
Ebbitt Express, 27
Go-Lo's, 18
Haad Thai, 8
Harry's, 30
Hunan Chinatown, 13
Jaleo, 36
John Harvard's Brew House, 29
Mayur Kabab House, 3
Mr. Yung's Restaurant, 19
New Big Wong Restaurant, 17
Old Ebbitt Grill, 27
Reeves, 26
Stoney's Restaurant, 1
Szechuan Gallery, 16
Tai Shan Restaurant, 14
Tony Sheng's Mongolian Restaurant, 15
Tony Sheng's Seafood Restaurant, 15

🛍 NIGHTLIFE
Capitol City Brewing Co., 9
Coco Loco, 10
DC Live, 34
Diva, 5
Fado, 11
Sky Terrace, 28
The Ritz, 35
Zei, 6

◯ SIGHTS
Discovery Channel Destination Store, 23
ESPNZone, 31
Federal Bureau of Investigation, 39
Ford's Theater, 33
Martin Luther King Jr. Library, 25
MCI Center, 23
National Aquarium, 42
National Archives, 38
National Building Museum, 21
National Law Enforcement Officers Memorial, 22
National Museum of Women in the Arts, 7
National Sports Gallery, 23
Navy Memorial & Heritage Center, 37
Old Patent Office Building, 24
Old Post Office, 40
Petersen House, 32
Ronald Reagan Building, 41

Farragut

⚑ ACCOMMODATIONS
Center City Hotel, 8
Farragut Lincoln Suites, 20
Governor's House Hotel, 6
Holiday Inn Downtown, 10
Marriot Residence Inn, 11
Quality Hotel and Suites, 7
Washington Int'l Hostel, 9

🍴 FOOD & DRINK
The Art Gallery Grille, 16
The Baja Grille, 24
Casa Blanca, 13
Famous Luigi's, 1
Il Pranzo, 18
Juice Joint Cafe, 12
Julia's Empanadas, 14

Sizzling Express, 15
Thai Kingdom, 25
Via Cuchina, 21
Vie de France, 17

🛍 NIGHTLIFE
The Madhatter, 3
Odds, 22

Ozio, 5
Relish, 19
Rumors, 2
Sign of the Whale, 4
Tequila Grill, 23

Foggy Bottom

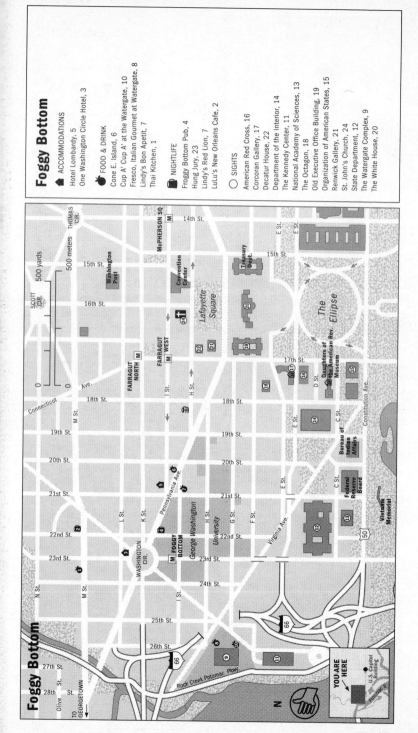

▲ ACCOMMODATIONS
Hotel Lombardy, 5
One Washington Circle Hotel, 3

● FOOD & DRINK
Cone E. Island, 6
Cup A' Cup A' at the Watergate, 10
Fresco, Italian Gourmet at Watergate, 8
Lindy's Bon Apetit, 7
Thai Kitchen, 1

■ NIGHTLIFE
Froggy Bottom Pub, 4
Hung Jury, 23
Lindy's Red Lion, 7
LuLu's New Orleans Cafe, 2

○ SIGHTS
American Red Cross, 16
Corcoran Gallery, 17
Decatur House, 22
Department of the Interior, 14
The Kennedy Center, 11
National Academy of Sciences, 13
The Octagon, 18
Old Executive Office Building, 19
Organization of American States, 15
Renwick Gallery, 21
St. John's Church, 24
State Department, 12
The Watergate Complex, 9
The White House, 20

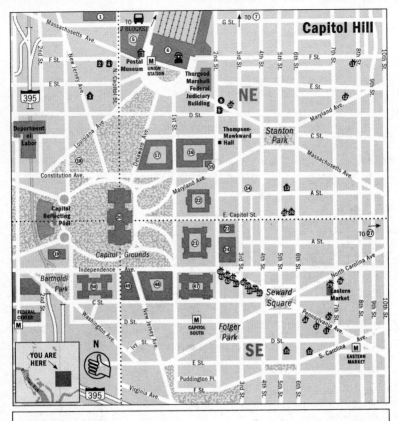

Capitol Hill

Capitol Hill

🏠 ACCOMMODATIONS

BullMoose, 13
Hereford House, 32
Holiday Inn on the Hill, 3
Maison Orleans, 35
William Penn House, 26

🍎 FOOD & DRINK

2nd St. Deli, 45
Anatolia, 33
Armands Chicago Pizzeria, 10
Banana Café and Piano Bar, 11
Bread and Chocolate, 30
Burrito Brothers, 46
Capitol Hill Jimmy T's, 25
The Dubliner, 4
Hawk 'n' Dove, 37
Hunan Dynasty, 43
Il Radiccho, 42
Kenny's Smoke House, 12
Le Bon Café, 44
The Market Lunch, 29
Misha's Deli, 28

Mr. Henry's Victorian Pub, 34
Roasters on the Hill, 31
Taverna the Greek Islands, 40

📷 NIGHTLIFE

Capitol Lounge, 41
The Dubliner, 4
Hawk 'n' Dove, 47
Kelley's "The Irish Times", 2
Politiki, 38
Red River Grill, 9
Tune Inn, 36
Xando, 39

⬤ SERVICES

Gas Station: Exxon, 8

◯ SIGHTS

Capital Children's Museum, 7
The Capitol, 20
Caring Institute, 14
Folger Shakespeare Library, 23
Government Printing Office, 1

House Office Building: Cannon, 48
House Office Building: Longworth, 49
House Office Building: Rayburn, 50
The Library of Congress: James
  Madison Bldg., 47
The Library of Congress: Jefferson
  Bldg., 21
The Library of Congress: John Adams
  Bldg., 24
Lincoln Park, 27
National Capitol Postal Station, 5
Senate Office Building: Dirksen/
  Hart, 16
Senate Office Building: Russel, 17
Sewall-Belmont House, 15
The Supreme Court, 22
Taft Memorial, 18
US Botanical Garden, 19
Union Station, 6

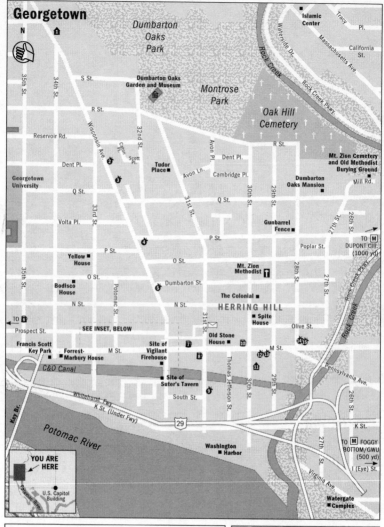

Georgetown

N

Dumbarton Oaks Park

Dumbarton Oaks Garden and Museum

Montrose Park

Oak Hill Cemetery

Islamic Center

Waterside Dr.

Rock Creek

Tracy Pl.

Massachusetts Ave.

California St.

Rock Creek Pkwy.

S St.

R St.

Reservoir Rd.

Wisconsin Ave.

35th St.

34th St.

Cajon St.

32nd St.

Scott Pl.

R St.

Dent Pl.

Mt. Zion Cemetery and Old Methodist Burying Ground

Mill Rd.

Georgetown University

Dent Pl.

Tudor Place

Avon Ln.

Avon Pl.

Cambridge Pl.

Dumbarton Oaks Mansion

Q St.

33rd St.

Q St.

31st St.

30th St.

29th St.

27th St.

26th St.

Volta Pl.

Gunbarrel Fence

P St.

P St.

O St.

Poplar St.

Yellow House

28th St.

27th St.

TO M DUPONT CIR (1000 yd)

35th St.

O St.

Dumbarton St.

Mt. Zion Methodist

Bodisco House

Potomac St.

N St.

N St.

HERRING HILL

The Colonial

Prospect St.

SEE INSET, BELOW

31st St.

Old Stone House

Spite House

Olive St.

Rock Creek

TO G

Francis Scott Key Park

Forrest-Marbury House

M St.

Site of Vigilant Firehouse

Thomas Jefferson St.

M St.

Pennsylvania Ave.

C&O Canal

Site of Suter's Tavern

South St.

30th St.

29th St.

26th St.

Key Br.

Whitehurst Fwy.

K St. (Under Fwy)

29

K St.

27th St.

Rock Creek Pkwy.

Potomac River

Washington Harbor

TO M FOGGY BOTTOM/GWU (500 yd)

I (Eye) St.

Virginia Ave.

YOU ARE HERE

U.S. Capitol Building

Watergate Complex

33rd St.

Potomac St.

Prospect St.

Wisconsin Ave.

M St.

Site of Vigilant Firehouse

Georgetown

ACCOMMODATIONS

Georgetown Suites, 11
Holiday Inn, 1

FOOD & DRINK

Aditi, 18
Amma Vegetarian Kitchen, 21
Au Pied du Cochon, 5
Bistro Med, 20
Booeymonger, 16
Burrito Bros., 25
Café La Ruche, 9
Dean and Deluca, 24
Fettoosh Express, 23

Furin's, 15
Georgetown Cafe, 3
Houston's, 31
Luciano's Cafe, 29
Myth.com Cybercafe, 26
Patisserie Poupon, 2
Quick Pita, 17
Saigon Inn, 13
San Marzano, 22
Thomas Sweet, 4
Vietnam-Georgetown Restaurant, 12
Wrap Works, 30
Zed's Ethiopian Cuisine, 14

NIGHTLIFE

Champions, 28
Garrett's, 10
J. Paul's, 27
Mr. Smith's, 8
Old Glory, 7
Rhino, 19
The Tombs, 6

Adams-Morgan

ACCOMMODATIONS

Adams Inn, 3
Kalorama Guest House, 19
Normandy Inn, 30
Taft Bridge Inn, 29
Washington Int'l Student Center, 18
Windsor Park Hotel, 31

FOOD & DRINK

El Tamarindo, 28
Julia's Empanadas, 10
Mama Ayesha's Calvert Café, 1
Meskerem, 23
Mixtec, 8
Mobay Café, 21
Pasta Mia Trattoria, 7
Perry's, 13
Red Sea, 9
Saigonnais, 27
So's Your Mom, 14
Star of Siam, 12
Tryst, 11

NIGHTLIFE

Blue Room, 25
Brass Monkey, 26
Bukom Café, 17
Chaos, 4
Chief Ike's Mambo Room, 4
Club Heaven and Club
Hell, 25
Millie & Al's, 20
Mr. Henry's, 15
Pandemonium, 4
Prive, 24
Toledo Lounge, 22
Tom Brazil, 16

SERVICES

Gas Station: Exxon, 2
Grocery: Safeway, 6
Pharmacy: CVS, 5

Shaw/U District

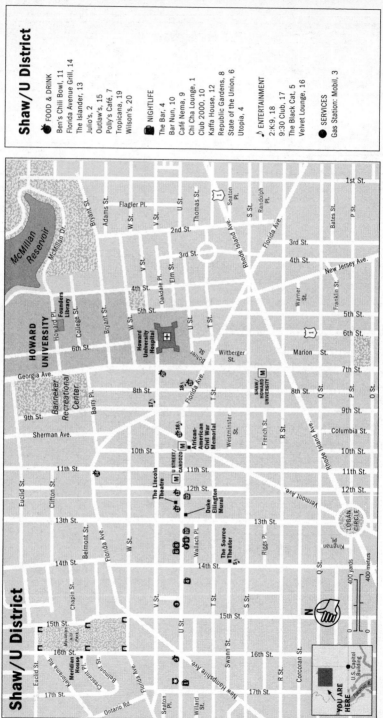

Shaw/U District

🍴 **FOOD & DRINK**
Ben's Chili Bowl, 11
Florida Avenue Grill, 14
The Islander, 13
Julio's, 2
Outlaw's, 15
Polly's Café, 7
Tropicana, 19
Wilson's, 20

🍸 **NIGHTLIFE**
The Bar, 4
Bar Nun, 10
Café Nema, 9
Chi Cha Lounge, 1
Club 2000, 10
Kaffa House, 12
Republic Gardens, 8
State of the Union, 6
Utopia, 4

🎵 **ENTERTAINMENT**
2:K9, 18
9:30 Club, 17
The Black Cat, 5
Velvet Lounge, 16

● **SERVICES**
Gas Station: Mobil, 3

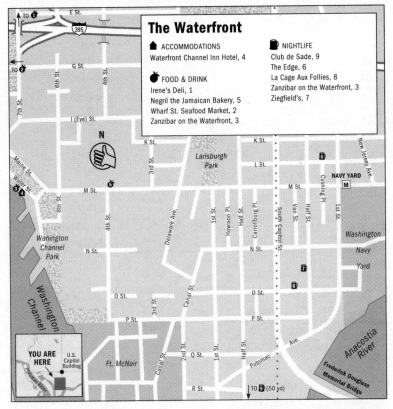

The Waterfront

ACCOMMODATIONS
Waterfront Channel Inn Hotel, 4

FOOD & DRINK
Irene's Deli, 1
Negril the Jamaican Bakery, 5
Wharf St. Seafood Market, 2
Zanzibar on the Waterfront, 3

NIGHTLIFE
Club de Sade, 9
The Edge, 6
La Cage Aux Follies, 8
Zanzibar on the Waterfront, 3
Ziegfield's, 7

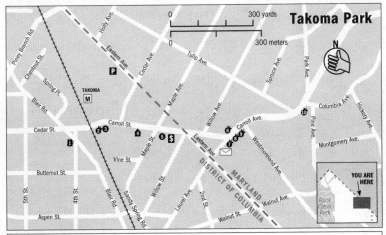

Takoma Park

ACCOMMODATIONS
India House Too, 4

FOOD & DRINK
Everyday Gourmet, 7

Mark's Kitchen, 6
Savory, 10
Spicy Delight, 2
Summer Delights, 8
Taliano's, 9

NIGHTLIFE
Takoma Station
Tavern, 1
Taliano's, 9

SERVICES
Pharmacy: CVS, 5
Laundromat, 3

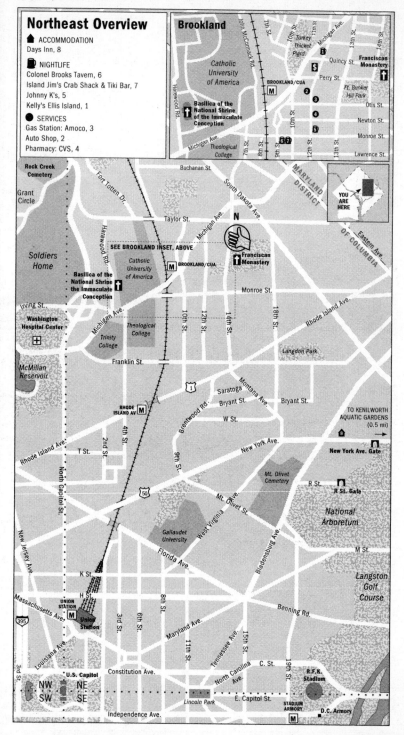

Northeast Overview

ACCOMMODATION
Days Inn, 8

NIGHTLIFE
Colonel Brooks Tavern, 6
Island Jim's Crab Shack & Tiki Bar, 7
Johnny K's, 5
Kelly's Ellis Island, 1

SERVICES
Gas Station: Amoco, 3
Auto Shop, 2
Pharmacy: CVS, 4

Brookland

Turkey Thicket Plgrd.
Michigan Ave.
Quincy St.
Franciscan Monastery
BROOKLAND/CUA
Perry St.
Ft. Bunker Hill Park
Otis St.
Newton St.
Monroe St.
Lawrence St.
10th St.
11th St.
12th St.
13th St.
14th St.
8th St.
9th St.
John McCormack Rd.
Catholic University of America
Basilica of the National Shrine of the Immaculate Conception
Michigan Ave. Theological College

YOU ARE HERE

MARYLAND
DISTRICT OF COLUMBIA
Eastern Ave.

Rock Creek Cemetery
Grant Circle
Soldiers Home
Irving St.
Washington Hospital Center
McMillan Reservoir

Buchanan St.
Taylor St.
South Dakota Ave.
Michigan Ave.
Fort Totten Dr.
Harewood Rd.

N
SEE BROOKLAND INSET, ABOVE
Catholic University of America
BROOKLAND/CUA
Franciscan Monastery
Basilica of the National Shrine the Immaculate Conception
Monroe St.
Rhode Island Ave.
Michigan Ave.
10th St.
12th St.
14th St.
18th St.
Trinity College
Theological College
Langdon Park
Franklin St.

RHODE ISLAND AV
4th St.
2nd St.
Brentwood Rd.
Saratoga
Bryant St.
W St.
Montana Ave.
Bryant St.
Rhode Island Ave.
T St.
New York Ave.
9th St.
Mt. Olivet Cemetery
R St.

TO KENILWORTH AQUATIC GARDENS (0.5 mi)
New York Ave. Gate
R St. Gate
National Arboretum

North Capitol St.
New Jersey Ave.
Mt. Olivet St.
West Virginia Ave.
Bladensburg Ave.
Gallaudet University
Florida Ave.
M St.
Langston Golf Course

K St.
H St.
UNION STATION
Union Station
Massachusetts Ave.
Louisiana Ave.
3rd St.
6th St.
8th St.
Maryland Ave.
11th St.
Tennessee Ave.
15th St.
19th St.
Benning Rd.
C. St.
R.F.K. Stadium

U.S. Capitol
NW NE
SW SE
Constitution Ave.
North Carolina Ave.
Lincoln Park
E. Capitol St.
STADIUM ARMORY
D.C. Armory
Independence Ave.

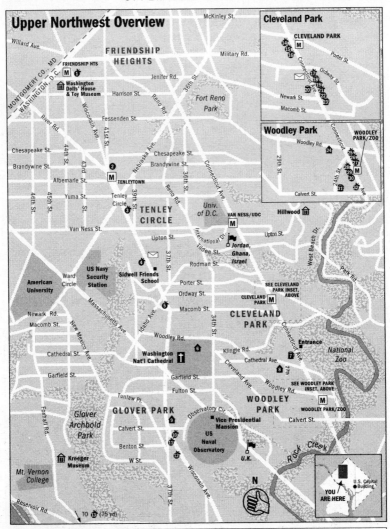

Upper Northwest Overview

Cleveland Park

Woodley Park

Upper Northwest Overview

🏠 ACCOMMODATIONS
College of Preachers at the
  Washington Nat'l Cathedral, 6
Kalorama Guest House at
  Woodley Park, 8
Savoy Hotel, 9
Woodley Park Guest House, 24

🍴 FOOD & DRINK
a.k.a. Frisco's, 3
Cactus Cantina, 5
Cafe Ole, 4
Entotto, 13
Faccia Luna, 12

Firehook Bakery & Coffeehouse, 19
Ivy's Place, 15
Jandara, 32
The Lebanese Taverna, 26
Maggiano's Little Italy, 1
Mama Maria and Enzio's, 10
Medaterra, 28
Nam Viet Pho 79, 17
Rocklands, 11
Saigon Gourmet Restaurant, 27
Spices Asian Restaurant & Sushi Bar, 21
Thai Town, 25
Yanni's, 16
Yenching Palace, 14

🍸 NIGHTLIFE
The Aroma Company, 18
Ireland's Four Provinces, 20
Murphy's of D.C., 31
Nanny O'Brien's, 23
Oxford Tavern "Zoo Bar", 7

● SERVICES
Laundromat, 30
Pharmacy: CVS, 29
Pharmacy: CVS, 22
Pharmacy: CVS, 2

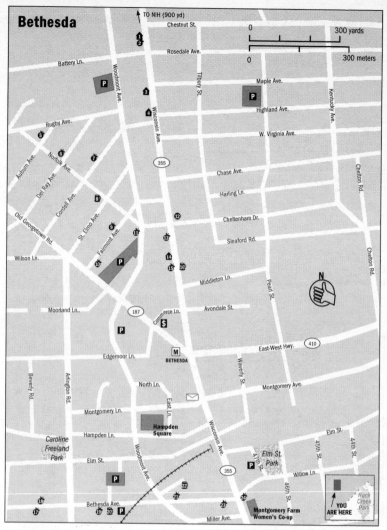

Bethesda

🏠 ACCOMMODATIONS
American Inn of Bethesda, 3
Bethesda Court Hotel, 14
The Bethesda Ramada, 1
Holiday Inn, 4

🍎 FOOD & DRINK
Aldo Cafe, 10
Bethesda Crab House, 17
Bob's Famous Homemade Ice
    Cream, 23
Chatter's, 2
Grapeseed, 7

Louisiana Express, 18
Paradise Restaurant, 24
Philadelphia Mike's, 15
Rio Grande Cafe, 9
Steamer's Seafood House, 5
Tako Grill, 13
Tara Thai, 19
Tastee Diner, 11
Thyme Square Cafe, 21
Tia Queta, 6

🍸 NIGHTLIFE
Bethesda Rock Bottom
    Brewery, 8

Bethesda Theater Cafe, 16
Lewie's, 22
Parker's, 20

⬤ SERVICES
Pharmacy: CVS, 12

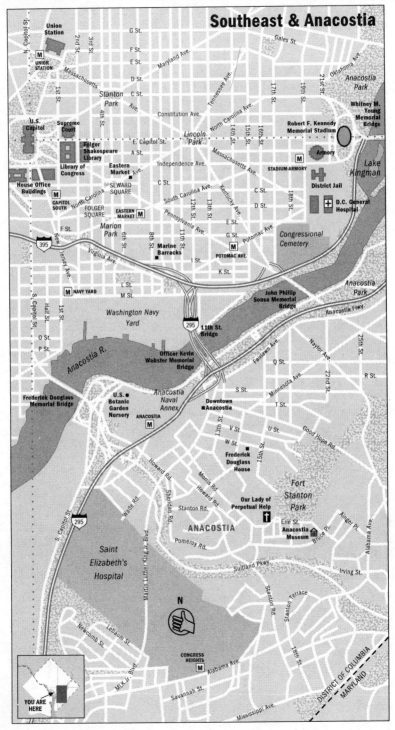

Southeast & Anacostia

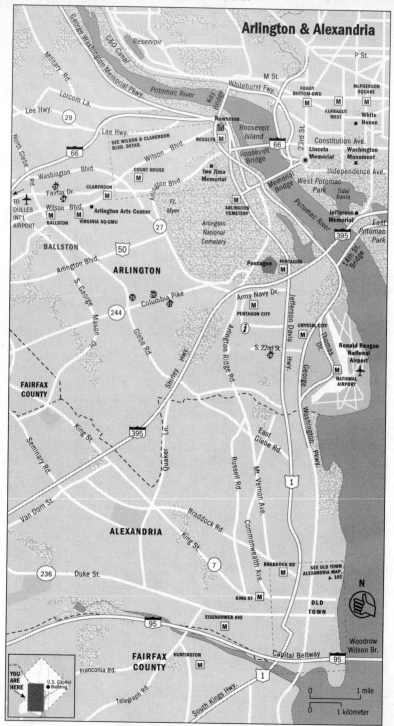

Arlington & Alexandria

🏠 ACCOMMODATIONS

Best Western Key Bridge, 21
Highlander Motor Inn, 1
Holiday Inn Westpark Hotel, 22
Quality Hotel, 15
Quality Inn Iwo Jima, 20

🍎 FOOD & DRINK

Atomic Grounds, 19
Bob & Edith's Diner, 27
Cafe Dalat, 4
Cafe Saigon, 5

Crystal Pallas Café & Grill, 28
Delhi Dhaba, 13
Food Factory, 23
Hard Times Cafe, 6
The Java Shack, 12
Kabul Caravan, 17
Lazy Sundae, 8
Little Viet Garden, 7
Queen Bee, 3
Red Hot and Blue, 18
Rocklands, 24
Silver Diner, 2

Steak Around, 14

🍺 NIGHTLIFE

Arlington Cinema 'N' Drafthouse, 26
Carpool, 24
Galaxy Hut, 11
Iota, 10
Ireland's Four Courts, 16
Whitlow's on Wilson, 9

⚫ SERVICES

Laundromat: Quality Wash, 25

Wilson & Clarendon Blvd.

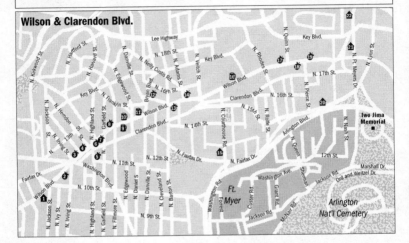